The History of the Christ

The History of the Christ

The Foundation
for New Testament Theology

Adolf Schlatter

Translated by
Andreas J. Köstenberger
1997

Original edition:
Die Geschichte des Christus
Stuttgart: Calwer Vereinsbuchhandlung
1923

A Division of Baker Book House Co
Grand Rapids, Michigan 49516

© 1997 by Andreas Köstenberger

Printed in the United States of America

Library of Congress Cataloging-in-Publication Data

Schlatter, Adolf von, 1852–1938.
    [Geschichte des Christus. English]
    The history of the Christ : the foundation for New Testament theology /
Adolf Schlatter : translated by Andreas J. Köstenberger.
       p.   cm.
    Includes bibliographical references.
    ISBN 0-8010-2089-1
    1. Jesus Christ—person and offices. I. Title.
BT202.S34513 1997
232—dc21   97-7452

For information abou academic books, resources for Christian leaders, and all new releases available from Baker Book House, visit our web site:
http://www.bakerbooks.com/

Contents

Translator's Preface

Schlatter's Appeal

Every aspiring scholar is on the lookout for models to emulate. Adolf Schlatter has been such a model for me. Unlike many of his contemporaries, he treated Scripture with respect and the confidence that it could be trusted to reveal God's word to his generation. Schlatter's thought is far-reaching, blending a remarkable grasp of the original languages with considerable interpretive skill, intuition, and synthetic power. His writing is at times convoluted, then again crisp and direct. Regarding the present work, Schlatter himself expressed the wish it could have been half as long.[1] He also recognized his work's lack of stylistic sophistication, which renders translation cumbersome at times. Indeed, more than once Schlatter has been declared virtually untranslatable.[2]

May this attempt to translate one of Schlatter's most significant works be judged with these limitations in mind. Every effort has been made to remain faithful to Schlatter's intentions—even wording—wherever possible. At the same time, we have sought to avoid wooden literalism, striving rather for an idiomatic, readable rendering that remains true to Schlatter while communicating to the contemporary reader. The tendency to impose on Schlatter gender-inclusive language has been resisted, since it appears anachronistic to revise Schlatter to satisfy the sensibilities of a later generation.[3]

A word regarding the translation of the original title, *Die Geschichte des Christus*, as *The History of the Christ*. The wording sounds as strange to modern American ears as it would have to Schlatter's contemporaries. The

---

1. Letter to his son Theodor on December 7, 1908, shortly after the completion of the manuscript on November 1 of the same year. See Werner Neuer, *Adolf Schlatter: Ein Leben für Theologie und Kirche* (Stuttgart: Calwer, 1996), 466.

2. Peter Stuhlmacher, "Foreword," in Adolf Schlatter, *Romans: The Righteousness of God,* trans. Siegfried S. Schatzmann (Peabody, Mass.: Hendrickson, 1995), x.

3. Cf. the present translator's forthcoming review of S. Schatzmann's translation of Schlatter's commentary on Romans in the *Journal of the Evangelical Theological Society.*

wedge driven between the historical Jesus and the Christ of faith lay deep, and Schlatter's choice of title strikes one therefore as deliberately provocative, even defiant, as if Schlatter were throwing down the gauntlet to the German scholarly establishment.[4] Hearing "history" and "Christ" mentioned in one breath would have violated established academic conventions of Schlatter's contemporaries, and the fact that it still does today is a telling testimony to the influence liberal German scholarship has had in North America in the twentieth century.

As is well known, the German word *Geschichte* may refer to either "history" or "story," and it is sometimes difficult to decide between these two renderings. As is already apparent in Schlatter's foreword to the first volume, he conceived of the task of New Testament theology as primarily a historical task, so that it seems justifiable to choose "history" as the proper rendering of *Geschichte* in the present instance. Indeed, the fact that the apostolic teaching is rooted in the history of Jesus Christ is the very foundation for Schlatter's programmatic division of his New Testament theology into two volumes. Moreover, it has been suggested that, when Schlatter entitled his work "Die Geschichte des *Christus*," he almost certainly meant to refer, not merely to "the Christ," but to "the Christ *who was* Jesus," a point that, incidentally, resembles closely that made by the Fourth Evangelist. If so, "The History of *Jesus Christ*" would reflect this contention more closely in English than "The History of the Christ." While there is an element of truth in this, it seemed advisable to allow the book itself to develop the identity of the Christ rather than to state it explicitly in the title. After all, Schlatter could have perfectly well called his book *Die Geschichte Jesu Christi* ("The History of Jesus Christ") had that been his desire.[5]

Brief mention should be made of a number of terms that presented serious challenges in translation. One such term was that of "Gemeinde." I have usually chosen the general English term "community," at times supplemented by a qualifier such as "*the Jewish* community," "*the early Christian* community," "the community *of Jesus' followers*," or the like. While these approximations add needed specificity to the otherwise vague (and often misleading) notion of "community," the term "Gemeinde" nevertheless remains notoriously difficult to translate, because the sense of "Gemeinde" is also reflected in English words like "church," "fellowship," or the term "God's people." It should also be noted that there is a difference between the German words "Gemeinde" (religious, cultural, or eth-

---

4. Walter Bauer, speaking for the German scholarly guild of Schlatter's day, chided the latter for failing to distinguish between the Jesus of history and the Christ of faith (review in *ThLZ* 48 [1923]: 78). On the latter distinction, see especially Martin Kähler, *The So-called Historical Jesus and the Historic Biblical Christ,* trans. Carl Braaten (Philadelphia: Fortress, 1964 [1892]).

5. Cf. Robert Morgan, *The Nature of New Testament Theology,* SBT 2/25 (Naperville, Ill.: Alec R. Allenson, 1973), 32–33, who translates *Die Geschichte des Christus* by "The History of the Christ" and contends "that the christological judgment that Jesus is the Christ [is] implicit in his [Schlatter's] title."

nic community) and "Gesellschaft" (a socio-political construct, "society"), and that Schlatter never uses the latter term. As Robert Yarbrough remarked to me in personal correspondence, Schlatter's use of "Gemeinde" makes perfect sense in the cozy confines of early twentieth-century Württemberg and the Lutheran state church found there. But today it tends to conjure up overtones of political and sociological jargon that were entirely absent from Schlatter's mind when he wrote. A related term is the word "Volk." It could be translated by "people," but in English this connotes an universal anthropological scope generally not in Schlatter's view. Therefore I chose the term "nation" as the closest English equivalent to underscore the ethnic dimension usually reflected in Schlatter's thinking. Another variant used at times is "the people *of Israel.*" Finally, Schlatter frequently refers to Jesus' "königliches Recht." This amounts to his "regal status," his status as king-elect, so to speak. But "right" also has the connotation of "claim" or "privilege," in the sense of a deserved, rightful, confirmed, but as of yet not yet universally acknowledged position. These are instances where the translator is reminded that translation is an imperfect exercise at approximation at best. In such instances where ambiguities remain the reader is therefore referred to the German original.

Finally, why was Schlatter's *New Testament Theology* chosen for translation, when several other significant works could have been selected? There remains, of course, a subjective element in such a selection. In the end, the translator felt, and others he consulted agreed, that the present work provides an ideal introduction to Schlatter's opus at large, perhaps supplemented by *Das christliche Dogma,* which features his systematic thought. While Schlatter also produced important monographs, such as *Der Glaube im Neuen Testament (Faith in the NT,* 1885), scholarly commentaries on Matthew (1929), John (1930), and other New Testament books, the devotional *Kennen wir Jesus? (Do We Know Jesus?,* 1937), and important historical and philosophical treatments, none of which have thus far been translated,[6] his *New Testament Theology,* perhaps like no other work by Schlatter, provides access to the totality of his theology, tracing in bold, broad strokes the movement of the gospel from its inconspicuous beginnings in the ministry of John the Baptist to the ministry of Jesus to the apostolic era, culminating in a grand synthesis of the New Testament period. For this reason the *New Testament Theology* was chosen.

Schlatter's Contribution

Until this day, Schlatter's incisive theological work has remained something of a well-kept secret among English-speaking theologians and bibli-

6. The sole exception is *Die Geschichte der ersten Christenheit* (1926), which was published as *The Church in the New Testament Period* in 1955.

cal scholars.[7] The Anglo-American scholarly guild has been extremely slow to award Schlatter the respect due him. During his lifetime, none of Schlatter's books were translated into English.[8] His true stature can be appreciated by the fact that (the first volume of) Kittel's massive *Theological Dictionary of the New Testament* is dedicated to Kittel's teacher—Adolf Schlatter.[9]

Schlatter was born on August 16, 1852, in St. Gallen, Switzerland. He died on May 19, 1938, in Tübingen, Germany, at the inception of the Second World War. His teaching career spanned more than forty years, with his most mature years spent at Tübingen (1898–1922).[10] In an age when liberal scholarship carried the day, Schlatter stood firm in his advocacy of a conservative approach to biblical interpretation and theology.[11] He was convinced that

7. See the brief quarter-page entries on Schlatter in the *Oxford Dictionary of the Christian Church,* ed. F. L. Cross and E. A. Livingstone (Oxford: Oxford University Press, 1974), 1243; and the *New Catholic Encyclopedia* (New York: McGraw-Hill, 1967), 12:1134, the latter excerpting the articles in the two German works *LexThK* and *RGG.* See also Ernst Käsemann, *New Testament Questions of Today* (Philadelphia: Fortress, 1969), 4–5, who deplores this neglect in an eulogy on Schlatter. But see now the forthcoming entries by Robert W. Yarbrough on Adolf Schlatter in the *Encyclopedia of Evangelical Biblical Scholars,* ed. Walter A. Elwell (Grand Rapids: Baker) and in *Major Bible Interpreters,* ed. Donald McKim (Downers Grove: InterVarsity).

8. Apparently the only essays by Schlatter to be translated in his lifetime were "The Attitude of German Protestant Theology to the Bible," *Constructive Quarterly* 2 (1914): 99–110 and two entries in the *Dictionary of the Apostolic Church,* ed. James Hastings (Edinburgh: T. & T. Clark, 1915 and 1918), entitled "Holy Spirit" (Vol.1, pp. 573–81) and "Paraclete" (Vol. 2, pp. 121–22). For a long time, the only posthumously translated work by Schlatter was *The Church in the New Testament Period,* trans. Paul P. Levertoff (London: SPCK, 1955). Recently Schlatter's commentary on Romans has been translated as well. See further Morgan, *Nature of NT Theology,* 117–66, translating Schlatter's essay "Die Theologie des Neuen Testaments und die Dogmatik" (first published in *Beiträge zur Förderung christlicher Theologie* 13 [1909], no. 2, pp. 7–82; reprinted in *Zur Theologie des Neuen Testaments und zur Dogmatik,* ed. Ulrich Luck [München: Christian Kaiser, 1969], 203–55).

9. For appreciations of Schlatter in English, see Peter Stuhlmacher, "Adolf Schlatter's Interpretation of Scripture," *New Testament Studies* 24 (1978): 433–46; idem, *Historical Criticism and Theological Interpretation of Scripture,* trans. Roy A. Harrisville (Philadelphia: Fortress, 1977), 46–48; idem, "Jesus of Nazareth as Christ of Faith," in *Jesus of Nazareth—Christ of Faith,* trans. Siegfried S. Schatzmann (Peabody, Mass.: Hendrickson, 1993), 1–38; and W. Ward Gasque, "The Promise of Adolf Schlatter," *Crux* 15, no. 2 (1979): 5–9. See also Gerhard Maier, *Biblical Hermeneutics,* trans. Robert W. Yarbrough (Wheaton, Ill.: Crossway, 1994), 352–57; and Werner Georg Kümmel, *The New Testament: The History of the Investigation of Its Problems,* trans. S. McLean Gilmour and Howard C. Kee (Nashville: Abingdon, 1972), 194–97.

10. For further information, see the popular biography by Werner Neuer, *Adolf Schlatter* (Wuppertal: R. Brockhaus, 1988); ET: *Adolf Schlatter: A Biography of Germany's Premier Biblical Theologian,* trans. Robert W. Yarbrough (Grand Rapids: Baker, 1996). See also Neuer's recent scholarly biography on Schlatter referred to in note 1 above.

11. A significant contemporary of Schlatter was Adolf Harnack, whose lifespan almost exactly equals Schlatter's (1851–1930). They overlapped in Berlin where Schlatter taught from 1893–98 and Harnack from 1889–1921. As Morgan remarks, Schlatter's chair in Berlin was established by the king of Prussia to counterbalance Harnack's influence following a controversy when Harnack told students he wished the church would give up using the Apostles' Creed (*Nature of NT Theology,* 172, n. 43). Morgan cites Schlatter as "the greatest conservative of the generation before Bultmann," who "stands outside the mainstream of the development of New Testament studies" (2), "perhaps the only 'conservative' New Testament scholar since Bengel who can be rated in the same class as Baur, Wrede, Bousset and Bultmann" (27).

biblical exegesis was the only proper foundation for systematic theology, and in this respect anticipated and influenced Karl Barth.[12]

While Schlatter may best be known for his commentaries on Matthew, John, or Romans,[13] his theological approach is given its most pronounced expression in the two-volume *Die Theologie des Neuen Testaments* (1909/10), written during his Tübingen years shortly after the death of his wife, Susanna, in 1907.[14] The agenda is already set in the unusually perceptive preface to the first volume. Schlatter claimed the primacy of historical research in New Testament theology, rejecting the intrusion of subjective, idealistic notions into the discipline. His insistence on the distinction between the two "horizons" of the biblical text, the ancient and the contemporary one, and his affirmation of the preeminence of the first horizon are as timely today as they were then. At the same time, Schlatter did not rest content with historical exegesis. He urged the pursuit of "the doctrinal task, through which we align ourselves with the teachings of the New Testament and through which we clarify whether or not and how and why we accept those teachings into our own spiritual lives, so that they are not only truth for the New Testament community, but also for us personally."[15]

In the end, Schlatter conceived of his task simply as "letting Jesus be who he was" and allowing him "to speak for himself."[16] Schlatter made every effort to keep his own apprehension of Jesus from being obfuscated by the views of contemporary scholars. His hermeneutical approach can be summed up by one phrase: "perceptive

12. In 1907, Karl Barth's father urged Barth to hear Schlatter: "He felt that it was time that, with my liberal tendencies, I should hear some sound 'positive' theology . . . so he sent me off to Tübingen, to Adolf Schlatter" (from a conversation with Tübingen students on March 2, 1964, quoted in Eberhard Busch, *Karl Barth: His Life from Letters and Autobiographical Texts,* trans. John Bowden [Philadelphia: Fortress, 1976], 42). However, Barth went to hear Schlatter very irregularly, and then only "with considerable resentment" (ibid., 43, quoting from the *Fakultätsalbum der Evangelisch-theologischen Fakultät Münster,* 1927). Indeed, Barth sneered at Schlatter's "talent for moving difficulties elegantly out of the way without really tackling them" (ibid., quoting from a letter to W. Spoendlin from November 4, 1907). Barth particularly could not bear the way Schlatter dealt with the Gospel of Matthew. Later in Barth's career, however, he expressed great admiration for Schlatter. Thus he wrote in a letter dated May 2, 1934: "Of course, in relation to you I will always remain a beginner and student." Cf. Werner Neuer, "Der Briefwechsel zwischen Karl Barth und Adolf Schlatter: Ein Beitrag zum 100. Geburtstag Karl Barths," *TBei* 17 (1986): 86–100 (letter cited on p. 99).

13. Schlatter's commentary *Der Evangelist Johannes* persistently aims to demonstrate the Jewish background for the Gospel of John, citing numerous Old Testament and Jewish parallels. Schlatter found an ally in the British scholar Edwyn Hoskyns (1884–1937) whose work *The Fourth Gospel* was posthumously published in 1940 (ed. F. N. Davey).

14. The subtitle for vol. 1 was *Das Wort Jesu* and for vol. 2 *Die Lehre der Apostel.* The second edition of Schlatter's *Theologie des Neuen Testaments* appeared in 1920/22 with new titles for vols. 1 (*Die Geschichte des Christus*) and 2 (*Die Theologie der Apostel*). A third volume entitled *Das christliche Dogma* outlining Schlatter's systematic thought was published in 1911 (2d ed. 1923). For a listing of reviews, including discussions by W. Bauer, R. Bultmann, M. Dibelius, H. Holtzmann, and H. Windisch, see Neuer, *Schlatter* (1996), 844; cf. also the critiques by Rudolf Bultmann in *Theology of the New Testament,* trans. Kendrick Grobel (New York: Charles Scribner's Sons, 1955), 2:248–51, and "Zur Geschichte der Paulus-Forschung," *Theologische Rundschau* NF 1 (1929): 52–53. Neuer also provides detailed autobiographical background information on Schlatter's writing of *Das Wort Jesu* and *Die Lehre der Apostel* (464–80).

15. See Schlatter, *Das Wort Jesu* (Calw/Stuttgart: Verlag der Vereinsbuchhandlung, 1909), 9.

16. ". . . laß ihn, wie er war; laß ihn reden." *An Theodor,* December 23, 1908; quoted in Neuer, *Schlatter* (1996), 466.

observation" (*Wahrnehmung* or *Beobachtung*).[17] For Schlatter, "every true theologian is first and foremost an observer."[18]

In an age when scholars had grown skeptical of the very possibility of finding the historical Jesus in and through the Gospel documents, Schlatter expressed his confidence that Jesus' person, teaching, and work could be gleaned and distinguished from what the New Testament writers proclaimed.[19] He rejected an arid scholasticism, an approach to scholarship that was primarily concerned with current critical fashions, statistics, and "purely historical" reconstruction, urging instead an holistic understanding of the time in which Jesus lived and an effort to understand his theology comprehensively.

Schlatter distrusted the contemporary proponents of source and form criticism as well as the history-of-religions school. He was well aware of the distorting effects of improper methodological presuppositions on the exegetical and theological task. Issuing a call to a scholarship of humility, Schlatter wrote, "The boundaries for his [the historian's] explanatory work are found where his grounded awareness ends. Historical thinking does not extend beyond that which is revealed by the available sources. Otherwise historical research would turn out novels."[20]

Think of it, Schlatter's sustained defense of a miracle-working Jesus and of his essential Jewishness in contrast to gnostic thought was written well before Bultmann, who is by many considered to be the most influential theologian of the twentieth century. If people had listened to Schlatter rather than Bultmann, biblical scholarship in the second half of the twentieth century might have taken quite a different course and been spared many cul-de-sacs in the process.

Schlatter's work is a telling statement on much that has happened since his day. While history is not likely to repeat itself in exactly the same way, there is much to learn from the insights of scholars of the past.[21] Many of the best arguments in the history of interpretation have never been refuted, just forgotten or ignored. Let

17. "Es gibt . . . für das menschliche Auge kein höheres Geschäft als das Sehen, durch das wir auffassen, was Jesus will und sagt." Schlatter, *Das Wort Jesu,* 5. Cited in Neuer, *Schlatter* (1996), 467. See also Gottfried Egg, *Adolf Schlatters kritische Position gezeigt an seiner Matthäusinterpretation* (Stuttgart: Calwer, 1968), 21–33. Stephen F. Dintaman, in his published dissertation *Creative Grace: Faith and History in the Theology of Adolf Schlatter* (New York: Peter Lang, 1993), 29, n. 7, concedes that an English translation of the term *Wahrnehmung* "which would adequately convey Schlatter's method has eluded me." He settles for "observation," realizing that this term by itself is too passive to convey Schlatter's thought. But "perception" or "perceptive observation" is a much better rendering. See the reviews of Dintaman's work in *Theologische Revue* by Werner Neuer and by Robert W. Yarbrough, *EQ* 68 (1996): 253–56.

18. "Jeder echte Theolog ist Beobachter." Schlatter, *Die philosophische Arbeit seit Cartesius nach ihrem ethischen und religiösen Ertrag,* 2d ed. (1910), 12. Cited in Schlatter, *Zur Theologie des Neuen Testaments und zur Dogmatik,* 12.

19. For a thorough analysis of Schlatter's treatment of the historical Jesus, cf. esp. Johannes Heinrich Schmid, *Erkenntnis des geschichtlichen Christus bei Martin Kähler und bei Adolf Schlatter* (Basel: Friedrich Reinhardt Verlag, 1978), 240–431.

20. Schlatter, *Wort Jesu,* 11.

21. See recently Cardinal Ratzinger, "Zur Lage von Glaube und Theologie heute," *IKZ Communio* 25 (1996): 359–72, who on p. 371, n.17 commends W. Neuer's recent biography of Schlatter and acknowledges the undiminished relevance of Schlatter's work for contemporary exegesis.

Schlatter's voice be heard again in a theological landscape that has seen some change, but one that is not so different that we can afford to neglect the prophetic words spoken by one of the greatest theologians of this century.

While the labors of translating Schlatter's German into passable English have been mine, and I alone bear ultimate responsibility for the final product, this project would not have seen the light of day without the wise encouragement of Rev. Robert Seale, the enthusiastic support of Jim Weaver at Baker Book House, and the committed, competent counsel and correction of Robert Yarbrough. My thanks also to Maria denBoer, editor at Baker, for her customary poise and unbureaucratic can-do attitude, and to Werner Neuer, eminent Schlatter biographer, who, at the occasion of a visit to Tübingen, extended his hospitality and shared some seminal insights regarding Schlatter that significantly improved this translation at several points. May the reader digest this work empathetically and with a sincere desire to enter into a deeper knowledge of Jesus, aided by the perceptions of a man whose entire life was passionately dedicated to this quest that in this life can always and only remain an open-ended task.[22]

Andreas J. Köstenberger

22. Cf. Schlatter's last work, the devotional *Kennen wir Jesus?*, which was published shortly before Schlatterr's eighty-fifth birthday and on whose revision schlatter worked in 1938 prior to his death.

Foreword to *Das Wort Jesu* (1909)

To those who have urged me to publish a theology of the New Testament I hereby give what I have. This, I hope, will soon be followed by a second volume entitled *Die Lehre der Apostel*. I consider New Testament theology to be a historical task in distinction from dogmatics, although this runs counter to the majority and the most influential portion of contemporary literature, which customarily ties the historical presentation directly to the polemic against New Testament Christianity. It does, however, appear desirable to me to retain in the church a tradition of New Testament statements that does not intermingle these with the interpreter's own judgments. Therefore I write neither as a reviewer of Jesus and his messengers nor as their admirer (they did not desire any laurels) nor as their opponent and critic. I rather consider it to be the historian's task to perceive what actually happened. In my view there is no higher calling for the human eye than perception which apprehends what Jesus desires and claims.

Since one's intellectual labors and the business of teaching are not yet completed with the accomplishment of the historical task, so that we are still faced with the challenge of measuring our own intellectual property by the concepts mediated to us by the New Testament with a view toward appropriating the latter, I intend to supplement my historical work with a volume entitled *Das christliche Dogma*. For a thorough discussion of the distinction between dogmatic and historical work and of the different objectives of New Testament theology I have used the *Beiträge zur Förderung christlicher Theologie* (1909), volume 2.[1]

The Objective of This Work

The New Testament writings present us with the task of identifying their teachings and of clarifying their origin. We customarily call this branch of his-

---

1. [See Morgan, *Nature of NT Theology*, 117–66.]

torical research "New Testament theology." By calling this field of *historical* work "theology," we affirm that its object of scrutiny is the statements about God and God's work contained in the New Testament. In speaking of "New Testament" theology, we are saying that it is not the interpreter's own theology or that of his church and times that is examined but rather the theology expressed by the New Testament itself.

It is the historical objective that should govern our conceptual work exclusively and completely, stretching our perceptive faculties to the limit. We turn away decisively from ourselves and our time to what was found in the men through whom the church came into being. Our main interest should be the thought as it was conceived *by them* and the truth that was valid *for them.* We want to see and obtain a thorough grasp of what happened historically and existed in another time. This is the internal disposition upon which the success of the work depends, the commitment which must consistently be renewed as the work proceeds. (Note that at this point we are not studying what the New Testament words mean *for us,* how they influence *our own* thoughts and actions, and whether or not and why they achieve over us the compelling authority of truth. At the proper time, however, this question will be very important.)

Indeed, the acquisition of historical knowledge is for no one the only goal to be attained. Apart from the historical task there remains, constantly and necessarily, a second one, the doctrinal task, through which we align ourselves with the teachings of the New Testament and clarify whether or not and how and why we accept those teachings into our own spiritual lives, so that they are not only truth for the New Testament community, but also for us personally. The distinction between these two activities thus turns out to be beneficial for both. Distortions in the perception of the subject also harm its appropriation, just as conversely improper procedures in the appropriation of the subject muddy its perception. I think here of recent richly amalgamated constructs, portrayals of Christ and of the apostles, which are partially formed by observation and partially by the interpreter's presuppositions. Through the latter, both the portrayal's fidelity to its object and its faith-generating power are certain to be negatively affected.

It comes as no surprise that historical research appears to be boring and worthless to a religiously shaken and jaded generation. Insofar as this generation frees itself from its Christian tradition, it rushes to polemics (to the extent that it wants to preserve it), to apologetics, and to dogmatics. However, it is only the "seeing" that turns away from one's own self that satisfies both our intellectual need and the need of our faith. There is nothing more necessary or encouraging for our faith than that we can see and hear. For we cannot improve on Paul's statement that defines the genesis of faith: It comes not from dreaming and speculating but from hearing.

Our task, then, can immediately be divided into two parts owing to the fact that the work of Jesus is clearly distinguished from the apostolic proclamation. By coming to understand Jesus' work we clarify for ourselves the most important factor that produced the doctrinal formation of the New Testament. Therefore the knowledge of Jesus is the foremost, indispensable component of New Testament theology. The second task consists in investigation of the convictions held by the first Christian community.

The essential characteristic of these concepts, with whose content and origin we are presently concerned, is that they are links in the chain of the history which was experienced and wrought by the people of New Testament times. These people did not attempt to separate their thinking from the way they lived. For this reason they did not even create the appearance of laying before us timeless insights independent of historical circumstances. Rather, their intellectual labors stand in conscious and complete connection with their choices and actions. They are grounded in their experiences, serving them as a means for directing their calling. Their thoughts are integral parts of their actions and hence of their history.

Therefore the task of New Testament theology is not exhausted with statistics which produce lists of the teachings of Jesus and of his disciples. This kind of procedure would predictably lead to a historically distorted picture, a compendium of abstract, timeless "doctrines" presented as the contents of a consciousness that was cut off from choices and actions. Jesus and his disciples, however, did not bear and transmit their ideas in this way. In order to observe rightly we must illumine the context which generated their thoughts and into which their thoughts immediately reentered as the basis of their work. To that extent the historian also has the task to explain, not just to report. He would lessen the grounded awareness provided by his subject if he did not also grasp the causal processes which make his subject visible. The boundaries for his explanatory work lie where his grounded awareness ends. Historical thinking does not extend beyond that which is revealed by the available sources. Otherwise historical research would turn out novels.

On account of this, New Testament theology stands in the closest relation to the kind of historical scholarship that refers to the events through which the church came into being. Among these, literary and linguistic criticism merit special attention. Even more than in the case of the early Christian community, it is impossible to abstract from Jesus' actions a so-called doctrine, since in his case word and work, assurance and will, formed a close-knit unity. To make this plain constitutes a major task of the first part of New Testament theology. Nevertheless, the objective is not identical with that pursued by the narrators of the "life of Jesus." What occupies us are not the events which make up the story of Jesus but the convictions upon which Jesus bases his word and work, convictions made visible through those words and works.

Our work is interdependent with that of literary criticism (so-called Introduction). All the real fruit yielded by literary-historical research, by which the time and form of our sources are illumined, directly impact the theological assessment of the history. At the same time, this assessment represents an indispensable tool for the literary-critical task. For the shape of the documents is profoundly conditioned by the internal religious history of the community.

If extrabiblical data existed about early Christian religious history that supported, for example, the now widespread understanding that John made up his stories like fairy tales, as it were, and that his Gospel is therefore worthless as a source for the history of Jesus, or the view that the heading "Matthew" attaches the apostolic authority to a compilation of internally diverse components, these judgments would intervene significantly in the work of New Testament theology. However, these views are not substantiated by observations of language, topography, history, and documentary attestation. They rather originate from history-of-religions considerations, lying to a large extent within the discipline of New Testament theology, on whose progress "Introduction" depends in all its more thorough investigations.

Two factors may suggest that it be advisable to extract Jesus' word solely from the Synoptics: respect for the contemporary mood of university religious faculties as well as the difficulty resulting from the relationship of the texts to one another. The simultaneous use of Matthew and John clearly does render the understanding of Matthew more difficult, and the sharp apprehension of what Matthew describes for us as Jesus' word and work is perhaps eased if we forget the Johannine expressions entirely at the outset. However, it is equally clear that the limitation of sources endangers historical perception. The fewer the statements that are acknowledged by the witnesses admitted, the more wide-ranging and daring will be the conjectures, and the imagination of historians will supplement the silence of witnesses. If we confront the fact that in the ancient church John overshadows Matthew, a corresponding truth is equally clear at the present time: The understanding of Matthew vanishes if one tries to do without John. Which of the Gospels we prefer to work from is far less decisive for the historical outcome than whether we leave out, say, John. Admittedly, to opt for Marcan priority is seriously ill-advised because the terser and leaner witness poses less resistance to imaginative reconstruction and conjecture than a fuller and richer one like Matthew.

Foreword to *Die Geschichte des Christus* (1920)

The knowledge of Jesus is the foremost, indispensable centerpiece of New Testament theology. When we strive to perceive the convictions set forth by the New Testament and to comprehend how they developed, we take the first step toward this goal by understanding the assurance Jesus bore within himself and how that assurance conditioned his every action. To grasp this is to grasp the most effective cause lying behind the formation of the church's teaching. For this reason I began my presentation of the theology of the New Testament published in 1909 with the portrayal of "the Word of Jesus."

I proceeded from the observation that the ideas of the New Testament received their uniqueness from being components of the history experienced and produced by the men of the New Testament. For they brought their thoughts into a conscious and complete connection with their will and action. Through what they experienced they gave their thoughts content and basis. They used their experience as the means to fulfill their calling. This rendered what we call their teachings components of their actions and thus their history. This law, which controlled the entire history of the early church, was most fully realized in Jesus' own ministry. Even less than in the case of the apostles is it possible in the case of Jesus to separate a "message" from his actions, since, in his case, the word and the work, the assurance and the will, form a closely connected unity. The task of crystallizing this phenomenon I called "a major task of the first part of New Testament theology."

By not merely repeating the earlier presentation in its old form and by giving it a second and, as far as I am concerned, final form, I heed the verdict that our comprehension of Jesus is rendered more difficult when individual teachings such as Jesus' statements regarding conversion to God, his disciples' and Israel's relationship to God, his own divine sonship and his regal aim, and the outcome of his earthly life and what would follow it, are merely set side by side. I hope that the reader will succeed more readily in perceiving the

21

unity binding everything that Jesus said and did when he pictures the interdependent activities of Jesus. Three deeds—that Jesus made John the Baptist's message his own, that he therefore called the community into the divine
kingdom, and that he thus took the cross upon himself—are the deeds of
Jesus that make up his history. To comprehend them is to lay hold of the
splendid riches of his word together with its unifying foundation.

Foreword to 1923 Edition of *Die Geschichte des Christus*

Since the characteristic of a historical work consists for me in the sincere effort
to listen to the sources, the verdict of the *Theologische Literaturzeitung*[1] that I
"only imagine myself to be a historian" does not cause me to change the title
of my presentation of Jesus. That verdict is based on the outlook that was the
inevitable outcome of idealistic religiosity: Only polemic against Jesus is "history." That same outlook follows the custom characterizing it since the time
of the Greeks: No other view but its own is "science." I have stated elsewhere
where I find the logical deception and the ethical deficiency of these traditions. The other verdict that the words and actions of Jesus in my presentation
become a unity only by the practice of imposing my own dogmatics and ethics onto him would be significant for me only if it could be demonstrated that
my dogmatics and ethics are my own invention rather than that which is giv-
en by Jesus and the church. This conviction does not remove my awareness
of the limitations afflicting my presentation. The new publication of my book
makes me painfully aware of these since I was able to correct them at only a
few places.

1. [Two reviews critical of Schlatter's approach to New Testament theology appeared in
this journal: the first by H. Holtzmann in 35 (1910): 299-303, the second by W. Bauer in 48
(1923): 77-80. Schlatter here makes reference to the review by Bauer who called Schlatter's
claim "to work as a historia" a "delusion."]

The Objective of This Work

As the disciples made their reminiscences of Jesus the permanent possession of the church, they worked according to the method of the Palestinian school, which preserved the memory of the fathers by passing on their "sayings" and "deeds." This is why the Gospels consist of sayings and anecdotes[1] that confront us in every case with a particular concrete incident from the life of Jesus. The saying expresses how he bound his disciples to his will in a particular case. The anecdote shows how a certain circumstance provided an occasion for his activity. This lends the Gospel accounts a value that nothing can replace or transcend.

The disciples' relatively small concern for the preservation of the chronological sequence, which is given expression by the texts' diversity, likewise is in accordance with Palestinian school custom. I want no part in the futile attempt of reconstructing a chronological sequence of Jesus' words and actions, since, by discussing the question of whether one of Jesus' sayings belongs to the time of his early or later ministry, we immediately distance ourselves from the sources, thereby exceeding the story's own boundaries and merely creating fictions. For the sources convey to us the sayings of Jesus because they discerned in them his abiding will. By confronting us with a wealth of individual, clearly comprehensible events, they call us to a scientific work which can bear fruit by making us think through the many individual sayings and activities of Jesus so that their causal effect becomes visible.

Thereby one's attention is directed toward the internal root, not toward the visible aspect of the events. But this aspect, too, can be reconstructed by the one who is familiar with Judaism and Palestine at the time of Jesus, reconstructed so that a new presentation, while it may not represent incontrovertible certainty, may nevertheless amount to more than fiction and approximate historical truth. Thus the stories can be made more vivid in our imagination and thereby support the grasp of internal realities. For me, however, the goal

---

1. Even John's Gospel retains a close affinity to this older method of presentation.

23

is not the fabrication of colorful images which stimulate the imagination but rather insight into the ground and the aim of Jesus' work.

The understanding of Jesus' story in the context of the history of Palestinian Judaism can take on great scientific value, since all the events which influenced the latter, such as the emergence of Hellenism, the development of the Rabbinate and of Pharisaism, the rule of the Herodians, and the way in which Judaism was integrated into the empire, also were components of the history of Jesus. I have, however, not reproduced my independent presentation of Jewish history but rather remain content here with short sketches of the situation which arose through the history of Jewish religion in the first century.

In the evaluation of the sources I agree with the judgment of those who produced the canon of the four Gospels at the transition from the first to the second century. The opposing assessments in the present literature derive from history-of-religions considerations rather than from observations gained from the language, topography, history, and documents themselves. These considerations find their refutation when we succeed in gleaning from the Gospel accounts a unified and comprehensible picture of Jesus' history.

The Preparation for Jesus' Work

I

1. The Expectation of the Anointed One

The first act by which Jesus stepped out of his village of Nazareth, out of the quiet life of a craftsman, and began his public ministry was his contact with John, whom people called by the surname "the Baptist." Jesus' conviction that God's word had come to the nation through John gave him the resolve with which he assumed its leadership. Perhaps we tend to imagine religious events in such a way that they affect merely the internal life of the individual. In seeking to understand Jesus, we must free ourselves from this view of religion. Jesus was not led by self-related motives,[1] not even in the purest form. It was rather events affecting the Jewish community that stirred Jesus to action that would seize the entire nation. These events received the power to influence decisively, not only the history of the Jews, but the entirety of world history, from the fact that they had their ground in the expectation of the "anointed king," the Christ.[2]

The work of the Baptist was, however, not the only precursor of Jesus' ministry. The news that John testified to the imminence of God's rule would never have brought about the turning point in his life unless Jesus himself had been prepared for it. For the Baptist's work imparted that depth to Jesus' very first public step that was thereafter characteristic of his conduct. It left no room for slow developments, unprepared groping, and indecisive interludes. Since the Baptist confronted the Jewish community with an elevated portrait of Christ that was directed toward certain goals, Jesus either had to reject it or

---

1. By "self-related" I mean that kind of will that seeks the enhancement of one's own life. As I use the term here it has neither positive nor negative connotation.
2. "Christ" translates the Syriac *Meschicha, Messias,* into Greek. The noun corresponding to "anointed" is "king."

receive it into his will; the situation required decisiveness. When he associated himself with the Baptist, he recognized his own calling to be the messianic work. Jesus did this without being hindered by the fact that the conception of the Christ held up by the Baptist for him and for the entire nation possessed supernatural proportion and that it connected the revelation of God's rule with the presence of the Christ. The decision to align himself with John, however, was preceded not only by Jesus' public participation in Jewish community life, however rich, pure, and effective we may imagine it to have been. It was also his own prior history that furnished the necessary assumptions upon which the beginning of his ministry was built.

His disciples pointed to this by combining birth narratives with their account of his words and works. One must not think that the authors of the Gospels provide us with late legends. By including these narratives they rather seek to report the kinds of events upon which the subsequent history is based. On account of these experiences and in the possession of these thoughts, John and Jesus, according to the Evangelists, accomplished their work. It becomes apparent by the manner and diversity of their presentation that the creative ability of the early Christian community, which rejoiced with excited gratitude in Jesus' work, came into play. Both accounts, each in their own way, provide splendid evidence for their poetic power. They possess, moreover, at the same time incomparable historical value, even if we deem the share of early Christian creativity in them to be considerable. For in them the powerful messianic expectation finds expression in the way in which the church related this expectation to Jesus' ministry, which was not by scribal interpretation. It was rather free of distinctive Pharisaic coloring, so that their expectation looked very much like it had been appropriated right out of the Old Testament. In this expectation of the Christ, Jesus and all those who participated in his work had lived from their youth onward, as the Christmas story indicates.

The power with which the hope connected with the name "Christ" moved history proceeded from the fact that it was *religious*,[3] that is, directed toward God. The Jewish community had realized by the events that had created it, through the call of the fathers and the exodus from Egypt, as well as through their preservation despite the guilt and death brought on by the Babylonian incursion, that God was their Savior. For this reason their hope demanded an act of God that would save the community and gained assurance by seizing upon the prophetic promise as the proclamation of God's will. As he had ruled them earlier through the sending of his messengers, he will reveal himself to the community again by ruling it through the Promised One. Therefore the Jewish community called him "God's Anointed," that is, the one whom God had appointed to the regal office. And for that same reason it saw the basis for his rule in the fact that in relation to God he possessed the rank of son.[4] Because of his relationship with God, because he is "the Holy One,"

3. I call an action "religious" when it receives its grounding through the concept of God.
4. Owing to Psalm 2 both names were already related to one another before Jesus; cf. John 1:49; Matt. 16:16; 26:63. See also Luke 1:32.

he receives kingly power whose purpose is the revelation and glorification of God (cf. Luke 1:17, 76; 2:14).

Of the two names with which the Jewish community described the Expected One, "Son of God" defined his relationship with God while "Christ" denoted his relationship to the nation. The former name placed him under God; the latter, above the nation as king. The former designated him as the recipient of divine love; the latter, as the mediator and dispenser of that love to all mankind. His relationship to the world and his relationship to God, however, exist simultaneously and substantiate one another reciprocally. In order for him to be Lord over God's people God makes him his Son, and because he is Son, he makes him Lord over God's people. The name "Christ" expresses the aim for which his communion with God is given him. The work of the Christ consists in the creation of the abiding, perfected community, and the work of the Son consists in the fact that through him the presence of God, connectedness with God, religion, arise. And because he is the Son and the Christ in unity, his rule gives rise to that kind of community which is united in God and set apart for him.

The preceding history of the nation had as a further result that its religious expectation was at the same time directed toward *ethical* goals.[5] For since the restoration of the Jewish nation in Persian times, the Law had increasingly acquired the power to control all expressions of its life. The Jewish community held the pervasive conviction, the all-encompassing dogma, that it would forfeit God's grace if it resisted his will. It possesses its share in God only by obeying him, for God is for what is good and against what is evil. Therefore the messianic hope also merged with the ethical aims of the nation, and this occurred in such a way that the negative as well as the positive effect of the Law determined what the work of the Promised One was expected to be. The Law showed the need for which the human being requires help. For out of the nation's opposition to God arises its poverty from which Christ liberates it. Through him, God sets the guilty free from their guilt and punishment (cf. Luke 1:77; Matt. 1:21). With similar effectiveness, the positive content of the Law determined the messianic concept, since it made doing God's will the calling of the Christ and of the Jewish community (cf. Luke 1:75). The Christ exercises his rule in obedience to God's commandment and produces that kind of community that consists of those who do the divine will.

The religious ground of the expectation directed toward the Christ made it universal and elevated it above all limitations. This expectation described both the gift granted by God and the circle of its recipients in absolute categories. The messianic idea aimed at a final goal with which divine grace reveals itself in its completeness and leads the community to completion. Nothing higher than the Christ is expected, but rather the abiding and eternal are desired from him (cf. Luke 1:33). This found expression in the teaching con-

5. "Ethical" I call that behavior which has its ground in the norms that are set for our will.

cerning the two ages. The course of history is divided into two halves by the sending of the Christ so that his advent ends the present human state and establishes a new world order. In view of those receiving the divine gift, the messianic idea was universal in all its forms, since it bestowed the promise not on individuals but on the community. God's work does not consist in the completion of many or of a few human beings. It rather creates the abiding community, and individuals in it and for it.

Protecting this truth against any variation was the concept of king. Since the community had up to this point been limited to the Jewish nation and had been particularistic in this respect, the messianic idea transcended it, but not in such a way that it aimed at its destruction, but rather at its fulfillment. This idea saw in the community's limitation not merely an incompleteness and an embarrassing weakness, but the means through which the fulfillment would be accomplished. Since the community's limitation up to that point had its ground in God's election, it determined that the hope would possess truth and the possibility of realization only as a religious hope, that is, only because it was directed toward God. The eschatological community will come into existence through God, not through human beings; through divine giving, not through human merit; through God's call that achieves his aim with kingly power, not through the exercise of human will. It thus becomes, however, the fellowship of all those whom God calls, and does not grant any preference to individuals. It rather creates an entity that will be united with God, thereby uniting its elements with one another. Through this it will become apparent that the small compass of the community up to that point was a beginning that was transcended by God's rule. God will bring this incipient rule to completion by forming out of all those who have entered eternal life a community bound together in God (cf. Luke 2:14, 32).

All events that had their ground in the messianic idea thus received an incomparable depth, since they simultaneously changed the history of religions, ethical history, and the entire constitution of the community. They strove in all directions to bring about a complete renewal of human life. They received their depth, however, not merely through the positive content of the goal entailed by the messianic idea, but also through the impact of contrasts to it. For the expectation of the Christ possessed the content that the Christmas story shows us only where the will is ruled by that certainty of God that received its grounding through the Scriptures. Besides Scripture, other influences were operative in Judaism that are apparent everywhere in human history. To the extent that those gained influence, they dragged the concept of Christ down into the service of irreligious, unethical, and particularistic aspirations. In that case, the sending of the new king should serve the glorification of the Jew and should help him to greatness, whereby the hope became godless. It should also satisfy the demand for more happiness, while being at best only loosely related to spiritual need. In this way, the idea lost its completeness and was supposed to apply only to Judaism, to the exclusion of the nations, while providing even for the Jews only a limited, temporal benefit. Before Jesus' ministry, these mutually contradictory aspirations were often intermingled in a confusing blend.

The pious will that longed for God's revelation and the selfish desire that longed for the Jew's greatness, the longing for happiness and that for righteousness, the thought of a goal that gives fulfillment and the wish for a partial, temporal improvement of the situation often occurred simultaneously without clear separation from one another. The distinction had to be made, however, when the one appeared who in earnest dependence on the Scriptures understood the kingly goal to be his calling.

The new Christian convictions that originated only through Jesus' demise do not, however, become apparent in the birth narrative. The Christ's office is rather described by the angel entirely from the standpoint of Old Testament expectation. What is to come is not anticipated. A preview of Jesus' cross is missing, as well as the Gentile church and the separation of God's rule into different stages that would distinguish among the earthly work of Jesus, his heavenly activity, and his return. The kind of expansion of hope caused by the expectation of the resurrection of the righteous, too, does not surface (cf. Luke 1:75). In the description of the office given to the Baptist, references to his baptism and his execution are missing. The account receives its form from the grateful joy that now God's promise is being fulfilled. It is significant that the disciples did not ground the ministries of the Baptist and Jesus in prophecies that already indicated their end. They rather claim that the expectations that they had nurtured in their youth were identical with the messianic hopes of the community. The break between them and Israel did not occur already in their youth but was their own doing.

2. The One Born of God

Prophecy pointed to the Christ's birth as the event through which God would provide salvation for the nation, and in the Septuagint version of Isaiah, the Promised One was described as the son of the virgin.[6] The disciples contend that this did not hinder, but rather strengthened Jesus' certitude; for as Joseph's fiancée Mary had received Jesus by the Spirit of God. She then learned the meaning of the miracle happening to her by the appearance of one of the highest angels of God, who proclaimed to her the commission given to her child. The account's major emphasis, God's creative activity at Jesus' origin, is also expressed by those words of Jesus that describe his share in God as eternal. When he spoke of his eternal life in God, he revered a miracle at the beginning of his human life that transcends by far the secrets surrounding the origin of human life in the natural order.

Jesus therefore laid hold of the kingly prerogative as his own, because he praised God as his Father, whereby he described God as the one who had given him life through his creative activity. For the notion that he had acquired sonship by himself, and that he had elevated himself to it by his piety,

6. The supposition that the Greek version of Isaiah could not have had any significance for the Galileans is inaccurate. Not the Hebrew but the Greek Bible had been the vernacular Bible for a long time.

cannot be used fruitfully by any historian, since it is a perceptible fact that Jesus glorified not himself, but God. Further, by "Son" he referred not to what he had made himself to be, but to what God had made him. By calling himself the Son of God, he derived, with complete assurance, his existence and his will, his vocation and his success, from God.

In appearing before the nation as the One promised in the Scriptures, he revealed that he did not trace God's presence with him from a certain day, but that he carried the idea of predestination within him and that he knew himself to be the one who was foreknown by God, the one to whom God's eye and will had been directed from the beginning. He thereby related God's father-hood to his entire life in unity and completeness and placed the beginning of his sonship at his birth.

Jesus did not, however, describe his share in God merely by the idea of pre-destination. For this idea draws a distinction between the divine thought and the subsequent process, since it understands the preexistent merely as an idea and what happened in history only as its temporal correlate. Jesus, however, described his unity with God as complete. He maintained, not merely regard-ing the divine counsel but even of God himself, that he was the active agent in Jesus' human existence. Jesus did not interpret his life as the mirror image of a divine thought but understood it in its concrete existence as God's work and possession. For his consciousness there were no disjunctions between himself and God.

The completeness of his divine sonship meant for Jesus that he was given unity of will with God so that he knew himself to be the one who did the en-tire will of God with complete obedience. This perfect unity of will, however, was for him one with the perfect unity of essence. This explains why he de-scribed himself as eternal. Jesus did not distinguish between unity of will and unity of essence but rather considered God's will and being as inseparable. Therefore he said that he existed before Abraham was, before the creation of the world; that he had come down from heaven, not from the earth; that he was in heaven even during his earthly life and that he ascended there because from there he had descended; that he was in the Father even while in the world; and that his death would result in his return to the glory which he had had with the Father (cf. John 3:13, 31; 17:5, 24; 8:58; Matt. 28:19).

Through such words, Jesus did not actually distinguish between something temporal and something eternal, something human and something divine. He rather claimed that he, as a unified person, participated in God's eternity. He did not single out individual thoughts as given to him by the Father nor individual decisions as worked in him by God.[7] He also did not use one of the concepts dispersed by gnosticism, that is, that in him a preexistent soul or a heavenly spirit or a divine power was present. Nor did he teach a promiscu-ous commingling with God, as if he felt merged with God, dissolved in God, or had absorbed God into himself. He rather understood God's effect on him

7. This would have led to his application of the concept of inspiration to characterize God's dealings with him. See also p. 129.

in the unity of his person and in his complete humanity in such a way as to view what he was as God's property. He did not thereby ignore the human condition; he had his origin by birth in time (John 18:37). Jesus did not transpose his "flesh" into heaven. Nevertheless, he regarded the life that was his nature and possession not as having come into being, but as eternal, because he belonged to God and lived in God. His claims went no further. We have no dominical statement transmitted that is designed to explain how his eternity and his birth counterbalance one another and how the temporal and historically conditioned could at the same time be eternal. Much less did he create formulas designed to clarify his relationship to God in his eternal glory.

Everyone understands why the verdict has prevailed that the statements made by the apostles regarding the eternal existence of Jesus were an exaggeration of his divine sonship, originating according to the pattern of myth. This myth is said to have been spawned by the desire for a God who would appear among humans. It is presumed that the disciples wished to strengthen faith in Jesus by this device while in fact they damaged recollection of him greatly, since they thus introduced into his portrayal a mystery that rendered the reconstruction of his history impossible.[8] In our judgment regarding the apostles' account we must, however, grant no place for any desire but the historical, which is directed only toward the facts and which poses no requirements whatsoever regarding how readily understandable these facts are to us. The hope is groundless that, after rejecting the statements of all disciples—of Matthew, of John, of Paul—and thus of the entire first generation of Christians, we will still be able to arrive at a "historical" knowledge of Jesus. In any case, this much is clear: John's account of the eternal Christ is not to be subsumed under the judgment that he concocted the report himself according to his own religious desires, because he sets Jesus' statement regarding his own eternity in relation to the reasons that caused Jesus' rejection by Capernaum and Jerusalem. Since Jesus associated himself with God so completely, Israel rejected him and his disciples believed in him. On this alone John predicates the entire weight of blame that Jesus bore. Does it make sense that John would place Jerusalem's guilt in the fact that she rejected a notion that John falsely ascribed to Jesus? It should not be doubted that it was indeed John's conviction that Jesus confessed himself to be the one who had come from above. Moreover, John was not alone in this opinion but had, as the Epistles show, the support of the entirety of primitive Christendom.

The disciples remained faithful to Jesus' statements regarding his divine sonship in that they never link the divine commission in which his work was grounded merely with his later accomplishments and destiny. They rather claimed that this commission had been granted to him through his birth. By birth, his disciples maintained, he is Lord over God's people and God's Son. This was their claim in presenting his birth as the preexistent one's entrance

8. In terms of literary criticism, this reasoning proceeds as follows: a teacher who falsely claimed the name of John incorporated Pauline Christology into an older tradition; the ending of Matthew is a foreign addition to that Gospel; and Luke 1 originated only after apostolic times.

into his human form of existence, as well as in describing his conception as the creative work of the Holy Spirit in his virgin mother. Other portrayals of the Christ than those that saw in his birth the process in which the divine work of grace occurred are not found in the New Testament.

If Jesus had been given a mystical and thus dualistic piety that related God's love to his "soul" while excluding his body and nature from communion with God, regarding the external course of his life as religiously inconsequential, we would, of course, need to separate everything said by the Christmas stories about Jesus' origins entirely from Jesus' own consciousness. Jesus, however, did not receive this kind of piety through his divine sonship but consistently placed himself with his entire being, body and soul, his internal life and his nature, into dependence upon God and devoted to his service. Therefore his divine sonship did not lead him into an asceticism that fought the body, and therefore he did not think of continuing to live as a glorified soul after his crucifixion but longed for resurrection that would transpose him comprehensively into complete communion with God in both body and soul. We know by this outcome how he conceived of the beginning of his divine sonship. It began by God giving him a body, just as it is completed by God restoring the body to him.

The suggestion that Jesus would have considered it a violation of his morality if the gracious act by which God gave him sonship had occurred already at his birth is also totally out of place in a historical analysis of his life. For the judgment that he would in that case no longer have himself to thank for his noblest deeds, because his personal accomplishment would have to be chalked up to mere physical cause and therefore be devalued, applies the very concept of liberty that Jesus rejected. He did not admire himself as the creator of his own life and will, least of all when he considered his relationship with the Father. He stood before God as one who received and took shape as God granted, not as one who bestowed gifts on himself. It was only from this dependence that the capacity for his own activity arose, albeit, of course, in personal perfection such that he put a genuine will into the service of his Father with complete love and without interruption, with the profound conviction that his communion with the Father was of a piece with the integrity of his will.

The firmness and completeness of that dependence are, however, by no means to be distanced from Jesus' consciousness, however one may conceive of its mediation, whether it was only spiritual or also physically conditioned, whether it originated in his birth or was realized only later. Under no circumstances is that quality of religious genius that elevates itself into divine sonship a concept that can be applied to Jesus. If Jesus had declared his body and his humanity merely to be an "appearance" by means of a gnostic, docetic doctrine of preexistence, the concept of eternity that Jesus bore in himself as a component of his sonship would have ruled out the reception of his sonship by birth. Jesus' thinking, however, was totally closed to such a concept. A look back to his birth as the beginning of his body and his earthly life was an essential part of his consciousness and was never extinguished or replaced by the concept of preexistence. This concept always gave rise to the question how Jesus' earthly, human life had originated. On the basis of his eternal communion with God, this question could only receive the answer that it had originated with God, just as it now consisted in God.

Likewise, the thought of the creative process that gave him the beginning of his earthly life did not contradict his concept of eternity as if the former had been superfluous in the light of the latter, constituting merely its repetition. For by the concept of eternity he expressed what he now and always is with the Father. He expressed how completely God was united with him, even now in his earthly life, which formed the basis for his exaltation as the Christ. All this was never expressed simply by the account of *how* he came to be. It always required an additional declaration that expressed *what* the one whom God had brought into being is by virtue of his relationship to God.

Of these two statements, neither was merely the repetition of the other, nor did either evolve merely through reciprocal conceptual development. If they originated with Jesus, they required facts to ground them: the statement regarding his conception called for a tradition regarding the process through which he came into existence; the assertion of preexistence, the fact of his communion with the Father that he now experienced within. Metaphysical issues—whether his being in the absolute sense of eternal existence would rule out his becoming; whether his becoming in the realism of his conception would rule out his being—are not to be intermingled with the observation of the history and the thoughts of Jesus. If his experiences gave him both convictions, then the metaphysical problem arising from these twin truths did not disturb him. Then he bore both in such a way that they mutually supported each other, because both made his divine sonship understandable according to their reality and completeness. The first truth did this by revealing that he came into being, with the full complement of natural attributes, as God's work; the second, by revealing that he received his entire internal life from God.

While Jesus described his birth as miraculous with the solemn words by which he called himself the eternal Son, his words fall short of depicting the kind of miracle he considered it to be. One may ask whether Jesus could not have conceived of the divine activity in connection with the natural mediation so that it did not nullify it but rather was executed through it. Was it not possible for Jesus to recognize in God the giver of his life without the names of father and mother losing for him their natural significance? This thought has received great power owing to the miracle that we prefer to avoid and also because the removal of the normal male function in the conception of Jesus presents itself as a crude bodily dramatization of the divine "Son" concept, a dramatization that distorts the metaphorical element in that concept by relating it in terms of a natural event. Postulating a miracle, it is clear, was never the result of a thought process in Jesus' mind. In looking back to his beginnings, he did not dream or speculate. It is just as certain, however, that he made miracle, together with the messianic aim, a consistent and essential component of his thoughts, and that he considered his sonship and his messianic office to have been revealed only when God worked that which was new and wonderful. If we remove every miraculous element from his beginning days, so that his public ministry follows an unknown youth, then the notion of miracle still crops up in his history later with his claim to messianic prerogative and capacity. Then, however, his claim will more easily yield to the historian who is all too eager to assign to it a dark, sickly color.

3. The Son of David

Prophecy transferred the kingdom that would bring the people of God to fulfillment to a descendant of David. This was no burden to Jesus, since the tradition was present in his family that it belonged to the house of David. Admittedly, the effort to make this clear by way of a genealogy failed, since the two ancestral tabulations included in the Gospels contradict each other. That Jesus himself had a part in this tradition, however, is apparent by the fact that he committed himself to the designation "Son of David" with the assurance that God would fulfill his promise in him. For the ancestors and the father of Jesus, however, a mystery still lay over the promise given to their line. This mystery was concealed by the future and remained completely impenetrable as far as God's highest grace, which brings the world to completion, is concerned.

While the narrative repeated by Luke lingers with Jesus' mother, who received her high calling in the obedience of faith, Matthew tells of the father and how surprising his share in the great divine work was for him. The miracle happening in his fiancée induced him to break his engagement, and he entered into marriage with Mary only in obedience to special divine direction. Thereby the Evangelist removes all self-made, presumptuous plans from Jesus' beginning. The child on which the lofty mission rests is put into a circle that preserved with living hope the promise given to the nation and his own family. Jesus' family, however, did not derive any self-exalting claims for itself from the promise nor use it to try to lever itself beyond its humble circumstances.

There is a deep connection between Jesus' ministry and the infancy narrative owing to the fact that natural and historical relations are not destroyed through the miracle. What significance, one may ask, did father and brothers and an inheritance (ostensibly established by an essentially uncertain genealogy) derived from David have for one who was generated by the Spirit? After all, his life was put onto a virtually supernatural plane through the miracle at his birth. Jesus' concept of God, however, rendered such a use of miracle forever impossible. For he never understood God's supremacy over the world as an antithesis against it, much less as contradictory to Scripture. What God does in the sending of the Christ is firmly linked with his preceding activity.

For this reason it is part of the Christmas story in both of its forms that Mary is chosen to be the mother of the Christ because she was the fiancée of a son of David. Thus the creative act that makes the Christ the Son of God unites with the fulfillment of the promise of the Son of David, and Jesus, when he was addressed as the Son of David, acknowledged his Davidic descent, confirming such pleas (e.g., Mark 10:47) by responding to them. Just as his Davidic heritage was not minimized by his exercise of lordship at God's right hand, so he did not deny his mother and brothers because he was the Son of the Father, descended from heaven. For he knew himself placed into these relationships by his Father. The rift between him and them originated only in the word of repentance and because of the cross.

4. The Anticipation of Elijah

Apart from the announcement of the Promised One, no other prophetic word had so strong an effect on the nation as Malachi's statement that before the great day of God Elijah would come. He would prepare for the divine work that the coming king would have to carry out. The Jewish people looked eagerly for Elijah's appearance, since it would visibly indicate the onset of the age to come. But even this aspect of messianic hope did not constitute an obstacle for Jesus. For his birth was that of a child called to prophetic activity.

In its treatment of the Baptist, too, the narrative preserved by Luke is grounded upon the assurance of God's rule, which knows the final outcome and assigns to the one called by John his work already at birth. Later the Baptist's ministry drew on inspirations that gave him the inner certainty he needed for it, and John the Evangelist expressed this strongly by denying any acquaintance on the part of the Baptist with Jesus, maintaining that the Baptist had acted only on the basis of the certainty he received by inspiration (John 1:33).

By adding the Lucan narrative, however, it becomes clear again that no mystical, ahistorical, and anatural conception of God's relation with his messengers originated in Jesus' proximity. The narrative is not based on any doubt regarding the clarity and certainty of the prophetic events. It maintains, however, that the events through which God's revelation is carried out do not occur merely in the realm of the soul but shape the entire history of the one called, including its external circumstances. God's rule does not express itself merely by moving the soul through a vision at a given point in time but rather by preparing the person and the destiny of its servants with everything that is important for it. Therefore the Baptist grew up in a way that he was equipped for his vocation.

Since the Baptist is given to his parents only at a time when their advanced age robbed them of any hope for a boy, his birth is described as a special act of divine grace. This grace, however, touches not only the parents, but the entire nation, since every member of the community's share in God is bound entirely to what is granted to the community. Thus the narrator looked back to the Old Testament accounts of the births of Isaac, Samson, and Samuel, who were also born by virtue of a special divine promise. For in the same way that God's rule was revealed among the fathers, the thoughts emerge by which his activity is interpreted in the present. That the Baptist was thereby elevated above that which was otherwise expected for pious Jews resulted from his participation in the messianic work. He is therefore not understood as a teacher, nor as merely a prophet enabled by illumination to speak God's word to the community. Here the man himself is God's gift, because by his activity he is to renew the condition of the community.

Since the messianic time has its characteristic in the fact that God's gracious and marvelous works are now taking place, its beginning consists in the fact that God gives life to the one who will serve him with word and deed in the revelation of his rule. Attention is drawn, however, only to the fact that God made the Baptist the instrument of his grace and granted to him the message of his kingdom. By contrast, how he received an eye for Israel's sin, how he became the enemy of Pharisaism, how he gained those convictions that separated him from the entire community and made him a preacher of repentance—none of this is explained by the sources' glance back at the Baptist's origins. The account sees in the Baptist's assurance regarding God's work the causal factor that determined his entire ministry. It also resulted in his preservation from evil and his opposition against sinful Israel. Here we can draw connecting lines to Jesus by virtue of the fact that he, too, understood the call to repentance to be gospel and placed neither the Baptist's nor his own vocation into the exposure of sin and proclamation of judgment. He placed it rather in the service of God's wisdom that reveals his greatness and grace (Matt. 11:19).

John's recent history connects with the established heritage of the Jewish nation in that he is given to a priest and announced to that priest in the temple as he carried out the incense sacrifice of the morning while those gathered in the temple court tarried in prayer. Here it becomes evident what seemed to the Jews to be its most magnificent property among all its possessions: the temple, which guaranteed to it God's presence and grace. It likewise authorized it to pray to God with confidence for the sake of the temple. This assessment of the temple comes to light again and again in Jesus' ministry. It towers as the magnificent sacrament that provides communion with God for the nation, everything that otherwise distinguishes this nation from all others. This special value of the temple is not based on the fact that the sacrifices or the feasts or the expertise in the Law were connected with it but rather that it is "the house of prayer" (Matt. 21:13; Luke 19:46; John 2:17). Thus the priest being stricken dumb brings a serious claim to light, a claim that God's work directs toward all associated with it. They have the obligation of subjecting themselves to the divine will in quiet and complete obedience, free from doubt or objection. Faith fully devoted to God, faith that waits for his work, turns out from the very beginning to be the right attitude for those who have a part in Jesus' earthly life. Thus expression is given to the rubric under which Jesus subsumes his entire activity.

Subsequent to the encounter of the two mothers and after John's birth, the first proclamation of the Christ takes place through his father's prophetic word. This proclamation praises the salvation given to the nation by his arrival. By the fact that the women are not merely passive observers of the events, the beginning of a movement becomes evident, a movement that Jesus continued through his activity and that came to a conclusion in the community of the apostles. The barrier that had formerly separated the woman from God's service falls. Of course, she had long participated busily in the synagogal community, but only in a secondary capacity, since only the man was considered to be fully subject to the Law, while the woman pursued her niche in worship as best she could. Her inalienable right in the community consisted in her motherly function. Since this, however, reached its highest significance in the fulfillment of community, and since now those two sons are born through whom God's rule is revealed, women, too, are called in a special way to testify to the divine grace, a testimony that never again becomes extinct in the community.

However close the connections are that relate these narratives to Jesus' work, they also contain features that point to the religious mood that preceded Jesus' work. Neither in Jesus' words nor in the community's behavior does one find the notion that a divine word is particularly holy and confirmed when the messenger is Gabriel. The conviction consistently accompanied Jesus that the heavenly host participated fully in his earthly ministry. He knows these heavenly beings to be near as spectators in all he does, as the bringers of the help and gift that his word of blessing grants to the people (John 1:51; Luke 15:7, 10; Matt. 18:10; Luke 16:22). The singling out of an individual angel, however, and the strengthening of confidence through the use of an angelic name is completely missing in Jesus' words. In Matthew, it is the dream that provides the means by which Jesus' parents receive divine guidance, and this stands in connection with thoughts rooted in the Jewish community. If the soul is separated by sleep from the body and the world, heavenly beings can approach it and grant to it the prophetic dream. Later, however, this concept disappears completely, both in the portrayal of Jesus and in the instruction he gave to his disciples. The sign punishing unbelief, too, corresponds nicely with the deep sincerity with which Jesus laid the claim on all that God must be believed. Yet there is no similar event in the later stages of the accounts of Jesus' life.

5. Nazareth and Bethlehem

According to Luke, Jesus' mother lived in Nazareth. This is confirmed by the Matthean narrative, which says that the parents settled with the child in Nazareth when the turmoil during Archelaus's reign rendered residence in Judea dangerous. Little Nazareth was not far from the southern part of the Galilean hill country that rises above the plain of Jezreel. We possess ancient data regarding that region since we have preserved Josephus's account of his activity in Galilee as a leader of the uprising against the Romans in the winter of A.D. 66–67. Many of the events at that time occurred in the neighborhood of Nazareth, for the capital of Jewish Galilee, Sepphoris, was located in close proximity north of Nazareth. Nazareth, however, is never mentioned in Josephus's account. It was so small that it did not achieve any significance in the Galileans' struggle against the Romans.

Nevertheless, the place was called a "city" in Galilean terminology. This indicates that the village was not the property of a single landlord but inhabited by free people. Apart from the little houses that were crowded closely together, a spring flowed from the foot of the mountain slope, which explains why a settlement was established at that location. East of the village rises the well-rounded peak of Mount Tabor, which was at that time the location of a fortress, and from the southwest Mount Carmel looks over the wide plain that was in Greek rather than Jewish hands. The Galilean villages, on the other hand, were inhabited during Jesus' time exclusively by Jews, and places of prayer were everywhere. In each location, worship proceeded according to Pharisaic principles.

Since the basis of the messianic kingdom in the ancient kingdom of Jerusalem was given expression in prophecy and in popular expectation by the fact that Bethlehem was connected with the birth of the Christ, it became a severe hindrance for Jesus' ministry that he was a Nazarene (John 1:46; 7:41, 52). The Jews' resistance against the church took the form of its persistent effort, ostensibly in the name of his own people, to remind everyone of Jesus' provenance from Nazareth. For Jesus' disciples, however, no offense was created by calling them "Nazarenes." For both narratives regarding Jesus' birth claim that, while Nazareth became his home, Jesus had nevertheless been born in Bethlehem. According to the Lucan account, it was owing to the tax legislation of the emperor and the decree of the official who administered the production of tax lists in Syria that Jesus' birth occurred in Bethlehem. Thus what was a major offense for every zealot-minded Jew became the means through which the prophetic word was fulfilled.

Matthew, on the other hand, did not place the Roman ruler but the Jewish king next to the newborn Christ, since Herod's wild, boundless craving for power, seeking the latter as an end in itself, stood in an irreconcilable contrast to the rule of God that provided Jesus with the framework for his activity. Thus the profound struggle Jesus entered the moment he began his ministry became immediately apparent. Thereby also a fundamental basis for Jesus' entire behavior is revealed. Jesus separated his kingly aim entirely from the power that the Herodians admired and possessed. Nevertheless, he went his way without fear. God protected his son from even a ruler as terrifying as Herod and later called him back to Israel after forced flight to Egypt.

At his birth Jesus is designated as the Christ in such a way that the first worshipers are led to him, as befits the messianic office's relation to the community. His first witnesses are the heavenly ones. Here it becomes evident how much heavenly beings meant for Jesus and for his disciples in the formula "heavenly kingdom." These beings did not come between God and the people nor between the Father and the Son. It is, however, an essential aspect of the glory of God's rule that it unites the heavenly with the earthly. The end of Jesus' earthly ministry unites harmoniously with signs that attend his birth. They blend together without tension in light of the fact that Jesus enjoyed God's good pleasure, yet placed himself among the repentant; that he knew

God's omnipotence to be with him, yet still suffered patiently without allowing himself to be enticed to forcible expression of power.

While there remains a stark contrast between the prophecies of the Christmas story and the later course of events, Jesus' way to the cross grows out of them in straightforward fashion. The Christ, of course, is revealed as the one to whom God leads the community. Angels call the worshipers, and the Spirit opens Simeon's mouth in the temple. A miraculous star calls the most dangerous opponent of Judaism and Christendom, the magician, to worship. However, it is only shepherds who are invited to seek the Christ. The dawn of the time of salvation is only revealed to a few individuals who long for it with great desire. No popular adulation is engendered. No sign occurs that renders faith unnecessary, nothing that would correspond to the Jewish and human conception of divine rulership. These narratives already contain the sobriety of Jesus' later work. His worshipers are selected according to the principle of complete grace, and indeed in such a way that the national vanity of Israel is not nurtured and that its sin becomes visible.

Likewise, by the fact that the memory of Herod who persecuted the newborn Christ was preserved in the Christian community, the story of Jesus' birth was linked to an Old Testament prototype, since the rescue of the newborn Moses despite the murder of children in Egypt and the rescue of the newborn Jesus despite the murder of children in Bethlehem are parallels. This parallelism was even clearer for the Judaism of Jesus' time than it is for us. For the story of Moses was often told in such a way that the prophecy of an Egyptian who foretold the birth of Israel's savior induced the Pharaoh to kill the Jewish boys,[9] just as in Matthew magicians proclaimed Jesus' birth to Herod and thus gave occasion to the murder of children. The recourse to Old Testament stories, however, was not added to Jesus' story after the fact at a later time but moved all those who had a part in it from the beginning. For every pious person sought the interpretation for all that remained mysterious in his history or that of his people in what Scripture reported concerning the divine governance. For the history of the Christ, it was the history of Moses, the "first redeemer," that served as the key to understanding the history of the one who would now bring complete redemption.

6. Jesus' Life in Nazareth

The circumstances in which Jesus lived until about the thirtieth year of his life did not indicate that he would be the one who was to come. Jesus' father Joseph provided for his family by working as a carpenter, producing the few wooden parts used in houses and other wooden devices. An intrinsic benefit of Jesus' father's trade might have been the fact that it often led him away from his own village so that his son who accompanied him would have re-

---

9. [Here Schlatter apparently has in mind traditions associated with the first chapter of Exodus.]

ceived a clear picture of his own people from the beginning. In the light of the memories and hope surfacing in the Christmas stories, however, it is no longer an impenetrable mystery how it could be that the one who was conscious of a unique sonship in relation to God and who rose to preeminence as the Lord of the eternal community dwelt for years quietly and happily in his own home and village. From God's signs that attended his advent and early life originated the quietness that is able to wait. He knew that he belonged to God with his entire life and being and that he did not have to pave his way himself, since God had put him in that place and would continue to lead him in a way confounding all human thoughts.

That selflessness that remains the characteristic of Jesus' entire work[10] was already given to him through his beginnings. The one conceived by God and led to Nazareth could do nothing for himself. He had to wait for God alone. Of course, a task of inconceivable magnitude resulted from the fact that Jesus, with his solemn limitless anticipation of the messianic future, had to reconcile himself to the stifling constraints of a Galilean carpenter's home. He was sufficient to the task and refrained from any selfish exploitation of the promise he knew was his. Every task creates by its solution qualities that correspond to the task's greatness. The effects that sprang from the challenge Jesus faced can be seen in the fruit of his life: the internalization of his will whereby he gave God his love; the distinction between God and personal well-being, for which deprivation did not disturb communion with God; the freedom from people that did not submit to the judgment and custom of the Jewish community and yet full and true solidarity with that same community; in a word: the victorious strength of the certainty of God that penetrated every movement of his will so that he could neither forsake God nor become disobedient to him. In order to live with messianic self-awareness in Nazareth, Jesus already needed that will which the temptation narrative describes as his own at the beginning of his ministry, a will that did not demand that circumstances suddenly change, a will that did not evade every obstacle by pointing to the divine promise and that longed for lordship only in that way appointed to God. Such a will found firm footing in the things his parents would have told him about his calling.

The only memory preserved from this time is linked with the completion of Jesus' twelfth year (Luke 2:41–52). From that time on he was, according to the interpretation of the Law prevalent in the Jewish community, obliged to the independent fulfillment of the divine commandments. Regarding those who were called early to the service of God (e.g., Samuel and Solomon), tradition held that their activity began after their twelfth year. Therefore his own looked at him with great expectation to see how he would now behave. According to custom, he went with his parents and other Galilean pilgrims to the Passover in Jerusalem. After the end of the festival week, however, he separated from his parents and remained with the

---

10. "Selfless" I call not that person who is nothing and has nothing but the one who is everything he is and does through the one from whom and for whom he lives.

teachers in the temple. There the parents who had left Jerusalem without him found him on the third day. He termed his mother's reproach groundless, since an inner urge drew him to that which pertained to his father. His behavior shows that he lived in the Jewish community in a loving manner, receiving from it what nurtured him internally. Its temple, its worship, its Scripture, its teachers were the means whereby the Father was revealed and present to him.

At the same time, however, it is evident that he distinguished himself from the rest of the Jewish community not only through his expectations for the future but through what God gave him for his present state in life. For he did not have a hidden God whom he hoped to find only later but a Father through whom and with whom he lived. Therefore he felt at home amidst what was his Father's possession. For this reason it was not merely the legal commandment that bound him to God. And thus the feast did not terminate for him at the hour when legal duty had ended. This freed him from custom and also from his parents. He did not, however, use the strength and inwardness of his sonship, which elevated him above worship ordered merely by the commandment, as a pretense for artificiality and iconoclasm, since he did not understand that sonship selfishly but found in it the incentive to obedience that preserves the divine commandment. Precisely for that reason, because he had to be in his father's house and because he could not part from him, he did not destroy his relationship with his parents but returned with them to Nazareth.

The account shows with what force repentance arose in those who knew Jesus, not because he acted as a moralist and polemicist—this the boy did as little as later the man—but because his behavior had such a piercing, illuminating effect that his own became conscious of their poverty through his union with God. We hear nothing of any of the additional events that filled his youth. There is only the single conflict with his parents at the pivotal point of how he and they understood true worship. The narrative thereby draws attention to the painful suffering that began early and pervaded Jesus' entire life. Even his parents did not know what the Father was for him despite their own relationship with God. In his central longing he ran up against an opposition that hindered communion with all those around him. The profit he derived from this later showed itself in his ability to suffer, an ability that made him open to pain without it overcoming him. He had the ability to suffer earnestly and at the same time to preserve the joy that originated in him precisely because of the manner in which he bore duress. Such an ability can only be acquired.

That he was capable of preserving his divine sonship in Nazareth shows that he steered clear of all gnostic, dualistic, or otherwise egoistic thoughts. He did not derive from that sonship any opposition to the natural order, nor did he opt out of any of the pressure it placed on him. Work for his family did not seem to him a defilement or weakening of his communion with God but rather its proof.

In one point alone he deviated, as far as we have records, from cultural expectation in a significant way: by not entering into marriage. The fact that the Jewish community was based on the entirety of its people rendered marriage a duty for everyone. Delaying marriage until later in life was discouraged. In a well-ordered household there lived not only the sons and the still unmarried daughters but also the young wives of the sons (Matt. 10:35). The decision made by Jesus in this respect certainly stems from his religious understanding. It is illumined by the word used to instruct his disciples regarding the propriety of renouncing marriage. According to Jesus, the one who made himself a eunuch for the sake of God's rule renounced marriage legitimately (Matt. 19:12). In this as in his boyhood debut in the temple his special vocation was revealed.

7. Jesus Foregoes Rabbinic Training

Even in his more mature years subsequent to the death of his father, Jesus did not seek acceptance into the rabbinate, although faith in Scripture connected him with it. He was a member of the Jewish community for the sake of the Scriptures, because the community stood under their direction. Therefore the community's worship was also his. He prayed its prayer with all the others. The sermon delivered by the community also gave him guidance. Even when the rabbinate had rejected him and he went to the cross, he conceded that it sat on the seat of Moses and that its word had to be heeded and put into practice by the community (Matt. 23:2).

The religious communion, indissoluble and complete, which connected him with the rabbinate, was characterized by the fact that for both Jesus and the rabbi, the doctrine of inspiration was normative in their interaction with Scripture. Thereby the origin and the aim of Scripture were interpreted according to the experience of the prophets, and the ministry of the Spirit was connected not merely with the word spoken by the prophet to his contemporaries but equally with his book through which he speaks to all generations. Likewise, as the rabbi read the Scriptures with the confidence that it made God and his will known, Jesus, too, heard God in the Scriptures and said with all the pious that their authors "spoke by the Holy Spirit" (Matt. 22:43). Therefore he answered the question of what one should do in the same way as everyone else: one should do what Scripture commands. And he answered the question what God will one day do for the world as did everyone else: he will do what the Scriptures promise.

From this it was immediately and clearly visible that Jesus did not produce his own religious language, just as he did not seek to gain insights that surprised through their novelty. Jesus rather produced his thoughts by using the convictions current in the Jewish community, and he spoke using the language already present there. Further, he did not merely participate in the use of religious language to the extent that it was already provided through Scripture. Without erecting a dichotomy between the past and the present, between the Holy Book and the nation, he took up within himself thoughts currently alive, even if they had originated only after the closing of the canon through subsequent intellectual labor.[11]

Therefore he also proceeded in the interpretation of Scripture like his contemporaries with whom he knew himself to be one when he applied Psalm 110 or Daniel's Son of Man to the Promised One or when he saw the saving power of faith illustrated by the brazen serpent. His proofs for the resurrection and for his right to heal on the Sabbath from the Law, the defense of his divine sonship from Psalm 82:6 and of his liberty from 1 Samuel 21:6 resemble the procedure of the teachers of the Law in the manner in which he drew analogies (Matt. 22:31; 12:3–5; John 7:22; 10:34; 3:14).

Nevertheless, he remained separate from the rabbinate and did not join a master as his disciple. This is apparent from the fact that he entirely avoided everything that could be considered "formal expertise in the Law." There is no tradition of an allegorical interpretation by Jesus, no interpretation on the basis of the use of the same word in several passages of Scripture, or similar artful techniques employed in rabbinic scriptural interpretation. His use of the Bible expresses the conviction that it communicates God's will clearly and that it does not receive its profundity through the art of its interpreters.

He did not lack the intelligence that would have enabled him to become a "disciple of the wise" and to enter into competition with the rabbinate. In sayings like the ones contained in the Sermon on the Mount one notes a remarkable intellectual capacity. The same holds true for the parables. Was not his inward possession, his consciousness of sonship, the strongest incentive to strive for knowledge? In Christendom, faith in the Christ immediately functioned as a powerful stimulus for intellectual labor, because, with the Christ, the final and highest were present, and the question of how what one possessed really would be the complete and eternal was immensely stretching for thought.

In Jesus, however, the effort to form a theory that would describe and explain God's work never took shape. His attention remained directed toward God's will, since he possessed God's sonship by doing it. He did not put the acquisition of knowledge in the place of obedience and love but persistently advocated the primacy of the will for our relationship with God. Unity with God is achieved by the fact that the person desires God's will, and desires it

---

11. The words current in the synagogue are found equally in Jesus' call to repentance and in his proclamation of God's rule. Conversion, to place faith in him, of little faith, good works, to gather treasures in heaven, the righteous who do not need conversion, debts, forgiveness of debts, to justify, to lead into temptation, offense, to confess one's sins, to make oneself lowly or exalted, light, truth, love, to do the truth, to love one another, to walk, our Father in heaven, the Father, kingdom of heaven and of God, to inherit God's kingdom, God's sons, God's will, to do the will of God, the hour, in God's name, to hallow God's name, from above, this world, the world to come, the anointed one, disciples, to follow as disciples, the Holy Spirit, the Scriptures, to fulfill the Scriptures, God's community, the house of God, the world, the nations of the world, the prince of the world, the accuser, the angels of the accuser, paraclete, judgment day, the last day, the resurrection of the dead, eternal life, paradise, the judgment of hell—all of these are phrases already current in Jewish piety.

in such a way that he does it. Out of this grows the assurance of God (John 7:17).

He thus forfeited greatness and personal self-glorification. The rabbinate taught by its example that the one who let his intellectual sharpness sparkle and his memory shine gained mastery over the community. But Jesus subsumed this self-centered use of knowledge under the rubric of "sin." The rabbis "spoke from themselves" and therefore also for themselves. This he could not do. His obedience toward the Father was one with his love, and this made him selfless.

8. The Rejection of Pharisaism

The distance that Jesus kept from the rabbinate presupposes that he was also always, and from the beginning, separated from the Pharisees. The Judaism of his day comprised various religious groups, sects among which the federation of the "separated ones" (Pharisees) was the mightiest. It had its origin in the extension of protocol developed for the priests in the temple to the community at large. This protocol was presented to all truly spiritually minded persons as the level of perfection they should strive to attain. The rabbinate was closely linked with this movement. Both of the movement's characteristics, the Pharisaic with its ethical focus and the scholarly stress of the rabbis, strengthened each other. The zeal for the Law produced the zeal for theological study, which in turn received its direction through the Pharisaic maxim that the fulfillment of the Law was the nation's most important concern and would determine its destiny.

For this reason the rule of "sages" over the Jewish community brought about their subjugation under the Pharisaic norms. Jesus kept his distance from Pharisaism, although he was connected with it in a firm commonality, not merely through isolated peripheral similarities but through fundamentally congruent convictions. The ruling conviction of the Pharisee was that the Scriptures called Israel to obedience. For Jesus, religion was the exercise of obedience, and to this aim he devoted his entire work and life. He did not make the perfect correctness of his thoughts the most important concern but elevated only three theses to dogmas, principles that without fail were to be heeded in the community: the uniqueness of God, the inspiration of Scripture, and the resurrection of the dead. Apart from this he allowed his thoughts liberty so that for many religious questions no clear decision could be reached or was desired. In his view, Scripture was not holy because it contained a theory of God, but rather because it proclaimed God's commandment to the community. Scripture is "law," and the doing of it was the community's highest priority. All teaching and learning exercised within the community were subordinated to this purpose.

This impulse of intense piety was consistently found not only among those who had contact with Jesus but also in Jesus himself. It was his firm possession and provided a firm guideline both for his behavior toward God and for his work in the community. His religion, too, consisted in the exercise of obedience, since he did not know himself to be the Son because he knew God's thoughts or because he was united with him through a certain power but because he did his will. Without the development and the power of Pharisaism, therefore, Jesus' history is inconceivable. This history presupposes that the community had learned to ask what it was required to do for God and how it should give him its will.

Pharisaism attempted to do this with great resolve. It considered Scripture to be the revelatory means through which God made his will known to the community and did not try to experience that will through an inner, subjective process but rather consulted Scripture at every turn to find information regarding proper conduct. Scripture was supplemented by hallowed custom, the "tradition of the elders," which was viewed as its interpretation and completion. How one should read and interpret Scripture was expressed by the principle of obedience: Scripture gives God's explanation of what one should do. All other holy things venerated by Pharisaism are derived from the sanctity of Scripture. The temple had such great sacramental significance because God had ordered it to be built in the Law. The priest is indispensable because God appointed him. The Pharisee approached the altar not with a sacrificial theory that sought to describe the inner meaning and effectiveness of the sacrifice; God commanded it and God demands obedience, therefore one approaches the altar. The laws of purification led him to scrupulous consciousness. An inner justification, however, was not necessary. He could even dispute that such an inner rationale existed. But this did not change the prescribed conduct: God commanded it. Venerable tradition, too, received its authority from the fact that it aided in the fulfillment of the biblical commandments and served to authenticate them.

This also produced a commonality between Jesus and Pharisaism. Jesus, too, both for himself and for all who asked, answered the question, "What should I do?" with "Keep the commandments," and "Have you not read . . . ?" His heavenly sending, likewise, which elevated him above the community, was grounded in Scripture and was therefore relevant and binding for the Pharisee as well. There was no dispute between Jesus and the Pharisees regarding whether God would send the Christ or not and whether the Jewish community needed him or not. There was no doubt concerning this, for Scripture said it. The dispute between them pertained to the question of whether Jesus' person and work were what Scripture promised and God willed or not.

For Pharisaism, religion became one and the same with the conduct of one's life. It did not treat personal conduct as a special function that stood beside other legitimate concerns; it regarded the practical service of God as comprising the whole scope of human duty. To obey God was the Pharisee's central desire and controlled his entire activity. Therefore his rules extended to the greatest and to the smallest matters. Their primary content, of course, pertained to the explicit commandments of Scripture. But to those was added a legal and moral system that ordered the entirety of life. The principle of obedience resulted in the fact that here no gradation between important and unimportant was admissible. Obedience rendered everything important. The most important thing of all, the holy city and the temple, were meaningless apart from obedience. All else was dispensable if the Jews had to be deprived of them in God's providence. Again, even the smallest thing received absolute value by the fact that with its accomplishment obedience to God took place.

Jesus likewise did not exercise his religion merely in breaks from the other pursuits of life but demanded from himself and from everyone that every thought and action be done for God. He knew nothing of a separation between religion and morality and therefore also nothing of a distinction between holy and profane time or between holy and profane love. He equated the two great commandments, one requiring love for God and the other love for others, since service rendered to others belongs to the service of God, while love for God rules everything. Thus Jesus ordered his behavior by the rule to which Pharisaism subjected itself as well. Luke did not distort the historical situation when he noted that the Pharisee answered Jesus' question regarding God's commandment in precisely the same way Jesus did (Luke 10:27; cf. Mark 12:32–34).

The struggle of the human will and its activity against God were felt deeply by Pharisaism. It was controlled by "the fear of sin." The pious are "those who fear sin." This thought ruled its entire practice. The purpose of the Law lies in its function of keeping Israel from sin. Therefore it is the obligation of the faithful to fight off sin in a persistent struggle. From this resulted a penitent attitude, one that acknowledged the need for forgiveness. And thus it was that the motif of justification moved to center stage. The description of typical religious outlooks reflected in the parable of the tax-collector and the Pharisee is confirmed by the Jewish sources. The one who is as guilty as a tax-collector must stand in the distance. The pious one judges him because God judges him. For the pious one, the aim is for God to "justify" him: he approaches the altar to receive justification. Not the question which of the two was justified before God was the new element in that narrative but only the answer given by Jesus. The Jewish community had learned the question in the school of Pharisaism. Jesus' verdict regarding the nation's condition as expressed in his preaching of repentance followed the Pharisaic train of thought very closely.

Pharisaism considered resurrection to be the future aim and fought for it so successfully that it succeeded in making it a dogma throughout the Jewish community. It rejected the immortality doctrine of the Hellenistic theologians. The Pharisee was not concerned with determining the qualities of the substance of the soul and of its future destiny. Pharisaism's distinctive is not a theory of the nature and the destinies of the soul but a willful, personal longing for "eternal life." God's kingdom will appear through God's creation of the community whose members live eternally. To belong to this number constitutes the personal hope of the individual. Reentry into the community will come about through resurrection. Whoever denies this therefore destroys the hope of Israel. The Pharisees abhorred those as heretics who disputed the resurrection.

This description of the human aim that transcends earthly life and gives the individual an eternal destiny deeply influenced messianic expectations. The portrayal of the Christ received a content that differed significantly depending on whether only a change in one's earthly circumstances was sought or whether one strove for the gain of eternal life, with hope directed toward that state in which sin and death would be no more. Jesus' promise, too, is based on the conviction that God's coming regal exercise of power would do away with not only sin but also death. It would consist not merely in his forgiveness but also in his bestowal of life.

The fact that resurrection leads to the final state of the community implied the view that death would not cause a person's destruction. For this, Pharisaism had the two terms "paradise" ("Garden of Eden," the place where God rewards the pious) and "gehenna" (the place where God's judgment falls on the godless). The relation of these terms to the doctrine of resurrection was not sharply established. In Jesus' time, one may still have thought of gehenna predominantly in terms of the eschatological judgment. At any rate, a person's destiny after death was no longer conceived of as some shadowy state. The age to come would rather reveal divine retribution for a person's work on earth. Jesus shared a closely similar hope. When he phrased his promise to the one who died next to him on the cross, "Today you will be with me in paradise," he expressed a thought that was known to the Jewish community from Pharisaism. The same holds true for the rich man who descends into torture after his death (Luke 23:43; 16:23).

Because the common ground shared by Jesus and Pharisaism extended to the core of their piety, he called Pharisaic piety a "righteousness." Compared with his own righteousness, however, he considered it to be small, poor, and weak, and he elevated his disciples above it, because it could not provide them with a share in God's rule (Matt. 5:20). His separation from Pharisaism was not merely a consequence of the Pharisees' rejection of his claim to be king, although their rejection of it completed the break, but it rather originated in his own behavior, which necessarily reached back beyond his public activity and even included his life in Nazareth. He therefore revealed his separation from the Pharisees by his very first step of associating with the Baptist and by joining those who were baptized by him. For by this act he smashed the Pharisaic ideal of holiness.

Since Pharisaic piety venerated the divine Law as the authority to which the Jewish community is subject, it deemed it necessary, in order to be obedient to God, to break fellowship with those who had sinned. The pious must put them to shame, because they would break the Law if they remained in fellowship with transgressors. They would violate God's honor if they did not distance themselves from sinners. This means of effecting and proving personal righteousness was rejected by Jesus when he desired baptism, because he thereby did what the guilty must do. This establishes that he had not pursued Pharisaic righteousness earlier in the course of contact with his fellow-villagers.

After becoming one of the baptized, he did not conduct his relation to the nation according to Pharisaic orders. By beginning his ministry only subsequent to baptism, he also distinguished his behavior toward God entirely from that of the Pharisees. Because the Law controlled their concept of God, they strove diligently to elevate themselves to God through the exercise of their own will. Jesus' inaugural experience, however, did not consist in a decision by which he offered himself to God and said, "I am your Son." It rather lay in his hearing of the declaration, "You are my Son." His sonship with God was an essential repudiation of Pharisaic requirements and conjectures, of the transformation of religion into the self-exaltation of man, of a perfectionism by which human beings elevate themselves to communion with God. He devoted his love not to himself but to the Father and did not strive to reveal man's greatness but God's. Therefore his service to God consisted in submitting to the will of God that had become so palpable to him and in following his call. But Jesus did not only assume this posture during his public ministry; it already characterized his conduct in Nazareth.

9. Jesus' Relationship to Hellenism

Beginning with the time when the Ptolemies and the Seleucids had ruled Judaism in Palestine, Judaism was continually exposed to Greek culture. From the end of the fourth century on, the Greek language and custom had penetrated the land with such power that it had in many places completely supplanted the ancient traditions. Around Galilee were now cities that were entirely Greek, some of which administered sizable regions. To the west, the region of Ptolemais bordered Galilee, and on the northern border of Upper Galilee was the region of Tyre. East of the Sea of Galilee were Hippos and Gadara, and Philoteria was located where the Jordan flowed out of the Sea of Galilee. The plain between Mount Tabor and Carmel was in Greek hands, and Scythopolis, the ancient Bethsean, was an entirely Greek city.

Only the pagan cities, however, had accepted Greek customs without resistance. Judaism's religious ties with Scripture had become so strong during Persian rule that it did not forsake the use of the Hebrew Holy Scriptures in worship, and this also strengthened the national language that was related to Hebrew, a Syrian dialect called Aramaic that had come to be used during Persian rule in the entire Near Eastern region. Therefore the Galilean villages became bilingual from the time that the king of Jerusalem, Alexander Jannaeus, conquered them and made them the exclusive possession of Judaism. For contact with the neighboring regions, Greek was indispensable.[12] Among themselves, however, they spoke Aramaic. It was the wish of all spiritually serious Jews to learn the Hebrew text as well.

If a father was faithful to Scripture, he read the holy texts aloud to his son from an early age. The Jewish community supported him in this by instituting everywhere organized instruction for boys. Regarding Jesus, we know that he prayed the Psalms in Aramaic, and that nothing hindered him as a twelve-

---

12. The Gospels indicate use of the Greek Bible, often even when their text is reworked according to the Hebrew text. Whether the reading of the Greek text still occurred in the Galilean communities of Jesus' time is not perfectly clear. Later the Pharisaic movement enforced everywhere the reading of the Hebrew text.

year-old from participating in the instruction given by the teachers of Jerusalem in the temple where the Hebrew text was discussed. Likewise, he was not prevented from entering into discussion with the procurator Pilate with whom only those were able to converse who spoke Greek (Matt. 27:46; Luke 2:46; John 18:33ff.). In all of this Jesus resembled his fellow-countrymen.

Hellenism was a significant factor in Jesus' earthly ministry, since the views Jesus rejected had their origin partly in Greek ways of thought. It was Greek thought that strengthened the tendency to make relationship with God a matter of knowledge and words. Zeal for study and the veneration of teachers that developed in Jerusalem would not have arisen in the form it did without Greek influence. "Teachings" (Talmud) were formulated in Jerusalem because the Greeks had science and thereby induced the Jew to reflect on the content of his teachings on God. In this the leading thinkers of Jerusalem set themselves, however, in conscious opposition to the Greeks, defending the national ideas and their tradition grounded in the Scriptures. At the same time they rejected Stoic concepts of God and a teaching about God that had been transformed into physiology according to the Aristotelian model. They wanted the teachings of Scripture, and those alone. Simply by the fact that Jerusalem's theologians created a different theology than those of Alexandria, they show that they were susceptible to Greek influence. Thus it came to pass that Jesus stood before the "wise," sages who possessed authority over the Jewish community; and thus it was that the entire community sat in the synagogue on the Sabbath and occupied itself with study and discussion. When Jesus praised it as God's magnanimity to have given insight to the weak rather than to the wise, and when he had the courage to be formally untaught despite the prevailing Greek conviction that considered knowledge to be the highest possession attainable, he did not merely confront the rabbinate; he also proved to be no slave of Hellenism.

The Greek had been led by his rational thought to a virtual rejection of the cult, and this resulted in a commonality with the convictions of Jesus, since Jesus, too, received his communion with God not through the existing religious structure but independently of priest and altar. No single word is extant, however, that would give rise to the supposition that he considered Greek thought to be an ally in his attack on the cult. He did not single out animal sacrifice, the temple, or the inherited priesthood from the rest of Judaism as weaknesses that needed to be rendered intelligible by reinterpretation. The value of service in the temple was, for Jesus, secured by Israel's call by God. On the other hand, it is not evident that Jesus marked out Greek thought as a more menacing opponent than other ideas contributing to the unbelieving behavior of the nation. While he did not appropriate Greek ideas, one also does not find in his words polemic against them.

The Jewish community's contact with the Greeks and Greek influence on Jewish culture also contributed to the transformation of piety into the striving for greatness, the desire for honor, and the exhibition of every pious act before the public eye. Once again, Jesus rejected Hellenism in its entirety when he himself willfully remained insignificant, describing the striving for greatness to his disciples as the sin that shut them out of God's kingdom, a sin from which they had to repent. In debunking Pharisaic merit he also dethroned Greek virtue.

Greek culture brought to the Jewish community political alertness and democratic activity. Now everyone shared keen interest in public concerns, and by virtue of the fact that the priest and the teachers stood under public supervision that granted them no prerogatives for which they did not also bear responsibility, there developed effective protection for everyone. Jesus' ministry was a beneficiary of this protection (Matt. 21:26; John 7:44–46; 12:19). The hustle and bustle of the common public life also gave his word a sense of pervasive urgency. The ideal of liberty had been planted in the Jewish community by the influence of the Greeks, and this ideal prepared and supported the freedom Jesus encouraged among his disciples. His reprimanding of self-seeking personal autonomy, however, would be misinterpreted if one understood Jesus merely in the light of the democratic mood of his time. For Jesus spoke out guided by that singular will that was unique to him, and he confronted the democratic use of power no less than that of the rulers.

Nevertheless, the disciples' appropriation of his thought was rendered easier by the fact that the Jewish communities had learned to administer their own affairs and to incorporate all of their citizenry into this administration. At the same time, this development contributed to the severe struggle that Jesus faced, since intense hatred readily resulted from the politics of that time, issuing also in the formation of parties. The Greek hated the Jew, the Jew hated the Greek. The more intense the contact and the dispute with paganism became, the more Jewish confidence transmogrified into fanaticism. The Jew, through a pathological emphasis on his unique status, asserted himself against the pagan world that was in many respects superior to his own. This was also reflected in the inner life of the Jewish community. Strife escalated among its parties. Disputes immediately became matters of life and death. Between Pharisaism and Sadduceeism stood the memory of a vicious civil war, and the struggle between the rabbinic teachers and the high priests was bitter and acrimonious. The contempt with which the Zealots regarded timid members of the Jewish community had already reached the point of unsheathed daggers. To this tattered, hate-filled community Jesus must proclaim God's rule. Once again he confronted a core conviction of Hellenism when he turned the rule "Hate your enemy" upside down and thus elevated his followers completely above the political strife and party dispute.

The fruitful elements added by Greek culture, on the other hand, included the fact that through its influence a discussion about immortality and resurrection had arisen and exercised a public impact. Greek thought contributed to the fact that under the influence of the knowledge of nature immortality was disputed. Yet under Greek auspices the longing for eternal fulfillment also became strong, not merely at the national but also at the individual level. The question of how much of this was derived from the Platonic and Stoic teachings of immortality and how much was taken from Oriental, Persian, or even Egyptian influences is irrelevant for Jesus' ministry, since it is inconceivable that he himself drew on ideas about this subject from regions beyond the immediate milieu of Judaism. It was already an accomplished fact at that time that an individual, in comparison with ancient times, set his sights higher, conceiving of the Jewish community's transfiguration in such a way that the preservation of the individual person was likewise connected with it. Thus Jesus did not need to plant the idea of immortality. The Jewish community had it and was open to a form of kingdom preaching according to which God's rule bestows eternal life on those to whom it is revealed.

Greek science and literature also contributed to the fact that psychological terms by which we account for the details and complexities of our mental state were sharpened and took on a more definitive content. Words designating the internal experience of processes such as faith, truth, love, repentance, sin, guilt, grace, and forgiveness were enriched, since Greek psychology and ethics awakened a heightened perception of internal dynamics. This enhanced self-observation that paid attention to personal sensibilities and clarified the nature of the soul. Not only Greek psychology but also the general development of thought and speech is apparent in what Jesus said. At the same time it is evident that he did not pursue new ideas from Greek sources, nor allow such ideas to have direct influence on him. Vaunted Greek "reason" is in Jesus nowhere to be seen. He did not grant thought a special competence or separate the internal life into a multitude of abilities. For Jesus, our ability to think is very far indeed from being our essential or sole attribute. Likewise, the core concepts of Greek ethics are entirely missing.[13] He did not polemicize against the technical advances used by the Greeks to enhance the external development of life, but he also did not esteem them as a gain of essential significance.[14] He conceived of the inner life as a strong unity, calling its subject according to Old Testament usage "the heart." This he considered not merely nor even predominantly the source of emotions; "the heart" is rather responsible for the formation of thought and volition. The term "soul" he used for that which bears the life principle, while the expression "flesh" designates life's natural basis and limitation in the Old Testament sense. The concept of spirit is enriched by his words only to the extent that it describes the divine activity. Joining spirit with truth, resulting in "spirit of truth," was not the result of Greek influence; the prototype for this idea was given with what was always expected from the divine spirit: he opens the eye and effects knowledge—he is, after all, the one who inspires the prophet. Beside the Old Testament language it was a novelty that now the bodily members had a unified name, "body." Through this a clear expression, "body and soul," was created for the external and internal in the human being. But the limitation inhering in the description of psychological and physiological phenomena, whereby a rift emerges between soul and body, between internal experience and externally effective action, and between the individual and the community, was entirely

13. Where Greek concepts such as idea, virtue, ideal human being, heroes, etc., are used in interpreting Jesus' word, a historically unusable potpourri is the result.

14. Jesus' view of nature, too, does not reveal any Greek influence, either in the way he conceived of the earth or in how he thought of the sun and the stars.

foreign to Jesus. His share in the fruits of the Greek intellectual heritage consisted merely in the fact that the concepts and words at the disposal of religious psychology were more developed in his time than in ancient times.[15]

The richer development of rhetoric, too, which the Greeks cultivated with eagerness, served Jesus as an effective tool. The Jewish community had long been accustomed to receiving instruction through didactic oral presentation. It corresponded to custom when Jesus presented his thoughts to the communities in coherent speech, so that all the Gospels say of individual discourses that they produced changes in the internal lives of the disciples. But here, too, Jesus' distance from Greek thought remained clear and great, because the Greek cultivated artful rhetoric for the sake of aesthetic enjoyment as such, while Jesus never spoke merely for the sake of artistic pleasure but rather transformed his word into the deed through which he combatted evil and brought divine grace to his listeners. With regard to his form of speech, too, as well as with regard to content, he kept himself entirely free from Greek rules and models.

10. The Beginning of God's Rule

Jesus' ministry was preceded by John's appearance before the nation as the herald of a divine message. He told the nation that a decisive alteration of its situation was at hand, one by which God would prove to be its king. John expressed the implications for people's behavior by calling for "conversion" and "repentance."

From the time that Christendom took its view of religion and science from the Greeks, it considered the Baptist's work in the light of the expectation that a new thought or theory appeared in it that offered the Jewish community insights that it had not possessed up to this point. What John set in motion, however, does not confront us with some intellectual's accomplishment serving a theoretical aim but with the deed of a man who had a will, was able to act, and demanded from the people a response—altered behavior toward God. His will was rooted in the certainty that God was at work, accomplishing that which would bring the fulfillment awaited by the nation. Since he wanted to turn its will and renew its practices, John urged the twin imperatives "repent" and "convert" in his preaching, terms that already had a firm hold among the Jewish people. He spoke to them in terms that they possessed and confronted them with aims that were immediately clear to them.

By this, and only by this, his ministry connected firmly with the religious situation and the prevalent messianic hope. Since the Law held firm sway, "good works" were the centerpiece of religion. Not in ideas, teachings, insights, attitudes, or mystical experiences of any kind did the Baptist's contem-

15. From Jesus' words one may name here the following concepts: the will with its clear demarcations from remaining internal proceedings; righteousness and love and their clear distinction; the strong development of the concept of honor; truth with its differentiation from wisdom; ignorance as the lessening of responsibility; faith; doubt; sorrow; hypocrisy; the differentiation between doubt and the refusal to believe and between little faith and unbelief.

poraries find the ingredient that would make the human being pious. The question that occupied all the pious continually was, "What must we do?" This was the subject of deliberation in all gatherings for worship. Therefore the Jewish community does not come to completion through the revelation of new teachings but by God's deed, which renews its condition and which grants to it transformed worship. Inasmuch as the Baptist's work consisted in the announcement of God's rule and the call to repentance, it found its place in the history of Palestinian Judaism as a constituent element of it.

For the pious of Jerusalem, the formula "kingdom of heaven" initially served the purpose of describing God's existing relationship to the nation. They thereby emphasized the special characteristic and the magnificent privilege of their ethnicity by recognizing its difference from "the nations of the world." Jerusalem's teachers said: God has established his kingdom with us through his revelation at Sinai by his word: "I am the Lord your God." Thereby God placed us under his rule, and every member of the community that confesses allegiance to the one God and Lord of Israel acknowledges God's kingdom for himself and for the entire nation.

The Pharisaic movement had made it an obligation for all the pious to confess belief in the one God of Israel morning and evening. The importance of this daily pledge to God was expressed thus: "We thereby take upon ourselves the kingdom of heaven." By the same formula the teachers also described what shape Israel's hope in the coming revelation of God should take. For God's rule is future as long as it is still resisted by humanity. Presently the "kingdom of the earth" still differed entirely from "the kingdom of heaven." For what those rulers "on the earth" accomplished did not bring the people what the heavenly powers possess.[16] When considering the resistance that God's rule encountered, the rabbinate thought especially of the pagan religions, peoples, and rulers. In the endtime, however, all these opposing elements would be overcome. Then God alone would rule, and no foreign power would harm the nation's existence. Then it would receive its complete form by the fact that God would act in victorious power and glory as its king.

By the proclamation of God's rule, the Baptist confirmed the verdict prevalent in the Jewish community regarding the situation prepared for it and the goal given to it. Like others, the Baptist said: God is our king; he will prove to be that because that's who he already is; because he made us his people, he will reveal through us that no one has power over us except him alone. The Baptist's work was based upon the fact that Israel was God's possession. With equal sincerity, however, he also confirmed the verdict that considered the present state of the nation to be in opposition to God's rule. The present situation constituted a danger and an emergency. What God's closeness would provide for Israel was still nowhere to be seen. Now, in John's preaching,

16. Jewish sources commonly used the plural "kingdom of the heavens"; in the same vein we speak here of "heavenly powers." Both expressions allude implicitly to the plethora of spirits who in glory and eternal life were thought to inhabit the various heavenly realms, rendering God's greatness visible there.

however, what God bestowed on the heavenly ones is also manifest on the earth and will become the possession of those who are obedient to God.

Only the Palestinian community, whose leaders were the teachers of Jerusalem, expressed their faith and hope in this way, while the largest part of Greek Jewry had made the concept of "providence" the centerpiece of their piety. Their aim thereby distanced itself from what the Palestinian community longed for. For the concept of "providence" limited God's guidance to the natural side of human life, to the situation that forms us from the outside, to our fate. This was subsumed under God's will and accepted from his hand. By contrast, the personal state of one's life was separated from one's relationship with God and assigned to the realm ruled by the human will that itself cares for these concerns. The one, however, who spoke of God's kingly rule described God's relation to mankind in such a way that it comprised the entire condition of his life, including his will. In confessing God's rule, he expressed his own will to obey God. Therefore it was only the concept of kingdom, not that of "providence," that produced an eschatology. Through providence, nature was given pious consideration. But no completed, eternal goal was forthcoming. The kingdom motif, on the other hand, subjected one's personal life to God, who for the sake of all that is godly wages war against all that is not. As a result, this motif gave rise to the hope that God will one day establish his right and power to rule in such a way that all mankind is subject to him.

Since the thought of divine rule was also linked with the question of what it would accomplish for and in the Jewish community—the protection, happiness, and life it would enjoy by being in God's kingdom—one could also understand the formula "God's kingdom" in relation to the place and the persons among whom God's regal activity reveals itself and creates its salvific results. The Baptist, however, when speaking of God's rule, directed people's view especially and primarily to that which God would do. Owing to its religious content, he used the phrase "heavenly kingdom." He utilized it to stir up spiritual renewal in the community, because this phrase did not refer to a human accomplishment or to Jewish privilege, but gave content to hope placed in God's action. By giving precedence to the proclamation of God's kingdom over all other longings for a glorious future, he protected it against selfish corruption.

Therefore the ministries of the Baptist and of Jesus are obscured when we borrow the phrase "the highest good" from the Greeks in order to interpret the promise of "the kingdom." For with John and Jesus, the heavenly kingdom was not a material good or a state somehow beyond the concrete acts of God and people or a human possession that could be acquired and enjoyed, as if the main thing were what the individual would gain for himself. God's rule was rather his activity that established parameters for the human condition. The "kingdom" did not set itself apart from God as a thing produced by him, just as it was not distinguished from the individual like a good attached to him, but it was God's personal interaction with people, and this in such a way that God determines his communion with them in all the fullness of his divine status. Therefore an obligation to love grew out of the proclamation of the kingdom, while the longing for a "highest good" stood in no clear and necessary contrast to selfish desire.

In fact, the "kingdom," when understood as the highest good, can powerfully entice the selfish will and promise it complete satisfaction. But because the Baptist and Jesus in their proclamation of God's rule did not speak of what the human being needs and desires but of the means by which God reveals himself and shows his greatness, they did not direct themselves to the desire for happiness but issued a call to repentance to the Jewish community that was designed to awaken love. If God reveals himself as king, people receive their aim beyond that which they desire for themselves. They now live no longer for themselves but for God, and indeed for the community God creates. Therefore the message of the kingdom was only understood and believed by those who converted to love.

In accordance with Jewish expectations, the Baptist proclaimed that the execution of judgment would be connected with the revelation of perfect grace. At this point, however, the Jewish concept of God was incomplete, and the teachers of Jerusalem were unable to overcome the uncertainty that confounded religious behavior. All agreed that righteousness was the characteristic of divine activity. There was also no doubt that God's will was to make known his grace; this was a certainty planted in the Jewish community by the Scriptures. But the sentiment that both norms, each inviolable, were in conflict was unavoidable. Contemporary theory contained various attempts to remove the struggle between grace and law as the expression of God's righteousness. It was said that God had two yardsticks, righteousness and mercy, and that he applied either according to his free counsel. Another view was that God punishes through secondary agents while he himself works only that which saves. Such theories, however, reveal only the awareness that grace and Law might stand in conflict; they offered no resolution to the impasse. The Baptist did not address this dilemma with the help of new theories but made it unambiguously clear that God's rule consisted simultaneously in the completeness of the righteousness effected by God and in the perfection of his grace. God's glory would be revealed through both in one unified act, providing fulfillment for the community.

Therefore the Baptist's message involved the proclamation of imminent wrath and impending judgment. But his horizon did not extend beyond Israel. He sought to confront the obstacle still hindering heaven's rule not in paganism, nor in the rule of the Roman emperor, nor in nature, but in Israel. Here was the evil imminently threatened by God's judgment. Thus he moved away from popular expectation and from the numerous apocalyptic scenarios created by it, since they were obsessed with historical and cosmic questions. Instead, the Baptist addressed the Jewish community solely regarding the issue of whether or not it did what was good in the sight of God. For the coming judgment would separate between the fruitful and barren trees, between wheat and chaff in Israel. God's rule produces the pure community from the currently existing one by removing the unrepentant and evildoers from it in judgment. All other concerns, such as what he might do with the nations or with nature, disappeared in the light of one great concern: that Israel withstand God's judgment. In the Baptist's view, there would be nowhere to hide from God's condemnation of evil. The fire by which he will remove the chaff cannot be extinguished, and no human power can resist it. As wielder of the thresher's fork Christ is poised above the community. Chaff and wheat are given into his hand. The ax will remove the barren tree.

But the proclamation of God's rule did not thereby turn merely into a threat against the community. For that same proclamation brings to the community the fullness of grace. The positive theme of the Baptist, not the negative one, constituted the major content of his message, and this positive message said that God would now create the complete community that would truly be consecrated to him. The Christ's highest office is not to ply the ax; he comes to establish fruitful trees. The gathering of the wheat into barns is the aim of his entire work. Although people were guilty and in need of repentance, the Baptist called them to eternal communion with God. By offering this to all, and by saying that guilt does not render one unworthy of the divine kingdom; by rather calling tax-collectors and prostitutes to communion with God and to his sanctified people (Matt. 21:32; Luke 3:12–14; 7:29–30), the proclamation of heavenly rule became the attestation of divine grace, a grace knowing no bounds. Only that lack of repentance that hardens itself against God's call is subject to fire and the ax.

Later in the church, presentations of the Baptist took root that understood him one-sidedly as a purveyor of threat and anxiety. This was justified in part by his fasting and the white-hot intensity of his call to repentance. There was also an understandable effort to stress the difference between the Baptist and Jesus. The accounts of Matthew and Luke as well as John show, however, that the Baptist bore within himself "joy made full" (John 3:29; Luke 1:14f., 76f.; Matt. 3:11). The earnestness of repentance and the fear of God did not obscure for him the positive content of the messianic concept. Even in repentance, as certainly as it demanded painful struggle, the Baptist saw not simply burden and misery. For it is joy for the community to give up its collective godless will. It is happiness to do away with its evil.

The community attains to its new condition through God's provision of a king. God's kingdom and the activity of the Anointed One were united in the Baptist's promise. God now acts upon Israel as its king by subjecting it to the Promised One. This promise also connected the Baptist with the community's hope, since the figure of the coming king possessed the brightest brilliance of all the concepts and images used to describe the goal of God's rule.

By placing the kingdom concept above the expectation of the Christ, the Baptist vigorously resisted a prevalent misconception. This error is commonly associated with religious experience and becomes especially noticeable when the religious impulse becomes dominant over human will. It is that God's gift is made available to man solely for the sake of enhancing his own life. This kind of "religion," however, does not suspend struggle with God; rather it intensifies it. If the awaited Christ had been "believed" without human will's subjection to God, then his activity would have found its goal in man. The result would have been a Christ who serves man, most of all the Jew, and who glorifies him rather than revealing God, showcasing not God's but man's and the Jew's greatness. But this would have been the mark of the spirit of the anti-Christ, not of the Christ. The proclamation of God's rule described the Christ, not man, as the one through whom God would rule and accomplish his will; hope was directed toward the work God would do in man to reconcile him with himself. To seek Christ as the proclamation offered him was to seek God's reconciliation with man and man's reconciliation through God and for God.

The promise of the Christ bound expectation of the kingdom inseparably to history. It ensured that this expectation would not dissipate into speculative abstraction. This tied hope to a historical process through which God's grace would manifest itself in the national experience within the prevailing circumstances. When their hope was allowed to drift from reality, it easily slipped, owing to its absolute aims, into a hostile antithesis to nature, deriving from God's supernatural sovereignty the destruction of nature, since the complete goal could only be reached when the world came to an end. But if God's kingdom were revealed and effected through the man whom he made to be his Anointed, the preservation of nature was included in God's purposes, and the completion of the world could not be understood in terms of its destruction. For now history became the sphere in which God's work occurred, and what developed was not a religion for a life beyond the present world, nor merely mysticism,[17] religion for souls. Rather, the individual, his life bound irrevocably to nature, becomes the recipient of divine grace, called to God and subjected to him.

By the Baptist's portrayal of the Christ it became clear how utterly serious he was in proclaiming the imminence of God's rule. For he linked the Christ's advent directly to his own work and expected that he himself would see him. His ministry would be brought to a close, in fact, with Christ's coming (Matt. 3:11).[18]

11. John the Baptist's View of the Christ

Since the portrayal of Christ was regarded as an aspect of eschatology, it received a greatness transcending all human measure. The Baptist described himself as incapable of being a partner in the Christ's work or even rendering him the smallest service. The Christ accomplishes his work alone. The impact of this statement regarding the Christ becomes apparent when one considers the iron will giving rise to the Baptist's activity. He spoke as the messenger of a divine word, elevated above popular and political authorities, fearless even

17. "Mystical" I call this kind of piety that seeks the process by which God reveals himself and by which he unites us with himself solely in one's own internal life. It renders history and nature religiously indifferent.

18. Matt. 11:2, too, confirms that John connected the message of the kingdom with the expectation of the Christ.

before the prince, waging single-handed warfare with the entire Jewish community. Jesus called him the greatest of all, one who towered above even God's noblest servants of ancient times (Matt. 11:11). Nevertheless, John explained that there was no comparing him with the Christ, since he did not deem what he was able to accomplish through his own work suitable to bring the eschatological community to completion. For this other means were necessary, not merely a preacher of repentance, also not merely a baptizer, but one with power to dispense the Spirit and fire.

The process we encounter here is typical for the entire sequence of events beginning with the Baptist. The consciousness of God created in him what we call "humility." It gave him a clear sense of the limitations imposed on him and of the smallness of the contribution granted to him (John 3:27–31). He thereby proved that his consciousness of God had freed him from self-will. Such will desires greatness, power, success, superiority over others. Only when it is done on account of God and for God's sake can even minor service be rightly aspired to and joyfully exercised. For then it does not possess greatness through the breadth of its own coverage but through the glory of the one for whom it is done. Further, the deprivation by which one renounces one's own greatness results in joy, since the deprivation assures that the one called by God is certain of God's greatness and that he desires for himself no other greatness than what God gives him.

John explains the Coming One's total superiority by the fact that he would act in the Holy Spirit (Matt. 3:11). He is the bearer and giver of the Spirit who proceeds from God. Since God gave him the divine Spirit as the means of his activity, the Baptist grounded the Coming One's regal status in his divine sonship. For the one who has God's Spirit is his Son (John 1:34). In this way the Baptist confirmed that expectation which Scripture had established in the Jewish community. The concept of the Spirit was the ordained means of expressing God's activity in the personal circumstances of human life and of saying that God generates the thought and will of man and grants him the strength to act. This is all the more true for the Christ, who was called "the Anointed One" because God's Spirit would rest on him. Prophetic pronouncements did not describe merely the Christ as the bearer of the divine Spirit; they also cast the endtime community as filled by him. This idea was intensified in Jesus' time by the fact that the resurrection of the dead was another key component in the fulfillment of the community, and resurrection comes about by the Spirit of God who brings new life to the dead. The current religious state of the nation confirmed this. For it deeply sensed its present poverty as it recalled the prophets to whom the divine Spirit had given the word that was definitive for the entire community. As the pious viewed the matter, the present was distinguished from the past and from the future by virtue of the fact that the community presently lacked the Holy Spirit. Therefore the Christ will have him and bestow him.

Together with the promise that the Christ would baptize in the Holy Spirit, the effective removal of sin was attributed to him. For the characteristic of cleansing from sin is essential to the notion of baptizing. The Christ will thus deal with sin differently than John, namely, in such a way that he over-comes it through the Holy Spirit and that he produces through him the com-munity that is freed from evil and shaped according to God's will. The ethical aim determined simultaneously the Baptist's concept of kingdom and his image of Christ. He put neither God's rule nor the Christ in the service of na-tional selfishness. His aim arose from the most holy possession of Israel, from that which the Law had given it. John desired God's will to be done by Israel; he longed for the appearance of that kind of humanity that would not sin. The Christ will replace the fallen and guilty community with one that lives in union with God through the Holy Spirit. His message received a solemn greatness by virtue of the fact that he moved the fulfillment of this compre-hensive prophecy directly into the present. To "you," the deeply estranged, those threatened by God's wrath, he will come. By the Spirit of God Christ will fashion into a holy community those who had been in danger of divine judgment, all but ready for the ax that was poised to fall.

12. John the Baptist's Sense of Mission

The certainty with which the Baptist applied God's rule in Christ to the present presupposes events that equal prophetic inspiration. The Jewish peo-ple therefore interpreted his ministry in such a way that they came to call him a prophet. But he did not use that term of himself, in keeping with his focus on the messianic age. He saw in the things then underway not the repetition of earlier events, nor the renewal of what the community once had, but some-thing new: fulfillment. He therefore refused completely to cast himself as the head of the community who would bring fulfillment. He also did not preach the names of those whom the Jewish community, on the basis of earlier pro-phetic proclamation, associated with the last days slated to arrive with the Christ.

His message is characterized by the fact that he did not speak of a multi-tude of coming ones. He expected only the Coming One in whose hand lay the entire work of God (Matt. 3:11; 11:2). Thereby John, like Jesus, proved his independence from the rabbinate and the legend (Haggada) cultivated by it. As the rabbinate created new law according to its discretion and unhesitat-ingly attributed to it the sanctity of divine commandment, rabbinic imagina-tion, too, took the liberty of interpreting God's work according to its wishes and of supplementing it. The self-exaltation that imposed onto God its own ideas and desires, however, could not stand up to the sincerity with which the Baptist judged the state of the nation and the certainty with which he ex-pected the coming work of God. The legendary constructs by which the rab-binate dramatically pictured coming events paled by comparison.

Liberation from the rabbinate also freed the Baptist in his encounter with Scripture, in whose authority the power of the rabbinate had its basis. The Baptist, too, acted on the basis of Scripture, for it was witness to the fact that Israel was the possession of the heavenly King, and it had prophesied that be-fore the great day of God on which the eternal King would come, the prophet would be sent to the nation who would prepare it for God's regal work. At the same time, however, the Baptist's work moved away from Scripture; for it spoke of the advent of Elijah, and Elijah he was not (John 1:20–23; cf. Matt. 3:3; 11:10; 17:10–13). His mission was something new, promised by Scripture and nevertheless not its copy but rather a new deed of God. This deed gave the Baptist assurance that it would fulfill what Scripture promised.

He also made use of a scriptural pronouncement that gave him a firm position before the Jewish community and that revealed to it the agreement of his work with God's counsel. He did not provide it with this confidence by appealing to his own internal experiences and inspirations but by appropriating Isaiah 40:3 as written for himself. He spoke as the "voice" promised to the nation that announced God's arrival.

This elevated him above the issue of miracles (John 10:41). If he had placed himself beside the ancient messengers of God as a prophet, a proof of his special office through signs would immediately have been required of him. Later, when the growing escalation of messianic expectations produced prophets, these were pushed immediately to the promise of signs by the doctrine firmly rooted in the Jewish community.[19] For the nation yielded to a divine proclamation in the consciousness that unconditional obedience would now be required of everyone. But it was necessary for the prophet to provide immediate proof of his sending if his message were to receive a hearing. This proof could only consist of a wonderful deed through which God's power intervened on his behalf in a way that was visible to all. Therefore the requirement was set that anyone who stepped before the Jewish community as a prophet must validate himself through a sign. Since the Baptist, however, did not desire anything for himself, no miracle was required of him, and he himself did not require it of himself but rather made the word and baptism the means of performing his task.

13. The Means of Salvation

Since God's regal work would take place very shortly, John called the nation to "repentance." By calling the content of his demand "repentance," the German word *Buße* expresses only inadequately what John and Jesus desired, since we think of *Buße* especially in terms of the condemnation of the wicked and of the painful memories brought about by sin. The Baptist's and Jesus' call to repentance, however, directed the Jewish community's view firmly toward the positive goal of the turning of the will toward the good will by which it ended its improper behavior and subjected itself to God. For the people to repent, therefore, did not mean to entertain thoughts that clarified sin for them. It also did not merely call them to adopt a gloomy mood that deplored their improper behavior. Rather, the decision called for by an appeal to "re-

19. Theudas promised his followers that he would separate the Jordan for them, and the Egyptian prophet promised that the walls of Jerusalem would collapse at his word. Cf. Jos., *Ant.*, 20.5.1.97–99; 20.8.6.167–72.

pentance" had always, whether people obeyed or not, the weight of the completed deed. "Conversion" is therefore a far better word to denote the "turn-around" required of Judaism by John. With the instruction to "turn around" John established rapport between himself and the Jewish nation in the same way as with his promise of God's impending rule. His commandment could not have come to the people as a surprise; for it did not ask them for something entirely new or previously unknown but applied a formula embedded in the piety of the day with the firm certainty of doctrine.

Because the Jewish community venerated the divine Law as its Lord, the consciousness of responsibility before God accompanied the community in its entire activity, and the community gained strong confidence in God from the zeal by which it strove for the fulfillment of the Law. For it consistently applied the concept of merit,[20] never before treated with as much earnestness as now in the classical time of the rabbinate. But alongside this proud self-worth with its resolve to fulfill the divine Law there arose at the same time a vivid fear of sin. This was frequently accompanied by a deep sense of the need for repentance in view of people's actual condition. The term "repentance," a command drawn from prophetic preaching, thus took on an official, doctrinal dimension. The Pharisaic movement made it the obligation of every pious person to include a sincere and repentant formula of confession in daily prayers. Fear of the guilt resting on the community thereby strengthened and enhanced Pharisaism, since each person sought to outdo the other in separating himself further from "sin." From the generation before the Baptist, the Psalms of Solomon and The Assumption of Moses provided hard, scolding sermons regarding the ethical state of the nation. It is thus understandable that the Baptist's thesis—the nation's need to turn from its sins—found much agreement.

He directed his call to repentance toward the community, not only to individuals, in accordance with the universal scope of messianic expectation. The "you" whom he called to repent were not a number of isolated individuals but the Jewish people with their uniform will and with their common guilt. In this, too, the Baptist thought like the entire Jewish community and the rabbinate. For true piety consisted for all contemporaries of Jesus in one's involvement in the community, not in separation from it. As was commonly acknowledged, Israel was a unity in God's sight. All of its members stood under the same obligation and had their lives in common. Therefore they also shared a common guilt if they sinned. But precisely by expecting conversion from everyone without exception, the Baptist distinguished himself from the rabbinate. For the rabbinate's proclamation of repentance, even when it became hard and passionate, always extended to only a part of the community, since it was based on the presupposition that Israel's worship proceeded according to God's will and was not fundamentally flawed, though many fell

---

20. The concept of merit obtains when we measure our actions according to their value for the other person and when we assess the reciprocal action that can be expected from the other person as a result of our actions.

short of their duty. In that case, however, there could never be a lack of those who upheld Israel's praise and glory before God; the fallen ones who required repentance stood as a special group beside the righteous and complete. The Baptist, however, did not exempt the righteous from his call to repentance but required their conversion with particular earnestness.[21] He considered those who were regarded by the community as paragons of righteousness to be especially guilty and corrupted. By beginning so resolutely the confrontation with Pharisaism, he underscored the validity of his call for repentance for every last person. For if Pharisaic piety had to be rejected, then the nation had to convert in its entirety, and not only individuals were lost but the Jewish people as a whole.

The Baptist did not consider the nation's guilt to lie solely in its religious shortcomings. This can be seen in his positive prescriptions for the converted that also reveal what he condemned as sin (Luke 3:10–14). However, he did not give the repentant new religious instructions. He rather sent the customs official back to his toll booth in order that he might be honest from now on. He did not take away the soldier's arms but required him from now on to abstain from violence and bribery. Even in those rules directed at no particular class or occupation, the Baptist did not introduce some new worship procedure, like increasing times of prayer or ordering a new thanksgiving or intensifying celebration of the Sabbath. To do so would have been to remain in agreement with the rabbinate, which expected help from such reforms in light of the guilty state of the community. The Baptist, however, required help from those who had possessions for the materially deprived. To let these suffer would be sin for them. The Baptist described repentance as turning from callousness to doing good, from selfish consumption to generosity, from violence to righteousness.

The Baptist rendered such judgments because he measured people's guilt from the perspective of the messianic hope. This hope stated that the community's fulfillment was already at hand. Therefore he required of Israel that it become a unified community, a closely knit nation, thereby ready to receive her king. When the hungry stood beside the affluent, and when those given power through the collection of tolls and the possession of arms consistently perpetrated injustice and inflicted misery in the community, the fabric of the community was clearly in tatters. The wrath of the coming king would of necessity turn against those who were responsible for these conditions.

The Jewish community suffered from deep division because its goods were distributed very unevenly among the various classes. A small part had great riches through the possession of large quantities of land and through commerce trade, while the majority lived in bitter poverty, since the dense settlement of the country had grown beyond the availability of goods and since, on top of the considerable religious contributions, a terrible tax burden lay upon

---

21. Matt. 3:7 is confirmed by 21:23–32. It was public knowledge in Jerusalem that the Baptist had also called the teaching and ruling heads of the community to repentance and baptism.

the nation. They therefore had an open ear for that part of messianic prophecy promising that, with the time of salvation, poverty would disappear because nature would be transformed, with grain and vine ripening in magnificent fullness for all. At that time the holy city and the land at large would be filled with all manner of bounty. For this reason first the Baptist and thereafter Jesus had to confront the question, both on account of the conditions in which the Jewish community lived and because of the thoughts that moved them, what they should say to the rich and to the poor in the service of divine grace. For this reason the call to repentance condemned from the outset that kind of corruption that arises from possessions.

From one saying of Jesus (Matt. 21:32) we learn that the Baptist's movement also led prostitutes to him and that he administered baptism to them. Thus he offered baptism not only to men but to women. In this, too, he locates himself within the existing religious situation, since the sanctification of the nation grounded in the divine will and work also conferred on women an indispensable place in the community. Therefore women, too, will belong to the transformed community and receive eternal life. The debased conditions of the present, however, were due largely to the unchecked indulgence of erotic desire. It was therefore an essential part of the conversion and renewal of the nation that the prostitute leave her sinful way.

By these demands the Baptist did not imply that he condoned the Jews' religious practices and theology. He rather expressed his sharp opposition in combatting the leading religious groups, both the Pharisees and the Sadducees, as corruptors of the Jewish community. If people did not keep even the simplest regulations of the Law and did not even carry out God's will in their relationships with one another, it was already obvious that their worship was defunct as well. Because the Baptist did not expect deliverance from the piety present in the Jewish community, he went into solitude, avoided communion with its leaders, and offered forgiveness not by the existing means of grace, the altar and other institutions provided for repentance, but through his own baptism.

While his requirements were simple, they nevertheless called the individual's entire will to repentance with radical sincerity. When the Baptist called the nation to a brotherly unity in which each cared for the other, he fought against deeply rooted desires. When he instructed the customs official to believe that precisely in the midst of his old associations and duties God had forgiven him and accepted him into his eternal community, although the entire nation was against him and condemned him, this looked like blasphemous effrontery. But John esteemed God higher than all others, considered God's grace and not people's severity as normative, and believed, not the righteous in the community, but the promise of God. Only a decisive, complete conversion that liberated the publican from everything previously considered holy and righteous enabled him to continue his old profession in the personal and joyful expectation of God's rule.

Since the repentance John preached received its content from the rule of love and of justice, he was supremely concerned with the "fruit of repentance" (Matt.

3:8). It made an indelible impression on the followers of the Baptist that he turned away in horror from certain ostensibly penitent men who desired baptism because he feared that they could not be saved. Why, if they desired baptism? The "fruit of repentance" will be absent from their lives, because they are not willing to turn their repentance into action, through which alone it becomes effective. This shows that the Baptist's eyes had been opened to the uselessness of the nation's liturgical exercises. He saw that its rituals merely covered its evil with a shining veneer. Meanwhile, it could not attain purification of its will.

The decisive clarity with which John rejected a repentance that produced only days and prayers of repentance also proves itself in the fact that he contested people's faith. The Jews' confidence in God was not based solely or primarily on their pious achievements but on the fact that the nation had come into being through God's call. It was therefore built upon circumcision and other sacraments that represented its ties with God. All those who opposed the Baptist and Jesus were convinced that God's electing grace had given Israel its privilege. This confidence must necessarily resist the call to repentance, since it was directed not merely to a few but to all. To endorse John's call would be to devalue the sacred possessions upon which the Jewish community's share in God was based.

The Baptist proved that the commandment to lead Israel to repentance possessed for him the untouchable sanctity of a divine order. It shattered Israel's confidence and distinguished between what it had received from God and what it did with God's assistance. The divine word given to it remained undisputed; the grace shown to it must not be misrepresented or denied. God chose Abraham, and his children constitute the community chosen by God. The prophecy given to Israel remains in force. Nevertheless God "is able to raise up from these stones children of Abraham." The Baptist rejected the community's confidence when it understood grace as excusing it from repentance and legitimizing evil, as if it and its corrupt ways were indispensable for God to fulfill his promise.

This spelled the end of a faith that declared itself free from obedience to God and derived an unethical result from God's promise. The Baptist's call to repentance, therefore, had the appearance of leading away from faith, since repentance and works were the tasks with which he charged the community. In truth, however, the Baptist inaugurated that series of events through which faith became the central act of piety. For by destroying false faith that subverted God's goodness into the legitimization of evil, that faith developed which was truly directed toward God and resulted in reconciliation to him.

John intensified his earthshaking proclamation by the practice of fasting, of which Jesus makes mention (Matt. 11:18). But Jesus, the best witness imaginable for the Baptist's attitude toward God, did not see in his fasting any damaging notions that would have lessened the value of the Baptist's call to repentance. He did not excuse the Baptist on account of his fasting, but he did charge the people who took offense at it.[22] The information that John contented himself with what the desert had to offer, wild honey and grasshop-

---

22. Jesus likewise did not object to the fasting of John's disciples. Cf. Matt. 9:15.

pers, makes clear that Jesus' disciples did not derive his fasting from some gnostic theory, through which he might have sought to construe nature in antithesis to God, since the aversion against meat was the inevitable consequence of such theories. Even Luke's account, which associates the Baptist's abstinence with the old Nazirite custom and therefore makes him abstain from wine, contradicts a gnostic interpretation of his fasting. All our data lead only to the established synagogue custom of connecting fasting with prayer and repentance. The guilty party had to humble himself before God by forsaking passions and enjoyment. Therefore the nation's annual day of repentance was a day of fasting, as were the Pharisees' two weekly days of prayer. Israel was faced with a decision on which her entrance into the world to come would depend. The Baptist regarded Israel's lostness as great and her obduracy profound. It was uncertain whether it would be possible to awaken the Jewish community, to bend the righteous and shatter their authority. Therefore the Baptist stood before God as prayerful supplicant; from the Jewish point of view to pray this way meant also to fast. Unceasing prayer and continual fasting were of a piece. At the same time, his fasting pointed unequivocally in the same direction as his call to repentance. Because the people sinned by seeking to amass riches for themselves while letting others languish in want, and since they desired in place of God only the goods of this age, the Baptist made it clear to all that his desire was directed completely and solely toward God. Through his fasting, he clearly showed to all the religious aim that was liberated from the desire for personal gratification.

A call to repentance understood as action focused from the beginning on its end. The initial act would mean nothing without followthrough. To John's call obedience was either rendered or denied. His call was therefore from the beginning accompanied by the question: what then? His message answered this question by maintaining that hard on the heels of the time given to the nation to repent would come the kingly revelation of God. This not only legitimized his right to call the Jewish people to decision so that they would separate from evil and subject themselves to God and clarified why he directed his demands to all and charged them to perform certain works; it also showed why the things he demanded from the people really constituted their return to God. How was the power of sin broken by all this? As the Jewish community prepared itself for the advent of the Christ, and because God's regal work would occur at that time, its repentance would result in salvation. By linking the call to repentance with the proclamation of God's kingdom, John united remorse with hope and faith, since he called the people's attention not only to their guilt and need for betterment but also pointed to God's gracious work by which their repentance would reach its goal: liberation from evil. Repentance would then result in renewal, because God would show himself to be their king.[23] This gave the preaching of baptism rich content:

---

23. The connection between repentance and God's work of salvation remains clear throughout the entire New Testament. A great theological shift resulted when they were rent asunder in the postapostolic church.

it described both the greatness of divine grace and the depth of Jewish guilt. It awakened a godward longing that transcended all that lay within the realm of human competence while at the same time calling for decisive personal response through which the nation would focus its entire will on changing its conduct. God's highest praise was coupled with profound horror in the face of present depravity. The simultaneous awakening of opposite moods, of pain and of joy, of greed and of gratitude, of fear and of confidence, both terms of each couplet receiving full emphasis and serving to ground the new will, constituted from the beginning a characteristic of early Christian history. Whoever focuses merely on the one or the other sentiment falsifies his reconstructions.

By itself, the call to repentance could easily degenerate into a retrogressive effort that longed for conditions once present but now forfeited through people's lostness; perhaps repentance would be the key to restoration.[24] Since the call to repentance, however, was grounded in the proclamation of God's rule, it was directed entirely toward the future. It had its aim not in any of various imaginable repristinations but strove to ready the nation for what was to come.

The grounding of John's call to repentance in the prophecy of the kingdom made it pure. The Baptist did not have to veil sin but could be entirely truthful and say the most severe word without bitterness, because he stood in the shadow of the greatest promise of all, one that determined his every motive and goal. He could call the theologians and priests "brood of vipers" and could stir up in his hearers the deepest revulsion, making them shudder within themselves. Yet this was without stirring up dispute or division that would break the community apart, and without plunging it into a despair by which the present condition would have become completely irremediable. For the purpose of the call to repentance was not the exposure of sin, nor was the call intermingled with that impure disposition that takes joy in the humiliation of the guilty. Rather it was issued in order that the greatest good might be granted and communion with God be achieved.

Only by linking the call to repentance with the proclamation of the divine rule did it receive that simplicity which turned people's entire potential for action to the most proximate ethical tasks. If the people proved to be obedient to God in that which lay within the realm of their knowledge and will power, they were assured of complete victory over evil. For then God's rule had set the nation free.

It is significant for the historical picture that we grasp the connection between God's rule and people's repentance in just the way the sources present it. If we defy the sources by having the Baptist launch an attempt to move God to exert his rule by pushing the Jewish people into repentance, we assume that he thought pharisaically. The thought easily emerged from Pharisaic piety that the kingdom could be forced by general repentance. Thus, for

---

24. See the phrase by which Jesus described people's expectation of Elijah: "He will restore all things" (Matt. 17:11).

example, it was said in Pharisaic circles, "If Israel kept only one single Sabbath, it would be redeemed," and the opinion was thereby expressed that God would have to redeem the nation if it could only be induced to obey him so completely that it would no longer have any transgressors in its midst to rob it of divine deliverance by their guilt. But the assurance with which the Baptist proclaimed God's regal self-disclosure and called for radical change set him apart entirely from Pharisaism. Because he expected God now to reveal his kingdom to the nation by dealing with it according to his grace and justice, he rejected the Jews' godlessness and callousness without reservation, considered the practical uselessness of Jewish piety to be guilt, shattered the prevailing religious arrogance, and attested to God's independence from all human will and work. This is why for John the question of how the nation related to God's work now underway took on supreme seriousness. If Israel failed to heed the call to repentance, it would experience God's rule as judgment and would fall prey to unquenchable fire. From this arose the concern that made John fast and pray for his people out of fear that they would exclude themselves from God's rule through their sin.

14. John's Baptism

Both of the convictions that provided the content of the Baptist's ministry found moving expression in the action that he charged them to perform. This was the ritual bath, baptism. The use of baptism for the purpose of preparing people for God's revelation was new to conventional piety, since current religion used the religious bath only for the removal of impurity and thus merely for the purpose of removing a particular external blemish. This was also the case when the proselyte received baptism for the first time, even though the significance of the bath was increased due to the fact that its reception, together with circumcision, constituted the condition for the proselyte's entrance into the Jewish community and his share in its salvific good.

By drawing a connection between the washing and sin, however, the Baptist rendered it an absolute act in which God's grace presented itself completely to the individual, and in which the person's entire behavior toward God was renewed. This meant that repetition of baptism was now disallowed. It became a once-for-all act, and for the same reason it necessitated a Baptizer, because this baptism had its basis in a divine message on whose proclamation its value rested. The conventional bath of purification, on the other hand, was administered by the person himself. Nevertheless, the removal of separation from God was already the act's aim for repeatable Jewish baptism. Another aim was the preservation of the person baptized in the sanctified community. Thus the new shape given to baptism by the Baptist tied in easily and intelligibly with the conventional custom.[25]

---

25. The connection with established custom is confirmed by the constancy of terminology. Βαπτίζεσθαι was not a new coinage, but the conventional term for the religious ablution.

The Baptist did not issue his call of repentance to the Jewish community merely through words but saw its fulfillment in an action. He understood repentance not in terms of a thought but a deed. By his call to baptism, the Baptist demanded that the nation decide how it wanted to respond to God, and that it would act in a way indicating its subjection to him. For his part God would prepare them for his rule by offering forgiveness of sins and liberating them from all that currently shamed it and separated it from him.

Skepticism toward reports that the Baptist baptized for the forgiveness of sins (Mark 1:4; cf. Luke 3:3)[26] must be rejected, because the bath was given for the sake of purity. Had it ended with a consideration of guilt without granting success to that repentance which provides assurance for the guilty that God removes his guilt, it would have been meaningless. However deep the nation's fall had been, in repentance John offered the means for it to reach God's kingdom. The Evangelists' account is confirmed by Jesus' word that John's baptism was from heaven (Matt. 21:25). He thereby excluded the thought that it was merely appended as an adornment to the Baptist's preaching. Jesus summarized John's entire ministry by the act of baptism, and that in such a way that the Baptist accomplished God's will by it by both calling the people impure and by declaring them cleansed.

The value of his baptism, of course, was limited by the fact that he did not designate himself the creator and sovereign of the new community. Since the Christ would only come in the future, the remission of sins, too, had a future dimension. In the end, that person would be freed from guilt who received the Christ. Not until Christ gathered the wheat would the sinner be entirely saved. John had no intention of elevating his ministry above that of the Christ. The revelation of the grace he brought to the Jewish community would rather be superseded by what the Christ would give. The preparatory significance John assigned to his entire ministry, however, did not trivialize the purity he granted to the repentant through his baptism, because he acted in the power of his sending through God and thus in the conviction that the Christ would not destroy his work but complete it. The same grace that empowered the Baptist to issue the call for the guilty to enter the eternal community will reappear in the Christ. Therefore the repentant person who accepted baptism from him should be assured that the Christ would accept him. Once placed into the purified and perfected community by the Christ, he will have experienced the forgiveness of sin in full measure.

Since the repentant person expressed his repentance publicly through baptism before God and men, confession was linked with it by concrete expressions (Matt. 3:6). Since, however, repentance did not merely consist of the acknowledgment of sinfulness and since it was grounded in the acceptance of divine forgiveness, the confession remained free from all regulation. We do not hear anything of a confessional rule, nothing of regulations regarding the things that should be confessed in order for repentance and baptism to be

26. The term "remission of sins" was not a theological innovation but reflected synagogal usage.

valid. This is a telling feature of the circumspectness with which the term "repentance" was used. No meritorious value was secretly attached to the sinner's remorse; rather that remorse signaled a sincere rejection of faith in human will and a turn to God's grace. Until God's grace was more fully revealed, the people were charged to return from baptism to their existing circumstances and do what was right in God's sight.

Baptism conferred on the relationship between the baptized person and God the quality of an internal, personal connectedness. But this did not erase the universalism of the messianic aim and the idea of divine might from the Baptist's consciousness of God; they remain essential to the concept of "God's rule," as is evidenced by his description of the coming Christ. That the concept of God had its content solely in power, however, so that it alone gave greatness to the promise, was out of the question. God's rule was not merely portrayed as a miracle with divine omnipotence creating a new state of affairs. In that case God's rule would have consisted merely in a demonstration of what his power could do. Nor did the concept of righteousness alone define and determine the relationship with God. As surely as his kingdom reveals itself in judgment and as it discloses his glory by working righteousness, the Baptist and those baptized by him did not expect that God would do no more than repay evil and establish justice. Such a one-sided interpretation was ruled out by the fact that John administered washing and forgiveness to the guilty. God's grace is made the foundation of relationship to him, as everyone came into the complete community by the forgiveness of sins. The onset of God's rule thus involves his gracious reconciliation of man with himself.

This altered the individual's relation to the community. Up to that point he received his relation to God through the community into which he was born. It prescribed for him its worship. Of course, he had to participate in the common heritage of the nation with his own piety but in such a way that his knowledge and will conformed to what had already been given to the community. To it belonged God's promise, and the individual shared in it as a member of the nation. Repentance, however, consisted of the individual's personal decision by which he separated himself from the established form of the community. Since access to God occurred through repentance, the life history of the individual and not the nation became the means by which this access was mediated.

This did not result in a denigration of the concept of community. For the Baptist's call to repentance was addressed to the community as a whole, and God's kingdom is brought about by the transformation and perfection of his community. As long as the kingdom concept was the focus, the community remained the dominant religious term. Yet the relation between the religion of the individual and that of the community was definitely rendered new through baptism. The community now consisted of those who submitted to God by their own decision. Belonging to the national community of Israel was not sufficient for attainment of eternal salvation. For the factors that made this salvation available now penetrated the inwardness and liberty of man's personal life.

The Baptist did not bring about a gathering of the converted into a messianic assembly. He stood by his conviction that it was not he who would reveal God's rule. He made only a start in founding a visible community, as those who had accepted baptism and thus received the claims of the kingdom were separated from the unrepentant by a visible sign. But this did not yet create a new community in the fullest sense, because the Baptist sent the baptized back into their existing circumstances with the counsel to act with integrity of will and wait for the Christ. This did not result in a visible public assemblage of the baptized, nor in anything resembling the establishment of a church or a sect.[27]

15. John the Baptist's Success

The Baptist stepped before the nation alone, not undergirded by one of the strong religious communities, not as a member of the rabbinate, not supported by his priestly privilege, although he was the son of a priest. He was upheld solely by his divine sending, and in this state he moved the entire Jewish community so that pilgrims gathered in all the villages to come to the Jordan. Jesus' words regarding the Baptist say as much. In Galilee Jesus asked his hearers without hesitation why they went to the Baptist. He did not also have to ask whether or not they had gone. Although not all may have opted for baptism, they had all been at the Jordan, and all were subject to Jesus' reproach that they no longer knew what they had searched for and received there. When he spoke about the Baptist with the leaders of the nation in Jerusalem, they refused to answer his question. They rightly anticipated that an attack on the Baptist would provoke such passionate indignation that no official authority, civic or religious, could prevent the crowd from serving swift and destructive justice on such slanderers as would dare dispute the Baptist's prophetic sending (Matt. 11:7–19; 21:23–27).

At that time, of course, the Baptist had already been killed by Herod. His martyrdom glorified his memory. It was a distinctive trait in the Jews' image of a prophet that he suffered and died for God's sake. This hallmark of the prophetic sending was now true of the Baptist. At the same time, the occasion of his execution spoke to people's consciences with unmistakable clarity. While all silently acquiesced because of the constraints of their situation, they nevertheless realized that what the ruler had done was sin and that the Baptist had clearly died for God's justice and commandment.

For this reason there remained therefore even after the end of the movement John spawned a circle of men in the Galilean villages, for example, in Capernaum, who were distinguished from the rest of the community as "the disciples of John." They were called this not merely because they had received

---

27. This is not rendered uncertain but is rather confirmed by the fact that beside the great number of baptized there also existed a circle of disciples of the Baptist. The phrase "disciple of the Baptist" by itself, admittedly, does not distinguish between those obedient to the call to repentance and those simply gathered around the Baptist. For the more narrow sense, cf. Matt. 11:2; 14:12; John 3:25.

his baptism but also because they were linked with one another by a distinctive religious observance, by prescribed fasting and their own prayer (Matt. 9:14; Luke 11:1).[28]

And so it was that the Baptist's memory continued into the subsequent generation, as the narrator informs us from whom Josephus took his report regarding John (*Ant.* 18.2.116–19). We hear from him that people in Galilee waited for the divine punishment to be visited upon the murderer of the prophet. When the king of the Nabateans, the father of Herod's first wife, vindicated the abomination laid upon his daughter by Herod's marriage to Herodias by starting a war and by defeating Herod's troops, the Jews saw this as the revenge for the blasphemy the ruler had committed by executing John. Even after the temple's destruction Jewish sources celebrated the Baptist with words of praise, though at that time the policy reigned in all of Judaism and in its entire literature, a policy developed primarily regarding pagan religions but now transferred to Christianity as well, that the Jew not speak of foreign worship. It was rather to be treated with complete silence. Not even then, however, was John reckoned among the apostate, and his memory was not conceded to the exclusive possession of Christianity.

The strong communion between Jerusalem and communities outside Jerusalem also resulted in the preservation of the Baptist's memory, not merely in Palestine but also in Greek settlements, so that his baptism continued to be performed. Twenty years after his death there were still circles in Alexandria and Ephesus whose religious behavior was determined by their having received "the baptism of John" (Acts 18:25; 19:3).

Nevertheless, Jesus declared the Baptist's movement to have been unsuccessful. While it showed many individuals the way to a share in God's kingdom, including some who had not been reached by the Pharisaic call to repentance and others from that stratum of society that the community was able only to humiliate and reject as apostate, no turn in the corporate attitude of the nation had occurred. The religious excitement that once precipitated baptismal gatherings at the Jordan passed from the scene without lasting effect (Matt. 11:7–19; John 5:35).

Where Greek convictions exerted influence, such as with the noble priestly families, the ideas used by Josephus to interpret John the Baptist ran counter to his own claims. Josephus transformed him into a teacher of virtue and made baptism a symbol of internal purity. To hear Josephus tell it, John dramatized the notion that first comes betterment of the soul, then purification of the body. This is how many an educated man in Jerusalem and Galilee thought about the movement of the Baptist. For under the influence of Greek thought an evaluation of religious ritual had spread even to the Jewish community that understood it as merely a symbolic portrayal of ethical truths. Greek thinkers could not conceive of actions through which a connection

---

28. It is not clear from our sources whether the Baptist's disciples also dispensed baptism. In favor of this are the following: (1) John's baptism spread into the Diaspora; (2) in the beginning Jesus' disciples, too, administered baptism to the penitent (Acts 18:25; 19:3; John 4:2).

with God could be established, and when the action sought to effect some supernatural eschatological aim, it appeared entirely overdone.[29] For this way
of thinking, the Baptist's preaching was rendered futile even when he was admired as a noble man murdered by Herod without reason.

Even stronger was the resistance by which Pharisaism opposed the Baptist.
It did not allow itself to be pulled away from the ancient holy objects of veneration, from the Law as the guide into righteousness and from the temple
and the forgiveness that could be found in it. The Baptist was a "reformer,"
and for this reason alone judgment was passed on him in the eyes of the majority of the nation and of its Pharisaic leaders. When John did not apply to
himself any of the names prophecy supplied in connection with the endtimes
but appealed to Isaiah 40:3, his authority was shattered (John 1:19–23).

In Jesus' view, the resistance to the Baptist indicated antagonism against
the radical nature of his demands, which did not countenance intermingling
of worship and the desire for happiness, of love for God and selfish lusts. "He
neither eats nor drinks," the people lamented. They castigated the complete
rejection of natural enjoyment as something absurd and likened it to the kind
of self-destruction that demons would bring about. They later evaded Jesus'
demand for them to acknowledge the heavenly origin of John's baptism and
the "faith," the unconditional assent and decisive obedience, which it signified. Yet some of them were presumably prepared to accept the substance of
the Baptist's preaching as correct and praiseworthy. Current piety's unholy
intertwining of worship and the demand for personal well-being, of love and
selfish lust, proved firm.

In the light of the demise of the Baptist's movement, the question of
whether Israel would allow herself to be saved took on renewed urgency.
Whoever continued the Baptist's work could not base his decision on the expectation of success. Such a decision was possible only as an act of obedience
yielding to the divine leading and independent of the question of outcome.
The Baptist, however, had already expressed in the face of his opponents' resistance why he was not shaken by the prospect that his work would fail. The
continued existence of the holy community was not tied to what Israel did.
For divine grace was one with the Creator's omnipotence, and the rule of God
had begun.

---

29. Both Philo and Josephus reflect this way of thinking.

The Turning Point in Jesus' Life

1. Jesus' Request for Baptism

When the message that promised the beginning of God's rule surged through the land, moving the Galileans to flock to John like the Judeans before them, Jesus, too, desired baptism. For he perceived God's word in the Baptist's proclamation and saw in the community's baptism its call to God. And since words are insufficient when God's grace is revealed, he did not acknowledge the Baptist's mission merely with words but did what God commanded the nation through John. As he later stood before the people, always free and solely guided by his assurance of God, so also the decision propelling him into his public ministry was an act of obedience by which he followed God's will.

Jesus expressed his judgment regarding the Baptist's mission, out of which his desire for baptism arose, again and again during the course of his ministry, as often as he was approached with the question of how he related to John. One occasion arose after John's imprisonment, when John demanded from him an explanation regarding his regal claims. He in no way altered his own attitude nor withdrew his unconditional support for the Baptist's work but praised John's greatness precisely at that time and held up before the nation what it had received through the Baptist's mission and what it had forfeited with its rejection of him.

A second occasion for Jesus to express his verdict regarding the Baptist arose from the stumbling block that the expectation of Elijah provided even for his contemporaries. The promise that the days of the Christ would begin with the appearance of Elijah directed expectation toward a renewal of the Jewish community that would occur as the effect of divine power and would therefore elevate God's messengers above all opposition. But for Jesus this expectation furnished no hope that his work would end in any other way than

73

by death. He rather used this word of Scripture, too, to confirm for both himself and his followers the will to the cross. He achieved this by declaring that the divine promise of the coming of Elijah had been fulfilled in the work of the Baptist.

A third word regarding the Baptist arose from Jesus' dispute with the leaders of Jerusalem when he frustrated their attempt to test him by the counterquestion whether it had been God or men who offered John's baptism to them. By demanding from them, prior to any further explanation, an acknowledgment of God's will in the granting of baptism with its call to repentance and its offer of divine forgiveness, he lent complete consistency to his behavior from beginning to end. Because he did not justify himself before those who did not believe that what the Baptist called their guilt was indeed their guilt in God's sight, so that the forgiveness offered through baptism was likewise from God, he sided unreservedly with the Baptist and rooted his own work in the fact that the call to the perfect grace of Israel's end time was granted by baptism (Matt. 11:7–19; 17:10–13; 21:23–32; cf. John 5:33–35).

Jesus confirmed his judgment that John had received his commission from God by conforming his own ministry to that of the Baptist. Like John, he acted in the conviction that God's rule had now begun and that it consists in the rule of the Christ. Also like John, Jesus ascribed to the Christ the vocation of judging evil and unrepentant Israel. Jesus also derived the regal claim of the Anointed One from his being gifted by the Holy Spirit, and he exercised that claim by liberating the community from sin and by granting it righteousness before God as well as eternal life. If any one of these principles had been absent from Jesus' work, it would have been separated from the baptismal preaching. But they all resurface with complete clarity in Jesus' work, just as he clearly preserved his unity with the Baptist in the principles and aims of the call to repentance. Jesus also knew of no other preparation for God's rule than repentance and required, like John, that the entire nation convert. He, too, confronted Pharisaism relentlessly and rejected the "righteous." For him, as for John, conversion consisted of those simple acts by which we bring our relationships with one another under the rule of love. He regarded his people's callousness as guilt and led those who had possessions to surrender them voluntarily. Like the Baptist, Jesus grounded his call to repentance in divine forgiveness and its power to obliterate all guilt, and he connected it with the washing given in his name. He condemned the faith that had degenerated into pride, freed God's grace from all Jewish claims, and made its aim the call of individuals. This produced a manifestation of divine grace, the very content and purpose of divine rule, which grants us inner union with God. Jesus incorporated all these norms previously present in the Baptist's ministry with conscious clarity and thereby demonstrated the sincerity of his allegiance to the Baptist. In calling the Baptist the one whom God had sent to prepare the way for him, Jesus spoke without pretense or posturing and with complete uprightness.

Through his identification with those who desired baptism Jesus now conducted himself as fully one with them, since the nation's sin had been made painfully plain to them. He had done the same in Nazareth. Rather than stepping away from his people onto a remote height, he stepped into their midst. For since they were guilty and endangered, he was tied to them in complete community. Because his assurance of God did not separate but connected him with sinners, he visibly lived out the truth of that forgiveness granted to them by God, the power of which determined their relationship to God. Because God forgave, Jesus, too, forgave, and he transformed his forgiveness into action by identifying with the accused and hurting community. In this way he participated actively in the Baptist's struggle against the nation's sin, validated the call to repentance for all, and showed all "righteous" persons their duty. If they had no need of conversion themselves, since they had remained in their father's house and service, there were still those who had fallen beside them. They should rejoice with the shepherd who finds what had been lost and join the father and brother in celebrating their reconciliation. If they were really "righteous," good trees who bore good fruit, possessing the treasure in themselves that made them capable of serving others, the call to repentance had even greater significance for them. For in that case they were identified all the more with the community. If, on the other hand, they despised it, their "righteousness" would be their downfall.

We know that it was not consciousness of his own sin that led him to baptism. For he continued his communion with sinners and his separation from the "righteous" until his death, but he never explained this separation in terms of conviction of sinfulness. The separation arose rather through the power and perfection of his love, which led him to the sick as the doctor, to the lost as the shepherd, to the barren fig tree as the painstaking gardener, and to the indignant as the saving exhorter (Matt. 9:12; Luke 15:4–7; 13:6–9; Matt. 21:37). The distinction that separated him as the pure one from the guilty never disappeared from his word. When he called himself God's Son and thus appropriated that property which the Jewish community praised as its precious inheritance,[1] he nevertheless consistently distinguished himself from it by using the name "Son of God" in the singular and by adding to it the designation "the only one" (John 3:18). He called himself the Son apart from whom the Father had no other and used the expression "my Father"[2] and "your father." In contrast, he did not use the name "father" for God in the same way for himself as for others, avoiding the expression "our father" that would have erased his distinctiveness relative to all others. The consistency with which all texts preserve this conception of his view of God reveals that it made a deep impression on the disciples that Jesus distinguished his relationship with God consistently and clearly from that enjoyed by others, including the sonship of God he gave to his disciples.

1. The community loved to use the name of the Father. "Our Father, who is in heaven" was a frequently used name for God. Therefore they also called themselves "the sons of God" (cf. John 8:41).
2. Instead of "my Father" Jesus also said simply "the Father" and "the Son." The terminology of calling one's own father simply "father" (*abba*) was well established.

The distinction Jesus made between himself and all others did not derive merely from the fact that the "son" concept gave him that regal will whereby he admittedly placed himself as unique over all, since the concept of "Christ" is inconceivable in the plural. But why could master and disciples, king and nation, not bow in shared sonship before their common father? It was not a difference in giftedness, commission, and function that necessitated separation of the fatherhood of God revealed in him from the fatherhood possessed by all. Such a difference would amount to the existence of strong beside weak, great beside minor sons of God. In his community, however, Jesus expressly denied such distinctions and elevated the common fatherhood of God above all (Matt. 23:9). Greatness and power were emphatically not the decisive aspect of relationship to God for him (Matt. 18:3; 19:14). His conduct receives its foundation only through the unbroken validity he assigned in his divine consciousness to ethical norms. God responds differently to the sinner than he does to the one who does his will. Only here, not in distinctions pertaining to power and calling, Jesus drew a line of separation that he utterly could not conceal. Evil must not be ascribed to God. By refusing to ascribe to God the same fatherly relationship to himself as obtains with us, he sanctified God's Law and preserved the boundary between sinners and the only one truly righteous.

When he contrasted the father with the two sons, the disobedient and the obedient one (Matt. 21:28–31; Luke 15:11–32), he used neither of them to depict himself but represented his own task and accomplishment by what the father did. That he did not group himself with the sons was in part the result of his being sent to call both the righteous and the lost to repentance. But the distinction did not arise from some higher level of power or knowledge on Jesus' part but from the fact that both sons had need of the word of repentance and both became sons only through conversion. His sonship, on the other hand, revealed itself in his fulfillment of God's will with respect to both. Because he addressed the disciples, too, as "you who are evil," it remained for them to "become God's sons" (Matt. 7:11; 5:45), while he claimed for himself origin from God and unhindered communion with him.

Jesus thereby proclaimed that both self-accusation and remorse for sin were absent from his consciousness. If he had perceived in himself anything godless either as a persistent condition or as sporadic interruptions of his communion with God, he, too, would have subsumed them under God's forgiveness. This would have preserved his communion with God despite an ungodly will. But then there would have been no need to distinguish his own sonship from that of others. Rather, the necessity would have arisen of equating himself with others, since he granted the need for forgiveness to them as part of what sonship entails. But as the "unique son" he had to distinguish himself from them if his unity with God truly did determine his entire will.

Jesus victoriously rejected the suspicion that his lack of repentance might be based on the loss of ethical judgment through the pervading earnestness of his call to repentance. In judging religious hypocrisy to be sin, he also placed himself under the rule of complete truthfulness. He ruthlessly exposed the abominableness of preaching repentance and seeking to convert others while simultaneously suspending the validity of the same principles for oneself (Matt. 7:3). Likewise, there is no statement whatsoever that extends the concept of guilt uniformly to both him and all others. His opponents sought constantly to convict him of sin in order to prove him wrong. But Jesus just as consistently rejected their assumption that he, too, was sinful. At the same time, Jesus denied praise to those who claimed for themselves divine sonship of God and hailed him as their father. He considered it his duty to destroy the lies of those who called themselves God's sons even though they hated and lied (John 8:41–44). With the same truthfulness that looked only to God and honored him, he separated himself from all others and maintained the uniqueness of his sonship.

That his call arose out of love and sought to produce communion, indeed a common sonship before God, between him and sinners, further proves that the difference he maintained between himself and them was for him a real and absolute necessity. Together with the claim of the uniqueness of his sonship he clearly revealed the complete selflessness of his love and thereby prevented the suspicion that this distinction was empty and the mere product of self-exaltation and vanity.

His word did not cause his disciples merely to recognize their guilt with profound sincerity. It also induced them to acknowledge continually and bluntly as they proclaimed the word of repentance to others that they would destroy themselves and their entire work if they failed to own up to their solidarity with them as sinners. If their recollection had been that Jesus expressed himself in similar manner, identifying with his hearers as a sinner himself, this would have touched their own consciousness (cf. Matt. 7:11). They did not preserve a single word, however, that added to "you who are evil" a joint confession, "we who are sinners." The gospel is rather based on the conviction that Jesus refused communion with human sin. For this reason the disciples present him as the one who was tempted and not as the one who sinned. And they describe to us the hours when he could not carry out his ethical opposition to the world without choice or struggle but rather found the will that was conformed to God's by overcoming his own contrary inclination. The intention and result of the disciples' portrait is that in these processes Jesus' purity is revealed in its entire magnitude.

Whether he punished or forgave, his word of repentance always expressed an unweakened consciousness of strength in view of his own will. He had come to fulfill the Law—which meant to love completely just as the father loves. He did not merely want to teach the Law, broken by all at every turn, but to do it. He had the will to do this—but also the ability (Matt. 5:17–19). This consciousness fulfilled all of his claims regarding his calling. When he knew God's rule to be present in what happened through him, he made visible once again his freedom from sin. For God's rule is not present because sin occurs but because his will is done. When he granted divine forgiveness to rank sinners, allowing them at his table with the promise that they would be God's guests, he expressed his freedom from sin. He called sinners to forgive

sinners those sins which they committed against one another, and he called
them to pray jointly to God that he would forgive them their debts. He himself, however, did not, like the sinners he addressed, petition God to forgive
him and them. He rather joined them at table in order to grant them divine
grace. His authority to forgive in God's name, however, cannot be separated
from the power to overcome sin. He never exercised forgiveness for any other
purpose than to sanctify and had the confidence that following him would
bring about such sanctification. "Follow me" is not the word of one who is
stumbling but of one who knows he is obeying God. By being able to trace
sin to its internal beginnings, to the point where it is intertwined with our nature, and by nonetheless not despairing of his power to overcome, he revealed
the comprehensiveness of his purity. He did not merely put himself above a
few sins but above all sin with the authority to forgive and to end it. By explaining his cross-encompassing will in terms of death for the forgiveness of
others, he once again revealed an unviolated conscience, one that does not
land him in the same situation as one who sins finds himself.

The same observation confronts us when we observe how he executed the
function of judge and when he broke off communion with the guilty. He pronounced these verdicts without fear, for they did not apply to him. When he
denied justification to the praying Pharisee, he did not also condemn himself;
he stood before God without arrogance. When he denied God's rule to his
disciples who longed for greatness, he was free from such longing in himself.
When he called the righteous who scoffed at the penitent to rejoice with him,
he rejoiced in them like the angels in heaven. He emphatically impressed
upon his disciples the principle that they should refrain from judging others,
since the law they invoked against others also applied to them. But he broke
off ties with the brood of vipers without the fear that his verdict would also
judge him. For he had no internal communion with those whom he thus
judged.

Only through the purity of his conscience was it possible for him to possess the regal will as he did. He elevated himself above all and nevertheless
remained the opponent of all arrogance. How would he have been able to
keep himself free from it when his difference from the others had no real
foundation? If he had based this difference on the strength of his intellect
or on the greatness of his power, a complacent sense of self-admiration
would inevitably have shown itself. Only because the purity of his will separated him from others was he able to uphold his regal status with complete
firmness, free from pride. He who is good stands above that which is evil.
The one who sins is a slave; the one who does not sin is the master. And how
could he forfeit all means of power without being shaken and without yielding to sorrow or doubt? His authority was based on his purity; evil does not
overcome what is good.

Only through a pure conscience was he able to unite justice with the grace
that we always observe in him. When he judged, he did it with a pristine will
that hated nothing but evil; therefore he could at the same time forgive and
be gracious. When he was gracious, he acted out of a pure will that hated evil;

therefore he could at the same time judge. A violated conscience resists justice, for it fears it, and injects weakness into grace, for it creates room for sin.

Without purity of conscience, doubt would have inevitably surfaced in Jesus' thought. How could he bear within himself the mystery of his identity without being shaken? Nobody recognized him; all contradicted him, and he still did not turn into a person who doubted or became immobilized by introspection. He turned into neither an apologist nor a dogmatician. For the difference separating the good from the evil will possesses a weight that is, quite simply, irrefragible. The impossibility of denying ethical norms was in the fiber of his being, and all of his certainties attached to this. Since he was free of all remorse for sin, he also was not plagued with doubt.

Jesus' statement by which he related God's activity and delight to his entire life and will is thus united with his entire conduct and word, with his call to repentance and his kingdom concept and his messianic identity, and with his resolve to bear the cross, in such a way that the entire Gospel account of Jesus would be dissolved by their denial.

We do not yet grasp the motive for his behavior with the notion that he did not conceive of repentance in terms of meditation; he rather longed for the new will that subjects itself to God, and this longing was united in him with a good conscience by the assurance of divine grace. Against this view is the fact that he gave to the disciples, too, inner peace by their bearing of his yoke; nevertheless, it always remained significant for them that their wills had been guilty of lapse and they must constantly guard against relapse. Therefore Jesus never played down the distinction he drew between himself and all others. There is not a single saying presenting the ethical task of Jesus and of the disciples as identical: Jesus never said things like "we want to deny ourselves," "we do not want to be anxious," and so on. This, too, reveals how Jesus conceived of the uniqueness of his sonship.

It has been suggested that we should divide Jesus' life into two periods, an earlier period where he still had an obscure divine consciousness for which the name of the Father remained too vast because he could not yet assimilate his internal possession as God's gift. Then came the later period that began with baptism. From that time on he knew himself to have come from God and to live for God, because he considered his baptism to be the complete extinction of his guilt. It gave him the joy of someone whose sins had been forgiven in his dealings with the community. This interpretation of his conduct founders on the fact that he did not instruct his disciples to deny or conceal their sinfulness. Instead, all whom he helped attain a secure faith in God's forgiveness he simultaneously urged to a remorse for sin, through which they might acknowledge their guilt and cry out for God's pardon.[3] If his baptism had extinguished his own guilt from his consciousness, he would have connected a magical conception with baptism and borne the thought within himself that his baptism annihilated his old nature and transformed him. Such ideas, however, do not remain without effect in one's consciousness. When they are

3. Regarding this the Lord's Prayer is the decisive document.

present, they determine with clear effects one's entire deportment toward God. In this, however, Jesus clearly and continually evidences the opposite of magic. He shows that he conceived of his relationship with God as *personal*[4] and that he was oriented toward the Father in his thought and will and was subordinate to him. When does he ever speak of material means through which he sought to attach himself or us to God? And in this entirely personally conceived relationship with God he never wavered. Through it he was the unique Son.

Only the nature of our own will that renders us ignorant of how love functions presents it as impossible for us that Jesus came with a pure will, not driven to baptism by his own need but for the sake of the community and as its member. Nevertheless, continual experience shows that community is not destroyed by a pure but by an evil will, and this not only when a person destroys it by hate but when man conceals himself, isolates himself, and turns inward upon himself. No such compulsion prevented Jesus from experiencing and promoting community. He did not merely speak of love but had it. He saw people's need as clearly as the Baptist. He saw the necessity of repentance and God's readiness to hear the repentant person's request for forgiveness and to redeem it with the regal working of his grace. Now, because God summoned the community, he knew himself summoned above all to seek God's kingdom and righteousness, for himself and for everyone; to confess the guilt of the community—he, who knew it fully—and to do what the divine word had prescribed as the way to the divine kingdom. He saw with entire clarity that he acted differently than other people, wherefore they took offense at his behavior. He was slandered for his friendly dealings with sinners (Matt. 11:19; 9:15) but could not desert them, though he did not find the reproach pleasant to bear. For he had been given rapport with sinners by God.

Jesus set aside the Baptist's concern that baptism was for sinners, not for the Christ, by designating his behavior as "righteousness." By this he claimed that baptism possessed for him unconditional ethical necessity (Matt. 3:15). Both in the terminology of the synagogue as in that of the New Testament, the term "righteousness" denotes unconditional endorsement so that a coherent, complete will is demanded of what is called "righteous." Jesus, by reckoning his baptism as part of his "righteousness," counted it as part of his duty toward God and the people.

Thus he accomplished "all righteousness." He would not have done his entire duty toward God and the community if he had preserved merely himself pure, decisively distanced from sinners. Now, however, he did it completely, when he united himself with them and made their need his. In the same vein the Baptist would not have fulfilled his calling entirely, either, had he baptized only the Jewish community and not the Christ. For he would have broken in two the forgiveness he must bring to the nation, would have attenuated the divine grace, if he had declared the Christ to be too exalted and holy ever to

---

4. "Personal" I call that kind of behavior that is recognized by one's consciousness so that thought and will are united in it.

enter into communion with sinners. Now when John baptized Jesus too, he separated himself entirely from Pharisaism. Now the old Jewish righteousness sank into oblivion, and the new, better, "all" righteousness (cf. Matt. 3:15) emerged.

The fact that comes to light here requires attentive perception on our part. The love by which Jesus acted was for him one with righteousness, one with obedience. For it completely determined the direction of his ministry, which received full confirmation through it. It makes an enormous difference for the way we conceive of Jesus whether he viewed his identification with sinners as an achievement that went beyond what he termed his duty, or whether he reckoned it as his righteousness. His later activity confirms that he never conceived of his communion with sinners differently than in such a way that it belonged to the "fulfillment of righteousness" for him. This he saw as his office.

He thereby evidenced a consciousness of struggle that transcends our condition, because love, when it seeks to enter into such a communion with sinners, must possess power not to defile itself by the corruption of others, and beyond that to bring them help and to overcome their evil. He was, however, upheld in his communion with the people right up until the cross by the brave assurance that he would conquer, not be conquered, and that he would extend himself with fruitful results, not toil in vain. This assurance received immediate confirmation through the result of his baptism. No sudden, theatrical change occurred with it, as if now his consciousness of guilt had vanished and the assurance of sonship suddenly surged forth brightly. The sign given to him at baptism rather stood in a clear, causal connection with the consciousness of strength that was the basis for his entrance into the community of those who received John's baptism.

2. The Sign That Summoned Jesus

As others' baptism directed their view not merely to their own condition but upward to God who forgave them and who called them into his kingdom, for Jesus, too, baptism did not end with a meditation regarding his own will and duty but with an experience that corresponded at a higher level to the grace that others received through baptism. God did not give him that grace which brings about forgiveness; he bestowed his good pleasure by which Jesus was his Son and heard and saw his love, while others had to believe it without seeing.

By hearing God's voice proclaim his good pleasure to him, and by seeing the Spirit, the gift given to him by his fatherly love, his experience stood in a clear connection with the spiritual possession of the Jewish community. That he heard the divine voice reminds one of those events that are passed on by Judaism under the title "daughter of the voice." This was the designation for manifold signs that indicated God's will, surprising words such as words of Scripture that gained an inner connection to the sign-conveying event. The phrase, however, appears also in the sense of an utterance from above that audibly touched those involved. In this form, the pious claimed, God's rule was granted to them even now, in distinction from the glorious past. When man requires divine guidance, God calls to him short individual words that show him God's will. There is no reason to doubt the connection between Jesus' experience and this concept. As his entire internal life, this experience arose from concepts that were not new but had been the property of the Jewish community. Jesus experienced God as he, a member of the community, conceived God to be. This community expected God's voice to speak to the pious in special circumstances; Jesus heard it. Its content renews the words of Scripture that portray the Promised One. Jesus is the one promised by the second Psalm and the one Isaiah described as the servant of the Lord with whom God is well pleased.

When God's love was revealed in this way by the coming of the "Spirit" who stirred up God's effective presence in his internal life, Jesus' self-consciousness remained in agreement with his people's expectation and the Baptist's proclamation, since the latter had announced it to be the glory of the Christ that he would work and baptize through the Spirit. No clear connection to Scripture or to other widespread conceptions, however, can be demonstrated regarding the visualization of the Spirit through the dove that descended from above. The only thing that is clear is that something filled with life became for him the picture of the Spirit, who did not appear to him as a force that could be visualized, for example, through light or fire, but as alive, since he creates life in his recipient. The important sentence "the Spirit gives life" was common property of Jesus and of Judaism.

The account does not see the event's importance in the fact that Jesus had now become the Son of God. For it does not give to Jesus his conversion or his call to God nor his reception into God's love. It rather reveals what he is, since God testifies to him that he is his Son, and therefore grants him now the Spirit through whom he is able to act in God. The disciples did not ascribe the "son" concept to Jesus in piecemeal fashion; they rather knew that he did not use it merely for individual parts of his life, because he was bound to God in the indivisible totality and unity of his self in the firmly intertwined course of his life. This remains true whether we look at the events not attributed directly to God and those that were effected by him in linear sequence, or whether we regard them in parallel fashion. Therefore we would also err if we considered Jesus' baptism to be the point in time when he laid hold of the kingly ideal for the first time. For a sonship of God from which no call arose would have been an entirely different will than the one that Jesus in fact had. He never enjoyed his closeness to God as merely a gift given to him for himself, and he never sought merely the enrichment of his own self. Rather, through his sonship he received the obligation to serve, without which the uniqueness of his sonship would have been transformed into an ugly monster. In that case there would have been difference between him and everyone else but no longer unity. It would have turned into the attempt to attach God's love to his person alone and to take it away from all others. Jesus never conceived of his sonship in this way, and he never applied it to live in a special relationship with God that belonged to him alone. In his own view, this would have been a sinful, because loveless, sonship of God, a contradiction like the delusions of which the "foolish and blind" teachers were guilty. But even though Jesus' sonship was always connected to the assurance that he must do God's work, it had not yet been shown to him whereby he had to accomplish it. Now, however, he received the divine instruction for which he had waited. Therefore the Baptist's message and the sign given to Jesus intervened in his life with summoning power.

For the one who considered his life to be God's work and gift, no self-appointed beginning of his ministry was possible; he had to wait until God called him. If we ascribe to him the notion that he did not need any special gift for his regal activity since he was, after all, God's Son, we once again introduce a harsh contradiction into his portrayal. For he gave his disciples a clear awareness of the greatness of the event that occurs when an individual wills what God wills, thinks what God thinks, and does what God does. He instilled in them the conviction that they needed for this the divine Spirit, however great their gifts might be, and that they could only receive the Spirit through God's ever new communion and gift. And now they could receive the entire regal work! It was when Jesus saw that God's Spirit was in him that he acted.[5]

His ministry thereby received in a decisive way conformity with the messianic idea, since this idea imposed upon all participants the absolute prohibition of their own initiative and grounded their entire work on obedience. Its aim was, after all, that God's rule would determine the state of the nation. Therefore those who served that rule as instruments had the obligation at every step to perceive fully the divine guidance and to obey it. They could do nothing of themselves; to act willfully would break the conviction that moved them. Here every arbitrary step was a fall. With the complete yielding of all self-effort was coupled the carefree attitude that rendered it independent from the calculation of success. If activity had the hallmark of obedience, if there was certainty regarding divine guidance, then the outcome was with God. Of course, whoever ascribes to the Baptist a divine consciousness that permits him to dare an assault on God, so that he will at last reveal his rule, will also explain the baptismal sign for Jesus as meaningless and reckon that Jesus himself dove into his messianic pursuit through a passionate stimulation of religious feeling. This theory, however, remains in persistent conflict with the disciples' own account.

The manner by which the disciples narrate Jesus' debut brought two things to expression. First, Jesus was independent from the baptismal sign since he did not receive his divine sonship from this alone but possessed it previously. Second, the sign possessed for him the inexhaustible importance of a divine declaration by which the Father showed him his will so that the event deter-

---

5. The tendency to render baptism worthless for Jesus derived its strength from Greek ideas about religion, which looked at Jesus merely for thoughts and found in the events merely symbolic presentations of ideas.

mined his entire ministry with causal power. This becomes apparent by the fact that we have no saying of Jesus in which he exploits the baptismal sign as a proof for his sending.[6] He did not base his sonship on this single moment which, after all, passes immediately into the past, and did not call himself the Son because he became such at one point in time but because he was the Son. He proved the Spirit not by telling how he came upon him but by speaking in him and by acting in him.[7] The event's importance for his history is revealed by the fact that its narration became a part of the gospel, whereby the disciples say that Jesus' work and their following of him were based on his baptism. Thus it was already from the beginning; for John said that the first disciples came to Jesus because the Spirit had descended upon him.

For Jesus' experience at his baptism, the phrase "vision" has gained currency. This does not of itself require a polemical response, since we do not have precise statements about the form of the event. The implication of the term "vision" is that Jesus' seeing and hearing were not necessarily caused by material processes but could also have originated simply as something Jesus experienced in his soul. Thereby, of course, the account does not become more comprehensible, since a movement of this kind in someone's psyche equals in its obscurity an event that was mediated naturally, especially because then both the Baptist and Jesus will have to have experienced just the same thing. The term "vision," however, takes on a fallacious nature for the historical work when it is connected with the thought that the event did not have any substantiation apart from some subjective inner process. Through this dogmatic judgment the explanation of what happened is brought into sharp contrast with what the experience was for the consciousness of the participants. This inevitably tends to transform the story from the form in which it was experienced by those concerned into the form which it "must have had" according to the judgment of the person seeking to explain it. From the course of religious history transpiring in Jesus' disciples one may observe clearly that the baptismal sign and related events, that is, the resurrection appearances and Jesus' transfiguration, remained distinct from any idea of human causation and that such events entered their consciousness with the same independence from their own will as any sense perception. The baptismal sign would never have become a part of the gospel and the event by which the Christ was revealed if a merely psychological concept of vision had been attached to the process, however distantly. The objectivity of what was experienced, in the sense that a basis was given for it that transcended psychological process and a divine action was experienced in it, constituted for Jesus and for the disciples the prerequisite for their entire assessment of the event.

If "visions" had entailed the notion that they originated in their recipients' somehow intensifying their inner lives to the point that ecstasy set in, it

6. John 5:37 possibly refers to Jesus' baptism but not exclusively so.

7. Jesus' behavior lent the apostolic preaching its form. The thesis that Jesus' sonship was based on the fact that God's Spirit determined his existence is found in all clarity in Paul's writings (Rom. 1:4; Gal. 4:6; Rom. 8:9). It is, however, nowhere substantiated by the story of Jesus' baptism, but by the fact that the Christ now grants the Spirit to his community.

would have shaped the religious disposition of Christianity with clarity. From the vision caused by self-effort, a mystical piety would have emerged that seeks the place of God's revelation, not in history and the world, but in one's inner life, inducing everyone to evoke within himself the experience that would produce his union with God, in which he could rest satisfied. For this kind of religion, God's external attestations to man are unnecessary. He would need no Scripture, no community, no history, no nature. The visionary retreats into himself, since that is where he can achieve his highest aim, unity with God, through his own method. Neither Jesus nor his disciples, however, have any relation to this kind of piety. Their relationship with God does not originate in their elevation to God but in the divine gift that determines the condition of a person's entire life from within and without. It is therefore a far-reaching distortion of history when the fact is obscured that the baptismal sign consisted of a sober apprehension. It came to Jesus and the Baptist just as they perceived any other event and equally removed from their own formative causation.

The manner by which Jesus now stepped before the nation was ordered by the fact that he had felt his chosen status as the one elevated above it at his baptism, when he confessed the guilt of the people before God and when he identified with those who asked for God's grace. A self-centered understanding of his privilege was incompatible with the interpretation that his chosen state originated from an act of repentance and humbling before God. That God privileged him could not separate him from the Jewish community now. For precisely his identification with it, which made him the people's advocate before God, was confirmed by the sign, placed under God's good pleasure, and counted as his righteousness. And so the rule assigned to him was service, God's service in the testimony to his grace, service rendered to the people in the removal of their guilt.

By the fact that the sign consisted of the sending of the Spirit and of the attestation of his sonship, his internal relationship with God, which determined his personal existence, was made the foundation for his entire work. The prospect of his rule was opened up for him, since, as the Son, he was connected by the Spirit with the one who now revealed his rule to the people. If he was connected with God through his Spirit, he was linked to the power that perfects all things, with the grace that reconciles, and with the righteousness that executes justice. To begin with, however, the sign determined neither the program of his mission, his regal dignity and exercise of power, nor anything future, but expressed God's attitude toward him. His relationship to the world was subordinated as the secondary and derived element of his relationship to God. Not his future greatness was guaranteed to him by the sign, which rather revealed how God now assessed him and what God now gave him. The sonship of God, which now determined his condition and had its characteristic in the fact that he was moved by God's Spirit, was made the ground of his ministry. With this any framing of the messianic goal was rejected that thought exclusively or even primarily of a change of the situation facing people and hankered for the transformation of the world. Primary is relatedness with God. From this arises mastery over the world and effect on it. The baptismal sign did not announce that God was readying material good for the nation but that the one now in their midst was ruled by God in his inner being. God's gift to the Jewish community consisted of the fact that the Son of God was with it. But the internal and upward direction of his will could not produce passive mysticism that could do without work. For the connection between the sign and the baptismal preaching did not allow for any uncertainty regarding what he should do. God now reveals his greatness to humanity in judgment and grace; for that reason the one gifted with his Spirit should make an end to their sin. He should gather the community that is truly God's, exempt from judgment and bound for eternal life. How he was to overcome sin and create the perfected community, the baptismal sign indicated by making certain his relationship to God. Jesus can overcome sin as he remains in the Father's good pleasure and thinks, chooses, and acts in his Spirit.

The baptismal sign was never presented in such a way that it had touched Jesus without affecting the Baptist as well, since no one spoke of God's voice and the appearance of the Spirit in the conviction that they had remained a mystery the Baptist could not grasp. Rather, the significance of the baptismal account was always, also in Mark, that the sign achieved its purpose and revealed the Christ, not merely for his own consciousness but also for the nation, and foremost for the one who must speak for him owing to his special commission. The fact that the baptismal account has as its only topic God's testimony to Jesus, however, clarifies Jesus' way of thinking and thus the entire course of events at a crucial point.

That Mark speaks only of God's sign, not of the Baptist's testimony for Jesus, that Matthew speaks only of the Baptist's objection to Jesus' baptism, not of the Baptist's testimony to him, arose from the religious framing of the concept of the Christ. This concept controlled the disciples, because Jesus himself had it and championed it effectively. It excluded that people would make Jesus the Christ and prove him to be such. The participants in this history demanded God's testimony regarding Messiahship. He alone gives to the Anointed One his regal privilege, and he alone reveals him. It is true that John helped bring out the significance that the Baptist's word had for the beginnings of Jesus. But he, too, expressly formulates the rule limiting his importance (John 5:34). If God sent his Spirit to Jesus, everything else the Baptist said and did for him retreated in the light of this fact's importance. From this kind of thinking developed the patience and the expectant rest through which Jesus, from the beginning, was protected from any premature and self-willed divulging of his privilege and goal.

3. The Temptation of Jesus

Jesus did not remain with John but first wandered into solitude. As in the birth narrative, the memory of Moses influences the disciples' account at this point. Before bringing the people the Law, Moses lived on Sinai for forty days in communion with God, entirely cut off from human communion and normal means of sustenance. It remains impossible to ascertain whether in Jesus' own spirit, too, lay the thought of Moses as an example to be emulated. The disciples considered the major issue in the events of those days to be that Jesus withstood Satan's temptation. This corresponds to the fact that Jesus, too, viewed his disciples' overcoming of temptation as a necessary part of their task (Matt. 6:13; 26:41; Luke 22:28, 31). By the fact that this necessity also extends to Jesus, his relationship to God is likewise subsumed under the rule of righteousness that is valid for all. For the term "temptation" belongs to those kinds of terms that express the validity of righteousness even within divine grace. Because man should have his own will, and indeed a good one, he is put in the position of having to develop it by testing. The divine grace granted to him does not exempt him from this. Rather, precisely due to the particular greatness of the grace given to him, it is necessary for its recipient to prove his subjection to God's will through his own resolve in temptation. Thereby the grace granted to him proves to be righteousness.

Jesus did not confer on human beings the power to tempt him. True, they incessantly tried to impose their views onto him and force him to honor their evil will and act like them. But the rejection of their impositions did not result in what Jesus termed his temptation, since they did not require of him a choice by which he confirmed his relationship to God. Toward the ill-will of man, his will was bound fast to God and possessed an unshakeable steadfastness. Nor did Jesus grant power to act as a tempter to a spirit or demon. Rather, he saw in Satan the opponent with whom he had to wrestle because from now on his regal calling made him the dispenser of grace for mankind. By this grace he deprived Satan of his privilege and power.

The process was rooted in the fact that Jesus saw a close relationship between the concept of "guilt" and the verdict of "sin." When he spoke of "sin," he condemned human behavior, both in what it willed and what it did, as reprehensible; by "guilt," however, he referred to our reprehensible behavior as the basis for necessary consequences that dishonor and defile us.

It is true that he did not make the description of guilt the major emphasis of his call to repentance, for he did not permit that self-seeking, corrupted form of repentance that seeks merely to escape the destruction deriving from evil. Therefore he directed people's gaze sincerely and uprightly to their reprehensible actions, not awakening the consciousness of guilt in his disciples by describing the punishment following sin as graphically as possible. Nor did he speak as the one who intensified the terror of the judgment by new revelations. Rather Jesus merely revived in them the conceptions and insights that were already confirmed convictions in the community.

Instead, when he took stock of the people's condition, his eye was also directed consistently toward the consequence the person prepared for himself through his evil will. Among the consequences of sin Jesus counted man's being handed over to the power of evil spirits. That is why he did not see an essential part of his regal calling in the description of Satan and his kingdom and in the unmasking of satanic sin but rather in the obliteration of the slavery that subjected mankind to Satan, the "prince of this world."

Jesus described Satan's relationship to God by calling him "the accuser," who wants man to be defiled by sin and who therefore calls upon God's righteousness against him. By placing him first as man's accuser before God, and only subsequently as tempter and corrupter of man, Jesus avoided a dualistic break in worldview. All of Satan's activity thus remains encompassed by God's righteousness and occurs merely within the realm given by it.

He approaches man as the tempter, inciting him to sinful action. Of those who heard the word without understanding, Jesus said that Satan robbed them. The despicable work of Satan is also not described here as the beginning of evil; for the inability to understand the word preceded it and was certainly condemned by Jesus as culpable, not merely as a natural foible. Satan has no power until man has turned away from God so that he is the cause of the judgment that befalls man. This, however, leads the human being into a permanent dependence on him that determines his inner character and makes him a child of Satan. Jesus considered lying and murder to be satanic. Being a child of Satan thus is rooted in the fact that man does not permit God to give him truth and love, but rather allows Satan to give him lies and hatred whereby his will takes on the same form as Satan's. Thus arises in him a steadfast evil that takes his individual decisions and creates an unalterable condition. From this dependence on evil results communion with him in ultimate death (Matt. 13:19, 38; John 8:44; Matt. 25:41). Jesus noted that he had acquired the right to destroy this human dependence on Satan by overcoming him first of all with reference to himself (Matt. 12:29), and he honored the duty thus imposed on him as the holy rule of divine righteousness.

It is instructive for Jesus' contact with his disciples and for the motives shaping the Gospel accounts that the internal aspect of the baptism is not represented at all, while in the case of Jesus' temptation an extended account makes clear where Jesus drew the boundary between the good and the depraved will. What the presence of the Holy Spirit meant for Jesus' consciousness, how he himself experienced the communion of his will with God and was blessed in it, his disciples did not address. On the other hand, they made visible what he called an assault on his purity, how he closed himself against sin and how he proved to be obedient to the Father. They were gripped by Jesus' call to repentance, and their allegiance to him was based on the fact that he "fulfilled righteousness."

They did not see the process by which Jesus preserved his close connection with God in an act of thought but in an act of decision. Not an assault on his thinking is described, but an assault on his will, not a moment when he doubted, nor even changes of wishes and hopes, but a choice by which he acquired for himself the perfected will that generates response. What he wanted to do when he stood hungry in the wilderness, when he looked into the abyss from the temple wall, when Satan offered his help—these situations thrust on him a decision, and his victory consisted in his act of obedience.

The questions he settled through these decisions did not emerge from his relation to people but from his relation to God, which as the decisive point of his life held priority over all other relationships. In the temptation, he had to prove how he conceived of his divine sonship and how he used it. By answering this question, all his relationships with other people, too, lost or received their validity. From the same viewpoint Jesus later looked at the temptation that the disciples had to overcome in connection with his cross. It was not the disciples' fitness for work or their competence that was tried then but their attitude toward God. The struggle they had to undergo likewise related to the preservation or loss of faith.

Rather than freeing himself from hunger in the wilderness by way of a miracle, Jesus completed an affirmation of God by which he remanded his life entirely and exclusively to God's will. He did nothing to preserve his life, because he needs nothing but a divine word. If God promises him life, Jesus can do without even bread. Jesus' conception of God lifted God above nature, and the supernaturalism of his piety is characterized as that which is indispensable for its purity and righteousness. He did not need to acquire bread but merely stay close to God, who is not bound to nature or its resources but governs it in the liberty of the Almighty. In order for his elevation of God over nature to remain pure, however, it was necessary that he not link any selfish desire with it. In the face of nature's painful demands his willingness to suffer hunger did not become a pretext for self-help but an occasion for submission to nature.

If he bore deprivation with unconditional confidence in God, this appeared to result directly in the fact that he did not merely not fear danger when it arose but sought it that he might experience the glory of God in all its greatness. Contrary to the thought that no danger could threaten the Son of God because God's promise put the angels at his disposal, Jesus held firm to the ruling majesty of God. Man must not put God to the test nor urge him to help by taking a self-initiated risk. That would be to obliterate the normal relation between him and God, man taking precedence and furnishing initiative and God bringing a happy ending to man's gamble. Jesus held fast to the rule of obedience that placed him under God's guidance. Thereby he did not break or limit the promise; his confidence in God remained boundless. But he found the condition for confidence in the principle that man act according to God's will. Only the one who obeys can believe, and the applicability of the promise is determined by the fact that God's will remains, and must remain, the will that prevails.

His kingly aim would lead him into battle with Satan. But he refused Satan's promise that by a single act of worship he would not merely free himself from his opposition but also assure himself of his help, because he devoted his entire will to the worship of God. He did not want to win the world by turning away from the Father and therefore could not soften his antagonism against Satan. He completely united the concept of universal kingship with the religious aim and gave the former its purpose through the latter. He placed God over everything. Only from this, but from this with great sincerity, arose his will to rule, the demand that the world be his and subject itself to him, whereby Satan's power over it would be terminated.

This presentation of Jesus' will makes visible his equality with the state of life given to all. Yet at the same time it clarifies his essential difference from it. The grasping for bread in hunger in every form that may be successful is human, as is the transformation of faith into a false confidence that dares all things, or the striving for power by all available means, including turning away from God. Likewise, what Jesus chose as the good will—confidence in God, obedience toward him, and love that adores him—does not completely transcend human consciousness. These are our human functions. Here we do not find a description of the temptation and of the victory of a superhuman being but the dire need that always plunges human lives into turmoil. The ethical struggle common to everyone comes here to its normal conclusion. At the same time, however, the process rose above common experience. For in Jesus' temptation, a sense of power that reckoned the miracle to be an attainable possibility and laid claim to rule the world transcended the normal human condition. Granted that the event's ties were close indeed to the common duty of all, so that we are here shown a sin and a righteousness that are human, still, in the clarity and strength by which Jesus' assurance of God rules the will and determines the point both where the temptation seized him and where it required decision, this portrayal of Jesus' will possesses a qualitative difference from all that otherwise takes place in history.

By this description of Jesus' piety the disciples expressed that he remained comprehensible to them and to the entire community even in the things that were decisive for his religion. For he exercised the same capacities that all agree comprise the essence of religion. The disciples found the difference between Jesus and other pious people in the fact that he put commandment in place of theory and will in place of wish, a will that was able to act and that did away with all those shortcuts and breaks through which the pious aim must be offset by the existing measure of life. Jesus, they say, lived out trust, obedience, love in full measure. Since he did not merely stand before them as an inscrutable mystery, neither did they resort to any docetic concepts, although they viewed him with the thought that he had come from heaven and that he was called to an eternal rule. Nevertheless, the Gospels are based on the conviction that Jesus' activity is comprehensible and that it is possible to understand what he wanted and did. Since he possessed his divine sonship in those kinds of forms that everyone understood to be pious, the disciples did not describe him as a foreign visitor to earth but as their master and friend, of the same nature as they were and understandable to them.

Historians who started with the presupposition that the experience of a Satanic incursion would have had no room in Jesus' consciousness sought to explain the temptation in light of Jewish messianic expectations. These would allegedly have forced Jesus to a decision.[8] It is, however, characteristic of the height Jesus occupied and to which he elevated his disciples that the conflict

---

8. Here Jesus' temptations are interpreted with the notion that in the first scene Jesus must decide whether to provide bread for the people, in the second whether the fall would provide him with the admiration of the spectators, and in the third whether he would dispense with the vision of a glorious future Jewish state. At the same time, this interpretation had ties with the intellectual tradition that does not understand that Jesus could have had other interests than the development and ordering of his own ideas. But the text views the act of Jesus' will and the action that arose from it as the effective power that determined everything that followed.

described for us here takes place far above the wishes cherished by Jewish teaching about the Christ. A split arose between Jesus' aim, on the one hand, and several other considerations, on the other. One of these was the contrasting assessment of the political situation in relation to the ultimate goal of the Jewish community. A second was the Jews' different estimation of their national constitution in contrast with the transnational, universal greatness of God's kingdom. A third split arose through the evaluation of Jewish righteousness and Jewish guilt in relation to God's commandment. A fourth may be traced to the veneration of the temple and sacrifice when compared to true personal worship. But none of these questions is dealt with here. We are not told that Jesus was tortured by the question whether a military operation against Rome might be part of his office, or whether Israel's righteousness would be so valuable that it compensated its guilt, or whether the temple was not indispensable and eternal. His temptation arose at a more profound level where the Jew did not seek it and where prevailing messianic doctrines did not extend. The struggle involved the basic will to piety. It involved confidence in, obedience to, and love for God. Even in the third temptation, where the struggle turns on the messianic world rule, no specifically Jewish viewpoint comes to light. For no one speculated that the Christ should assure himself of Satan's help, not even those who were able to celebrate a "son of the star" as the Christ.

With this decision Jesus cast off all popular flattening of the messianic aim and its distortion into an anti-Christianity that pits man against God. By subordinating his use of power to his assurance of God and by rendering it selfless and one with obedience, and by using his power entirely for the glorification of God, he said goodbye to that usurpation of heaven's power that sought to bring about Jewish glory, goodbye to a Christ who would not be Son of God but rebel against God. The inseparability of the Christ's office and divine sonship and the inseparability of divine sonship from the love of God were secured by Jesus' decision. His separation from Pharisaic righteousness was thereby also confirmed. If Jesus had embraced that will that deduced from divine sonship the rejection of suffering and claimed full authority to venture every risk and grasped for power by every means, he would have become like those "righteous" ones whose goodness culminated in self-admiration, who made demands of God and sought to enlist him in their service. By rejecting the selfish abuse of his sonship, he demonstrated why he was opposed to Pharisaic righteousness.

The norms to which Jesus thus subjected himself guided him in his entire work. We find him always in that complete confidence in God that needed nothing else for life than a divine word, and this in such a way that his confidence in the divine life-giving love rendered him free from selfish passion and incapable of anxiety or self-interest, so that he subjected himself to every natural order. He permanently united his confidence with the rule that made obedience his calling and that considered his sonship never to be an exemption from obedience, and his obedience never to be an infringement of his filial privilege. Therefore self-willed decisions regarding himself or the world always remained foreign to him. Likewise, he always considered the aim of the regal will the fundamental act of religious devotion, that is, the worship of

God and the veneration of his name. He subsumed messianism and religiosity under one and the same will.

Regarding God's will—what his confidence should expect from God, what his obedience should do, and what his love should present to God as its service—Jesus searched the Scriptures. The description of his temptation indicates that he did not appeal merely to Scripture when he sought to communicate with the community but also when he had to come to a personal decision that would assure continued obedience to God. Even in the throes of testing he arrived at a decision by gleaning from a biblical saying what would be good and godly. In this way he proved himself to be a member of the Jewish community, as he went beyond merely relating messianic prophecy to himself and seeking Scripture's guidance for special tasks he faced. Rather, he grounded his resolve in biblical words that showed all members of the community what their obligation to God was. He thus did not extract from the Bible this or that piece as destined for him while leaving the rest aside but subjected himself to it with complete subordination so that he accepted the responsibility to fulfill what it required of all.

He proved the completeness of his confidence in Scripture by the fact that the single word of Scripture was sufficient by itself to substantiate his decision. He did not base his decision at the first temptation upon an extensive meditation about the biblical concept of miracle and nature, at the second temptation upon an investigation of what Scripture promises to faith, at the third temptation upon a general consideration of how the world rule of the Christ should be understood according to the prophets. He rather resorted to single, concrete sentences in Scripture and attached to them his entire assent.

At the same time, however, he knew better than to think himself obliged and authorized to obey every biblical quotation, because the abominable will of the tempter, too, based itself on Scripture. Jesus was therefore not merely confronted with a guiding word of Scripture but also with a word that was used to subvert him. The rejection of the misused quote by which Satan wanted to push him into sin occurs by Jesus' countering of misquoted Scripture with another word of Scripture. Obedience toward one word that would break the other would be wrong. He could not be so believing that he was unbelieving toward the other word; he could not practice obedience by simultaneously transgressing what Scripture said. Scripture is illumined by Scripture and thus also delimited and determined in its use. His confidence that the single word of Scripture would guide him correctly was based on the fact that he was willing to be obedient to the entire Scripture. Individual words taken by themselves could lead to foolishness and sin but only when the will failed to pay attention to other parallel instructions.

Since God spoke to him in Scripture, he concluded his deliberations with the quotation. Beyond this, he did not ask further questions, and every form of doubt, every resistance, was now over. His attention was directed solely toward the question of which word of Scripture would provide him with divine guidance for his actions. Once it was clear which passage should be applied, obedience took over. Jesus always linked the assurance of God with obedience, not with theory. He did not find in Scripture the impetus for far-reaching intellectual speculation but the motive for his will and for his work. He did not cite Scripture in order to interpret it but to do it.

His use of Scripture did not change during the course of his work. He used it in the same way at the defense of the temptation as when he clarified for himself the necessity of his death. In that case as well he arrived at the decision by becoming certain of the agreement of his will with Scripture, and then, too, he placed Scripture beside Scripture. For there was no doubt that Scripture accorded to the Christ dominion and glory. But he did, however, not want to appropriate words that spoke about the glory of the king in such a way as at the same time to reject those that spoke of the suffering of the servant of God.

The account closes with the hint of an experience that confirmed as correct and wholesome that renunciation of all self-will which he had exercised in trusting obedience. Angels brought him the food he needed and which he did not get himself by appealing to his sonship. Even though here invention interwove with the disciples' memory, it reveals an indispensable, effective part of Jesus' history to which the progress of his work was tied. He forsook, was deprived, and suffered not in the conviction that his share in the divine help that grants him life and glory would be hindered or lessened thereby. Precisely as the one who foregoes his privilege he obtains the full possession of what God's almighty hand presents to him. This rendered Jesus' obedience joyful and gave it its completeness.

4. The Renewed Encounter with the Baptist

From solitude, Jesus returned to the Baptist, and at this meeting John designated him as the Promised One for those who were with him: "This is the one" (John 1:30). Thus the messianic idea was transformed from an expectation into a declaration revealing what was present. While possessing absolute content, the idea no longer floated above temporal processes in unattainable heights. Now promise and history had become one. The event received its significance by the height to which the concept of the Christ had been elevated. When linked to David, it could be appropriated by a man skilled in war. The more, however, the concept of the Christ took on a religious content, and the more God's grace and glory became the hallmark of the messianic period, the greater the step became from the ideal concept to a real human being, from hope to history. The Baptist took this step first, not Jesus. Jesus' regal appearance began with the Baptist's testimony, not with his testimony to himself, since Jesus possessed from the beginning the inability to work for himself, an inability that always remained characteristic of him because it was inherent in the idea of God that animated him. Only God could reveal him and make him the Lord of the community. Only the success God gave him was true success, in Jesus' view.

This fits well with the fact that the Baptist did not interrupt his ministry or alter it, although with the conviction that Jesus was the Promised One the great epoch had begun.[9] This illustrates the seriousness with which these men conceived of the obedience they owed to God, seriousness that was free from hollow excitement. They were barred from all self-initiated adventure. The Baptist did not throw away the mandate of preparing Israel for God's rule. Indeed, the Christ had come, but the community had not yet been gathered around him. How he would effect this, the Baptist waited to see, and he kept maintaining that he could not help the Christ in his work. This appears to be so much the only thing possible, and so totally taken for granted, that it is reported initially without any discussion.[10]

The first of the three sentences by which John presents to us the Baptist's testimony regarding Jesus are known to us through Matthew: he will baptize with the Spirit, not with water. The Baptist maintained his complete subordination to the Christ that barred him from any collaboration with him even when Jesus, the Nazarene, the carpenter, stood before him without any means of power. The second saying called him the Lamb of God that takes away the sin of the world, and the third described him as the Preexistent One who was before the Baptist, even though he now came after him (John 1:33, 29, 30).

The Baptist saw the content of Jesus' calling profoundly shaped by the ethical predicament of the Jewish community. Thus the new word remained parallel with the messianic saying passed on by Matthew. Even now, he did not speak of social and naturally caused needs, for the Christ's work that must precede all other things consists in this: that sin must be atoned for. Since the verdict of "sin" implies that God's condemnation rests on human behavior, sin is removed by the provision of forgiveness in effective power so that a new condition of life results.[11] The Baptist, however, did not characterize Jesus' work as a struggle, nor did he describe it as a wrestling with the powers of evil. The thought that Jesus was the Promised One was linked with solemn joy: he would bring an end to the ethical predicament, make guilt disappear, and produce the pure community.

This is what Jesus effects as the Lamb that belongs to God. A lamb that belongs to God was a daily occurrence in religious practice, for the lamb destined for the altar is God's. The portrayal of the servant of God who suffers like a lamb, too, was known to both men.[12] Rich significance was thus not absent from this portrayal. It described Jesus as God's possession, as the Holy One who was completely yielded to him and who was placed entirely in his service. Therefore, since God has chosen him for himself in order to be his with all of his obedience and his love, he has the authority to forgive, to absolve from guilt, and to create the pure community he will baptize with the Spirit.

---

9. This is evident not only in John 1 and 3 but also from the fact that the circle of his disciples still existed at his death (Matt. 11:2; 14:12). It was only the Baptist's arrest, not Jesus' baptism, which occasioned the end of John's preaching.

10. Only later did the Baptist explain in a speech to his disciples in John's Gospel why he did not see in Jesus' own ministry a lessening but the fulfillment of his own mission (3:27–36).

11. How John understood the words is indicated by 1 John 3:5.

12. The Baptist did not read merely Isaiah 40, and Jesus did not read merely Isaiah 61 (John 1:23; Luke 4:18).

All thoughts of Jesus' work were thereby separated from those that did not link the rule of the Promised One with the internal need of man originating in his guilt and that therefore desired from him merely the power by which Jesus would subjugate the world to himself. Beyond power, Jesus has a yet higher office arising from his relation to God and giving him a holiness that is comparable to the one possessed by the lamb destined for the altar. But the Baptist did not merely distance the popular wishes from Jesus' aim but also clarified more precisely his own prophecy in an important way. The portrayal of the Christ that presented him as the one who administered the ax and the winnowing fork, as the one who cuts off the barren trees and burns the chaff, was not thereby contradicted as Jesus too always saw the hallmark of divine rule to lie in righteousness and power. To the contrary, the newer picture expressed the fact that, with the proclamation of the ruling and judging Christ, not everything was said that was needed by the community and that the Promised One would give it. That proclamation did not yet fully describe what had to happen first and what now constituted Jesus' task. It did not consist in subjugating the world to himself but in subjecting himself to God; not in receiving rule from God but in yielding his life to God. He thereby effected, not the annihilation of transgressors, but the pardoning of the guilty. The name "God's Lamb" not only described what God would give him but also what he would give God, and thus the basis was noted on which he must place his power. He was therefore not elevated above the community but placed within it. Since, as the lamb belonging to God, he became the shepherd appointed by God, his elevation above the community was rooted in his identification with it, and his rule from his service. Since he rendered this service, however, as God's lamb, the Baptist bowed before him at that time as completely as when he had only spoken of the Coming One. He made this clear by the statement expressing the Christ's eternity. Although Jesus did not give any evidence by his external appearance but remained unknown and powerless in John's presence, he was nevertheless exalted above all since he had divine origin and a heavenly nature.[13]

The new element expressed by these statements of the Baptist had been anticipated by the complete renunciation of all claims to human righteousness that he executed by his call to repentance. No one felt the inadequacy and defilement of all human work as he did. The teaching office and the priesthood of Israel had failed; no man could help. Aid could come only from above, and from there he expected it with complete certainty. The one who came after him would bring an end to sin. How could he do this? He descended from God.[14]

This formation of the conception of Christ, giving preeminence to the Christ's religious function in the service of forgiving grace, followed seam-

13. Thus it is assured that the circle around the Baptist and around Jesus did not from the beginning think merely of a ministry of Jesus that would do no more than simply prepare the heavenly kingdom perhaps via a prophetic office like that of Moses. For with the presence of the Eternal One God's rule has arrived.

14. The statement that John's Gospel fancifully conformed the Baptist's prophecy regarding the Lamb of God and the concept of eternity to his own image of Christ is possible only when one understands him as nothing more than a religious poet.

lessly from the preceding events. In encountering Jesus, what was evident to everyone was the upward orientation of Jesus' life by which he presented his love to God and was able to give up whatever he must. And for this reason he possessed God's good pleasure and was exalted above the community through the sign when at his baptism he identified with the repentant. Thus he did not stand above the flock but in its midst, not comparable to the shepherd but to the lamb, but as the lamb that was God's property, and he exercised that abandonment which forsakes everything for God's sake. As a result God granted to him power to give the people what they needed and what the Baptist could not give them: liberation from guilt.

No less clear is the unity between this beginning and later events. The aims formulated here remained Jesus' aims during his entire ministry. What the Baptist said regarding the ruling and judging Christ, he placed in the future. He was not yet willing to ply his ax but rather sought to reconcile. He did not yet wish to burn the chaff but went after the lost, since his calling was to administer grace. His relationship to the Baptist's proclamation was admittedly no more difficult than it was to Scripture. That he heard God's word from the prophets and that he identified completely with them did not render him unfree. Likewise, he understood his obedience in relation to the Baptist not as enslavement but followed the path he himself had recognized as the one shown by the Father.

Nevertheless, it was significant for Jesus' own consciousness and for his disciples' following of him that he could agree without reservation with those words of the Baptist that expressed the next task that needed to be fulfilled, and that he heard in them the divine will that was valid for him. Jesus saw his first task in belonging completely to the Father, and the purpose of his calling in liberating man from sin. As the Baptist linked in his message the power that is able to take away the sin of the world with the selflessness that does not desire anything but to be God's possession, Jesus, too, never had a will directed toward power that was not connected with this selflessness, nor a humility that was not accompanied by this power-wielding will.

While the Baptist did not place him above the community but in its midst, Jesus likewise did not consider himself merely to be the Lord but always also the member of the community. He did not think of himself merely as the builder who builds God's house but also as the stone used to build it, not merely as the sower but also as the grain of wheat that falls into the ground. In this, he did not see any obfuscation of his regal status. As the stone is the cornerstone that bears God's house, and as the grain of wheat is the rich fruit that creates the messianic community, the Lamb brings the sin of the world to an end and thus reveals God's rule. Jesus always saw the basis of his rule over the community in his identification with it and united it with the service he rendered.

In this word of the Baptist, however, one can also observe that Jesus did not give up his freedom, nor shape his inner life according to alien patterns. The phrase "Lamb of God" clarified his calling for him by way of religious practice, which is why it has no parallel in Jesus' own sayings. In order to express what love thinks and does, Jesus did not use such words, which were taken from the service of the altar. He likewise did not often resort to the concept of holiness in depicting discipleship.[15] Even in his portrayal of love rendered to God, he took his illustrations primarily from human relationships, from the son who entirely obeys the father, from the slave who serves tirelessly. He called the life he gave to God in death a ransom, not a sacrifice. Even regarding the future he spoke not of the heavenly priestly service of the disciples, but of their meal with him and of their share in judgment on the thrones beside him (Luke 17:7; Matt. 20:28; 26:29; 8:11; 19:28).

What caused him to avoid priestly phrases? He lived in God's love and did not seek to obtain it by rendering his service to his brothers. He refused love to turn upon itself and therefore did not give it a rich store of terms by which its dignity and its accomplishments were described. He turned his followers away from the material objects used in religious worship and instructed them to make their will the sacrifice by which they praised God. Even the call to repentance led him into a continual struggle against priestly ritual, since the Jewish community had emptied it of its meaning and kept its heart far from God. It called for sacrifice while sanctioning harshness against others, defiling that sacrifice through a pride that sought to make God its debtor by the gifts it presented to him. Therefore the Baptist's word retained its own coloring beside the words of Jesus. This, however, did not keep the Baptist's word from accompanying Jesus and his disciples throughout their entire history and from clarifying for them the divine will with increasing certainty.

The Baptist's word also showed Jesus the way to the cross. Indeed, the saying is not cast as prophecy that would describe something yet to come. It rather announces what had just happened to the world. The Baptist ascribed to Jesus at that time the ability and dignity to be the Holy One, and to make himself the effective sacrifice, by which he would obtain divine grace for humanity. He thereby expressed what he would give to those who followed him. Only when a lamb is made God's property is it destined for the altar. By using this designation, the Baptist did not separate Jesus' suffering and dying from his calling. He testified to his regal status in such a way that it was not in opposition to his will to the cross but rather provided it with its rationale.

This did not result from some theoretical construction but from the fact that both the Baptist and Jesus had in view the chasm by which the one who could not agree to Israel's sin but must overcome it was separated from the nation, and how difficult his confrontation with the world would be. Moreover, both conceived of the consecration by which Jesus made himself God's possession in terms of a complete obedience that did not refuse God anything but yielded to him even if he required suffering and death. We must not doubt the Baptist's determined sincerity that did not shy away from death. Without this sincerity, he could not have issued the call to repentance the way he did. Likewise it is clear that in John's message Jesus was able to frame the

15. The closest parallel to the Baptist's saying is the use of the term "holy" for the relationships of Jesus and of the disciples to God (John 10:36; 17:19, 17).

goal of his regal will, since we do not know him any other way than as the one who withheld nothing from God. This preview of the final outcome, however, did not make Jesus into an intellectual or into a system builder, because he was God's lamb and wanted to be that with determined will. God alone disposes over his lamb; only thus it is his own. He will show him how he has to serve him, and Jesus will be prepared to do whatever is asked of him.

The Baptist removed the offense of Jesus' powerlessness before the people by describing him as the Preexistent One (John 1:30; 3:31). Anyone who separates the Baptist's statement from Jesus' own declarations regarding his eternity can give them a gnostic interpretation according to which Jesus' regal status would be based on a divine being, earlier existent in heaven, who was now present in him. This interpretation, however, is precluded by the fact that the Baptist described the one who came from heaven as God's Lamb. The concept of sacrifice was never comprehensible to those who understood sonship of God as having a share in divine powers. This concept comes to the fore only where the surrender of one's will to God is made the essential characteristic of sonship. A holiness that is comparable to the one possessed by the lamb belonging to God does not originate from the reception of powers or substances but through the love that yields itself completely to God. On this love the Baptist based Jesus' regal status. This is confirmed by the fact that he described the Preexistent One also as the recipient of the Spirit.

The saying recorded by John overlaps with the prophetic word regarding the Christ in Matthew, because both point to a complete difference between the Christ and the Baptist, going far beyond a merely relative difference in gifting and success. Only to the Christ did the Baptist's prophetic word ascribe the establishment of the eternal community through judgment and pardon, whereby he was lifted out of human dimensions and placed in a relationship to God that made him the bearer of the entire divine activity.

To what extent the form by which the Baptist expressed the Christ's majesty and described his unity with God has precedents in Palestinian tradition regarding the Promised One can no longer be ascertained with precision. The account preserved for us regarding the messianic concepts of the Jewish community is too fragmentary and too unclear. This is partly because the eschatological thesis of the rabbinate never received dogmatic definiteness and validity but retained a fluid diversity and indeterminacy. And it is also partly because passionate rabbinic opposition to the church rendered Jewish tradition uncertain in important places, such as in the interpretation of Psalm 110 or Isaiah 53.

In the Greek Psalter, the concept of preexistence was clearly linked with the Christ (Ps. 110:3: "Out of my bosom I generated you before the morning star was made"), and it is not a matter of indifference that the same Psalm 110, which also otherwise effectively determined Jesus' thoughts regarding his kingly aim, ascribes to the Christ an existence with God before the foundation of the world. The messianic title "dawning from on high" in Zechariah's prophecy (Luke 1:78; cf. 24:49) also provides an answer to the question of where the Christ originated. Jeremiah and Zechariah made "dawning" the name of the Promised One, from whom it is now said that he would come from heaven, just as the power that the disciples receive through the Spirit comes from on high, from heaven. This had an undoubted effect on messianic conceptions in Palestinian tradition, so that the idea of preexistence was not bound up with messianic expectation as a fixed dogma. Preexistence was not the single all-determining doctrine inherited by the Baptist and Jesus.

If the Baptist's word ascribed to Jesus the heavenly and eternal manner of his life in God, and if he read in Psalm 110 or in the name for the Christ "the dawning," a testimony to the eternity of the Promised One, this doubtless forcefully strengthened his concept of the Son. Nevertheless, Jesus' statement regarding his divine sonship was more than a mere transposition of a biblical statement or of the Christology articulated by the Baptist. His consciousness as the eternal Son required grounding in his own existential situation. It found this grounding in the power by which his entire thought and will, fixed intently on his Father, originated.

5. The Separation from John the Baptist

After this Jesus separated once and for all from the Baptist; he no longer did his work united with him. In the same way that the Baptist continued his own work in obedience to the calling given him, Jesus revealed the commission issued to him by giving his work its own new beginning.

In an address to the Galileans Jesus pointed to the difference that was apparent to all between his behavior and that of the Baptist: "The Baptist did not eat nor drink; the Son of Man eats and drinks" (Matt. 11:19). Jesus laid aside the rule of fasting to which the Baptist subjected both himself and his disciples. For it concealed his relationship with God and also did not accurately represent either to his disciples or to the entire nation how Jesus wanted to order their behavior toward God. For the rule of fasting continually focused attention on personal misery and guilt and made repentance the decisive event upon which a share in God's rule depended. From this arose grief, sorrow, and fear that transformed prayer into pleading petition and hope into a painful longing born out of deprivation. Jesus' sonship and the call to his regal work, however, made the major element of his message not people's agony but God's power, not people's corruption but God's will to create something new.

Since Jesus made his opposition to sin complete by judging it as guilt, he told the entire nation as well as every individual that sin destroyed their lives. "The soul," the bearer of life, will be taken away from the one who sins; therefore sin makes him dead, and the gate through which the people pass leads them to destruction (Matt. 16:26; Luke 13:3, 9; Matt. 7:13; Luke 15:24; Matt. 8:22). In this judgment, too, he remained in close agreement with the Baptist, since he, like the Baptist, wrestled with people's death and corruption in everything he said and did. Therefore his message also instilled the fear of God. But this did not introduce a rupture into his concept of God so that the justice that orders death and the grace that creates life fought against one another. He rather saw justice and grace as united in God's rule. This occurred through the fact that grace determines the aim of divine activity. Therefore he did not merely direct people's view toward their own condition but directed it away from their behavior and toward God's work, thus creating through his message not merely fear but also faith, and creating fear in such a way that it would lead to faith. He thus placed the individual before God not merely as the petitioner but also as the recipient. Therefore he also provided the poor the promise that God was revealing himself to them with the riches of his regal activity, whereby he also conferred a joyful gratitude upon poverty (Matt. 5:3; Luke 6:20; Matt. 11:5). This spelled the end of ritual fasting, for those who realized what was happening there now began that feast which prohibited miserable lament (Matt. 9:15).

Under this rule he also brought life that is mediated to man by nature. Now the grateful reception of the gifts granted to us by nature became the characteristic of those called to God's kingdom. Just as Jesus erected no dichotomy between justice and grace in his divine consciousness, he also did not stand in opposition to nature so that he viewed its corporeality or its laws as a weakening of its dependence on God. He did not direct his attention to nature for its own sake, and he did not ask what it would be or accomplish by itself. He rather considered it as merely the means by which God gives man his gifts. He also did not make the fact that God was the Creator of nature the major emphasis of his teaching about God; for nature does not yet give us the communion with God that love desires.

The widespread name of God, "Creator," also lived within Jesus in its entire weight (Matt. 19:4). It formed the prerequisite for all that he said about God. But he placed it lower in importance than the name "Father," by which he denoted not merely the beginning of our life in God nor merely God's provision for our destiny but promised us God's personal connection with us. This promise, however, would not have been possible for him nor would he have been able to give his own concept of the Son its completeness if he had separated nature from God as unworthy of him. He did, however, see in it the work of his Father and moved within it with a joyful, grateful disposition. The sun, he said, is God's, and it rises because he causes it to rise. All experience God's goodness in sunlight and rain. And in the beauty of the lily, Jesus saw God's work, proclaiming to all that God does not merely grant them the necessities of life but also magnificence. His Father did not care merely for human beings but also for every bird, ordering its life span (Matt. 5:45; 6:26, 28–30; 10:29).

The misery nature creates for our religious behavior by putting us to death was also a great weight upon him. When hunger seized him in the wilderness, or when looking from the temple wall down the cliff pictured for him the danger of a fall, this provided for him the occasion of a temptation (Matt. 4:3, 6). He must even then hold fast believingly and obediently to the glory of God that creates life. When at Lazarus's grave the sisters wept, he wept with them (John 11:35). Therefore he surrounded the entire process of nature, even that which causes us to die, with the assurance of God, and he accepted it as God's order set for us and valid for this world. When the bird falls dead to the ground, it happens with God's knowledge and will, and when the disciple has to die, God gives him over to death. Likewise, he viewed his own death as arranged for him by God. The jubilant joy of life characteristic of him did not drive him to an antagonism toward our mortality. For life is God's gift, and his gifts are not wrung out of him or attained by sheer demand. If he does not grant them but gives men over to death, this underscores God's judgment that separates the sinner from him and exhorts us to return to him. To find God is to forego death; for union with God is life without death (Matt. 10:28–30; Luke 13:1–5; Matt. 22:32; John 8:51; 11:26).

Nature's man-threatening component, "snakes and scorpions and the entire army of the enemy," Jesus likened to Satan, whom he called the archetypical destroyer of life (Luke 10:19; John 8:44). But this did not lead Jesus into a dualism or to a theory that attempted to explain the side of nature that appears harsh to us. It is an admittedly peculiar proof for the power with which Jesus limited his thought that we have not a single word from him about the origin of death. For even when he made it Satan's chief characteristic, that which typified his rebellion against God, that he was a murderer from the beginning, he did not explain how human dying fit into the all-encompassing divine moral order. He rather showed how much we should fear and avoid hate and why it burned especially hot against the one who told the truth.

Jesus' judgments regarding the human body and the processes occurring in it had special importance for the grateful, joyful relationship he sustained with nature, since opposition to nature was always directed foremost against these processes. Because we have received from God soul and body, Jesus called food and clothing comparatively smaller gifts that God provided with all the more certainty since he had granted us such great gifts (Matt. 6:25). God had bound woman and man indissolubly to one another (Matt. 19:6). That the human being receives food through the mouth and that he eliminates what is useless does not result in any religious difficulty and does not defile the human being (Matt. 15:17). It is not the natural processes independent of us that separate us from God; rather, from our "heart" emerge the things that devalue us. In his divine consciousness, Jesus had the ability to unite not merely without bias but with glad consent and positive participation all that was natural. Without this conviction, his share in physical life would have implied consciousness of defilement and separation from God within him.

With the phrase "flesh" or "flesh and blood" he joined the larger community in describing man in contradistinction to God. But he expressed here not merely the distance, but also the contrast between man and God. By the phrase "born of woman" he evoked, as did common usage, a reminiscence of the limitation and weakness inherent to us above which no human greatness can rise (Matt. 16:17; 26:41; John 3:6; Matt. 11:11). By basing his statement describing the human being's distance from God only on the human condition, he showed that he did not already deduce that distance simply from our share in nature. In that case he would have referred to general characteristics belonging to the entire created order to denote the human predicament. This predicament originates first of all in the realm of human life, not because we are part of the natural order alone.

Even the verdict Jesus pronounced on "the world" does not alter his largely positive stance toward nature. For this verdict located the contrast with God not in nature but in the unified shape of human behavior that is common to all.

As a result of these convictions Jesus did not continue the struggle against our natural disposition to which the Baptist's practice of fasting was devoted. It thus disappeared from the circle of Jesus' disciples. Fasting, however, was not the only thing that separated Jesus from the Baptist. Even more important was the fact that John had revealed his opposition against people's behavior by dwelling not among the Jewish community but in the desert and by demanding from the people that they come out to him. Jesus, on the other hand, maintained the resolve that had led him to dwell in the midst of those who had been baptized. He remained even now united with the Jewish community, returning to it, submitting himself to the custom valid for it, and carrying his message into its worship gatherings. He thereby exercised his regal prerogative that authorized him to say of the community that it had been given to him by the Father and that it was his possession.

The term "patriotism" is insufficient for an understanding of what he did. It is true that his decision grew out of his love for his people; this love, however, was constrained by a love for God that lent his behavior its greatness. His loyalty to the Jewish community was his obligation not merely because of the Jewish people themselves but because of the Father, and it was not merely patriotism but religion. This gives due recognition to the phrase once used by the Enlightenment, "Jesus' accommodation to his contemporaries." His behavior was indeed based on the desire to be accessible and comprehensible for the Jewish community. It did not, however, emerge from a calculated, artificial effort to conceal his inner difference from others. He rather honored the community created by God even more than nature and was therefore drawn to it by its dire need.

If Jesus had fraternized with gnostic religionists who said of themselves that a heavenly power or something similar was manifest in them, he could have left Israel to its own devices and found a following apart from the old community that would have served to reveal his own greatness. But because he appropriated the prerogatives of the promised king, he was there for Israel, born for its sake and equipped for its sake by what God gave him. Therefore he did not remain in the desert but began his work in Galilee.

He also distanced himself from the work of the Baptist by separating the call to repentance from baptism. According to John's report, baptism was continued by Jesus' disciples only at the outset, when Jesus remained for a while in Judea after his first activity in Jerusalem (John 3:22; 4:1–2). It disappears, however, in Galilee. The sign with its prophetic significance served Jesus as his tool no longer. Since the uniqueness of baptism was essential to it, and since it was designed to reveal the completeness of divine grace, it was incapable of repetition. Those who longed repentantly for God's rule had received it from the Baptist. Now Jesus granted them forgiveness, not again through washing, but through his word.

The Baptist was not shaken by Jesus' separation from him. He preserved his readiness to subordinate himself to the Christ even at a time when Jesus began his work in separation from him (John 3:27–36), by announcing to his disciples that Jesus was the Son of God who would prepare the feast for the community and grant it eternal life.

6. The Call of the First Disciples

According to all accounts, Jesus' participation in baptism was followed by the establishment of a circle of disciples. This act of Jesus gave them precedence in all that he did for the entire community. As different as Matthew's and John's narratives are at this point, they agree in this: the first thing Jesus did in his messianic authority was to call disciples.

We have in our Gospels three narratives regarding how the first disciples came to Jesus. Each of these emphasizes one particular motive that led them into communion with Jesus (Matt. 4:18–22 = Mark 1:16–20; Luke 5:1–11; John 1:35–2:11). In Matthew, Jesus calls fishermen working by the lake to follow him. Thus their complete obedience is made the characteristic of their communion with him. The disciple follows Jesus by leaving the old entirely and without hesitation. He gives up his possessions and does not tolerate any division of his love, yielding to Jesus unconditionally.

In the narrative preserved by Luke, the communion between Jesus and the first four disciples began by Jesus' use of Peter's boat as he spoke on the lake. Thereafter Jesus showed them his power to give them everything they needed by a miraculous catch of fish and thus won their confidence. They saw that with him they would be well cared for, body and soul, in their personal lives and in the callings he extended to them. In view of the divine activity, Peter felt and confessed his own guilt that made him, sinful man that he was, unworthy of communion with Jesus. But Jesus called him and thereby acted toward him as the one who forgives. Precisely because the consciousness of his guilt was awake in Peter, he was useful for Jesus, and his attachment to him was firm.

Both narratives stand in vivid contrast to one another. The former describes the abandonment that leaves everything, the latter, God's power that grants everything; the former, the obedience that readies itself for any service, the latter, thanksgiving for the kindness that frees them from any care; the former, the decisiveness that brings complete sacrifice, the latter, the consciousness of guilt that rejoices in Jesus' forgiveness. But Luke, in the final sentence of his narrative, already links both descriptions of discipleship to form a unity. One's own free decision that accepted the call and thanksgiving for the received gift, the preparedness to selfless sacrifice and the confidence of divine help, did not conflict with one another but together led to the disciples' attachment to Jesus. What led them to him was not a notion of self-gratification that does not wish to forsake and obey, but merely to receive and enjoy. The entire commitment Jesus demanded always shaped their contact with him. However, they also did not enter communion with him with cares regarding how they would support themselves, or cares deriving from their guilt, or cares regarding feelings of inadequacy for his service. They rather affirmed their confidence in divine help, since they saw in what they experienced with him that God was with him.

According to John, Jesus found the first disciples among those who, due to the baptismal preaching, repentantly waited for God's kingdom. Thus his connection with the Baptist also proved itself in the establishment of his circle of disciples. Where the Baptist found obedience, there also developed faith in the Christ. At the founding of Jesus' band of disciples, as also in his entire account, John speaks solely of faith. He places faith above everything that the disciple receives for himself and above everything that he does for Jesus. Faith is therefore the greatest thing Jesus grants to the disciple, since through faith he links him internally with himself. In this internally produced unity with the Christ consists, for John, Jesus' work. John presupposes the founding of a closed circle in the subsequent presentation. But he does not narrate it. Since Jesus gave his permanent communion to those whom he united with himself through faith, the circle of disciples developed from the first believers. John explains the firmness characteristic of the disciples' association with Jesus by showing the religious basis for that firmness in Jesus' action. He traces people's attitude toward Jesus, whether faith or hatred, not merely to their will, but to the divine activity. This pattern had particular validity at the founding of the core group of Jesus' disciples, owing to the importance this circle had for Jesus' work. Therefore he expected that the Father would lead those to him whom he could draw to himself. He considered those who came to him to be God's gift and received before their encounter with him an illumination through which the Father showed them to him. He immediately called Simon "the rock," and Nathanael he had "seen" before he came to Jesus. Thereby his call became not an attempt that could possibly fail, but a powerful action that bore certainty within itself.

Since the disciples saw in him the Christ, and therefore the one who had God's Spirit within him, they dealt with him in the understanding that his eye would also see what was concealed and what went on within a person (cf. Luke 7:39; Matt. 26:68: if Jesus was the Christ, he needed to be able to say who struck him). This immediately injected into their dealings with Jesus complete truthfulness and ended all religious hypocrisy. With him "they walked in the light." This put them in a reverential distance to him that can always be observed in their dealings with him. At the same time, their allegiance to him was confirmed. Since Jesus knew what they were, the fear disappeared that their communion with him could fall apart. When they were amazed about their call and why he had granted it to them and not to others, the clarity of his view gave them the courage to believe in it without doubt or fear, since he had known them, after all, from the beginning.

But this means that the first disciples' attachment to Jesus was not bereft of all natural mediation, nor had it been effected in a solely miraculous way.

The Baptist's share in their call already connected it to preceding events. Since the Baptist made known who Jesus was, Andrew and John chose to follow him; the two subsequent disciples, Simon and James, were induced to come to Jesus because they were the brothers of those who followed him first. Philip was connected to Simon through their common home town, and they already had had a previous relationship with Nathanael, all being Galileans. Jesus did not place arbitrary qualifications on God's work, as if it had to be entirely miraculous without the cooperation of natural relationships. Even when these natural relationships led disciples to him, the Father had led these disciples to him.

John also explains by way of a sign how the disciples' faith in Jesus grew firm. At a wedding in which they participated after their return to Galilee in Cana, the home of Nathanael, Jesus provided wine and thus brought the feast to completion when the bridegroom could not bring it to an end himself. Similar to the catch of fish, he thus presented himself to the disciples as their provider who had help for every need and who prepared for them the feast that had now begun with God's regal activity. Together with the joyous conviction, however, that Jesus would fulfill the request, even when it made great demands, and could furnish everything that human wishes and popular myths of regal glory ever told, this wedding feast instilled in the disciples the conviction that they should not yet expect the revelation of his glory since "his hour" had not yet come. The hour of his celebration had not even come by his provision of wine for the feast in miraculous power and goodness. The disciples also learned that his communion with them did not reduce him to dependence on them and did not allow them to transform their hopes into claims he had to obey. John expressed this emphatically in telling of Jesus' denial of his mother's request. When, in jubilant joy over the revelation of his regal status, she wanted to push Jesus to the miracle, he affirmed brusquely and unequivocally that it was not her role to lead him. If even his mother lost the right of expressing her wishes as commands he must obey, the disciples were entirely obliged to believe in him by receiving what Jesus gave them apart from any claims.

How we answer the question of whether John's portrayal should be rejected or linked with that of Matthew largely determines the picture we have of Jesus. If we had to consider the events spoken of by Matthew and Mark when Jesus called the disciples away from their circumstances through his command and obliged them entirely at their first encounter with him without their having any previous knowledge of him, the supposition could hardly be rejected that Jesus, by requiring blind obedience, predicated his disciples' loyalty upon a coincidence or, from his standpoint, a miracle that had no connection with nature. If we put both accounts together, however, Jesus directed his call to the disciples at a time when they knew what they stood to gain if they came, and what they would lose if they rejected his call. In that case, a deliberate decision, fully aware of the issues involved, constituted the basis of their discipleship. Through the relationship of both texts to one another, it becomes probable that the development of faith in the disciples should be distinguished from their entrance into permanent disciple-ship of Jesus. Their first encounter with Jesus at the Jordan was followed by an act of Jesus in Galilee by which he granted them the rights and duties of discipleship. It was then that he showed them that their old circumstances had irrevocably changed. From now on their following of him would be their sole vocation.

Matthew's narration is parallel with pericopes in other Gospels that like-wise portray the determination that Jesus' call required of those to whom it was issued. From these elements one can gather how Matthew understood his narrative. Matthew's own entrance into following Jesus as well as Jesus' nego-tiation with those who wanted to follow him when he left Capernaum stood under the same viewpoint as the call of the first four disciples (Matt. 9:9; 8:18–22; Luke 9:61–62). Here one cannot speak of blind obedience and co-incidental encounters. The men whom Jesus confronted with the decision of leaving everything behind and of yielding completely to him knew what was involved in their coming to him. Thus tradition includes two parables that warn explicitly of unadvised entrance into discipleship (Luke 14:25–35). Whoever wants to build a tower or wage war should first count the cost. This is the complete opposite of the exploitation of a momentary mood that bases one's entire discipleship upon a sudden welling up of emotion. Such a tactic is ruled out owing to the weightiness of the renunciation it requires and the greatness of guilt that arises when mood no longer suffices. Salt that has be-come bland is entirely contemptible. These passages indicate how the disci-ples understood what took place at their decision to follow Jesus.

The internal difference in the accounts reveals already at the beginning of discipleship a fact that retained great significance for the disciples' future min-istry: Jesus made his companions independent in their piety and protected them against one-dimensional spirituality and facile imitation. The piety of one man consisted of his sincerity of repentance that put the act of deter-mined obedience over everything else. That of another was characterized by a faith expressing itself as gratitude for the grace he received. The piety of a third acquired unity with God in his believing identification with Jesus. These were different religious types, and they did not originate only later but were evoked and guarded by Jesus himself in his followers. We should, of course, not think that he awakened in them an intentional reflection on their own pe-culiarity. For it is a predominant characteristic of the Gospel account that it does not linger over individual disciples and does not individualize their view. It thereby expresses that Jesus gathered them into a united group to which he issued the same word of repentance and to which he gave the same task of proclamation. Jesus did, however, give to each one religious independence by submitting his entire dealings with them to the rule of truth. Truth immedi-ately brought with it freedom, and freedom could not be in short supply among Jesus' circle because he conceived of repentance as the transition from selfish will to selfless love. For love, however, freedom is indispensable, whether we speak of love for others or love for oneself. Love has freedom and gives freedom, since it makes all abilities subservient to the service of God, both personal abilities and the abilities of those to whom it grants its help and gift. That Jesus gave to the community he founded its basis in love is proven by his leading it into freedom.

In calling his disciples Jesus did not achieve an elevation above the community by a visible attestation of his kingly aim. For by living together with disciples, he used an existing form of religious interaction. His novel work remained thereby in agreement with his initial step of identifying with those who accepted John's baptism. The external uniformity with existing form, however, covered an essential difference that distanced the disciples' relationship to Jesus decisively from the usual one between rabbi and disciples. Usually the authority of the one who became a rabbi did not consist in his personal character but was based on his training in the Scriptures, on his knowledge of Hebrew and the Bible, and on the fact that he himself had been the disciple of a famous teacher with whom he had practiced the fulfillment of the Law so that he could now serve as an example to others. The disciples, however, did not follow Jesus on account of a theory that also existed without him or on account of some theory or because of a tradition that had other witnesses besides Jesus. For their allegiance to him was brought about by the word that called them to repentance. They heard in Jesus' command God's will, heard in his judgment God's judgment, and received through his forgiveness God's forgiveness. By obeying his call, they were granted God's grace and a share in his rule. They considered Jesus' communion with them to be God's grace, since they saw in him the Christ. The entire account of the disciples' dealings with Jesus is built upon the proposition that whoever stood in communion with him knew who he was, the Christ. For the account does not contain a single pericope where Jesus' disciples ask him about his aim or where they still seek to find out whether he was the Promised One or not. But since Jesus united his invitation to the kingdom with the call to repentance, their following of him had not been effected solely by the hope that expected from him the revelation of his regal glory. This would not by itself have overcome the weighty challenge posed by his poverty and suffering of persecution, and especially his ethical demands. They did, however, seek in him the one "who takes away the sin of mankind," and from this longing arose an internal allegiance to him that created unity between him and them and kept them firmly tied to him. Accordingly, the Gospel story does not know of a single moment when the disciples doubted Jesus. They went with him all the way to the cross.

Together with the call to receive divine gifts, Jesus gave them from the beginning the obligation to serve. They should become "fishers of men" (Matt. 4:19), not merely sharers of his joy who celebrated his feast as friends of the bridegroom but co-workers who bore his gifts to others and rendered them widely effective. By calling Simon the "rock" at the very outset, he did not prophesy to him merely that he would be integrated into God's building but also that he would become a pillar of strength for others. We know from Matthew 16:18 how the disciples understood the simile surrounding the term "rock" whereby, for those who are concerned with facts, any doubts regarding

The History of the Christ

the name's meaning are removed. This rules out the view that Jesus described Peter's character with this simile, be it in an affirming or warning fashion. For the disciples associated the "rock" with the building Jesus had to build; Jesus built God's house upon that rock. For the disciples, Peter was a vocational name, parallel with "fishers of men" and the shepherd "who tends Jesus' sheep" (John 21:16).

In Israel the concept of "God's house" belonged to the elementary framework of religious thought; Israel was "God's house" as the community called and sanctified by him. Latent in Christ's commission was the notion that he would build God's house since in creating a living social fellowship he was doing exactly that. The question arose who would make a start and to whom the continuation of Jesus' work would be entrusted. From that conception of his commission and his office that Jesus himself obeyed, the goal that should lead the disciples in their dealings with him immediately emerged. Since he was sent in order to produce the community, he needed those who would serve him. Therefore the disciples, through whom the beginning of his community was given, were indispensable. That is why he gave precedence to calling them over any other deed and recognized in Simon the one whom God had given him so that the community would follow him.

7. Parting Company with Nazareth

The prophecy that God's rule would now begin was valid for the nation as a unified whole, and the call to repentance was directed toward those who wanted to pull away from the prevailing evil and be freed from their common guilt. Therefore no doubt appeared to attach to the question as to where Jesus must do his work, since the nation had in Jerusalem a center that tied all of its parts together into a firm unity. Jerusalem's importance for the entire nation was not grounded in political or natural circumstances but in religious ones, since it was the chosen city. In it the temple in particular possessed sacramental value as the place chosen by God. Yet Jesus did not make Jerusalem his place of residence, since he saw how the Baptist's call to repentance had been directed largely in vain to the Jewish people. He was eventually confirmed in his decision to work primarily in Galilee by the arrest of the Baptist. By going to Galilee and remaining there, Jesus postponed further decision, while in Jerusalem his work immediately resulted in a clash with the religious leaders. Thereby he also continued the story of his youth without a break; he knew himself to be made a Nazarene by God's guidance and saw this guidance also confirmed by the fact that his disciples were Galileans.

When he presented himself in his hometown of Nazareth as the Promised One, he clearly revealed to it what he included and what he excluded from his regal vocation (Luke 4:16–30). Since he could read and interpret the prophetic texts according to the order of worship, he read Isaiah 61:1ff. not merely as a prophecy but claimed that the prophet's prophecy was being fulfilled and granted to the community, thus achieving what the Baptist had described as his calling: he would take away people's sin. He did not confront the Nazarenes with his regal name, for he did not appear before them as the one who demanded, nor did he desire their adulation or support. He stood before them as the one who gave, as the one who brought freedom to the captives and forgiveness to the ones in bondage, as that servant of God of whom the prophet had spoken. The second part of Isaiah served him toward this end, since he could apply the prophecy found there directly to himself and to his work without having to point to something still future. Jesus was now called to God's service that the servant of the Lord described there should exercise, and this rendered his word the complete divine gift. As the bringer of the gracious divine word and as the called evangelist he stood before the community, and therefore he was the Christ; for the liberation and forgiveness had been obtained, since he proclaimed them in God's name.

The Nazarenes, however, took offense, owing to their familiarity with Jesus. In their understanding, the divine commission would give to the one who had it a mysterious, almost spooky manner. Therefore Jesus was refuted by the fact that he had been placed into the natural and historical contexts of a human life. This thought reared up against Jesus not merely in Nazareth but everywhere; it received, however, particular strength in Nazareth, since everyone knew him there.[16] The decision required of him on account of this objection profoundly impacted the way he framed his kingly aim. Jesus replied that the truth of his human life substantiated his divine sonship and rendered him fit for his regal work. Thus his vocation did not require some magical dissociation from his natural surroundings. Therefore he was the Son of God and the Son of Man with the same unified and complete will, without any contradiction arising for him from this. Because he was a man, he was the Christ. He did not despise his flesh but praised it as the means by which he exercised his service to God and by which God accomplished his work.

Since the Jewish community responded to the attestation of his commission by attacking him, he was confronted with the question of miracles. But he could not call upon God's power for his own ends. He thus united complete selflessness with his kingly aim. Even when those with whom he had spent his youth broke ties with him, self-help was a procedure impossible for him. This rendered him incomprehensible to others; for according to the standards of public morality, self-help was an obligation and the condition by which alone he would deserve confidence. A doctor who cannot heal himself is put to shame. Jesus, however, took this offense upon himself. He was here subject to a law that had absolute necessity for him. He could not demand. As he did not demand anything from the nation, he did not demand anything from the Father. He stood before the Jewish community as the one who gave and before God as the one who received. Neither here nor there did he appear as the one who demanded. He thus united the power to rule with the granting of liberty while also bringing his assurance and confidence to their highest revelation. Trust in him should not be created by a separate sign but by what his

---

16. Regarding Capernaum, see John 6:42; regarding Jerusalem, see John 7:27; therein stirs the docetic element in Pharisaic Christology.

word created in people. By placing himself on this high level, he proved that he knew himself to be the bearer of the divine word and the worker of the divine work so that God was to be recognized in him. He thus earnestly affirmed his commission by God.

His messianic concept was now immediately tested severely by the Nazarenes' rejection of him. Israel and the Promised One, the Christ and the community, were concepts that complemented one another; that they could be severed from each other was inconceivable to all. What was there left of the Christ if the Jewish community rejected him? This train of thought was even sharpened in Nazareth on account of the fact that all those relationships were severed there that had been grounded in his natural communion with them. He bore the rupture without being shaken, however, since he did not doubt the success and victory of God's rule. He quoted examples from the history of the prophets, of Elijah who was sent to the Gentile woman and of Elisha who healed the Syrian. These examples proved that God's work is not destroyed by Israel's unbelief. The question that reached into the future regarding when and how God's call would come to the Gentiles was thereby not yet addressed. Jesus merely maintained by this word what he now had to regard as his work, and he was certain that he should not open himself up to the fear that everything was lost when Israel was lost, as if God were powerless without the Jew. God would find his own as he had always done up to this point, even when Israel hardened itself in unbelief. Jesus' entire conduct was based on this certainty. He stood there in complete peace, in the certainty that the Jewish community was now faced with the great decision that would lead it either into God's kingdom or into separation from him. He neither flattered the nation nor lured it with artificial means. He was not at the mercy of the hearers of his message. If they accepted it, this was their salvation. If they rejected it, God's rule did not depend on their decision.

The final scene of that exchange also revealed an important characteristic of the way he regarded his kingship: namely, that it included his being prepared to suffer. If he did not want to subject himself to the Jewish community but wanted to place himself above it freely, he had to be prepared for the fact that the nation would attack him, not merely verbally, but violently. In Nazareth, a passionate act of judgment resulted, since the blasphemer was to be pushed over a cliff. The religious justice of Jewish communities had become hard, seeing its most important task in protecting God's honor against any attack, destroying everyone who threatened it. Therefore Jesus' proclamation entailed the continual danger of death. Precisely because the Jewish community was religiously zealous, there were only two possibilities for it: if he deserved the messianic name, he was worthy of unconditional faith and the rule was his; if he, however, used the name without justification, he had to die. This procedure shows that Jesus decisively seized the goal described with the title "Lamb of God." Since he was prepared to go the path of Elijah who was driven by Israel's resistance to the Gentiles, he already stood close to the realization that his way was foreshadowed for him in Jonah, whom God delivered from "death" to send to the Gentiles (Matt. 12:39).

8. Residence in Capernaum

Since Jesus considered constructive interchange with the Nazarenes to be impossible, he made Capernaum his residence. This was Galilee's farthermost northeast corner and was the northernmost village on the western shore of the Sea of Galilee. The village was situated close to the Jewish border but still within it and was a closed Jewish community. We gain more precise knowledge of the population of the plain of Genezar at the time of the revolt against Rome. At that time it proved its complete commitment to the Law and its readiness to venture anything for Israel's freedom and God's rule. The community of Capernaum failed to achieve the goal of every Jewish community—to obtain complete uniformity and not to admit any Gentile inhabitants—only in that Herodian military were stationed in this border town. In addition, the officer who commanded it was Greek in his religious preference.

Jesus' decision to settle in Capernaum originated also from the gravity of the conflict into which he saw himself placed. Since he was here directly at the Jewish border, he easily reached Gentile territory through a brief stroll or through a journey across the lake. Here he could interrupt the confrontation with the Jewish community at any time by leaving the region. The Isaianic word quoted by Matthew (Matt. 4:13–16), too, influenced Jesus' decision, since Jesus knew the book of Isaiah as well as Matthew did. Nevertheless, Jesus did not exercise obedience toward the prophetic word in such a way that it pushed aside all other considerations. His obedience to Scripture did not render him blind to the real circumstances that influenced the course of events.

Jesus' retreat to Galilee did not entail an abandonment of his universal aim through which he applied his commission to the entire nation and thus especially to Jerusalem. Yet he strongly emphasized by this decision that the call to repentance was directed to the individual and that it should be freed from the existing community. For the eschatological community had to separate itself from guilty Israel by way of a new beginning. However, although Jerusalem had become the home of the "brood of vipers," the seedbed of resistance against God, the seat of Pharisaic dissolution of the Law and the distortion of religious worship that corrupted the nation, it nevertheless remained the holy city in which his Father's house stood. What Jerusalem therefore meant to him becomes visible by the fact that after he judged his work in Galilee to be concluded he considered the journey to Jerusalem to be a virtual necessity, despite the certainty that death awaited him there. He had no notion that he could complete his work without the journey to Jerusalem, or that he could die elsewhere. The concepts of "Jerusalem" and of "the cross" were firmly connected in his mind. This was based upon the significance Jerusalem had for the entire nation. What happened for and through Israel could not be accomplished in Capernaum or Sepphoris but constituted part of Israel's history by the fact that it happened in Jerusalem.

Jesus remained in touch with Jerusalem and with the entire nation even in Galilee, since his reputation caused many to come to Capernaum. In the same way the Baptist had moved the entire nation, even though he dwelt in the desert. Accordingly, Jesus did not wander restlessly from one village to the next, although he practiced itinerant preaching and often spoke in the worship gatherings of the Galilean villages. He rather acquired a firm residence so that everyone could easily find him. The feasts provided him opportunities to reach the entire nation. Since Jesus' participation in the feasts was prescribed through custom, the older accounts did not consider it necessary to explain the background to Jesus' lament that he had often called Jerusalem to himself. But "you were unwilling," he sadly declared (Matt. 23:37). This statement bears the entire weight of ascribed guilt. Jerusalem did not want to return, since Jesus remained distant from it, and it did not know him. This verdict, however, could not be based merely upon the work of the final days of Jesus' ministry when Jesus acted in the conviction that the outcome of his confrontation with Israel had been decided and the fall of Jerusalem could not be averted. Luke also did not understand this lament of Jesus in such a way, since he placed it already before his final arrival in Jerusalem (Luke 13:34). Jesus' lament also goes beyond the proposal that his work in Galilee was by itself intended to call Jerusalem to faith, because what he said and did in Galilee also moved Jerusalem, and since many Jerusalemites visited him there. This proposal has no merit. Jesus said clearly that he wooed the holy city directly and visibly with faithful persistence, albeit in vain.

The Offer of God's Grace to Israel

1. The Call to God through the Word

Jesus did not have in mind a technique or method by which the conversion of Capernaum, Galilee, and Jerusalem could be effected.[1] Technique can only regulate and enhance human performance; but in conversion to God, Jesus did not see merely a human decision. For Jesus, conversion pointed to God, who gives his grace to the individual. The forgiveness Jesus offered to the guilty nation was God's action having its ground in God's own will. Some kind of didactic, liturgical, magical, or ascetic sleight of hand would have been totally out of place. Jesus had no special procedure by which to manipulate God's will and activity. His certainty of God entirely excluded such thoughts.

Therefore it was the word that was his means of work. He proceeded thus, however, not because he did not yet have anything greater or more effective, but because, according to his judgment, in the word God gives testimony to the individual regarding himself. The individual needs nothing else and cannot receive anything greater than God's word. By bringing the call of God to the Jewish community, Jesus did not intend to describe or to explain or merely to prophesy God's rule to it. He rather produced it for the nation through the word. For God's rule went into effect through his proclamation. Those who had rebelled against God were saved as they heeded his word. He did not merely express forgiveness but gave it by pronouncing it, and he did not merely predict judgment but executed it by issuing the verdict. For Jesus did not separate the word of God from God but considered himself to be united with God through his word by a genuine, faithful will. This made his word the highest power and the complete good.

---

1. The condition of the first community confirms the data about Jesus. It, too, knew nothing of a technique or method by which conversion could be effected.

113

Some, not heeding the religious and thus realistic version of the word as Jesus plied it, have transformed the offer of forgiveness merely into a promise and repentance into a wrestling for a future goal. The disciples' statements regarding Jesus' conduct, however, are very definite in this respect. The disciple resembles the slave whose debt is forgiven, and thereby he stands in the king's service and is equal to the son whom the father has forgiven and grants the full filial right. When Jesus justified one of the two persons who prayed in the temple but not the other, he delivered a verdict he regarded as valid. Whoever prays like the tax-collector should believe that he is justified, and whoever prays like the Pharisee should know that he is refused justification (Luke 18:14). Because Jesus did not consider his word to be mere preparation, to be followed only subsequently by the divine gift, but because it accomplished the connection with God and was itself the gift with which God's grace was received, God's rule was in Jesus' view already present through the Baptist's proclamation (Matt. 11:12; Luke 16:16). That is why he stepped before the friends of his youth in Nazareth with the declaration that the prophecy was fulfilled in their hearing. By listening to him they possessed what the prophet had promised, because God's grace is obtained by being proclaimed. Therefore Capernaum, too, was lifted to heaven through what he told it, for God's rule consists of the presentation of his word. He ascribed to the word power to make man clean and holy, for through it God's name is given its content for man. The accuracy of the interpretation given to the parable of the sower by the Gospels, that is, that the seed is the word, is proved by the fact that we do not see Jesus use any other means, and that he also did not leave anything other than his word behind for his friends. But even his word he did not leave behind in such a way that he merely communicated thought to them. Rather, by the word he facilitated for them a religious effectiveness through which they could lead men to God. Through the word, they would effect man's binding or loosing (Luke 4:21; Matt. 13:19; John 15:3; 17:17, 6, 7; Matt. 10:13–15; 16:18–19; 28:19).

Through this estimation of the word Jesus rose above the Baptist, since he thereby united the two concepts that comprise the content of the baptismal preaching: God's kingdom and conversion. He made this connection more firmly and completely than the Baptist had done. In the Baptist's statement regarding the Christ and his doubt of Jesus (Matt. 3:11; 11:2), a greater tension becomes apparent between these dual aims of the baptismal preaching than existed in Jesus' thought world. With the Baptist, the time of repentance as preparation was distinguished from the time of glory God's deed would bring in response to the conversion of the Jewish people. But what John separated, Jesus united. Through conversion, man comes to God and is given all he needs. He receives eternal life. By forsaking evil and doing good, man experiences God's rule, and his perfect grace becomes personal reality. Like John Jesus held that the goal toward which his entire will was oriented lay in the future. But his prophecies all contain a statement regarding the present by which he clarified and confirmed the individual's relationship to God that had now been secured. He did not merely speak as someone who warned and who is able to announce a future calamity nor as the giver of rosy hopes that grant a preview of coming happiness. He rather prophesied because the decision by which he confronted his hearers received its significance from the fact that the eternal good was obtained or lost by it.

Jesus arrived at this estimation of the word because God's activity and goodness had for him complete reality. He did not seek to generate preconditions that would bring God to man or make God his father. He rather saw in God the entire readiness to open himself up to man and to accept him into his fellowship. In this way man was given the complete gift in being given the divine word, since it uttered (and thereby secured) the sincere and genuine love of God.

By making his work the presentation of the word, Jesus knew himself to be in harmony with prophecy. For it furnished him with the term "evangelist."[2] Already the prophet said that salvation would appear with the word proclaiming God's grace. For Jesus, this was confirmed through his divine sonship. This ruled out any seeking of the work of God's grace merely in the future. He was authorized to call people to God by that authority he already possessed as Son and Christ, and thus the word did not become only a prophecy but also "God's good news" that expressed what God did and gave. That is how conversion became man's redemption.

Love, and only love, with its complete trust, treasures the word as tantamount to the gift. Through his own high estimation of the word Jesus rendered his activity completely religious. Only that man could be satisfied with the word who was concerned for God, and for God alone. He was given everything with the word that issued the call to God. When, however, selfish desires stirred in messianism, desires longing for the glorification of the Jew and seeing the most important characteristic of the messianic era in the bliss it afforded, the Christ could no longer limit himself to the word but had to have power as his tool. So great was the need that it would yield only to power, and power alone would elevate the community to the kind of glory it desired. This was not Jesus' view of things. By effecting man's connection with God through the word, he set himself apart fundamentally and irreconcilably from all self-centered efforts, and he determined that his aim was, earnestly and entirely, not the glorification of man, but the revelation of God.

His ethical goal was one with his religious one. He put the giving of one's will to God above all man can experience. If he had striven for a transformation of nature or of political conditions, the word would have been insufficient for his purposes; he would have had to change the situation by use of power. Since, however, he wanted to give men good will, and since he did not consider anything to be of greater magnitude, necessity, or blessedness than that man become a doer of the divine will, he used the word as his tool. In this manner he treated man as a person who determines his relationship to

---

2. Synagogal interpretation also saw in Isaiah 52:7 a designation for the Christ. The supposition that it was only the disciples who connected the term "good news" with Jesus' word is possible only when the repentance required by Jesus is twisted into a work of repentance that initially remained without success.

God through his will and determines it correctly when he gives his will to
God. So, through his call to repentance, Jesus remained subservient to divine
grace. Resorting to forceful means might have sufficed to judge evildoers, but
it could not have effected their conversion.

By his high regard for the word as the revelation of God's grace yielding
eternal fruit, Jesus did not sell out to intellectualism, as if the community's
fulfillment would come about through a new teaching or theology. This
would have moved the point of contact between God and man to the realm
of the intellect. Jesus never created the illusion that he knew of a theology
sufficient to save in itself. For the word grants reconciliation with God because it expresses the divine will and subjects the will of man to it. Jesus knew
himself to be an evangelist, not the proclaimer of a divine wisdom or interpreter of divine secrets. Since the word creates God's personal relationship to
a person and of the person to God, this goal is also its boundary. Every question transcending this boundary was rebuffed. For Jesus the decisive event lay
in man's hearing, in his being sought by divine grace, and in accepting and
obeying God's call. By considering the word to be the revelation of God, he
expressed his utter opposition against Greek and Pharisaic intellectualism.

From this, of course, developed a mighty contrast. For now the greatest
simplification of the word stood beside Jesus' estimation of it as the means
through which God's rule grants its eternal and perfect gifts. Alongside the religious tradition that prevailed in the Jewish community, and beside the Old
Testament canon, Jesus' word looked meager, since it remained completely
framed by the two statements of the baptismal saying.[3] Jesus himself, however, did not succumb to this contrast, since he saw the greatness of his word
in the fact that it unveiled how God was currently working on man and showing him how he must order his behavior toward God. Since his word, both
the word of repentance and the offer of the kingdom, revealed what was occurring at that time, it possessed for Jesus the characteristic and transcendent
majesty of truth.

Since Jesus respected man's free will, and since he therefore did not think
of grace as overcoming and overpowering man, he juxtaposed this estimation
of the word with the expectation that it might be spoken and heard in vain.
The field receiving the seed was not always also the one that bore fruit, and
the guests who had been invited to the feast were not those who celebrated it.
Therefore he also separated the terms "called" and "chosen." Many were
called in vain. The one who had been called had received the word; for the
one chosen, God's deed that united him with God was fulfilled. Jesus never
sought the reason why God's call was separated from his election in the inef-
fectiveness of the divine call, as if God's will had not been one with his word,
but this dichotomy could only originate through sin. The ones who had been
invited lost their share in the feast through foolishness; the ones who had been

3. With John this contrast takes on an intensified expression: the word that was God became flesh. When it is expressed, however, it converges with the statement regarding Jesus' divine sonship.

called lost their reward through their unfaithfulness. Those who allowed themselves to be invited while at the same time despising the grace shown to them, like the king's guests without festive clothes, end up in prison. By distinguishing the chosen from the called, Jesus made clear that, for him, God's work consisted simultaneously in the execution of judgment and in the extension of grace.

2. The Regal Activity of God

Jesus' primary and ultimate idea, the thought with which he began and conducted all his thinking, was the idea of God. If we consider his relation to nature, or his verdict on people, or the aims he set for himself or for his community, or the aims in which he saw the consummation of world events, it was always his consciousness of God that was the basis for his statements and that produced his judgments. Since nature is God's, it imparted a sense of order and joy to him. He loved Israel as the holy community; but Israel was the holy community through no one but God. He made the one who repented to be his brother; but he was converted through submission to God. He ascribed saving power to faith; but faith has such power through God. The Son is placed by God into communion with him, and the kingdom of heaven is the community's fulfillment and the giving of life through God.

His thinking and willing traversed such vast expanses that the illusion arose that they bore inherent irreconcilable differences. He lived joyfully in nature and at the same time willed miracles; he was obedient to Scripture and free from it; he identified with his people and still was in a position to reject them; he united with his disciples in eternal communion and yet was determined to judge them. He addressed himself to the human will and gave it, in good and evil, the power to effect an individual's destiny. At the same time he subjected everything completely to the divine government, executed justice and granted grace, required works and granted everything to faith, wanted glory and at the same time renunciation, desired dominion for himself and at the same time liberation for others. It is, however, crystal clear what moved him to these apparently irreconcilable goals. He always obeyed the same incentive; his thought always received its impetus through the concept of God. He was joyfully submitted to nature, for it is God's work; and he elevated himself in his actions above all natural possibilities, for in almighty help, God is revealed and magnified. What had been written guided him, for here God spoke; and he said more than what had been written, for God also was speaking at that time. He was an Israelite, for God had sanctified the community for himself, and he judged Israel because he considered God's justice holy. The disciples were indispensable for him, for God's work was carried out through them. Therefore, however, he also awakened in them the fear of falling and of eternal death; for above them, too, stood God's justice. He affirmed human will, for God desires a person's love from the will and gave to it his Law; and God's will is done in everything, for the power and rule are his. Justice is accomplished, for God is perfect in goodness and hostile to evil; and for the same reason he brought to all complete grace. Therefore life arises only from good works, for God never becomes the friend of evil; and faith obtains God's gift, for God is good and destroys no confidence that trusts in his grace. Jesus desired glory, for God reveals his glory, and he joyfully abandoned everything in complete poverty and humility, despising death; for he did not desire glory for himself and did not prepare it through his own activity but sought it in God. He had the regal will, for everything must be subjected to God, and he wanted to serve and lead to liberty, for God's rule is the demonstration of his grace that grants to the human being life, power, and glory. What Jesus said and did was, without the thought of God, a chaos of contradictions, and it is easy to play off one of his sayings against another; with the thought of God, however, there is unity, and the beams pointing in vastly different directions now all proceed from the same source of light. Therefore the proclamation of the "kingdom of heaven" stood above all that Jesus discussed with the community and that he required of it. With this proclamation, Jesus did not present the nation with a "good" it was to receive at that time but he lifted it above its own desires and showed to it God's activity.

When he had his disciples request, "Your kingdom come," he did not make the subject of their request a human condition, be it that of an individual, that he might feel blessed, or that of the community, that their lifestyle be raised, but he directed their desire to God's rule, just as he directed it to God's name that should be exalted and to God's will that should be done. When he illustrated through his parables what the "kingdom of heaven" was, he did not describe a place or condition of blessedness to which humanity should be led; he rather showed his disciples how God dealt with people and how he acted in present and coming history. Therefore he set alongside God's kingdom as a promise of equal significance God's fatherhood, and he thus also related to the community's consciousness of God, since it, too, praised God simultaneously as its king and as its father. When it called God "our Father who is in the heavens," it thought of the same events through which God had made himself the king of the nation. Since he had created the nation through the election of the fathers and the exodus from Egypt, he was its father, and from this also resulted the continuing care he exercised on behalf of the nation. Within the community, the individual had now also a part in God's fatherly love. The name "father" for God, however, now took on a clear relation to the internal condition of individuals through the personal call of persons who united themselves of their own accord with the will of God.

For neither for the Jews nor for Jesus was there any tension between the name "King" and the name "Father." When he called God "King," he described the foundation of the community to be God's work. When he called God "Father," he thus indicated that God also gave his love to all individuals. The name "Father" served to testify to the divine goodness, the name "King" to the divine righteousness. The former term was associated with the offer of divine forgiveness; the latter, with the proclamation of divine judgment. God's house and God's kingdom, however, are one and the same, and those who share in God's rule are his sons. When, in Jesus' parables, it is at one time the father who forgives the guilty son and then the king who forgives the failing servant, the one term was no weaker an expression for God's grace than the other (Luke 15:22; Matt. 18:27). While in the former case the father grants the filial right to the repentant son, the king in the latter instance retains the guilty in his service; God's gift of grace was described in both situations. While the son was dead while separated from the father, the slave who had been faithless toward the king was thrown into prison; both conditions signify lostness. The names of "King" and "Father" unite in the description of the divine work, since grace and righteousness, the foundation of life in the individual and the establishment of the eternal community both constitute the uniform divine will and are carried out through the same divine work.

Therefore John in his Gospel portrayed Jesus, without any misrepresentation of Jesus and with expert representation of his word, exclusively as the one who revealed God's fatherhood and who made a person a child of God while deemphasizing the kingdom concept. For the revelation of the fatherhood of God is completely one with the revelation of his rule. The condition that the religious aim of Jesus that is secured through the proclamation of the kingdom be recognized without reductionism was entirely sufficient for John, since for him the Son lived, spoke, and worked for the Father and had his aim in humanity's becoming subject to God. John's Christ is the way to God.

Another phrase by which Jesus explained the kingdom of God was the "new covenant." While, when thinking of God's rule, one thinks of the divine work by which the community receives life in all its fullness, the term "covenant" spoke of the determination of the divine will upon which its connection with God is based. The currently valid order of Jesus' day was not adequate to bring the Jewish community to completion. To rectify this, a new divine will was revealed that gave communion with God a new content (Matt. 26:28).[4]

By wanting God's rule, Jesus completely identified the goals of the individual and of the community, even that of the world, and gave the same answer to both questions. What is the outcome of a person's life? And what is the goal of world history? What the individual needed to desire for himself was to see God's rule as his protection and life, and this also gives the world's course its aim. Jesus did hold out two hopes, one desiring the final result of a human life and the other the completion of creation. "God will reign"; this Jesus made the comprehensive depiction of the last things; this names the concluding procedure by which each individual's life and world history will come to completion. Thereby he regulated and purified both the individual's drive toward happiness and thirst for life and the community's corporate self-cen-

---

4. The prophetic formula does not, of course, come into play for the first time at the institution of the Lord's Supper. One should distinguish between the idea of a contract and a "covenant." The term "covenant" remains the best word for translation, since the thought is tied to the determination of the divine will that the community receive the covenant with complete gratitude and total obedience. "Testament" is distorting, since the idea of a "final will that is valid beyond death" is entirely missing. The "covenant" differs from the "law" because the law only determines what the community has to do while the covenant determines what God does for it.

teredness. He made the object of his promise neither individuals' eternal happiness, nor the preservation of the nation's ethnic heritage, nor the transformation of nature to unimagined power and beauty. The individuals' happiness was included in it, as was the glorification of the community. But above both Jesus set the fact that God would appear in his full nature and greatness and that he would reveal his own glory. Everything man desired and obtained for himself was thus subsumed under the larger idea under which Jesus gathered man's entire longing: that God would act upon mankind according to the measure of his divine being.

In determining the goal that the community had ahead of it, he told it at the same time through the message of the kingdom what its present misery consisted in: it was subject to powers opposed to God. That foreign powers could do their work upon it, however, was only possible because it had until that time been separated from God and did not yet possess his grace. Everything that still separated it from God, however, was now taken care of by God's regal activity. With Jesus, this contrast had an ethical dimension. God's rule was carried out by the overcoming of sin.[5] What opposed it was, according to Jesus' parable, the dullness that did not accept the word, the softness that yielded to persecution, the desire for sensual goods. In this enumeration of the opponents of God's rule, Jesus did not think of natural law or of political circumstances. The thorns choking the seed are of a different kind. The judgment linked with God's rule consisted therefore of the separation of God's children from the children of the evil one.

Since for Jesus, however, evil did not have its origin and existence merely in humanity but had ties with the supernatural, God's opposition to sin also meant opposition to Satan, who is overcome as the accuser, tempter, and destroyer of life. As a third element, Jesus linked with this the elimination of death. He set God's revelation in contrast to a person's dying and made the promise of life parallel to the proclamation of God's kingdom. To obtain life and to obtain God's rule is one and the same thing. The promise, "he has eternal life," has no lesser content than, "he will share in God's rule" (Matt. 7:14; 18:8; 19:16–19; 25:46; Luke 10:25; John 5:24).[6] With this, Jesus remained one with the understanding of hope already present in the Jewish community, since it expected the end of death and the resurrection. As sin and death were related to one another as cause and effect, so righteousness and life are once again linked causally in God's activity.

Since death also is one of the things ended by God's rule, this rule stands over against nature in a contrast that became even more profound, because not merely dying but also sin were interwoven with human nature. Victory over it therefore also required a renewal of nature, and the desire awakened by Jesus did not long for the preservation of the present form of human existence but for a new life of a higher kind. Since the opposition of God's rule to the

---

5. This can also be observed in the parallel terms. The sons are separated from the father and considered dead by him on account of sin, and a new covenant is necessary since the community's sins stand between it and God. The new covenant makes their sins forgiven ones.

6. Matt. 16:18, too, i.e. the community's victory over the gates of Hades, belongs here.

existing condition thus extended to the entire world order, it became the revelation of an omnipotence that changed and renewed everything in heaven and on earth. Jesus' promise clearly expressed this conviction (Matt. 24:29). From this, however, did not result a crass materialization of the message of the kingdom such that the construction of a new world made up its essential content. Its center always remained the pardoning of man. The conflict in a person's conduct toward God ended by God's rule does not arise from nature, which Jesus honored even in its present form as God's creation. Nature effects in man its aim, eternal life. Therefore the thesis is false that Jesus, by announcing God's rule, preached the collapse of the world. Not collapse, but life was the key word of the message of the kingdom. It indicated that God would render his will effective "on earth *as in heaven.*" This is not negation of the world but its fulfillment.

Since therefore the message of the kingdom always and essentially had a prophetic sense, since the dethronement of the powers that resisted God's rule did not occur in the present, God's reign was also linked in Jesus' message with the distinction between two kinds of world (aeons).[7] Not "this world" but "the coming world" was characterized by the reality of God's reign. The kingdom had come when judgment had made an end to evil powers of either earthly or heavenly kind, and when resurrection had freed the individual from death, and when the transformed state it brings about also had redeemed him from what now created for him ethical dilemmas. Then God would give him his Spirit by whom he would stand in communion and unity with God and by which he would also be united with the heavenly spirits. All pain arising from nature would then be removed from the homeland of the righteous. They would be like the angels, receiving comfort for all they had had to suffer, sharing in righteousness, lords of the earth since they would be sons of God who would see him (Matt. 5:3–10; 13:40–43, 49; 16:27; 20:21; 22:30; 24:31; 25:1–46).

Thereby, however, Jesus did not merely move the community's share in God's rule into the future. He already confirmed it now for those who obeyed the call to repentance. This gave the decision with which Jesus confronted the individual the urgency that God's rule with its eternal good would at that time be won or lost. It followed from the manner by which he esteemed the divine word that he set forth its proclamation as a promise in the strict sense: not only later and under certain conditions would God's rule manifest itself upon those whom he called: they had it already at that time and participated in it. They were not merely enjoined to hope for eternal life; they already had it. Therefore Jesus' message was the "evangel," the message of God's act—and in particular that God was bringing the consummation to pass. Therefore, however, Jesus' message was at the same time also prophecy and produced with faith also hope, a complete hope that possessed assurance. Jesus' concept of God excluded, however, that the hope he gave to his disciples looked into the

---

7. The separation and naming of both worlds were available to Jesus in existing terminology in the same way as the kingdom concept.

distance as if dreaming, making God's rule an illusion that had no basis in the present and that thus fled into another world. He rather gave all words that portrayed it, strictly and entirely, the characteristic of revelation by which he revealed to his hearers that activity of God that was at work in them and determined their present. Jesus kept his word from all abstractions and illusions, not in spite of the concept of the kingdom, but through it. Since God's rule exists and is imminent, since it exists in glory and approaches so as to fulfill its existence, Jesus was custodian of a "now" that was filled with true religion, a present time that granted him communion with God. Therefore he did not search for a religion but had it and did not need to ignore his experience and resort to dreams when he wanted to be concerned for the things of God. He rather found in the experienced event the material that completely filled the horizon of his love for God. He would not, however, have had any present time determined by God if he had not also had a future that shone for him in the brightness of God's glory, just as he also saw God's rule already in the past (Matt. 21:33–34; 23:13). Only a future full of God's revelation would complete what God did at that time.[8]

That Jesus bound together what transpired in the present as well as its future fulfillment into the one term "kingdom of God" did not create confusion on the part of his hearers or disciples. The kingdom concept had this shape in every version of it. Whatever might become the content of the messianic idea, he set the present in a strong causal relation to the final end, and he did not tolerate any portrayal of the future that was completely separated from the existing condition of the community and that merely erected another world. For the Anointed One is sent to the existing community to bring perfect grace and final redemption to it. He comes, because the community had had its king in God from the beginning, was founded and preserved by his rule, and received from his rule whatever constituted its possession. The present form of God's rule therefore also guaranteed to it victorious safe passage through all that still hindered it. God's rule rendered hope certain and assured. There thus arose no tension between the affirmation of God's rule based on current observations and kingdom hope that focused on expectation. These substantiated and confirmed one another. The more faithful the community was in its affirmation of God's regal activity in the present, the stronger and more certain also its desire for God's future activity.

Another connection between Jesus' view of the future and the present was that God's reign reveals his verdict on mankind. God's final act of judgment brings to completion the work that was now begun by man. The connection between the end and the existing condition of the community did not, however, arise merely from the principle of reward and punishment but equally from the offer of grace, since its new dispensation fulfilled what the grace shown earlier to the community had begun. The more the concept of God

---

8. The presentation by the Gospels is confirmed by the apostolic letters, which did not separate Christian teaching into two parts, a doctrine of present salvation and one of the coming redemption. They rather show with strict uniformity of their goal in Jesus that perfect grace which comprises present and future.

was the decisive center of the concept of the kingdom so that it directed the view away from the circumstances of the nation to what God's grace granted to the Jewish people, the firmer became the unity between the present and the final form of God's rule. For only human history degenerates into the contrasts of sin and righteousness, death and life, misery and blessedness; God in his grace is always the Perfect One. The aim of Jesus' sayings and parables therefore consisted solely in an effort to show who could gain a share in the kingdom and how one could obtain assurance now rather than only later. The kingdom was announced to the nation for the very purpose that it should receive it. Only the unbelief that considered the divine word to be empty held, in Jesus' judgment, the idea that the kingdom could not yet be obtained. This was the way those whom Jesus likened to hard soil conceived of the kingdom because they did not understand the message of the kingdom and thus disregarded it.

The key aspect of Jesus' proclamation of God's rule was therefore the saying by which Jesus indicated through which procedures God was now manifesting it and of what man's transposition into his kingdom consisted. Without this information, the concept of the kingdom would have remained an apocalyptic or doctrinal dream; with it, however, it seized the will and became able to determine one's conduct of life. At this point there developed the difference between Jesus and the rabbinate that is never captured by mere formal definitions of the term. Jesus substantiated his statement that God showed himself to be king at that time, not merely through the Law that had existed since Moses but through his sending. Since he connected with his sending not limited but complete grace, one could now gain the kingdom by obeying its call. Therefore the offer of the kingdom consisted of the call to repentance. This call showed the guilty where he had to turn, to Jesus (Matt. 11:28). And because repentance led the guilty into communion with the Christ, it separated him effectively and eternally from his sin and made him a member of the holy community that the Christ created and would complete. God's rule was thereby not future but present. The one who believed in the Christ had acquired God's grace. He thus shared in the kingdom and eternal life, was complete, and had attained the goal. Thereby also he was given hope, because the Christ's office brought with it the consummation, and it was clear that this must still be waited and hoped for, as long as his work consisted of the call to repentance, thus making him the hidden and rejected one.

Jesus' hearers bore within themselves the phrase, "All of Israel has a share in the world to come," which gradually grew into a fixed doctrine in the Jewish community. Jesus' offer of the kingdom was distinguished from this statement by the fact that he separated the kingdom more strongly from the present than the rabbinate did, and since he simultaneously set it into the present more visibly and more powerfully than the rabbinate did. The Jewish phrase was based upon the community's righteousness. Jesus shattered this conviction. The verdict was thus not incorrect that Jesus heightened the eschatological power of the kingdom concept and that he separated it from the present; the new element in his teaching consisted of the fact that he destroyed the satisfaction with which the Jewish community evaluated its own religious condition. He thereby deprived it of the confidence with which it already laid claim to the kingdom by confronting it with a decision by his call to repentance. Jesus distanced the kingdom from the present and made it a goal remaining to be sought. Thus the forces resisting the kingdom—sin, death, and Satan—became more visible than they did in the consciousness of Jesus' contemporaries. But in all this the matter is being viewed one-sidedly. Jesus simultaneously represented the regal ministry of God, the possibility of perceiving and of obtaining his work, with an assurance that all others lacked, because he linked these with his own sending, of which he said that it comprised both the present and the coming time and that it executed God's entire will.

This did not arise merely from the fact that he leapt in his thoughts over the short period that still separated him from the final end, considering it negligible.[9] For this interim was by no means empty for Jesus, and only if it had been empty would it have disappeared as insignificant. In this interim, Israel would make its decision for or against God, and for his disciples it would be a time of work filled with the deep sincerity of their duty to service. If the offer of the kingdom had no other basis than the thought that it would not be long until it came, hope must sink into a morass of uncertainty in view of the events facing Jesus in the immediate future. If we ask further why Jesus considered the time to be short, we are again referred to his statement regarding himself. Since the revelation of God's rule was entrusted to him as the Anointed One, it would come soon. It was, however, tied to "this generation" since it was related to Jesus' sending. Regarding this question, however, there is no room for speculation. Jesus said why he considered God's rule to be present. The man who spoke the word in such a way that it called others to the kingdom and who sowed the mustard seed in such a way that the final end resulted from it, and the shepherd who gathered the community—these were not mysterious figures. They were him.

This lent Jesus' thought regarding the end its characteristic that distinguished it from that of his contemporaries. Future longing can be born out of pain, out of despair over the present, or out of the consciousness of being forsaken by God. A view of the future as the dawning of the day that chases the night away corresponded, in Jesus' time, with an awareness of the night that had overshadowed the Jewish community. Or future longing can develop on account of God's gift, not because of being forsaken by God, but because of fellowship with him and enjoyment of his presence rather than exclusion from his grace. Then the future brought revelation and stability to the present. The former view produced an eschatology of lament calling for theodicy and announced opposition to the existing order. The latter was the joyful eschatology that praised God's greatness and prophesied the completion of the existing order. Jesus' hope was not a child of doubt and pain but was born of the

---

9. This interpretation was attractive to those who did not ascribe the messianic idea to Jesus or saw in it merely an ineffectual addition to his actual way of thinking.

assurance of God. Although he saw the distance between existing conditions and the final aim more sharply than the lamenting eschatologists, he could have participated in their doubts and protests only if he had doubted his sonship and his commission. From those, however, emerged thanksgiving for the complete grace that was now offered to the nation. God's feast is celebrated; all who do his bidding have a share in it.

Both verdicts, that the present is filled with divine grace and that the present is only preparatory for the future perfect state, recur in Jesus' statements regarding his disciples. His community is God's kingdom as certainly as they are his servants and sons. For God's kingdom is not a place or thing; it is people upon whom he exercises his kingly prerogative. His rule is revealed by the fact that the Christ gathers the community that belongs to him. Therefore the parables dealing with God's rule portrayed the conditions in Jesus' community, and what he and his own experienced. With equal clarity, however, Jesus excluded the notion that God's kingdom was equivalent to the circle of his disciples, not merely because the eschatological community would be larger, but also since the disciple, too, can fall, and since the call to repentance also retained its complete seriousness for him.[10] For whatever the disciple possessed, his being son and servant of God and justified, he had through the word. Out of this came the hope and effort that could not rest in his present possession but saw that the goal still lay ahead.

There have been efforts to demonstrate that Jesus' word here points to a movement, be it that he gradually emphasized more and more sharply the presence of the kingdom in connection with the clearer statement regarding his regal status, or that the eschatological idea had receded in view of the approaching end and with the vanishing of initial hopes. But these efforts trafficked in mere speculations. In the words preserved for us we always have a twofold reality before us: that Jesus injected the richest content of the promise into the present and made it achievable for his disciples, and that these final aims towered over everything they could experience now. But this means that the question posed to all by his call to repentance still remained open for all.

3. Jesus' Statements Regarding Himself

In order to obtain its share in God's rule, the Jewish community had to find its point of contact with Jesus, and Jesus aided the nation in this by showing it that he was God's son. On the other hand, he did not step before it with the regal name. Otherwise he would have stood before it as the one who demanded its absolute obedience for himself. He did not, however, desire people's subjection to his own power but its free and complete unity with him. Therefore he showed it instead the basis for his regal status: his close relationship with God.

Jesus acted thus because the two convictions guiding him, his divine sonship and his office as the Christ, interpenetrated each other. This made his

10. See p. 239.

disposition toward the world and toward God an inseparable unity. His communion with God gave him his vocation, duty, and work. Likewise, his work
and rule took place completely within the framework of his relationship with
God; it was his worship, his religion. Because he understood his sonship messianically and obtained his office through it, he did not conceive of it as an
enhancement of his own life and did not make it the subject of his own enjoyment. It became for him the basis for action, since he existed for the community because he was the Son, and what God was for him was revealed in
the things he did and provided for humanity. This lent his relationship with
God its greatness, because it was not limited to the content of his own life but
encompassed all that he must accomplish with man. It conferred depth and
strength on his dealings with others, since he had his ground and aim in his
communion with the Father.

Because he bore the Son concept within him, no other vocational choice
had room in him but the regal one. That is why he also subjected his word to
the rule that to acknowledge his sonship was at once to see clearly the regal status that was his. As the Christ, he took the role of mediator between God and
the world since it was to receive God's rule through Christ's rule, God's forgiveness through Christ's forgiveness, God's gift through Christ's help. However, he did not see in the ministry of mediator a goal to which he still needed
to aspire. For the Christ concept possessed for him the same immediate certainty as did the concept of Son. He had the power and the obligation to be
the mediator of grace for people, for he was the Son who did not merely seek
God but had him and who did not merely seek to obtain his gift but possessed
it and could therefore give it to the community. As the Son, he knew that the
Father gave him his complete love, and this love was perfected by his work in
him so that his work was accompplished through the Son. The carefree assurance with which Jesus considered his relationship with the Father comprised
therefore also his mediatorial office as well as the office of the Christ. He did
not have to acquire it but already had it since he was the Son. Jesus' carefree
assurance also eliminated the need of developing a theory in order to explain
the transfer of God's work to him. The principle of love was completely sufficient in this regard, since love leads to the commonality of activity. But in all
this Jesus expressed merely that idea which was part and parcel of his divine
consciousness.

His communion with God was a person-to-person exchange, since he saw
the Father in divine self-sufficiency over him while at the same time possessing a life of his own. Therefore his disposition toward God was love, and his
closeness to him was the commonality of will that arose because he wanted
the will of the Father with all of his own will. This made him selfless; it was
impossible for him to find the goal of his work in his own possession and success. Since his selflessness, however, originated from love, he was completely
free from the fear that he might by that love render his claim doubtful or harm
his honor. His gospel was therefore the proclamation of God's rule, and he
did not need to call undue attention to himself. Through the Lord's prayer,
he turned his disciples' desire toward God's name, rule, and will, and did not

command them to pray: sanctify the name of your Son and bring about the kingdom of your Son. The thought that he would thus give up his own name, rule, and will never occurred to him, since it was God from whom he desired his glory with pure rejection of any selfish drives. He justified the repentant tax-collector without insisting on a connection between repentance and his own sending. To the one who praised him as good and sought instruction that would lead to eternal life Jesus responded that no one was good except God, but that God was truly and fully good and that his commandments in their simple clarity would surely lead him. In ways readily accessible to us he invested love with promise and could describe the community's fulfillment in such a way as to place it with the patriarchs at God's festive table. But with the revelation of his selflessness he always combined the revelation of his power without obscuring or changing it. Through the Lord's Prayer, he gave his disciples the confidence that God would sanctify his name to them. He would reveal his lordship and fulfill his will in them, because they were his disciples. The one who prayed like the tax-collector heard from Jesus that he was justified and must believe him that it was so. The one to whom he revealed God as the only one who was good he called to himself with an absolute promise and an equally unconditional demand. He referred everyone's love to himself not only when they knew him and strove to honor him but because he rejoiced in every goodness through which God's will was done. For his will was accomplished when God's will came to pass.

Therefore we also do not have any word of Jesus about his baptism, his youth, or his birth. Because he planted faith and obedience, as did the Baptist, through the word of the kingdom and of repentance, he did not transform the acknowledgment of the Son of God into an enumeration of events through which he had developed. His word called hearers to that decision by which they had to decide for him or against him; his word gave a basis for their decision not through the past, and still less through hidden and mysterious means, but through that by which Jesus proved to them God's grace. The divine work they perceived provided them with the basis for their decision by which they determined their relationship to God's rule. The basis was not the concealed beginning but the revealed result of his sending, not what the Son received in his inner life from the Father but what he was for those around him. Jesus never abandoned this realism in his concept of God, a concept that seized the present and conferred causal power on the process that fulfilled it, whether resulting in communion with God or separation from him. We therefore have no word from him that describes and uses as a self-justifying proof an hour that brought him a new beginning with fertile power. Likewise, he gave no explanation designed to make his divine sonship understandable, not even when he expressed its eternal completeness.

If human life had become empty for Jesus, and if the work with which his condition presented him had become meaningless apart from his eternal communion with God, history of religions data from elsewhere would provide plenty of analogies. From these originated the expectation that Jesus, if he had really known himself to be the Eternal One, would have had to speak, not from his human consciousness, but from his heavenly memory, not about the obligation brought to him at that time by the need of the Jews, but about what had been known to him through his tenure in heaven. The facts, however, preclude this conclusion. According to all witnesses, Jesus' message did not consist in a description of heaven or of God's nature or of the glory of his preexistence but rather in the claim that he had been sent to mankind and was calling it to himself. Accordingly, he did not point to what he had once been in unity with God but to what he now was for humanity by virtue of that unity. Therefore he never made his eternity the topic of instruction, with the theoretical purpose of fleshing out christological doctrine as fully as possible.

It is true that John says that Jesus carried this certainty continually within himself, and it was so powerful that it either became the basis for his inner life or was not found in him at all. Jesus is not transformed thereby, however, from the one who had lived in the Father into the one who had his goal in the development and proclamation of a doctrine of pre-existence. According to the Johannine account, Jesus relied on this truth merely for the substantiation of the faith, without pressing it into the service of intellectualism for which it was useless since it remained a complete enigma. In his confrontation with the Jewish community, which kept him quite separate from God in its thinking and saw nothing in him but his visible humanity and therefore refused faith in his promise on account of his youth, Jesus spoke his "I am", by which he united himself completely with God. But this saying retained the unmitigated audacity of a mystery that excluded any comprehension. And when he explained to the nation how he fit his dying into his messianic work and how he made his flesh their bread of life, and when he readied himself for death and saw in it his entrance into God's glory and the basis for his permanent presence with his disciples, he rested his word upon the certainty of his eternity.[11]

By having its basis in his divine sonship, his kingly aim became the lofty truth under which all else was subsumed. Because he was one with God, he stated that everything had been entrusted to him, since everything that was to God belonged to him as well (Matt. 11:27; Luke 15:31; John 17:10). Therefore Jesus also clarified the connection between his sonship and his rule by the term "heir," which had been given to him by Psalm 2 and relates directly to the way he compared his relationship to God with human sonship (Matt. 21:38). Since God's domain, whose heir the Son is, does not consist of things but of the community called by him, the community is also the Son's domain since it belongs to God. Its obedience, faith, and honor belong to him since they belong to the Father. This thought related to the future in the same way that God's rule still belonged to the future. Nevertheless, the analogy from inheritance law did not produce the connection between sonship and his regal

11. For an academician who does mental work as his profession it may appear incredible that Jesus was able to control his thinking to such a degree that he bore the thought of eternity within himself without introspection and the formation of theories. However, our task is not to shape him according to our image but to observe who he was.

aim; it only clarified it. It had for Jesus immediate validity since he considered God's love that had been given to him to be complete.

The connection of sonship with the kingly aim, however, also gave him that inwardness which rendered Jesus capable of any deprivation. For the concept of "Son" extended his duty to the community's deepest concerns. There was no higher perspective from which it could be contemplated than that it consisted of sons of God. This was not to relate God's grace to an isolated event; rather, the entire condition of humanity was given its origin and aim in God, and to this end Jesus devoted his ministry. Since being God's Son was not merely his property but also the gift he gave the community, no other conception of his office than the regal one was possible for him. On this account, however, he isolated it from all selfish and sensual aims. He could retain it even when only his associates acknowledged it and when the cross was prepared for him precisely for the sake of his regal office. For all happiness and obligation derived and originated from his divine sonship. From it the community is renewed in all its circumstances and was brought to completion. Because he had it, he was the Christ even on the cross and through the cross.

Since he considered his union with God to be complete, he did not present himself to the Jewish community as a prophet and did not substantiate the validity of his word through the concept of inspiration. We do not have any saying of Jesus with the prophetic formula "Thus says the Lord." He was prevented from this not merely by the enthusiastic reception given to the concept of inspiration by the community, since it taught that the prophet had to lapse into complete passivity so that he could say God's word, similar to the lyre played by an artist. Thus it did not concede that the divine word entered into the prophet but demanded that he merely relay it without it actually entering him. More acceptable concepts of inspiration were conceivable, yet Jesus did not use even these. For the concept of inspiration restricts God's dealings with man to isolated processes set apart from man's normal condition and occurring merely in connection with special commissions. This fell short of what Jesus possessed within himself as his sonship and what he showed the community. For that sonship granted him complete and permanent communion with God. By the name "Son," he did not merely apply God's participation in his life to his consciousness so that he would be given thoughts and words but uniformly and entirely to his "self." He knew himself to be determined by God, not merely in individual insights, but in his will and work. Therefore God was for him not merely the one who inspires but the one who generates, and therefore he did not express his vocation by the name of a prophet but by that of the Christ.

Therefore also the phrase "ecstatic" does not apply to Jesus, since this concept, too, is dualistic, and divides his consciousness into processes that exclude one another. It is appealing because Jesus' consciousness remains unique, and because it is not equivalent to the one given to us. But it is unsuitable because it connotes a sudden, abrupt movement of the inner life that is contrary to nature, and this contradicts Jesus' statements regarding himself. Indeed, not infrequently processes may have surfaced in Jesus' life, such as in prayer, which psychology of religion may designate as "ecstasies." The entire stock of his statements, however, makes clear that these were not elevated from his permanent consciousness as isolated climaxes so that his assurance of God was based solely or predominantly upon them. His abiding, complete communion with God encompassed his waking life and occurred in natural ways just as it encompassed all isolated events.

John's account is at this point exactly parallel to Matthew's. Since John shows Jesus' communion with the Father by way of his individual actions, a parallel emerges to the process of inspiration, but not in such a way that John interpreted Jesus' sonship as a series of inspirations and ecstasies. The continual, waking course of his inner life is not devalued. It rather constitutes a major part of John's memory of Jesus that Jesus received the word and commandment of the Father in a consciousness that was in control of itself, and that he now proclaimed and fulfilled it by the free act of obedient love. Therefore no oscillation in his inner life arose from particular attestations of God, as if he entered into contact with God here but lost contact there, now being with the Father but then again being alone. His communion with God is rather described as constant, and precisely because it is, it becomes visible and effective in concrete experiences. As everything in John, being and act are here not brought into a mutual tension; rather, essence generates act, revealing and upholding itself through it.

The closeness with God he felt as sonship did not consist merely in the fact that God gave him norms for his will. Jesus ascribed to himself a complete communion of will with the Father that was a communion of life and therefore also gave him a part in the Father's power and activity. For this reason he used the image borrowed from the servant in order to awaken and to regulate the disciples' vocational will. But he never used it for his own relationship to God. He stood before the people as their servant and before God as the Son. The servant, of course, is completely tied to his master, belongs to him as his possession, and does his entire work for him. Therefore the image was useful for Jesus in order to clarify for the disciples their relationship to him and to God. When compared with sonship, however, the communion between servant and master remained incomplete, since it was grounded, not in nature, but merely in the will of the master, not in generation, but merely in a legal relationship. It therefore could also be dissolved, since the master could give the servant away, and the dependence was not based on liberty, since the slave did not receive knowledge but merely command and had to render obedience without love being expected from him (John 8:35; 15:15).[12] Therefore Jesus did not call his relationship with God servanthood but sonship, and therefore his regal will originated from it.

Since, as the Son, he was the mediator between God and the nation, God himself accomplished the mediation between himself and it. It did not come into being through something foreign to God. For the Son's activity was

---

12. By the same token Jesus does not use the concept of reward for his own relationship to God, although for him, too, the fulfillment of his service is the condition for his glorification.

based on what he had received and provided for the community what God himself had granted him in the first place. Therefore Jesus' concept of mediator did not place God at a distance from himself or from the community but effected its unity with him. Thus Jesus did not express his aim using the concept of priest, although he did read Psalm 110, in which the Promised One is described as the eternal priest, as the divine word destined for him. For the priest dwells in the community and appears before God as its representative in order to seek for it divine grace and to obtain for it its gifts. Jesus' thought, however, did not have its starting point in the Jewish community but in God, not in its separation from God that renders it poor and needy but in God's closeness to him that enabled him to offer his gifts to it. Therefore he clarified his vocation for the nation by comparing himself with the temple rather than with the priest since the temple was the place where the Jewish community found God and where it received his forgiving grace (Matt. 12:6; John 2:19).[13]

If the concept of Christ had been separated from the concept of Son, the Christ could have easily been considered the one who acted on God's behalf, which would have led to the question of what constituted his contribution to the glorification of God. Jesus' word, however, never took that direction. He never placed himself independently beside the Father and never thought of God as the recipient and of himself as the giver but continually proceeded from God's complete readiness to give to the community everything it needed. He also proceeded from his complete dependence upon the Father by which he drew his entire activity from him. Since the vinegrower had planted the vine, it would grow and bear fruit for him.[14]

Of these two convictions of Jesus, one is not to be regarded as the basic and dominant one and the other merely derived and subordinate. It was incorrect to derive the filial consciousness exclusively from the consciousness of the office. This occurs in the view that Jesus understood his sonship "theocratically," whereby it is suggested that he had awakened within himself self-confidence through the magnitude of his accomplishment for the community so that God was present for him in special closeness. Then he would have lost the internal property he had in relation to God and that was not dissolved in his relation to mankind. While his office as the Christ with a large portion of its accomplishments still belonged to the future, his sonship was not merely a prophecy, and it did not merely derive from his successes. It rather was his present possession through the Father's gift, and he saw in it the basis for his power. Since closeness with God became for the one who had it the beginning and root for all experience and activity, the concept of "Son" takes priority. But the basis proves to be such by producing its consequence. Therefore Jesus was the Son through the fulfillment of his vocation and stood in the Father's

13. Regarding the lack of priestly formulations, see p. 96.
14. The Christology of the apostles confirms the account regarding Jesus' position. It, too, places the Christ into unity with the Father and turns him toward humanity as the bearer of the divine gift.

love since he became the Christ for the world. His work for humanity laid the foundation for what God was for him.

Since Jesus was Son in the sense that he was the Christ, he was opposed both to the Jewish version of the regal office and to the gnostic understanding of the Sonship of God. The former lay behind him since he was not turned away from God and to the world by his kingly aim but turned to God since he possessed and exercised his regal prerogative as the Son. Therefore he was protected from any selfish distortion of power and could never succumb to the will of replacing God's rule. For him, victory over the world was obedience toward God, and submission to God was power over the world. Therefore it could receive boundlessness and completeness, not by the attenuation but only at the revelation of the uniqueness and majesty of God.

Jesus' opposition to gnostic concepts was equally complete. When, according to widespread gnostic thought, a heavenly being or a divine power was thought to have been present in a human being of ancient times or the present, a miracle of nature resulted whereby the person thus privileged enjoyed the peculiar phenomenon of his supernatural nature in self-admiration and presented it to others for the same purpose. If Jesus had had any similarity with the gnostic founders of religion, he would have made the knowledge of divine activity by which he originated the center of religion and would have required people to admire the divine miracle that stood before them in his person. Jesus, however, lived because he knew himself to be given sonship in order to be the Christ, not for himself but on account of mankind in the Father. His sonship did not pull him away from mankind but to it and rendered him one with it, since he had to complete his work for it. For he was the Son for the purpose of being the shepherd of the flock and the physician of the sick.

Jesus' connection with the Baptist already showed him to be opposed to gnostic thought. The objection was widely held in the Jewish community that Malachi's pronouncement of Elijah did not speak of the Baptist since he was not Elijah. According to Jesus' judgment, however, people's unwillingness to repent was not justified by the fact that Elijah did not come down from heaven but that the prophet had been selected from the community. He, too, possessed his sonship of God in his human life, not through the supernatural character of his nature, but through the glory of his work. That the Baptist likewise proved to be the promised messenger of God by his word and not by the mystery of his nature thus corresponded to his own relationship to God. By fashioning its tools from the midst of the community, divine grace revealed its perfection.

When it later became his task to prove his divine sonship in the temptation, it once again became apparent that he did not understand it in a gnostic sense. For divine substances or powers are not subject to temptation but create their effects to the extent they are present of necessity. Only will is tempted, not powers. The divine sonship revealed to us by the account of Jesus' temptation is characterized by the fact that he yields his confidence, obedience, and love to God by way of a conscious decision.

Nowhere does the portrayal of Jesus deviate from this line of reasoning. Jesus never described his relationship to God by way of material categories but always exclusively in personal terms. Only this made it possible for Jesus's regal will to reveal itself as selfless, humble love. The gnostically conceived sonship demands to be admired and needs great success for its validation. If relationship to God is based on the concept of power, humility is impossible, because power reveals itself in great effects, in rule, not service. Jesus, on the other hand, who knew himself to be given his communion of will with God by his sonship and who received by it his vocation for the world, recognized God's greatness and the glory of his vocation even in seemingly insignificant labor and had his goal not in admiration that elevated him but in the faith he established by humbly helping the weak and guilty.

The gnostic concept of "son" and the enthusiastic concept of the spirit that desires from the divine spirit the overcoming and suspension of human consciousness and will belong together. Both remained foreign to Jesus. Jesus distinguished between his inner life and the Holy Spirit. He looked up to the Spirit as to the strength by which he received the ability to do miracles. Therefore he called the blasphemy of the Spirit the most severe, unpardonable attack on God, while, as long as the blasphemy was merely directed toward himself, he granted forgiveness (Matt. 12:28, 31). He therefore hoped for the Spirit on behalf of his disciples and saw in its arrival a greater gift than the one he had procured for them through his earthly work. The promise of the Spirit gave him comfort that showed his disciples the healing effect of his cross (John 14:16; 16:7).

The differentiation between the Spirit and his own life, however, did not result in Jesus sensing a contrast between them and in seeking to suppress his personal life in order to sense and enhance the Spirit within himself. In his temptation, he proved to be the bearer of the Spirit by distancing himself from evil will by his own decision and by yielding to God with all his trust, and when working miracles he revealed the Holy Spirit by granting the request with clear consciousness and free will. He did not link his anointing by the Spirit with his sonship but had that anointing as Son in such a way that he possessed his own conscious life and activity as given to him by God.

This is linked closely with the fact that Jesus reminded the community of his vocation by calling himself "the Son of Man." This name of Jesus is not only used in the Gospels, where it has a clear relation to the content of the phrase. For the formulation was considered by them to be a designation of Jesus by which he indicated that he spoke regarding himself.[15] The phrase "son of a man" signified in everyday usage about as much as our "someone" or "one." Thereby, however, Jesus' self-designation is not explained, since he

15. For Jesus' contemporaries, the use of the third person in a statement regarding oneself was less conspicuous than it is for us. The phrase, "that man," that is, "I," was common. Of course, Jesus' self-designation is not merely taken from ordinary usage and cannot be explained by the intention to use the word "I" directly. What the parallel with everyday usage implies is merely that this expression was not all that far removed from the usual modesty in Jesus' speech and that it did not appear peculiar or artificial to his hearers.

gave the phrase special meaning similar to his two other names, "Son of David" and "Son of God." This altered its sense profoundly. A son of David and the Son of David, a son of God and the Son of God, are not identical. "The" Son of David is the one who is set apart from all other sons of David and for whom all are waiting. Every pious person called himself a son of God; but no one could say, "I am the Son of God." Thus everyone was "a son of a man" while no one was "the Son of Man."

The name has a clear relation to prophecy, in particular to Daniel 7:13 ("One like a son of man") and to Psalm 8:4 ("What is a son of man that you should visit him?"). Daniel's word is the major passage; the second reference, however, is thereby not rendered meaningless, for prophecy is understood as a unity. Judaism read Daniel's vision attentively[16] and determined from it the expectation of the Christ. One also finds "the Son of Man" in Jewish apocalypses as a designation for the Christ. If we apply Jesus' name to prophecy, the uniqueness of this Son of Man results from the fact that he alone was the Promised One. As he was the one chosen from among the many sons of David, he also was the one among the many sons of men whom prophecy had proclaimed.

Palestinian literature agrees, however, with the disciples' report by the fact that "the Son of Man" was not a firm name for the Christ in ordinary usage. This is already evident in the Gospels by the clear distinction in the use of "Christ" and "Son of Man." The one who described himself as the Son of Man always raised the question whether he likewise used the name of Christ for himself, while the latter designation allowed no further question but determined unambiguously what Jesus demanded as his right and promised as his gift (Matt. 16:13).[17] The name was thus merely messianic title as little as the name "Son of God," nor even merely a quotation from prophecy, although it doubtless reminded people of the one who "comes on the clouds of heaven."

The name "the Son of Man" constituted a clear parallel to the other name of Jesus, "the Son of God," and it is impossible that these two self-designations lay side by side in Jesus' consciousness without being related to one another. After all, Jesus used this self-designation to express not merely an isolated aim but who he was and wanted to be. At the same time, both designations pointed to one another through their stark contrast in both form and content. Jesus knew himself to be linked with God and with humanity through his origin so that this dual connection gave him the measure of his life and the goal of his work. By "Son of God" he said that he had his life from and for God. When he simultaneously called himself the Son of Man, he said that he had and wanted to have his life from and for man. While the one name expressed his

16. The question whether Daniel's presentation and its interpretation were influenced by the synagogue through Babylonian traditions does not pertain to the history of Jesus but that of the synagogue.

17. Paul indirectly confirms the evidence provided by the Gospels. The fact that he never uses the term "Son of Man" allows the conclusion that he did not consider this name to be equivalent to the term "Christ."

closeness to God, the other expressed his closeness to man. This double communion determined what he was and did. Everything that he experienced and accomplished depended on the fact that he originated from God and from humanity and that he belonged to God and to humanity. Therefore he was not merely one among many people but "the Son of Man," since he was at the same time "the Son of God." His uniqueness in the one respect explained his uniqueness in the other. That no one shared with him his divine sonship also made his relationship to man incomparable and gave him a position as man that no one had except him.

A conflict between the two bases of his life would have resulted only if Jesus had understood divine sonship in a selfish way and used it for his own exaltation. In that case, he would have turned away from humanity for its own sake. Since, however, he understood it messianically, he was united with humanity through it. His rule over it was based on the fact that he belonged to it; his sending for it placed him in an existential unity with it.

By stressing this self-designation again and again, Jesus pointed to the characteristic that gave him direction at every step in great and small things. He pointed to what everyone immediately noticed to be mysterious and offensive about him when they remained distant from him, or as holy and great, albeit mysterious, when they were connected with him. The question was always there of how he conceived of his divine sonship given his relationship to humanity. Did he derive from it his incorporation into human life or his separation from it? Did he, as the Son of God, want to be a human being, with all that origin from humanity entails, or not? The decision by which he placed himself among those baptized and his overcoming of temptation were both already based upon the clear resolution of this question. As his work progressed, it received ever greater depth and an escalating seriousness, climaxing in his way to the cross. It was and continually remained his will to lead a human life in the strength of his communion with God, and precisely because he led this life in communion with God he was "the" Son of Man. This did not restrict his right to want what otherwise no one was permitted to desire, and to do what no one else could do. No exclusion of God's gifts, by which he might have retreated to a life of ordinary human proportions was entailed by this train of thought. In order to be the Promised One, he needed special proofs of God's love. But everything he would receive from such proofs entered into his human condition of life and did not destroy it. He knows the Father, but in the way that a human being can know him; he obeys him as a human will is able; he does God's work in the way that a human being can accomplish it.

In this appeared the greatness of divine grace, and this is why he invested his entire will in this name. It thus becomes apparent how much God esteemed man and how high he exalted him. "The Son of Man has authority to forgive sins on earth." What initially had been the sole prerogative of the invisible God in heaven, Jesus, the man, was able to do on earth, and thus God's forgiveness was revealed, became effective, and was experienced and believed by the sinner. "The Son of Man will come in the glory of his Father"—such a great thing God has destined for man. At the same time arose from his closeness to humanity the difficulty of his vocation, the obligation to obedience and service, and the necessity of suffering and death. "The Son of Man is put to death." The designation "Son of David" provides a parallel for the manner in which Jesus united consciousness of strength and weakness, exaltation and humiliation, passion and suffering. This name, too, expressed the greatness of his sending. At the same time, however, Jesus saw a contrast between his origin from David's family and his destination for the heavenly throne. Likewise, he focused his entire will upon that aim of his life which he expressed by the name "the Son of Man," without reluctance and with complete gratitude. And with that same name he praised the glory of his sending. He simultaneously expressed by it what burdened him as weakness and pressure. In both cases, what linked the two names was the fact that they stood in contrast to his status of Son of God. This name alone spoke only of his power, not also of his weakness, only of what he possessed, not also of what he lacked, only of his blessedness, not also of his suffering.

Someone with confidence in his reasoning prowess may conclude that Jesus called himself "the son of Adam" and clarified his position within humanity and his task for it by looking back to paradise. Although he was aware of the first chapters of the Bible, we do not have a single saying of Jesus that explains his sending through Adam's nature and deed. He looked forward to God's aim and described his task not by what once was and happened but through Israel's guilt and need, which were evident all around him, and through God's glory, which he had above him. Therefore it is improbable that he thought exclusively or even predominantly of the primal man by his use of "Son of Man," whether of the perfection with which Adam proceeded from God or of his fall.[18] Jesus' self-designation received its significance from God's ultimate lordship, which will end the present crisis by giving heavenly power to the man fashioned and sent by him. He made himself one with human life as it now existed, guilty and judged by God's righteousness, and loved and called to God by his grace.

18. Even less should one think of the gnostic speculation according to which God had created an original human being *(Urmensch)* before the world that he had kept with himself in heaven and now sent to earth. For "the Son of Man" is preceded by other human beings from whom he originated; it is not the name of the original human being. The assertion that the term "son" in this usage is entirely without significance is also incorrect for Syrian and entirely for Greek. Thus the speculation is refuted that Jesus stepped before the people as the primal human being, since there is not a single saying that describes the miracle in his nature, discusses the mysteries of the transcendent sphere, or deals with the process of creation. The gnostic form of thought and will and that of Jesus and the Gospels stood in such a definitive contrast that no sound historian can blend them; its only support is mere hunch. John and Paul, too, knew nothing of such a statement by Jesus. John explains Jesus' concept of eternity by the fact that God's word had made him (1:14), and Paul, while linking his Christology with Gen. 1:26, did not base this upon a reference to "the Son of Man."

4. The Decision Demanded by Jesus

Jesus made clear to Capernaum, which he had adopted as his own town, and to all to whom his itinerant preaching led him or who traveled to him, that the decision for God he required from them would occur by their ceasing to do evil and resolving to do good. By making this requirement, he did not add a different, limiting, and constraining word to the "good news," the proclamation of the kingdom. Even when inviting people to repent, he spoke to them as "the evangelist," because he did not consider it to be a calamity but a joyful work that the individual should forsake evil and find the good will by which he desired God's will (Luke 15:7, 10).

How Jesus targeted the will of the people in order to subject it to the divine commandment is seen in the Sermon on the Mount. For the days the disciples spent with Jesus in the Galilean mountains became for them an adventure, since Jesus showed them there the difference between his will and what up until that point had been considered to be righteousness. None of the words, however, that are part of the Sermon on the Mount dealt merely with his hearers' thoughts. Each served the purpose of awakening in them the decision that would correct their actions. Therefore Jesus concluded that discourse with the parable that demanded obedience from the hearer who "did his words" and gave to that hearer his promise.

In order to show Capernaum what he required from it as conversion he turned to its tax-collectors and made one of them his follower who accompanied him everywhere (Matthew: Matt. 9:9; Levi: Mark 2:14). The city saw in the tax-collector's renunciation of everything he had previously loved the sincerity of his call to repentance and in Jesus' extension of fellowship to him the authority by which he forgave the guilty. Another man, Simon, whom he also made one of his followers, received the nickname "Zealot" (Luke 6:15). His call into the apostolic circle and the giving of his name resulted in a parallel to Matthew "the tax-collector." Since the zealot and the tax-collector constituted the harshest contrast that existed in Judaism, Jesus, by connecting both with himself and with one another in his apostolic circle, showed the circle of his followers that repentance was necessary for all its groups and that God's grace was given to all.

Since the Passover arrived soon after his settlement in Capernaum, he appeared before Jerusalem and before the community gathered there for the feast. He showed to it the necessity of repentance by attacking the market that was held there in the outer court of the temple for the sake of the cult. Owing to the cult's importance for the piety of the entire nation and especially for the holy city, Jesus linked the call to repentance here with an event directly impinging on the cult. Because the city honored the temple as its most precious treasure, since it guaranteed God's gracious presence, and because it saw in the temple service the major part of its obligation, the cult's corruption disrupted every aspect of the city's life. Even now, however, Jesus completely avoided all doctrinal instruction regarding the nature and the value of the temple. He merely selected the market from the multitude of sinister things attached to the cult and focused on it the decision whether the nation would recognize and end the sinful nature of its worship or whether it would defend it against him. He did not allow Jerusalem to make the call to repentance merely a meditation or discussion, but demanded obedience and put the merchants to flight.

By locating conversion in the deed by which blameworthy conduct finds its end, Jesus took upon himself the obligation of showing the people through clear and reasonable instructions how they could put away sin and become obedient to God. His teaching could therefore not imitate the Greeks, who expected help from the knowledge of good, into which they sought to introduce people through general concepts. For these concepts remained abstract ideals separate from reality, and abstract ideals were incompatible with the aim of the call to repentance.

Likewise, Jesus could not follow the way of the priesthood and the teachers of Jerusalem in their instruction of the community. In order to erect clear boundaries against sin, these had become casuists, dissecting the duty of the pious into an unending series of limited accomplishments, and setting for each an exact measure by way of a completely determined formula. By none of these individual accomplishments, however, did they achieve what Jesus wanted to give to the community, which was the separation from evil and the good will that desires the will of God.

Was there a third alternative beside the two already existing forms of ethical instruction, beside the concepts of virtue derived from Greek science and the casuistic rules stemming from the temple? The requirements Jesus directed toward the Jewish community were entirely separate from Greek abstractions and entirely concrete. They were, however, equally far removed from the rules of the experts in the Law. When he showed to the disciples in the Galilean hills what sin was, he denied them the anger that originated in dispute and hate, the dishonoring of the woman for the sake of passionate lust, and the use of the divine name as a pretense for a lack of truthfulness. Thus the disciple found out what Jesus rejected and how he must convert. He came to know how he could become obedient to him.

To purify worship he did not present the community of his followers with general exhortations but denied the disciples any public display of religious activities, removing the market from the temple and denying the altar to the person who did injustice to others. This completely described the turn to which he sought to lead the hearer. He never resorted to casuistry, however, not even when he spoke of the seating order at a festive table or the guests to be invited to the meal (Luke 14:7–14). For his requirements did not confront his disciples with all sorts of aims but always with just the same one. His demands regarding relations to God and others called lovelessness sin and love good. By clarifying the contrast between lovelessness and love through his individual requirements, he transformed obedience toward his concrete, individual command into the complete rejection of lovelessness. Complete turning to love was shown to be God's will. This effected a change of the will that truly broke with evil.

After John has presented what Jesus required from the entire nation by depicting Jesus' attack upon the temple market, he puts two individuals before Jesus, expressing in the selection of these two examples the universality of the call to repentance. A teacher of Jerusalem and a Samaritan woman, the most worthy and pious and the most ordinary member of the community, stand before him. He extends the same love to both and applies to both the call to repentance with the same justice. He deprived the rabbi of the certainty with which he expected God's perfect gifts for Israel. For Jesus placed his hope in God alone. Those whom God made his children by his Spirit would obtain it. From this contrast also arose a conflict in their christological concepts, having its root in the ethical sphere. The aim of the Spirit coming to human beings and making them fit for God's rule was not reached by the execution of judgment and the use of power but by the cross. For man is won only when he is brought to faith, and Jesus led him to faith through the cross. But the condition for believing association with him lies in right conduct, in the doing of the truth. Then man's work is not evil because he does it from within himself but good because he accomplishes it in God. From one's turning to truth, to the good, and to God, arises faith in Jesus, since the person thereby separates himself from the darkness and comes to the light.

The first part of the conversation explains what Jesus expected from God's regal activity. Subsequently, his conclusion provided a parallel to what the other disciples called "conversion." Beside the doer of the word to whom the promise of the Sermon on the Mount was directed and the doer of the divine will whom Jesus called his brother, here stands one who does his work in God and therefore comes to the light regarding the Christ. Both elements are one. Jesus directed his call to repentance also to the teacher since he did not do the truth he knew. By requiring obedience for truth to be present, Jesus lent profound and clear expression to the concrete call to repentance that demanded from the individual the entire will that turned into action. In Jesus' judgment, man made the decision that determined his relation to the Christ through his attitude toward the norms he possessed as clear, certain truth within himself.

After promising the woman from the heretical community that was cut off from Israel the water that would fulfill her desire, he showed her the greatness of the promise that granted her life by proving that he was the one who knew her appalling history. Here, too, he effected conversion by sanctifying the ethical norm; having a man who was not her husband was sin. Jesus operated as the light that exposed evil in its blameworthiness, and he urged the woman to decide whether to move away from him or toward him. What separated her from him he removed by elevating her above the dispute regarding temples that had become the major aspect of religion in the Samaritan community. He denied abiding value to both forms of religious worship, the one exercised in Jerusalem and the one on Mount Gerizim. Neither had its basis in the Spirit and in the truth, so neither corresponded to that worship which was desired by the Father. He confronted the woman with her need to make a decision for him so that she would affirm his promise of being the Christ. By telling her who it was that confronted her with her sin and nevertheless kindly

extended the highest forgiveness to her, he made divine grace an experience
for her that connected her to him as one who believed.

Many mistakes in the interpretation of Jesus' history are removed when we
succeed in truly apprehending that his ethical pronouncements are not med-
itations on ethical problems but parts of his call to repentance. He left us no
treatises rooted in the sphere of ethical theory. Those who ascribed to him the
attempt to create a new ethical teaching original to him thought unhistori-
cally. The ethical sayings of Jesus are particularly full of parallels with Jewish
tradition, and this corresponds to their purpose of bringing the nation to the
decision to forsake what he rejected. The clearer the hearer came to an understanding of what he should obey, the more ease and certainty Jesus had in effecting such a decision.

In his call to repentance Jesus found support in the strongest and holiest
conviction of Judaism, one that lent it its unity and penetrated all of its expressions of life. This was that God had given his Law to the nation, and this
Law possessed unalterable validity. For Jesus' call to repentance was an unconditional claim. He did not explain the decision to which he led the individual
by calculations of success that weighed a greater or lesser amount of good and
bad things. The repudiation he demanded of what he called "sin" was total,
and the obedience to what he called righteous and good was likewise comprehensive. If he had admitted relative measurements or worked with the concept of development or gradual perfection, he would have spoken with the nation about the deficiencies from which it still suffered, about the progress in
knowledge or virtue or blessedness it was still capable of, about those elements
in its teaching, its custom, and its law that still required improvement, about
where its thinking did not yet reach the truth of God, where its activity was
still imperfect, and where its measure of life was still capable of elevation.
Jesus' word never went this route; it always required a decisive, complete assent that tolerated no procrastination. Therefore a complete contrast arose
from his preaching. Jesus entirely dissolved the community that resisted the
call to repentance and founded it completely on those who obeyed him.

His disciples considered the absoluteness of his judgments and claims to be
the new element that encountered them in contrast to their previous piety. He
completely rejected the evil that sought to dishonor and to harm the individual, not merely owing to the damage it caused, but even when it was still entirely concealed in our inner life, and he considered love to be good for its own
sake, not merely owing to the advantage it brought to others or to ourselves.
He therefore freed it from all limitations, both from those we give to the
neighbor, so that love cannot be destroyed by his hostility, and from those we
express to God, so that the service of God should be free from any selfish consideration, focused solely and exclusively on God. In the case of those who
wanted to follow him, he ensured that they understood the absoluteness of his
requirements by shattering entirely their longing for happiness and money
and their connection to the custom of the Jewish community (Matt. 8:19–22;
Luke 9:61–62; 14:25–35).

When someone thought that by accompanying him he would ensure his own happiness, he confronted this with the declaration that he was completely poor and that he could offer nothing to his followers. If following Jesus, according to the opinion of the one who sought him, still allowed other loyalties, and this following did not grant complete freedom from the community's judgment, he did not permit it. Owing to reasons that are easily understood, the disciples preserved in their memory a case when he freed a man who was prepared to follow him even from the duty of piety toward the deceased father. No longing for happiness, no esteem of another duty, no second desire beside obedience was allowed. Everything fell by the wayside; he turned the entire will of those who followed him toward what he required of them.

It was important for all that Jesus secured the absoluteness of the call to repentance by applying it also to his mother and brothers, as John portrayed at the very beginning of Jesus' ministry in his dealings with his own mother (John 2:4). The woman who transferred her admiration for Jesus to the body of his mother, since such a son would be the pride and joy of his mother (Luke 11:27), spoke completely from the Jewish community's way of thinking. Everyone, even his own followers, presented him with this train of thought, in the expectation that he would share it and that he would make it his aim to use his greatness to glorify his own mother. But he preserved the absolute validity of the call to repentance by applying it also to the selfish claims of his own and by subjecting them likewise to the rule that God's word must be heard and that God's will must be done (Matt. 12:49–50). Only in this manner came about that close relationship with him that made a person his brother. John held the absolute manner of Jesus' call to repentance up to the Jewish community in a way that was equally clear as Matthew's, since he framed it in the contrasts of truth and lie, love and hate, and spirit and flesh. The turning to one of these opposites amounts to the decisive, complete turning away from the other.

Jesus' call to repentance took on its categorical certainty by being grounded in that idea which shone always at the bottom of Jesus' soul; it was religious, that is, it originated from his assurance of God. What he demanded made God's will known; when he judged, he expressed what God rejected (Matt. 7:21; 12:50; 15:3; 19:6). From the concept of God, however, arose the absolute connections that seize the human being entirely, not merely his limited or partial will but his entire will. That is why community was fatally jeopardized if dispute arose at this point. Likewise, unity, if obtained here, was obtained completely. Since Jesus' requirement had a religious foundation, he did not treat the nation as ignorant regarding good and evil but expected it to see the blameworthiness of its conduct and to know what it had to forsake. By demanding that Israel give to God what was due him, he implied that Israel knew what it kept from God, though it belonged to him.

He was not, of course, unaware of the confusion in people's ethical judgment that necessitated instruction concerning what was sinful. This confusion arose from the sophistry that wanted to justify evil as good in order to maintain its own righteousness. Since their legal commandments instructed the Jews to shrink away only from complete evil, Jesus told his disciples that unrighteous anger was likewise sin, and when Peter sought a limit for his forgiveness, he showed him that and why such a refusal to forgive would also amount to sin. He refuted the ingenuity that seeks in the term "neighbor" a cover-up for lovelessness by the example of the Samaritan and showed by a proof from Scripture the corrupt custom to be sin that exposed the woman to the man's arbitrary treatment (Matt. 5:21f.; 18:21f.; Luke 10:29; Matt. 19:3–8).

Since it was, however, false education and sophistry, hypocrisy and lying, which led the individual to consider evil to be good, these misconceptions confirmed his conviction that the knowledge of God's will was a given for the community. Regarding the ordering of man's conduct, Jesus was therefore able to refer each to what he would want done to himself, since he would have secure guidance in this, which would lead him to the fulfillment of God's will, even into the entire Law, if he did not erect a wrong distinction between himself and others. Regarding the question of what one should do to obtain eternal life, he therefore had nothing but an answer that put the question to shame, because he never conceded that ignorance concerning good was righteous. The questioner knows the good, just as he knows the one who is good, yet the good remains unknown to him until he knows him who is good. He knows where he should turn: "Keep the commandments" (Matt. 7:12; 19:17; Luke 10:25–37). Therefore he did not tell Nicodemus, "Seek truth, learn and understand it," but, "Do it." He knows what is bad and what is good, and that only the one who does the good does his works in God. Jesus sought the condition for Israel's following of him not in his own or anybody else's discovery of God's will; the decisive act consisted, according to his own judgment, not of an act of the mind. What rather was at issue was the question which will the individual wanted to do, his own or that of God (John 3:20–21; 7:17).

This conviction arose equally from the religious substantiation of the call to repentance and from the categorical way in which it was phrased. Through God's presence the human being was placed in the light, and the call to repentance was only necessary for him since he did not have God's word abiding within himself (John 5:38). Since God was good and resisted all evil, ignorance regarding sin was only conceivable in the case of complete distance from God. Therefore the instructions regarding what was good and evil were themselves part of the call to repentance and were necessary only because the nation resisted the will of God.

How do the keepers of the vineyard know their duty? They know who owns the vineyard, and those who are invited into the presence of the king know what honor and obedience they owe to their king. The righteous brother knows what he has to do when his fallen brother returns because he knows what he owes to the father. The person knows whether he comes in his own name or in the name of God, whether he enters the flock as a thief and robber over the wall or whether he is let in through the door by the gatekeeper, whether he is from the truth and from God and does his work in God or not (John 5:43; 10:1; 8:47; 18:37; 3:21). In Jesus' judgment, ethical insight is present with the possession of the knowledge of God.

Jesus did not consider it necessary to examine the processes that lead the individual to reject his conduct as sinful. He did not separate between elements that should be attributed to nature and factors that pertained to conscience, aspects that related to Scripture or to his own word. He had the confidence that he functioned as a light upon man and would give people the ability to see so that they would truly apprehend the contrast between their own will and God's will, with the result that they would attain to the knowledge they needed for their conversion to God. For this, however, they did not need an examination of what functioned as a source of light within them but needed merely to face their own evil in all its despicableness.

Jesus made repentance available to the nation to the extent he could, giving the call to repentance the most simple form conceivable, and placing it directly within common understanding and ability. For he saw in the removal of the unrighteousness one person commits toward another the value of return to God. Of the two great commandments, he confronted the scribe with the one that required him to love his neighbor with the promise that he would obtain eternal life. Regarding the Samaritan and the priest and the Levite he showed when one fulfilled this commandment and when one did not. He thereby made explicit both religious lack (the scribe) and fullness (the Samaritan). Although the Samaritan did not come from the temple, the teacher should still learn from him how to do God's will so as to receive eternal life. He did not reproach the rich man in his torment that he had forgotten God but that he had allowed Lazarus to perish.

While he stated at the conclusion of that same parable that the rich man, in his harshness, had refused obedience to Moses and the prophets, these appear here as witnesses for the love commandment in its simple applications. That the rich man did not merely act against his intuition but against the scriptural commandment well known to him aggravates his guilt. For the other rich man, too, who asked him for a work that would bring him eternal life, Jesus held up the commandments of the second table of the Decalogue. The entire Law and the Prophets are fulfilled when we give to people what belongs to them, as we know to do from what we wish for ourselves.

Jesus did not expose the dichotomy between the tradition and God's commandment by referring to the impoverished state of their religious prescriptions but by pointing to the fact that Jewish custom freed a person in certain cases from the commandment that required honor to one's father and mother. He thus restored a simple, uncontroversial norm to first place in the esteem of the community and did not converse with the representatives of tradition about their religious regulations and their exegetical follies but forgave them everything. What he did not forgive, however, was that they could command a son under certain circumstances that he should allow his father to go hungry on account of God.

Even in his concluding verdict regarding the Jewish nation he applies the same norms to it. The weighty matters in the Law are judgment, mercy, and faithfulness. The one who neglects those, even while conscientiously tithing his spices, did not merely nullify his entire obedience to the Law but became culpable. He called the Pharisee's meal impure despite all washings on account of robbery and gluttony. The thoughts of the heart that shame the person before God are those that militate against the second table of the Decalogue.

In the Sermon on the Mount he clarified for his disciples through the same norms his opposition toward the prevalent piety of their day. The better righteousness does not come from the realm of the cult or theology but is attained by the overcoming of unrighteous anger, immorality, lying, revengefulness, and hate. The seriousness with which he withstood such evil that we do to others also became evident in the severity of his threat. When he spoke of improper almsgiving, praying, and fasting in which God was not given the honor due him, he claimed that such worship was futile. But the threat of judgment in hell was given not there but when he warned of the angry word that put the other person to shame. The call to decisive resistance in order to keep the entire body from being cast into hell is set side by side with lust that dishonors women (Luke 10:25–37; 16:19–31; Matt. 19:18–19; 7:12; 15:3–6; 23:23, 25; 15:19; 5:22, 29).

This cannot stem merely from the fact that Jesus' call to repentance had aroused his hearers' consciences regarding gross sins, since in this respect there was no difference between his public discourse and his instruction of the disciples. Jesus did not call the disciples to confess in prayer how much their love of God had accomplished but that they had forgiven their neighbor. And in his final word to the disciples Jesus formulated the norm by which he would judge all people: his grace would look with favor on the simple demonstrations of kindness with which we help one another (Matt. 6:12; 25:31–46).

If we proceed from the analogies provided by the history of religions, it would not be strange if in the case of Jesus, the strength of his concept of God lay in the fact that all other relations became worthless for him. Since, however, he bore within himself the concept of the Son and of the Christ in powerful unity, his call to repentance demonstrates the opposite procedure, one that did not separate but rather united closeness to God with humanity, that made the human being worthy and valuable for him rather than indifferent so that he became the guardian of those relations that unite us with one another. For him, this did not amount to a weakening but to the accomplishment of the religious aim served by his call to repentance. It is God who desires goodness for man, just as God acts kindly toward him. In the same way Jesus, by representing the right of the individual against the one who infringed upon it, promoted God's will.

The religious seriousness of sin came to full expression in the images he used in his call to repentance. The son refuses obedience to the father; the slave grabs for himself what belongs to his master; the guests despise the invitation of the king. What Jesus considered to be the things of God that Israel should have given him but in fact withheld from him, we know from the first requests of the Lord's Prayer. It used God's call for its own honor, sought in God's rule its own happiness, and even in its worship merely did its own will, nurturing its own pride by it. It did not have God's love that was concerned for what was God's. Moreover, as it placed the gifts of God—his knowledge, his commandment, his promise—into the service of its own selfish desire, and as it sought, not God's, but its own glory, it also received the offer of the fulfillment of the promise in vain. For it did not desire what God provided. It despised his grace.

By the image of the guests Jesus created an especially sharp formula for the sin of the Jewish community, since here its rebellion is directed against God's goodness, not against his commanding severity. Even in man's rebellion against God there are places where he sins in such a way that he falls irretrievably from grace. Since Jesus saw in the divine Spirit the greatest gift of God, he considered a person lost when he had the operation of the Spirit in view and nevertheless was able to blaspheme him (Matt. 12:31). He pronounced judgment over Jerusalem because it had always stoned the prophets, and he described people's sin toward God for Peter by the ten thousand talents beside which man's guilt toward one another pales by comparison.

By directing his call to repentance toward the unrighteousness that took place among men, Jesus did not intend to deny their religious guilt or to minimize it. The opposite is true: he thereby proved it. When even the smallest commandment was trampled under foot, and when the most evident demonstration of love was impossible for man, this proved how great his resistance to God really was. How could "an evil and perverse generation" serve God? How could a priest fulfill priestly service when he did not even help a dying person? How could those really pray who were capable of taking the widow's house away from her? They merely pretend to pray, he said (Matt. 12:39; Mark 12:40). What made their behavior so horrible was not only that a human being perished; it was godlessness.

Jesus saw the things that justified God's wrath and judgment not merely in man's incalculable guilt before God but in the small guilt that accrues between people. Peter was forgiven his great debt to God because he asked for forgiveness. But if he later choked his fellow-servant, he deserved imprisonment. Worship became sin, an occasion for stumbling and sin, when it confirmed the worshiper's evil. If he was unable to reconcile his wrong toward others and nevertheless wanted to sacrifice, Jesus sent him away from the altar since it was impossible to bribe God and since one could not procure God's favor unless the brother had received what was due him. That the oath continued to be valid when it was used to refuse parents the help they needed, Jesus called the abolishment of the Law. Those who brought sacrifices to God rather than showing kindness toward others he confronted with Hosea 6:6, and he placed the priest below the Samaritan when he let the wounded person languish where he lay (Matt. 5:23–24; 15:4–6; 9:13; 12:7; Luke 10:31).

According to the same principle, Jesus led people to a decision for or against him at the market in the temple. He rejected the market since Israel brought its greed for profit even into the sanctuary and unfolded it there without shame. They made his father's house a business and used worship for the sake of amassing riches (John 2:16). He called it sin that people esteemed the temple for the sake of the vast business that was connected with it owing to its economic importance for the city and called a cult corrupt that served the purpose of people's own enrichment.

The reproach pierced even deeper: the Jews had made the temple into a robber's den. As for Jeremiah, so in Jesus' usage the idea behind the cave probably was that it provided protection for the robber, from which he could stage his next crime. Israel was using the temple to secure God's protection for its evil way, not to forsake evil and return to God. The temple covered the nation against God's wrath and granted them the security that allowed them to continue their sin without being punished. The market therefore had to be at the temple so that everyone had the gift close at hand by which he wanted to buy security, and therefore the nation's calamity grew out of the cult.

The authorization to give this form to his call to repentance came for Jesus from his desire to effect man's salvation. Since man must escape judgment and come to God, Jesus placed the decision by which each decided for or against God into the circumstances that called him immediately to choice and action, to that good which he could presently do, that evil which he could immediately forsake. This Jesus could do since God's grace was revealed in the call to repentance.

Jesus therefore did not consider it to be the task of the call to repentance to reveal all evil in its darkest depths. He thus freed it from its harshness. He did not use the whip in the temple against those who sacrificed at the altar nor against the priests but was content when the Jews at the market understood what contaminated its worship. He did not confront man with all his spiritual poverty, from the dark ideas he harbors regarding God's kingdom to the perversion of his natural instincts, but showed him the ill-will that he is capable of destroying. He can exercise righteousness and kindness toward his brother and do away with the unrighteousness he has done to him and forgive what he himself has suffered. Because he could do it, he also should do it. Jesus gave this requirement the full weight of a condition for the person's share in God's rule. But he also made this requirement rich with promise.

The entire Gospel account shows how strongly and consistently Jesus was able to subject his disciples to the rule of this principle. Although the call to repentance brought him continually into contact with the most ordinary of people generally and Jews in particular, the effort to lay bare the vulgar and seamy is entirely foreign to the Gospel record. That occasion where a most despicable misdeed clamored for Jesus' condemnation arose from the fact that the Pharisees brought the adulteress to him with a cruel lust that hankered for the death penalty. It is, however, no coincidence that this account, as valuable to us as it is, is preserved for us through another tradition than that found in the Gospels (John 8:1–11). When Jesus let Lazarus die by the dogs in front of the rich man's door, he did, of course, give his picture dramatic clarity. But sensationalism is avoided; he did not dwell on the tale's gory aspects. The rich "lived all days gloriously and in joy"; that sufficed.

The description of sin given to us by the Gospels is, of course, entirely sufficient to illustrate the horror with which Jesus viewed the nation, a horror expressed by the flaming denunciation "brood of vipers." But the account accomplishes this primarily by bringing noble figures, humanly speaking, into contact with Jesus and thus subjecting them to his call to repentance. The rich man who inquired about the work by which he could acquire eternal life; the woman who praised his mother; the man who called him to be a judge against his brother; Martha who strove to serve Jesus and therefore resented her sister—these are not ignoble figures. The impact of Jesus' call to repentance becomes visible in each case precisely by the fact that it contradicted those wishes everyone had. The entire account obtained its form through Jesus' pronouncement that the call to repentance was based on forgiveness and therefore did not needlessly shame man or brutally unmask his evil but gave him that will by which he freed himself from evil and became obedient to God.

If a transgressor allowed himself to be moved by Jesus to condemn his evil, he was ready for the confession of his "debts." The use of monetary debt (ὀφείλημα-*choba*; Matt. 6:12; 18:23–35; Luke 7:41–42) was common in Jewish piety as a dramatization of the relationship with God into which the man entered through his evil actions. By using this imagery, Jesus expressed the irrevocability of the obligation into which the ethical norm placed man before God, so that the necessity of punishment arose when the norm was violated. The debtor could release himself from the creditor in no other way than by payment of the debt. Especially when speaking of the forgiveness that dissolved this bondage and obliterated the consequences of sin, Jesus required the repentant person to remain conscious of the greatness of his request for forgiveness from God. He must realize that he asked for grace he could not obtain by himself, just as the debtor is unable to erase the debt that God alone, in the omnipotence of his own goodness, is able to deal with. Jesus made this confession a necessary condition for God's forgiveness. The guilty person had to acknowledge that the divine will requiring the good could not be bent or broken but was absolutely valid, and that therefore the breaking of the same led to the individual's loss of divine favor and separation from God. This was a loss for which only God, not man, could compensate. Jesus never thought of repentance apart from this conviction. If it was missing, the act would be a renewed falling into sin, a new robbery of God, and not a turning from evil.

But since Jesus did not make his call to repentance a description of human misery, he also did not make confession the unmasking of sin, as if this were the condition for reconciliation with God. Confession always appeared as in the Lord's Prayer, both in the portrayals of repentance (as in the case of the prodigal son, the tax-collector in the temple, and the slave found guilty by the king) and in the narratives that describe how Jesus won people to himself (such as Peter who, as a sinful human being, felt unworthy of fellowship with him, or Zacchaeus, the sinful woman, the Samaritan woman, or the money-changer). Confession was highlighted everywhere in such a way that the divine grace gave it its form. It required acknowledgment of God's will in its righteousness. But it directed its view not backward but forward, and granted the guilty new closeness with God, covering all that was so heinous (Luke 15:21; 18:13; Matt. 18:26; Luke 5:8; 19:8; 7:38; John 4:29; Luke 23:41).

Therefore Jesus' aim did not result in some titillating enterprise that sought to move people by stirring up emotional tempests. The Gospels would not possess the serenity peculiar to them if Jesus' own work had not had this same characteristic. After all, he wanted to induce the hearer to right action, and he would not arrive at this through excitement but only by seizing clearly evident norms with determination.

5. The Repentance of the Pious

Jesus considered the Jewish people, and individual communities comprising them such as Capernaum and especially Jerusalem, to be units that had a common will and were capable of common activity (Capernaum, Chorazin, Bethsaida: Matt. 11:20–24; Nazareth: 13:57; Jerusalem: 23:37; cf. 10:14–15). These units were the addressees of his indictment. Their common will was reprehensible, and they were the recipients of the call to God. The nation should convert to him. The sign of repentance in the temple demanded conversion not from individual priests or worshipers alone; it required a decision for Jesus from the entire Jewish community. In the parables portraying Israel's guilt, Jesus attributed to the nation a uniform will. A single barren fig tree became the image for the entire community, and no distinction was made between those vinegrowers who remained true to their master and those who helped themselves to his produce. Likewise, no difference was made between the guests who were prepared for the king's feast and those who rejected his invitation. "The generation" was evil and immoral.

How can a community act? One could expect Jesus to place the decision into the hands of the authorities. Their importance for the destiny of the nation is not overlooked; John strongly emphasized the Jewish community's dependence upon its leaders (John 7:26, 48). The court of the prince is a seedbed of godlessness (Matt. 14:1–12; Mark 8:15). The Jewish community resembles a flock without a shepherd, a ripe wheatfield without workers (Matt. 9:36–38), and these images do not even reveal its entire misery: thieves and robbers steal in among the flock and abuse the sheep at their whim.

The religious leaders whom the Jewish community obeyed did not have their authority from God. The gatekeeper had not let them in to the sheep by the gate. Their authority stemmed from their selfish greed for power, and they fulfilled their office not as servants of God but for the sake of their own greatness and gain (John 10:1, 8–10).[19] Nevertheless, Jesus did not restrict his call to repentance to the leaders. He did not seek the nation's guilt solely with them and did not make its conversion dependent merely upon the repentance of the men who ruled it (Jesus did not ask anything of Antipas except that he

---

19. The image of the vinegrowers is often understood along the same lines as the thieves stealing in amongst the flock. In the case of the vinegrowers, the only interpretation I can accept as possible is the one that likens them to the community.

give him time: Luke 13:32–33). He did not separate them from the community but placed them within it and attributed to it a competence regarding the things of God and an obligation to personal action.

The pious, on the other hand, had greatest significance for the community's decision. Jesus laid the responsibility for the community's destiny upon them, for upon their decision depended the judgment of all. Therefore Jesus directed his call to repentance to them with special urgency. In Capernaum, there was a Pharisaic group separate from the majority of the community whose members were known by everyone. On the other hand, there was a group of men who were publicly known as sinners and who had been excluded from fellowship by the major part of the community. Jesus issued his call to repentance with its complete forgiveness and its unconditional requirement to both groups. The community's conversion, however, was not yet accomplished by the sinners' turning to Jesus. It would have been achieved only if the righteous had subjected themselves to him, and this was rendered impossible since the righteous resisted him, for they had the authority that was heeded by the community.

It was only common wisdom prevailing in the community, which conferred on the call of tax-collectors an outstanding importance in Jesus' work. In contrast, Jesus' dealings with his disciples did not reveal that Jesus made any distinction between those called "sinners" by the community and others regarding their need for grace. Such a singling out of individuals as particular sinners would have lessened the completeness of his forgiveness and diminished everyone's confidence in his grace, since genuine forgiveness entirely extinguishes the consequences of sin and thus effects equality for all. It is therefore an important testimony to Jesus' conduct that the Gospel record reveals the greatness and necessity of Jesus' forgiveness not with regard to Matthew or some other particular "sinner" but concerning Peter.[20]

The disciples emphasized so strongly that the call to repentance was also directed toward the righteous that only few pieces of tradition deal with that disdain for God and one's neighbor which presented itself clearly as sin and was judged by public opinion (Luke 16:19–20.; Mark 12:40; John 4:18). This was also influenced by the fact that Jesus did not seek to shame a person through the exposure of his sin. Where sin is recognized, love remains silent. This, however, was not the only motive that shaped the account. Apparently the disciples ascribed special significance to Jesus' confrontation with the righteous, making the understanding of his will and of his cross dependent upon one's agreement with this struggle.[21] Jesus did not speak of those who left God's vineyard and who forsook his service but about the sin of those who administered that service for their gain rather than God's. Jesus pitched the Sermon on the Mount against those who condemned murder and avoided

---

20. This report of Jesus' conduct is confirmed by the practice of the early church, for it upheld the equality of all before God in its midst. There was no special group of "sinners" in it.

21. Another possible influence upon the form of the texts may be the fact that Christendom seeks in them such words of Jesus as are valid for itself, not those by which he judges the ones who are outside.

adultery as sin, not against those who murdered and followed every lust; against those who fought for their right, not against those who demanded in boundless revengefulness another's life for an eye; against those who loved the friend, not against the selfish who loved merely themselves; against those who were ready benefactors and fasted and prayed, not against those who neglected to do so. The same tactic is repeated in the case of the Sabbath, purity, and service in the temple. We have no word against those who broke the Sabbath but merely against those who sanctified it most strictly.[22] The sign of repentance in the temple was not directed against those who despised sacrifices but against the market everyone considered necessary for the glorious operation of worship. The controversy regarding the forgiveness of sins was begun not by those who did not esteem it but by those who wanted to protect it as God's prerogative against the desecration allegedly committed by Jesus. Not a rich person who gloried in his wealth but one who longed for eternal life he set in relation to God's rule as a camel to the eye of a needle. He portrayed the son who left the father for the sake of the other son, who had always remained with his father and promised him obedience verbally. Jesus was at pains to show the "righteous" son his sin. Likewise, the encounter with the sinful woman and the adulteress were recounted so that the sin of the righteous might be exposed (Matt. 21:33–44; 5:21, 28, 43; 6:1, 5, 16; 12:1; 21:12; 9:3; 21:29–31; Luke 15:11–32; 7:36–50; John 8:1–11).

The same perspective shapes the account of Jesus' dealings with his disciples. He told the parable of the slave who was thrown into prison not to a disciple who was unwilling to forgive but to one who was prepared to forgive seven times on the same day. He shattered the hopes, not of sluggards who showed no concern for God's rule, but of those who longed for greatness before God; not of the faithless, but of those who asked him to increase their faith (Matt. 18:21, 1; Luke 17:5).

Jesus did not call the pious to repentance simply because he rejected their sin but also because he condemned their righteousness. It was not his calling to call the righteous. He praised the father because he refused to give insight to the wise and hid his work from them. The worshipers of God who served him with much prayer, fasting, and almsgiving he sent away empty. The son who never transgressed his father's commandment and who was in his house with full filial rights he separated from God. The one who thanked God for his own piety was the one who was not justified. The one who only needed a small debt forgiven, Jesus confronted with his lovelessness, since forgiveness was in vain unless he also received love. Those who were obedient to their master's call and worked all day were those who rebelled against him and complained; and those who had promised to be fully obedient to the father and had agreed to do his will were those who disobeyed (Matt. 9:13; 11:25; 6:1f.; Luke 15:29f.; 18:11ff.; 7:41f.; Matt. 20:1ff.; 21:28).

---

22. A saying directed toward someone who broke the Sabbath was passed on in the early church not by way of the Gospels but through another tradition.

We do not come to understand what Jesus did when we empty the term "righteous" so that it no longer contains the complete sincerity of ethical consent. If it is transformed into an irony, the condemnation of sinners whom Jesus set beside the righteous also loses its seriousness. The sick of whom he spoke were in his judgment seriously ill. With equal certainty, the healthy were healthy. Jesus conceded to the righteous that they truly obeyed God and that they did what he commanded. They acted according to Scripture and therefore stood beside the fallen ones like the healthy beside the sick, like the flock that remained with the shepherd beside the lost sheep, like the one who only owed little next to the one who could not pay back a great debt.

Whoever obscures this verdict slips on the other side of the contrast into an idealization of sin that distorts Jesus' own judgment. Flattery directed toward the tax-collector who was in truth noble and generous is abhorrent. Jesus had the ethical contrast in sharp view, on the one hand frivolity, disdain of God, greed, and violence, true rather than merely apparent guilt; on the other hand devotion to God, attention to his commandment, zeal in his service, true rather than merely apparent righteousness not just before others but before God. Only insofar as they lacked hypocrisy that denied evil, flagrant sinners possessed a virtue that Jesus honored. Evil, however, does not become pure by being practiced openly. Through openness it perhaps becomes possible to heal evil. But it is not therefore justified.

Jesus' accusation against the righteous held that they, in order to maintain their own righteousness, did not sustain their contradiction against sin consistently enough but also took pleasure in evil. They agreed with it, justified it, and found it compatible with the divine law. Jesus showed his disciples by the fundamental norms upon which those dealings were based that the righteous neglected the sweeping domain of sin in its nascent and covert forms and declared such sins legitimate while Jesus himself extended the scope of sin to the entire evil act. This rendered their righteousness narrow and small. He could, however, offer them divine forgiveness for this if they did not fall by using their righteousness as an occasion to sin. Doing right is accompanied by temptation since it awakens in us a strong self-consciousness. For the pious person this results in the temptation to rebel against God and to praise not God but oneself. Jesus did not tell them that their good deeds were lies. They rather slipped into pride by really doing what God told them to do. From their good they fell into sin, and they experienced a fall from their righteousness, since they no longer bowed before God regarding themselves but now withstood him, defending their right and power against God and representing their will before him. Thus, in the final analysis, their pious activity no longer served to subject "the righteous" to God but encouraged them to stand against him.[23]

Therefore they no longer resembled that servant who, when returning home from working in the field, considers it as his obvious duty to serve the

---

23. The significance attained by the concept of merit in religious theory shows the strength of these tempting blandishments.

master also at the table. Even less did they know the pain of the kind of love
that does everything it can do and nevertheless does not rest content but re-
gards itself as unworthy. They rather looked back to the work they had done
and admired themselves, excusing themselves from the obligation to serve
(Luke 17:7–10).

The proud attempt pervading their piety hardened them in their dealings
with others since pride chokes love. The pious person, for the sake of his own
elevation, could not go without the humiliation of those without piety. He
rather exercised his holiness by subjecting sinners to himself. Thereby he
spoiled his preaching of repentance, no matter how zealously he proclaimed
it to sinners. He also did not overcome sin in this way but sinned even in his
preaching of repentance, since, by the way he judged others, he entered into
a dispute with God. He also stirred up sin in others when he did not lift them
up through his judgment but rather trampled them under foot.

The harshness designed to increase his righteousness was coupled with lack
of genuineness. In order to illumine this contrast, he had to act out his piety
like a play-actor and to conceal his commonality with sinners. Himself he glorified; them he painted black. In himself evil was justified; in others it was
subject to condemnation. He saw the splinter in others while being oblivious
to the log he himself lugged about.

In all words spoken against the righteous it is unambiguously clear that
Jesus rejected them, because of the outcome of their do-gooding. The righteous in Capernaum whom Jesus refused to call prohibited him from doing
for sinners what the doctor did for the sick, and they resisted God's grace that
became a stumbling block to them since they admired themselves. The "righteous" who did not need conversion did not want to rejoice like the angels in
Jesus' gathering of the fallen, while their righteousness and greatness paled in
comparison with those of the angels. They therefore resembled the older
brother who argued with his father for the sake of his own righteousness while
rejecting his brother, or the person who prayed in the temple while despising
the one who had fled to God's grace, or the debtor with the small debt who
ridiculed the great love of those who had large debts, or the workers who did
their entire duty and complained against the master because he was gracious
even toward the least. The righteous whom Jesus refused any further wages
cared only for their own honor; the pious rich person who admired himself
for his obedience rejected following Jesus; and the false disciples allow themselves to break the Law on account of the greatness of their religious accomplishments (Matt. 9:11–13; Luke 15:7, 20ff.; 18:11; 7:39; Matt. 20:11; 6:1;
19:16–22; 7:21–23). Thus religion was turned into its opposite, the monster
of an impious piety, by which the person glorified himself rather than God
and corrupted rather than assisted his fellow man.

Jesus did not blame the righteous for fearing divine punishment and for
longing for divine reward. The basic concept of the Law that regulated piety
in its entirety—that human will mattered for God and that God's behavior
toward the individual corresponded to his work—was Jesus' unshakeable
conviction (Matt. 5:12, 46; 6:2; 10:41–42; 18:35; 24:45; 25:21, 30, 35–36,

42–43). Therefore he agreed with the rabbinate that there was no proof of God's rule without the demonstration that God was the righteous one, no longing for his rule that did not desire to see God's righteousness in operation, and no share in it apart from righteousness. Jesus' proclamation of God's rule, too, was at the same time the announcement of judgment, and he often used the rule of retribution as a guiding norm: the one who did not forgive would not receive forgiveness from God; the one who judged would be judged by God; God would be merciful toward the merciful and would do good to those who did good to others. The harsh individual would find God to be harsh, while the kind person would find him to be kind (Matt. 6:33; 5:22; 6:14–15; 7:1–2; Luke 16:9–12, 25).

By emphasizing this, Jesus did, however, not entangle himself in a contradiction that would force us to the historical reconstruction that he was not yet able to separate his concept of God from the concept of merit and righteousness, because his contemporaries were controlled by the concept of merit. For he destroyed the Pharisaic use of the concept of merit with deliberate clarity. He did this, however, not by an abstract discussion of the relationship between divine and human will, because his weapon was not the formation of theory. He rather encouraged everyone to condemn his own conduct. In turn, when evil was sincerely forsaken the threat of divine retribution ceased.

This stands in close connection with the fact that Jesus turned faith and love truly to God and freed them from being preoccupied with one's own value and accomplishments. A faith that still measured its own strength and tied its own greatness to God's grace, Jesus did not call "faith." Faith was only where God's grace was affirmed that interceded for the individual. He likewise did not concede that love was considered love when it still calculated how much it has already accomplished and how great was its reward. True love possesses an inexhaustible willingness to serve. It does not recount before God the value of its achievement but senses its lack of value and laments its own slightness. The faithful servant was the one who felt "worthless" (Luke 17:5–10).

To a person's sincere, unconditional turning to God corresponded God's sincere intercession for the individual. Jesus' God did not merely follow the rule of retribution. It was thus not dependent upon the preceding human work, as if God had merely been the observer and critic of human performance. He was the father, the one who gave life, because it was his will that his sons should live. He has complete grace and can forgive in the creative omnipotence of the one who blots out what has happened and separates the evil deed from its evil consequences. Jesus thus showed with unparalleled clarity that the concept of merit entered into conflict with God's rule. For merit does not want to forgive even though God forgives. It wants to humiliate where God honors, despise where he loves, and sow corruption where he gives life, because it denies the liberty and greatness of divine love. Again and again it excuses and justifies what God's judgment condemns, as it defends its own unrighteousness and sets aside God's righteousness.

When Jesus spoke out against the concept of merit, however, he did not attack God's commandment. He fought the notion of merit because and to the extent it distorted love and intermingled it with selfishness, not because he denied the will or depreciated ethical obligations, as if allowing them merely a preparatory, exclusively human validity. He considered them to be God's commandments that did not set aside but executed and realized his rule. Therefore he insisted that God would punish, since he sincerely hated ill-will, and that God would reward since he sincerely loved good will.

He called disregard for God's reward impious and thereby differed from the community's piety that did not seek its reward with God but rewarded itself and did not desire the greatness and honor given by God but elevated itself (Matt. 6:1; John 5:44). If an individual disregarded God's reward, he based his hope merely on his own strength and accomplishment, as if he did not need God's work for the achievement of his own goal. Jesus did not set the proud use of the concept of merit and the disregard for God's reward side by side as opposites but saw both concepts to be interwoven with one another and fought against both. By seeing in God's work the condition for all that a human being could obtain, he gained, being fully confident of God's rewarding faithfulness, at the same time the ability to serve selflessly without looking toward success, as well as the freedom from all reflection upon the greatness of the work that did not allow him to think of anything but his work. He eluded the concern for success, for it lay in God's hand. His confidence in God's reward also arose from this. Since the reward lay in God's hand, every service bore fruit, and every breach of service incurred punishment.

Emphasizing punishment while downplaying reward could appeal only to those who transformed repentance into nothing more than a painful mood. In their mind it was enough for the repentant person to be set free from judgment and punishment; expecting reward was out of the question. But Jesus did not conceive of repentance merely as a sense of moral impotence nor merely the cry of a despairing person. He did not replace ill-will with lack of any will but with good will. If the son wanted to return home, he had to decide to serve the father, even if merely as a hired hand. The one who asked for his debt to be forgiven also had to determine not to increase it by being unwilling to forgive the debt of another. Together with forgiveness, he also had to seek preservation and salvation from evil. Since Jesus did not conceive of a repentance that was not also obedience, he did not jettison the concept of reward.

He did not see any conflict between forgiveness and the execution of justice. For in forgiveness God did not measure human performance but acted upon man according to his own kindness. Here he dealt with "his own" according to his authority as the one who epitomizes generosity (Matt. 20:15). The goal of forgiveness, however, consists in making its recipient a doer of God's will. Jesus did not conceive of it merely as the removal of the painful consequences of sin, nor merely as the release from punishment. He sanctified through his forgiveness and thereby opened the way to obedience. His opponents and accusers, of course, attributed to him a forgiveness that conflicted with righteousness, because it allegedly spared evil and thus favored it. Jesus, however, consistently rejected this charge. When Jerusalem's teachers brought an adulteress to him, suspecting him, the friend of sinners, of breaking the law and justifying sin, he demonstrated the purity of his forgiveness and his conformity to justice by extending the condemnation of sin to all, including the accusers. The guilty one is, on account of her sin, worthy of death. This, however, also applies to everyone else's sin. This showed that his forgiveness was based upon the observance of divine righteousness. He did not extend it because he cherished sin but because he cherished releasing people from it. Where forgiveness, however, did not overcome evil but strengthened it, he took it away again, even threatening Peter with this (John 8:7; Matt. 18:21, 35).

While he did not take offense at the expectation of reward and the fear of punishment, he considered it to be an abuse of the concept of righteousness that the "righteous" used it merely to express their own self-assessment. Whoever called himself righteous expressed his conviction that God received him with favor and endorsed his conduct. Jesus did not merely call the righteous' practice of justifying themselves a foolish, useless enterprise; he considered it sinful, since man thereby assumed a privilege that belonged to God alone. They are justified only when God justifies them and when they partake of God's righteousness vouchsafed by his verdict and revealed by his rule. This was no innovation over against the theory of the Pharisees, since they, too, based their righteousness upon God's approving verdict. This is exactly why Jesus charged them with justifying themselves and allowing their selfish desire to usurp what properly belonged to God alone. Therefore he demanded from his disciples that their desire should have its aim not in their own but in God's righteousness, just as it also was their duty to ask not for their own but for God's rule (Matt. 6:33; Luke 16:15; 18:14; Matt. 5:6).[24]

6. The Offer of Reconciliation

Jesus could describe repentance as the liberation from evil, since his call to repentance had its ground in the divine forgiveness that had become for those who repented an attainable present state and reality through the divine sonship included in the messianic office. He attributed to his forgiveness the power of removing entirely the separation from God that originated through sin and of providing complete restoration for the guilty. With complete joy he described divine grace to all not merely as a future aim they should strive to attain in long exercise of penance and obedience but as something he granted to them. His disciples and his opponents realized this with particular clarity in Capernaum, when he expressly declared his forgiveness to a lame man who, overcoming all obstacles, had been lowered to him through a roof (Matt. 9:2).

24. The religious conception of justification became the characteristic of the Christian community.

This should not be considered an exception to his usual behavior. He claimed and exercised the right of calling every repentant person with complete effectiveness and thus continually practiced forgiveness. He showed to all not merely silent patience but forgiveness, whether they were righteous or repentant, disciples or opponents, because his word dispersed evil with a clarity that was recognizable for all. Nevertheless, he continually ordered his communion with those around him not according to their evil but according to God's grace. It is, of course, possible that the behavior of the lame man provided an occasion whereby Jesus took explicit steps to underscore that he granted him forgiveness. More dangerous and tenacious than the obstacles that may have rendered the lame man's faith a formidable challenge was that status of the concept of God revealed in the antagonism of those teachers who opposed Jesus' work. Therefore the disciples did not speak of the former while giving full expression to the religious leaders' rage at his forgiving act.

Current teaching in the Jewish community rendered God's forgiveness a mystery that eluded human understanding. Since only God was able to grant it, it became uncertain whether one had it or not. Thus no faith in God was possible, and all proofs of his grace experienced by man were misunderstood, shortcircuited, or perverted with respect to their purpose. Physical help was, of course, requested from God, and no one protested against the healing of a sick person; whether his sin could be forgiven, however, remained uncertain. Jesus destroyed these disjointed thoughts about God, which expected healing without forgiveness from him and requested from him the gracious operation of destiny but denied that love for the person which united him with God because it forgave his sin. He maintained that he was prepared and able to help because he had the authority to forgive. This is the very reality that exposed the reason for his help, goodness, and overall friendly demeanor toward sinners.

Since Jesus did not reduce repentance to a mood, forgiveness also did not consist for him merely of an emotion. It was rather that deed of God by which he established communion with the guilty, who experienced it through Christ's uniting them with him. He who was known by all as the enemy of evil therefore brought about conversions by relating to the fallen with the friendliness of genuine love. Therefore it was for him an important event that he granted them table fellowship, whether as guests at his table or as a guest in their house. By giving them his bread or receiving theirs, he made clear that he dismissed the guilt that separated them from him. Thus he effected Zacchaeus's conversion by inviting himself to be his guest and thanked him for his hospitality by covering his guilt and shame, forgiving his sin (Matt. 9:10; 11:19; Luke 15:2; 19:5).

He thus described the purpose of his mission by the statement that he offered forgiveness to those who had rebelled against God. If they listened to him and gave God what was God's they would be forgiven and be fashioned into a holy community. The two portrayals of Jesus' work portrayed in parallel fashion by Matthew, the exhortation to those who robbed God and the invitation of guests, should not be separated by time. The obligation to service and the promise of blessedness had been given jointly to Israel, and Jesus, by bringing people to obedience, also led them to receive the divine gifts whereby it was revealed that they were forgiven.

What he was able to give to the repentant he therefore represented by the festive meal that the father prepared for the prodigal (Luke 15:11–32). The rationalistic interpretation of this image that related it to the feeling of blessedness arising from repentance when it is exercised strongly enough runs counter to Jesus' thought. His attention was directed solely to what he did for those in debt. God granted them joy and honor by Jesus' acceptance. With the second part of the picture, likewise, he did not merely promise to the righteous who sinned his complete readiness to forgive but actually forgave them. The righteous brother's objection was directed against the one who returned. For Jesus' "righteous" detractors denied him the right to forgive. And the father drew close to the prodigal; for Jesus justified divine forgiveness and thus also offered it in all its splendor to the hardened "righteous."[25] His listeners were not to ask where the shepherd was who cared for the lost sheep. This had occurred through Jesus' deed before their very eyes. Likewise, his exhortation to joy did not merely have in view a future point in time or merely represent a timeless possibility; people were exhorted to joy on account of what Jesus did right then, and if they had joy they would do what the angels did. He showed to his disciples what they possessed by virtue of their calling by the example of the king who graciously forgave the debt to his servant.

His readiness to forgive remained entirely intact despite his battle with the sins of the "righteous." In the course of that battle he continually proved his readiness to forgive. He did not contrast their sin with a purer form of piety, nor compare their deficient righteousness to a more complete obedience. He rather placed the praying Pharisee beside the tax-collector who was weighed down by his guilt, and set the son who did not leave his father beside the one who had squandered his inheritance. He juxtaposed the one who owed a small amount with the one who could not pay a greater debt and contrasted the righteous people of Israel, from whom the kingdom was taken, with the pagan soldier who obtained it. The fact that great sin did not remove his communion with sinners, and that he dealt mercifully with frivolity, perversity, and obduracy, revealed that when he denied communion to the righteous despite their pious efforts, he did this in the service of divine grace.

Once he granted forgiveness to a fallen woman whom the Jewish community shunned as sinner by accepting her homage and gratitude. At the same time he offered it to his Pharisaic host. He did not tell him a parable that denied him forgiveness as if the debtor who owed only little was not forgiven his debt. He, too, was granted forgiveness, for Jesus kept communion with him despite his Pharisaism and his lovelessness, and he confronted him with the

25. This becomes evident by the fact that the parable apparently lacks an ending. What will the complaining brother do now? Jesus only previews that he will raise objections to his father. This picture finds its completion necessarily in both the prediction of his death and the parable of the vinegrowers. It is, however, developed in Luke 15 only as far as corresponds to the occasion Luke records and is not already made a prophecy.

latter only when he objected to the repentant woman. He granted forgiveness to the rich young ruler by promising him eternal life if he kept the commandments while at the same time exposing the sin he committed by his restlessness and arrogance that violated the commandment. For God "is good," and therefore the rule also remained valid for him, despite his ignorance of God, that the one who keeps his commandment finds eternal life. And even when he revealed that his love of God was mere pretense and that his affection was actually set on his wealth, Jesus loved him and prospects remained open for him. Even the one who was last could still become first (Luke 7:44–47; Matt. 19:17; Mark 10:21; Matt. 19:30).

Jesus did not merely conceive of forgiveness as restitution nor the return of what had been lost. It did not merely restore the earlier broken relationship to the guilty but rendered the communion more profound and firm through its restoration. Love grew strong by overcoming the other's guilt. The shepherd rejoiced in the sheep he found again more than in those for whom he did not have to search, and the father prepared a feast for the prodigal rather than for the one who lived with him. This, according to Jesus, was not simply a human sentiment. In this way, he said, those in heaven rejoice. Matthew also expressed in his brief, serious manner that Jesus issued his call to the rebellious at the same time he invited them to the feast. Thus the call to repentance did not merely grant a return to submission to God that had existed previously but led to a new communion with God that surpassed everything previous.

By the offer of forgiveness the call to repentance received its purity and effective power. Jesus, like the Baptist, was able to place all due stress on that call, without harshness, since the granting of forgiveness was his first and last mandate. True, it was when he showed the brood of vipers what made them worthy of this designation that he first sowed separation between them and himself. But his intention was not to despise and condemn them but to approach them with the intent of establishing the relationship that would make them God's servants and guests. Therefore he also was able to spur on each penitent person's will to the greatest sacrifice and most sincere work without thereby transforming religion into moralism or making performance the major element of religion. For all work and effort to which Jesus enabled an individual were predicated upon the granting of divine grace.

7. The New Commandment

Jesus considered love to be the goodwill demanded by God. That is why he also exercised forgiveness. He deemed the power of forgiveness, of raising up and sanctifying a person, to be that it produced love. When he was scolded for this, he justified his forgiveness by insisting that it would produce, not moral hardening, and not renewed indebtedness, but love (Luke 7:42; Matt. 18:33; 6:12). Therefore Jesus demanded from his disciples that they should ask God for forgiveness after they themselves had forgiven, for forgiveness that does not produce love is in vain. But such vanity could come about only by way of a sinful decision; if a person showed upright conduct, love received

produced love, and by the granting of forgiveness goodwill was awakened, because the one for whom the father prepared the feast at his return would now
remain with him.

On love Jesus bestowed promise (Matt. 5:7, 9, 44–48; 6:14, 20; 7:1; 18:5,
35; 19:17–19, 21; 25:35–40; Luke 6:35–38; 10:37; 12:33; 14:14; 16:1–9). If
he had refused to grant it, he would have obliterated his call to repentance. If
he had not been able to name for the Jewish community a goodwill that had
God's good pleasure and his promise, he would have made repentance torture, and the call to repentance would no longer have been "good news." He
therefore proclaimed that God's rule would be the portion of all the merciful,
of all those who forgave, and of all those who gave good gifts to others. The
Christ united himself with all those who were kind. After attributing causal
power to man's evil conduct, he did the same with his goodwill, not because
he had forgotten the concept of guilt or in order to renew the doctrine of
merit, but rather because he sincerely opposed man's propensity for sinning
and thus showed him the conduct by which he had God's good pleasure.

He derived the necessity of love not from the view that evil was not really
totally despicable, so that the right kind of human effort could serve as penance or compensation; nor from the view that God's will was limited with regard to forgiveness so that human kindness must first be shown before there
could be divine mercy. It was rather Jesus' position that God was always one
with the ethical norms that conform to goodness and always opposed to evil,
even and especially when he forgives. Jesus considered fellowship with God
that produced or protected evil impossible. The one who loves God loves the
one who is good and the good itself and can make God his own by no other
way than affirming what is good. He therefore could not receive forgiveness
except by exercising it and could not demand it solely for himself while denying it to others. If God separates the destructive consequences of the evil done
from the one who makes the petition, that person also must leave the evil
done to him behind and forgive. In order to forgive he must love. In subjecting his forgiveness to this rule, Jesus did not exercise it in the service of sin but
of righteousness.

The determination with which Jesus demanded forgiveness cannot be derived from singular motives such as his special softness or sensitivity or from
a preference for the special virtue of being a peacemaker.[26] When he urged
forgiveness, he did not speak of an isolated task with which the individual
might occupy himself occasionally beside his other purposes in life but of that
kind of conduct that has always been indispensable for the establishment and
preservation of communion among ourselves. Its disruptions are constantly
apparent; community in every relationship can be preserved only by forgiveness. This does not result in a negative procedure, merely in defense against

26. This formula was a mixed construct that used the Hellenistic point of view in order to
interpret Jesus and therefore often hindered understanding of him. For the one who sees his
task in the enhancement of his own powers via an ethic of virtue, being a peacemaker remains
an isolated virtue of subordinate significance. It also makes a difference whether a person's aim
is set beyond himself, that is, in his service of God and his neighbor, or not.

evil, but through forgiveness we preserve communion even when there has
been rupture, because we deny evil its consequences and remove its destructive effects. By preserving communion we deepen and complete it.

Jesus initially directed love toward God with a coherent, complete will. In
all earnestness he called this the foremost commandment. The first longing
Jesus awakened in the disciple was directed toward the honoring of the divine
name, rule, and will. That was love for God, not the cultivation of human interests for their own sake apart from our relationship with God. As foolish as
the thought was that the individual would be harmed if God's will was done,
and as certain as these requests were able and ought to capture everything we
strive for, there was no mention here of those things that belonged to human
beings but of what pertained to God. All human needs were subsumed under
the one aim: that God would receive what was due him, the honor due his
name, the revelation of his power to all, and the doing of his will by all. Jesus
confronts the concern about daily needs with that will that asks for God's rule
and righteousness. Those are "the things of God." In dealing with the disciples, it was Jesus' goal to get them to the point where they were concerned for
what was God's in contrast to what was man's. "Give to God what is God's"—
his entire call to repentance was grounded in this desire.

In the Sermon on the Mount he considered "righteousness" to be what the
disciples did for God. He assigned to it the pure kind of complete love that
considered God alone. It remained the final goal of the service of humanity
to which the disciples were obligated as the light of the world and as the salt
of the earth that people praised their Father on account of them. Jesus directed their view not merely toward the need of those who depended on their
service nor merely toward the value of the gift they offered but placed the entire weight in their service on the Father's name. He showed them by the
harsh slave that every attack upon a fellow-slave amounted at the same time
to an attack upon the king, since whoever corrupted the fellow-servant resisted the king's grace. He expressed the same idea when he contrasted the
contempt of the little ones with the way that God honored the angels who
serve them, or when he compared the wrath of the righteous with the joy of
the heavenly ones or derived love's perfection from the completeness of divine
love (Matt. 22:37–38; 6:9–10, 33; 16:23; 22:21; 6:1–6, 16–18; 5:16; 18:32–
33, 10; Luke 15; Matt. 5:44–48).

Love for God, however, is immediately also love for people. It thereby
proves its genuineness by transcending all selfish motives. Only the love that
is intermingled with selfishness thinks only of itself when it thinks of God. To
the extent that it really turns away from its own self to God, it has God in view
as the one through whom and for whom all live. Thus it is due all that is
God's, not merely one's own self but the neighbor as ourselves. This does not
mean that a divided will arises that turns away from God to man. Love for
one's neighbor is planted into the heart turned entirely to God as the second
commandment and does not thereby lead us away from our love for God. It
has its ground and place in love for God rather than existing alongside it.

For this very reason Jesus assigned to relationships between people an independent value, not merely in his evaluation of sin, but also in his promise. But it would be wrong to conclude that Jesus measured love merely by a religious standard since it belonged first and foremost to God, as if he had examined every good deed with regard to the extent to which it was grounded in its remembrance of God and to which it arose out of love for him. He rather blessed the mercy, forgiveness, and giving that we exercise in human circumstances and promised it divine mercy, forgiveness, and pardon, not merely with those who were without religion but also with his own disciples. By this he proved that he ordered our relationship with God and with one another truly according to the rule of love. For when thinking of love, he did not think of the depreciation of human life for God's sake or of an absorption or vanishing of human interests in the love of God. He saw love as giving value to man. He saw to it that his work had its goal in man.

Since love for God is the great love, it also gives our ties with human beings their measure since it forms their basis. Both communion and freedom originate from it. It does not merely liberate people from things that receive their value merely by serving love as means and tools (this is evident in Jesus' confrontation of the rich; see p. 166). It also provides us with independence in all human relationships, both against attack and hatred of others and against their attraction to us with its bondage and power. According to Jesus, every love toward man that breaks love toward God becomes sin. Therefore whoever loves human beings more than Christ sins, be it parents or children. In the conflict Jesus placed his disciples with the world, it became their duty even to despise their neighbors, since they had to be able to deny their desires, to fear their advice, to hurt them, and to break communion with them (Matt. 10:37; Luke 14:26).

Jesus did not consider such conflicts to be merely a destiny to which the disciples should yield passively but made it his personally resolved duty to fight this fight against all those he loved, all who loved him, and even against himself. The clarity with which Jesus thought regarding the issue of love and the completeness of his love have their measure in the simultaneous validity of both rules, that is, "to love the enemies" and "to hate parents and children." They are inseparable and can only be understood jointly. The power of the association that cannot be disturbed, not even by the enmity of the other party, and the power of the separation that is not thwarted even by the richest and most intimate relationships, coexist side by side; for they have the same basis. The direction of one's entire love toward God renders it possible for every human communion to be dissolved and makes any disturbance of it ineffectual. Nothing unnatural originates from it, neither harshness that despises parents and neglects children in the place of piety nor gullibility and carefreeness in the contact with the enemy that cover up and thus support evil. What Jesus wanted was the position of complete freedom without slavery because of either the hostility or the friendship of others.

Since Jesus considered that kind of action to be love that had its goal in the well-being of others, he made its characteristic attribute a selfless manner that was perfect when love was complete. He did not yield to the scruples that love, through its selflessness, might jeopardize our own happiness or life. The kind of love that consumes a person's inner life and leaves no goal or desire that would provide him with the meaning of his own life would be a nonsensical procedure in Jesus' view. Love cannot yield this result in relation to God since God is good and himself the one who gives, the one who grants man life and who preserves and perfects him. Love that did not seek or receive anything from God would deny what God's love desires and produces. If that were the case, God's will would be presented as complete selfishness that absorbs everything; Jesus conceived of God's love as a genuine doing of good by which the individual received his life and his strength. Therefore Jesus was convinced that every sacrifice offered to God would be richly rewarded and that one's life would not be lost for his sake without being thereby won. This is evidenced not merely by the eternal outcome of life but already in one's present relationship with God (Matt. 6:4).

According to Jesus, love also does not lead to any damage in one's own life in the relation to one's neighbor. In this regard, too, it remains the complete opposite of self-destruction. For the ordering of these relationships Jesus used the formula given by the Law, "to love one's neighbor as oneself." Love for one another was required by his new commandment given to his disciples. The goal of our submission to others is their equal position with us. This is not obscured by the requirement also to love one's enemy, by which Jesus clarified the contrast between genuine love and that kind of love that is bound and polluted by selfish desires. He led his disciples away from hate completely, and they proved that they truly had been freed from it when hatred directed against them was unable to awaken hatred in them. Complete, limitless patience was indispensable for this. Without it they could not be freed from hatred against those who attacked them. It is impossible to separate the completeness of patience from the completeness of love. By this he admittedly established completely separation from evil without, however, teaching the devaluation and destruction of one's own life. To love one's enemy does not mean to support him in practicing his evil and destroying us. To be able to bear everything does not mean to incite others to hurt us. The absolute rejection of all evil and of all injustice remained free from all challenge by the rule of complete patience and love.

As in complete patience, love also proves its pure selflessness through its pervasive separation from greed for honor, possession, and even life. But even when Jesus lent sharpest expression to the contrast between love and selfish desires, he protected it from the unnaturalness that slides into self-destruction, since he emphasized the value of material things expressly and precisely when people forsake them by promising gain to the deprived. Through this he explicitly combatted the fear that we harm ourselves through love. In regard to other people, of course, the completion of communion is often hindered by the fact that love is not merely given but also received. Otherwise it would not be necessary to talk about love for one's enemy or about forgiveness and patience. But love for others is comprehended by love for God and for this reason is fruitful in the greatest degree.

8. Jesus' Dispute with the Galileans

The exhortation to repent directed to the Jewish community by Jesus rendered his work a confrontation everywhere, including Capernaum. It would not have become such if he had merely sought to describe and to reveal evil with his call to repentance. But since he sought to move the individual away from sin to God, appealing to his will, a wrestling began between him and his listeners in which each pummelled the other with blow and counterblow. There would also have been no conflict if he had counted merely the judicial office as his mandate and if he had been content to expose sin by condemning it and by withdrawing from fellowship with sinners. But since he suspended the execution of justice as long as the call to repentance was in effect, he approached man with it rather than withdrawing from him. He entered into fellowship with him rather than distancing himself, seeking reconciliation. Since this reconciliation could only be effected by the conversion of the sinner, Jesus' work took on all the characteristics of a confrontation, and the determination with which the call to repentance was issued excluded all forms of compromise. If Jesus had restricted himself to relative verdicts, union between him and the Jewish community could have been maintained, even though he scolded its condition harshly. However, he did nothing to reduce the radical nature of the decision with which he confronted the nation.

Everything depended upon the fact that he fought the struggle peacefully rather than sliding into argumentativeness. The greatness of his aim of wanting to lead the Jewish community back to God also lent greatest significance to the manner in which he formulated the call to repentance. If by entering the fight he had ceased to be the peacemaker for his people, he would have obscured for them his regal calling; for the making of peace for the nation was inseparably linked with the name of the Christ. He first guarded the fight against unnecessary escalations by leaving the customs of the Jewish community intact and by maintaining contact with everyone, including the Pharisees. By this, however, the confrontation was simultaneously rendered more intense.

He would have made his task easier if he had avoided the Jewish community as the Baptist had done. By "eating and drinking" with all, he also planted the word of repentance in his personal contact with individuals. Luke makes this clear by locating the sayings of Jesus that condemn Pharisaism at a meal where Jesus was the guest of a Pharisee (Luke 11:37–52; cf. Luke 14). The information that Jesus did not merely issue his call to repentance publicly but also in personal contact with the individual is indispensable for an accurate picture of Jesus. That could have been dismissed as untrue if he had only been described as the great communicator who attacked opponents publicly but failed to issue his call to repentance in the personal sphere. He stood, however, for the same norms that he spoke about publicly when he was the guest of a Pharisaic host.

He injected peace into the conflict by offering reconciliation to those who fought against God. Thus he led the community of his followers into peace with God. He also produced peace among individuals by leading them into love. The things he forbade his disciples in the Sermon on the Mount—anger, lust desiring the foreign woman, lying, abuse of rights for the purpose of justifying oneself, the intermingling of love and hatred—by such things they robbed themselves and others of peace. Likewise, the righteous who elevated themselves because of their own righteousness lost their peace, as did those who sought treasures on earth or who burdened themselves with sorrow or who acted toward one another as judges. The disciples observed that he removed the conflict from them and created peace between them.

This excluded the use of force as one of his methods; he also prohibited his disciples from exercising it (Matt. 9:16–17; 7:6). Force would have produced strife. One should not patch up the garment in such a way that it tears even more severely, and one should not store wine in such a way that wine and wineskins are ruined. Allegiance to him should be grounded internally, because he sought to be whole and true. Therefore he did not demand anyone to subject himself by force, and he protected all in their religious freedom before they believed in him. He termed a mishmash of old and new highly damaging.

His patience did not cause a watering down of the call to repentance that would have avoided all struggle. For his call to repentance was based upon the conviction that the old and the new differed by a clear contrast that was evident to all. The communion with existing piety into which he placed himself ensured that his attack of others was understood as an attack solely directed toward evil. Merely against this, not against the natural manner of man or against the religious inheritance of the Israelite, did he direct his opposition. He made this clear to all by maintaining religious and natural contact with them.

What caused the rift between him and the Galileans was this: he forgave the guilty.

As much as his call to repentance often hurt individuals, driving them to active protest against him, the attack against Jesus was mounted, not owing to the harshness of his demands, but owing to his forgiveness. Not the harsh but the gracious element of the call to repentance incited the Galileans against him, not the fact that Jesus called Capernaum evil and impure but that he completely overlooked sin in his dealings with those who repented. This resulted from the fact that the inner situation of the Jewish community was determined by Pharisaism. The consciences were awake; sin was feared; there was a readiness to do difficult things and to suffer for God's sake. "What is God's work in order that we may do it?" they asked, ready to undergo whatever he might demand (John 6:28).

This zeal, however, was interwoven with a concept of righteousness that rejected grace and therefore took offense at the calling of Matthew. They resisted seeing in Jesus' forgiveness God's will and revelation, and suspicion against Jesus immediately arose by which they desecrated the central procedure of his inner life. This suspicion did not merely come to light when they spoke of him as a "glutton and drunkard, a friend of tax-collectors and sinners" but also when the Baptist's disciples were concerned about the fact that they never saw his disciples fast. At this point the rabbis also felt the depth of his consciousness of being called. So they directed their attack against this part of his ministry (Matt. 9:3, 11, 14; 11:19; John 8:1–11; Luke 7:39; 15:1; 19:7).

From a human point of view it was natural that the Jewish community conducted its confrontation with him not merely by defending itself but also by accusing him. It rejected his call to repentance by suspecting sin in him, and the righteous did this with particular passion. After all, in their own judgment, they represented the cause of righteousness against him. Even when he did not accuse them, he continually challenged their aims by his conduct, aims they pursued with the confidence by which righteousness must be defended.

The personal turn that the conflict took did not elude Jesus. For by defending the rightness of his actions he defended the commission given him by the Father whom he obeyed, and he simultaneously protected his disciples by refuting charges as their "advocate" that also pertained to them and that had the potential of shaking their confidence. He therefore relentlessly rejected all attacks that were directed against himself. When they assailed his forgiveness or spotted the devil in his works or called his behavior on the Sabbath sin or challenged his freedom from tradition, he maintained that he acted in communion with the Father and that he had Scripture on his side. In this way he exposed the sin they committed by attacking him.

This entailed the danger that the confrontation would degenerate into a battle for the honor due those who were fighting. Both sides found within themselves the normal behavior toward God and fought therefore with the same weapons against one another. They called him a transgressor of the Law; he accused them of the same. They detected in him boundless pride that claimed what belonged to God alone; he revealed as pride the sin of the righteous by which they usurp what belongs to God. They called him a blasphemer because he wanted to destroy the temple; he called them corruptors of the temple who had made a robber's den out of it. They said he lacked validation from God since he refused their demand for signs; he said they were separated from God since he did not draw them to himself. Did not charge stand against charge, argument against argument? What was the truth here? Jesus, however, kept the conflict from being obscured by insisting until the end that it did not arise from his own conduct but that it was the consequence of their false piety. Their separation from God was revealed in their opposition toward him. The one who prayed like the Pharisee in the temple could not rejoice with the angels that he called sinners to God. The one who treasured evil in his heart saw the devil where God revealed his rule. Therefore he never made his defense merely a discussion of his relationship to God and his office but combined it with the call to repentance.

This call had two goals that stood in a certain tension with one another. The completeness of his forgiveness resulted in the conviction that no guilt resting on the Jewish community could separate it from God's kingdom but that it stumbled solely by rejecting the reconciliation of God it had now been offered. It became subject to judgment merely owing to its rebellion against Christ. This thought is paramount for John. "If I had not come, they would not be guilty of sin" (John 15:22, 24). Likewise, Jesus said that Capernaum and Jerusalem would stumble owing to their rejection of him, the Son and heir (Matt. 11:20–24; 21:37–39; 23:27; cf. Luke 19:14, 27). At the same time, however, the call to repentance sought to underscore that the rejection of him had its basis in the fact that Israel persisted in rebellion against God, not only at that time, but from long ago through a long chain of sins. Therefore Jesus substantiated his woes against the nation not merely by the fact that they had rejected him but by the guilt that arose in the realm of its own knowledge, in the sphere of their own religion. That his word remained fruitless for them was a result of their breaking of the Law, their Jewish sin, and not first of all because of the offense they took at him (Matt. 23).

9. Jesus' Dispute with the Rich

Jesus saw in wealth the ground of grave sin since it attracted the heart of the one who possessed it so that the heart was on earth while it should have been in heaven with God. It was there, however, only when the individual had with God what he recognized to be his treasure and possession. What Jesus had against the rich, however, was that they slid into complete dependence on their wealth. Thus there arose an absolute contrast that forced the individual to a decision, since he must become either God's slave or the slave of his possessions. Jesus desired for a person to belong entirely to God. The relationship with him was all-consuming. With similar complete allegiance, however, wealth captured the rich, since from it, too, grew love that determined the way he conducted his life. Therefore Jesus considered wealth corrupt, since it robbed the individual of love for God, thus making him godless (Matt. 6:21, 24).[27]

In agreement with what we know of Jesus' call to repentance elsewhere, he portrayed in no less harsh terms the hardness in a person's conduct arising from wealth. In the story of Lazarus, he constrasted the rich man with the poor man twice, first so that Lazarus was the needy one who waited for the crumbs, then so that the rich person was the petitioner who pleaded for a drop of water. When the rich person could have given, he did not give anything. When he had to ask, he did not receive anything. Jesus linked both events by

---

27. In contemporary usage, "mammon" was, without negative connotation, the common word, not merely for wealth, but for all kinds of possessions, whether great or small. It meant something like our term "property."

a causal relationship: since he had not given anyhing, he did not receive any-thing. Since he let Lazarus die in misery, his request was not heard either. Thus it was ordered by divine righteousness.

Thereby is expressed what made wealth dangerous in relation to people. By it the rich person was preoccupied with his own welfare and grew hard toward others. Likewise, Jesus described the farmer who had an unexpectedly rich harvest as controlled by a will that was merely concerned for the securing of one's own livelihood for one's own enjoyment (Luke 12:15–21). Thus the unity Jesus introduced between love for God and love for one's neighbor also proved to be true in the evaluation of wealth. Since the one who loved mammon no longer loved his neighbor, mammon's slave was no longer the slave of God. What Jesus demanded on account of God was at the same time re-quired for the sake of man, and what he demanded for the sake of man, he demanded for God.

Jesus applied the same norms to the steward who had been unfaithful to-ward his master. He had been unfaithful, and this because his only response to those who owed him money was to demand repayment. In contrast to this generally condoned conduct, Jesus praised renunciation as the right use of wealth, corresponding to the will of the one who gave it. However, he did not conceive of renunciation as the destruction of material goods but as their use for the well-being of others, and since wealth strengthened the energetic ac-tivity of love, he called it a means of gaining eternal life.

This verdict regarding wealth implied that Jesus' help for the poor did not consist of liberating them from poverty. The disciples said he had shown com-plete mercy to the sick and dying. But they never speak of his efforts to im-prove social conditions. The question of life moved him; whether the individ-ual died or lived, whether he was weak or vigorous—these things mattered to Jesus. Therefore he required from his disciples that kind of help for the poor that removed from them the misery that directly threatened their life. As was Jewish custom, he therefore counted "alms" together with prayer and fasting as part of the "righteousness" of the pious (Matt. 6:2; Luke 11:41; 12:33; John 13:29).

On the other hand, there is no record that he made a poor person rich by way of a miracle. We rather hear that he rejected the one who expected him to be the guardian of righteousness by doing away with the unbearable injus-tice of his brother's taking advantage of him (Luke 12:13). He did not con-sider it part of his vocation to make sure that everyone received the property due him. When he encountered a funeral procession on his way to Nain bear-ing the only son of a widow, her poverty evoked mercy in him. He did not, however, help her by giving her money but by restoring her son. In Jerusalem, he saw a widow sacrifice her last penny to God and praised her profusely, but we hear nothing of his bringing an end to her poverty (Luke 7:13; Mark 12:42).

Love that was capable of giving all was in his eyes the greatest wealth a per-son could obtain. We therefore also do not have a word of Jesus regarding the issue of slavery. Slavery, of course, was in the Jewish realm no longer a pressing issue since there were merely pagan slaves in affluent households. He did, however, immediately encounter these slaves in his dealings with the pagan population. He gave to the slave of the centurion who was based in Capernaum his health; he did not, however, demand his release.[28] This had its basis not in a lack of empathy for the misery that accompanied poverty. When he placed the poor beside the blind, lame, leprous, and dead, or with the hungry, weeping, and outcasts, it is clear that he considered poverty to be an evil (Matt. 11:5; Luke 6:20–22; 14:13).

As he recognized in his ability to heal the sick the glorious demonstration of divine grace, he also saw it in his ability to help the poor. Helping them, however, did not consist of making them rich but of telling them the good news he was able to bring to them for the same reason he also helped the sick. Because they suffered on account of their poverty, God cared for them with his glorious grace and granted them his eternal gifts. Thus they were helped even though they remained poor. For in such a way they received "the treasure in heaven," that is, God's grace and joy in him.

Poverty oppresses the individual by burdening him with sorrow, and this Jesus called a blight (Matt. 6:25, 34). But he thought here less of the dark moods with which our lack of foresight into the future can torture us than of the hot desire that it incites in us. This militates against the highest desire by which we should long for God's rule and righteousness. For this reason Jesus helped the poor person by taking sorrow away from him, not by a change in his circumstances, but by calling him to faith. He extinguished the godless thoughts and wishes attached to poverty and thus made the poor man glad by subjecting him to God's kindness. Thus poverty became itself something good like the renouncing of anything by which love for God was active and proved itself. Jesus formulated his thoughts in complete clarity when he called the one who forsook his wealth perfect and when he praised the poor person on account of his poverty. For on account of this both were rich in God.

He did not fight the sins stemming from wealth and poverty merely with words but remained poor himself from a free, persistent will, and made his followers poor as well. Otherwise he would not have been able to awaken in the rich person the courage to forsake his wealth and in the poor person the courage to faith. Because he counted poverty to be part of his mandate, he bore it joyfully, since he valued it as genuine wealth. The renunciation he exercised had the sweetness of love in it that could leave behind everything for God's sake. He did not connect with it an essentially selfish glorification of poverty as if to set it in contrast with the burdens of culture or to praise the freedom enjoyed by the one who has nothing. His attitude retained its natural form and was open to the uncomfortable in renunciation. When he told the one who offered to follow him that he had nothing to offer him, not even what the animals had, he did not think that this prospect would lure the dis-

28. In this regard, too, our Gospel tradition is identical with the one possessed by Paul. Paul knew a word of the Lord that prohibited the facile dismissal of wives; he did not, however, have one that demanded the release of slaves. Paul possessed as little as we do social legislation of Jesus, an important point.

ciple; he rather confronted him with the difficulty of his decision (Matt. 8:20; cf. Luke 22:35; Matt. 19:27 also speaks of the gravity of the decision leading to the disciples' following Jesus). This was not an ode to the sweetness and glory of poverty nor, of course, a lament regarding the situation he had chosen by his free will. He destroyed any expectation in his followers that he would bring them wealth and happiness in the conviction that this was absolutely essential for them and the only means by which he could inspire in them the ability and industry to serve him. Only thus did he free them from Israel's traditions that combined faith in God unscrupulously with the accumulation of wealth and that sought the blessing it wanted to receive from God by becoming rich. The pious person wanted to experience the compensation for his worship, just as the godless should experience the condemnation of his godlessness. Since Israel thereby polluted its love and service of God and needed to be called to turn from money back to God, it became the duty of Jesus and of his disciples to separate what Israel had joined and to show to everyone that they neither desired nor gained money by the divine word. After Jesus had excoriated the temple's money-changers, he did not then grant to his own the connection of profit motives with their profession (Matt. 10:8–10 will be treated under the sending of the disciples). Just as he considered it to be an important decision when a rich person renounced his wealth, however, he viewed it as an important task to ensure that the disciple remained in poverty. He achieved its perfection only by God's omnipotence. When, however, the good God gives him the love of God, poverty becomes gain for him precisely because it is difficult. For love proves its strength by what it forsakes.

Therefore when a historian categorizes Jesus as an ascetic, he obscures his concept of love. For the aim described as "asceticism" belonged to Greek ethic, originating from an ethical school of thought that had been formed without, or even in contrast to, the concept of love. This ethic rather made the goal the formation and ultimate perfection of our personality, which entailed the renunciation of everything that weakens or harms us.[29] An ascetic ethic that has its aim in the enhancement of one's own life to its maximum potential and that calculates the necessary means to achieve it of necessity gives weight to the measure and the form of one's possessions. It creates measurements that indicate from what point onward wealth is harmful.

From Jesus we do not have a single statement along the lines of "this or that you may not own." For his judgment always related to a person's attitude toward what he has, to the direction of his love, whether it turned to wealth or to God and his neighbor. By using the word "Mammon," he did not delineate how much property an individual was allowed to have. The word was not even suitable for this. He rather laid his entire emphasis upon the slavery entailed by wealth, regardless of what it consisted in and how small or how large it was. The contrasting results in the cases of the steward and the rich person contrasted with Lazarus—where he showed how wealth became a blessing in

---

29. This is another area where the hybrid intellectual constructs that interpreted Jesus' conduct using Greek formulas were a rich source of false inferences.

one instance and a curse in another—are merely a function of their different attitudes toward the needy. This yields an essentially different aim than that of the ascetic, who seeks help and harm in things.

The arrangement of the sayings dealing with money yields clear hints of how the disciples conceived of Jesus' attitude regarding this topic. The one of whom Jesus demanded complete poverty is set beside the one whom he freed from the pious duty toward his father. He thereby no more demanded the destruction of the family than he insinuated that possessions are evil in themselves. The second saying places love beside love, communion beside communion, love for one's father beside love for God, and fellowship with one's relatives beside fellowship with Jesus. If tension resulted between those, Jesus did not leave the decision ambiguous but turned the individual entirely to God.

Thus wealth became a person's enemy by drawing his love away from God. The rich man who could not decide to renounce his possessions succeeds in the Gospel record those who considered it their legitimate right to dismiss their wives and those who had little esteem for children. Here, too, the connection between these stories is probably in view and characteristic for the way in which the disciples understood Jesus' word. That one should send away one's wife and have little esteem for children while zealously clinging to one's wealth are choices of a self-centered will. Jesus reversed all these judgments and required his disciples to retain their wives and to extend God's grace to children while permitting them to renounce their possessions. His opposition to human ways of thinking always arose from the same basis. Human beings reverse their love, deny it where they should give it, and grant it where they should not do so. They love their wealth and take it away from others and from God.

Therefore the phrase "renunciation of the world" is an inadequate description of Jesus' will as is the phrase "asceticism," at least as long as one conceives of the "world" that Jesus supposedly intended to destroy the natural world. He did not renounce it but decried that will of the individual that transformed the natural good into a curse for himself by turning away from God for its sake. Of course, he also combatted the worship of wealth by pointing to the ephemeral nature of both possessions and those who possess as well as to the contrast between this world and the afterlife (Matt. 6:19–20; Luke 12:15–21, 16 [not merely Lazarus, but also the steward]). By this, however, he did not depreciate our present life since the higher goods he placed above the tangible ones do not become ours merely in the afterlife but already in this world. Jesus showed to the individual who lives in nature and is dependent upon it (not to a person who does not exist until the age to come) how he could find true wealth obtained from God, and how he could be freed from tormenting anxiety by trusting God.

Therefore Jesus' attitude toward wealth left the grateful appreciation and use of nature that we otherwise find with him entirely intact. He does not reverse the phrase that the things that make an individual evil come from the heart. For there also arises the danger of wealth, not in material possessions, but in what the individual makes of them. John, too, did not know any ascetic rules of Jesus, since he considered any instruction regarding possessions relating to one's body to be unnecessary. It would not have been unnecessary if ascetic rules had held sway, since these would have then become conditions for the possession of salvation. One's right attitude toward the "world" was for John one's ethical posture, and he did not conceive of the "world" in terms of things but in terms of people with their joint expressions of will and their conduct of life. John merely rejected false love whereby he agreed with Matthew, testifying as clearly as Matthew did to Jesus' aim.[30]

These demands were connected with the dawn of God's rule in the same way as the other parts of the call to repentance. The anticipation of the coming judgment strengthened opposition against all evil and fortified people against the enticements of wealth, while joy in the eternal and perfect good strengthened that love that gladly renounces everything for God's sake. Those who connected Jesus' confrontation of the rich with his promise, so that a disillusioned pessimism arose from it that destroyed the joy and the possession of the present in the intention of enhancing the desire for the coming world, worked with presuppositions that are foreign to the texts. If Jesus traced the misery of the afterlife to sinful happiness in this world, and when he likewise assigned an eternal reward to the good deed done in this life, when he showed the rich person his foolishness by pointing out that he would remain separated from God on account of his wealth while freedom from possessions yielded readiness and prepared the disciple for the arrival of his master (Luke 12:34–35), then he used the same motives for the renunciation of sexual lust, for the patience and love to be given to the brother, and for the courage to martyrdom, in short, for the entire yielding of one's will to God's and the entire yielding of one's life to God's service in power.

The natural needs of everyday life remained thereby entirely acknowledged. Jesus' prayer dealt with the issue of food and drink not merely as unavoidable but made it his disciples' duty to ask God for their lives' sustenance and to expect that he would grant them their bread. Thus Jesus warded off from his followers that kind of godlessness that arose from the individual separating his natural needs from his relationship to God, giving himself to them in work and pleasure without thereby remembering God. When the disciple, on the other hand, made these requests the content of his prayer, he separated them from the anxiety they normally caused, placed them under the guidance of faith, purified them from their excess, and measured his desire for daily needs by what he really needed. Thus he gained for himself the ability of the first, great love that asks for the things of God. That this love, however, should limit or choke the desire for the sustenance of one's own life was incompatible with Jesus' thought. The will directed toward God's rule rather

---

30. Paul had access to sayings of Jesus that spoke against mammon. For the saying in 1 Cor. 9:14 that expressly authorizes those who administer the word to be supported by the community cannot be separated from Jesus' dispute with the rich. Paul, however, knew nothing of ascetic rules of Jesus. He rather subsumed this issue under the concept of liberty.

lent the request for the sustenance of one's life its depth and reason as well as, admittedly, its proportion.

The words that assure disciples freedom from anxiety are not intended differently. The poor person who is given faith and the rich person who is given God's love are not exempt from those activities by which they procure their livelihood. Human labor was not replaced by miracle, and one's own laziness was not supported by divine care. By pointing to the birds and the lilies, it is not those who are made examples for the disciples. Rather, what God does for the birds and lilies is made, by an argument from the lesser to the greater, the basis for the disciples' own behavior. By shattering the power of false passion and by making room for the highest love, Jesus neither depreciated nor rendered despicable the natural functions by which we make our livelihood. Nor did he merely moderate and calm them but simultaneously strengthened them, since the faith Jesus gave to the poor and to the rich person will be shown to be God's gift in their appreciation of their apportioned work as each cares for his own life within the divine order.[31]

He also did not do this as a loner, nor limit it to himself but offered his instruction and example as the member of a firmly linked community whose love he expressly extended to natural need and misery. The love he was talking about fed the hungry, cared for the wounded, and prepared the festive meal also for the poor and cripples (Luke 14:13). Since he placed the disciple into the community of his followers, help was available for natural needs, and a commonality comes into being where the overflow of one covers the lack of another (Matt. 25:35–36; Luke 10:33; Matt. 19:29). Jesus' instruction on the proper use of money merely fleshed out the concept of love. This concept, however, it developed in pure perfection. Beyond this he gave no concrete directives on how one should use one's money for the brethren. He merely told the rich young ruler to give to the poor. Subsequent to his repentance, Zacchaeus gave half of his wealth to those he had harmed (Luke 19:8). How he ordered his circumstances remained subject to his own discretion; Jesus did not regulate his conduct. Thus it becomes evident at an important point how exclusively Jesus was concerned with the internal effect he wanted to evoke by the call to repentance. Not the quantity of one's performance, but the turning of one's will to God in pure love was the one thing he desired for God. Thereby was God given his due.[32]

Whether we misinterpret or interpret correctly Jesus' evaluation of wealth shows itself by those words by which he measured the value of life and death, honor and dishonor, ruling and serving, knowledge and ignorance, marriage and celibacy, the family and freedom from it. Against all these goods that come from the natural order of our lives he directed the same complete denial that separated one's desire from them and elevated them above it, as in the

31. Paul and Barnabas associated their voluntary poverty not with begging but with their own work. Thereby it becomes evident how Jesus' words were understood by his followers.

32. Just as little does one find in the Gospel records sayings regarding the early church ordering the use of property for fellow-believers. It is completely certain that the disciples did not possess any economic rules from Jesus.

case of wealth. The disciple had to be in a position to die, to suffer shame, and to renounce rule. He possessed no native wisdom that could secure him to God. He could renounce marriage if given the gift and had to shatter all dependencies upon relatives and nation. The reason that made this renunciation one's duty was always the same: these goods corrupted the disciple when he yielded his obedience for their sake and thus did not fulfill his duties as a disciple, and their renunciation became his gain when he renounced them for God's sake and when his love for God was revealed in his renunciation.

Jesus' thought, however, was never that life or marriage or family or national origin or knowledge or honor or power were corrupt in and of themselves. They were such for the one who placed them above God and who seized them in such a way that he thereby denied the Christ. He therefore protected them with an absolute esteem when they were attacked by ill-will. To the one who refused his father honor and support he quoted the saying that the one who shamed father would be guilty of death. To those who were married he said that God had brought them together and that the one who broke his own marriage or who touched another sinned. To be put to shame was felt to be an acute form of suffering, and Jesus strengthened those who had to bear shame by the highest promises.

One cannot speak of the depreciation of earthly life by Jesus when he constantly rooted its preservation in God's creative power. But here, too, he thought of the kind of renunciation that forsook those goods not merely as burdens but as sacrificial means to the joy that accompanied every service of God. As he let the disciple be poor with joy, he instructed him to suffer shame joyfully and to renounce power with his entire will, being not the first but the last. This will directed toward renunciation is made possible by Jesus' inclusion of the completion of all of these goods in his promise. By his commandment calling the disciple to die he did not instill in them a longing for death; he rather directed them to die in order to gain life, just as he called them to be poor in order to become rich. He did not make lack of dignity or the breaking of the law their goal but rather called them to forsake their right for the sake of righteousness in order that they might receive and retain their righteousness from God. He told them not to fear shame for the sake of honor since God honored those who obeyed him. He told them that they would gain true greatness and real power by limiting themselves to the small service that renounced greatness and promised to his little ones the highest knowledge that could be effected in them: that which came by God's revelation. For those who left behind everything, even their own, those who allowed themselves to be expelled from the holy nation of Israel, he opened his community with its multitude of kinsmen. The phrase "renunciation of the world" would thus spoil Jesus' thought here, since it conceals that he granted the highest positive evaluation to the individual, including everything that belongs to the necessities of his life and happiness. As in the case of wealth, he did not require the renunciation of all of these goods because he strove for their annihilation but because he elevated God with an absolute exaltation and because he assigned all goods their wholeness only when the will directed toward God stood freely and entirely above them and controlled them (Matt. 10:39; 16:25; 5:39; 20:26–27; 11:25; 19:12).

10. The Helper in God's Power

Regarding God's kingdom Jesus' view was directed toward goals that could only be realized by the creative act of omnipotent grace. By proclaiming the messianic message he presented himself to the world as the one who worked through God, and what he worked was life. For God's rule dispelled death. Therefore the Gospel record never consisted merely of Jesus' words but always also of stories that described his powerful activity by which he became the protector and giver of life. In John, too, where we find the highest esteem for the Word since John emphasized Jesus' unity with God through the Word, this did not lead to a depreciation of Jesus' work. It remained the indispensable, even decisive, motive to faith. "If I do not do the works of my Father, do not believe me" (John 10:37; 14:11). For the word disintegrates when it is not linked with the power to accomplish the work.

The attempt to find a miracle-free Gospel as the first form of Christian tradition to which only later miracle accounts were attached has no chance of success, since the Christ concept too would need to be kept far removed from this "original Gospel." By omitting works and limiting oneself to mere teaching Jesus' regal will would fall by the wayside. His consciousness of power that was revealed in the signs he performed and his claim to rule were inextricably linked, and with the impossibility of removing them from Jesus' story is also established that the miracle was not merely attached to it at a later point. It is not just the passion story that is inextricably linked with the miracle, since it is not merely the crucifixion alone that, together with the resurrection, designates Jesus as the Christ. Rather, the proclamation of his second coming likewise describes him categorically as the worker of miracles. Disciples who did not proclaim Jesus as the risen and returning one are nothing more than an absurd legend.

The indissoluble connection between miracles and the story of Jesus is also confirmed by the account of the miracles itself, since it is such an integral part of the entire tradition that no story devoid of miracles can be separated from the texts by historical methods. Even in material such as that arranged by Matthew in chapters 11 and 12, which have all the characteristics of earliest tradition, the concept of miracle is inextricably intertwined. What is it that can substantiate doubts regarding the account of the query of the Baptist when considered by itself? Is it supposed to have been construed owing to a dogmatic need? The Baptist's question has an entirely transparent reason, both in the facts as in the conflict between the traditional concept of the Christ and Jesus' behavior. Jesus' answer has, at any rate, all the signs of the form of will characteristic for him: the lack of any demonstration, the combination of a claim to power with selflessness, the categorical ethical sincerity, the messianism on the way to the cross. But the miracle cannot be separated from this vignette. The Baptist's disciples hear and see his signs and are to report them accordingly to him. If we eliminate the answer, the entire piece disintegrates. No one in the Christian community ever spoke about the Baptist's doubts without also telling about the answer Jesus gave him, and this answer includes the reference to miracle (Matt. 11:2–6).

The denunciation of Capernaum, Bethsaida, and Chorazin does not derive merely from those who knew the circumstances at the Sea of Galilee owing to its topographical information. It leads us also by its content so specifically into Jesus' heated disputes that the removal of this saying will be difficult for any historian. The saying is inextricably linked with miracle. On account of the miracles, Tyre and Sidon will be treated less severely than those communities that had Jesus in their midst (Matt. 11:20–24). We cannot eliminate the Sabbath controversy from the tradition without entirely obscuring Jesus' history. For the Sabbath, in turn, it is essential that Jesus performed his healings on it. Jesus' answer to the accusation that he worked them through Beelzebub, likewise, cannot be judged to be a legend after the fact. How could a religious need invent a situation in which Jesus defended himself against the accusation that he stood in communion with Satan? The event, in turn, is unthinkable without the sign. Thus Jesus was not scolded because of his morality or because he attacked Pharisaism. The charge arose from the fact that he did what no one else could do, and people searched for an explanation for the power given to him. Likewise, the rejection of those who demanded signs from him includes the concept of miracle. Jesus' refusal is not substantiated by his inability to work miracles, as if he had no power beyond what nature granted, but by the evil of this generation. Jesus rejected the demand for a sign because he did not want to give it, not because he could not give it (Matt. 12:10, 22–24, 38–39). In the same manner, the account of miracles is everywhere inextricably interwoven with tradition.

Because the story of Jesus was never available to Christendom in any other form than the one that reported his signs, enhancements of the miraculous events are in individual cases possible and probable (e.g., Mark 5:11; Matt. 21:19; 17:27). But all these instances, however numerous we may consider them to be, assume the account of the miracles to be an essential part of the gospel. Since Christianity was certain that Jesus had acted in miraculous power, the miraculous nature of the events was presumably occasionally elevated and injected even where it had not been present from the beginning. Since, however, such enhancements of miracle stories are only consequences of those stories, they do not explain and refute them.

The close connection between the signs and the words is essential for the historical verdict. If the reports had assigned Jesus unusual power merely in his actions, doubts regarding them would be justified. A miracle story about someone who proves to be poor and weak in his own inner life would present itself as legendary. In Jesus' case, however, word and deed together have a unique power, and he does not transcend the form of existence possible for us merely by his actions but also in his thoughts and choices. For we do not and cannot have this divine consciousness that he bore within himself. We do not stand in this unhindered confidence toward God, this complete closeness to

him that does not contain any division or separation. The fact that the loftiness of his word is accompanied by a parallel loftiness of his ministry renders
both plausible, and their uniformity lends the story of Jesus, despite the miraculous nature of both his thought and actions, its intelligibility and its coherent naturalness. John was led by a proper judgment to accentuate powerfully this parallelism between Jesus' word and his signs.

Later the miracle stories of the Gospels are corroborated by the miracles of
the apostles. If the Lord did not do any signs, neither did the disciples. If, on
the other hand, they acted in the assurance that God's omnipotence would
come to their aid, we know that they had miracle stories in their gospel. It is
impossible to remove the sign from the account of Paul and Peter, and thus
it is firm how old the miracle stories of Jesus are, that is, as old as the apostolate. The sign belonged to the gospel that Paul heard, just as it belongs to ours.

If the miracle stories are considered to be later additions to the original
reminiscences, the midrash of the synagogue would provide a parallel for
their interpretation, since the synagogue partly exaggerated the miracle without scruples regarding the history of the fathers and in part freely invented
it. According to this theory, the legend originated from the Old Testament
narratives and the concept of revelation supported by them. Since, for Christianity, miracles appeared to be indispensable for Jesus' messiahship, it attributed them to him by a dogmatic conclusion.

This stimulus did not come from the attitude of contemporary pious persons and teachers, since they did not appear nor were venerated as miracle-
workers. It is not a historical concept that the working of miracles was expected from every pious person. No one pushed Jesus into the role of miracle-worker or would have attached a miracle story to a memory of him if he
had merely conducted himself as a pious person like all the others. Of the
celebrated teachers of Jerusalem and Javne—Hillel, Gamaliel, Yohanan ben
Zakkai, or Akiba—there are no miracle stories. What is reported from the
Pharisaic circle as special grace are answers to prayer, such as on the sick bed
or for the end of a drought or in other need whereby individual pious persons could develop the reputation of a special power in prayer so that their
intercession was solicited even from afar. To this could be added dreams,
voices, also prophetic words that mediated to them special guidance from
God.[33] What we know about Jewish exorcists differs from the accounts
about Jesus decisively, especially since the Jewish exorcist always worked
with material means to which the miraculous effect was linked. He did not
ascribe the latter to himself but to the formula he spoke, the ring he had, or
similar means. Magic always played a part in this.[34] None of this goes be-

33. The Jewish objection against the Gospels was not that the rabbis could do the same things
Jesus did but that the Gospel stories were invented or that Jesus had worked with sleight of hand
or with magic. Cf. the disputation of a Jew against Jewish Christianity repeated by Celsus.

34. The claim that Jesus placed himself in Matt. 12:27 beside Jewish exorcists misinterprets
the text. Jesus set himself apart from the Jewish exorcists by calling them "sons" of blasphemers.
Precisely because the deeds of the exorcists were not done by the Spirit or God while still being
praised as God's work, they would be judges of those who call the Spirit of God diabolical.

yond what recurs in the church repeatedly. It provided a firm connection between the miracle story and what Jesus' contemporaries thought and did; it does not, however, constitute a parallel. The manner in which Jesus' ministry is described remains particularly different from such alleged parallels since what they report as "miraculous" was not done but merely received by those who experienced it.

Old Testament miracle accounts did, however, influence Jesus' story significantly when he claimed to hold the messianic office, but only then. The Jewish messianic concept included the miracle. "Our fathers received the manna; what will you perform?" This portrait of the Galileans is richly confirmed by Jewish sources and illumines the situation of Jesus and of his disciples. The miracle of Scripture provided the norm of how a revelation of God occured, and its characteristic was the creative omnipotence that knew how to produce everything that served its purposes in instantaneous fashion. Therefore the concept of miracle was immediately brought to Jesus by his environment, since it was known how God authenticated his messengers and what he granted them. Even the fact that the rabbinate did not have the power to do miracles could strengthen the desire for such miracles, since this lack revealed the limitations of its calling and "the absence of the Holy Spirit." Whoever transcended the teaching profession by a special commission, however, had to prove his higher claim by showing that he possessed what was lacking in the rabbis but had characterized the Old Testament bearers of revelation.

Isolated accommodations of the Gospel narratives to Old Testament stories are probable (Matt. 4:2; 21:7; 27:34), but the substance of the accounts cannot be explained by this motif.

The interpretation of the miracle story as mere imitation of the Old Testament model falters in light of the fact that such an imitation of Old Testament models is not recognizable in Jesus' words. They are above the suspicion of being artificial constructs formed according to scriptural patterns (see the discussion of Matt. 27:46, p. 372). The same can be said about the major elements in the course of Jesus' history, such as his baptism, his call to repentance, his proclamation of the kingdom of God, his cross, and his resurrection. None of these things is an imitation of the Old Testament. The thought that Jesus' work has to be an imitation of Old Testament events and words cannot be observed in the circle of the disciples at all. For them the conviction that Scripture expressed God's will, which would be fulfilled without question, was connected with the certainty that God's rule could not be calculated in advance but had to be accepted in faith and obedience as it happened. This applies wholly to the sending of the Christ, who did not merely repeat old things but brought fulfillment.

The miracle story, too, is free of slavish dependence on the Old Testament. The raisings from the dead told concerning Jesus resemble those of Elijah and Elisha merely in the fact that in both cases dead people were awakened. But they reveal no particular accommodation to the Old Testament pattern. We do not have here the one who prays and who throws himself onto the corpse; Jesus does not achieve divine help by way of wrestling in prayer but acts with certainty, and every time the situation is completely individualized. The characteristics of Jesus' miracles that are sharply accentuated in the Gospels stand in marked contrast to the prevailing concept of miracles. The foregoing of self-help, his refusal to use miracle in the fight against enemies and for the sake of personal glorification, and the pure naturalness of Jesus together with his evocation of divine creative power are not shaped according to the model of tradition. The disciples were conscious of this, since they depict the Jewish desire for miracles as causing a sharp dispute with Jesus, and they are proven right by the fact that the will expressed in Jesus' signs was not the Jewish one, as little as the one expressed by his words.

Of similar originality is the external shape of these actions. In each instance they are placed into a particular situation and motivated by it. When, for example, the question is discussed before the lame man whether it was God's prerogative alone to forgive sins or whether Jesus, too, could have authority on earth to do this, this does not copy an Old Testament situation. Jesus' deed is rather put into the situation brought about by the rabbinate of the first century, and this situation is portrayed with concrete and controllable accuracy. The miracle cannot be separated from this portrait that clarifies for us the nature of the faith of Jesus' contemporaries. Without it, it has lost the reason for its existence. If this method is supposed to explain the narrative regarding Jesus, it should also be applicable to the signs of the apostles. They can, however, not be understood as an imitation of the Old Testament but are completely individualized. They are neither developed from patterns in the Old Testament nor from patterns in the Gospels.

The men who are supposed to have proclaimed a non-miracle-working Christ, legends gradually attaching later to their message as its alleged proof, do not fit into any point of early Christian history, as if their supposed proof was gradually attached to their message in form of legends. Whoever seeks to observe the religious condition of the first century will be at a loss where to find the men who did not consider the miracle to be a gift from God, worthy of the highest esteem. All had their canon in the Old Testament and took from it the content of their concept of God. This did not yield the rational mood that desires for everything to proceed along the fixed course of nature. Regarding the expectation of the Christ, they all directed their hope to an absolute aim that transcended the boundaries set for our own power. Where are we supposed to find historical grounds for a messianic idea making no use of miracle?

A theory like the above lent strength to another kind of explanation that not merely considered the miracle story to be the product of imagination but that wants to understand how faith in miracles took hold in Jesus himself and in his followers and therefore searched in the accounts for a historical "core." To this it is supposedly enabled by the power of faith. Jesus stood in the confidence of the omnipotent rule of God. Likewise, those who call upon his help are controlled by faith that, after all, the Gospel account itself considers the indispensable condition for the possibility of miracles. Such psychological powers could lead to peculiar results, such as in the case of hysterical or otherwise neurologically abnormal people. After all, a large share of miracle stories deal with psychological disturbances. Thus it supposedly is significant that Mark begins his account of miracles with the healing of a demoniac. Jesus could easily have exercised a strong influence upon such sick people and could have effected their temporary soothing. For they were moved by the strongest religious impressions, since they supposed they had the Christ in front of them. That Jesus counted on the Creator God was readily affirmed. Accordingly, he himself acted creatively as a miracle-worker and also appeared as such to his environment, while the procedure itself did not transcend the mechanically controlled natural process.

Moreover, it supposedly was intrinsic to faith that the result of these activities was not observed. After having been called upon by the leper, Jesus sent him assuredly to the priest; the result was committed to God and did not cause Jesus any further concern. No one had diagnosed that the leprosy had really disappeared. Not to be concerned about such statements, it is said, would be an essential characteristic of faith. One may also count on a series of coincidences that can easily gain great significance regarding faith in miracles, such as in the story of the miraculous feeding. The disciples remembered a festive meal that Jesus held with those who had come to him. The estimated number of people fed must at any rate be dismissed since it is exaggerated, as was common for Jewish numbers. The meal had given the impression that Jesus here provided bread for the community. No one had asked where it had come from. One should put in this category especially those signs by which the accounts allowed faith in miracles to arise in the circle of disciples, such as the great catch of fish or the surprisingly large amount of wine; here coincidence could easily have played a part.

It is impossible to extend historical verification to isolated free-standing incidents. Jesus' own integrity, however, is the subject of a secure observation that controls our own judgment. The interpretation of the miracle story attacks Jesus' integrity when it ascribes to him a faith that operates in a vacuum without concern for truth so that he promises, for example, healing to the leper without caring whether healing was actually effected or not. Jesus, it is argued, assumed that God would be concerned about this, and therefore confidently sent him to Jerusalem whereby he was removed from his own view. Such a faith is ethically suspect; for it renders one blind and indifferent toward reality. It thus becomes daydreaming and harshness toward those who are deceived. An inviolable ethical norm demands that faith should not close but rather open the eyes of a believer and that it should not separate him from reality but rather connect him with it, not merely out of consideration for others but for the sake of faith itself, since a faith that is indifferent to outcome is internally corrupt and no longer that entire yes to God that Jesus called faith. For even if inner uncertainty had no part in this indifference that concealed the actual event, this form of faith would merely have revealed its calming effect, while hamstringing any truly moving and stimulating impact. A healthy faith cannot part with the assurance that the gift requested by it was received and that help had been given, to the extent that it sincerely desired the good requested.

How Jesus conceived of and evoked the act of faith, however, is not removed from our observation, since the foundational forms of his inner life become visible in his entire life conduct. It is possible to judge whether in Jesus' case faith blinded the ability to see or not, whether he was closed to actual reality or whether he devoted sharp observation to it, whether he fought with postulates of faith against the actual course of events and maintained, and in God's name demanded, what was excluded by the way things naturally happened or not. Jesus was not preoccupied with the construction of a dream world in the name of faith, as is proved by the fact that he idealized neither the Jews nor his disciples nor his own success nor the outcome of his life. Those who see in the concept of God at its very root merely a construct of the imagination will, of course, evaluate this differently. According to them, Jesus moved with his entire thought and intention in a dream world. By this, of course, the entire Gospel record, not merely the miracle stories, is separated from the realm of real life and transposed into the sphere of psychological malformation by virtue of its lack of intelligibility and predictability.

Jesus' belief in spirits appears to provide evidence for the phenomenon that his faith created alleged realities beyond actual reality. In the same way that Jesus' commands to the spirits had merely subjective basis, and an examination of to what extent in a given instance spiritual powers were a possibility is out of the question. He did not need any objective confirmation for all his "miracles" apart from the subjective occasion. The task of understanding "miracle" would be completed for him and us by the fact that his claim of working miracles should be understood in psychological terms. But against all this it must be pointed out that, in relation to the otherworldly spirit world, Jesus, like everyone else, confronted a mystery that he also treated as such. In the case of a miracle within the natural sphere, however, the issue was that of observable effects that he could not ignore as irrelevant without proving himself to be a dreamer. Here his ideas would have had to withstand the control of visible events, and these ideas would have become sinister if he had withdrawn them from those events or maintained them in contradiction to these.

This theory likewise does not adequately account for the actual events. It views the causal factor for what occurred at that time in the psychological power of faith, contrary to Jesus' thoroughly vouchsafed own disposition. He spoke of faith with those who asked him, and these were often different from those who required and received healing. Owing to the faith of the centurion, his slave was healed; owing to the faith of the mother, the daughter was restored; owing to the faith of the father, the sick or already dead child had become well. One therefore cannot explain the events by recourse to the psychological impact of faith on the spiritually sick. The standard by which Jesus assessed the indispensable nature of faith was simply an ethical rather than physical one.

This evaluation of the psychological power of faith involves the idea that spiritual disorders are more easily healed than physical ones. Since, however, spiritual processes have characteristics of their own, like actions performed through natural processes, this consideration procures its probability by way of the supposition that these "miracles" did not produce any real effects. When the abnormal symptoms temporarily retreated, it was nevertheless completely uncertain how the sick person would feel the next day. Not faith but unbelief is established by appearances that continually fade again, perhaps also a forced increasing desire to do miracles, but never the certainty that the Gospel record credits to Jesus and by which the disciples affirm his sending by the father. It is beyond doubt that Jesus wanted to help from sincere motives and that he did not merely long for theatrical effects. If so, he needed the same certitude and power to lift inner disorders as to remove physical diseases. Both had as their prerequisite the collaboration of the creative power of God.

The disciples claimed that Jesus had the will to act in God's power if those whose body was ailing and whose life was thereby in jeopardy and burdened asked for his help. He did not do the signs of his own initiative in order to authenticate his word or to prove his legitimacy, nor did he himself urge those who suffered to come to him. Generally he refrained from taking the initiative. When life was requested from him, however, he did not retreat from the painful misery of death by way of passive empathy but rendered assistance. Matthew's account of Jesus' response is very specific in this regard (Matt. 8 and 9). Even when he acted of his own initiative without having been asked, his deed never turned into an arbitrary demonstration of divine power, but always had its motive in the respective situation (such was the case at Nain in Luke 7:13, with the signs narrated by John in 5:6 and 9:4, and at the great meal in the desert in Matt. 14:16).

When his help was solicited, he did not look for natural means, since he confronted the destruction of life for which no natural help was available. He rather turned to the omnipotence of God, in the conviction that the creative activity of God was with him and would procure success for his word. Thus he answered a leper who called upon him for help: "I am willing; be clean." For he did not consider divine help to be doubtful or limited but affirmed it as given to him with certitude and as more than adequate for every need. The narratives arranged in Matthew 8 and 9 indicate that nothing that disturbs human life, neither sickness nor storm, neither nature nor spirits, neither guilt nor death, set limits to his help but that he knew himself to be authorized to hear every request and to grant his own complete protection.

The members of the community that were tormented most severely were the demoniacs, whose suffering was terribly heightened by the theory that sought to explain it. Since this theory possessed the power of a public verdict, those who suffered did not seek to elude it. Even they traced what they experienced to the presence, perhaps even residence, of tormenting spirits within them to whose power they had been subjected (Mark 5:9). This idea was an old one in the Orient, while, according to our sources, it only gained currency in the Jewish community during Hellenistic times, since those times strongly heightened the inclination to attach to those conditions a definitive explanation and to establish a definitive theory for its treatment.

Not every disease was traced back to a "spirit." Outside and within the Gospel tradition a distinction was made between diseases that were based on physical functions and those that were attributed to invisible influences. No one, for example, called a leper a demoniac. Possession became a possibility especially when ethical abnormalities accompanied the disease, such as anger, destructive tendencies that were directed against others or against one's own life, together with an abnormal increase in strength.

Jesus neither removed the interpretation of these conditions by way of a rational critique nor did he seek new insights regarding them. He confronted them solely with the assurance of God that maintained his authority over all of man's adversaries and who extended his grace even to the most severe disorders. He therefore remained averse also here to all speculative theories. In Josephus one reads that such spirits were souls of the deceased. This idea has a Hellenistic flavor, and it is doubtful to what extent it had currency in the Jewish community. There is no reason to attribute such thoughts to Jesus.

The fact that he subjected the spirits to the rule of Satan whose kingdom they constituted (Matt. 12:25) suggests that they were of a different kind than human souls, but one cannot reach a firm conclusion from this saying, since deceased souls, if they are evil, too, could be subjected to Satan's rule. When sending out his disciples, Jesus saw Satan fall from heaven prior to the exorcism of the spirits (Luke 10:18). Regarding the connection between those spirits and Satan, attention is given entirely to the basic ethical law that the destructive power of spirits is only possible through God's execution of justice, and liberation from them only through the granting of divine grace that coincides with the rejection of the accuser. By thinking of Satan's power in connection with the tormenting effects of the spirits, Jesus placed ethical need above physical need and designated evil as the reason for the power of these influences. Humanity would have no invisible foes if there were no power of evil in the supernatural realm. But Jesus did not discuss the kind and origin of these spirits. This is confirmed by the fact that the disciples did not know any names that Jesus had given to spirits.[35]

To leave those to their own devices who knew themselves to be controlled by destructive spirits was impossible for Jesus because of his consciousness of God and of being the Son. It would have resulted in a disruption of his affirmation of God if his power to help had come to an end at a point where the

---

35. "Legion" in Mark 5:9 is no proper name that might stand in relation to other terminology. The rhetorically powerful portrayal of a spirit chased away from human beings who searches for a place of rest in the wilderness in Matt. 12:43 merely serves the purpose of heightening the power of the call to repentance. It seeks to impress upon the listener that, by having been offered the kingdom, he has experienced the greatest thing possible, but that rejection of that offer does not invalidate it but results in even greater calamity than the one that oppresses the community already. The extension of possession to animals cannot be supported by Matt. 8:31. The narrative emphasizes that Jesus' power over spirits could be observed in a visible event, not merely in the transformation of the possessed, but also in an external event that showed how powerful those spirits were and that they had really been exorcised by Jesus.

spirits worked their destructive effects, while the messianic aim spoke at the same time of total grace that worked the complete liberation of man from all corruption. To this end certitude was indispensable so that he was allowed and able to defend persons not merely against natural calamity but also against supernatural influences. In this way he also completed the call to repentance in a way that made a great impression upon the Jewish community. He brought the summons to God to all, even to those who were under the power of Satan. He offered reconciliation to all and made the return to God a reality for them.

By taking this kind of approach to those issues, Jesus liberated his disciples from all superstitious fear. If we wish that he had rejected all belief in spirits with a cool air of superiority, we hardly understand what it took for him and for his disciples to overcome the difficulties that resulted from the idea of the supernatural. Nothing less than that fearless peace regarding all that may be found there and that is not felt by our own consciousness could give them the position held by Jesus, that is, the recourse to God's protection that extends over all mysteries. The powerlessness of rational criticism in the face of such fearful conditions was based on the fact that it could never provide an explanation that could cope with the mystery. That mystery stepped into the foreground with its darkness and pain so that such criticism was often enough unable to cope with it. Jesus, on the other hand, had and provided in this regard something complete, not by rational deliberations whether there were spirits or not, but by being grounded in God whereby a complete certitude was reached since his grace is perfect. On account of this those pressures that the enigma attached to the disorders of the inner life can lay upon an individual were lifted. In view of the power over spirits Jesus claimed to possess, the disciples moved freely in Gentile territory. They passed by paganism without fear of demons since Christ shielded them.

These healings had special significance for Jesus because in his dealings with those who were possessed his regal name found expression. The name of Christ was directly linked to the idea that Jesus was the liberator from corrupting spirits and that his word would protect the individual against all satanic power. This was absolute power, complete grace. Those who were possessed no longer stood within the community's firm connections and therefore immediately expressed the impact Jesus made upon them, while the normal Jew waited for his teacher and did nothing before everyone followed. But since the possessed one had despaired entirely of himself and of all human help, he operated in fear and hope with absolute ideas. Thus it happened that when he felt himself to be in Jesus' power, he took recourse to the highest, the regal name.

This happened for the first time soon after he ahd taken up residence in Capernaum, subsequent to a Sabbath worship service in the community's place of prayer. But Jesus suppressed the demons' proclamation of his divine sonship and of his regal status. He did not desire the testimony of spirits but the faith of human beings and demonstrated his regal status by granting Israel return to God. Thus he revealed in his conduct toward demons the selfless-

ness of his activity and his complete dependence upon God. The miracle did
not happen for his own sake but for the sake of those whom he helped, and
from his Father alone he expected his glory. God, however, does not speak
through demons but glorifies his Son himself. Jesus waited for this testimony.

While honoring God as the one who controlled everything that happened
to the individual and in nature, he did not conclude that he could disregard
nature, since it, like the wonderful creation of life, had come into being
through divine activity. Therefore the naturalness of Jesus was not jeopardized by his miraculous work. The later experiences of the church show the
greatness of this procedure, since miracle-workers easily gave room to the impression that they could disregard or shatter nature. Jesus, on the other hand,
after doing the sign, subjected himself again completely to the natural order.
He obeyed it and commanded it, and both derived from the same reasoning.

He did not fear nature since God was greater than it, and he commanded
it, not because it produced ungodly things, but because it was God's work.
Therefore he could not hate it but rejoiced in it and was subject to it, and his
miraculous help did not lead him away from it, since, after all, it was in the
miracle that the power and grace of the one who had created nature were revealed. He therefore grounded his disciples' faith in like manner in miracle
and nature. By the perception that in nature everything, even the smallest, is
provided for, the disciple should gain the faith that would liberate him from
anxiety, and he should attain to the same goal, that is, the carefreeness of faith,
by the fact that God's creative power had given him bread (Matt. 6:26–30
along with 16:8–10).

These contrasting elements in Jesus' behavior, that he now wanted to act
free from all natural conditions, then immediately thereafter to subject himself entirely to them, were strongly felt to be an enigma by those who saw him
at the cross: he mightily helped others—now he died in agony (Matt. 27:42).
But the simultaneous validity of the norms that guided Jesus were a mystery,
not for him but for the Jews given their viewpoint, since his will was directed
not toward divine power (as theirs was) but toward fellowship with God. In
the same way that he shattered the demand for a miracle in others, the claim
that his life should merely be grounded in miracle remained entirely distant
to him. He was concerned for God, not for the form of divine activity,
whether immediate or mediate through nature. What mattered was that
God's life-giving grace would be effective.

Since Jesus' actions resulted from sincere mercy, they initially had their
purpose in themselves. They intended to remove a need that awakened Jesus'
mercy. This is not obscured in John's account that connected the signs with
the basic idea of Jesus, whereby John made those signs effective for the faith
of his readers. Therefore he led their thoughts from the feeding to the bread
of life, from the healing of the man born blind to the granting of the ability
to see, from the raising of Lazarus to the giving of eternal life. By this, however, Jesus' deed is not drained of that purpose that produced it in the first
instance. Therefore the meal still remains foremost of all the removal of hunger, the healing of the blind man the liberation from blindness, and he re-

stored the brother to the mourning women. Each deed, however, transcended its occasion, and John achieved through his presentation the purpose of showing that Jesus' signs revealed what should move the entire community and attach its faith to Jesus.

This, however, had been the custom in the community from the beginning. The help granted to the individual had always been considered important for all, or it would not have been told. Its imperishable significance arose from the fact that those acts of Jesus grew from his fundamental convictions and made them effective. Therefore they were operative far beyond their occasion, not because this was despised as insignificant or because it did not attract Jesus' entire love, but precisely because Jesus poured his entire love into those needs and because he provided help for them in such a way that he made his relationship to God fruitful for the petitioner. Since he approached the individual need with which he was confronted with his entire soul and strength, he revealed the full extent of who he was right down to the deepest foundations of his activity.

These experiences revealed and confirmed God's communion with him, even to himself. Even the strongest inner life cannot replace the external experience with which it is confronted. Only dreaming lets human life consist merely of one's inner life. When a tension arises between what lies within and the external world, and the former is not supported and confirmed by the latter, so that one's self-consciousness must preserve itself merely by itself without being protected by perception and experience, severe struggles inevitably result. If, on the other hand, we receive guidance that coheres from without and from within, we thus obtain assurance. Jesus, too, was subject to this law of human life so that the experience by which he saw God's grace protect and create life through him had serious significance. The internal certitude of his sonship did not render the experience of divine power and grace worthless for him but rather made it valuable and fruitful.

Through these acts his sonship was revealed. Since he performed them through God's power and grace, they revealed the unhindered wholeness of his relationship to the Father. He could ask for and receive all things from him, and the goodness that acted for and through him was boundless. Therefore the accounts emphasize both: that the work Jesus did was received by him, and that they were his works rather than appearing beyond, beside, or above him. Jesus rejected the demand for God to work something miraculous apart from him in order to authenticate him. For such a demand would have denied him trust and thus was unbelief. Faith turns to God in supplication and has its basis in what he himself does. What reveals him is not what takes place for the benefit of the supplicant but what God does. Jesus was enabled by God to the deeds that he performed out of his mercy by his own will. It was God's gift, first for himself, and through him for the one who requested it. For this reason he said, regarding the signs, that God's spirit worked them through himself and that they were mediated through his prayer and were God's answer to it (Matt. 12:28; John 11:41; Mark 7:34; 5:19).

Together with his sonship, his messianic office was revealed through these deeds. For by granting the requests of the petitioners, even though the request transcended the limits of human capability, he possessed and realized the regal will. As always, Jesus demonstrated at the same time his entire sovereignty and his complete selflessness—his sovereignty since he took recourse to God's omnipotence, his selflessness since he made it subservient to mercy. In this way he showed himself to be the one who fulfilled Scripture. The community saw in him God once again as it saw him in his previous revelation. The same perfection of God's power and grace that had once been revealed to it now had been revealed through him once again.

Thus the signs became an essential link in the proclamation of God's rule. In them the petitioner had experienced God's activity in such a way that it was mere goodness, that it ended every need, that it created life, that it removed all guilt, and that it granted complete forgiveness. This happened through the Christ, not merely supernaturally while he destroyed human history—that would not be God's rule nor God's regal providence for man for the purpose of establishing the community who knows him—but the man Jesus who had been put in the midst of the Jewish community performed these deeds that bore within them complete grace and by which God answered his prayer despite human guilt. The one who experienced God in such a way stood under his rule and saw his regal activity for his people. Thereby the proclamation of his kingdom did not merely become eschatology but occurred in the present.

Since the completion of divine rule also entails the inauguration of a new, more glorious world, Jesus possibly also related miracle to this thought, revealing with joy that the Father had not created nature for death and torture to take abiding residence but in order that his glory that provides life and joy might be revealed in it. Since he honored nature as God's work, he gave it his love, and therefore it could become his aim to show already then that he was given power over nature, power that removed from it what was hard and imperfect. This train of thought, however, is nowhere given explicit formulation (it is perhaps alluded to in Luke 10:19; cf. also John 11:25: "I am the resurrection") and remains at any rate subordinated to the simple main idea that "nothing" would be impossible for the Father, since his ability to give and to help would be more than sufficient for every need. Through the greatness of his doing good occurs the glorification of the Father and the Son.

Jesus' helpful deeds thereby also entered into effective connection with the call to repentance. Jesus saw the greatness of Capernaum's guilt in the fact that it had seen his works without being brought to repentance (Matt. 11:21; likewise, John links the signs with the call to repentance to Capernaum and Jerusalem: see chapters 5, 6, 9, 11). In revealing the divine activity and help to the nation by his signs, he powerfully strengthened the call to repentance, since every clarification of God separated from evil and bound to his will, just as he also showed God's reconciling grace through his signs. Because God revealed himself through him actively to the community, it was shown thereby its obligation to leave what he rejected and to obey what he told it to do.

When conversion did not occur and the divine gift did not have the result of separating its recipient from evil, it had been robbed of its purpose. This idea should not be replaced by another kind of idea, that is, that Jesus had added the miracles to his ethical teaching later as an authentication of his authority. He never thought of a merely formal confirmation of his teaching office.

Together with repentance he also created faith through his works. Since he granted the request for help, he produced by it a personal relationship between himself and its recipient. He did not merely exercise his power nor merely give gifts, desired or undesired, but turned his mercy and love to those who trusted him. On account of this the miracle remained in inner agreement with the aim of the call to repentance. Just as he moved everyone through it personally and made each person's decision, by which he would reject evil and desire good, the condition for his relationship to God, the petitioner's own deliberate turning to Jesus remained the indispensable prerequisite for Jesus' act of help. By transforming his request into a confession of faith, the petitioner recognized Jesus' sending, submitted to his power and goodness, and thereby arrived at inner allegiance to him.

If faith in him was denied, Jesus did not bring about these effects. He refused to overcome unbelief by the demonstration of his power and confirmed it in the same manner as faith. Since unbelief expected nothing from him, it received nothing, just as faith received what it sought from him. Jesus respected the position into which the individual placed himself toward him. He thereby purified the exercise of his power from all violence that robbed others of their liberty. This, too, united righteousness and grace in a uniform will. By rejecting unbelief, he executed his judicial office even in the demonstration of his mercy.

For this reason he always bristled at the demand for miracles. He heard only the request; the demand he utterly scorned, since it is only faith, not unbelief, that receives the sign. The diligence with which both Matthew and John emphasize this point reveals that they saw in this an essential characteristic of Jesus' conduct. Both note that the granting and the refusal of a sign cannot be separated from one another or assigned to different times but that they arose from a uniform will (Matt. 12:38–40; 16:1–4; John 2:3–4, 18–19; 4:48; 6:30.[36]

Jesus judged the demand for a sign to be the expression of a sinful will. Its refusal therefore became a necessity. His decision was not merely arbitrary. He could not expect from God the fulfillment of such a desire. A faith that expected a miracle from God even under those circumstances was an impossibility for him. He could not accept the demand for a miracle because it proceeded from "a perverse and adulterous generation." Its malice and impurity stood in a causal connection with its demand for a miracle. It resulted from the fact that faith was impossible for them, that God's righteousness became

36. Matthew juxtaposes the miracle that causes the Pharisees to call Jesus a servant of Beelzebub with the demand for a sign that Jesus refuses—a carefully weighed contrast. Parallel to this is the refusal of a sign after the miraculous feedings of the multitude, also in John.

merely an occasion for fear and antagonism, and God's grace merely an opportunity for doubt. Therefore they only yielded to power and desired it only because it helped them out of their misery. In the fact that they claimed for themselves the divine gift and power together with their evil will, Jesus saw boundless arrogance and a break with all piety. Thus the sign, were he to perform it, would dishonor God and reward evil and result in confirming the individual in it.

The decision thus made by Jesus separated Israel from him and brought him the cross. That he was aware that his refusal to use the miracle as his defense would lead him into death comes to light in the fact that he connected the refusal of a sign with the reference to his end. The sign that they will receive is represented by the story of Jonah, who sank into death and was saved. It consisted of the fact that he would rebuild the destroyed temple. He does not give manna from heaven but his flesh for the world. If he had acquiesced to their demands, he would have revoked his judgment regarding Pharisaism at a major point and obscured his call to repentance. He could not concede that there was another way to God apart from repentance, namely, the proof of power that overcame unbelief. Only by crushing these demands could he reveal God's rule rather than that of the Jew who wanted to make God's miraculous power subservient to himself. That Jesus rendered the boundary between faith and demand, between the desire for a sign that glorified God and for a sign that dishonored him, inviolable par excellence, John expressed in no uncertain terms in the woes against the Pharisees and then by Jesus' refusal to accede to his mother's request at his very first sign (John 2:3–4). Here where Jesus was confronted with an expectation that was filled with boundless confidence, he closed himself precisely for this reason to any presumption that claimed his power for the wishes of his relatives.

By refusing the sign he did not refuse mercy. For the love he gave to others stood under the rule of God's love. An action that strengthened the individual in evil was no mercy. He also did not move away from Scripture through this. For while it described God's revelation as the proof of his glorious power, it simultaneously said that Israel could not merely by power be made to be a sanctified community. For it described its resistance against God despite the signs it saw. The fathers had eaten the manna in the wilderness and still had died (John 6:58). According to Scripture, the miracle could not be used to replace repentance.

Jesus could take this position only by acting in the selflessness of genuine love. He himself was the one who worked with what he had received from the Father, and he thereby also received for himself the divine testimony that confirmed his sonship to him. Thereby, however, the use of miracle was not permitted him for his own glorification but rather was denied him. Therefore he did not exhibit those he had healed like trophies; sent the leper to the priest and the healed Gadarene to his home; and, to the amazement of his disciples, left when the crowd pressed toward him (Matt. 8:4; Mark 5:19; 1:35). In working miracles he remained in a pure way exclusively and completely the one who gave and served, the one who gained nothing for himself, neither honor nor gifts nor protection. By this the liberty of his renunciation was revealed. For he himself remained poor, without possessions or protection, although he gave others life.

Thus the miracle became possible for him only by his ability to die. The manner by which he did it, only for others, not for himself, incited hatred against him; it did not, however, cast him down. By the power with which his work spoke for him the Jewish community and its leaders were forced to decide for or against him. The call to faith that the miracle entailed also brought with it the incentive for confirmed unbelief. It forced those in whom it did not establish faith to unbelief toward him. Both Matthew and John strongly emphasized the relationship between Jesus' crucifixion and his miracles. On account of his miracles he was suspected to be a servant of the devil, and on account of the raising of Lazarus the Sanhedrin decreed his execution (Matt. 12:22–24; John 11:46–53).

Since he did not defend himself with the miracle, he also did not use it for the execution of judgment but merely in the service of benevolent grace. It was that gracious will of God that he wanted to reveal through his works. He was not motivated by a desire for revenge, even though he bore the greatest consciousness of power within himself (Luke 9:52–56). The curse of the fig tree does not obscure the message of the Gospels in this regard (Matt. 21:19). That curse, of course, turned the law's statute against the one whom Jesus had warned in vain and was spoken on the assumption that God would confirm it just as he did merciful pronouncements. Just as the fig tree denied food to him who was hungry, Israel caused him pain and death since it let him work and ask in vain. Therefore it had to fall; the barren trees must be removed. Since, however, he executed the judicial will by this act merely upon the tree rather than upon people who withstood him, the sign in its pointed, prophetic manner remained parallel to the words of judgment regarding the destruction of the temple, the vinegrowers, and the guests, and did not deny his mercy any more than those words did.

While the will that produced Jesus' actions could not remain mysterious to those who received it, his impact in the realm of nature retains its complete incomprehensibility in our accounts. It is not merely our contemporary image of nature that provides here a rationale for astonishment and offense. For the fixed nature of the natural processes has always determined human consciousness. The profound impression made by those events upon Jesus' contemporaries as well as the impression made ever since was based precisely upon this conflict. John described this clash for us graphically by narrating the investigation caused by the healing of the man born blind (John 9:13–34). It is not only the modern consciousness that considers it impossible for a dead person to rise, and it was always judged that a leper would remain leprous. Even Jesus himself held to this view as long as nothing other than the natural process was operative. The value of these events consisted precisely in the fact that thinking limited to nature had to reject miracles, since it was only able to accept them by allowing itself to be reminded of God. They posed the question of

God in complete clarity. For there was only one who worked effects that produced life: God.

Therefore the miracle story of the Gospels omits any discussion of this miraculous process. God's creative acts are above any attempt to comprehend them. The moment, however, a miracle story is the child of imagination, the tendency emerges to illumine the mystery that causes amazement and to conceive of a way by which the miraculous result could be achieved. One of the oldest examples for this in the realm of interpretation of the Gospel story is the reference in the Gospel of the Hebrews, where Jesus is miraculously transported to a mountain and where he now explains how this happened. The Holy Spirit transported him there on only a single hair, for the event is miraculous, but on one hair he bore him. Now we know how the matter became possible. That the accounts of the disciples do not yield a single parallel derives from Jesus' own attitude, from the determined sincerity by which he bowed before everything that belonged to God. For him the miracle was a creative act of God. There was no room for speculation. The discipline by which he tamed the imagination of his disciples is also significant for the verdict regarding the testimony to miracle.

It is important for the evaluation of the Gospel record that the will revealed by Jesus' miracle cannot be challenged. It would be nonsense to doubt his majesty and purity, be it in a religious respect when one considers Jesus' attitude toward God, be it in an ethical respect when one thinks of the manner in which he thus related to people. One cannot call it ethically reproachable to help a leper the way Jesus did. If only we could do it! A dispute can only arise regarding the physical rather than ethical message of the account, regarding whether such an effect could have been achieved or not and whether or not such an ability is conceivable. Whoever denies the possibility of success, however, also disapproves, of course, the will directed toward it, since the will becomes blameworthy when it strives for the impossible. But the disapproving verdict stems merely from the physiological point of view. It conceives of our connection to nature in relation to an attitude that is reported regarding Jesus and thus produces an absurdity. If one, however, concedes the possibility of the event, the manner in which Jesus did and used the sign possesses an ethical majesty that is beyond reproach.

The will that is revealed in Jesus' works and the one revealed in his words are the same. In both we find an absolute affirmation of God that conceives of him as the giver of all good things and that removes anything human and natural that is assigned power and legitimacy beside God as entirely worthless and powerless. In both we find love to be the ground from which the entire attitude arises, love that is selfless and strong and that does not spare one's own life but makes one's entire ability fruitful for others. In both one finds the regulation of love that serves others by obedience toward God, so that it completely honors ethical norms. In both one finds the highest exaltation to the greatest activity connected with the entire renunciation of all selfish gain and honor. In both work and word there is the will to the cross. This would never have come to pass if Jesus' words and the miracle story had come from different sources, the former from the first, the latter from a later generation, nor if the former had come from Jesus while the latter had its origin merely from his disciples. Such an origin in different sources would always result in a notable rupture between the two major components of the gospel.

The more we reinterpret the miracle record or seek to distance it from the course of history, the farther we distance ourselves from the real events. We must grant Jesus his own concept of miracle from a historical point of view whether we like it or not, with the simple decisiveness that the disciples grant to him. He expected God to help him beyond all impossibilities in the creative omnipotence of his grace and was convinced that his concept of miracle was confirmed by what happened through him.

11. The One Who Prayed

Prayer undergirded and sustained Jesus' ministry. Therefore it is not only his ministry but also the prayer that upheld it that demands careful attention by the historian. Jesus did not merely participate in the prayer of the community but cultivated it as a major part of his own life, since the disciples spoke of his continual prayer through the night (Luke 6:12; Matt. 14:23; Mark 1:35; 6:46; Luke 5:16; 9:18; 11:1). We know this not only by his preserved prayers but also by the instruction he gave to his disciples for their own prayer, since, by assuring the correctness and answerability of their prayer, he also provided information regarding his own.

According to Jewish custom, he gave thanks at every meal and for all other divine gifts (Matt. 14:19: 15:36; Mark 6:41; 8:6–7; John 6:11). Likewise, the divine activity that apportioned him personally his success and accomplishments became reason for thanksgiving, even when it placed him in concealment, made his work futile, or prepared the cross for him (Matt. 11:25). Therefore he also desired to develop a spirit of thanksgiving in those he helped. If it failed to arise, he called this guilt. He desired God's praise as the fruit of his entire work, praise that did not merely appear to him as an ornament added externally to the divine activity and human experience. Rather, God seeks praise, and when an individual praises and thanks him, a necessary act occurs, full of truth and power. He therefore showed his disciples that it should be their highest aim for God to be praised on account of their works (Luke 17:18; Matt. 21:16; 5:16), and he considered it his own aim to produce the kinds of worshipers God desired (John 4:23).

Everything that would eventually be a ground for thanksgiving he first of all made the object of his prayer. He gave the request and the thanksgiving in his prayer the same completeness and content. In the same way that he gave thanks for the bread, he also asked for it. He also asked for equipping necessary to his calling, as well as for the signs, since they were God's gift, and since his confidence in miracles was based upon the fact that the Father always listened to him. He also asked for the gathering of disciples, since one should ask God for workers for the harvest, just as he thanked the Father for those whom the Father gave him (John 11:41–42; Luke 6:12; Matt. 9:38; John

17:9). By directing his call to repentance to the community, he did what the gardener does who pleads for the barren tree. The forgiveness by which he blotted out Peter's denial and preserved him in the dominical fellowship was preceded by his intercession, by which he secured for Peter from the Father his preservation in faith (Luke 13:6–9; 22:31–32). Through intercession, his word and work for the disciples received their highest fulfillment.

Analogous to the way he viewed his messianic office, he expected from his praying that it would not end with his death. He would confirm his closeness with his disciples before the Father by interceding for them and would secure for them the Spirit by his intercession (Matt. 10:32; John 14:16). By his petitions, he did not, however, merely pray for others but also gained his own preservation in communion with God. In his thinking here there was no room for a separation between person and office. His final prayer in John was foremost of all a request for glory for himself since his own glorification was one with the completion of his commission. Particularly when "his soul was disturbed" and when he had to control disparate moods within himself, he attained peace within himself by the petition that desired the glorification of God's name and the completion of God's will (John 17:5; 12:27; Matt. 26:39).

Jesus knew no tension between thanksgiving and petition, not seeing in one a lower form of prayer than in the other. The reason for this was Jesus' refusal to set God's work in contrast to man's work and to see one limited by the other. Therefore he never stood before God merely as the one who received or as the one who desired and acted himself. He rather gained his own work from God's. This was played out in the way in which he assigned to thanksgiving the end of the divine work, and to the petition the beginning of his. In his statements regarding prayer, however, the exhortations to prayer are dominant owing to the greater challenge the petition presented to his disciples' faith (Matt. 7:7; Luke 11:5–8; 18:1–8; Matt. 21:22; John 14:13–14; 15:7).

He therefore gave unconditional promise to petition, which reveals that he linked with prayer the certainty of an answer. "You always hear me." He did not practice it as an experiment but rather presented to God in prayer the complete affirmation of his own love and gift. Therefore the assurance, "Father, I am willing," was not merely a wish or a longing but a settled will. It embodied the Son's and the Christ's consciousness of power. Therefore he promised the disciples the answer to their prayers when they were based upon his own name (John 17:24; 14:13; 15:16; 16:23), since, when he identified with them before the Father, he thereby effected their inclusion in God's grace, just as their rejection would result from the withdrawal of his communion with them.

He did not point to the success of his intercession by giving a particular assurance; it possessed intrinsic certitude. Therefore it was the power that he set against Satan's accusations. Even the greeting by which, according to custom, one wished peace to those whose house one entered, he invested with the certainty that it was not merely a wish but that it would bring them peace, for the request would be fulfilled (Matt. 10:32–33; Luke 22:31–32; 10:5–6). Therefore he placed the blessing on the same level as prayer. Through blessing he offered divine grace to others, obviously considering it fruitful and effective. Since he blessed the children, God's rule would include them as well (Matt. 19:13).

Since Jesus' prayer embodied the certitude of God and of the power given to him, it simultaneously strove for two aims: it praised God alone and sought in God alone its success, while at the same time investing the desire of the one who prayed with absolute value, since his prayer would ultimately be fulfilled by God. Jesus' prayer had as its key characteristic that it united both aims with entire clarity rather than bringing them into a necessary conflict. This shows that it was motivated by love; for the struggle between self-assertion and the affirmation of God comes to an end only through love.

By centering his prayer on God he obliterated any notion that prayer was necessary because of weakness or harshness on the part of God. Prayer originated in faith; without faith, it became sin and therefore lost all potential of being answered. Jesus called pagan the thought that prayer helped a need within God, whether one thought of a need of his intellect, as if he learned of a need only through a person's prayer, or whether one thought of a need in his will, as if it was only prayer that encouraged and moved him to kindness (Matt. 21:22; 6:8; 7:11).

His attitude toward those who called upon him followed the same rule. He did not allow himself to be asked merely because the Father was unavailable. Rather, the needy person may and should ask Jesus for help, since God may and should be called upon for help, and since God had sent him to offer his kindness. When he revealed his own name to his disciples as the ground for their prayer, he did not thereby give them the idea that God was powerless or unwilling apart from his name. For his name's power of grounding their prayer and of making it answerable stemmed from the fact that it was the Father who had sent Jesus and who had led them into union with him. The idea that prayer to Jesus would be a replacement of prayer to God has nothing to do with Jesus. Through the Lord's Prayer he rather made the call to the Father the prayer of his community.

But Jesus' assurance of God did not result in the outlook that asking and thanksgiving were unimportant. To the contrary, he inferred that they were necessary and would be confirmed and fulfilled by God's direction. He did not stop praying because the Father already knew what he needed. Rather, that was the very reason why he prayed. He considered the conclusion to be inhuman that deduced from God's perfection the uselessness of prayer. This would have conceived of God as devoid of love. This, in turn, Jesus considered to be contrary to nature. After all, every child petitioned his father! In substantiating the need for prayer, he deliberately went beyond human kindness to that kind of asking that did not give up when confronted with a reluctant giver or an unjust judge, an asking that ultimately overcame even them. By this he wanted to convey to the disciple how deeply he would dishonor God by prayerlessness (Matt. 7:11; Luke 11:5–8; 18:1–8). This did not, however, lead him to conceive of a theory regarding the way in which God would incorporate human will into his own and how he would realize it in his providence. The idea that God was good was completely sufficient for him to substantiate the power of prayer.

Just as the necessity of prayer does not arise from a lack in God, Jesus also did not conceive of its success in terms of obliging God to act. Jesus' God is free to give even when not asked and free to ignore the requests of those he rejects (Matt. 5:45; 7:21). For the unconditional nature of answered prayer does not transfer power in a matter into the hand of the one who prays. Jesus exercised the same liberty regarding those who asked him. When he considered the request appropriate and therefore gave since he was asked, this did not prevent him from granting forgiveness of sins together with the healing of the body without having been asked. This also did not mean that the request became bondage for him so that he lost the authority to reject it: "You do not know what you are asking for" (Matt. 9:2; John 5:6; Matt. 20:22). This, however, did not result in a reversal or limitation of the unconditional promise he had given to prayer; for "one is good," God, in everything he does (the certitude of prayer is that of faith; see p. 200).

The content of his prayer received thereby a boundless breadth, for it comprised the inexhaustible wealth of divine grace. Therefore the curse had to be eliminated from the disciples' prayer. The oneness of divine righteousness with God's grace meant that the disciples could only bring their prayer to God for rather than against others. Likewise, Jesus did not stand before God as the accuser of his opponents in order to inform him of their guilt or to call down his judgment upon them. For his commission had been given to him by divine grace. Even when he instructed the oppressed community to seek shelter with God as the just judge by praying, he did not view its prayer apart from the certitude that the execution of divine justice would at the same time be the revelation of complete grace (Mark 11:25; John 5:45; Luke 18:1–7; Matt. 21:22). If, however, prayer was united with it, nothing was impossible for it, not even the moving of a mountain.

At the same time, however, Jesus drew firm and narrow boundaries for prayer. Since he gave it the certainty of an answer and since he based it upon faith, speculations and far-reaching fantasies had no room in it. It can never become God's counsel to present to him freely invented possibilities and new aims instead of what had been assigned by God to the person who prays. The Lord's Prayer reveals how Jesus enabled praying to be certain. None of his phrases—that God's rule should come, that God cared for human beings even more than for the birds and the lilies and that he would give them their bread, that he would forgive all debts and would set them free from all evil—expressed the primary wish of the person who prayed. Every one of these phrases is rooted foremost with all clarity in Jesus' own promise, and since each represents an aspect of God's promise to the disciples, it also becomes the content of his petition and confirms it.

The disciples became obedient to this rule of Jesus by linking the promise given for prayer with their calling. Matthew placed them in the Sermon on the Mount in the midst of those sayings that demand boundless love for others and in the discourse regarding the community beside its task to overcome evil by loosing and binding. John, too, links it with the work assigned to the disciples (Matt. 7:7; 18:19; John 14:13 along with v. 12). Their service gave their prayer its content and at the same time power before God. Jesus' prayer, too, is remarkable for its modest, concrete manner. He prayed at the cross, not for the salvation of mankind, but for the forgiveness of those who crucified him. In Gethsemane, he prayed, not for the new covenant or the reconciliation of the world, but for the will to be able to accept death from God's hand.

His prayer shows no trace of an attempt to advise God what to do by enumerating ways, for example, how he could snatch him up to heaven or enable him to escape. It looks merely to the decision which that hour demanded from Jesus, whether he now wanted to enter suffering or not, and sought for his decision the grounding in God's regal will. He made his prayer pure and chaste by not even concerning himself with the possibilities that would have taken on significance only when the liberating word came from above, opening up another way than the one he saw before him.

The prayer that expresses Jesus' final thoughts in John, too, remains exclusively limited to the concerns necessitated by his current situation. Since he faced the cross, he needed to be lifted up to God who would glorify him. Regarding those whom God had given him he needed their preservation in communion with him. To this was added merely the anticipation of those who would believe in his name through them. The prayer did not develop a program or concern itself with the future church or with eschatological events. The situation in which he stood with his own at that time, at the threshold of death, provided the material for his prayer (Matt. 26:39; Luke 23:34; John 17:5, 11, 15, 17, 20).

The assurance of God upon which he based his prayer liberated it from any artificiality, be it rhetorical or ascetic. The modesty with which Jesus prayed also entailed his following of the existing custom for prayer. The praise of God for the illumination of the ignorant begins, as original and lively as it is, with the phrase taken over from tradition, "I praise you, Lord," and concludes with the agreement with God's will in a form that likewise corresponds to current usage.

The Lord's Prayer, too, drew from already existing forms of prayer in its address of God. This coincided with the fact that Jesus framed his prayer according to the pattern of the Psalms (Matt. 11:25; 27:46; Luke 23:46). He also freed prayer from fixed methods by loosening its connection with fasting. While he did not dispute the existing custom for prayer even at that point (so that the disciples gladly connected persistent prayer with fasting later on), he did not impose any set pattern of fasting either on himself or on his disciples (Matt. 9:14–15; 11:19).

As unadorned as Jesus' prayer was, it was nevertheless the high point of his experience. He did not perform it hurriedly or perfunctorily, because it epitomized his whole character and spiritual possession. The Lord's Prayer provides no grounds for objections to the way in which John described Jesus' praying in this regard. Since the other texts also speak of nights Jesus spent praying, they likewise testify to the fact that he incorporated into his conversation with God all the knowledge he bore within himself. Since Jesus' prayer was based upon the assurance of God, it was based upon whatever clarified for him God's work and helped him realize God's will. The more clearly the praying person remembers this will, the more certain his praying will become, and the more certainly his will will turn into prayer.

Since Jesus directed prayer to God, he turned it away from the public eye. The latter merely tempted the person who prayed to turn his view and will away from God to other people, making the motive for his prayer the honor he would be given. This, in turn, would render that person's prayers worthless before God. Therefore prayer remained for Jesus the final and richest product he sought to promote with his work. By enabling the disciples to pray through his name, he had reached his goal and had created the messianic community, just as he gave his work its fulfillment by presenting himself to God while praying for his own (Matt. 18:19–20; 21:22; John 16:23–24). Thus prayer became not merely the internal possession of the individual but also the characteristic of the community. It became not merely the hidden root of life but at the same time the manifest product by which God's name receives honor.

Jesus separated the concept of merit entirely from prayer. Since it was rooted in the certitude of faith and the desire of love, it did not present itself as some individual virtuoso performance but was itself God's gift that he worked within the person. Pure prayer that longed for God and was characterized by truth was worked by God's Spirit (John 4:23–24). Jesus was only able to pray this way by feeling no tension between his regard for God and regard for his own life. This reveals the personal nature of his relationship to God and shows that in that relationship he possessed the obedience that is grounded in love. His love for God gave him his selfless connection to God. At the same time it gave him the energy of a will that was conscious of its righteousness and power and able to act in unity with God.

12. The Establishment of Faith

In his dealings with those who sought from him the omnipotent help of God, Jesus made faith the decisive process by which the human being received his share in God's grace. The Jewish community and its teachers likewise did not lack the concept of "faith," since Scripture provided it and since no concept of Scripture remained irrelevant for the community of that day. A passage such as Genesis 15:6 was read with care. Therefore the teachers' usage provides also at this point parallels to Jesus' words.[37] Faith, however, was not elevated as the foundational process above the other religious functions and was not given decisive significance in and of itself. When the scriptural passages were interpreted that dealt with faith or unbelief, faith was explicitly

---

37. A collection of such parallels is found in *Glaube im Neuen Testament*, 3d ed., 588–600, 609.

mentioned. For one's own piety, however, it remained an aspect of love or repentance that was given no further consideration.

The "completely righteous person" exercised his service for God by the love of God that made him obedient to his commandments, without it being said that he believed in God. The duty of those who had sinned consisted of repentance, which does not mean expressly that the attitude by which they received freedom from guilt was faith. The sincerity with which the Jewish community dispensed of all its religious obligations it also displayed in its exercise of faith. It understood faith as confidence in the divine providence, since it honored God as the benevolent shaper of its destiny; as confidence in Scripture whose word it accepted as the divine word; as confidence in the divine justice that would reward the service rendered to God. The Gospels present the strength of Jewish faith in moving terms, and in this they are abundantly confirmed by the Pharisaic literature. The widow who offered her last pieces of copper to God expressed great confidence in him (Mark 12:42–43).

Nevertheless, Jesus called the community unbelieving (Matt. 17:17), not because it simply did not believe in God in specific cases—this yielded it reproach for its "little faith"—but since it resolutely rejected Jesus' call to faith and quenched the impetus to faith it was given. In its faith, likewise, it paid attention only to what faith could give it. It therefore continually leaned on what it thought, desired, and did, finding reason for confidence in itself, in its own teaching and work, and perhaps also in the greatness and meritoriousness of its faith (Luke 17:5). But this was to deny faith to God. Since it knew itself to be separated from God in its inner condition of life, it did not dare to claim his grace for its guilt; the doubt that resulted demonstrated remarkable resilience and power (it revealed this in its rejection of Jesus' forgiveness; see pp. 156, 164). When confidence in men takes root, a pride arises that wants to dispose of God's gift and help, because it supports itself by its own greatness.

Jesus liberated those who accepted his word from the doubt that resisted God. He gave them the confidence in the divine calling that granted the guilty forgiveness and God's eternal gifts. He destroyed the proud and arrogant kind of faith in them by awakening at the same time the fear of God. Even this fear could not remain what it had been in the community but needed purification, since it had been twisted around to focus on man rather than God like all of their piety, and since it was dominated only by the fear of the evil that might befall a person. As long as one's internal separation from God had not been removed, fear was not the fear of God but a selfish bondage by which the individual feared for the loss of his happiness or life. Jesus purified this fear of God by relating it to God and by giving it its basis in God's judgment (Matt. 10:28; 18:35; 20:16; 22:11–14; 24:45–25:30). In this way he also ended the conflict between fear and faith. When it was truly God whose holy and righteous will man feared, this fear drove him away from himself and turned his eye to the divine work, leading him to the petition by which he yielded himself believingly to God.

Jesus purified and strengthened faith, not by allowing it to disappear behind the religious works that proceeded from it but by investing it with the promise that made it the staple that provides for us communion with God. He showed the disciples that faith that was the attitude that united them with God (Mark 1:15). Faith brought about this result because Jesus did not merely proclaim divine help but also granted it, and this provision was experienced not only by those who called upon him in their need but especially by the disciples whom he summoned to help others, whereby God's grace and help also became their own experience. Jesus, however, gave this help only to faith, and without faith he denied it.

Faith was the only thing Jesus demanded from the one who desired divine help from him (Mark 5:36). He expressed its all-sufficiency for the reception of any help in the strongest terms conceivable. As long as it was found, however tiny, nothing would be impossible for the disciple; then he would be free and ruler of the world. Jesus deliberately invented impossible-sounding promises such as "to move mountains" or "to cast the fig tree into the sea" in order to remove any form of limitation from God's gift (Matt. 17:20; 21:21; Luke 17:5–6; Paul, too, knew the expression: 1 Cor. 13:2; parallel with it Matt. 8:2, 10, 26; 9:2, 22, 29). The power of God that removed all obstacles was active on behalf of the disciple if he had faith.

Jesus related these promises to the specific decisions regarding which the disciples turned to divine goodness. Therefore he told them when they were incapable of healing in his absence that they had no faith, not even the smallest amount. By this he did not dispute their conviction of his regal status and their decision to follow him. He rather confronted them with the fact that this conviction of theirs did not prevent them from considering God's help to be unavailable in their concrete situation and from considering Jesus' commission to be impossible to execute. They did not believe, since they failed to avail themselves of God's help regarding the need that called for their help at that moment. Jesus did not call faith an abstract conception of God's grace or an undetermined preparedness to rely on him. He rather considered it to be the characteristic of faith that the assurance of God would determine the conduct of the disciples, and this in such a way that they would see in him the one who was at work for them by his complete grace.

Jesus saw the opposite of faith not merely in the refusal of faith, that is, in unbelief, but already in the internal struggle in which contrasting deliberations and desires clashed with one another (Matt. 21:21). Thereby he made certainty the characteristic of faith. Faith is not a matter of isolated special demonstrations of trust; rather, it determines the entire behavior of a person, because he now knows who Jesus is to him and that he grants him God's gift precisely through faith. That faith produced an abiding conviction and a confirmed will and was assured by the fact that absolute messianic categories were applied to Jesus' work. The one who called him the Christ did not merely expect from him an isolated gift but described him as the one who took away sin and death, who created the eschatological community, and who granted the complete gift. This certainty, however, ordered the entire behavior of the individual and placed him in a new relationship with God that encompassed everything he received and did.

This is the all-important thought in John's account about Jesus, since he presents a particularly telling testimony for the clarity and strength with which Jesus created faith in his disciples. For in John's Gospel, the only goal of Jesus' entire work is that faith which is set on him. John claims that the establishment of faith was the aim toward which Jesus' entire word and work were directed. He thus referred faith entirely and exclusively to Jesus and placed no other action beside or above faith. Faith is honored as the highest of all functions that make up our life, and Jesus is described as the one object among all objects of faith in whom faith placed results in contact with God and attainment of life.

In Jesus' dealings with petitioners, faith received all kinds of content according to the various circumstances that provided them with the desire for divine help. For John, however, faith is always the following of Jesus in acknowledgment of his divine sonship by which God's entire grace is received. In this way John also expresses powerfully that Jesus transformed faith into a perfected confidence, so that even if it was as small as a mustard seed it could be certain of the help God grants. For he describes faith as the possession of eternal life. By it one obtains salvation; sin and death have passed away, and complete communion with God is obtained. Faith does not, however, receive its assurance by what the individual perceives in himself, as if confidence lay in the sense of sinlessness and immortality received. Assurance comes solely by what the Christ is, since the Christ is the only means to fulfill God's commission. Since his gift is eternal life, the believer has it. He will not have it or obtain it only under certain conditions at a later point, since Jesus, in John as in Matthew, made faith the complete, unambiguous appropriation of divine grace.

By looking at the concrete expressions of faith that desired helping kindness from him and by looking away entirely from his own greatness and strength, while still giving the entire promise even to the smallest amount of faith, Jesus linked the call to faith with both the call to repentance and the commandment to love. By repentance Jesus did not think of general sinfulness but of the concrete damage that corrupted his listeners, setting against that damage the definite act of obedience, even if it only accomplished little by itself, if only it sincerely subjected itself to the divine commandment. By love he did not merely think of great achievement of actions borne out in concrete human conditions; it was to such love that he granted unlimited promise. Like repentance and love, Jesus also situated God's grace in the real course of human history by the promise given to faith. He conferred that grace upon the first, most simple expression of faith as long as what he saw emerging was genuine faith that trusted in God. Jesus always acted on the basis of God's complete kindness and therefore invested man's smallest gesture of devotion to God with God's greatest boon, his complete grace. He thereby also consciously and completely repudiated the concept of merit in his evaluation of faith and liberated the disciple from himself and his own inability.

If it had been Jesus' judgment that the present was completely devoid of divine assurances, so that he sought God's rule solely in the future, or if he had separated God's will from his word, not already gaining closeness with God from the divine word, or if he had placed his service to God into something other than love, tying the reception of salvation to singular material performances—in all these instances, Jesus' statements regarding faith would not have been possible. They are closely tied to the basic framework of his call to repentance and to the announcement of God's rule. Faith receives all things because God acts in his regal grace upon the individual, and faith alone overcomes a person's separation from God, since God calls the person to himself by his word and unites him internally with himself in his personal condition of life.

The assurance that Jesus made a characteristic of faith received its manner and limitation from the way in which it related to God's work. It thus did not clarify calculable effects of a natural process but God's will and work. For that reason it entailed submission to God and to Christ, since Jesus did not permit any self-exaltation that would have elevated the petitioner above himself and God. Precisely as one who believed, the petitioner subjected himself to the will of the one upon whom he called and thus acknowledged his right to rule. Nevertheless, faith is assurance since it possesses in God complete grace and help. This is why the disciple was not to doubt even in specific instances that God stood at his side with power and grace that could move mountains, poised to give aid (this is also confirmed by Jesus' statements regarding prayer; see p. 194).

By promising God's perfect gift to faith, Jesus placed everyone in the same position before God and opened the community to everyone. Thereby all limitations were removed from it. The Gentile, however, reached faith with more difficulty than the Jew, the confirmed reprobate than the righteous, and the one who was not called into discipleship than the one who had been placed into the fellowship of Jesus. Everything that caused separation from Jesus and removed the petitioner from him also rendered faith more difficult for him. Therefore Jesus called it "great faith" when the Gentile despite obstacles called upon him with assurance. He evaluated the one who was crucified beside him and pleaded for his grace similarly. When, on the other hand, a disciple who had been called stood there without trust and behaved, for example, in a storm in such a way as he would earlier have conducted himself apart from communion with Jesus, or when he despaired due to lack of bread, Jesus rejected this as unbelief, since his call enabled, and thus also obliged, the disciple to faith (Matt. 8:10; 15:28; Luke 23:42; Matt. 8:26; 16:8). These differences stemming from the different circumstances of individuals did not by themselves do away with the equal position of all. For to the extent that faith was present Jesus answered with limitless giving. He saw his calling in the undermining of no one's willingness to trust. If anyone sought God's grace, he received it. To reach for the gift was to acquire it. He established the principle, "Let it be to you according to your faith," without restriction.

Among the greatest marvels of Jesus' life is that his promise for faith was as unconditional as his demand for repentance. His two rules appear to grind against one another in irreconcilable tension. By the word of repentance he sanctified God's Law as inviolable and demanded that the individual should do away with his evil will. If, on the other hand, he found faith, he made no moral demands, did not examine the petitioner, and did not ask what kind of guilt or repentance he could show in his life, or whether his conversion was complete or not. In this case he did not admit the question of whether the believer was worthy in light of the work accomplished by him or not. The individual rather had God's grace as soon as he sought it by faith in Jesus. That Jesus was at the same time the one who worked repentance and faith shows how truly and magnificently God's forgiveness was present to him and how completely he lived in the conviction that God was good. God's kindness granted faith a hearing, and this same kindness required that that person separate himself from his evil. Since this kindness forgave, it was possible for Jesus to give the promise to faith without restriction. He therefore made his opposition to Pharisaism complete since, by focusing on faith, he pulled man completely away from focusing on his own work, since he now possessed the ground of his relationship with God no longer within himself but in God.

Jesus also liberated faith from all intellectual claims and did not examine the orthodoxy of those who approached him for help. This is demonstrated by the fact that he conceded great faith to Gentiles, however inadequate their ideas about God and Christ. Their conduct was faith, since they comprehended God's help in him with certainty. The independence Jesus granted to faith in relation to the other functions did not render those worthless or do away with their effective share in the development and perseverance of faith. Faith remained in an effective connection with the act of knowing, since insight into Jesus' office and his relationship to God gave the individual the ground for faith.

Whoever saw in him God's rule was called to faith, and the clearer and stronger this realization developed, the stronger was the incentive given to faith and the greater the person's enablement to it. The Jew, on the other hand, was kept from faith by his sinister thoughts and defective Christology. In order to trust Jesus he first had to shatter ideas that had been passed on to him and controlled him, ideas regarding the Christ and God's rule. He could come to faith only by overcoming the fantastic element in his theology. Thus the relationship between faith and thought was closely intertwined. Clear thought and strong faith or confused thought and the thwarting of faith accompanied one another.

The relationship between faith on the one hand and conversion and obedience on the other was equally firm, since Jesus granted unconditional validity to the demand for repentance. If this requirement was rejected, faith was impossible, since the one who disputed his demand could not trust him. He could trust only by agreeing with Jesus when he rejected his own conduct and by seeing in his offer of repentance the extension of divine grace. By this he also had received the highest proof for Jesus' credibility. The one for whom Jesus became the reconciler with God had trusted him. More-over, repentance was grounded in faith, since the believer, as certainly as he saw in him God's grace and desired it, knew that Jesus was justified in de-manding obedience.

The relationships between faith and repentance and between faith and knowledge operate in the same way in John as they do in Matthew. Even though John did not use the term "repentance," there is no doubt that in John, too, faith determines an individual's ethical conduct and following Jesus also entails the forsaking of evil, even though John does not use the term "repent." If that were taken to show that Jesus actually never called to repen-tance, so that faith should perhaps replace Jesus' moral demands, this would be a gross distortion of his word. It remains, however, entirely clear in John that Jesus stood in complete opposition to all evil and that he redeemed his own from it.

The irreconcilable opposites of love and hate, truth and lie, light and dark-ness, and life and death, shape John's entire presentation, and it does not re-main in doubt where Jesus stood in this faith and where he placed those who believed in him. A mixture of truth and lie, of love and hate, of Christ and the world, of God and the devil is impossible for John. For the one who believes in Jesus the choice regarding this contrast does not remain open, as if one could follow Jesus while still oscillating between love and hate, lie and truth, or God and the devil. The place of the believer in Jesus is firm: it is with Christ, that is, in the truth, in love, in the Spirit, in God.

The means by which the ethical result is reached and resistance against evil is achieved is in John precisely one's position of faith. When he presented Jesus' preaching of repentance simply by revealing why faith became impos-sible for Israel, this was not because his ethical will was weaker, his rejection of sin set aside, or the sanctity of the divine will obscured in his view of God. It was due rather to the fact that, for John, Jesus linked separation from evil and grounding in love directly with the existence of faith. For John, the eth-ical and the religious properties of the believer converge entirely, and the eth-ical and the religious aims are reached by the same process—through faith in Jesus. This conviction arose directly from Jesus' ministry, from the conver-gence of his preaching of the kingdom with his call to repentance. John learned from Jesus that there was no closeness to God that did not end one's ethical misery, and that did so effectively.

John also preserves entirely the distinction between faith on the one hand and knowledge and theory on the other. He does not provide us with doctrine in the place of faith, nor with a faith that is believed (this shift occurred quickly in the church owing to pressure from Greek thought). His faith, too, is the following of the Christ as he reveals himself in word and work, not the repetition of a formula. That John presented with vigor equal to Matthew's Jesus' resolute resistance toward religious intellectualism was the direct result of faith, because faith is not a single act of thought or a flawless set of teachings about God or Christ but moves the individual in his inner condition of life and turns him to Christ. It does so not merely by a transformation of his thoughts but also by a movement of his will that controls the person entirely and uniformly since he trusts in the veracity and goodness of Jesus.

Jesus demanded that people trust him as they trusted God and did not allow any conditional request or unmet expectations, which he called unbelief (Mark 9:22–24). This did not, however, lead to a division in one's faith, as if now a faith directed toward Jesus was placed beside that presented to God. Faith rather directs itself, by an undivided act, toward God in Jesus. Precisely because Jesus wanted to prevent faith from being separated from God and from being directed to anything beside God, he insisted that the faith exercised in him be completely one with the trust given to God. He did not permit any separation between himself and the Father but presented himself to the petitioner as the one who acted upon him in God's name and who granted the divine gifts to him. God should be sought and found in him. That is why those sinned who stood before him in uncertainty rather than faith.[38] By turning faith in its entirety toward himself, he revealed his sonship and actively exercised his messianic claim. The request directed toward him received thereby all the characteristics of a prayer whose truth and accuracy were based on the fact that the one who made the request saw the power and grace of God as present and effective in the Christ.

John portrayed the religious nature of faith, its focus on God, as powerfully as Matthew. For the believer placed his trust in Jesus in the understanding that Jesus came from above, that he spoke the Father's word and accomplished his work, and that trust in him was placed in the one who sent him. Therefore John also considered unbelief in Jesus to be reprehensible, since it rejected God and amounted to godlessness.

Since Jesus awakened and responded to faith, he consistently trampled under foot the disciples' efforts to admire or to celebrate him. He shaped his teaching, miracles, and the testimony to his regal status in such a way that they could not venerate his greatness. He wanted more than admiration, even faith, since he wanted what the individual owed to God, and God did not yet receive what was due him as long as he was merely admired. Thus he separated his own rule from all domineering, selfish exercise of power. By awakening faith in the disciple, he subjected him to himself, not by coercion but by free will, not for the sake of his humiliation, but for the sake of his reception of the divine gift, not for the purpose of making him blind but in order to instill in him the assurance of God, not to make him faint but to empower him. He exercised his rule by grounding it in faith, exercising it in the service of divine grace.

Jesus' words regarding faith would have remained ineffective had the disciples not continually realized that he himself exemplified a complete trust in God. In every situation he grasped the helping power of God without limits

---

38. Since faith was placed only in the reception and preservation of an idea, it has been said that, for Jesus, faith consisted of faith in God; for the apostles, however, it was related to Christ. From Jesus' viewpoint, it is absurd to say that when faith expected particular help from him it was directed, not toward him, but toward God, and that when faith expected the messianic work from him it was directed toward him rather than God.

and assumed his availability to help. Assistance is thus available even when it is not yet experienced, and it would be sin to doubt it. Therefore he excluded in his dealings with God any attempt to manipulate him, such as to move him to kindness or to guide his activity. By doing so, he elevated himself above all judgments that judged solely according to what was visible. By the standards of human thought, Jesus' situation contradicted the grace and promise of God: if only the visible was considered, he was poor, powerless, a fool, and a lost man. His confidence was directed solely toward God, not toward his own experience or what he already possessed or experienced. This struggle took on incomparable gravity because his path led to the cross. He clung to the notion that he had God on his side, even though everyone was against him. He was at peace with God even in the midst of the most severe suffering. He knew his life to be in God's sure hands even though he himself would die. He saw himself called to be a giver of grace even though he experienced judgment and knew himself to be the mighty reconciler of the community before God even though God took everything away from him.

Nevertheless, the disciples, while claiming that Jesus enabled and required them to believe, did not speak of Jesus' own faith. John also did not speak in those terms, even though he had rich phrases for Jesus' piety and described faith as that process by which Jesus united the disciples with himself. But he applied the concept of faith only to Jesus' attitude toward others: "He did not entrust himself to them." Regarding Jesus' attitude toward God he said that Jesus heard, loved, knew, and saw him, not that he trusted in him (John 2:24; 8:26, 40; 15:15; 10:18; 15:10; 14:31; 10:15; 17:25; 3:11; 6:46; 8:38). Since he derived the rule for the disciples' attitude from Jesus' own attitude toward the Father, one might expect the phrase, "Believe in me as I believe in the Father." This phrase, however, is not found in John.

Once again, the difference between Jesus' dealings with God and our piety becomes apparent with full force in the fact that Jesus did not designate faith as the decisive process that characterized his own relationship with God. As believers, we achieve allegiance to God despite obstacles by overcoming barriers. The believer turns his thought and will away from himself and toward divine goodness in the understanding that there is a separation between God and himself that can be overcome by trusting in him. Difficulties arise for us both in the sphere of thought and in the realm of volition: in the former since trust is necessary in the one who is invisible and since we do not know his will and work; in the latter since trust needs to be exercised in the one before whom we are subject to condemnation, guilty, and liable to punishment.

Since Jesus did not speak of his own internal struggle with God, he also did not speak of his own faith. Those two facts belong together, that is, that the confession of sins and the expression of faith likewise are both lacking in Jesus. He also conceived of God's hiddenness differently in the case of the disciples than in his own case. Where they had faith, he had the "knowledge of the Father," which he claimed to possess uniquely. His statements regarding himself direct our own view therefore immediately toward what his unity with the Father granted him as his calling and work.

Thus the term "faith," as used by the community and by Jesus himself, was to be directed to those attestations of God that encountered the individual from the outside. On this account Jesus used the term for the attitude of those who approached him with their requests in order to receive God's help from him. Jesus himself, however, did not enter into relationship with God by receiving any external testimony of divine grace. He rather possessed the assurance of God through his internal condition of life. He expressed its immediacy through the phrase that he knew or saw God and presented himself to the community and to the disciples as "the witness." From this arose their rather than his duty to believe in God.

13. Jesus the Israelite

Jesus gave his call to repentance and his help grounded in God's almighty grace to Israel, the community created by God. In this community he honored the work of his Father. He knew himself connected with those who had once instructed God's people in God's service and had ruled them, not merely by their Scriptures but through a living fellowship. He saw the greatness of his regal status in the fact that he was elevated above them as their Lord. The king of Israel, David, honors him as his Lord; Isaiah saw his glory; Abraham rejoiced to see his day. Moses accused Israel before God on account of its unbelief in Jesus, as he once accused it in the wilderness of breaking faith with God. Elijah and Moses assisted him, and at the revelation of the divine glory, all chosen ones will be united with the fathers at God's table (Matt. 22:43; John 12:41; 8:56; 5:45; Matt. 17:3; 8:11; Luke 16:22).

However, he also gave his entire strength to the sinful generation that now constituted the community, although he was not prevented from dealing with Greeks by any external barrier. Every time he looked eastward across the lake, he saw the towers and walls of Greek cities, and when the confrontation with the Jews escalated, he often set foot on pagan soil. Even then, however, he confirmed with flawless insistence that Israel's separation from the Gentiles was holy, and he related his sending exclusively to Israel. When a Greek, such as the centurion living in Capernaum, approached him with faith, he answered him, but even then the process received depth by the fact that he simultaneously preserved his close connection with Israel. The centurion was right not to bring him into his house but merely to desire his word. Jesus told the Canaanite woman that he would not break faith with Israel, calling her attitude "faith" only when she tied her request to the complete acknowledgment of the separation that divided him from Gentiles; then, of course, he granted her request. Even to the Samaritans who, after all, stood in closer proximity to the Jews than to the Gentiles and who believed in him, he merely granted two days, since he devoted his entire work to Israel and did not want to cause any offense (Matt. 8:8–10; 15:21–28; John 4:39–40). He was united with Israel in life and in death, and the completeness of divine grace that authorized him to grant the requests even of Gentiles and of Samaritans had its initial revelation in the fact that he called Israel.

He demanded the same faithfulness even to the point of martyrdom for Israel from the disciples, although no external necessity forced them to forsake their own lives. For beyond the open and nearby border, the asylums that granted them protection were continually in view. It was God, however, who separated Israel from the Gentiles, and therefore he also placed his disciples into the community, even though they stood there as sheep among wolves and God's message needed to be proclaimed to the world (Matt. 10:5, 16–23).

Together with the grateful esteem of what the Jew had received from God, however, Jesus was led from the beginning by the certainty that the community needed a new beginning since he had called it to repentance. By his call to repentance he gave himself complete independence from the nation. He stood freely above it, strong enough to let it fall and to limit himself to the few men who followed him, in the confidence that the community would emerge from them and that his own would be the ones for whom God's rule would be revealed. Already when the community in Nazareth rejected him because he spoke to it with messianic authority, he reminded it of the fact that Gentiles received divine help when Israel had rejected the prophets. He was protected against the suspicion that he persevered faithfully toward his people by some motive other than a religious one or by another consideration than the thought of God's election, by which he had set Israel apart for himself. Jesus' motive is evident by the clarity with which he judged the sin of the Jews and by which he spoke his verdict when it resisted his word. He thus proved that his devotion to the Jewish community did not render him its slave. When its leaders called his sonship of God blasphemy, this did not throw him into doubt or despair. He became a lonely man, honored by no one as the Promised One except by his followers. All considered his loneliness to be proof to the contrary; it did not cause him to doubt himself. He was able to do what his contemporaries considered impossible: he condemned Israel and separated from it without crumbling himself. Israel fell; he did not. Israel's demise was not his, nor was it the end of his kingdom.

From the very beginning, his work had led him on a course that separated him thoroughly from Judaism,[39] since the latter had a strong interest in the public nature and greatness of God's rule. It used the world as a stage on which Israel's glorification would be played out. No adherent to Judaism compared God's work with a man who put a mustard seed into the garden or with a hidden treasure. At the very minimum, the ten lost tribes would need to be gathered from the entire Diaspora. When Jesus rejected any thoughts aspiring to greatness and saw his work in turning the Jewry gathered in Palestine away from their sin and back to God, he did not think merely in terms of Judaism but revealed his opposition to Jewish longing. Since they were the chosen community while now resembling a flock without a shepherd, it was

39. By "Judaism" I refer to that form of Jewish piety that frames the relationship between God and the nation in such a way that the nation's preservation and glorification were God's purposes.

his duty to save what could be saved, and all other thoughts retreated in the light of this concern (Matt. 9:36; 10:6).[40]

Jesus' work did not receive this limitation from his final aim or from the conception of God's rule. He always designated the universal aim in terms of the "kingdom of God." Since God was the Creator of nature and the one who directed history, his rule extended to all of humanity. The rabbinate, too, expected from God's rule that at that time all idols would fall and God's glory would be revealed to mankind, while it would often stress fanatically that God's rule would bring ruin to the Gentiles and would cause them to repent because they had put idols in God's place and had trampled Israel under foot. Therefore God's kingdom would never be an event touching merely the Jews. It always brought humanity to its goal, and the thought, likewise, was not out of reach for the Jews that not all the Gentiles would find their end in hell but that there were also those among them who feared God. As Jesus' hearers thought of the proclamation of God's rule in terms of predictions regarding the end of the world, Jesus also did not merely contrast Capernaum or Jerusalem with heaven but the earth or the world without limitation. His kingdom would be revealed by the fact that "God's will was done on earth." Therefore he made his disciples the salt of the earth and the light of the world and sent them, because Israel rejected its calling, to all who would receive them, just as he himself had his goal in being revealed to all on the clouds of heaven.

The limitation of his work is likewise not due to a limited conception of divine grace. He did not focus on the Jews because the Gentiles' guilt was too great for the gospel. Conversely, we must not burden him with the idea that other nations, such as the Greeks, were more noble and pure than evil Israel. He saw in Israel's sin that of mankind and thus considered Israel as belonging to the world in its attitude toward God. Was the Jerusalem temple alone a marketplace, and were there angry men only among the Jews? His work was altogether free from any basis in the notion of merit. As he did not remain with Israel as if to do so would be particularly virtuous, he did not avoid the Greeks because he judged their sin to be unforgivable. He was able to forgive Israel's sin only through the completeness of divine grace. This grace was also able to forgive the guilt of the Gentiles. The call to repentance rather took on particular seriousness for Israel since guilt grows with the grace received, and because only those who have been entrusted with his gifts can rob God of what rightfully belongs to him.

Therefore Sodom would be judged less severely than Capernaum; even Tyre would have repented (Matt. 10:15; 12:41–42; 11:21–24). But neither the completeness of divine grace, which enabled Jesus to deal with all human guilt and need nor Israel's unrepentant attitude, which opposed the revelation of God's rule to it and sought to thwart Jesus' assertion of his regal sta-

40. In support of the notion that Jesus, too, thought of a gathering of the ten tribes in the endtimes, one may adduce the twelve apostles and the twelve thrones. This promise, however, was not given major significance in prophecy, much less for practice.

tus, altered his close relationship with Israel. He drew only one implication from the community's resistance: the will to the cross. The thought of going into exile (John 7:35) or the thought that he could protect himself against the Jews through Gentiles such as Pilate did not exist for him. If Israel wanted to kill him, it belonged to his calling that he allow himself to be killed. His woes over Capernaum and Jerusalem embodied the realization that his path would lead to the cross as well as the readiness to go there, and this lent his judgment internal greatness. When he realized his own people would not respond, he yielded himself to death and thus unconditionally honored God's righteousness. By completing his close connection with Israel, he simultaneously revealed the difference between what is called "Judaism" and himself.

His relationship to Israel was also not based merely upon what God had given it earlier. For Jesus, as for the rabbinate, Israel's holiness was valid and effective before God. God considers Israel to be his possession and the vineyard that he built for himself. He therefore sends to it the Son in order that he might subject those to him who rebelled. He opened for them the treasures of his rule in order that they might rejoice in his feast, because he had promised it to them.

Israel's relationship with God, of course, was based upon what had happened earlier. In the days of the fathers, God had built his vineyard, and Israel had received the invitation to the feast through the prophets. Jesus, however, never construed his concept of God merely from reminiscences but extended God's work into the present. He saw in God the readiness to prove his love and faithfulness to Israel and to give his gifts to it. Therefore Jesus' relationship to the community was a direct result of his divine sonship and of his office as the Christ. (The thought that he was a Jew despite being God's Son was foreign to Jesus.)

Jesus could not forsake Israel because he was the Son. He set his entire will on the high aim of revealing God's trustworthiness and faithfulness to Israel. Since God had chosen it, it was the good pleasure of the Son to confirm this election and to bring God's gifts to those he had chosen. If he should work in vain and die, and if his disciples might die as well, he did whatever he could to free God from any reproach. Indeed, no reproach fell on him since the Son fulfilled the word given to Israel with the faithfulness that took death upon itself.

Jesus' thought was thus one with the idea that Israel was made his nation and flock by his regal prerogative. When he proclaimed the call to repentance or placed himself among the vinegrowers or wooed his lost sheep, he fought for what was his own so that his property would not spoil and so that his regal status would be upheld. That he could not relinquish his kingly aim nor separate from Israel, that he could not remain silent and avoid the cross, this was for his consciousness one and the same act.

Therefore he also was not afraid of setting up an obstacle for the establishment of the perfected community by his work upon Israel. He accomplished the task given to him without speculation how it would end but also without doubts whether Israel would follow or not. Moreover, since he bore within himself the certainty of death, he was certain of the fact that, now that Israel had spurned God's gift, others would be invited. By giving his life for Israel, he did not render the execution of his commission by his disciples, to whom he gave the task of proclaiming his message among the nations, more difficult. For in his disciples' eyes Jesus' Jewishness did not stand in contrast to his regal office but was rather its prerequisite. His close relationship with Israel revealed to them the completeness of his obedience, the selflessness of his love toward the Father, and the greatness of his forgiving grace that he had shown Israel even when it rejected him. The condition without which there would never have been any preaching to the Gentiles is this: Jesus' cross was understood to be the revelation of the love of the Christ and of God. In the case of his disciples, Jesus achieved this by not allowing anything to separate him from Israel.

14. The Fulfillment of Scripture

Since Scripture was the bond of unity that tied the Jewish community together in its different segments, the close ties yet freedom of Jesus' relationship to the community are likewise revealed in his use of Scripture.

By demanding repentance from Israel, he acted at the same time in accordance with Scripture and independently from it. He rejected Jewish worship as sinful, since it invalidated Scripture, while he could not break Scripture. His call to repentance was an affirmation of the Law against the community that, since it knew God's will through the Law, did not act in ignorance but committed sin, and that therefore did not need instruction but repentance and forgiveness. He separated himself and his followers from their disobedience by obeying Scripture and by fulfilling the Law while all others broke it (Matt. 5:17–19; 15:3; Luke 10:26; 16:29; John 10:35).

At the same time, the call to repentance led him away from Scripture beyond the Law. On the one hand, he did not permit Israel to seek in Scripture the cause for its fall and to shift blame from itself to God, to the inadequacy of his revelation and the incompleteness of his Law. On the other hand, the fact that Israel's Law had not kept it from falling and had become the occasion for its corrupt worship revealed that the ancient word brought by the earliest messengers of God was insufficient and not God's final gift to the community. Corporate return to God could not consist merely of returning to Scripture but occurred when God's people became obedient to the one who protected it from the abuse of Scripture, and who removed what had made such abuse possible, thus fulfilling Scripture's intention.

The same rule for the use of Scripture resulted from Jesus' messianic concept, since he looked simultaneously backward to what had already existed and forward to what would be complete. Since Scripture gave the expectation of the Christ to him and to the entire community, the messianic idea could not effect any break with Scripture. Then Jesus would have destroyed the foundation that bore him. By sending the Christ God confirmed Scripture, and Jesus, by beginning the work of the Promised One, submitted to it in complete readiness to obedience.

At the same time, however, he stood above it through his office as the Christ, since God revealed himself through the Christ by new grace that leads the community to fulfillment. The messianic work was accomplished by the Son to whom the Father did not speak merely through that word which he once had given to his messengers and which the entire community had learned without recognizing the Father. But Jesus knew the Father, because his dealings with God were not mediated only by Scripture, and this led to his freedom in understanding Scripture.

His canon, as that of his contemporaries, consisted of "the Law and the Prophets" (Matt. 5:17; 7:12; 11:13; 22:40; cf. Luke 24:44: Law, Prophets, and Psalms). The third part of the canon, the poetic books, was not omitted by this expression, since the prophets were speaking there as well and since Jesus had high esteem for the prophetic significance of the Psalter. Statements from the Psalms stood at the top of the sayings by which he understood himself called to suffer. That this third group of Old Testament books was not firmly delineated and that these books were less authoritative than the other parts of the canon corresponds to the condition of the synagogue. Jesus did not produce anything new here; we have no list of canonical books from him.[41]

In his dealings with the Jewish community, Jesus used Scripture as the effective means to elicit its agreement. By quoting Scripture, he defended himself against attacks and protected what still remained mysterious about him. Countering his opponents, he referred to Psalms 110:1 and 82:6, while we do not hear how he interpreted the Psalter for the disciples. We learn how Jesus interpreted Malachi 4:3 only because the disciples allowed themselves to be intimidated by the objection of the rabbinate. Since he had not yet made clear by the parable of the vinegrowers that he would be the Lord of the new community, he expressed this by the word of Scripture that made the rejected stone the cornerstone of the new building. He did not tell his detractors that heavenly and eternal glory would be prepared for him in his own words, but with the two sayings that elevated the Promised One to God's throne and onto the clouds of heaven (Matt. 22:41–44; John 10:34; Matt. 17:10–13; 21:42; 26:64).

Likewise, he used Scripture as a weapon when he went on the offense against custom and tradition. When objections were raised against his conduct on the Sabbath, he responded by asking what Scripture said about David and what Hosea 6:6 was talking about. When he was confronted with the issue of divorce, he let Scripture provide the answer; for everything should remain the way God had made it in the beginning. When he attacked the market in the temple, he quoted the words of Scripture, words that made the tem-

---

41. The conduct of the early Christian church corresponds at this not unimportant point to the Gospel record; one does not find in it any effort to determine the exact composition of the canon.

ple the house of prayer and condemned Israel's abuse of it. And when the elders denied him honor and only children praised him, he rejoiced because Scripture had predicted it (Matt. 12:3; 19:4; 21:13, 16).

We see, then, that he did not conceal the liberty he had toward Scripture but exercised it before everyone's eyes and despite all objections, even though this resulted in Israel's demise and his own death. When he used the Sabbath in order to do good, this did not impinge merely on the rabbinic interpretation of the Law but on the Law itself. He carried out the struggle against Pharisaism so completely that the statement in Scripture upon which Pharisaism based itself was done away with. Everyone knew that the Sabbath commandment did not read, "You should not do any evil on the Sabbath" but "You should not do anything on the Sabbath." When doing good even on the Sabbath became one's duty, and when Sabbath regulation ceased to be a hindrance to the work of love, the wording of the rabbinic Sabbath commandment had been set aside.

Likewise, he did away with a large portion of the Mosaic Law in matters of purity by postulating that nothing that entered the mouth made a person unclean. When he exempted the sons from the temple tax since only their underlings paid it, this interfered profoundly with the present existence of the cult since the Law imposed the payment of holy gifts upon all the members of the community. The same can be said of Jesus' verdict that the Mosaic arrangement of marriage merely revealed people's hard-heartedness. Since the regulations on marriage had great importance for the life of the entire community, the reproach that those regulations did not perform God's will but were rather grounded in the corrupt condition of Israel went deep (Matt. 12:12; 15:1–20; 17:26; 19:8).

His free, new will is not demonstrated merely by isolated sayings; rather, his entire conduct arose from it. When he protected piety against greedy contamination by setting almsgiving, praying, and fasting into the private sphere, he moved away from Scripture that made worship the public concern of the community. When he consistently excluded casuistry, he moved away from Scripture that adjudicated numerous cases by concrete legal rulings. When he removed all those limitations from ethical judgment that were intended to leave at least some room for evil in people's lives, he did this with the express declaration that he was not revoking merely what his contemporaries said but what the ancients were told whom God had given the Law at Sinai and to whom Moses had proclaimed it. He did not thereby belittle Scripture but stated explicitly that it was finally he and not solely Scripture who judged evil completely and demanded perfect love.

When he made his disciples a brotherhood that had no teacher and leader other than himself, he did away with the old didactic office, and by tying his disciples' expectation solely to his own revelation, he set aside large portions of ancient prophecy (Matt. 6:1–6, 16–18; 5:21, 27, 33, 38, 43; 23:8–10). He did not make his disciples exegetes of Scripture and did not assign to them the task of interpreting the biblical books to the community. Rather, a new word of God was coming to the community through them, and he considered it his first and foremost calling to give this new word to them.

Whoever considers it promising to remove any apparent contradictions by means of literary-critical analysis of the texts can choose to eliminate statements that express Jesus' submission to Scripture as later editions. The theory here would be that later Judaism distorted Jesus' portrait in favor of its own preference. Another route would be to eliminate those statements that depict Jesus' freedom. This would entail the theory that later ideas have intruded into reports about Jesus; only Paul's work and the mission among the Greeks brought liberation from the Law. But it is impossible to separate the records in such a way that Jesus' appeal to Scripture can be put on one side and his free words and deeds on the other. For Jesus united the two norms continually and inseparably.

By eliminating his appeal to Scripture one destroys the account of his cross. It was an essential characteristic of Jesus' way to death that he embarked on it in the certainty that he thereby showed obedience to Scripture and that he thus fulfilled what it had predicted. Likewise, the deed at the cross revealed Jesus' liberty; for by it he made an end to the old community. "Do not weep for me, weep for yourselves!" Jerusalem was falling. Israel's history had come to an end; something new was beginning. By establishing his kingdom by way of the cross Jesus placed himself above the old order of the community and above its Law while nevertheless proving to be obedient to Scripture by the same act, dying in the certitude that Scripture had assigned suffering to all servants of God.

Jesus' appeal to Scripture can also not be removed from the dispute with Pharisaism, because it was only through Scripture that his opposition to it became a call to repentance. Jesus did not criticize it through the idea that the morality of the Old Testament was still incomplete and that progress beyond it was still possible. This would no longer have been the word of repentance declaring the Pharisees so guilty that their guilt resulted in the loss of the divine kingdom. Jesus' verdict was as follows: you knew through Scripture what is good before God, and you did not do it. Nevertheless, Jesus' confrontation with Pharisaism did not turn into an exegetical investigation that sought to determine the meaning of the biblical commandments, whether they should be interpreted pharisaically or not. Rather, the phrase, "But I say to you," settled the dispute.

Jesus spoke as the one who proclaimed God's will, who had the authority to tell them what was good before God, and who thereby transcended even that part of Scripture affirmed by the Pharisee. He was the Lord of the Sabbath, from whom one was to learn how it should be properly observed (Matt. 12:8). Small critical operations do not provide us with an accurate understanding of Jesus here. It can only be gained by paying attention to his sonship and his office as the Christ. When these are concealed, Jesus' relationship to Scripture becomes unintelligible, and continual contradiction with the sources and thus also the effort to dissect them become unavoidable.

Many are preoccupied by the thought that since Jesus used the concept of inspiration, and because Scripture was linked with complete obedience rendered to God, Jesus had no room for an independence that enabled him to set words of Scripture aside as no longer valid. This idea, however, overlooks that Jesus received his freedom precisely from knowing himself placed before God through Scripture, not merely before the Book. Jesus' freedom lay in the train of thought formulated by the concept of inspiration expressing that God could be heard exclusively and completely in Scripture. By experiencing God's will and work through Scripture, he received confirmation of his own closeness to God rather than finding the latter weakened or replaced. Of course, he thus deepened his separation from the community, since the latter related to God merely through Scripture and since the only way in which it was able to show its faith to God consisted of its faith in Scripture.

That explains why exegesis was the major component of its worship. But had this also been true for him, he would not have been the Son. He understood Scripture, not because he spoke from within himself but because he spoke from the Father (John 7:15–18). By this, however, the proclamation of that word given to him by God took the place of the interpretation of Scripture.[42] The new discourse and the new work of God that Israel now experienced through him could, however, neither effect the destruction of the old nor merely preserve the status quo. The community that will abide forever would not have had to be called and gathered if Israel had already achieved its goal. Both convictions became one by the fact that the entire truth and power of the old attestation of God remained preserved in the new. Jesus' liberty entailed the certainty that he expressed by his commandment, without reduction or misrepresentation, that will of God which was revealed in the old commandment. God did this, of course, no longer in the same way he had the service of himself to the old community but as the Christ was able to express it. Nevertheless, it was a way that revealed God's unity in entire clarity and that revealed the same righteousness and goodness to the community as were revealed in Old Testament times.

In his own view, Jesus did not effect the dissolution but the fulfillment of the Law when, by offering reconciliation, he placed himself above the Law. After all, it was not the breaking of the Law that in itself caused the people to perish. Rather, this violation was forgiven and its condemnation expressed only when the people rejected reconciliation with God it was now offered. For the Law, too, included both elements, condemnation of sin and the testimony of divine grace for the sinner. When the tax-collector sought forgiveness in God's temple, this was not against the Law, and when the Christ declared him righteous by his regal authority, he fulfilled the Law.

If Jesus did not see the completion of the call to repentance in some restoration of the old commandment that had been broken but in the establish-

---

42. Because this was Jesus' stance toward Scripture, a new Testament was formed. Had he merely been an exegete, the Old Testament alone would have remained the canon.

ment of the new commandment that called the repentant to love and gave them the promise, then he knew himself to be free from any contradiction with the Law, because he saw in it, too, the testimony to divine love. Thereby, of course, arose a new worship of God, since he now summarized all commandments in a single will (Matt. 22:37–40), so that instead of the many there arose one duty that comprised the entire human activity. Thus the evaluation of the individual pieces of the Law was a profound alteration of traditional usage.

Injunctions now had their value no longer by themselves but received meaning by providing love with the means of accomplishing its work. Thus all material religious means were reduced to the internal relationship with God rooted in one's will. Since Jesus, however, measured the significance or insignificance, dispensability or necessity of the individual injunction by its relationship to the love commandment, he knew himself to be free from any contradiction with the Law. For he derived the standard by which he measured those things from the Law.[43]

He prohibited the disciples from dismissing their wives so that they might obey the will of God given to them in Scripture. When he saw in the Mosaic Law a testimony of Israel's resistance against God in this regard, he accused the Pharisee of blindness concerning the intention of the Law and ignorance of the struggle it waged against human evil. Otherwise he would not have claimed the right to dismiss his wife as his fair due.

When he removed the difference between clean and unclean things, he did not intend to declare a person's defilement as harmless but rather sought to fulfill what the Law of purity desired. For what really renders a person unclean and guilty before God comes from the heart, and Jesus established the true meaning of separation from these things by removing the concern for unclean things from the community. If he exempted the sons from the holy tax, he did not remove them from God but rather provided them with the means of honoring God as their Lord. Thus the community received the effective way of worshiping God as God's sons render it to him.

For the disciples Jesus' treatment of the Sabbath commandment was particularly instructive when it came to Jesus' relationship to the Law. Since the Sabbath recurred within short intervals, it intervened profoundly in one's course of life. A man's piety was measured by the way he celebrated the Sabbath. Therefore Jesus insistently revealed the difference between his will and the customary observance of the Law at this point. This difference arose from Jesus' subsuming of the Sabbath commandment under the rule of love, whereby he did not permit people to use the Sabbath as an occasion for harshness or for the refusal to love. He did not recognize the prohibition of doing good on the Sabbath to be divine. He did not call a worship that hindered love obedience to God's will. Thereby he simultaneously removed the exter-

---

43. Jesus' attitude toward Scripture would admittedly have been impossible if the call to repentance had originated from the desire to restore the past. But Jesus had his aim in what was to come; see p. 66.

nalization of the judgment by which every violation of an injunction was immediately considered to be sin without consideration for the internal processes. By subsuming the Sabbath under the love commandment, however, he did not break the Law, since the latter demanded that Israel love God. In this way he underscored all the more Israel's duty to place God and his service above all earthly concerns, including the service of resting from one's earthly work. For the individual does not obtain rest by the violation of love and the refusal to do good, just as he does not stand in God's service merely by doing nothing.

Jesus' call to repentance also affected the cult, since God's rule cannot reveal itself without procuring for the community a new form of worship. The better righteousness demanded by him also entailed better prayer. With Jesus' judgment of Israel the temple fell as well, and Jesus was able to do so since he granted "more than the temple" and since he would rebuild it. For only through him is that worship possible which the Father requires (Matt. 12:6; 26:61; John 2:19, 21; 4:21–24).

But Jesus' renewal of the cult by no means casts doubts on the fact that he saw in the Mosaic Law, as did everyone, that testimony of God that had created the community and that determined its relationship to God. God's vineyard originated by his giving of the Law to Israel. Therefore he entered into the sanctuary as the house of his Father where the one who prayed aright received justification. Whoever gave to his brother what belonged to him was permitted to approach the altar with his own sacrifice, and Jesus sent the leper to the altar according to the regulation of the Law (Matt. 5:24; 8:4; Luke 2:49; John 2:16; Matt. 21:13; Luke 18:10; Matt. 5:35).

Jesus maintained the conviction that he in his behavior toward the Father observed cultic requirements in complete truthfulness. He also produced suitable cult observance among his disciples. When he put himself in the place of the temple, it was his sincere opinion that what the temple granted to the Jewish community by its attestation of the presence and grace of God was given even more effectively by his own commission. He agreed with the Jewish community that God's temple was indestructible, though he did not ascribe this sanctity to the house built of stones (Matt. 12:6; John 2:19). By acting in complete obedience to God, not only prayer but also sacrifice took on serious reality for him. This applied not only to his joy that rendered the cult a feast but also to those things he had to forego. His sacrifice did not remain limited to internal processes but surrendered to God all he had, even his own body and blood. He therefore transcended the animal sacrifice, the temple building, and the priests serving them, by a higher worship without, however, despising the former as groundless and without purpose, since the ruling of the Law that the individual should give what he has to God in order to receive God's gifts also regulated his own communion with the Father.

The name of Christ by which he expressed his aim did not lead him to formulate a theory that gathered Old Testament statements regarding the Christ and interpreted them in relation to his own work. Many statements that had messianic significance both for him and for his contemporaries are never mentioned. Jesus' appeal to Scripture is the clearest when his daily lot concealed his regal status and set him at odds with the Jewish community. He found support in Scripture against what appeared to be true and against the judgment of the nation, and therefore it was for him and for the disciples a major matter that Scripture prophesied his way to the cross (Matt. 26:24, 31, 54, 56; Luke 18:31; 22:37; 24:27, 44, 46; John 2:17; 13:18; 15:25; 17:12).

On the other hand, one never detects in him the effort to copy prophecy by doing whatever it said regarding the Christ and nothing else. He therefore did not merely retain his opposition toward intellectualism but also revealed his liberty toward Scripture, accomplishing the work assigned to him by the Father in the assurance that nothing in prophecy had crumbled and that God would fulfill his entire word. Only thus it was possible that he did not assume any rule in the form of a civil kingdom despite Isaiah 9, that he did not execute judgment despite Isaiah 11, and that he did not present himself as a priest despite Psalm 110. Only thus was it possible, in a word, for him to go to the cross.

When he preferred the prophecy regarding suffering over the words by which Scripture described the greatness of the coming king, resorting, not to Isaiah 9, but to Psalms 22 and 69, he did not yield the prophecy regarding his glory as if it were fleshly and ungodly but acted in the conviction that he would procure the glory of divine rule precisely by the way of suffering. In such a way he would prepare regal majesty and the eternal community for himself. He never entertained the thought that his messianic aim would result in a shortening and weakening of what Scripture had promised. He believed that he would be the Christ also in glory since he was the Christ by the yielding of his life on the cross, and that he would not be able to be the Christ in glory if he refused the cross and was unable to fulfill the words of Scripture that referred to it.

When he tied his disciples completely to himself and made it their sole profession to follow him, he did not mean to detract them from Scripture. They would fulfill it by obeying him and by doing the service he assigned them. He did not equip them by way of abstract concepts and theories for the task he thus assigned them but referred them to God's government. How the Law was fulfilled by his word, how the old community was renewed in the new one, and how prophecy was fulfilled by his cross was not brought about and revealed by didactic formulas but by God's progressive work. Therefore he compared the disciples with the steward who possessed as a part of his treasure both old and new and who used both (Matt. 13:52). He succeeded in assuring that the disciples' attitude toward Scripture had the same characteristics as his own: complete confidence in them that obeyed it and liberty from it that understood and applied it with a view to the Christ.[44]

---

44. The attitude of the apostolic community proves the accuracy of the presentation of Jesus' attitude toward the Bible given by the Gospels.

15. The Dispute with the Pharisees

Since Jesus always remained separate from Pharisaism, and because his separation from it had already taken place from the first stages of his ministry, the Gospel record does not contain any information regarding the beginning of Jesus' dispute with the Pharisees. It rather presupposes in the first accounts that there was a break with them and that it was irremediable. Already the Sermon on the Mount substantiated the requirements Jesus directed toward the disciples by the explanation that they would remain divorced from God's rule unless they had something better than what Pharisaism was able to give them (Matt. 5:20). In John, too, Jesus' first discourse with Nicodemus already expressed his opposition against Pharisaism with strong determination.

With similar certainty, however, the Gospels reveal that he did not see his dispute with Pharisaism as the aim of his work and the content of his discourses. He initiated the struggle by freeing himself and his disciples from Pharisaic regulations and did this in clear awareness of the ensuing consequences. Since Pharisaism demanded from the entire community submission to its leadership and discipline, it considered Jesus to be sinning by eluding its jurisdiction. Jesus, on the other hand, was not content with justifying himself but conducted his defense by an attack that destroyed the entire Pharisaic piety.

The disciples' penetrating understanding of these events is revealed as they recount Jesus' opposition to Pharisaism as epitomized in its regulation that people wash their hands before meals (Matt. 15:1–20). Since this regulation was typical for Pharisaism, which was supremely concerned with a system of purifications that were in and of themselves not merely inoffensive but understandable and useful, the controversy surrounding this issue reveals the ground and depth of the contrast between Jesus and this leading Jewish sect.

Jesus refused to obey the Pharisaic tradition since it led to transgression of God's commandment. He stated not only that the disputing of God's good will was inherent in the veneration of tradition but that such disputing arose from that veneration and was demanded by it. In his view, the question was whether one should obey God or the elders. The question was answered in a way that his ruling was beyond dispute even for the Pharisee's conscience. Jesus did not claim that the hand-washing regulation was in itself in conflict with God's commandment; he rejected it because it was part of a tradition whose entire right of existence he denied. And he denied it because it included regulations that demanded what was sinful.

Jesus proved this to the Pharisees by the regulation that a son who by the oath of Corban refused the father his help would be required to keep his oath. On account of such things Jesus cast aspersions on the entire system. These regulations would have been impossible if they had really desired to do God's commandment. They arose merely from the fact that the tradition had become an independent authority that sought to compel obedience for itself. Thus the innocent regulation also became harmful, and it was therefore not without danger, since it pursued a different aim than God's law. While the latter resisted that kind of impurity that came from the heart, the purification rites took attention away from it, replacing it with a man-made purity by which true impurity was not prevented. Even when Jesus tied his argumentation to the Pharisaic viewpoint by justifying his ministry on the Sabbath by current custom or by relating his power over spirits to the things done by Jewish exorcists (Matt. 12:5, 12; Luke 13:15; 14:5; John 7:22–23; Matt. 12:27), this never implied acceptance of the Pharisaic regulation. He did not tell the Pharisees that they could agree with him and remain Pharisees too. He destroyed even the pretense by which they concealed their accusations and exposed the true motive that compelled them to contradict him.

Therefore he also did not differentiate within the party and did not divide the Pharisees into good and bad Pharisees (cf. Mark 12:34; Luke 10:27–28),[45] although there were, of course, great differences that arise in the course of human life even under the rule of a common thought world. He rather judged the value of the system rather than the particular results to which it led individuals and did not merely reject individual aspects of the system but the entire piety regulated by it. Therefore he also did not participate in the differences between teachers and schools. He criticized neither Shammai nor Hillel, for he considered the fundamental idea of the entire system to be false.

Jesus measured the sin of Pharisaism by the same norms that elsewhere determined his call to repentance. He called it sin that the Pharisee defined piety as a combination of an arrogant self-esteem that elevated itself before God and harshness toward others. He rejected the Pharisaic Sabbath since it forbid kindness on the Sabbath (Matt. 12:12; Mark 3:4; Luke 13:15–16; 14:5; John 7:23). The entire system is condemned when it can forbid a son the support of his father once he has taken an oath, or can authorize a "righteous" man to dismiss his wife at will or to pervert his right as creditor of a widow (Matt. 15:5–6; 19:3; Mark 12:40).

The Pharisee shamed the repentant and gratuitously condemned the innocent (Matt. 9:13; 12:7; Luke 15:25–32; 18:9–13). The uncontrolled indulgence in wild sensual desires easily attached itself to pride (unchastity: Matt. 12:39; greed: Luke 16:14; Mark 12:40). From this resulted persistent untruthfulness. Since the Pharisee came close to equating love with hate, repentance with the justification of sin, and the confession of God with selfish ambition, he had to resort to pretense. Thereby he poisoned the religious community he had cultivated, particularly in his own circles but also to a great extent the whole community. His entire worship became hypocritical, and its purpose was bent away from God to personal greatness. It therefore also distorted the concept of power and turned it into tyranny, ruling over the community by suppressing it and by manufacturing its own fame.

Thus Pharisaism did for the Jewish community what the thief did for the flock, robbing what was God's (Matt. 23:2–12; John 10:1–11; Matt. 15:13–14). Jesus' reproach, however, was never merely that such sins occur in Pharisaism, but that they were produced by its piety and substantiated and covered

45. That there were also reprehensible kinds of Pharisaism, the rabbinate has always acknowledged.

by its worship. Pharisaism refused love to God and others because of its holiness in the name of God. Therefore Jesus denied the Pharisees their inner relationship to God. He did not see God's work there; the individual's own will was operative. God had not planted this plant; those are not shepherds whom the gatekeeper allowed to enter. They grasped for power with selfish and self-appointed ambition.

Even in his condemnation of Pharisaism Jesus remained entirely prepared to forgive. This he proved initially by not escalating the struggle through exaggeration. When they portray him on the Sabbath, the disciples reveal his opponents' righteousness and thereby the plausibility of his case without any effort to conceal it. They did not single out from the Pharisaic Sabbath observance one of the many curiosities and exaggerations that had always given occasion to mockery and had provided a basis for comfortable polemic. Jesus' attack focused on the place where the Pharisees had Scripture on their side, and by rejecting the way in which the Pharisees determined God's will in Scripture, Jesus revealed the contrast separating him from them in its entire depth.

The same situation is revealed by the discussion regarding purity, since it, too, did not expose merely the myopic, scrupulous side of Pharisaism but grounded its condemnation in a reasonable pronouncement that stood in clear connection with Scripture. The case, too, by which Jesus proved the conflict between tradition and God's commandment did not entail any exaggeration. The Pharisaic law book tells of such a case in Beth-horon.[46] The judgment would be false that Jesus grounded his objection against Pharisaism in a trivial matter. This story indicates that the village knew at the time of sons who no longer supported their fathers and that it saw this as their duty because they had now spoken the calamitous word. The son would have loved to invite his father to his wedding but was not permitted to do so; this would have been sin. That religion and morality were here publicly turned against each other and that love was refused to another person for the sake of God's honor is self-evident.

In the portrayal of the praying Pharisee and of the elder brother the brightest light falls, without a bitter word, upon what Jesus called the Pharisaic sin. The complaining brother is granted most emphatically his filial right in the father's house. When Jesus called the needlessly multiplied prayer of the Pharisees "babbling," this picture is, of course, telling, and the barb is sharp. But Jesus did not deny the fact that the Pharisee tried to pray, and the idea that he would procure an answer by multiplying his prayer did not do him injustice (Matt. 6:7).

The rule to "love one's friend, hate one's enemy" (Matt. 5:43) was hardly formulated by a Pharisee in this clear form. No historian, however, speaks of Jesus doing an injustice to the Old Testament Scripture or even to the Pharisees by referring to it. In his day the entire Jewish community, of course,

---

46. After the end of the war against Hadrian, Beth-horon belonged to the area forbidden to Jews. The event thus presumably still belongs to the first century.

already celebrated Purim with great enthusiasm. The concluding verdict in Matthew 23 admittedly bears powerful pathos that senses the gravity attached to this verdict. But here, too, the Pharisaic peculiarities, their tithing of cummin or the washings of cups, are not mocked but are expressly granted them, and wrath is directed merely toward the things by which evil revealed itself. None of these pronouncements is without rich attestation in Jewish literature.[47]

But Jesus did not merely direct his attack toward the rule of truthfulness and righteousness but continually offered complete forgiveness even to the Pharisee. He broke with him not despite his ability to forgive but because he wanted to forgive, while the Pharisee did not permit him to forgive others or desire forgiveness for himself. For Jesus wanted to forgive completely by effecting repentance by his forgiveness and by freeing the forgiven person from evil. Since the Pharisee, however, considered his sin to be part of his piety, he refused repentance and rejected forgiveness. This determined the outcome of all subsequent events. Jesus' condemnation did not fall on the impious or ignorant but on the pious and instructed members of Israel. It did not pertain to the things they perceived to be their sin and weakness but to the things that appeared to them to be their holiness and advantage. The break took on serious proportions since Jesus saw in Pharisaism the end result of Israel's history. It was the best the Jewish community had to offer, and this best was the reversal of piety into the glorification of man, a righteousness resulting in evil. Since Pharisaism, however, had already won the Jewish community over to its views and tied its fate to itself, this struggle did not concern merely a group of people who had strayed and could no longer be brought back into line but concerned the entire nation. The blind man led the blind man into a pit (Matt. 15:14).

It is equally clear why Jesus' separation from Pharisaism did not estrange him from the entire Jewish community and why he remained a Jew with all his heart. He did not grant to the Pharisee that he had become what he was through the teaching and instruction of God and that he heard and exercised the word of Scripture with a clear conscience. Jesus never conceded that God's word and grace had created those evil saints that glorified themselves on account of their piety. Therefore his condemnation of Pharisaism and his association with the Jewish community were one and the same. Because he was truly a Jew, he was not a Pharisee. The same reason that substantiated his communion with the latter also explained his opposition to the former. He was one with the work of the Father and thus separated from those who spoiled it. From the same consciousness of God that made him his son arose on the one hand his association and on the other his rejection.

The antagonism between Jesus and Pharisaism was also transferred to the Christ concept. The claim that the Christ was understood politically by the

47. The objection in 23:4 that the Pharisee bound heavy loads only for others can sound strange only for those who do not understand what Jesus called heavy loads.

Pharisees and unpolitically by Jesus merely scratches the surface.[48] It easily misinterprets Pharisaism's sincerity toward God. It is true that Pharisaism proudly contrasted the "kingdom of God" with the Roman world rulers. When God sat down on his throne, the arrogant rule of man who made himself God would erode and the community's condition of slavery would cease. By this, however, the Pharisee's concept of the kingdom did not lose the idea of God. It remained a major part of his expectation that God would make his greatness known. Pharisaic eschatology never became a mere political dream.

On the other hand, Jesus also was not pleased with the rule of the Herods and the Romans. When he was told about Pilate's bloody work upon the Galileans, probably in the opinion that he was called to vindicate them and to resist Pilate's violent acts, he, of course, refused resistance against Pilate. However, by placing his rule beside the collapse of the tower in Siloam, he called it a misfortune through which the community should become fruitful by leading it to repentance. He did not call the tetrarch a lion or a wolf but merely a fox; still, he resembled a wild animal (Luke 13:1–5, 32). The fact that his kingdom was not of this world and that it was not procured for him by his servants fighting on his behalf but rather had its ground solely in God's rule did not indicate that his government would leave the condition of this world unchanged (John 18:36). According to his promise, the divine rule would do away with the power of all other rulers. Jesus' separation from the Pharisees' messianic idea did not arise from the differing evaluation of political conditions but was the consequence of a deeper conflict.

In its hope Pharisaism also adhered to that will that elevates man and wants to make God subservient to him and thus demanded that God bring about Israel's glorification by his final revelation. Jesus contradicted this: God's kingdom glorifies God. This already finds full expression in the Lord's Prayer. A prayer that focuses on the final consummation without reaching for the victory, glory, and rule of the Jews does away with Pharisaism. Jesus' love for God did not permit the wish for the destruction of the nation or the world; for God rules by his grace and glorifies himself to those who receive that grace by his gifts. But Jesus' will was sincerely devoted to him, the Giver, not merely his gifts, and did not seek merely the help by which the human condition was elevated but God himself.

Therefore Jesus' promise does not contain any attachment on the part of God to Israel's present condition, while, for Pharisaism, the indestructible continuing existence of the present community was the axiom that determined its entire hope. It therefore clung to the present signs of election—the temple, circumcision, the holiness of Jerusalem and Palestine—and turned the prophetic notion of judgment exclusively toward the Gentiles, extending this to include those who lived as Gentiles within the Jewish community.

---

48. If we define politics as a skill in forming societies that makes no use of religious and ethical norms, we use a concept in interpreting Jesus that did not exist in his thinking. Not even the Pharisees thought politically in that sense. Both grounded the community on an entity that originated not merely by skill or compulsion but by a commonality of will resulting in a political union.

Jesus affirmed the divine working of righteousness in its pure justice for all, and foremost of all for those who were called to God, be it the Jewish people or his own community.

Therefore eschatology was linked for him with the needs that Pharisaism did not relate to hope, or in any case did not do so with sufficient urgency. Since God's rule brought about the destruction of all evil, the need for forgiveness arose for that help which would end sin in man. In this respect Pharisaism referred everyone to the capacity of his freedom; Israel produced its own righteousness before God by its obedience to the Law. The work that remained for the Christ was that of changing the situation that weighed down the Jewish community. Jesus, on the other hand, was the Christ because he took away the sin of the world. This of necessity resulted in a different estimation of the political aspirations of the Jews.

Thereby eschatology was also cleansed from its sensual element. For Pharisaism, the hope of eternal life retained a physiological dimension. After all, it was a nature miracle that provided immortality for the community, since the ethical question stood independently beside the hope of eternal life and was accomplished first of all by a person's own righteousness and the acknowledgment of that righteousness by the divine verdict. But for Jesus, no dualism could be tolerated here. Sin and death would cease together; righteousness and life were given jointly by God. The promise, however, was not broken into an assortment of isolated goods, as if the religious and ethical dilemmas and the problem of life were solvable by themselves. Humanity's fall and its restoration would occur by the indivisible grace of God that brought man to God and thus also to righteousness, kindness, and life.

As long as egotism shapes hope, sensuality always lingers within it. Since God was supposed to glorify the Jew, the entire process ended in a good life that took on more or less sensual features, although it must be recognized that Pharisaism here preserved a certain degree of modesty. The images of the future did not arouse sexual passion. The esteem for money, too, rather took on the shape of treasures being so readily available that the craving for wealth was extinguished since all would obtain it effortlessly. Jesus' promise, on the other hand, also did not merely have a spiritual dimension but was a teaching about resurrection, thus comprising nature and spirit, body and soul. The eternal aim would not be reached by way of the destruction of nature and of the body but by its renewal to an enhanced form of life.

Nevertheless, the contrast surfacing at this point between Jesus and Pharisaism is important. It received clear definition by the discussion of the resurrection (Matt. 22:23–33). While the Pharisee taught the return of the dead to the present condition and did not combine a much higher stage of life with the state of resurrection, for Jesus it meant the reception of a qualitatively different, higher form of life that would bring liberation from one's present needs and passions. As he already quieted sensual passions by referring them to a higher joy in God, and as he "told the poor the good news" believing that they received by it what would bless them in their poverty, so his vision of the future also directed people's love toward what was God's, toward a life similar to that of the angels, whereby sensual lust was eliminated.

This deeply affected the understanding of the concept of the Spirit. That "the Spirit gave life" was an axiom Jesus shared with Pharisaism. When the life by which the Spirit revived the dead, however, merely restored the present condition, no second birth was necessary, since the Spirit in this case did not have anything to offer those who were alive, nothing that intrinsically altered their relationship to God. Since Jesus, on the other hand, rejected the concept of restoration with regard to the perfection of the community, he could no longer attach it directly to the present condition of the human being in the carefree style of Pharisaism, as if the person possessed already all characteristics that would lead him to perfection. The new understanding of resurrection and the new shape of his ethic that he expressed by way of the phrase "spiritual birth" were the complementary links of a uniform train of thought.

For Christology, serious hope in God made room for humanness, while Pharisaism sought in the revelation of divine power the new element that was still missing in the present and that would bring about the consummation of all things. This eliminated ethical characteristics from their concept of the Christ and made omnipotence the essential trait by which he would destroy Israel's enemies and make Jerusalem the place of all joy. Thereby the understanding of Christ inevitably took on a docetic tendency. For Jesus, on the other hand, there was even room in his filial relationship for a genuine, real human life, since he did not view God merely with regard to his power but foremost of all with regard to his grace. He could be a man in such a way as to be with the Father; he could be the Son in such a way as to be able to be a man. For the decisive point at which communion with God occurred lay for him in the personal act of life. Being known by the Father meant to stand in his love; knowing the Father meant to love him. But he also had the complete love of God characteristic of the Son of God in his human course of life and on the way to the cross.

The bifurcation of the concept of Christ deepened on both sides that separation that had arisen in elementary religious and ethical norms. The Pharisee rejected an ethic that led to this messianism, and Jesus subjected Pharisaic piety entirely to condemnation, since it failed to recognize his commission from God and did not merely fail to help him in his work but even resisted him with all its strength. Thus two clear, complete refusals clashed with one another. The Pharisee did not desire what Jesus had, at any rate not in such a way that it appeared to him as the complete salvation and the fulfillment of the messianic aim. Jesus did not desire what the Pharisee longed for, at any rate not in such a way that he considered it to be essential to God's glorification and to the fulfillment of humanity. Therefore the preaching of the kingdom became a forensic verdict that shattered Pharisaism's claim to God's grace and kingdom.

Because the dispute with Pharisaism determined Jesus' history and the history of Christendom from the beginning, Pharisaism participated actively in it, since the opponent influenced the movement that acquired its property by defeating the other side. The widespread resistance to the fact that Christianity would be inconceivable apart from Pharisaism's rule over the Jewish community, and that it received its history and teaching by borrowing from it or in interaction with it, hindered the understanding of New Testament history in all its processes and produced a multitude of fantasies that draw a connection between foreign pagan or gnostic ideas and Christian convictions. This way of thinking, however, is supported merely by the conventional caricatures of Pharisaism that remain blind to its religious zeal. These misconceptions, in turn, are frequently due to the fact that the religious tendency of the interpreters was essentially thoroughly Pharisaic so that the critic stood on Pharisaism's side in Jesus' dispute with it. Then a distorted picture of Pharisaism had to be created against which the call of repentance was directed so that Jesus' polemic would not also pertain to one's own religiosity.

Pharisaism's relationship to Christianity became strong because the dispute with the former could not merely be conducted by a total rejection of the latter. Rather, its truth and its righteousness had to be separated from the things that constituted its sin. It was precisely this struggle that achieved the complete, effective union with the truth in Pharisaism. Since Jesus was confronted with Pharisaism as a religion of obedience that nevertheless ended in a dispute with God, he achieved victory over it by holding his sonship of God in obedience, but now in real obedience. Since he was confronted with religious pride in Pharisaism, he was obliged to humility in his entire conduct, since he could demonstrate the sinfulness of pride merely by being humble as the Son. Therefore he also provided effective power for the ideal of humility that was also held by Pharisaism. Since Pharisaism took its occasion for sin from Scripture, Jesus became subject to it and at the same time free from it. He lent the dispute its complete seriousness by denying eternal validity even to the things in Scripture that served Pharisaism as support.

16. Jesus' Opposition toward the Scribes

Jesus proved the sincerity of his condemnation of Pharisaism by publicly breaking with the rabbinate. Now it had become entirely clear that his call of repentance was directed to all. If there were blemishes in the conduct of the righteous, the thought was still possible that their teaching nevertheless was beyond reproach, drawn from Scripture, and sanctified by centuries-old tradition. But when Jesus accused the teachers as well, no one in Israel was righteous before him. Luke revealed the Jewish community's depth of irritation with Jesus' challenge of the sacrosanct authority of the scribes by the case of the teacher who recognized Jesus' attack upon Pharisaism and who nevertheless considered it to be impossible that Jesus also wanted to confront the scribes (Luke 11:45).

But even when he attacked the rabbinate, he did not change the call to repentance into a teaching and did not confront theology with theology. The concept of merit used by Pharisaism continually bore within itself the seed of what one calls a worldview. It led to certain conceptions of the relationship between God's will and activity to man's will and activity. It raised, since it set righteousness and love in contrast to each other, the question of final norms that had permanent validity, and produced, since it tied the individual completely to the regulations given to the Jewish community, the question regarding the relation between public law and the duty of the individual. In his dispute with the Pharisees, however, Jesus merely wanted to reveal the blameworthiness of their conduct, without ever addressing the theoretical basis for their practice. He reached his goal when it was clear that their self-serving admiration of their own accomplishments was to be rejected and that a righteousness without love that enslaved the individual and separated him from God was corrupt. He did not, however, define the concepts of "merit" and "reward" and did not derive righteousness from divine grace. He did not secure the inviolable liberty of the individual against the pressure of the community by a theoretical construction of the normal community. True, he spoke seriously about the danger of the false teaching by which Pharisaism became bad leaven and against whose subconscious power even Jesus' own disciples were not immune (Matt. 16:12; 15:14; Luke 12:1), and his condemnation also extended to its teachers. But he refused to use the same method as his opponents to overcome them. By acting in the kind of love that turned the will away from man to God, by uniting in his deed grace with righteousness, and by living in the kind of liberty that did not allow any other witness for one's inner life, much less any other judge than God alone, he revealed to his opponents the blameworthiness of their will by placing his and their wills side by side and freeing his disciples from the errant wills of his opponents. On the other hand, he did not himself assume the role of sage. John reveals this in his own way even more clearly than Matthew. Although he succeeds in giving his presentation a coherent unity, it does not contain any theology of Jesus nor any attempts at developing a theory that aspired to a totality of insight. John merely provides Jesus' statement "I am" that determined people's relationship to him on the basis of his communion with the Father.

But the community could attain conversion only if it received new ideas, and Jesus provided those to the extent that they were a prerequisite for its conversion. Therefore the words that formulate his call of repentance have at the same time the highest educational value. They impart, however, the teaching to the hearer in such a way as was necessary for the substantiation of goodwill, not for the transformation of a volitional matter into an intellectual one.

He saw in the deeds of the teachers the same contradiction that corrupted Pharisaism. They represented the divine Law with passionate zeal in their preaching, instruction, and judgment. The inner unity with God's will, however, remained out of their reach, and they did succeed at avoiding contradiction of God's commandment (Matt. 23:3–4). They urged the Jewish community to continual prayer and were themselves incapable of prayer, they, the "babblers." They obliged them daily to love God with their whole strength and continually displayed their own arrogance. They demanded the unblemished preservation of purity and did not see what rendered them unclean. Worse, by combining holy teaching with an unholy will, they corrupted not merely themselves but also the community they had tied to their leadership. Because they did not approach God, they also barred the rest of the nation from doing so. Therefore Jesus compared them in his parable not with the shepherd but with the robber and thief (Matt. 23:13; Luke 11:52; John 10:8, 10).

For this reason Jesus praised the Father for taking his revelation away from the wise on account of their wisdom and for giving it to the seemingly unqualified (Matt. 11:25). It was crystal clear that the cross would result for him from this. By thanking God nevertheless for this shaping of his revelation, he expressed that he was able to perceive God's glory in it. God's greatness and grace appeared in the fact that he did not do his work in order to provide man material for his thinking but in order that man do what even an ignorant person can do: to believe in God and obey him. By denying glory to the wise, God revealed his majesty but also the completeness of his grace, and for this Jesus thanked him.

The same line of thought informed him from the beginning of his ministry. He already separated himself from the scribes by making fishermen his first disciples and expected from God that he would reveal himself to the unlettered. He believed that repentance would destroy even a decadent theological tradition so that a refutation of its individual pronouncements would not be necessary. Foolish teaching would end together with bad morals, and illusory notions would come to an end together with the perverted will. With a new will new thoughts develop. This also comforted him concerning to his disciples' use of Scripture, although Scripture always created a need for instruction and erudition. Since they recognized his commission and kept his word, they would also understand Scripture in agreement with God's work.[49]

In this way Jesus won a complete victory over scribal tradition. The rule the scribes exercised over the Jewish community by way of developing casuistry and the rule the Jewish community exercised over individuals were incompatible with the aim of Jesus. It created a lack of liberty since it imposed the rule determining one's actions upon everyone externally. And since it could not describe and measure the internal process but merely determined the visible, material side of the action, it inevitably subordinated the internal to the external performance and transformed the internal service of God into the accomplishment of the work prescribed by the regulation.

In the Gospels, casuistry has completely disappeared. It does not even appear in such a way that Jesus still had to liberate his disciples from it; they are set free.[50] One thing, of course, we find out clearly: how Jesus set them free.

49. The way in which the New Testament interprets the Old Testament will frequently reflect Jesus' own interpretations. They cannot be separated from those of the disciples. He never gave a survey of Old Testament teaching to his disciples.
50. The two exceptions where issues leaning toward casuistry were brought to Jesus, that is, whether or not forgiving another person seven times would free someone from any further obligation to do so, and whether or not a man was entitled to dismiss his wife for any and every reason (Matt. 18:21; 19:3), have ample motivation. The requirement of unconditional forgiveness is a difficult pronouncement, and the accurate Pharisaic formulation of the issue of marriage reveals entirely the contrast between the petitioners and Jesus.

The question, "How many times of prayer are there?" was silenced by the word, "No multiplying of words." The question, "How does one tithe garden produce?" was dealt with when only foreigners, not God's sons, needed to pay taxes. "What is not allowed on the Sabbath?" "Anything evil," Jesus said. "When is it permissible to dismiss one's wife?" He replied, "Never." "When is an oath valid?" His answer: "Always."

Owing to the fact that Jesus held his disciples entirely to the rule of love, casuistry was dead. Thus it happened that the disciples formed a close-knit community without detailed regulations for repentance and confession that elaborated on what was sinful, without a list of duties by which their service for God and for their neighbor would be fulfilled, without a statement of faith or confession that enumerated forbidden and correct thoughts, without a liturgy that set standards for prayer, without a constitution that assigned to everyone his rights and duties, and without any legislation of the complete practice of freedom.

Even apart from the power of Jewish tradition one might expect that the conditions for casuistry developed to the smallest detail were available to the disciples as nowhere else. The terms by which they expressed their dependence upon Jesus were absolute. Their subjection to him was complete and possessed complete sincerity of religion: God revealed himself in him; God's will was accomplished through him. Even if the example of the synagogue had remained ineffectual, could there have arisen anything in the disciples but the effort to imitate Jesus and to determine how he acted in every situation in order to have rules for their own behavior?

But not a single piece of the Gospels, be it Matthew or John, has a casuistic, halakhic aim. Not a single story was formed and told for the purpose of the community's imitation of Jesus' behavior. The obedience rendered to Jesus by his disciples had a separate root and a different content. Their obedience arose from faith, from that complete subjection to him that did not place him beside the disciples but elevated him above them and recognized that he had been sent to do a work that no one did but him. Their obedience had their own work as its content, that calling which they must fulfill at their own place with their own strength in the exercise of their own love. It remains, however, highly remarkable that Jesus was able to liberate the disciples so completely from the scribal interpretation of Scripture.[51]

Didactic narrative (haggada), too, the second achievement of scribal erudition, Jesus rejected entirely. When he used biblical history and referred to David, Solomon, Jonah, Moses, or Abraham, or told the story of Lot, Noah, or Adam, nothing appears but the biblical story without any scribal addition or coloring. There is, of course, a clear connection with tradition in Jesus' calling the murder of Zachariah in the temple a particularly severe guilt, but here, too, there is no sign of the legend of the bloody stain in the temple that could not be removed (Matt. 23:25; the rabbinate, too, considered the murder of

51. Whoever removes the aim of the Christ from Jesus' history will never explain why he was not used by his disciples as an example in great and small matters.

Zachariah a particularly grave offense). Since he did not merely criticize the legendary constructs of the rabbinate from time to time but was opposed to the entire enterprise, he carried out a radical removal of the tradition by which the scribes surrounded the text of Scripture and liberated the disciples from the arbitrary dreaming of tradition. This was also significant for the way in which he and his disciples looked at his own history. Neither Jesus' history nor his commandment was turned into a new haggada.

The Gospel record reveals in all its parts a remarkable restraint of the imagination. The poetic power of the Christmas story is admirable owing to its clear yet tender transparency. Equally noteworthy, however, are the boundaries that constrained poetic formation even in the treatment of these issues. Luke graphically portrayed how the Baptist's commission was already given at his birth. But this suffices. The decisive turning point in the Baptist's life by which he stepped from the desert before the nation and received the certainty that the Jewish community now needed to be told of God's kingdom and of repentance remains concealed. "God's Word came to John" (Luke 3:2). That is enough, even though, if this were merely the poetry of the community or of individuals, the apocalypses provide ample examples for a gripping portrayal of the prophetic experience. Not a single piece of the Gospel record narrates a conversation between Mary and Joseph, none leads us to Nazareth during Jesus' youth. The account of Jesus' baptism indicates that Jesus was given a glimpse of heaven at that time. Any portrayal of the "open heaven" is missing, likewise any depiction of his inner experience when the Spirit filled him and assured him in complete joy of his sonship. The temptation narrative directs attention exclusively to the judgment by which Jesus discerned evil and goodwill while the external matters of the event remain obscure. This would have been a fascinating topic for the poet: the Christ struggling with Satan, executing the divine act of overcoming him! It is known that the imagination is stirred both by evil and by mystery. Here, however, it is strictly regulated so that the text leaves unanswered all questions regarding the course of events, showing us merely Jesus' will by which he resisted evil. The same observation can be made regarding the accounts of Jesus' miracles and the Easter story.

The shape of the Gospel records reveals Jesus' profound effect upon the disciples. This bridling of the imagination in favor of a will grounded in simple, clear norms amounted to a departure from a strong Jewish tradition at a crucial point. The procedure cannot be explained by Jesus' lack of imagination. His illustrations revealed a magnificent imagination, and many of his actions, such as the footwashing, showed great ability in shaping thought by way of a visual image. His intransigence regarding scribal tradition was motivated internally also at this point. It signifies a departure from religious insincerity that toyed with God and therefore also with reality. He invested his own dealings with God and with his disciples with the sincerity of the truth and of duty. Therefore he eliminated all things that served merely pleasure. He did not enhance the call to repentance by delightful images of heaven or fear-inspiring portraits of hell. He did not poetically represent the beauty and blessedness of brotherly love uniting the community or of the love for God by which he was devoted to the Father. He had imagination and used and evoked it also in his disciples. He disciplined himself strictly, however, by turning its entire attention to the regulation of its will rather than to religious enjoyment.

17. The Refutation of Smaller Heresies

Jesus had more in common with the Zealots than with any other group.[52] The impetus he received from this direction reached back into his youth since the Zealot movement had always had its home in Galilee. Galileans were the founders and leaders of the group called "Zealots." They did not separate from the Pharisees on account of a theory but owing to the aims of their will. Both movements elevated Israel above the Gentiles and viewed its subjection to Gentile rulers as despicable. They considered Israel's integration into the Roman state a calamity and a punishment for Israel's guilt.

Therefore the Pharisaic prayer asks for God's kingdom in the opinion that it would be the end of Roman rule. But the Pharisee accommodated himself to the situation and exercised faith in God by leaving it to him to alter people's circumstances. He prayed but did not participate in revolution since God alone could bring about the time of salvation. There were, however, also pious people who did not consider Israel's duty to be done merely by this hope but who added practice to their conviction, not merely binding others with heavy loads but also wanting to carry them themselves. These appropriated the honorific designation "Zealots." They urged the Jewish community to deny obedience to any other master but God. This matter took on particular practical significance in the area of taxation.

Jesus' struggle with the Pharisees contains certain points of comparison with that of the Zealots. The Zealot, too, was motivated by his faith in God's rule and by his desire for it to be revealed and based his conduct on its acknowledgment. He, too, felt the lack of truthfulness and the barrenness of Pharisaism, the contradiction between its pious words and the actual condition to which it led the Jewish community. Since, however, the Zealots wanted to heal this condition even by transcending Pharisaism, Jesus' pronouncements against the Pharisees met Zealot convictions head-on, too. By his decision regarding taxation, Jesus revealed both what united him with the Zealots and what divided him from them (Matt. 22:19–21). Their desire that God's property should remain God's also was his will. But a person should give to God exactly what was his rather than declaring holy by his own authority what did not originate from God and what was not desired by him. In Jesus' judgment, the Zealot transferred his desire from his serious aim to what was esteemed by sinful passion. Since he considered it to be incompatible with

52. There is nothing Pharisaic in the New Testament teaching. One is reminded of the Zealots, however, in John's account, not merely by his prophecy regarding the Roman rulers of the world but also by his judgment regarding gnosticism and Judaism.

God's rule and Israel's holiness that the Roman ruler demanded money from him, he did not see the true sanctuaries Israel should esteem and did not perceive whereby Israel broke faith with God and refused him what was his. Thus the Zealot, too, achieved merely another piety by which the individual fought for his desires, desiring to satisfy national egotism and to make God subservient to his own aspirations.

Once faithlessness toward God ceases, liberty toward the world has come. Jesus did not have to achieve freedom by the sword. He had it, since he had power over money and over all the things of the world and since he could use them with a clear conscience. Therefore he also could give to Caesar what he demanded. Since the Zealot did not give his love to God but remained enslaved by money, he ran into conflict with the emperor and got himself into the dilemma that drove him into revolution and demise. If the Zealot desired to obey God not merely by his words but in deed and to honor him alone as his master, Jesus likewise did not lead his followers to a faith without deeds that remained mere theory shattered by compromise with the existing circumstances. For God's rule drafted the individual entirely into service and made him the doer of God's will. But that kind of work by which Jesus brought faith to its truth and fruition was free from arrogance and was not a self-appointed, arbitrary service of God but rather served divine grace and righteousness. Therefore his service of God did not bring him into contention with anyone.

The Zealot, on the other hand, was hardened, like the Pharisee, by his own piety. While the Pharisee used the whip, the Zealot worked with the dagger. From his service of God Jesus gained complete patience that did not resist evil. Zealotism provided sufficient occasion for him to command his disciples nonresistance from the beginning. They had heard often enough that one's faithfulness toward God required that one not spare one's own life, particularly, however, that one destroyed the godless, and when the messianic idea moved the minds, Zealot ideals immediately reared their head. Since, however, Jesus, too, brought his disciples into complete and harsh opposition to their environment, he drew the final consequence, the requirement of martyrdom, no less decisively than the Zealots, who became famous by their immovable attitude in the face of death. For him, however, the condition for winning the victory lay in steering clear of hate, and his followers achieved such freedom from hate solely by that complete patience that is able to bear and to forgive everything.

Whoever is astonished by these pronouncements of Jesus misjudges the situation in which he found himself with his disciples. It required their readiness to patience and, with equal urgency, their deliverance from hate. Without these they were not protected from Zealot ideas. To begin with, there were among his listeners none who understood words such as "to lose one's soul" and "to take one's cross" better and seized it more readily than the Zealots. Martyrdom, however, remained for them a harsh, mysterious providence of God, to which the individual could merely yield. Jesus, on the other hand, by going to the cross as the Christ and by clinging to his kingly aim in his dying and by including in his commission, not the judgment of others, but his own death, thus revealing God's rule, separated his community entirely from Zealotism.

Other splits on the part of the community arose from the fact that, in contact with Oriental practices, sacramental methods of healing had developed. There were a number of such parties; the most famous were the Essenes. They distanced themselves from the Pharisaic movement, which championed as religion that the pious should do good works and procure the accomplishment of the Law. They looked for means to grant the individual a mysterious, magical, but nevertheless in their opinion real share in divinity, thus providing him with powers by which human nature would be transformed into immortality. This should also help him gain those insights that penetrated into the sphere of heavenly beings and powers and that provided a basis for dealing with them. It was especially the continually repeated bath that was used as a sacramental consecration. These thoughts resulted in "gnosis" in its many forms.

That Jesus never participated in such sects becomes apparent by the manner of his divine sonship, which did not have any gaps he sought to fill by holy things or physical consecration. He had the Father internally with him in his personal existence, and his communion with him was real since it was personal and spiritual, and therefore it was separate from the entire realm of magic. The longing that resorted to magic could also not arise among his followers, for they became God's sons by submitting to him with their love.

The sacramental groups lent content to their concept of God through concepts of nature in combination with the fact that they pursued the possession of "powers" as the aim of their efforts. This reveals that their concept of God entailed the sentiment of distance and separation from God. By sacred baths and an ascetic lifestyle the individual attempted to rise to the hidden, transcendent God. Religion was conceived of as a person's rising up to God. Merely the methods varied in these groups; the basic characteristic remained constant: an ascetic lifestyle or human self-effort led to one's transformation according to the divine order.

Jesus' message regarding God's rule represented a clearly developed contrast to these teachings. God did not act or exist in inapproachable distance and passivity but influenced history and created the community of those who knew him. It was not that the human being rose up to God but that God came to him. The individual did not work for God's grace but God gave it to him. This grace was granted by God's "call" rather than being won by magic. The community consisted of the guests who were invited to the feast. Their invitation gave them a share in God's gift. This constituted a clear contrast in the respective concepts of God continually maintained by Jesus, one that tolerated no intermingling of these theories.

Their stance toward Scripture differed as well. All of these groups were religious conglomerates combining Jewish and pagan elements. It is of subordinate importance where the foreign elements originated. This mixture did not consist merely of the fact that foreign ideas were attached to the concept of

God but showed itself with equal clarity in ethical norms. They always formulated some sort of an ethic of virtue that had as its goal the enhancement
of human powers. Jesus' piety was no religious medley but true to Scripture.
He was a Jew, nothing but a Jew, and was untouched by Hellenism even in
his ethical norms. The separatist tendencies found in those groups were also
entirely missing from him.

There is therefore no borrowing from Essene regulations in the establishment of his circle of disciples. Jesus did not require his disciples to take an
oath. He did not compose a manual of discipline for them, did not give them
any holy books of their own, did not prohibit them from going to the temple,
did not prescribe a particular religious practice for them, and did not equip
them with a particular method of sanctification. Echoes of what we learn regarding the Essenes in Josephus are found only in the moral sphere, since the
Essenes also were Jews. The points of contact between Jesus' ethical pronouncements and the moral of Pharisaism are, however, much more clear and
complete.

Nor are Jesus' sacraments, baptism and the Lord's Supper, patterned after
the gnostic movement. Regarding baptism, the Gospel records maintain of
the Baptist that he was a preacher of repentance and that he invested baptism
with clearly defined ethical ideas without, however, working with physical
concepts. Baptism was intended to bring about a person's conversion from sin
to God, and this was the way in which Jesus also gave it to his disciples. While
the change was significant that it was now given in Jesus' name in connection
with the Christ who had come, thereby no longer merely including hope but
faith, the act's basic form had not changed. Its relation to repentance and the
forgiveness of sins was not severed. Regarding the Lord's Supper, a relationship to the gnostic religions can be suspected only when the church's celebration of the Lord's Supper is cut off entirely from Jesus' own act. For Jesus' verdict regarding the basis and the fruit of his death had no relationship to
gnostic conceptions.

We do not find a special group of apocalypticists in the Jewish community.
What we now call "apocalyptic" was a branch of the haggada, the exegetical
science prevalent at the time. The material of apocalyptic originated from its
practice of interpreting, expanding, and systematizing prophecy according to
certain rules. To this end the writers put themselves into the place of the ancient prophet. That the authors of these treatises had visionary experiences
themselves is improbable owing to the concealment by which they hid behind
foreign prophets' names. A particular strand of piety cannot be detected in
these documents. They contain numerous parallels to the rabbinic tradition
where it deals with prophetic topics. They are inconsistent even where they
differ from one another, reflecting merely the ideas of their authors.

Whether Jesus read such "books of haggada," as the Palestinians called
them, or not is outside our scope of knowledge. One cannot consider it impossible that 1 Enoch was available in Nazareth as well and that the Jewish
community there also read portions from, for example, the Book of Jubilees.
Several indisputable facts prevent us, however, from finding in apocalyptic

books a similar or even greater source for Jesus' spiritual life than in Scripture, for his distance from Pharisaic expectation and his opposition to haggada transferred fully to the apocalypses. Jesus did not engage in an effort to synthesize of all future-referring ideas into a cohesive picture, and we do not have a single concrete parallel to individual statements in the apocalypses. Not one of Jesus' statements, for example, is reminiscent of 1 Enoch. Not even that sentence in Enoch based on Genesis 6 (the fall of angels) is reflected in Jesus' words. That signs are expected before the final revelation of God and that these would consist of great misery was no particular characteristic of apocalypses. This understanding was widespread in the Jewish community on the basis of the prophetic description of the Day of the Lord. Not one of the events that occurred in the apocalypses as signs of the final day was also named by Jesus. The apocalypses looked at the same time backward to past history and linked the final things with them to a uniform picture. Jesus' prophecy, on the other hand, was exclusively devoted to the present and demonstrated how the end would develop from it.[53]

The major issue occupying apocalyptic, that is, when God's rule would appear, Jesus fought earnestly in his disciples. He expected the emergence of a false prophecy whose characteristic would be the condensation of hope to self-appointed statements that promised the time of salvation at that time. The promise that the consummation would occur right then, however, is an essential mark of apocalyptic. When it is robbed of its anonymity and understood as a message brought courageously before the community, we have what Jesus rejected, rather than admired, as false prophecy. Likewise, the observation cannot be made that Jesus ever addressed a special group that allegedly possessed more religiosity than the great mass of people and that would be more receptive to God's rule. We always meet only one firm thought in him: that Israel is the chosen nation as well as the people who broke faith with God. We do not hear anything about a differentiation between a group that was blessed in a special way, a group that saw visions and received visits from angels, and ordinary pious people. The call to repentance is issued unconditionally to all, and only the Pharisees are singled out for special attention, because their decision determined the conduct of the Jewish community.

Jesus' consciousness of his calling provided the occasion for a particularly hard-fought struggle with the priests, since he rose with his kingly aim above the existing offices. If he was "more than the temple," he was completely higher than the priests whose holiness and service were tied to the temple. They were not, however, prepared to recognize his regal status. But since Jesus did not base his dealings with the Jewish community on his designation as the Christ but on his call to repentance, he did not clash particularly with the priesthood. His rejection of Pharisaism implies no common ground with the

---

53. In the same way that Jesus attributed to the community a uniform communal life extending from its beginning to its present that would produce its final, ripe fruit (Matt. 23:31, 35, 37), the entire community had the same thought. Pharisaism, too, conceived of Israel as a unity.

priesthood, although the ruling priests were Sadducees and were likewise engaged in a struggle with the Pharisees. Their objection to it, however, did not do away with the weakness addressed by Jesus since their piety strengthened selfish desires no less than Pharisaism did. Moreover, it incorporated a rational Greek element that distanced it from Jesus even more than the Pharisees. When the Sadducees saw in him the Pharisaic teaching on the resurrection and proved to him that it was inconceivable, he did not merely assert that he did not desire to make natural life eternal nor deny the common element uniting him with the Pharisees. He rather protected the teaching of the resurrection with Scripture, in fact precisely with their major portion of Scripture, the Pentateuch, just as a Pharisaic teacher would have done. The Sadducees' concept of God reduced to nature he called impoverished and their interpretation of Scripture bland (Matt. 22:29–32).

18. The Commissioning of the Twelve Messengers

When the reports coming from Galilee regarding Jesus' ministry moved the entire nation and when the masses crowded around him in Capernaum, Jesus led those who followed him into the Galilean mountains, and there he established the group of the Twelve. Mark alone narrates this as the result of those days. But Matthew, too, who began a summary of Jesus' message by the word he gave to his disciples, emphasizes as an important event the fact that the disciples distinguished themselves at that time from the rest of Jesus' listeners (Matt. 5:1; par. Mark 3:13–19).[54]

It is clearly visible that the men Jesus bound to himself appropriated his call to repentance with honest determination.[55] A clear proof for this is the fact that the concept of merit remains entirely separate from the report regarding their dealings with Jesus. It does not celebrate them as the heroes who participated in Jesus' work from the beginning and who remained faithful to him unto death, although the idea of the office he gave to the Twelve with their selection permeates the entire presentation and their service is praised in the highest language. They are distinguished in the Gospels from all other believers. The concept of office, however, remains entirely free from any self-centered use and is not grounded in the disciples' greatness but in the fact that Jesus made them his witnesses and gave them his word. The eradication of the concept of merit signifies, however, the entire acceptance of those norms that determined Jesus' call to repentance.

If the disciples had subsumed their self-consciousness under the concept of merit, they also would have celebrated Jesus as the great hero, and the pathos giving rise to the Gospels would have been their admiration for him. The Jewish community suggested this idea to them with a force that appears almost

54. Mark 3:13 derives from Matt. 5:1, and Mark 3:7–8 from Matt. 4:25. This was also Luke's judgment regarding the relationship of both texts since he combined the portion from Mark with the Sermon on the Mount (6:12–7:1).

55. This observation largely determines the historical judgment regarding the events by which Christianity came into being.

irresistible since it venerated all men of Scripture as heroes.[56] The Gospels, however, are clearly different in this regard; they grow out of faith, and the disciples saw clearly the internal difference between faith and admiration. For they portray Jesus' opposition to the admiration shown him, an opposition he expressed both in his verbal proclamation and in his signs (Mark 10:17, 18; Luke 11:27; John 7:15, 16).[57] How could Jesus create a circle of disciples that did not fawningly admire him? He clearly awakened strong feelings in the disciples. In Matthew, these are held back by the energy of a will that pours all its energies into ethical norms. In John, they are released more freely also into the full range of what he says. But the intensity of emotion that the memory of Jesus awakened in the disciples never rendered their narrative sentimental. Not one bit of it shows the disciples immersed into the sweetness of messianic hopes. The jubilant act of prayer recounted of Jesus pertained to the rejection of the wise! The depiction of the disciples as the friends of the bridegroom with whom he desired to celebrate his feast constituted the answer to an accusation that doubted his ethical sincerity. One is reminded of the report regarding Jesus' farewell—there are no tears—or of the entire crucifixion narrative. At the event where strong, overflowing love was expressed, the anointing of Jesus at Bethany, the disciples evidence an almost pathetic sobriety and are prepared to criticize sharply any sentimental expressions. This signified the determined departure from pleasure and the complete allegiance of desires to ethical aims, which shows how strongly Jesus' call to repentance lived in them (Matt. 11:25; 9:15; 26:8–9).

We possess a valuable witness to the disciples' way of thinking in the fact that Jesus, when asked to teach them a prayer that would distinguish them as a community, gave them the Lord's Prayer. By it Jesus considered his disciples capable of a will that elevated itself, free from all selfish desires, to the things by which God is glorified, to the holiness of God's name, the revelation of his rule, and the fulfillment of his will. He invested them with a strong sense of value, so that they asked for their lives to be preserved. But the complete renunciation of everything is included in this will that leaves behind any sensual desire. Repentance is awakened in them, and they stand before God as those who confess their sins. They do this, however, in prayer, believingly, in the confidence that God will forgive their sins and that any thought of penance by which they could atone for their own sins was excluded. Since they desired divine grace, they freed themselves from grudges and hate and were prepared to act toward others according to the rule of love. No arrogance attached itself to the consciousness of their special status; one detects rather the fear that testing still lay ahead of them, the fear that they will not be strong enough to resist temptation. They had a realistic stance toward the danger inherent in human life through its contact with evil, and this drove them to seek divine help. Since Jesus could expect his disciples to pray the Lord's Prayer, we know that

56. The Palestinian midrash, the archaeology of Josephus, Philo's portrayals of biblical history, and the entire apocalyptic literature agree in this.

57. If the disciples had celebrated Jesus as a hero, the crucifixion would have been inevitably conceived of as something tragic. This, however, did not happen; see p. 373.

his call to repentance had been received by them. The one who could pray it was converted.

The individual instances where the disciples are in conflict with Jesus' will also make an important contribution to the resolution of this issue. Since Jesus' word was one of repentance, we do not have any stories that praise the disciples but merely ones that judge what was sinful in them. What is revealed thereby, however, are not low desires. More than the conflicts that arose by the surprising course of Jesus' work,[58] more than his condemnation of Pharisaism and the way in which he did miracles and was ready for the cross, the disciples' objections that were directed against Jesus' ethic show their condition most tellingly, since they reveal how far their agreement with Jesus' word of repentance went.

Peter wanted to forgive much, but forgiveness still had to be limited. John did not understand the patience by which Jesus allowed himself to be chased away by the Samaritans. By their religious performance the disciples nurtured an elevated self-consciousness, and when they were outdone by others, they resented it. They were concerned regarding the weakness of their faith and saw in its greatness the condition for divine help. When bread was lacking, they considered this to be an important matter. When Jesus was occupied with children, they viewed this as an unnecessary preoccupation. They were startled by the idea of the indissolubility of marriage, and Jesus' verdict that called the rich unfit for God's rule moved them to the fearful question of who then would be able to be saved, since they did not yet see past human powerlessness to the omnipotence of divine grace (Matt. 18:21; Luke 9:54; Matt. 18:1; 19:27; Luke 22:24; Matt. 20:24; Luke 17:5; Matt. 16:7; 19:13, 10, 25).

None of these objections provides an occasion for surprise, even when we do not pay attention to the concrete context that tied them to the traditional ethics of that setting. Doubtless these portions were incorporated into the Gospel record for the purpose of revealing the profound contrast in which Jesus' will stood to the will of the disciples, and this purpose is superbly fulfilled. None of these doubts, however, was born from a low, unclean will. They rather originated from the unconditional love, humility, and faith Jesus desired and show that the disciples sincerely considered and obeyed Jesus' ideas and that they therefore perceived how far he stood above their own thoughts. This is also proved by Peter's denial that is completely unsuitable for denigrating the disciples. The way in which the unconditional truthfulness and obligation to confess is assumed even in the night of suffering and the fact that the concealment of discipleship exercised by Peter is judged to be sin shows how immovably Jesus' norms were anchored in the disciples.

Therefore it was with complete confidence that Jesus also gave them the promise by which he completed the call to repentance: they would experience God's rule, they had eternal life, their names were recorded in heaven, their entire guilt was forgiven and they were made God's slaves, they were granted

---

58. The disciples' scruples answered in Matthew 13 are considered in the discussion of the Sermon by the Lake. Regarding their objection to Jesus' readiness to the cross, see p. 290.

sonship with God, they were the called and chosen, they had attained the treasure that transcended all goods, they had complete joy, they were invited to God's meal and would celebrate the feast with Jesus as the friends of the bridegroom (Matt. 5:3–4; 7:21; 9:15; 13:44–46; 18:27; 19:14, 28; 20:1–2; 20–23; 22:14; Luke 10:20; 15:22–24).

This lent their allegiance to him a firmness that could not be compared with any other disciple relationship, since what they expected from him depended completely upon his own person. For his relationship with God—what God was for him and he for God—was intended to benefit them. Therefore person was here tied to person in life purpose and eternal aim, not in an isolated concern but eternally and completely. In other circles of disciples, the follower always departed again from the master when he had become equal to him, and when he persisted at his side piously until his death, his master's death constituted no major loss for him. After all, he had learned what the master had to give. In Jesus' approach to discipleship, on the other hand, he himself was what the disciples were looking for, and the reason for their fellowship with him consisted of what he himself had been given by God. Therefore the resulting ties were indissoluble. The one who came to him always followed him. Therefore the phrase "follow me" became at the same time the comprehensive commandment and the absolute promise by which everything was expressed that Jesus had to say and that the disciples had to do (Matt. 8:22; 9:9; 10:38; 16:24; 19:21, 27, 28; Mark 9:38). The love rooted in this fellowship took on the absolute manner of love for God.

According to the rule that entirely determined Jesus' fellowship with his disciples, he made their invitation to God's feast at the same time their call to serve. He used diverse images, some seemingly contradictory, to describe what they were to become through him. They were seeds and were at the same time harvesters, belonged to the flock and were simultaneously shepherds, received instruction and taught, would be judged and would judge Israel, needed forgiveness and forgave others (Matt. 13:1–9, 24–30; 9:37–38; John 4:35–38; Luke 12:32; John 10:1–12; 21:15; Matt. 13:52; 16:27; 19:28; 18:23–27; 16:19; 18:18). One symbol expressed their membership in the community, another their active participation in Jesus' work. The words designed for them were therefore never mere promises and never mere phrases of obligation but continually united promise with duty. He brought them the light in order that they themselves might be light and might let it shine and that they might be salt that salts others. He acted toward them like the father who told his son to go to work or like the one who hired day-laborers at the market. They were the shepherds he provided for the community. If the disciple refused to do his service, he would be thrown in jail (Matt. 5:16; 21:28–32; 20:1–16; 18:35; John 4:35–38; 10:1–11; 15:1–6). In this he did not see a lessening of the joy that was due them as the friends of the bridegroom, but rather their testing. For in his eyes, the service of God was not a burden or misery but glory and joy. They received rest by taking his yoke upon them. Those who waited for the beginning of the feast with burning lamps and those who were stewards of their master's talents did not represent different groups of discipleship. Neither images applied only at different times; both described jointly what membership in the circle of disciples always entailed (Matt. 11:28–30; 25:1–30).

Therefore the piety Jesus gave to his disciples did not merely consist of receiving or of working but of both, and this in such a way that one was conditioned by the other. Only by what the disciple received was he able to do his work, and only by doing his work did he possess what he received. Thus he acted according to the great commandment in the love of God that now received its content for him through his relationship with Jesus and through his obligation to serve. The firmness of the rule that the circle of disciples grounded its community in the work of ministry resulted not merely from Jesus' own aim that rendered the disciples indispensable for him but, no less urgently, from the concern for the pure, pious conduct of the disciples themselves. If they refused communion in ministry, their messianic hope inevitably fell into selfish and arrogant corruption. It was accompanied by the same temptation that had arisen for the righteous from their own righteousness by which they fell. Since they approached him with the prospects of the highest goods and honors as those who were chosen before all others, they, too, were in danger of committing robbery of God by desiring God's gift merely for their own happiness, of admiring themselves in the greatness of their own work, of subjecting others to themselves and of receiving, apparently in their zeal for God's justice, the satisfaction of vengeance. The greater the grace granted to them, the more despicable and corrupt their conduct would become if they strengthened by it their selfish will (Luke 12:47). The means by which Jesus protected them did not consist of laming their will, either by weakening their hope for God's glory or by weakening their zeal for God's Law (Matt. 20:22–23). He rather stretched both to the uttermost but protected them by bringing the word of repentance to a clear expression in them. Belonging to God's rule meant to depart from evil, and this entailed that they direct their desire for God's gifts at the same time decisively toward their service and that they understand the feast prepared for them in terms of their obligation for ministry.

He thereby transformed his disciples' piety into a striving for an aim that they still had before them. By granting them possession of eternal boon through his promise, he did not transfer them into a state of rest that merely enjoyed and gave thanks. He rather placed both pronouncements, the one that gave them the eternal gift and the one that transformed it into an aim for which they strove, side by side. God had put them in his kingdom, and they had to seek it. They were his sons and had to become his sons by obeying God's love. They had received eternal life and had to pass through the gate that would lead to life. They had received forgiveness and were to ask for it and to do what would procure it for them. Since they did what he required from the rich young ruler, they were complete and were to watch and pray in order not to fall (Matt. 13:11, 52; 16:19 and 5:20; 6:33; Luke 13:24; Matt. 19:29; John 3:16 and Matt. 7:14; Matt. 17:26; Luke 15:11 with Matt. 5:45; Matt. 18:27 and 6:12; Matt. 19:21 and 26:41).[59]

The aim was not still in the future merely because the disciples were confronted with external obstacles they had to overcome. Those were admittedly serious in Jesus' judgment. Much seed wasted away through the scorching sun of persecution and was choked by the thorns of sinful lust. But Jesus grounded the striving he awakened in the disciples even more deeply, not merely by an external impetus but directly from God's gift, not merely by what they still lacked but by what they were granted, not merely by their inadequacy and weakness but by their completeness and strength. What is the value of a piece of property one does not need, of salt that is tasteless, or of light when it does not shine? What is a talent when it is not used for the acquisition of more talents, or a branch that does not bear fruit (Matt. 13:12; 5:13–16; 25:27–29; John 15:2)? From the internal wealth of the gift granted to them arose their calling, for it embodied a richness that was revealed and effective only by their work. Jesus' thought took this direction because he never conceived of man as an isolated being but always as a part of the community, and with connection to it stemmed immediately the call to work. The salt-starved earth waited for the disciples; the world deprived of light needed them to shine theirs; and by imparting God's gifts to others and by fulfilling his will with respect to them, they completed their own goal. They gained life for themselves by performing together with Jesus the work of the harvesters (John 4:36).

The disciples could evade their calling and fall. Since Jesus saw in love the will that was good, he could judge no differently. For by Jesus' awakening of love in his disciples, their nature had not been changed but the ethical struggle had been made their abiding task. Since they were thus not merely placed in contrast to the world but also had to deny their own will, the possibility remained that they would fall, and alongside the certainty given them by Jesus' promise stepped uncertainty, and alongside faith stepped fear. From the beginning, Jesus vehemently resisted the idea that entrance into discipleship by itself would already grant salvation. Not every seed bears fruit, and weeds grow in the field as well. The fishnet catches all kinds of things. Faithful and faithless servants serve him; foolish and wise guests are invited; the salt can be tasteless, the light concealed; and the disciples who receive forgiveness can nevertheless end up in jail.

Moreover, since the gift received by the disciples was greater than that received by others, their debt, too, will be greater than others' debts. When expressing such warnings with great sincerity, however, he did not expect these warnings to weaken the disciples' allegiance to him, nor that they would cool their love and shake their confidence. For a disciple had not even been impacted by his call to repentance if he failed to understand that Jesus could not depart from God for the sake of the disciples. Doing God's will was his first priority and love for God his first commandment. Therefore every disciple

---

59. The Gospel records are confirmed by the Epistles. For the piety of the early Christians is based on the simultaneous validity of both truths: that salvation has been achieved and results in a perfected state of trust; and that salvation constitutes the aim toward which one's entire energy must be directed.

understood that Jesus would reject him when he rejected God's will, because Jesus did not deny the Father on account of men and did not obey the sinful desire of the disciple. Thereby he did not, however, lessen the love he gave to them; he rather perfected it.

By confronting them with the possibility of their fall Jesus did not cast doubt on their conversion to God, nor did he render their allegiance to him worthless. Since God's genuine and complete grace granted them their call, they were placed into a firm and effective union with him that entailed complete victory over evil. Therefore their conversion was not merely a wish or an attempt but led them to their goal. From now on God's regal work was at work for them.[60]

How did Jesus equip his disciples for service? The means by which he facilitated their work consisted merely of the free and continual access he granted them. The accounts know nothing of a formal preparation for their work, any more than they imply that Jesus used some "method" of conversion. Therefore we do not hear anything of lessons, of sentences he had them memorize, of religious activities he drilled them in, or any other methods. He saw their vocational ability merely and completely in their piety, in giving them for themselves their closeness to God. As he did not ground his own relationship to God in material things, there also was nothing of this kind that equipped them for their ministry. God's work was not done by artificial means. From looking to God Jesus acquired complete freedom from anxiety. He let the disciples grow as the branch grows on the vine. He also could not enable them to work together with him merely by sharing his thoughts with them. The use of the name "disciple" for their communion with him does not prove that he intended to give them nothing but instruction. Of course they should learn from him, but not merely insights; they rather were to learn how to obey God. His influence on them was directed toward the entire person, not merely toward their cognition but also toward their will.

Jesus placed only few into this personal fellowship with him, and thereby the establishment of discipleship was unambiguously separated from the foundation of the messianic community. He did not begin by forming a new community out of those who accepted his word but saw his vocation in the wooing work upon Israel that would lead to repentance. Since he accused it of making religious fellowship the seduction to untruthfulness and to the perversion of desire that turned away from God to the social position of the individual, he did not bring those who followed him into a relationship with one another that was visible and close, thus helping them to develop that internal focus that rendered them free toward the Jewish community and turned them to God alone. The gathering of the perfected community he expected from his revelation in glory. When God's rule came, it would unite with him the chosen ones from all the earth (Matt. 24:31).

---

60. The early Christians, likewise, connected the confidence that the ethical question was now solved, with the never-ending ethical struggle, thus preserving the position Jesus had given his disciples.

In order to bring his word to Israel, he separated from his followers a closed circle of twelve men, thus giving their service the characteristic of an office.[61] How he combined their office with his own, he expressed by calling them his "messengers" (Matt. 10:2, 5, 16; Mark 3:14; Luke 6:13).[62] Their vocation thus consisted of bringing his word to Israel. Their number looked back to Israel's old constitution while simultaneously looking forward to the final form of the messianic community (Matt. 19:28). The twelve messengers were designed for the entire nation of Israel, for all of its tribes, and the fruit of their labor will be the complete, new Israel instead of the present small and scattered community. Rules that ordered the relationship of the Twelve to the other disciples were unnecessary in Jesus' view. As he conceived of honor, rule, and office, no legislation was necessary to secure the preeminence of those who had been chosen or to protect other believers from them. Such rules become indispensable only when the office is conceived of selfishly and is therefore directed against the community. Jesus saw the privilege of the office given by him in the increased service and its power in the greatness of its performance, and this performance, in turn, was based upon the gift he granted them.

Among the Twelve he gave preeminence to Peter, thus confirming the promise by which he had accepted him. Therefore the Gospel record names Peter almost exclusively insofar as details of Jesus' dealings with the disciples are reported. He demonstrated his will to all by being understood by Peter. We would, however, have to distance ourselves from the facts regarding Jesus' history in order to link with Peter's preeminence a selfishly framed idea of authority by which he was exempt from all of Jesus' norms. Jesus did not assign to anyone an office that did not have its law in love, that hindered the work of others, and that incapacitated the community. By placing Peter above the others, he intended to strengthen the disciples' and the community's unity. There was one God, one Christ, and one community (Matt. 23:8–10). It was part of this thought that he also gave to one the apostolate with special preeminence.

At the same time he extended his special friendship to John. The data John provides regarding his relationship to Jesus show that his privilege lay in a different direction than that of Peter. The services this particular disciple was able to perform for Jesus personally, by which he proved his loyalty and love, resulted in the special treatment of John while Peter's privilege arose from Jesus entrusting to him the care for his community.[63]

---

61. An "office" develops when individuals are authorized to perform those functions that are indispensable to the foundation and preservation of the community.

62. The designation "apostle" has the same unadorned plainness that characterized all of Jesus' actions. The indication of John 13:16 that the name and the function of an apostle were as familiar to Jews as that of a slave is amply confirmed by Jewish literature. One preferably used an authorized representative in one's dealings with others and called him "apostle." The administration of public and religious affairs likewise required the sending of trusted "messengers" in a variety of ways.

63. Jesus entrusted his mother to John and his community to Peter. John's participation in the ejection of the betrayer and in Peter's denial conveys the same sentiment (John 13:23–29; 18:15–16; 19:25–27).

Since Jesus did not subject the disciples to his commandment merely externally, he did not treat them all in the same way but suited his word to their situation. It made a deep impression on the disciples' memory that his dealings with Peter differed from the way in which he treated James and John. The stories where Peter is featured as taking action, such as his effort to bring Jesus back to Capernaum, his sinking into the lake, his objection to Jesus' liberty on the issue of purity, his contradiction of Jesus' decision to go to his death, his conduct at the transfiguration and at the collection of the temple tax, his objection to the comprehensiveness of forgiveness, his question regarding the reward of the disciples, his astonishment over the power of Jesus' curse, his contradiction against Jesus' self-humbling, his sleep and sword stroke in Gethsemane, and especially his denial in the night of suffering, all these incidents portray how the disciple learned to believe in Jesus and to obey him by overcoming his own human ideas and wishes (Mark 1:36; Matt. 14:28; 15:15; 16:22; 17:4, 24; 19:27; Mark 11:21; John 13:6; Matt. 26:40, 58).

These stories resemble the narratives where the two brothers are the ones who act, where we see their desire to destroy the Samaritan village that had refused hospitality to Jesus, their request for Jesus to let them participate in his judgment before all others by giving them the two thrones next to him, and John's prohibition against the one who believed in Jesus' power over the spirits but who did not follow him (Luke 9:54; Matt. 20:20; Mark 9:38). Their love toward Jesus exceeded its usual boundaries. While the Gospels demonstrate by Peter's example how Jesus overcame the kind of doubt and lovelessness that arose from human ways of thought, they use James and John to portray how he protected their new ideas, their hope and love for him, against selfish desires based on their own initiative and prematurely demanding the judgment and coming glory.

When he gave the office to the Twelve, Jesus gave priority to the promise over his commandment and provided it with universal greatness. For he promised God's regal activity to all who lacked divine help. Now God began to work for them and gave them his eternal gifts because they needed them. He thereby freed the calling of his messengers from any sectarian limitation. God's rule comprised all the poor, suffering, merciful, pure, and righteous, and so it also extended to the office he gave them. This did not, of course, free them from poverty, shame, and death. But they were called to joyful suffering, since it did not jeopardize but rather substantiated their possession of divine grace.[64] Their suffering arose from the service they owed to humanity, since they did not receive what Jesus gave to them merely for themselves but for the world. Therefore it was their holy duty to make what they received effective for others.

This was not, however, followed by any presentation of their special office, neither of the assignment of particular religious mandates nor the command to evangelistic work. For it was not by official acts of the disciples that God's

---

64. The idea contained in Matt. 5:11–12 powerfully expresses that form of the Beatitudes found in Luke.

present action in regal glory upon man was revealed but by the disappearance of all that put the individual to shame and that divided the community. Wrath and injustice had come to an end as well as the desire that dishonored the woman, lying, arguing, and hate, ambition that corrupted worship, greed, anxiety, and the condemnation of others. For his disciples had as their characteristic that they had turned away from all evil and that they had been brought to pure, complete love. They could not do justice to their calling by singular, particular functions; they fulfilled it by acting in love. For God's kingdom was revealed by the emergence of that community that was united in complete love.

Against the manner in which Jesus conferred on love the status of completeness it is often objected that it effects the setting aside of law without which the selflessness of love must lead to self-destruction.[65] This verdict, however, receives its force only by cutting off the love commandment from Jesus' call to repentance. If we forget his pronouncement that gives over to judgment that person who is angry with his brother and vilifies him, and overlook the verdict that denies fellowship to the one who persists in injustice, treating him like a tax-collector or Gentile, limitless patience does indeed produce lawlessness. Love is thereby robbed of its ethical aim. It has become indifferent toward good and evil and thus has been softened.

Ethical norms, however, had inviolable validity for Jesus and were therefore assumed to be valid and effective in every demonstration of love. His love called for justice and proved its truth and completeness not by breaking but by achieving justice, thus creating communion and serving the well-being of others. Jesus rejected the Jewish community's traditional use of the lex talionis not because he hated the law but because he hated injustice. The law of retribution did indeed lawfully curtail that thirst for injustice which trampled others underfoot in retaliation for injustice suffered. But it simultaneously used the Law as a weapon against the one who attacked it. It wanted to destroy him through the Law, refused to exercise forbearance, resorted to the Law to justify the struggle against the one who violated it, and refused to forgive him. This resulted in a Law that was perverted into injustice. Jesus did not allow his disciples this self-serving use of the Law that transformed it into a means to harm one's neighbor. Nor did he attribute such an understanding of the Law to God.

By liberating love from this alleged obligation, he ordered his disciples' dealings with others in such a way that it corresponded to their relationship with God based upon the freedom and the completeness of divine grace. As they should conceive of God's attitude toward them as limitless and free from the obligation to retaliate, they also should exercise patience and goodwill in their dealings with others, corresponding to the perfection of their heavenly Father. By this was also assured that their conduct would never favor the

---

65. The question regarding "law" arises concerning Jesus' words merely when law is understood to be the sum of those volitional norms that are assigned absolute validity so that they function as ethical concepts. If law is considered to be the way by which we arrange our dealings with each other, Jesus did not speak of law at all, just as he did not talk about "culture."

breaking of the Law but rather overcome and prevent it. If they could not prevent lawbreaking in others, they could at least honor the Law themselves. They exercised forbearance in the assurance that their right lay in God's hands, that it was protected by him, and that he also placed individuals in the service of his execution of justice. Therefore Jesus stood before his disciples as the one who was not merely called to forgive but also to judge. He commanded them as well not merely to release but also to bind and to conduct the struggle against offensive behavior, not merely by overcoming their own passion but also by assuring uprightness in their dealings with one another (Matt. 18:6, 8 along with 5:29). The condition for this was entirely that love regulate one's actions. Without this, according to Jesus, there was no justice, no overcoming of evil, and no creation of community.

Right alongside the disciples' unity with one another, and with Israel in complete love, Jesus placed the separation that not only divided them from the old community but also produced in their own midst the contrast between genuine and false piety. They cannot join the crowd; their path is the narrow one. It requires from them the courage to stand alone. They also have to be on guard against false prophets, and false disciples will appear that Jesus will judge, since they simultaneously glorify him and break God's Law. Jesus' listeners can be divided into wise and foolish ones, and only those are wise who do his word.

Thus the idea is destroyed immediately at the establishment of the office of "disciple" that entrance into discipleship was by itself the possession of salvation, that it was already achieved by one's separation from Judaism. Both theses, that there was no salvation outside of the disciples and that there was no corruption within the same, are rejected, the former by the Beatitudes that promise God's help to all who need it, the latter by the conclusion that threatens judgment to all who do not obey God's will. Therefore Jesus did not express the disciples' separation from the synagogue by an external structure, nor did he sketch out a constitution for his community nor create any external characteristics for Christianity.[66] What caused the fall of the old community brought death also for the disciples if they did not separate themselves internally from it by treating basic ethical questions differently.

Therefore any faith directed toward Jesus is immediately depreciated which frees itself from ethical norms, and the illusion is destroyed that the possession of Jesus' word by itself is already gain. It becomes gain when acted upon. But he did not thereby put his disciples in a condition of fear and uncertainty; he rather gave them courage that was sure of its goal. If they must separate from the crowd and their path becomes narrow, this will not result in any wavering, for thus they obtain life. They are not defenselessly handed over to temptation, since every tree is known by its fruit, and Jesus' word grants his listeners a firm position and secure protection as they do it. Jesus did, however, from the be-

---

66. The only initiative toward the establishment of a particular Christian custom contained in Jesus' extant discourse is the Lord's Prayer, and it has nothing in common with sectarian undertakings but rather destroys them at the very root.

ginning prevent the disciples' separation from the old community from turning into religious skirmishes or Christian fanaticism. By calling his disciples to complete obedience consisting of pure love, he made it impossible for them to boast of their religious possession, to despise others, and to fight over preeminence regarding communities and religions.

Because it stands independently beside that given by Matthew, the form of the discourse preserved by Luke provides a second important testimony for the way in which the disciples understood and applied the Sermon on the Mount.[67] In this form Jesus' contradiction against the things that were created by the Law in the Jewish community does not immediately become visible. Luke did not portray Jesus at the occasion of his calling of the Twelve as a fighter who condemned the Jews and who liberated the disciples from the prevailing form of piety but merely repeated the positive conclusion by which Jesus' instruction ended: the description of perfect love to which Jesus' call obliged the disciples and in which their community should have its characteristic feature. Reflection on the later condition of Christianity had influence on this version of the discourse. At the same time, however, ideas become effective that determine the discourse also in Matthew and that can be considered characteristic of Jesus. It is maintained that Jesus made the positive yield of repentance, that is, the new will that obeys God, the major emphasis. Therefore the discourse does not dwell on what Jesus judges to be sin but on what he said about the disciples' love. Likewise, the early Christian community maintains that it was not Jesus' intention to make the disciples polemicists against Judaism. For he did not conduct his struggle with it as an end in itself but in order that God's will might be fulfilled and that that kind of community might develop that loved sincerely rather than arguing, and that had in view the greatness of its own task without, however, boasting of its religious preeminence.

By the manner in which Luke connected the love commandment with the parallels to the conclusion of the discourse in Matthew, he also expressed strongly that Jesus' love commandment told the disciples how they should fulfill their vocational and teaching obligation. In this version Jesus' pronouncements are reminiscent of the responsibility attached to the disciples' service and of the danger of failure accompanying it. They awaken the community's concern for love and how it should exercise its service correctly. Any idea of a religious technique that could have its effect independently of the ethical, personal character of the disciple remains rejected. The condition for his effectiveness consists of the fact that he has within himself the treasure from which he can give the good gift to others. Therefore it is based entirely on his doing of Jesus' word.

With jubilant confidence Jesus attacked human nature in this discourse. Since he rejected evil not merely in its public result but also in its secret beginnings, every disciple understood that Jesus did not address merely isolated problems that arise and pass in history. With each of these words he sought

---

67. Only beginning with Luke 6:39 are connections to Matthew's text likely.

to remove wrath or grant women complete protection or reject inadequate patience and halfhearted love or separate all pretense from piety or reject striving for wealth and anxiety. He fought against natural human instincts and placed every disciple in a persistent struggle against himself. He did not give to his disciples phrases depicting the blameworthy condition of man, since his word never merely served a theoretical, theological aim. He reminded them, however, that the "heart" produced what dishonored the individual, and that this ability did not reside merely in some hearts but in every heart. He also reminded them of the fact that man's sin originated from the fact that he was of "flesh and blood," wherefore help did not arise for him from what "the flesh" produced or performed but from God alone (Matt. 15:19; 16:17; John 3:6; 6:63).

Not only nature, however, but also people's sharing of a common life lent to the passion Jesus rejected its general spread and its irresistible nature. Therefore Jesus freed the disciples from what "the ancients" had been told, to whom every Jew looked up with highest respect as to the generation counted worthy of divine revelation. Thereby he reminded others of the power by which history moves individuals and how it gives a common will not merely to those who live together as a community at a given time but also to the resulting generations of the nation as they merge into a unified whole. Therefore Jesus did not consider the guilt of those who lived in his day merely to be the product of their own will but at the same time the result of Israel's earlier guilt. In his depiction of the vinegrowers he viewed what happened to him in relation to what had happened to the prophets, not merely from the perspective that similar things repeated themselves, but by using a causal concept that what happened then was rooted in what had happened earlier. The sons, he said, complete the sins of their fathers, so that all the innocent blood shed on earth gathers into a collective guilt (Matt. 21:33–41; 23:32, 35, 37). For he viewed the individual human being as a member of the world (*olam*, κόσμος: Matt. 18:7; cf. 16:26; αἰών: Matt. 13:22; Luke 16:8; 20:34; cf. the concept of "world" in John).

Therefore Jesus' commandment was intelligible only for those who saw its religious foundation, its connection with God's rule. Otherwise the objection could not be rejected that Jesus demanded the impossible when he struggled against human nature and when he resisted what history had produced. How could he nevertheless hope and demand for evil to end and link this hope with the simple actions with which he connected it: our forgiveness, help, and love by which we do good to one another? Everyone who had merely man's being and will power in view declared Jesus' commandment to be impossible to fulfill. But Jesus proclaimed God's rule, by which God would act upon man as redeemer, perfecting him toward eternal life. From this arose the promise always included in the word of repentance that presented freedom from evil to man as something attainable and as an assured aim. God will rule over those very persons, whose hearts produce evil thoughts, in such a way that his will will be done to and through them, on earth as it is in heaven.

Only by the fact that Jesus did not, when issuing his commandment, think only of what the human will was capable, arose the comprehensive terms "conversion," "forgiveness," or "justification." For human ability produces merely broken results and limited achievements, because we find in ourselves competing wills. Jesus, however, saw in conversion by which the individual withdrew and separated his will from his evil the emergence of God's communion with the repentant person. It therefore constituted the return of the lost sheep to the flock, the renewed entrance of the prodigal into the father's house, the reception of the justifying verdict of God by the guilty and the resurrection of the dead to eternal life (Luke 15:6–7; 18:14; 15:24; John 5:24). Therefore Jesus applied the term "perfect," by which Judaism described the aim of its ethical striving, to his disciples.[68] If the rich man forsook his wealth and entered into Jesus' discipleship, he would be perfect, and the disciples were perfect since they exercised complete patience, forgiveness, and love (Matt. 19:21; 5:48). The struggle with their own nature did not prevent them from placing their entire will into obedience, and above the perfection of their conduct stood for Jesus the perfection of divine love. This love confirmed the disciples' allegiance to Jesus and secured for them their aim.

By not permitting his disciples to doubt whether or not his commandment prohibiting natural desire could be fulfilled, he effected his confidence in God that conceived of God always as present also in them. That ill-will has natural reasons did not move him to denigrate nature. He judged man's will, not the nature that helps man also to goodness. Jesus called it natural for the father to be good to the child who made request (Matt. 7:11) and for the brother to rejoice in the return of his errant sibling. God, however, is close to man not merely through nature but also in his internal life.

The sons who live in the father's house are able to serve him. Jesus thus ascribed to man a mixed condition that arises from the fact that even the sinful human being does not fall from God's hand or lose entirely the connection with God's good will. Jesus did not further address the issue of the will, as little as he determined the sources of light from which human insights originate. His commandment approached the disciples with the confidence that each could use his will to subject it to God's will. What helped him was not that he understood how his will came to be but that he used it to obey, and Jesus helped him do this by making the regally active divine grace available to the disciple through communion with him.

Therefore Jesus also maintained the categorization of people into righteous and unrighteous, good and evil individuals. He separated them like good and bad trees, of which the former can only produce good fruit and the latter only bad. One has within himself a good treasure and draws his word from it, the other one has an evil treasure and draws from it (Matt. 5:45; 7:17–18; 12:33–35). How these pronouncements can be reconciled with the radical judg-

---

68. In synagogue usage, the term "perfection" did not pertain to the measure of power but to the relationship to the divine norm. The perfectly just or the perfectly godless were those whose ethical conduct increased to the full measure and aim, whether to perfect agreement with God's will or to complete opposition to it.

ments of those who pursue evil to the extent that it intermingles with our nature remains unintelligible when we do not keep in mind Jesus' concept of God as the ground of all his ethical judgments. His assurance of God did not permit him to render his ethical norms merely an ideal or requirement. They are one with God's will, which is the real power that already determines a person's existence and even more that of the disciple. Therefore there are good people. For the good God is present and rules, and through him a person is good and entirely separated from evil and thus also from those who are evil. No inconsistency was thereby introduced, however, into the call to repentance; Jesus did not address it merely to individuals who were especially guilty rather than to all. For he located the disciple's goodness in his persistent obedience rather than in a natural condition existing in him apart from his own will. To this end the disciple must distance himself from his own will, deny himself, lead the struggle against what was offensive, and remain alert. Since Jesus' word called him to this struggle and enabled him in it, he received with it God's gift that made him perfect.

19. The Disciples' Partnership with Jesus

Already at the time when Jesus directed the call of God to the Galileans, he also sent out his disciples. The first whom he put in his service in such a way were the Twelve. Thereby the disciples powerfully expressed their complete submission to Jesus by speaking merely of the fact that Jesus had sent them (Matt. 10:7; Mark 6:12 merely supplements the older account). The early church was told nothing more about their experience or achievements, since they considered the basis of their authority and ministry to be solely that they had received their commission from him. Their confidence that knew itself authorized to word and sign was not based on their own success.

Jesus thus was able to transfer his selfless kind of love, which does not seek its own advantage, to the disciples. Just as he did not place himself beside the Father or prepare for himself an honor of his own beside that of the Father, the disciples likewise learned not to place themselves beside Jesus nor to seek an honor other than that they did Jesus' will. Therefore the disciple disappeared from the gospel. The disciples' communion with Jesus found expression in the fact that they appeared as his messengers and that they were not ashamed of him. Jesus attached their eternal destiny to whether they acknowledged or denied him. He did not, however, make it their profession to bawl out his name as the Christ or to gather the nation around him in order that it should pay homage to him. His aim regarding the commission of his disciples remained the same as with his own word: the nation's view should be turned upward to God and to the ultimate goal. From this resulted the call to repentance.[69]

To that call he added the authorization to help, particularly for those who felt hounded or controlled by spirits. Thereby his name found public acknowledgment, since the disciples grounded their commands to the spirits in the name of Jesus (Mark 9:38; Matt. 7:22). But he deflected all further speculations from their work and made it correspond to his by making it their aim merely to show the people the great decision they had to make in order that everyone would know that he had access to God's rule. The discourse does not address the question of what will happen to those who prepared themselves for it or how the disciples were to instruct believers, establish communities, or reform worship or custom. Neither did they receive the mandate or instruction to gather a community. Just as Jesus placed himself within the existing community and had his aim in providing for it what it had been promised with God's kingdom, he ordered the work of his disciples. Therefore the rule also applied to them by which he limited his own work exclusively to Israel. He did not even visit the Jewish communities of the Diaspora that were very numerous in the neighboring Greek cities (Matt. 10:5; cf. Luke 10:1).

He made a major aspect of their office as messengers the refusal of remuneration. As he did, they found generous arms extended toward them that eagerly offered them rich gifts, because they awakened by their promise of the kingdom profound loyalty and gratitude in those who received it. And if anyone doubted whether or not the share in God's rule might move a Jew to put his financial resources at his disciples' disposal, the miraculous sign easily had this effect. Man expresses gratitude when saved from sickness or insanity. Already in the Sermon on the Mount the rule not to gather treasures on earth applied first of all to his messengers, who had to undertake the greatest work without seeking any profit for themselves because they were not to have their motivation in financial rewards that would corrupt their work.

This rule was expressly affirmed for their travels in his service. Since they came without provisions of their own and since they would leave as poor as they had come, they were not open to the suspicion that they proclaimed God's rule for the sake of profit. By doing their work free of charge, they would confirm the call to repentance that exhorted Israel to convert from money to God. These rules, likewise, arose from Jesus' struggle against the false love of man. He did not thereby describe poverty as the perfect state, by which they had the guarantee of eternal life. For he did not assume that those who received these rules would forsake their possessions. He rather expected that they had possessions and that they would give to the disciples what they needed.

If we were to interpret these pronouncements from an ascetic point of view, Jesus would create by them the class of those who practiced complete renunciation. They would be superior to those who exercised the incomplete piety of laymen. This thought, however, would contradict the assured absolute version of the call to repentance that prohibited for all everything that Jesus called sin. These rules, on the other hand, can be integrated seamlessly into the universally valid call to repentance, since the disciples showed to all

---

69. Matt. 10:7; Mark 6:12 mentions the call to repentance explicitly. Matthew merely speaks of the proclamation of God's rule. For that proclamation tells Israel what it could not discover by itself and had to be told until God's rule arrived. Nevertheless, Matthew could expect us to understand from what had gone before to what end the testimony of the approaching revelation of God had to move the listener.

by the selflessness of their own complete renunciation how they should be concerned with what is God's and how they should put their love rendered to God above all that their possessions meant to them. By not having or desiring anything, the disciple prepares those who receive him to renounce their own possessions and to give to others. Israel's conversion had been rendered impossible if the disciple, too, had sought financial gain rather than proving to be free from earthly longings so that the love directed toward God determined his entire work purely and victoriously. He was not thereby put into an unnatural situation nor made dependent on begging or continued miracles of provision. He rather was to receive his daily necessities from those to whom he came by Jesus' commission, not as a gift of mercy but according to the rule of righteousness.

The renunciation required by Jesus of his disciples extended farther still. Not merely were Jesus' followers not to use their service for the acquisition of wealth, they were to yield their very lives.[70] The disciples' collaboration with him entailed fellowship in sufferings and struggles. He entirely excluded the calculation of success from their work and thus separated them from any compulsion by which they might have compelled people's conversion. Their task was merely that faithfulness which was able to die. If Israel did not listen to them, this did not free them from the obligation to tell it of the great things God was doing. Precisely because Israel was headed for a great fall, their sending was necessary so that Israel knew what it was doing.

But the obligation of "bearing one's cross" and of a total renunciation of worldly gain, happiness, and life, did not mean that the disciples' sending happened in vain, nor that it merely served the purpose of divine judgment by revealing and fulfilling Israel's guilt. There were also homes and communities that received them, so that they brought to them God's peace, and they brought the one who received their word into an effective connection with Christ and with God. He was received when they were received, and the good deed rendered to them, even the smallest one, would receive its reward. With their fellowship in suffering, Jesus simultaneously gave them their share in his religious power. Thereby he invested their work with the confidence that they should not merely promise or describe the eternal good to people but that they should grant it to them.

Jesus considered the disciples' internal separation from Israel to be accomplished. They stood freely before the Jewish community, no longer intimidated by Pharisaism and the rabbinate, religiously separated from Israel and tied exclusively to Jesus. Therefore he spoke with them merely about those kinds of temptations that resulted from natural passions, from the desire for wealth, and from concern for their livelihood. Since these always remained dangerous for them, Jesus created the gripping phrases "to deny oneself" and "to take up one's cross" for the new will he gave to them (Matt. 16:24; 10:38;

---

70. For the connection between his words regarding martyrdom and the sending of the disciples in Matthew, cf. Luke 10:3. The texts know nothing of an oscillation in Jesus' mood so that he sought to effect people's conversion at that time by a violent assault.

Luke 14:27). By these he described a person's complete and permanent turning away from his own self and from those around him, by which he became foreign to himself and to others. He no longer listened to human ideas and wishes but was able to act contrary to himself and others, similar to the one who is condemned to die and who sets out on the road to his own death by taking up his cross, whereby he frees himself from all the world holds for him.

Even then, Jesus did not provide them with theoretical, dogmatic equipment for their work or make their topic the christological motif, even though the disciples were confronted with religious theories in dealing with the people that led to all kinds of objections, and even though they now had to be able to provide information regarding his aim and legitimacy and regarding the basis for their discipleship. But even then all theoretical new constructs remained entirely taboo. The disciples did not receive for their task a doctrine they must proclaim to the community.[71] It rather had to be clear to them that the question they awakened in people had its answer not in concepts or discussions but merely in the facts by which God's activity was revealed to the listener. God did not make his kingdom known in words or phrases but by providing repentance for the individual's sin and help for his abject need.

Only from this conception of his aim resulted the necessity for Jesus to equate his disciples immediately with those who take up their crosses and sacrifice their lives. If, in commissioning his disciples to issue the call to repentance, he had had in mind an ethical theory describing human or Jewish sin, it would not have been necessary to equip them immediately with the kind of courage that was prepared to die. But because Jesus lent absolute sincerity to his call to repentance even in the mouth of his messengers, rendering it a deed and therefore also producing the deed, be it obedience or renunciation, he freed them from the start from any aversion to suffering and from the concern for their own livelihood. He collapsed the present and the final realities into a single perspective in the way in which he thought about God's rule and promised to end their difficult struggle by his return. If he had not had his aim in God's kingdom, his promise given to his disciples regarding their work would not have been possible. They had the religious authority and ability to turn man toward God, because their work was not based upon thoughts and words but on God's rule.

While Jesus entirely set aside the didactic aim, he required their complete attention for the ethical uprightness of their conduct. At their commissioning, as already during the Sermon on the Mount, the disciples felt deeply how sincerely Jesus' concern was directed toward the fact that they not sin in their work, so that they would not be corrupted themselves but keep the faith, and that they would fear God, not men, proving to Jesus their entire love that sacrificed everything for his sake.

The ethical danger into which they were placed by their suffering is weighed with great sobriety, and the motives that would strengthen them to

---

71. Those thinking in Greek categories were therefore never satisfied with the content of the commissioning discourse.

overcome are developed carefully. In their suffering they experience the same thing he does. They should remember the judicial majesty of God, who reveals every mystery and whose judgment will destroy their lives completely. At the same time, they should keep in mind the protection given to them by his constant presence and understand clearly that their closeness to Jesus depended on their faithfulness since he would reject them if they gave up their work by being reluctant to suffer. That they respond correctly was considered to be the indispensable condition for the administration of their office.

Thereby the question regarding their own share in the kingdom and the question regarding the performance of their service are completely united. Thus Jesus rendered it impossible for their commission to be linked with a proud consciousness of their office and for their suffering to be tied to an excited happiness in martyrdom. Nevertheless, he did not give them over to doubt and despair but with the fear of God gave them faith that received powerful strength and steadfastness by the contrast between their destiny and their message.

With the ethic formulated in this discourse Jesus' followers went into the Jewish villages, soberly and free from sentimentality, dogmatism, and fanaticism, and at the same time fearlessly, separated from all selfish aspirations, and borne along by the conviction that they performed a service from which eternal life resulted for themselves and for their listeners. While we should remember that the Evangelist, too, becomes visible by this shaping of reminiscences in a tendency directed toward ethos and practice, this insight is abused when it is used to cast doubt on the historical value of his data. Matthew presented Jesus from the viewpoint of his religious possession but he presented him rather than himself, and him by what the community had received from him. In its personally shaped version, the discourse also reveals the direction and strength of Jesus' impact upon the disciples in a peculiar way. It shows how completely he elevated them above a merely scribal way of thought and how he turned their concern to their faithfulness, which he confirmed by liberating them from all other desires through their complete association with him.

The sending out of the Twelve is often used as a proof for the fact that Jesus placed his dealings with the disciples under a "pedagogical" perspective.[72] The phrase "education" can be applied to him since he had love as his rule and since it frees others by helping them to gain strength and to be active on their own, thus drawing their measure and aim from their need and ability. The formation of the Gospels clearly reveals the relationship Jesus established between his word and the internal history his disciples experienced in their communion with him.

This communion is the basis of the sequence of the discourses into which Matthew arranged Jesus' word. The Sermon on the Mount precedes the discourse at the occasion of their commission, because the disciple must know

---

72. Our school system lent the idea convincing power. Moreover, the tradition that Jesus from the start combined the disciples' possession of salvation with the obligation to service renders the observation more difficult.

Jesus' will before he can serve him as messenger to the people, and only when they have served him does he show them how God regally reveals himself upon them and through them. Only then does he testify to them about his end, since he revealed to them first of all the glory of God's grace in what they experienced before he asked them to follow him all the way to death. Then he also provided them with the rules by which he made their communion pure and fruitful, and with the hope that was able to wait for him.

A similar viewpoint livens up the Johannine account. For John, the disciples' union with Jesus is that work by which he performs his task. John begins by telling how that union came about. Jesus' separation from Judaism results in the fact that the disciples alone are his possession, and only through the words of farewell is expressed what unites them with him forever. But the movement in Jesus' word was not dependent merely upon the disciples' development but also upon Jesus' own relationship to God. It was not only for the disciples' sake that he did not make the future clear to them until the time for decision was right. He was prevented from this also for his own sake since he was bound to God's guidance by obedience and patience.

The understanding that he sent out his disciples also in order that experience would school their eye, so that insight would develop from their actions, therefore does not inject into the process any aspect that is foreign to the disciples. The discourse connected with their commission shows the insight about which Jesus assumed above all that it would be mediated to them through their work: the insight into the necessity of his cross. Now they themselves entered into the struggle with Israel's refusal to repent and experienced how the wolves dealt with the lamb. By taking up their cross they also learned why he bore his. But the guiding aim in their commission was not the gain the disciples themselves would derive from their work, just as he himself sought nothing for himself. He did not consider his disciples' ministry to be one of the activities that are rendered successful by the development of intellectual or technical skills. For in Jesus' view one does not learn telling the community God's message and acting in God's name by education. As he had called the disciples for the sake of the people, he also sent them out for the sake of the people in order that God's rule would be proclaimed to it by all possible means.

20. The Answer to John the Baptist's Inquiry

John the Baptist's ministry was ended by a violent act of the king, who had received from Augustus not merely Galilee but also the area east of the Jordan that was occupied by the Jews. Because he condemned the king's marriage to Herodias—who had left her former husband in order to become the wife of a ruling Herodian—in the name of the divine judgment that rejects adultery as sin, John disappeared in the jail of Macharus, the fortress beyond the Dead Sea. From his imprisonment he intervened once more effectively in Jesus' history by requesting from him a clarification of his messianic commission

(Matt. 11:2–6). By his answer to John's request Jesus clarified his own position, and this also was an important event for Jesus' own disciples.[73]

The Baptist's request did not derail Jesus nor did it move him to change his course of action. He did not consider it part of his calling to save the Baptist nor to attempt to free him, perhaps by intervening with the king. He expected John, as he did his disciples, "to take up his cross." Likewise, he was not shaken by the Baptist's doubts regarding whether or not God's power would intervene for him in the way necessary for the vindication of his kingly aim. After all, God's power was revealed, since he was able to help those who needed help in the service of almighty grace. He thanked God for the work he had given him and left no room for discontent or craving for a greater role. He did not reproach God for holding back or for failing to reveal his power and grace. For what God worked through him would, in his judgment, provide a firm basis for belief both for the Baptist and for everyone else.

This procedure clearly reveals the significance his ability to help had for him. His commission could not be substantiated merely by the insight and the richness of his word. He needed the assurance that "the Father was at work" and that he acted as the Giver of all help. Therefore the miracle was inextricably linked to his consciousness of office, and, in his view, this was so great and clear that any doubt in his commission amounted to sin. The same conviction was expressed by his answer to those who demanded a miracle from him. The divine activity was as obvious and clear as the signs indicating the weather (Matt. 16:3; Luke 12:54).

This new clarification of his ministry was linked with the developments leading up to that point into the unity of a clearly recognizable will. As in Nazareth, he based his legitimacy on the fact that he could help. He did not demand anything for himself, nothing but faith. Therefore he also avoided the designation "Christ." Just as he praised his word as God's gift in Nazareth, he saw even there proof for his own calling in the fact that he made the poor rich through his word. He was the Christ, because he was the evangelist ("good news bearer"), and his works revealed that he performed this task by God's commission. He did not yield his liberty to anyone, not even to the Baptist. No one told him what to do. He also never permitted the disciples to ask him a trying question. They were not to ask him, "Are you the Christ?" He asked them whether or not they thought he was, and thereby their confession of him became pure (Matt. 16:15; cf. John 10:24–25).

The gravity of the decision by which he rejected the Baptist's request moved him as well. He revealed this to all by giving the promise to those who did not take offense at him. Since he wanted to prove his regal status merely by helping, and since he was determined not to invoke God's judicial authority against the king but rather expected the Baptist to perform his final service, since the path of renunciation and humiliation had for him the necessity of God's will, the danger arose for the others that he would become for them the

---

73. Therefore this event becomes a part of the Gospel tradition, not out of a polemical tendency against the Baptist, even less for the purpose of nurturing secret doubts regarding Jesus.

occasion for sin and the reason for their fall. When God's power intervened for him merely by helping the poor and suffering rather than by protecting his messengers and by shattering their opponents, the Jewish community turned away from him. The Baptist's wavering showed how serious the danger of offense was for all. The words of praise Jesus spoke at that time regarding him exclude that he suspected in him a sensual, selfish desire. Where such a desire is present, however, offense occurs. Then the seed is choked by the heat of the sun and by thistles. Even then, however, Jesus looked at the Baptist, who called him the greatest of all and saw God's wisdom performing its work by his ministry, with gratitude. But even the greatest was in danger of sinning against God on account of Jesus.

What brought about the offense? No one was as equipped as the Baptist to understand Jesus' call to repentance and his way to the cross. For he, too, had wrestled with the nation's sin and now faced death in his struggle with the brood of vipers. He, too, had asked for God's forgiveness for the people and had seen the greatness of his own office in the fact that he could promise forgiveness to the nation. Nevertheless, he was seized by the anxiety that Jesus might be humbling himself to such an extent that the kingly aim was unattainable for him.[74] Why? Power and judgment, John was sure, were indispensable characteristics of the Promised One.

When the Baptist confronted the king with his sin, he also had acted as the forerunner of the Anointed One in order to save the king from Christ's judgment and to make ready the Jewish community for him since it was barred from repentance when the powerful sinned with impunity. If the Christ for whom John did his work and yielded his life now nevertheless was allowing him to perish, this supplied ample material for doubt in human thinking whether Jesus in his limitless patience would grant the community what it needed or not since, after all, evil appeared to be victorious. Who should still believe, who should still stand up for God's Law and commandment, who should still reject sin, when the Christ remained silent? Only because he recognized him to be the Lamb of God was he still able to maintain the thought that Jesus could be the Christ. But did he take away sin? Was this still that forgiveness which overcomes it rather than that which is weakness? The call to repentance disintegrates when it is separated from judgment, and forgiveness degenerates into deception when it is unable to destroy evil.

The certainty with which the promise was given enhanced the possibility of offense. From the beginning of his work the Baptist possessed the promise that he would see the Christ and his kingdom. Now his time was over, and he still had not yet seen him in his victory. He could no longer wait. Could God's promise fail? Did Jesus, by failing to reveal himself, refuse John what he was entitled to see on the basis of God's promise? He did not ask him for a powerful deed or his own liberation but merely for the word that would attest to his calling, merely for the regal name that would reveal him as the fulfillment of the promise. He would believe him when he spoke it. He knew that God

74. He had already expressed something similar at Jesus' baptism (Matt. 3:14).

had given him his Spirit without measure. But if he did not speak it, the danger of offense was acute. This danger arose from Jesus' calmness that expected everything from God and did nothing for himself.

The Baptist had contact with his own disciples even while in prison, and he saw in them how the blow dealt him shattered their confidence in God. They could not believe in the one whom he had proclaimed to them as the Promised One: Was it merely their own fault? Could anyone believe in him when he remained silent? How could someone be the Christ who concealed himself from Israel?

According to Jesus' verdict, the possibility of offense arose from the greatest thing he had, the completeness of his faith and love. It arose from the fact that he let God speak for himself rather than speaking of himself and that he merely wanted to help and to give. Since he could not allow this to happen, he became the ruler by enduring, the overcomer of evil by suffering. Therefore the possibility of offense could not be eliminated. But above the gravity of this pronouncement he placed the comfort that the one who overcame this offense would be blessed. He thereby gave to the promise the most expansive conceivable application. It belonged to anyone who did not find in him an occasion to sin and did not enter into dispute with God for his sake. The turning away of offense admittedly had its positive prerequisite in God's work being recognized in him, and in God being given thanks and being believed for his sake. Thus Jesus united a solemn expression of his regal status with a moment of most profound renunciation.

It is impossible to understand this event as the first contact between John and Jesus, as if John's query might have had the intention of winning Jesus for the messianic idea against which he may have rebelled. It need not be argued further that this is not the thrust of the texts. But even if we look at this portion in isolation, it does not tolerate this interpretation. For Jesus' warning against offense is as little an encouragement for initial faith as when Jesus told his disciples that they would fall on account of his cross (Matt. 26:31). Even by pointing to the divine power that was visible in his actions, he did not provide confirmation for a fledgling faith but reached out his hand to the one who was wavering. Since John was mystified by Jesus' silence and tolerance, he was to consider that God's power was revealed in his activity in such a way that it helped those who were in dire need. By having and using power to help rather than to judge, he offered those who saw and heard it no ground for offense. Admittedly this also paved his way to the cross.

The thought, the sign that the Baptist had received, and the great words by which he had described Jesus' commission rendered wavering impossible for him, so that one account destroys the other if one does not know the doubt but merely the denial. Genuine doubt, in contrast to rejection, presupposes faith, which the Baptist expressed even in that moment by being determined to give him the messianic designation even now at Jesus' own word. The faith thus extended to Jesus by the Baptist needed a reason. His offense at Jesus was entirely substantiated by the events and does not have the smallest obscurity to it. Weighty and subject to explanation was merely the Baptist's readiness to place Israel's entire destiny into Jesus' hand even now, if he would now merely declare that he was called to bear their trust. John's faith was based on what he had experienced earlier. We know, however, from rich experience that there is no faith that is entirely safe from doubt since, when facts and faith appear to contradict each other, facts have the power to overpower human judgment and to shake the affirmation based upon previous experience. The very fact that the Baptist knew Jesus as the Christ shook his faith, since he now had to connect the absolute messianic aim with Jesus' self-imposed limitation of serving the needy.

While Jesus did nothing for himself but let God alone speak for himself, he testified to the Baptist's greatness and confronted the Jewish community with what it had received from him and had rejected by rejecting him.[75] He thereby maintained the call to repentance as the solely possible and completely sufficient preparation for God's rule. Jesus did not derive any reproach against the Baptist from the fact that his work was not crowned with a success that it could and should have accomplished. The connection between his calling and the dawning of God's rule did not become doubtful for him owing to his disappearance in jail. Even less does one hear a reproach against God's rule. That the Baptist, and with him Jesus, too, had to work in vain and must be ready to die, resulted from the impenitence of the nation, from its childish behavior that criticized and thus marginalized God's messengers, even though his grace granted them the greatest thing they could receive. According to Jesus' verdict, the nation's impenitence arose not from the fact that his works were too small. Rather it was precisely his works that occasioned the great guilt of those who enjoyed his presence. Likewise, he did not witness to his own calling. While he did not pronounce the name of Christ, he praised his own sonship of God in all its glory. The fact that he was gentle and humble and that he did not counter people's evil with his own power to rule authorized him to call all those to himself for whom obedience toward God's will had become a strenuous task and a pressing burden and to give them rest (Matt. 11:7–30).

By refusing to use the name "Christ" to those who demanded it from him and by simultaneously testifying to his divine sonship in its completeness and uniqueness he did not act arbitrarily. By his sonship he expressed what God was for him, and this conviction was for him above any confusion or denial. Confessing the Father he considered to be his public duty. To this end it was necessary for his hearers to fulfill the condition of understanding, because they also had a consciousness of God in their own measure and were thus able to judge what was divine and what was not, whether he spoke from himself or came from the Father. If they had no eye for this, they thereby revealed their own godlessness. The substantiation for the requirement with which he confronted them by the name of Christ, on the other hand, was provided only when they discerned his divine sonship. His relationship to the world, as he determined it by the messianic idea, was the secondary and derived relationship, unable to come to expression and unformulated as long as his connec-

75. The event is entirely parallel to the Johannine account of Jesus' beginnings. At that time Jesus remained silent, and the Baptist testified regarding him. Now that the Baptist was virtually silenced, Jesus testified to the Baptist's commission, but not to himself.

tion with God was disputed. At the same time it transcended the present because of the eschatological significance of the Christ concept. That he had in God the basis and the giver of his entire existence, however, was what was present to him and what he experienced, what he was allowed to testify and to defend against those who failed to recognize God's work.

Even the way in which the Baptist suffered death became an effective part of the history of Jesus and of his disciples. Since the king had given orders for his death at a feast after the princess had made him pliable by the attractions of his dancing daughter, it was clear that the Baptist died on account of his denunciation of sin in the execution of the call to repentance. It was not the significance of this event that it awakened Jesus or his disciples from a daydream by the collapse of selfish hopes. In their readiness to suffer, however, they never looked merely to man or to princes, priests, or the nation, but they were turned toward God, asking what he would do, and now his will emerged clearly that the messengers of his rule, the preachers of his gospel, would meet death. For Jesus' disciples, the Baptist's end was a serious test, but thereby also an effective demonstration of their faith. When Jesus could soon thereafter expect them to follow him to Jerusalem without the prophecy of his death scattering them, the fate of the Baptist bore fruit also in this course of events.

21. Interpreting God's Work

A discourse Jesus gave at the Sea of Galilee about God's rule possessed timeless importance for the disciples since he provided them thereby with an understanding of his aim (Matt. 13:1–52). It brought to light his own determinative convictions: God's rule occurred through the word; it now stood with evil in an inevitable, irresolvable conflict; it revealed itself in small and hidden events; it required complete renunciation and entire devotion; it issued a call to all without damaging the execution of justice. None of these affirmations was new. They rather were the foundation upon which Jesus' entire work was based. Jesus always revealed his religious estimation of the word, an estimation that united God's call with closeness to him. And he always placed the obligation to repent also upon the disciples, destroying the confidence that presumed to have the guarantee of salvation already at the entrance into discipleship.[76] A love for detail that perceived God's glory in small things had always been a characteristic

---

76. The oft-assailed parable of the wheat and the tares likewise expresses a thought that is strongly attested to originate in Jesus. If the notion is removed from him that separation was to take place even among his disciples, the Sermon on the Mount, the commissioning discourse, and the addresses to his disciples in Matthew 18 and 24 need to be thoroughly reworked. Also, it would be necessary to remove from his parables the foolish listener, the merciless servant, the complaining ones who were first, the man without a festive robe, the faithless steward, the foolish guests, and the lazy servant. Only ignorance of Jesus' situation can excuse the verdict that these portraits were occasioned only at a later point. The pronouncement that all of Israel had a part in God's kingdom immediately produced the other pronouncement: if not all of Israel, then at any rate all of Jesus' disciples! Jesus had ample reason to contradict this notion. The limitation of this parable to church discipline is incorrect for the same reason that it is inaccurate to limit the parable of the treasure and the pearl to Mammon or that of the fishing net to the Gentile question..

of Jesus. With equal insistence he allowed God's rule to issue in the claim that desired from man his entire love with its ability to renounce everything. He always freed the call from all conditions and at the same time inviolably put in place the rule of righteousness. The parable of the seed that grew without the farmer's aid likewise expressed a truth consistently represented by Jesus. In his proclamation of God's rule he did not establish restlessness and impatience but faith that waited with confidence for God's work (Mark 4:26–29).

Nevertheless, he revealed by these parables "the mysteries of God's rule" (Matt. 13:11). For in those teachings of Jesus originated the scruples and objections that troubled even the disciples. When he saw in the word the means by which God granted his eternal and complete gifts, could the word reveal God's rule, overcome men's resistance, and produce the pure community? When Jesus put his whole love into the small work and forsook every effort at greatness, how could the consummation of the world come out of these small events? And could God's glorious revelation be present when renunciation and loss of life followed from it? When Jesus directed his call to all and rejected for himself the work of judgment, how could God's rule be present before the judgment occurred? And was justice not jeopardized when grace was extended to all? And how did the obligation to faith and patience originate from God's rule, which produced what was perfect?

The objections Jesus answered here show how internal and how profound the disciples' unity with him already was at this point. Their scruples arose from the fact that what happened and became visible at that point stood in contrast to the absolute content of the promise. He, too, saw in this the mystery of divine government. In order to illustrate the connection and unity he developed his similes. The word has opponents, he conceded, which may overcome it, like the seed is overcome. Nevertheless, the sower is able to bring in a harvest. Good and evil also coexist in his community, just as weeds can be sown in the field. Nevertheless, the pure community is developing. What he does is inconspicuous like the sowing of a mustard seed or the mixing of leaven with flour. Nevertheless, great things are being accomplished. In order to gain the treasure and the pearl one has to sell everything. Nevertheless, they result in incomparable gain. The catch of fish happens without discrimination. Nevertheless, separation occurs. What stood in strict unity with Jesus' other discourses was that these, too, had nothing to do with abstract concepts but were solely directed toward what now had to happen through Jesus and the disciples. How his work related to his kingly aim and bore within itself the glory of divine government, so that the consummation would arise from it, this the parables depicted. All of these things he made believable and imaginable for the disciples through the analogies he used.

That Jesus had already separated his disciples entirely from popular expectations is not visible merely by the fact that they understood him but already by the fact that these questions were found in them. What is here felt and explained as a mystery of God's activity does not lie where the apocalypticists sought it. Jesus did not provide them with a gnostic description of theophany nor an explanation of how God would reveal himself in his glory or how he would change the world and create conditions of life for those who lived eternally. Any sensual shaping of future images in order to stimulate imagination or even thought was excluded. The discourse presupposes that the disciples believed that complete grace and the eternal gift would be granted through Jesus' ministry. Therefore they were burdened by the contrast between what appeared externally and what happened internally, what occurred at that time and what would one day be true, and they considered any idea that alleviated this tension to be an improvement. Since Jesus did not derive this contrast from a physical necessity but from the struggle of human nature against God's rule, the opposition to the Jewish mood that considered God's omnipotence to be necessary merely for the establishment of the heavenly kingdom was intensified. The disciples, on the other hand, understood how Jesus' commandment and warning resulted from his kingly aim and how the ethical dimension of his ministry was tied to God's grace and rule.

The discourse created an even greater rift between Jesus and the nation, not merely through its content, which Jesus had always spoken of openly, but also by his refusal to interpret the parables for his audience. The manner in which he shaped and used them was in complete agreement with custom and created an entirely suitable means for the understanding of his word. In Jesus' view, his procedure did not deviate from what the other teachers did. When a rabbi told a parable, he always stated the event he explained by the analogy he created. Most Jewish parables were created for the purpose of interpreting Scripture. The interpreter added to what it said regarding God's conduct the comparison, "What does this matter resemble? A human king who dealt with his people in such a way or a human father who dealt with his son in such a way." Thereby the relationship between the picture and the matter always remained clear.

In Jesus' view, his parables functioned the same way. After all, he told his listener where the answer lay if he sought the parable's interpretation—that it explained to him God's rule. Jesus was not talking about irrelevant things but about what happened at that time, not about unknown things but about what his hearers themselves experienced. This, however, was only the case in Jesus' perspective, and he did not forget this when he told the parables to them. One part of his audience saw nothing of God's regal activity. The truths Jesus explained to them were not present for them, and for those who saw nothing of God's present exercise of his rule the parables remained empty and meaningless. They received merely the image that clarified what was portrayed for the one who personally had eyes to see it.

Jesus' procedure had nothing to do with secrecy or allegorizing deeper meaning. Jesus maintained the thesis that every good parable interpreted itself. Thus he refused to interpret the parables for his larger audience and provided an interpretation for the disciples merely as remedial lessons in order to instruct them to understand his pictures by themselves. For the person who was unable to do this the parable did not exist. It was transparent only for those who saw what Jesus called God's rule in the present events. Only polemically did one speak of a desire to be intelligent or of gnostic mysteries that were to provide the initiated with the privilege of special insight. Jesus' images interpreted themselves immediately piece by piece once it was recognized of what he spoke. Another reason he did not interpret them himself was because he did not believe he could show someone God's rule merely by words. The listener's experience had to come first. For only then did the concept have its place and value. The one upon whom God's grace did its work had in the word the gift by which he understood what happened to him.

Thereby he brought the form by which he showed the community God's rule into connection with his calling as a judge. He could not merely give but also had to forsake, and the latter was his duty no less than the former, as also the prophet had not been sent to open Israel's eyes but to close them. Had he thought of the mysteries of God's rule in terms of the apocalypticists, the seriousness with which he treated the themes they discussed would admittedly have been absurd. But that seriousness makes perfect sense in light of the sole subject of the discourse: how Jesus created eternal results despite being opposed and concealed.

Precisely the nature of God's rule that he illumined by his parables hindered him from showing it to all. If he had been able to do this, he would no longer have been the one who merely planted a mustard seed in the garden, and the treasure would not have been hidden or be available only at the highest cost. It would also no longer have been possible to extend a calling to everyone; the act of judgment would have had to happen immediately. There would also have been no barren ground, no heat of the sun, and no thistles by which the seed was choked. Jesus did not avoid the struggle he depicted in the parables, as if he stood in contradiction to his own commission. This was rather the way in which God revealed his glory.

Jesus' refusal to interpret his speech clashed hard with the Jewish community's desire, since it waited eagerly for the revelation of God's rule once told that it was about to begin. The desire to find out how God's kingdom would be revealed became strong when Jesus' ministry was in some way related to the messianic aim. By refusing this desire, in that he divided the listeners into those who saw God's activity and those who did not, Jesus did not separate the preaching of the kingdom from the rule of love, as little as by the other words and deeds that praised and executed the divine judicial office.

Whoever sees the root for this shaping of the kingdom preaching in Jesus' hostility toward the Jewish community follows suspicions of his own making. Jesus' preaching admittedly did reveal his sincere conviction that the entire nation would be seized and shattered by God's judging activity. This, however, is amply explained by the aim and the result of his call to repentance. Only novels have room for poetic inspirations of Jesus by which he might have depicted the blessedness and beauty of heaven for a delighted crowd. Even then he subjected the execution of justice to God's grace. For he did not stand before the community merely as the one who took but first of all as the one who gave. He gave "to those who had." That God's rule would make known the glory of his complete grace he expressed precisely in this kind of speech as his firm conviction, since it said that what God did with the Jewish community at that time would lead it to the highest aim and grant it eternal good. And he acted graciously also by refusing to use violent means of working the crowd. Open discussion would only have created hostility. If his listeners had understood what he meant by the sower and the pearl, the end of the kingdom preaching would have consisted of dispute, blasphemy, and an assault upon his life. By using parables, he softened controversy, spared his listeners bitterness, and prolonged the time given to him and to them.

At the same time, this procedure provided the disciples with an understanding of the reserve with which Jesus spoke about his kingly office, since the attestation of his regal status fell necessarily under the same rule to which he knew himself tied when he spoke of God's kingdom. If he had shown God's rule unconditionally to all, this would have meant that he also would have praised his own messianic office before all in bright publicity. For the visible kingdom and the revealed Christ are identical. If the community was capable of seeing God's rule, it was also able to receive the Christ. If Jesus, however, had to retreat into hiding, this had the result that the proclamation of the kingdom was not understandable for all. For whoever did not see the presence of the Promised One also did not see the presence of God's kingdom. By showing God's rule only to those to whom it was given and by concealing it from those who did not see, Jesus made clear why he did not openly announce his regal office before the community at large.

Jesus' Way to the Cross

1. The Judgment of the Jewish Community

Since Jesus' offer of repentance required action, there inevitably came a time when the Jewish community either removed or retained its evil will and Jesus either granted it forgiveness or pronounced its judgment. He therefore saw the execution of justice not merely as coming in the future but placed it in the same way into the present as the granting of forgiveness to those who returned to God. What happened was not merely calling but also rejection, not merely illumination but also blinding (Matt. 9:13; 11:25; 13:11; John 3:18, 19; 9:39). Since he called the nation to God's grace as the one who forgave, he did nothing to protect himself or to overcome his opponents by force. But he condemned the rejection of his word as the loss of the kingdom and handed the unrepentant over to death since he considered the execution of judgment to be part of the Father's work and thus also of his regal office.

In view of the benefits granted by reconciliation with God and of the destruction resulting from judgment, the condemning verdict became an immeasurably difficult act. It was the verdict of death for the entirety of the Jewish community and for all who were affected by its sin. The barren fig tree was cut down, and the temple was destroyed, when Jesus was not permitted to purify it (Luke 13:6–9; Matt. 21:19; John 2:19; Matt. 24:2; 23:38; Luke 19:41–44; 23:28–31).

One could expect his word to become increasingly the depiction of the punishment that the divine wrath would bring upon the guilty. But he never replaced the verdict by which ill-will was rejected and overcome by the deliberation on its destructive consequences. The scribe, in order to turn from his lovelessness, had to be able to see by the example of the priest and the Samaritan what mercy and mercilessness were. Jesus did not add any elaboration of heavenly bliss or hellish misery. Those who nourished their pride by their prayer were admittedly to consider that they would not re-

ceive any reward. But the expectation was presented to them unambiguously that they should understand that love was pure only when it was selfless and that their eying of honor before men corrupted their entire worship.
While he told Nicodemus that death or redemption was at issue, he demanded for him to realize at the same time that truth deserved obedience
because it was truth. Since he did not seek to avoid the impending doom by
depicting the terrors of judgment, he did not develop the concepts portraying the end of the individual sinner and of the sinful world beyond their traditional form (Gehenna: Matt. 5:22, 29; 10:28; 18:9; 23:15, 33; fiery fur-
nace: 13:42, 50; eternal fire: 18:8; 25:41; darkness: 8:12; 22:13; 25:30;
prison: 5:25; 18:34).

Already before Jesus' time, the term "Gehenna," the name of the deep val-
ley at the foot of the temple mountain where the worship of Moloch was carried out, had been applied to God's judgment, in contrast to Zion. This designation was first linked eschatologically with the theophany near and in
Jerusalem. Later it was separated from eschatology as a designation of that
place of judgment where death would lead the godless. At what level the concept was present in Jesus' words cannot be determined with certainty. His
statement that the entire person, not merely his spirit, but spirit and body
with all its members, would perish in Gehenna is reminiscent of the eschatological version. The living or risen ones who appear before the judge suffer
their punishment in Gehenna, body and soul.

The torture experienced by the rich man after his death, on the other
hand, is not considered to be a judgment in Gehenna. He suffers this punishment at the place of the dead, Hades. Nevertheless, this passage shows
that Jesus connected the corruption arising from evil not merely with the
eschatological event but already with the soul's departure from the body.
Moreover, even when the concept has an eschatological flavor, the geographical dimension has notably retreated into the background. Otherwise
the locality of his return would also be depicted with Jesus' second coming
occurring in Jerusalem or on the Mount of Olives. Since this emphasis is
entirely missing, it appears assured that he also did not tie the judgment to
the place near Jerusalem.

Following the prophetic words, he named fire as a means of judgment.
But here, too, we do not receive positive teachings or extensive depictions.
The idea that the fires of judgment would destroy those who were handed
over to them is implied when he contrasted the attempt to justify oneself
with the body's corruption, with all its members that had been nurtured and
cultivated by sin, and when he compared the death perpetrated by man with
that death which also faced the soul in Gehenna and thus entirely destroyed
the guilty. The final statement in Matthew, on the other hand, reminds one
of an ongoing punishment, since there fire is prepared, not merely for
human beings, but also for the devil and his angels, and since the punishment is called eternal in complete contrast to eternal life (Matt. 5:29; 10:28;
25:41, 46).

In his report regarding what Jesus called the consequences and the punishment of sin, John emphasized from the various images and phrases that portrayed the tragic end of human life merely the thought of death that is used interchangeably with the equivalent phrases "corruption" or "perishing." By this, however, John did not use a dualistic psychology that referred the term "death" merely to the corruption of the body while considering the possibility of an independent existence of the soul. He rather thought of the human being as a unity.

According to John, what dies on account of sin and suffers the loss of life is the human being itself. Since, however, he promises the believer complete liberation from death even though the believer, likewise, would suffer the corruption of the body, Jesus turned attention away from the physical side of the process, considering someone's death or life to be solely what was prepared for the person inwardly. Since the execution of justice already extended into the present and was completed on the day of judgment, Jesus lent the idea of death, just like his statements regarding life and God's rule, at the same time a relation to a person's present condition and to his future destiny (John 3:16; 6:49–50; 8:51; 11:25; Matt. 8:22; Luke 15:24).

As difficult as the negative judgment became in view of the death it brought to a person, it is nevertheless completely certain that Jesus pronounced it over the Jewish community. When he had the conviction that Capernaum and the adjacent villages to whom he had given his word with particular richness and who had been touched by each of his actions directly would not change their conduct, he responded to their impenitence with condemnation, whereby Israel's end was sealed.

For he did not reject Capernaum with the thought that its conduct was an exception and that the success of the call to repentance was more favorable in other places. The particular gravity Capernaum's guilt had in his eyes resulted from the fact that he had granted it divine grace particularly clearly and richly. Therefore Jesus' judgment pertained to "this generation," and for this reason Jesus said that the path to life was found only by few, and those who had been called previously were not also those who had been chosen (Matt. 11:20–24; 12:41, 42, 45; 8:12; 21:41; 22:8, 14; 7:13–14; Luke 13:24–27).

In this verdict he possessed the certainty that his own commission would lead him to the cross. He did not stand on the sidelines when he spoke the verdict of death regarding the nation but remained close to it even when it died. He kept himself pure from the selfish hardness that assigned corruption to the guilty while separating himself from them. He was the first who subjected himself to the consequences resulting from Israel's fall. Up to that point he had demanded that it should decide for God. From this requirement grew the demand directed toward himself that he should present his life to God. By going to death, he proved that he did not separate himself from the people of God when they fell and that he did not deny the good news when it assigned him the cross.

This did not result in any wavering on the part of Jesus. John said that Jesus directed his view toward the cross in his entire ministry, although he placed the announcement of Jesus' death at the same time as Matthew.[1] The picture Matthew gives us of Jesus' ministry does not differ significantly from this. For the Sermon on the Mount begins immediately with the disciples' preparation for suffering and with the mandate of ministry to the world. They are lonely, and their path is narrow. They need to protect themselves against false prophets by their own insight, and there develops in their circle room for a false Christianity that retains for itself a Christian facade by its confession and its works that will be destroyed only at the second coming. The commissioning discourse places the disciples in a struggle with unbelieving Israel that demands martyrdom from them, whose end will only come through the second coming. The portrayal of God's rule clearly places an extended period of time between the present, where that rule occurs through the word and where it remains hidden and requires renunciation, and the revelation of its glory.

In the discussion of the disciples' exemption from fasting that belongs to Capernaum, Jesus distinguished between two periods in the disciples' lives: the time of celebration in the bridegroom's presence and the time of fasting when he would be taken away. For himself, however, he already connected the preview of its end with the first festive time and hinted, to the surprise of the pious whom he gave the impression of carelessness, that he bore a burden and that he placed it upon his followers who did not suspect its gravity (Matt. 9:15). But what that event consisted in that would take away the bridegroom, he did not already depict at that time, nor did he base the disciples' communion with him from the beginning on the proclamation of his end. This agrees with the fact that reference to his death regularly occurred when he was asked to show a sign to justify his authority (Matt. 12:39; 16:1; John 2:18–19; 6:51).

Therefore Jesus' beginnings—his baptism, his withdrawal to Galilee, the Sermon on the Mount, and the selection of the Twelve—are as quiet and unassuming as his cross, and his final actions—the farewell from his disciples, the Last Supper, the statements before his judges—are as certain of God and of his power as his first steps. Whoever wants to divide Jesus' words and actions into two groups, optimistic at first, pessimistic in the final period, does so as a poet. Not a single sentence has come down to us that would necessitate apologetic efforts to reconcile a saying of Jesus with his will to the cross. By linking the offer of the kingdom with the call to repentance, he made his readiness to suffer the basis for his entire work, without which the struggle against the error of the nation would be inconceivable.

This struggle endangered his life from the beginning, and beside the call to repentance stood from the beginning the question where it would all lead. If the nation resisted him, Jesus claimed, righteousness would be accomplished!

---

1. The discourse in Jerusalem (chap. 5) does not yet contain it. It occurs in Capernaum after the feeding in the desert, and the older account places it at this time. After leaving Galilee, Jesus speaks about his death also in Jerusalem. The use of the brazen serpent to explain how Jesus would effect the faith that was now denied him and how he would make it the ground of life (3:14) is doubtless based on the idea of the cross. The passage, however, does not make this the topic of the speech but shows whereof the condition for Israel's salvation consisted. Regarding John the Baptist's statement in 1:29, see pp. 93–97.

He did not thereby think of the possibilities entertained by those who think of him without the will to the cross: Might he forget about the call to repentance and just keep silent? Might he separate the disciples from the Jewish community and make them into a sect? Might he construe for himself a marvelous exit such as being translated to heaven by God? Since he saw in the call to repentance the truth and God's will, and since he maintained both his opposition to evil and his offer of reconciliation, this resulted directly in the will to the cross. This did not alter his ministry up to that point but rather gave to it its fulfillment.

When the Jewish community killed him, there arose, of course, something new: for it, a new, more serious guilt; for him, a new, more profound forgiveness, since despite their action he granted the community the call to God. His relationship to God was crowned with a new, more profound obedience. The new element, however, did not consist of the fact that he placed his sonship only then in the purview of obedience or that he linked renunciation only then with the regal will. For he always possessed in his relationship to God the separation from all that desired to rival or oppose God and was therefore always able to sever any communion, to sacrifice every good, and to sell everything for the sake of the one pearl. He brought this to completion by accepting the cross from God.

Thus he gave to God what was God's. In this way arose "the suffering Christ," a new concept whose novelty incited not only John the Baptist and his own brothers but even the disciples against him. Before Jesus, no one thought that the tie between Israel and the Christ could be severed and that the place of his rule would not be Jerusalem but God's throne. But Jesus' thought did not take this turn from direct inspiration nor from a theoretical construct occasioned by a sudden flash of insight. It rather developed as a consequence of his linking of the call to repentance with the proclamation of the kingdom. Thereby he brought together into a clear unity what up until that point appeared to be a contradiction.

How could he simultaneously be the Christ and the hidden one? How did he create the eternal community while nevertheless being compelled to transfer the proclamation of the kingdom to his disciples? How could he perform miracles that did not promote his welfare but merely incited hatred against him? How could he require the confession of his regal name solely from the Twelve? He resolved these mysteries for his disciples when he told them that dying belonged to his work, because his rule over the community was identical with his obedience to God, and his obedience would be perfected by his death.

Therefore the ethical values stemming from the will to the cross emerge in his work already at the beginning, before he gave the disciples the prediction of his cross. He strengthened them for suffering immediately, as soon as he gave them a share in his work, and thereby provided them with the indispensable equipping for that work, since only thus were they protected from religious dispute and fanatical violence. His own example served to illustrate this: "a disciple is not above the master."

Since he himself was able to suffer, he also made his disciples capable of it
without shaking their relationship to God. From the beginning he battled
competition for greatness among his disciples, a battle that was possible for
him only because of his own example. By possessing the regal will in such a
way that he made it at the same time selfless, so that it did not awaken any
desire for greatness, he was able to will his cross. He made forgiveness the basis
of the disciples' communion with one another. For he himself exercised it. It
is impossible to have a desire to forgive without having a will to suffer.

When the nation rejected him, this resulted in the strongest motivation to
refuse forgiveness to it and to suspend communion with it. By refusing to be
taken over by this motivation but by yielding to it and by allowing himself to
be killed by it, he remained the one who forgave, consistent with the rule that
guided his actions from the beginning. He gave to the disciples the inner right
to expect a miracle from God without using it for their own protection or
honor according to the rule he first instituted for himself. By performing miracles merely for others rather than for himself he was on the way to the cross.

It is therefore highly unlikely that the supposition that the genesis of Jesus'
certainty of death inaugurated a distinct period in his inner life comes closer
to historical truth than the Gospel account. The conviction that Israel did not
want to convert, upon which his verdict regarding his own end depended, did
not arise merely through a single event but through what he continually had
before him. The power of resistance by which the collective will of the nation
confronted him was always visible, and he never laid aside his call to repentance as if it was uttered in vain, not even when he predicted his death. He
always proved himself effective with individuals, even when the community
broke apart. Since Jesus did not yet speak of his end, the first time even received a festive element, since the disciples rejoiced from their heart with him
at God's rule. It simultaneously had a particular gravity, however, that disappeared with the clear preview of the end.

When Jesus proclaimed God's rule, calling the nation to repentance and
including the kingly aim in his vocation without knowing how it would end,
submissive to God and satisfied to know that it would end the way God
wanted it to, not making any plans but being totally available to God, this was
removed from a merely human will as much as Jesus' conduct in his final
time, when he bore the preview of his death within himself in such a way that
he did not extinguish his joy in God and did not become indifferent to man.
The gravity of his task extended equally to the beginning and to the end of his
ministry. He allowed the fruit of his labor to ripen, and to the extent that his
final decisions drew near, his judgment regarding his end also was confirmed.
This finds expression in the Gospel account in the way by which Jesus' predictions of his death are substantiated not by a particular event but merely by
Jesus' desire to leave Galilee and to go to Jerusalem. Thereby the time of decision approached, and from this also arose the necessity to open the disciples'
eyes so that they, too, saw the end.

2. Jesus Parts Company with Jerusalem

Jesus also judged Jerusalem. When he was in the city for a feast, he helped a sick man who had been waiting there in vain for divine help for thirty-eight years. He did this in the halls beside a pond to which people attributed healing power when the water was stirred for an unknown reason. At the same time, however, he revealed, as always, that the Sabbath did not prevent him from working. Therefore he instructed the one he had healed to take his bed with him as he left the hall, whereby the commandment was violated that no burden should be carried on the Sabbath. The healed man immediately retreated fearfully in the face of the Jerusalemites' rejection, laying the responsibility for the breaking of the Sabbath on Jesus, even though Jesus had warned him at an encounter in the temple not to worsen his fate by a renewed falling into sin. Thereby what Jesus had done for the sick man lost any significance for Jerusalem's leaders, because they now paid attention merely to what they called Jesus' sin. For them he was condemned, since he broke the Sabbath.

The struggle intensified because Jesus appealed to the work of his Father regarding his conduct and thus expressed his complete freedom from the commandment and the casuistry attached to it. Thus the Jerusalemites were confronted with the question whether a relationship with God like the one portrayed by Jesus was possible for man, and whether it was permissible or boundless arrogance. Therefore the situation required of Jesus that he show them his communion with God in such a way that its ethical correctness became clear at the same time. The greatness of his commission had to become visible but in such a way that his submission to God was safeguarded and the suspicion averted that this idea amounted to a dishonoring of God (John 5:18–37).

Jesus achieved this by using the simile inherent in the name of a son and by explaining God's relation to him by the relationship existing between a father and a son, transferring this relationship in highest purity and effectiveness to his communion with God. God's disposition toward him was that of a father in its fullest sense, and he acted toward him in a fatherly manner. Likewise, Jesus' disposition toward the Father was that of a child and he acted toward the Father as a son.

From this simple analogy arose for him the entire messianic office and at the same time his complete subjection to God. For the relationship between the Father and the Son rendered the Son dependent upon the Father. He was bound to what he perceived and received in his dealings with the Father. His characteristic was the inability to do anything from himself. Therein Jesus saw the condition and the law of his entire ministry. He could not act when the Father did not act or desire when the Father did not command him or think when the Father did not instruct him. As the Son he knew selfish undertakings were out of the question. But through this powerlessness came his ability to do great works, to give life to the dead, and to execute judgment. For his relationship with the Father did not put him into an empty dependence but brought about that the Father showed him everything he himself did. The Father made him effective, because it was the will and joy of the Father for the Son to act like the Father and to complete his work.

From the same perspective he viewed the question of how he should prove his claim. Even the testimony regarding him received its distinctive mark by the decisive fact of his complete dependence upon God. He could not ground his claim in an experience that took place at a distance from God by winning others' loyalty by his eloquence or intellectual power or miracles. God alone could prove the accuracy of his claim. It is not man here who speaks the decisive word, not John the Baptist, not even Jesus, but only the Father, who alone could establish faith in him. Whoever bears God's witness to him has had Jesus' testimony attested. Where the Father remained silent, Jesus could not speak, nor could he present himself when God did not do so. He did, however, speak in the assurance that this witnessing activity of God was actually occurring. God's testimony vouchsafed his claim.

How was it possible, then, that God's testimony did not move Jerusalem to faith? In order to show this to his opponents Jesus revealed to them the contrast that separated their will from his, thus showing them the reason for their division. Jerusalem's fame for being God's community, of knowing him, and of possessing his word, was null and void since the Jewish community internally resisted God and since it had neither his word nor his love. Jesus' opponents' zeal for Scripture and its study disintegrated because they declined to obey it when they were called to decision. Scripture spoke of him and called them to him as the giver of eternal life.

By separating themselves from him they proved that their desire for eternal life was merely Pharisaic pretense, overshadowed by an entirely different desire, namely, their selfish will that sought their own greatness and glory. They desired their own glory rather than God's. Thereby John described the same event that is portrayed by the accounts of Jesus' ministry in Galilee. Jesus rejected the Jew's selfish grasp for his own greatness and revealed to him the false contradiction into which he fell by seeking to cover up his internal alienation from God by the pomp with which he pursued the veneration of the Law and exhibited his faithfulness to Scripture. This contrast excluded any understanding between Jesus and his Judean audience and bore the necessity for Jesus to pronounce judgment over Jerusalem.

3. The Feeding of the Multitude

When Jesus left the Jewish side of the lake and went to the Golan, into the mountainous and wooded area east of the lake between the region of the Greek city of Hippo and the large village of Bethsaida belonging to Philip the tetrarch, crowds followed him, driven by the desire to experience everything he did. After giving them his word in continual interaction with the changing groups of listeners, he provided a meal for them, undergirded by God's rich resources. As he cared for the disciples, he also assumed the responsibility of caring for the entire community.

He gave to it whatever it needed and presented himself to it as the one who offered God's complete gift: the word and bread. By lending powerful expression to his regal commission, he simultaneously removed from his activity any resemblance to the glitter of human authorities. What the nation and the disciples experienced at that point received its depth essentially from the fact that at the same time Jesus' poverty was revealed, since he hosted his many guests with the sparse existing supplies of bread and fish. They saw that his share in God's glory transformed his poverty into wealth that was able to give everything to everyone.

After Jesus' regal action, the messianic idea as the Jew bore it within himself came to the fore in those who had been his guests. For them the time appeared to have come to make Jesus king, because they could not imagine that it was not their prerogative to prepare his rule for him. Jesus' sign gave them the courage to dare everything for him, and they considered their number sufficiently large to overcome all obstacles since, after all, God's power was visibly present. Therefore Jesus separated his disciples from the crowd that acclaimed him and sent them back to the Jewish shore of the lake. They obediently followed his command. After this he, too, left those he had fed and went into solitude. But he separated himself only from the crowd. He wanted to show his disciples that nothing separated him from them. Therefore he desired and received from the Father the power to unite with them immediately and went across the lake.

After the disciples had overcome the terror and amazement that Jesus' presence, effected in such a miraculous way, caused them, Peter felt deeply how profoundly Jesus elevated them by granting them and not the whole nation his fellowship. He grasped demandingly for his share in Jesus' glorious power. It was his desire to stand beside Jesus on the water, borne, like him, by God's power. When Jesus called him to himself, because what the Father had given him was indeed given for his followers, and because his communion with them was total, the inner difference that separated the disciples from Jesus became apparent. In the face of the waves and the storm God's power vanished for Peter, and the visible danger moved him more strongly than the call of Jesus. He was not free from nature's impact upon him and was not entirely and exclusively dependent on God. Thus Peter, and with him all the disciples, experienced with particularly effective clarity that their share in the glorious rule of Jesus was based on faith and that the faith that tied their entire will indivisibly to Jesus transcended their own abilities.

What happened on the other side of the lake came to a conclusion in the synagogue of Capernaum. When those who had participated in the meal also arrived there, a discussion arose in which Jesus showed to his town that his work would result in his own death (John 6:25–66). On the one hand, the judgment of the rabbinate and the Pharisees' objection did not possess equally decisive significance for the Galileans as they did for Jerusalem. They did not give up on Jesus because they considered him to be a sinner and because they defended their view of the law against his; they rather acclaimed him on account of his works, and they were ready to follow him if only he continually exercised the power and care evidenced by his signs. But on the other hand, Jesus confronted them with the fact that he was not able to awaken a higher desire within them, and he directed their longing toward the living bread that would give them imperishable life and that was given them by God through the presence of the Christ. When they asked how he intended to fulfill this promise, he named faith as that attitude by which his kingly power would become effective for them.

At this point the insurmountable division between Capernaum and himself was revealed, for they rejected his invitation to believe in him. In their view he was not yet justified in such a demand, because his vocation remained too uncertain and his works too small. They had the fantastic world of legend in mind while Jesus stood before them in the bright light of a human history that appeared to put him on equal footing with everyone around him. Their attack, however, did not shake him, since he knew himself to be completely dependent upon God's activity. He could therefore not add any kind of compulsion to his promise, whether external or internal, by which he might subject them to himself. There was no other way than by faith. He rejected any selfish activity, because he depended on God's work. Faith in him was worked by God and could therefore not be produced by skill or force. For this reason Jesus also lent indestructible firmness to communion with him. Those who had been given him by God had an inviolable value in his eyes; for by breaking faith with his disciples he would also have broken faith with the Father who brought them to him.

Since the Galileans were not satisfied with the bread he offered them, considering trust in him to be impossible since he was a human being in an entirely natural way whose origin and home were known to everyone, he proclaimed to them the greatest thing he still had left to do: he would feed them with his own flesh. They despised him because he was flesh and because he was clothed in human fashion. They thought that it was possible merely to believe in the glory of God, in the one who fed them with manna like the fathers. Jesus objected that his own flesh was what would nourish them to eternal life. He glorified it as the means of giving eternal life and thus of fulfilling the messianic work, including their resurrection on the last day.

Since he could give them this greater thing merely through his own death, he clarified this idea by juxtaposing flesh with blood. By surrendering his own flesh and blood, he yielded life and thereby became bread for them. Since they remained separated from him and he could not overcome their resistance, the cross resulted for him; but his commission was thereby not thwarted; in this way he rather fulfilled it. The result of his death for them was life, and his flesh that rendered him mortal became the food that nourished them. He saw in his human nature the means to his service and regal work since he yielded it to death and thereby established his eternal association with his own, creating the messianic community of those who lived forever, those who were called to resurrection.

As he yielded entirely to the will of God that sent him forth, and as he sacrificed even the ultimate resource, his body and his blood, for him, he also would unite completely with those who came to him. He would grant them a commonality that transferred everything he was to them, giving them a share in his own life. Therefore he framed his promise that he would create life for them by his death, not merely in such a way that he would give his flesh for the world but that they would eat his flesh and drink his blood, making this the condition without which they would not obtain life. This was a puzzling mystery for his listeners; for him, on the other hand, it was the greatest expression of the glory of his commission, which revealed itself in the life-giving power of his death. The bitter obscurity of his word pointed to the mystery of his own history that now had to be revealed step by step. The Father had indeed called him to greater things than to give them bread, namely, to die for them. By being subjected to death, however, his flesh and blood were not destroyed. Rather, "You will eat and drink this"; for this was the food for believers by which he gave to them eternal life.

According to this account he did not part from Capernaum without telling the community how he included his death in his vocation and how he thus united it with his claim to their faith. This could only be accomplished by new, surprising utterances. For his thought and action were new. All rejected as nonsensical and impossible that he could be the Christ when he was rejected by the nation. This idea was as distasteful to them as the invitation to eat his flesh and to drink his blood. However, they needed to recognize his death as the action of divine grace that by his flesh and blood helped them to life. Therefore he did not avoid the offense created by his statement. For it indicated that the enigma of his own end had become clear for him. He agreed with God's will that led him to the cross and was certain that all drawn to him by God would agree with him and thank him for the surrender of the Christ, because their life would result from his death.

As a result of this discussion it was not merely the community of Capernaum that rejected him. There also occurred a division among his own disciples. Jesus sought to strengthen them by the promise that he would ascend to the Father and referred them to the Spirit-based power of his word. Since his word was Spirit, it was not destroyed or emptied of its power by his death but granted life. These words should not be understood as a kind of disclaimer by which he retracted his pronouncements regarding his flesh and blood. Both convictions simultaneously grounded Jesus' will to the cross, the one that the historical deed he performed as an earthly person with his body possessed divine necessity and salvific power, and the other that the effect of his death was based on his exaltation to the Father. He became the Christ by yielding his flesh and his spirit, by entering death and by going to the Father.

These convictions coexisted in Jesus' consciousness without contradiction, as certainties that operated simultaneously. He did not thereby depreciate the earthly process by putting it in a heavenly perspective nor declare what he did with his body to be ephemeral because supplemented by the life-giving power of the Spirit. Neither element here would be conceivable without the other; neither would be therapeutic for mankind by itself. A death that was not a departure to the Father would have been his demise; flesh not effectively tied to the Spirit would have been to no avail. But the heavenly gift originated for the world in the fact that he did in his flesh on earth the will of God and thus procured the Spirit, going to the Father and availing himself thereby of his presence in the community. Since he did not conceive of his death in terms of an escape into the afterlife, however, he did not move his disciples' faith from his human person and earthly history to heavenly processes and powers but gave their faith its basis in his own death. But even through this glimpse of a transcendent heavenly mediation of his ministry he was no longer able to retain the larger circle of disciples.

The picture we receive of the result of Jesus' call to repentance and its connection with the will to the cross in John on the one hand, and the older accounts in the Synoptics on the other, reveal a firm unity. John, likewise, says that Jesus was particularly close to Capernaum, emphasizing that his break with this community determined his own judgment regarding his end. He spoke with it about the most profound things that moved him, even about the reason why he readied himself for the cross and why he recognized in it the fulfillment of his work. The Jewish nation, however, remained aloof from him for reasons that also according to Matthew resulted in its condemnation by Jesus. The issue of the bread controlled them and provided the content for the expectation that they directed toward God. Since Jesus could not free them from their sensual desires, they also defended their Pharisaic conviction against him. In their piety, too, they remained the selfish ones who "do God's work" while declaring it impossible that anyone might subject himself believingly to Jesus. The sensual tendency in their will that longed for affluence and well-being and the self-confidence that sought to establish God's kingdom through its own will-power had the same root. By the fact that one will raised itself up against Jesus, the other one likewise joined battle.

Therefore the issue of miracles received decisive importance for their judgment regarding Jesus. The fact that he did miracles attracted them to him. That he did not do them in the way they demanded separated them from him. For them the miracle was not what it was for Jesus, that is, merely a means to the revelation of God; it rather was the final goal. Therefore they took offense at his humanity and gave up on him when he counted his death to be the fulfillment of the promise. In their view, God's rule was manifested by miraculous power. Just as he had done from the very beginning when, without seeking to manipulate the community, he had not tried to sew new patches of cloth on the old garment; he also confirmed their verdict now and told them that they lacked the inner prerequisite necessary for their association with him, because God did not draw them to himself. Through God he knew himself to be separated from them, and he based his will to the cross upon this result of his work in Capernaum.

By telling the community in Capernaum that life would originate from his death, bread from his flesh, and reunion with his disciples from his separation, he expressed the purpose and the value he saw in the cross in the same way as he did on the last evening at the farewell from his disciples. The parallel between these words and Jesus' Last Supper raised strong misgivings about the former. Did John manufacture a discourse by Jesus about the Last Supper, perhaps to remove the objection often raised against the eating of Jesus' body and the drinking of his blood, perhaps in order to secure a mystical deepening for the community's celebration through his particular Christology?

The difficulties attached to Jesus' concept of "eating my body, drinking my blood," however, remain without solution by this discourse. It merely maintains, ready for battle and harshly, the thesis that Jesus' flesh has the power to procure salvation and life and that it should be eaten by the community. Any allegorizing "spiritualization" of these words not merely violates the actual pronouncements but also separates them from their original occasion. The Galileans did not object to a figurative reference to flesh nor did they direct their objection toward a concept or a spiritual process but toward the fact that Jesus also stood before them in flesh and blood in the plain sense of the phrase, that is, in his complete humanity, since these appeared to them incapable of revealing the glory of God. This same flesh that was despised by others Jesus praised as the means by which he fulfilled his commission and created eternal life. Accordingly, John also does not say that Jesus reconciled the Jewish community, or at least the disciples, by his idea. The discourse rather ends in the only way it could have: not with the removal but with the creation of offense, not with insight into Jesus' aim but with amazement regarding its obscurity and in protest against its unreasonableness.

That by these words John undeniably thought of Jesus' Last Supper and of the religious act of the church does not yet make a doctrine regarding the Last Supper. The meal held by the community of Jesus' followers is not addressed at all. If we had no other account, we would not learn from these words alone that the community of believers enjoyed bread and wine in order to receive Jesus' body and blood and that it grounded its action in Jesus' institution. This, of course, becomes apparent by the fact that John did not derive Jesus' final act from a sudden impulse but that he found expressed in it what lent Jesus' will to the cross its ground and content from the beginning. One can therefore call his presentation apologetic in the sense that every discussion about the concept of the Last Supper is apologetic, because the conception of "eating Jesus' body and drinking his blood" always results in harsh offense. John, however, defends that Last Supper merely by testifying that the pronouncement regarding the Last Supper was Jesus' own pronouncement that expressed his own will.

The thought that his body was the means by which he procured life for the community by yielding it to death must not be separated as a strange intrusion from the convictions controlling Jesus' consciousness. The meal belonged to the images graphically developed within the community by which the complete proof of divine grace was described. Jesus, however, did not tie people's blessedness to material gifts but based everything on their allegiance to him. He prepared the meal for his own by uniting them with himself, and the fundamental act that rendered their communion with him eternal was his death, which would confirm and complete what he granted his disciples at that time.

In the meantime, their discipleship was revealed in the fact that they shared his meal and that they received their bread and cup from his hand, and he gave forgiveness to those who were ready to repent by allowing them to participate in his meal. This, however, did not come to an end by the cross but was granted to them by his death in new power. The term "cup" was a commonly used designation for what God gave to man. It indicated that God's work entered the person's inner parts and determined his inner condition so that he had within himself what God gave him and sensed how he drank and tasted the contents of the cup. God, however, gave the cup to the community by Jesus' hand, and the process that made him the giver of God's grace was his cross.

Jesus described his own calling and that of his disciples as being the light of the world and thereby expressed that he did not cling to his own possession but made it a gift that entered into others and was planted into them as something they possessed themselves. As light entered into others by his word and made them see, his life entered them like bread and made them alive, and this he effected by dying for them. Since he said "light and salt," it is daring to maintain that he could not have said "light and bread." He described the effect of his word by a seed and its potential for growth, a power that renewed the human being, as he had also used the analogy of the leaven. Food is an image not vastly different from seed and leaven. All of these images were based on the fact that he did not think of God as one who was absent but that he knew himself to be internally united with him and thought of him also in relation to others as entering into an analogous relationship. From the internality of God's work arose the internality of the community that Jesus promised to his disciples as the fruit of his death.

4. The Disciples' Confession of Jesus' Kingship

When Jesus was set to depart from Galilee because the lack of response to his ministry had become evident, he brought about his disciples' confession of his regal status (Matt. 16:13–28). He did this on a trip that led him to the north far beyond the boundaries of Galilee, near Caesarea which belonged to Philip the tetrarch. The city was located beside a famous cave, at that time consecrated to the god Pan, from which a strong spring flows that is a source of the Jordan. Jesus stood there at the boundary of the land that had once been given to Israel as a possession. Had he continued farther, he would have stepped into Greek territory. But it was not there that the field where he had to sow his seed was located. The greatest thing in his work for Israel was still ahead of him: that trip to Jerusalem that would bring about the decision.

After first ascertaining by his question that even those who had been impacted by his word, and who found great words full of living hope and fantastic imagination for the mystery they sensed in him, did not recognize in him the one in whom the promise would find its fulfillment, he desired from his disciples the confession of his regal status without which their communion with him would have fallen apart. He could make the final decision and complete his work in Jerusalem by his death only when he had the certainty that there were disciples who would guard his word and gather his community. Without these his death would amount to a surrender of his aim. Were he entirely alone, he would also stand God-forsaken. If, on the other hand, the disciples acknowledged his regal name, he had reached the aim of his commission and was ready to take the final step.

He confronted even his disciples with the new demand that they move toward the cross with him only if they believed in him with that complete confidence which developed through the messianic idea and trusted him to perfect the community for eternity. Only then they would remain associated with him both before his death and beyond it. No weaker term such as teacher or prophet was still sufficient, because death would have brought his calling to an end if he had not received any greater commission. The name of Christ alone instituted a community that would remain even if he died. It alone was sufficiently powerful to release them entirely from the old community. If they were to accompany him to the cross, they had to give up anything that Israel up to that time had considered to be established truth; the value of Israel's entire mechanism to achieve righteousness plummeted. Once, however, it had been determined that Jesus was the Christ, there was no longer any sacrifice too difficult for the disciple.

He required the confession only from them, not from Capernaum or any other group of people, since it did not occur to him to make the word of repentance optional. Since the people rejected it and subjected him to death on account of it, the messianic community originated by way of a new beginning rather than by Israel's worship of him. It was brought into being by the action of the disciples. He would become the Christ for Israel by being the Christ for the disciples.

By this act, too, Jesus remained true to himself, both by not admitting any public proclamation of his kingdom and by requiring his disciples to acknowledge him as the Christ at that time. For this demand was firmly grounded in the preceding events. Jesus had depicted his calling to the disciples as equal to those who had come before the Jewish community with a divine commission in former times and who still spoke to it by the Scriptures. Therefore his parable of the sending of the Son follows the one about the sending of the servants and has the same goal. Nevertheless, he had assigned the title of "prophet" to his disciples while not using it for himself, and he had already said regarding John the Baptist's office that it transcended the prophetic one (Matt. 5:12; 7:22; 11:9–14; Luke 16:16). The Christ stood above the prophets because the regal vocation was related to the entire condition of the community, uniting word and deed and not merely increasing the community's insight but rather renewing it. The Christ was not merely the one who spoke in the name of God but the one who performed the divine work since God's kingdom consisted of God's work. By continually exceeding the greatest the Jewish community had possessed up until that time he confirmed the disciples' assurance that he was the Christ.

The office of the Christ required him to produce the complete community, and Jesus' entire work was directed toward this aim. The disciples saw that he was not occupied with himself in order to make himself religious, that he also did not merely care for "souls" in order to produce in them a religious condition or institute a group around him like the head of a sect he indoctrinated with his own ideas. They continually saw that he lived for others, for them and for every member of the nation, and that it was his aim to make them members of that community that is God's. Owing to the facts that his commandment required obedience and his grace forgave them, they experienced his rule. For he executed upon them the regal act in bright clarity by procuring for them reconciliation with God, by removing their debts, and by removing their sin. Likewise, he acted like a king by refusing forgiveness through the judging act.

The calling that assigned him the messianic office, however, did not merely consist of the turning away of sin by forgiveness or punishment. Without these, of course, the community of his followers could not be established. However, it did not need and receive the Christ merely because it was sinful, but because God gave his gifts to it through him. He united it and rendered it the service that was well-pleasing to God. By his rule it experienced God's work as it did in no other way, and in his glory it perceived God's greatness. This was made clear to the disciples not only by his signs, as important as they doubtless were for their persuasion, but also by the communion into which he placed them with himself and with one another. He linked them through a new kind of love. They did not know it from their former experience, and what they had in one another was more than friendship or brotherly love; it was God's love. The disciples felt that their own circle was as different from the rest of the community as day was from night; with him, they "walked in the light."

Since the messianic idea was based on the pronouncement that God had promised the Christ, a reference back to the Old Testament was essential for him. The disciples continually saw Jesus following the Scripture in word and deed. They observed that he sought to bring Scripture and the community established by it to fulfillment. Since he was not led solely by prophetic words but possessed his own established relationship with God, this rendered his regal prerogative not unclear but on the contrary certain. For the concept of the Christ an eschatological preview was equally essential as the review of Israel's history and Scripture. But the disciples also saw the former continually in Jesus, because God's rule transcended the present condition of the world and would not be completed "at this time." Moreover, Jesus' promise is so notoriously powerful that it is not strange that the disciples considered it to be the guarantee of the perfect goal and that they desired nothing else than what Jesus promised them would happen.

Since the Christ worked everything God had prescribed for the community's eternal life, the concept of the Christ was conceivable only in the singular. He did not have others beside him who took turns with him or who shared his work with him but he remained forever as he led the community to its eternal perfection. He never gave his hope an egotistical expression, as if speaking of the way in which God would transfer him from his earthly need and from death into a blessed life. When he spoke of the future, he depicted himself as the one who gave, as the one who ushered the disciples into life and the kingdom, not as the one who received it merely for himself. And he spoke exclusively about himself.[2] For he thought of himself as the giver of the eternal gift. Thereby he expressed the Christ concept.

According to Matthew, he explained to us by the preceding discourses how Jesus established the messianic confession of his disciples. When he spoke after the selection of the Twelve about the aim of their communion with him, he did not elaborate on christological topics. He did not exercise the messianic office by discussing, explaining, and defending it, but by separating them from their sin and by extending good will to them. This, however, did not lead to a darkening of his regal status for his disciples but rather to its revelation. They saw it by what he considered to be sin or righteousness and by who he said would participate in God's rule. For thus he created the community that was God's.

The disciples perceived that he stood before them as the leader appointed for them by God on account of such words. They understood that he acted, not from a kind of piety by which he thought of how he himself might come to God and find obedience to God's will together with others. They felt the separation he established between himself and Israel in the way he acted powerfully by such words rather than merely teaching, by refusing to reward the falsely righteous rather than merely warning them, and by assuring those who performed the divine will, without, however, striving with and beside them for God's good pleasure. By his word of repentance, they also realized why he did not permit them to proclaim his regal name publicly. Since he was not satisfied with what the ancients had previously been told, it was an open question whether or not Israel would attain God's kingdom. Thus the community that acknowledged him as its Lord still had to be established. As long as Israel, however, rejected the word of repentance, he could not desire to be acknowledged by anyone but his own disciples.

Because the aims expressed by the Sermon on the Mount also determined his own activity, the disciples saw by it that he subjected his activity to the rule of love with the same sincerity he demonstrated in his condemnation of Jewish piety and in his requirements for his disciples. For he thereby purified it from being the glorification of his commission solely for the purpose of his own exaltation. They saw that he did not merely demand love from others but that he himself rendered it to God and to others by using his word to help them and to give pure love to them.

The commissioning discourse stood in the same relation to Jesus' kingly will as the Sermon on the Mount. It, too, was completely based on his regal status and was inconceivable without it. Even now that he made their communion with him their joint work and called them also to do what he himself did, they stood in complete submission, not beside, but under him. The idea that Christianity was the result of the joint work of Jesus and of his disciples, that their

---

2. In the portrayal of the parousia, not even a separate revelation of God is juxtaposed with Jesus' revelation.

thought supported his, that their will strengthened his, that their work magnified his, did not exist in the minds of the disciples. Their activity was based on what they received, and they received what they acquired not directly on account of their own relationship with God but from Jesus. By granting them God's gifts, however, Jesus presented himself to them as the Christ.

Therefore they understood that Israel's attitude toward them would determine its eternal destiny, both of those who accepted them and of those who rejected them. They knew that he expected martyrdom from them, that there was for them no situation in which they could deny or forsake him, that he would take care of them before God in such a way that his advocacy of them placed them in God's grace, just as the one whom he denied was rejected by God, and that they were given all power in his name, even the power that subjected the spirits to them. By not sending them out to proclaim his regal name he removed any offense from them, a concern for him since he placed them together with himself into the severe confrontation with Israel. Only when this struggle had come to an end would the revelation of his glory occur, and their commissioning showed that they were strong enough to overcome the severe offense that resulted from the break between Jesus and the Jewish community. When he pronounced woes over Capernaum, the disciples did not leave him but saw in his judgment the divine justice that was indispensable for the revelation of his grace.

By his discourse on God's rule, he confirmed to them both his regal commission and the necessity of concealing it from Israel, the former since it revealed to them the glory of God's rule by Jesus' work, the latter since it showed them by its form and content that it was not yet realized but occurred in secret. Since they believed that God's grace was given by his word, that it was inseparably linked with the revelation of his justice, that God's glory was revealed even in small events, and that the reception of his gift called them to every sacrifice, it is no longer incomprehensible that they withstood the pressure laid upon them by everyone's opposition, and that they did not already consider him refuted by the fact that it was them alone who acknowledged his right to rule. They were rather able to bear the mystery that the larger Jewish community rejected him and that Jesus bore its rejection, desiring only that he was recognized and acknowledged as the Christ by them.

Of the common messianic names, it was the phrase "the Son of David" that was most easily applicable for Jesus' environment since it was less defined than the designation "the Anointed." "Son of David" did not already speak of the ruling power given to him by God but merely of his legitimate right to do so implicit in his descent from David. The disciples saw in Jesus' attitude toward this designation that he never denied his kingly aim, because he confirmed that the name "the Son of David" was due him while not using it in order to elevate himself (Matt. 9:27; 15:22; 20:30).

Regarding the value of their communion with him, he had created various phrases: they celebrated his feast with him, the bridegroom, as his friends; they were his servants who managed his household or his possessions. He was the shepherd of God's flock and gathered what had been lost, the builder who built God's community, the sower who sowed seeds in God's field, the harvester who brought in the harvest, the fisherman who gathered the community, the messenger of grace who led the rebels back to God and who, upon their faith, built from them the sanctified community. He granted them more than what the temple gave them, placing them in God's presence and granting them the means for proper worship. He revealed God to them. While they did not see God's presence and rule without him, they perceived it through him, because he wanted to show it to them (Matt. 9:15; 22:2; 25:32; 24:45; 25:14; Luke 19:13; 15:4; John 10:12; Matt. 16:18; 13:3, 24; 9:37; 13:41, 47; 21:37–38; 12:6; John 2:19; Matt. 11:27). What else should the disciples expect from the Christ? He thus described to them the messianic work as done for them.

The larger community also provided him with the image of warfare. This imagery, however, is missing in Jesus' use of pictures.[3] He avoided it because God's power did not bring the one he sent into a struggle with his adversaries that found its analogy in warfare. In order to portray the way in which he rejected what God rejected, he used the images of the judge and of the shepherd, leaving his authority intact while at the same time clarifying why he withheld grace, that is, because his rule executed justice (Matt. 7:22; 16:27; 25:32; John 10:3). The fact, however, that he did not use illustrations of warfare did not shake the disciples' confidence in his regal power.

Often Jesus took from an entire chain of concepts only its most simple characteristic—he had been sent by God (Matt. 10:40; 15:24; John 3:17; 5:36; 6:29, 57; 7:29; 8:42; 10:36; 11:42; 17:3, 8; 20:21). He thereby expressed the certainty of his call and his demand for his listeners to believe, yet in such a way that the hearer was diverted from questions that transcended the present and focused on what Jesus now said and did. The substance of his commission would be revealed in the progression of the divine work. The concept of sending, however, served directly to prepare the concept of the Christ since Jesus did not relate the divine commission to individual words and accomplishments but uniformly to his entire work. In the entirety of his word, work, and destiny, and with his entire life, he was controlled by the commission given to him. This convergence of function and person, of office and life, lent him the kind of uniqueness he described by using the messianic name. Its ground was no secret to the disciples since Jesus never concealed his divine sonship.

It is equally clear why even then Jesus' question still possessed for the disciples the full weight of a question, not one that they dared to direct to him—for he did not allow himself to be interrogated by them—but one that he had to direct to them. For he had entirely prevented not merely the utterance of his formulaic title, nor merely dispensed with kingly trappings, but refused emphatically to fight for his own recognition. And he forbid them to do the same. From the nation's perspective the idea of his messiahship was thereby rendered impossible, for it thought in terms of the throne. It linked with this

3. Only in Luke 14:31 is the image of warfare borrowed, there, however, not in order to portray what he himself does but to show what the disciple ought to do.

the idea that he must strive for his own recognition and rule. Instead, he had done nothing to enforce his regal status since establishing his circle of disciples besides calling the Jewish community to repentance.

Were the disciples nonetheless certain? For them no less than for John the Baptist, the possibility remained to take offense at him. The demand he made upon them by his conduct was great. He expected them to understand that genuine rule did not seek its proof in titles, gestures, external insignia, or forms, and that it did not desire its own advantage. He was the Christ since God gave him power, not because man celebrated him as such. He desired their acknowledgment of his regal office for their own sake, because they thereby would be granted God's grace and because their faith represented God's work in them, not because he wanted to base his rule upon them. Since he expected much of them, it was a genuine, serious question when he asked them to express their own verdict regarding him.

Peter's confession that Jesus was the Christ also expressed the disciples' strong and great hope. If Jesus showed his regal status only to them, contrary to their own expectation, his promise helped them understand that this (for them) surprising turn of events nevertheless did not separate them from him, because it allowed his present concealment and humble state to be followed by his revelation. The disciples committed themselves to him in the understanding that he now received honor merely from them, but that later he would be revealed to all. The promise alone, however, would not yet have given sufficient reason for that decision which separated the disciples from the larger community and caused them to attach their destiny to Jesus' regal name in contradiction to all, unless they had taken Jesus' side in his struggle against Israel's sin. Israel must agree with Jesus as the representative of God's will and witness to the divine grace that reconciled them to God in contrast to their disobedience. Jesus' answer to Peter's confession demonstrates that he considered it to be the expression of a confirmed faith, and that this had originated in the disciples, because Jesus' word had transformed their agreement with Jesus. It had grown into a religious and thus indissoluble connection as the proclamation of God's will, as the extension of divine forgiveness, and as the liberation from divine judgment.

Jesus considered the regal name given to him by Peter to be God's revelation to him. Precisely because for human eyes a royal homage merely by his twelve followers with their deliberate separation from the people would have been a nonsensical procedure, so that an outsider who might have observed it would have ridiculed it, the disciples' confession was valuable for Jesus as the confirmation of his assurance and the ground of his complete gratitude. This result was brought about not by "flesh and blood," not by human thought or will. Human will judged differently and did not believe what Peter confessed. The conviction that Jesus, despite his concealment and powerlessness, was nevertheless the Lord and Creator of the eternal community was given by God alone, and therefore Jesus recognized in the disciples' acknowledgment of his rule the foundation of his genuine, eternal kingdom.

Precisely because in his situation "flesh and blood" failed, and man did not see anything of his glory and power, while the disciples were present who recognized it, it was evident that God had granted him lordship. The "mystery" that repeatedly causes objections against Jesus' conduct is merely the fact that he treated God as a reality and that he expected his own rule from God's, nothing different from that, as if he understood messianism piously, so that power had value for him only if it was given to him. For the same reason, however, he absolutely confirmed the messianic name when it was applied to him. Since faith in him could develop only through God's revelatory activity that confirmed his identity, it became, once it had arisen, unconditional assent to him.

It is, of course, transparent why Jesus' concept that he was king, more than his filial consciousness, causes not merely dogmatic but also historical disputes. The greatness of the messianic aim stirs amazement. By the fact that Jesus' filial consciousness was a unique process that transcended our measure of life, some observers manage the thought more readily that piety after all easily allows peculiar ideas to develop. Religious moods cannot be controlled. Perhaps Jesus was especially gifted religiously, a religious genius, or burdened by illusory ideas. By his will to rule, however, he intervened in the condition of the world, and from this arose the question whether or not his conduct was conceivable within a human life.

The negation of this question immediately follows when Jesus' pious rationale for his conduct is covered or eliminated as inconsequential.[4] Jesus' significance, it is then argued, consists of his new ethic or in his renunciation of the world or in his religious individualism, factors by which it would be incompatible for him to possess the messianic idea. This is the way in which one's own constructions, rather than observations, are made. When, in studying Jesus' teaching, one fails to give proper attention to the will that gave birth to it, and when one understands it not as calling the individual from sin to God but misinterprets it as ethic or theology, then, of course, the regal will should be denied him, since it has no room in a thinker who has merely intellectual goals in mind. Therefore rationalism was always confronted with the necessity of disputing Jesus' regal activity. This necessity, however, falls aside once one notes that Jesus' word confronts us with his activity, by which he sought to end sin and reconcile to God.

If one hears only the denunciations addressed by Jesus toward human conduct, the messianic idea once again is in contradiction to his aim. For renunciation and the will to rule wage war against one another. This objection is rendered baseless, however, when one perceives the positive thesis from which Jesus' denunciations proceeded. Toward God, he bore within himself complete affirmation. This gave him both absolute opposition to selfish dominance as a person desires it and the will to rule expressed by the messianic name that wanted to reveal God's rule by his own. The inward nature of that religious thought which turned the individual as a person toward God with

4. However the historian may judge the value of the idea of God doctrinally, as a historian he commits a mistake when he excludes it from the scientific equation. For it was the power that determined everything in Jesus' conduct. The mistake is made frequently that the historian renders the idea of God without significance for Jesus merely because it is insignificant for the historian.

his personal attitude and which also freed him from the pressure of the community becomes an incompatible contradiction to the kingly aim only when
individualism is understood in terms of selfish desire that seeks to enhance the
individual's measure of power by the destruction of the larger community.
But whoever ascribes to Jesus the aim of turning the individual toward himself and of destroying the community needs to remove the love commandment from his will, not merely brotherly love but also the love of God that
does not permit anyone to claim God merely for himself. Jesus, however, did
not break up the Jewish community in the name of "personality" in order to
render the individual stronger or happier by his isolation but in the name of
God, because it rebelled against God. From this same root also grew his regal
will by which he built the new community out of the old from his disciples.

The changes in the Gospel accounts necessitated by the theories refuted
above are extensive. Jesus' concept of the kingdom has to be eliminated, for
now the reference of God's rule to the present is without substantiation. Likewise, the miracle story and the rationale for faith have to go, since these pre-
suppose his consciousness of power. The call to repentance has lost its place,
since the extension of forgiveness to the guilty is a kingly act. The institution
of the circle of disciples no longer has any foundation, since, without confession of the Christ, it has lost its reason for existence. Moreover, since the fact
can hardly be removed that Jesus bore the cross as the Christ, his use of the
messianic name becomes his accommodation to an idea that was foreign to
him, a concept that was imposed upon him by the disciples or that was attributed to him by tradition while Jesus never united his will with it.

None of Jesus' actions, however, lend themselves less to the explanation that
they were based on accommodation to an idea foreign to him than his use of
the Christ name. The kingly aim requires the whole man. Whoever does not
sincerely possess the will to power does not have it, especially where the concept
of kingship is conceived of religiously and where power is desired as apportioned by God. That religious goals do not permit half-hearted assent but result
in unconditional commitment, Jesus himself taught with greatest clarity. Whoever attributes to him an ambiguous, haphazard relationship with the messianic
name brings him in conflict with the basic principle he affirmed for all religious
relationships. For he always desired perfect love and complete obedience toward
God. That he also rendered those in the exercise of his office as king he proved
by dying on account of his designation as the Christ.

The new content given to the messianic name by Jesus was for him no arbitrary transformation of it which could lend support to the verdict that he labo-
riously and incompletely appropriated a concept that remained foreign to him.
What the Jewish community expected from the "Anointed," that he be the king
appointed by God by whose rule the consummation would be brought to completion and by whom the endtime would come, he claimed of himself without
any scruples. By uniting the word of the kingdom with that of repentance and
by thus giving his regal office as its goal the removal of sin, he did, of course,
relate the concept of the Christ to ideas that were different from popular expectations. From his perspective, however, this was not a transformation of the

messianic idea, as little as its religious version by which he subjected his rule entirely to God's will. For for him Scripture determined one's entire relation to God. It stipulated that God's relationship with the individual would effect the ethical norm, which is why Israel could think of no communion with God that did not include obedience to his commandment, nor conceive of any separation from God other than that caused by evil. By uniting his call to repentance with the preaching of the kingdom, Jesus, in his own judgment, subjected his office and work to the same basic principle that the larger community recognized and had to recognize for its own relationship to God if it did not want to destroy its own foundation, God's Law. What he desired and accomplished by this was simply to distinguish the Christ completely and clearly from what he called a false Christ (Matt. 24:24).

Therefore Jesus confirmed his regal status even then exclusively to his disciples and enjoined them not to speak with others about his messianic identity. In both directions he agreed with the result that had come about through his ministry. The nation did not acknowledge who he was; this the disciple could and should not change. The disciple knew him and in this had to perceive the divine grace granted to him. The prerequisite for his entrance into death consisted of both facts. His disciples, however, needed at that time a definite, express prohibition in order to find a way to process the fact that he did not present himself to the larger community as king.

On the other hand, he described to the disciples their commission at that time in all its greatness and thus helped them understand why he desired solely from them that they recognize in him their eternal Lord. By them he established his community, since God gave them to him so that they might be his messengers. The greatness of his own office lent greatness to that of his messengers, and this office was fully brought to light by Jesus' death. Therefore he juxtaposed the declaration, "You are Peter," with Peter's confession, "You are the Christ." In this way he confirmed to Peter his office, which remained unshaken by Jesus' death, and was in fact rather brought to completion, just as was Jesus' own messianic office. As Peter, he would uphold God's house as the rock upholds the building. To this end he received that authority which the Christ alone could give him: the key to God's rule, and the power to bind and to loose with divine validity. The symbolic element in this saying took its cue from the act of the judge, who bound the guilty and who loosed the one cleared of wrongdoing.[5]

By use of an image drawn from the legal realm, the new procedure remained in close unity with the way in which Jesus had ordered his relationship with the disciples up to that point. Their greatness did not consist of an insight or in a religious experience that remained limited to them and that could be described by a mystical formula, although Jesus described the faith

5. The established use of the rabbinate for the phrases "binding" and "loosing" was for the formulation of laws by which something was prohibited or permitted. This use of the phrase, however, is derived from the concrete binding and loosing exercised by the judge. In Jewish usage, likewise, the concrete use of the phrase persists beside the derivative usage into later periods. The term "loosing" was common, for example, for the lifting of a ban.

by which Peter had attained certainty about Jesus' regal status as God's revelation to him. The glory he possessed rather was his service, and this service consisted of the effort of bringing those who listened to his message into an effectual relationship to God's grace and to God's judgment. He issued to them the call to God in such a way that it was effectual; he had the power to proclaim God's forgiveness in such a way that it was received, to wipe away guilt in such a way that it was eradicated and liberty was given to the individual, thereby loosing in such a way that the loosing was granted by God. Effectual in like manner is the execution of justice entailed by his work. When Jesus' messenger is rejected, assignment of guilt and separation from God ensue. Thereby the binding and the exclusion from God's kingdom occur.

Even this did not result in a new aim for the disciple's work but merely transferred to him what Jesus always had considered to be the permanently valid law of God's rule and of his own ministry. Because freedom or bondage, the gaining of life or the falling into death, reconciliation with God or separation from him ensued from his activity, his messenger, too, when giving grace by which he "loosed," at the same time effected the rejection of the unrepentant, by which he "bound." The faith rendered the apostle was rendered to the Christ and in him to God and led to the reception of the divine gift. The unbelief directed toward the apostle was directed toward the Christ and in him to God, resulting in the loss of the divine gift. Jesus wanted his messenger to act in the certainty that the giving of life and the execution of justice resulted from his work and that God's rule was revealed through him.[6]

The apostle's work received this glory and power by the fact that Jesus would complete his work only when his death had occurred. While Peter was the foundation on which the community would be built, Jesus himself would build it, and it belonged to him as having been called by him and to him. The thought of a replacement of Jesus' ministry through that of the apostle remains excluded. To the contrary, Jesus ascribed significance to the office of his messenger because he had the certainty that he would fulfill his calling by his death and would exercise his rule subsequent to it. On account of what he himself was and did, his messenger effected the revelation of God's grace and of divine judgment.

Just as Jesus' will was jointly directed toward the goal of kingship and toward the cross, however, he deepened, by helping his disciples to a grateful appreciation of their office, at the same time their freedom from selfish desire.

---

6. The dogmatic interpretation of the formula "binding and loosing" that thought of it in terms of religious legislation brought the apostle's activity and that of the community (Matt. 18:18) into sharp conflict with Jesus. All of Pharisaism that was completely rejected by Jesus is characterized by a casuistry that looses, that is, permits, an action and binds another, that is, declares it to be prohibited. The Pharisaic interpretation of the formula is also contradicted by the early Christian community's conduct, in which there is no trace of an apostolic law-giving setting forth permitted and prohibited things and having the sanctity of a divine commandment. Neither did Jesus in Matt. 18:18 institute a particular sacrament so that Peter had to loose or bind Israel by an act of confession and by a formula of absolution. For cultic forms have no room in the realism of Jesus' work, which granted the highest gifts of grace while simultaneously serving the indestructible divine law.

He also strengthened their ability to forsake their lives for his sake (Matt. 16:24–27). They found protection against the temptation arising from their dignity and power solely by the complete renunciation that buried all their own desires.

If the church has accustomed itself to thinking here merely of sensual desires, pleasure, and greed, it hardly understands correctly what moved Jesus and his followers at that time. The aims that made their lives significant and that could awaken in them selfish desires were of a higher kind. With the apostolate they had received a calling that transcended all boundaries. They viewed the world as their field of work and humanity as those whom they had to win. Their great office and work appeared to require of them that they spare themselves carefully, since work appeared jeopardized if dying became necessary for them. But no focus on possible successes, no attention to their calling that might aim at still greater things, was permitted to cause them to care for themselves and for the preservation of their lives to the extent that they refused obedience to God. Their confidence that God was working through them found its indispensable complement in the persistent turning away from their own self, because also for them the indissoluble connection between sin and death was valid, a connection by which the one who sinned lost his soul and thereby his life. No ministry or success of any stature, not even if they could point to a converted world as the fruit of their labors, would protect them from the fact that Christ would defend God's justice against them and surrender them to death if they sinned.

This appears to result in an unbearable contradiction. Jesus had just described them as the ones who helped others receive life while then referring to them as those who themselves died. At one time he called them the ones who proclaimed God's judgment to others, at another as those who were judged themselves. But Jesus did not permit them to bear within them only the former thought; he instilled into them emphatically also the latter. Yet he added the promise that faithfulness which was ready to die would not bring them any loss. They rather would gain life through death and would tend well their interests by denying themselves, because he would reveal the glory of God's rule upon those who proved themselves faithful.

Here John places Jesus' first saying regarding the disciple who switched to the side of Jesus' enemies (John 6:70). Since Jesus excluded one of his disciples from the certainty that God had given them to Jesus as his own possession so that the progress of his work depended on them, the justice that effected death was executed in his own circle, not merely by Israel's separation from him and by the fact that many listeners rejected his word, but by the fact that he rejected one of those he had chosen as given over to Satan.

The contrast ensuing from juxtaposing John's account with that of Matthew shows how profoundly these events were experienced by Jesus and by his followers. In Matthew, the disciples' confession of Jesus' regal identity is followed by the preview of the greatness and blessedness of the apostolate, of the highest gifts and aims of the gospel given to the apostle as effective power. In

John, the story is followed by the revelation of evil in its most severe consequence: the turning of faith into betrayal, the power of Satan that thwarts the
calling of the Christ and that transforms the disciple himself into a Satan. In
Matthew, complete joy and gratitude for God's work find expression; in
John, shuddering before the power of evil and the humiliation that must bear
the heavy load of human history and must honor God by affirming even
God's judging act.

Both events result from the same reality. Jesus, in his dealings with his disciples, sought their complete personal allegiance to him. He did not merely
treat them as students who had to learn a concept or as servants who had to
take care of some business. He desired their love and trust in him, because he
desired them for God, and he gave their communion with him the complete
depth of religion and of communion with God. If that communion was
proven true, it would result in the anticipation of the religious office in the
highest sense. If it was finally torn, this would lead to a revelation of the power
by which man could resist God. Fear of the impartial majesty of the divine
judgment was thus juxtaposed alongside faith, because it became clear that
even the greatest divine gift did not replace the upright decision and that
Jesus' grace was received in vain by the one who resisted it.[7]

Already at that time the severity of the event consisted of the strength of
doubts it was able to evoke. Was not Judas's resistance against Jesus proof that
Jesus' choice of him was wrong? Would it not be kinder for Jesus to release
him from their relationship in order to prevent at least the most severe consequence and so as not to assign to him a task that he could not fulfill, of going
to Jerusalem with him? The disciples' account reveals that Jesus unconditionally honored, even in his relationship with Judas, the sanctity of the ethical
law and that he did not retreat from evil so as to restrict it as much as possible
or cover it up. God's righteousness is done by allowing everything to come to
full fruition. A person's will is confirmed, for good as for evil. Therefore unbelief, like faith, receives what it desires, and the petitioner receives the unconditional promise, while the blasphemer receives the unconditional word
of judgment. Jesus did not doubt the necessity of the divine execution of judgment but acted in the certainty that that divine law bore within itself its purpose and that it had to be done. Therefore he confronted evil with an unlimited ability to endure, an ability that persists in patience until the final
moment, so that the disciples were able to betray him without hearing a harsh
word from him. The controlling norms of the call to repentance that oblige
him to honor the individual in his ethical liberty even when he hardened his
ill-will, as completely led Jesus when one of his own died on account of it as
it did in his relationship to Israel. Even though the pressing severity of the
event was enhanced, because here it was not merely God's previous call but
the grace given by the Christ that fell prey to the power of evil, Jesus sancti-

7. Regarding this, too, the later position of the apostles confirms the Gospel account. They
simultaneously possessed the certainty that they would bring to humanity the word of the kingdom, and the resistance against religious arrogance. This dual resolve cleansed them from all
self-admiration and placed them into the fear of God.

fied, here as there, God's righteousness, and spoke a curse over his disciple as he did over the unrepentant community, not reluctantly or defiantly but resolutely. Yet he did not lift the communion with him as long as sin occurred only inwardly. For he did not judge the desire but the completed work.

The disciples said that Judas was greedy for money (Matt. 26:15; John 12:6), thus comparing his fall to the fall of those guests who rejected the invitation to the feast on account of earthly gain or to Israel's vanity that rejected God's service in order to serve Mammon. It is entirely transparent that a disciple who longed for tangible things or happiness had to break faith with Jesus and to fall. Equally clear is that Judas was bound to Jesus by a strong desire. For his betrayal to the leaders of Judaism did not break an obligatory relationship that was inseparable on account of natural compulsion but a communion that was based exclusively on pure love. The disciple whose love grew cold could leave Jesus at any time. Since Judas did not arrive at the decision to forsake his discipleship, one misinterprets his story by considering it to be an example of vice. It was a particularly profound part of the history of religion, a struggle between the assurance of God and the desire that resisted it.

Therefore Judas did not even break openly with Jesus when he betrayed him to death. He did not find courage to fanaticism, and he did not call Jesus a false Christ. For a person breaks openly with such pretender, even if that person initially allowed himself to be deceived by him. Since, however, in Jewish thought regarding the Christ, the longing for wealth and the craving for heavenly rule were not set in antithesis to one another, offense at Jesus could easily occur from a sincere desire for God and his rule, while simultaneously being fueled by the longing for the fulfillment of one's own selfish desires. But Jesus' word and action confronted such piety with a decision. Earthly and heavenly treasures stood in opposition to one another, and their allegiance to the Christ placed even the disciples on the way to the cross. This was a new insight for all, an insight that no one embraced without internal wavering. In the case of Judas, too, the courage to attack Jesus that was born out of hatred may well have been preceded by many an internal struggle. When the prophecy of his death, however, cut off the hope that Jesus would fulfill the selfish desires of his followers, and when the course of events confirmed that prophecy, the kind of hatred could develop from this struggle that drew from the bitter feeling of disappointment the will to destroy him.

If we want to understand Jesus' dealings with his disciples, we must not forget the process evident in Judas. If it is discussed why Jesus made a hidden treasure out of God's rule; why he urged complete renunciation with this determined sincerity, wanting to accept the rich man only if he renounced his wealth; why he omitted any inspiring, winsome presentation of his regal status while underscoring exclusively the seriousness of the present—in all this the fact is not irrelevant that he had beside him the man in whom the earthly and the divine love wrestled with one another to such an extent that the former gained an overpowering strength that resisted even daily fellowship with Jesus. By distinguishing clearly between what belonged to human beings and what belonged to God, Jesus protected the other disciples from Judas's course and ensured that he alone stumbled because of him.

5. The Disciples' Instruction Regarding Jesus' Demise

When Jesus conveyed the certainty of his death to his disciples, they initially refused to believe him. Subsequently, however, they proved that their union with Jesus could not be destroyed. As they perceived that he looked toward the cross with a resolute will, their objections subsided. But even then their obedience remained incomplete and coerced. They acquiesced and went with him because he demanded it. They did not obscure this contrast between Jesus and themselves but rather called attention to it with serious intentionality. They thereby informed the church that the severity of what they went through determined their religious position with lasting effects.

Jesus took the pressure exerted upon the disciples by the anticipation of his execution seriously; he, too, felt it. For this very reason he did not allow the end to come unexpectedly upon them but suggested to them already in Galilee that it would inevitably ensue. If it had encountered them unawares, it would have been devastating. Since all their ideas about God's rule and Jesus' regal work were subject to revision, he himself induced the necessary change in their attitude toward him by announcing his death to them.

It was apparently self-evident, from Jesus' perspective at least, that eudaemonistic considerations played no part in his considerations at all. There is no word of Jesus or of the disciples that complains about the pain or the shame of the cross or that expresses that resistance to death which arises from the natural desire for life. Natural motives, however, which produce our human longing and thoughts, of course played a continual part in the entire process. But in Jesus' dealings with his disciples it was clear from the start that these longings had no part in the resolution of the issue posed by the cross.

Religious considerations, too, rendered the cross difficult and contributed to the fact that it initially appeared unimaginable to the disciples. Would it not destroy both the existing divine work and the divine promise? Jesus' crucifixion was the act of the nation and was decided by its leaders. That Israel killed the Christ, however, was its fall. This was the one issue that rendered Jesus' idea of death incredible to the disciples. His cross tore them away from Israel, and their entire religious condition rebelled against this.

This train of thought also comes to light by the fact that what was considered the most difficult thing regarding Jesus' demise was his being handed over to the Gentiles as well as the form of his execution, crucifixion. He ended up on the cross as the one rejected by Israel, leaving it for Gentiles to judge him. The cross was rendered particularly difficult not by the special shame and pain accompanying the crucifixion but by the fact that it was for everyone the visible sign of the Christ's rejection by Israel and thus of the fall of the elect Jewish community.

The forward-looking thoughts of the disciples that were devoted to the coming rule of God also were completely altered by Jesus' certainty of death.

They imagined him in the glory of his complete sonship as the one whom nothing separated from the Father, feeling the triumphal assurance of the one who had power over death. It appeared impossible to them that his work could result in a conclusion other than the revelation of God's rule. Now, with the cross, divine sonship was separated from power, communion with God from the possession of life, the office given by God from the possibility of its fulfillment, the regal status from final victory. This required a humbling before God that far transcended what the disciples had attained up to that point, a humbling whose severity was acknowledged also by Jesus. For he had previously imparted to them the concept of the kingdom without the anticipation of his death, while simultaneously now helping them through his prophetic words to unite with his will.

When the disciples' representative, Peter, expressed their objection to his prediction, he showed them that he obeyed the Father with his will to the cross. He thus saw in the cross not merely an opportunity but a necessity, not a bitter fate but a duty he seized decisively (Matt. 16:22–23). He did not partially agree with the disciples' thoughts, deploring that circumstances rendered their hopes without chance for fulfillment, but trampled them under foot because, by yielding to them, he would have ceased to obey God. Therefore he called the disciple a Satan, an accuser, since his counsel entailed the accusation that his divine sonship had become a delusion and that his confidence in the Father had failed. He perceived the correctness of his death-oriented will by turning his thoughts and desires toward the things that were God's, while Peter directed his thoughts toward the things that were man's, even when he claimed God's protection for Jesus. As long as the disciple took his aim from what man was to receive through God's rule and through the sending of the Christ, the Christ's cross appeared to be a calamity. The desire arose that the Master would preserve the disciples, shield Israel from this guilt and judgment, and confer God's gift on Israel without the Christ's death. In these considerations, however, the things that were God's, such as divine righteousness, grace, and rule, were forgotten.

Jesus' will to the cross, on the other hand, revealed love for God that was intent on the revelation of God's greatness, the execution of God's justice, and the operation of God's grace. For this reason he expected his disciples to understand him and to remain his disciples even then. For his entire word and work served the goal that they would be concerned for the things of God. He wanted to lead them, also, to that love of God which truly honored God as God, a love beyond the life of man and free from selfish desire, free also from cheap happiness, power-grabbing, and striving for greatness. They were to know through their fellowship with him that a piety which longed for the things that elevated man became sin, that a Christ who served only men was not the Christ of God, and that he came so that they would render to God what was his. Because Peter here once again resisted the meaning and aim of Jesus' call to repentance, he was not taught but reprimanded and threatened with expulsion from the community of Jesus' followers if he persisted in his thinking. This was an object lesson for him in why Jesus had to die. For he

saw in himself the profundity of the contrast that separated Jesus' will from
that of the disciples. Since even the disciple longed merely for the things that
gave life, happiness, and greatness to man rather than thinking of the things
of God, it was Jesus' vocation to reveal how God was honored and what genuine love and complete obedience were. Thereby he transformed the disciple
who himself stood in conflict with God into the one who knew liberation
from guilt and sin and who could give it to others.

At this moment, Jesus revealed his opposition against intellectualism with
particular clarity. He did not relate to God by seeking to understand God's
will before he obeyed. In view of his death, he therefore did not need a doctrine depicting the outcome according to its content, rationale, and significance. The norms resulting from love for God were clear to him as the final
and certain component upon which he based his actions. Therefore it was sufficient for him even then to illumine the contrast of wills by word and deed
that existed between those who strove for their own preservation and glorification and the one who accepted the cross from God. Thereby the longing of
love was fulfilled simultaneously with the desire of obedience. Since his cross-
focused will was founded in his love for God, he did not make a show of it.
The sacrifice remained pure by his refusal to calculate and admire its greatness. He subjected himself to the principle that the left hand should not know
what the right hand was doing when giving a gift, even when giving the greatest gift of all.

It is an established fact that Jesus' crucifixion seemed to his disciples to be
the demonstration of perfect love. As peculiar as this may appear to us, it cannot be brushed aside. Already Jesus' first pronouncement regarding his death,
however, shows how it came to be. He revealed to them that he did the deed
of the cross in the love of the Son to the Father. By this he gave them an adequate understanding of what he did. The suspicion was rendered impossible
for them that his will was rooted in weakness of faith, in a lack of trust in God,
in a darkening and weakening of his communion with God. They were made
to realize the necessity and fruitfulness of his cross, since he had to be rejected
by those who fought for their own cause on account of his love for God, and
since he could not die in vain for them but would procure the greatest success,
because what is done out of love for God cannot happen in vain.

The other sayings linked by Matthew and Mark with the announcement
of his end spoke of the necessity of death. They spoke not in such a way that
they weakened the obedience Jesus required from the disciples by construct-
ing around him a theory that could easily have degenerated into a theodicy
but in such a way that Jesus obliged them to discipleship on his way to the
cross (Matt. 16:24–27). In that which he obliged them, however, he also revealed to them his own will. By liberating them entirely from themselves and
by enabling them to forsake their own lives, he revealed that he, too, placed
his entire will into the idea of death; by making their loss of life their gain of
life, he showed that he, too, did not abandon his commission by desiring the
cross but that he intended thereby to fulfill it. It was true both for the disciples

and for him that he did not self-destruct when he readied himself for dying. His way to the cross was also for him the way to life.

He expressed this so strongly that one may with some justification wonder whether Jesus underestimated the value of money, work, marriage, law, or country. It is impossible to believe, however, that he underestimated life and that he had a longing for death that resulted in a pessimistic denial of life. Nevertheless, it was his greatest deed, beside which all of his other works pale by comparison, that he gave himself to death voluntarily. But he made it completely clear that his will was something entirely different than abandoning his office and his work. He did not act out of ennui but embodied the complete affirmation of life. For him, this was no abstract concept. He did not think of the preservation of his spiritual substance or of an empty self separate from his calling. His promise to the disciples, too, was not conceived of in an abstract fashion but promised them that the life they would gain by dying would preserve everything for them. It would complete what they now were as his apostles and what they acquired for themselves through their work. Likewise, the preservation he wanted to gain for himself by his cross pertained for him to his concrete relation to the Father and to the world. As the Christ, he would not disappear through his death but attain to life. In such a way he would fulfill his calling, upward to the Father and outward to the world.

Therefore he linked the prediction of his execution with resurrection on the third day. He did not see merely the cross but pointed at the same time to a new kind of life that the Father would give him. This assurance cannot be separated from Jesus' will to the cross, just as the promise of life for the disciples cannot be separated from their calling to martyrdom. That the promise for the disciples remained distinct from the expectation Jesus had in regard to his own end corresponded to the continual distinction he made between himself and them. The promise that they would "save and preserve their soul" did not say anything about the way in which God's care would be operative upon the dead disciple, how and where he would continue to live after having been faithful until the final act of renunciation. For himself, on the other hand, Jesus elevated the thought beyond this uncertainty because he persisted in his commission. This meant that the question for him was not at all how he himself would be saved and attain eternal life, but how he would fulfill the Father's will for humanity and how he would prepare the promised end for it, so that God's rule would be revealed through him. Therefore he did not think just of his soul with regard to his own end but of the renewal of his person, not in the indefinite future but immediately subsequent to his death, a renewal by which he would continue his work and preserve his communion with the disciples.

Once again, the differences in kind between Matthew's and John's accounts reveal the profundity of events. When Matthew tells us how Jesus prepared his disciples for the way to Jerusalem, the motif of obedience controls the entire discourse. It is God's will! This excluded any question regarding the reason or purpose of his will. The disciples had to obey, just as Jesus himself obeyed. Jesus' will to the cross, according to Matthew, sprang from his Godward perspective, from his desire to preserve for God what was due him. For the disciples, for Israel, and for mankind, his cross brought the greatest loss. But he cannot be concerned with man. For his cross is the service of God, bowing before God, the effort to honor God in his gracious righteousness. For this reason Jesus even longed for the cross. That is how Jesus was; but this is not yet the entire account of Jesus' resolve.

What John says regarding the way in which Jesus provided for Capernaum and for his disciples a foretaste of his end destroys nothing of what we learn from Matthew. By depicting his flesh as the nurturing food and his blood as the true drink Jesus did not create a theory that looked past God's will for another basis for justifying himself. "I give my flesh": Jesus expressed this as his own deed, thus showing the community the position in which he saw himself in relation to it. No disciple pictures Jesus asking whether his aim could be reached by some other means or why it was necessary to make his blood a drink for man and his flesh food. His death rather became his own free act by the fact that he thereby did God's will. Especially in Capernaum Jesus expressed his complete commitment to God in strong terms. Since he could not achieve anything unless the Father turned people to him, he also could nourish them with his own flesh and blood only when he accomplished God's will by the cross. John expressed with utmost clarity that Jesus did not glorify himself in his death but the Father, and that he expected glory from his death because God would become great and glorious through him.

The obedience exercised by Jesus in his will to the cross was, however, not coerced but one with love. Matthew impressed this upon the church by the contrast between Jesus and Peter. Peter obeyed under compulsion, Jesus voluntarily. Being concerned for the things of God meant to love God, and when Jesus did this by yielding his life, this was pure, unconditional love. But this love knew (however little it needed more basis than that it did God's will) that God's will was good and perfect even if it gave the Son over to death. What according to Matthew were "the things of God" for which Jesus longed in his death we know through the Lord's Prayer. We know that these things had nothing to do with God's self-preservation but that they arose from God's relation to the world, from his rule and his call to man.

By uniting love with obedience in his desire for the cross and by not allowing any division between them, Jesus completely separated what he did from any experiment of effecting God's grace and of establishing the new community by an atoning act. His entry into death was admittedly a cultic act in the highest sense, but not in the pagan form of an effect imposed upon God from below but in such a way that his cultic function consisted of the performance of the recognized divine will. Therefore love for the Father and love for humanity remained one in him even then.

On this account the words proclaiming the cross are in Matthew directly linked to the attestation of his work as king. He cared for the things that were God's by establishing that community which was freed and no longer captive behind the gates of Hades. Not despite the fact that he was the Christ but because of it he faced death, and not despite his death but through it did he build the eternal community.

This brings us to the pronouncement by which Jesus, according to John, took leave from Capernaum and, according to Matthew, from the disciples: his slain body, he said, was the bread of life. In John, too, Jesus' sacrifice remains entirely separate from the pagan concept of sacrifice. For Jesus did not remove himself from God when he died, as if his death had its aim in a process that would have had to originate in God; he rather placed himself into complete dependence upon God, for which reason his success consisted in what he gave to humanity. Just as light, in Jesus' view, does not need to be created by God but is his attribute and radiates from him into the world, revealing God to it, life, too, does not need to be established in God. The individual, on the other hand, needs it and receives it through Jesus' crucified body.

It is the definite testimony of the disciples that the prediction of death did not produce any change in Jesus' work with the nation or with the disciples. If we object that Jesus would no longer have been capable of working and loving once he was certain of his death, we think of the weakness of our own will. But because he went into death, because he sought what was God's, the certainty of the cross did not bring joy, love, and work to an end for him. What was done for God bore power and blessedness in itself. He saw in his end not the victory of human or satanic evil but perceived that thus God's grace and righteousness would become effective. This did not result in fatigue or abandonment for the time left for him and the service still to be rendered. Because Jesus made his death a service of God, he bore it joyfully and freely.

The disciples' wavering at Jesus' death cannot be used to counter their testimony that he had kept reminding them of it since the departure from Galilee. In their conduct during the final events, after all, it was not only their resistance to his cross but also their allegiance to Jesus that became apparent. When he told the leaders of Jerusalem the story of the son whom the vinegrowers murdered, the disciples did not step aside in terror, and when he called them to eat his body and to drink his blood because he brought them the new covenant, they did not turn away in unbelief. The kinds of events by which the disciples portrayed their unbelieving conduct at Jesus' death, too, show simultaneously that they were sincerely devoted to him. Only in that night did Peter conceal his discipleship; before this, no disciple ever said a word that denied his relationship with Jesus, and this although his death had long been within their purview. Those who said, "We hoped he would redeem Israel" (Luke 24:21) were without hope at that time; but even then suspicion regarding Jesus' sending from God had no room in them. The women who wanted to honor his dead body considered him dead, but their veneration of him had not been destroyed by his cross. Of these two events, only the disciples' state of belief is difficult to understand; it is self-explanatory that they broke down at Jesus' death. This merely reveals that reality is more important than our ideas. Only after his arrest did they leave him, precisely when his execution was no longer merely an idea but reality. That the disciples, however, remained together until Jesus' arrest, and that they were not estranged from one another through the approaching end, did not come about without Jesus' help. This help consisted of Jesus' weaning them from their dreams of glory and his showing them through open discussion regarding his end that he himself bore death without breaking apart, because he died in the power of his commission and of his office as king. Therefore they stuck with him.

6. The Sign Given to Jesus Personally

While Jesus usually revealed God's mercy powerfully to others, the disciples told in connection with the prediction of his death of an event where God's unhindered communion with him appeared to him directly. The sign occurred away from the community, even from the disciples, in the Galilean hill country. Only the three closest to him were witnesses to this event. In contrast to the dying that destroyed his body and shamed him, he received radiant light. His clothes became shining white, like those worn by revellers or saints. In contrast to the condemnation to which he was subjected by present Israel, Moses and Elijah appeared to him, and offsetting the rejection by men appeared the sign of the proximity of God, the bright cloud and divine voice giving testimony to him as the Son. As was the case at his baptism and resurrection, it was solely his personal closeness to the Father that the sign revealed. For it did not effect any change in his situation or place any tangible means of power into his hands. The disciples' view was directed toward Jesus' actual condition of life, toward what God made Jesus to be.

The event has connections both to the disciples' confession of Jesus' kingship and to the prediction of his death. After they had confessed the Christ, Jesus' transfiguration served as the confirmation for their confession, for they saw the heavenly glory upon him. Likewise, it guaranteed them the promise Jesus had given them in anticipation of his end. They saw how dear he was to God by the fact that God's glory was available to him; their hope clung to the fact that he died and would rise while performing his task. At the same time, the event revealed the greatness of renunciation Jesus took upon himself through the way to the cross. By stepping from so intimate a communion with God that he was capable of transfiguration into the pain and struggle of the cross, the liberty and greatness of the will to the cross became apparent. Because this thought moved the disciples, their narrative formed a stark contrast between what happened on the mountain and what occurred with the disciples. From a condition of blessedness, Jesus descended to the unrepentant community with its faithless way of life; from the company of perfected righteous men he returned to the wavering disciples. That he took this upon himself was the free decision of complete love. It was therefore not natural necessity that forced him to die; even less did death face him because the Father forsook him. He was so close to him that he already saw his own glory, and yet he humbled himself to the cross, precisely because God was present to him in a way made visible at the transfiguration.

His desire for the cross was strongly rooted in the contrast between what he possessed with the Father and what men did to him. He had to deny himself to remain with that faithless generation, and he longed for his death because it would lead him into the Father's glory. Was this early Christian poetry designed to visualize the passion story and the loftiness of the deed on the cross for the community? The event is not merely miraculous but has at the same time connections with concepts current in the synagogue. The rational interpretation of nature and of man spread by the Sadducean priests did not permit any exemption to the rule that our life ended with death. Therefore they interpreted even what Scripture said about Elijah's and Enoch's assumption to heaven as describing their deaths and contended that Moses was most certainly not taken up to heaven.

On the other hand, that portion of the nation that was opposed to the Greek worldview in line with Pharisaic teaching occupied itself all the more eagerly with those who had been taken up to God. To Enoch and Elijah were added the likes of Ezra, Baruch, and Moses. If then the disciples and thereafter all of Christendom had to familiarize themselves with Jesus' death, could they fail to think of those who had in previous times been transported up to God? Did they perhaps thus strengthen their own faith in Jesus' continual existence in heaven by stirring up, through the story of the appearances of Moses and Elijah, their certitude that these, too, really lived with God? In that case, the imagination of the nation occupied itself with those who had been taken up to God not only because they were considered to be privileged friends of God and acquainted with his counsel, but also because they were presumably assigned a new task in the endtime, since they would return to the earth with and perhaps already before the Christ. That Moses and Elijah came to Jesus corresponded to the Jewish expectation that made them associates of the Messiah.

Moreover, the manner in which the heavenly glory is revealed upon Christ's body is reminiscent of the pictures by which transfigured persons are usually portrayed. Likewise, the characteristics of God's presence, such as the cloud and the voice, follow existing conceptions. This account, too, as everything that we are told about Jesus, is clearly influenced by existing thought forms.

The verdict here depends upon the judgment we render regarding Jesus' demise and regarding miracle reports in general. Whoever rejects the resurrection story and limits Jesus' religion to spiritual processes also will reject the transfiguration account. It is conceivable only when a unity with God was revealed upon Jesus that encompassed him in his entire condition, soul and body. The judgment regarding Jesus' resurrection therefore necessarily comes into play at this point. The same can be said regarding miracle stories according to which Jesus acted in the certitude that God's power would also transform natural processes. Whoever considers it improbable that this confidence of Jesus corresponded to reality will lay the transfiguration aside. If Jesus, however, in the course of his ministry to others, ushered in divine effects that affected people's natural condition and not just the state of their souls, it can no longer be considered impossible that he also experienced such effects with reference to himself.

Even when one explains the account by his community's desire to remind itself of the greatness of its crucified Lord, it remains a rich documentation of Jesus' effect upon it. For the community did not take the will portrayed by the incident from its own imagination but knew it because it saw that will in Jesus. Here God's glory was in operation, not for the sake of sparing others suffering, nor for the sake of making its recipient happy—this was what Peter thought of the transfiguration in the story and therefore he was considered to be without understanding—but as a fortifying for the cross, so that the will to the cross might be free and complete. Nowhere but in him did the disciples see the will that turned willingly away from the transfiguration to the humility of earthly labor, to patience with the incompetence of the disciples and the nation's failure to understand, to mercy on the desolate.

7. The Task of the New Community

Still in Capernaum, Jesus once spoke with his disciples about their conduct toward one another in such a powerful way that this instruction provided forever the rule for their community. The occasion was the disciples' desire for him to name the one whom God would make the greatest at the revelation of his lordship. The rule of the Law and the teaching regarding merit lent the desire for greatness considerable strength, so that the question of who would outdo the others by his religious achievements and be the greatest was continually discussed in Jewish circles. It also immediately received practical importance, since everyone's place in the community depended upon his greatness.

The desire for greatness, however, appeared to be entirely confirmed by the promise of God's rule. It made those great who attained to it and gave different degrees of greatness according to one's measure of calling and work. But when the disciples presented their question to Jesus, he used it to annihilate in them the longing for greatness entirely. For it resisted God's rule, rendered one blind to it, and robbed those who yielded to it of their share in it. The disciples' question revealed that they needed to repent. Jesus illustrated the aim to which they were to turn by a child. Thereby Jesus demanded from the disciples the renunciation of exhibition of their strength and assertion of their significance, not only in their dealings with God but also in their dealings with one another. He thus applied to them the same standard by which he judged the Jew "righteous." The self-admiration that considered one's own religious conduct to be superior and that enjoyed and exhibited it was considered by him to be sin in the case of his own followers just as in Judaism. Greatness belonged to the things "that were God's" and that people should leave to God.

This rule had greatest significance for the disciples' common life, since a religious community acts differently depending on whether it exhibits its worship and admires its ethical achievements or whether it transfers the aim of its longing from itself to God and thus protects itself against self-admiration. Obedience to Jesus' rule extends the scope of its work, since it is now capable of honoring even small things and of using its power to help the weak. Jesus' rule produced in his community liberty and equality. It was not because he rebelled against the differences that existed between people or because he sought to conceal those differences that equality became his aim. He did not confront the longing for greatness with the pronouncement that all were equal but placed a child before the disciples, who stood not on the same level but beneath them. He called those who had fallen fallen, the righteous righteous, the small and weak small and weak, and the great and strong great and strong. Since he continually treated ethical norms as valid, it was not merely quantitative differences of strength that resulted from them, but also absolute, qualitative contrasts. And this was not merely in such a way that the basic disposition of people varied, so that one was wicked and the other good, but also so that good and evil became significant factors within the community and within individual life, since here, too, good and evil appeared continually and needed to be judged accordingly.

Jesus likewise did not conceal differences in power. He rather revealed already in the institution of the religious office that he did not expect the same from everyone in his service. In the parables of the field that produces fruit and of the talents, he expressly stated that not every hearer was able to make the word effective for others to the same degree, because the disciples' share in his gift was measured differently. Nevertheless, the obligation to serve remained constant for everyone, and the smallness of the gift never justified lovelessness. Yet Jesus still produced equality in his community, since, once the effort of procuring greatness for oneself was eliminated, the tendency toward portraying others as small fell by the wayside as well. Once self-admiration was obliterated, so was the contempt of the weak, and since it was replaced by help for them, this resulted in a continual leveling of differences. The righteous did not separate himself from the one who had fallen but united with him by forgiving him and lifting him up to his level. The strong one did not place himself above but below the weak, serving him and allowing him to share in his privilege. Thus the community was liberated, since there was no rule in it. Therefore Jesus developed no rule by which he ordered people's relationships to one another, although he gave to the apostles the religious office in the highest sense.

Why the liberty of everyone coexisted with the power of the office, why it did not push others down to idleness and dependency, becomes immediately clear by the fact that Jesus did not tolerate any greatness in his community. An office that is liberated from greatness is no danger for other people's liberty and leaves their responsibility and activity intact. Such an office is rather exercised by liberating others and by strengthening them in their activity since greatness consists of service. Therefore a brotherhood developed out of those who jointly obeyed Jesus, a union of free and equal peers. This resulted directly from Jesus' concept of love, from the fact that he did not unite his disciples by common property or by a common work but through love. Love claims and affects man and places the same value on each person, even the weak and lapsed, that the righteous and strong bestow on themselves (Matt. 7:12; 22:39). Thus all become equal, and all are free (Matt. 23:8–12).[8]

With the struggle against the will that craved for greatness Jesus linked instruction for believers who were united in brotherhood. This instruction no longer dealt with the disciples' calling regarding the entire nation, as the commissioning discourse had done, but gave them the aims they were to achieve in their dealings with one another. The community existed for the weak and small. It did not merely tolerate them but esteemed and helped them. Mercy was coupled with the readiness to serve the small. Jesus made his community into a fellowship where love toward the lost and endangered was at home. His community's completeness did not consist of the fact that it did not have any weak people in it but that it was able to bear them up, not in the fact that it rejected the guilty but that it led them back to God. This picture of the church stood in the same contrast to the ideals of the time regarding the glorified final state of the nation as Jesus' cross did to the ruling power of the Expected One.

Helping love is given the greatest promise: it is rendered to the Christ himself. How can the disciples continue to offer him their love and attain to closeness with him when they order and perform their communion and work without him after his death? Jesus did not give them the mediation of God's omnipresence as a means that would also make the Christ omnipresent, nor a religious act by which they would be able to touch him at his heavenly abode, but the demonstration of love to the small. For it preserved the disciple in fellowship with the Lord as a service rendered to him.

Since the disciples' dealings with one another were rooted in love, those dealings were characterized by ethical sincerity without exemption, for in Jesus' view love never worked evil. His followers were therefore linked with one another for the sake of the joint struggle against sin, and the one who caused another, particularly the small, to sin, was subjected to the most severe judgment. Therefore the circle of disciples also received a rule for the discipline to be exercised by it. By this discipline the evil found in its midst could be uncovered and removed (Matt. 18:15). Parallels in Jewish literature show that Jesus was not at all moved by the thought that he had to invent his own new law for his community. What it needed was merely that it used the given ethical insights and that it acted accordingly with all sincerity. His rule of discipline prevented the shaming of the one who had fallen; discipline included mercy. Therefore it was initially the personal, secret admonition that was required. Only then was the matter brought before the community, and even

---

8. The condition of the first community confirms here the Gospels at an important point. That community repudiated self-glorification as folly and sin, even in Hellenistic areas. For this reason it also had equality and liberty. To explain the Gospels as legend while lauding the Christian communities a few years after Jesus' death for their liberty and equality is a historical misjudgment. Two opposite misinterpretations continually cling at this point to Jesus' word: either one eliminates the apostolate for the sake of the liberated community, or the free community for the sake of the apostolate; either Matthew 18 or Matthew 16:18 are neglected. Both misinterpretations fail to understand Jesus' concept of service.

at that time for the purpose of preserving the sinner for the community of disciples. There was no room for a kind of justice that worked merely in negative terms, one that could do no more than dishonor and exclude. Until the time when it was impossible to preserve communion, it remained open to the one who had sinned. Simultaneously, however, it was noted that the community could not tolerate evil. If the sinner broke God's Law with persistent resolve, communion with him was lifted; he became for it "as a tax-collector or Gentile."[9] Thus the same law was valid in the circle of disciples that Jesus himself kept in his dealings with all: God was not to be denied on account of man; association with God rendered any community, even the one uniting the disciples with one another, subject to suspension, for they were brothers of the Christ who did the will of God.

The connection of concern for the lost and weak with serious discipline that did not leave any room for evil was possible for the community since it could forgive, and this did not merely constitute its privilege but also its inviolable obligation. Therefore Jesus concluded the discourse by the threat that the disciple would be thrown into prison if he dishonored a fellow-slave by failing to forgive. Without that capacity, discipline, by which they jointly opposed evil, would be entirely elusive. It embodied the willingness to forgive at its root, for it wanted to overcome evil by liberating its perpetrator from it. Only thus developed in the community that kind of honesty without which discipline became unattainable. The refusal to forgive always led to hypocrisy, the desire to cover up evil, the demise of trust. By exercising genuine forgiveness, the community rendered its dealings authentic. Now it became possible to address the effects of a lapse and to protect discipline against the kind of tyranny that crushed the weak. Community was rendered impossible only by that evil which rejected forgiveness in an unrepentant attitude.

These ethical aims alone provide the contents for the circle of disciples. We hear nothing of a technical apparatus for the attainment of certain religious or social successes.[10] Jesus' conception of religion once again proves to be entirely personal in its approach. Since the love awakened by Jesus was directed toward man and included his natural needs, the community also helped its members considerably in the acquisition of their daily needs (Matt. 19:29; Mark 10:29–30). But not a single word reminds one of this. There is not even a reference to the inward happiness and the riches of the joy that spring from the community. Once again the whole focus is placed upon the ethical calling. This, however, entirely excluded the individual's self-sufficiency from Jesus' perspective. The thought of a perfection or holiness for which man should strive by himself is completely missing. The task for everyone lies, not in his internal experiences, but entirely in the relationships into which he enters

9. Those who attributed to Jesus an admiration for high-minded tax-collectors considered this ruling incredible. But there is no contradiction with the call of Matthew or Zacchaeus. Jesus called them to himself precisely in order that they would no longer stand before God and men "as tax-collectors or Gentiles."

10. The first community strove for the same ethical aims as are depicted in this discourse, without any religious technique.

with the brethren. Obedience to Jesus occurs through concrete actions, and those have their place, not in one's isolated individual existence, but in dealings with others.

The convictions that lent the circle of disciples unity are also in this case not discussed for their own sake but are treated as the prerequisite for their ethical work. The disciples pledge allegiance to the Christ, they have in his name what unites them, and they believe in him. Their faith is directed permanently toward him, so that it controls their entire conduct and becomes their defining characteristic. Jesus' promise belongs to it; for he acts as judge of those who believe in him, as the one who avenges any attempts at luring them into temptation. While they may be small, without intellectual power, and without great works, they are still associated with him, because they direct their trust toward him, and they are his possession for whose protection he exercises his office as a judge (Matt. 18:20, 6). But by believing in Jesus the community is not merely turned backward to the past but also has the Christ present in its midst. He is at every assembly that has its basis in his name. There is as little an effort to formulate a theory that seeks to explain his omnipresence as when Jesus describes himself as the one who builds the new community (cf. Matt. 18:20 with 16:18). But this did not cause the conviction to lose anything of its all-encompassing power, by which it determined the entire conduct of the community. The thought remained far from it that it was left to itself and separated from Christ. He is with it.

By this it is given the right to pray; it owes the answers to its prayers to the Christ's association with it. He is the advocate who makes its prayer answerable, and by him it has that grace of God from which its right to pray originates. This results in that great confidence by which it recognizes in the weak and lost the subjects of its service and gives its life for them. The power necessary for this is available for it, since it can ask, and it can ask since it is united in Christ's name and has him with it (Matt. 18:19–20).

Likewise, the community has the ability to forgive since it has itself received God's forgiveness. Since Peter has been forgiven all of his sins, it becomes sin for him to take revenge on his fellow-servant and to torture him. Forgiveness is not described as a future aim the disciples still have to attain. They have it, not apart from Christ, but by the fact that Christ has called them to himself. Thereby their immeasurable guilt is canceled, and they are put in God's service as his servants in spite of it. The certainty of justification that constitutes the final word of Jesus' call to repentance is made the basis for the community. Yet this occurred not in such a way that the gain and cultivation of certainty became the community's aim, but in such a way that it was understood to be the basis of their duty, because it could only be preserved if it had the power to determine the disciples' conduct toward one another.

Jesus places complete confidence in the community's forgiveness that it would grant God's forgiveness and would execute God's judgment by its own judgment. Its loosing is loosing before God, its binding before God (Matt. 18:18). If a brother's unrighteousness compels the community to oppose him, his relationship to God is at stake together with his share in the community.

If he leaves because he does not want to forsake his sin, he is judged by God; if he permits himself to be severed from his sin by the brethren, he has God's forgiveness. Thereby the community is instructed to attribute completeness to the forgiveness granted to it by virtue of the fact that it continually subjects its concrete, particular sins to it. Yet a theory by which Jesus divided the completeness of grace into daily justifications or an institution that effects reconciliation with God anew every time it performs its rituals, or a casuistry that sought to delimit the validity of law and of grace in relation to one another, did not originate with Jesus. He smashed such casuistry when he denied the question whether or not forgiveness would be exhausted after granting it seven times.

The community's equality and liberty has its basis in the uniqueness of God and of Christ. By his rule it is free from all other authorities and desires to wield no rule itself but rather submits itself in the assurance that its submission is its greatness. Jesus made this the motivation from which the community's entire constitution resulted. He did not represent this, however, in a theoretical discussion (Matt. 23:8–12). Thus the community, similar to Christ, embodies the contrast that is mysteriously held in tension: it grasps simultaneously for the smallest and for the greatest, hiding the greatest in the smallest and revealing the smallest as the greatest. Since it is not a community of the strong and perfect but rather is open to the weak and exists for their sake, it unites an external inconspicuousness with an internal completeness. It is inconspicuous in its service, by which it proves helpful for the lost. Successes that change the world do not belong to its duties. Its greatness and honor consist of doing what the shepherd does who goes after the lost sheep. With the abandonment of external power, however, comes the ethical perfection, a condition of faith that is assured of God and certain of its forgiveness, that therefore has love not as an aim that is sought in vain or that is celebrated in words only but as a motivation for action, a love that unites man not merely with his fellowman but also with God.

The rules ordering their relationship to the surrounding world agree with those regulating the internal organization of the disciples. Matthew cites one such rule that determines the disciples' conduct toward the synagogue (Matt. 17:24–27). They are free from the religious taxes levied on the Jews, for the community consists of sons of God whose worship is no longer limited to services valued in monetary terms required of the community by old regulations. At the same time, it is required to avoid giving offense and therefore does not break the custom but submits to it, even when it has been freed from the custom through its own relationship to God. By this, too, Jesus made an all-embracing contrast the characteristic of his followers. They stand above the Law and at the same time are subject to it, they are free from it and fulfill it. They are free from it on account of the Christ whose divine sonship has renewed their relationship to God; they fulfill it for the sake of Israel that condemns the breaking of the Law as sinful apostasy and therefore would take serious offense at the disciples' liberty, rendering access to the Christ more difficult.

At the same time Jesus gave his disciples the confidence that their surrender of liberty would not harm them. Peter receives the coin no one was entitled to demand from him and that he must nevertheless pay to Israel from the riches of God, to whom also harks the fish. Even if legend may have added the fish to the powerful commandment of Jesus that subjected his own's entire dealings with the Jews to the rule of surrendering love, legend grasped historical fact incomparably better than its critics. The giving of offense was not prevented by a forced subjection to Jewish demands. Surrender accomplished its goal only when it occurred resolutely and cheerfully. Only faith, however, could cheerfully surrender its own right and the expression of its own conviction, and this required the certainty for the disciples that divine grace would help them when they went the path of renunciation. Jesus did not give them merely the weighty commandment that was full of sacrifices but also what made "his load light" for them: a confidence in the rich God.

Mark recounts in this context that John prohibited a Jew from using Jesus' power over the spirits when confronting demons without, however, actually following Jesus. John insisted that he receive Jesus' approval (Mark 9:38–40). This ruling ordered the disciples' relationship to those who joined themselves to Jesus but not to the disciples. They could have easily followed the tendency not to accept any faith in the Christ as genuine and wholesome which originated beyond their own community. Against John, however, who had difficulty in accepting an undecided, wavering attitude, Jesus maintained that his rule and grace did not end at the boundary of his circle of disciples. He upheld any trust rendered to him, any obedience that did God's will. Thus the circle of disciples received the twofold task of appropriating Jesus' great promise and to base their community on it, while not limiting Jesus' power and kingdom to their own circle. They were rather to honor his regal authority, which made him, even beyond their own fellowship, the Savior of all with whom his name met acceptance.

8. The Dispute at the Feasts in Jerusalem

When Jesus finally broke off his dealings with the Galileans, he did not immediately force the issue in Jerusalem but spent some time with the Jewish communities east of the Jordan located in the region called Perea by the Jews. Luke reports that he also visited a larger number of Judean villages, and John recounts that the Jewish village called Ephraim was Jesus' residence prior to the last Passover and Jesus' fateful course of action. This village was close to the Samaritan border at the foot of the hill country beside the uninhabited district descending to the Jordan. On this account it granted Jesus security similar to Capernaum.

Before he himself entered a village, he first sent two of his disciples. Therefore he did not appoint merely the Twelve to be his messengers but enlisted seventy men. They were not to cross the country as a large group but were to go two by two so that they could disperse to the villages he wanted to enter (Luke 10:1–20). By the increased number, which had a relation to Israel's old constitution similar to that of the "twelve" apostles, he now expressed the increased urgency of calling the nation since it was confronted with the final decision and his death was near. Their instruction consisted of the same sayings as the instruction of the Twelve at their commissioning. The identical nature of those instructions reveals that these sayings were to be set apart by the disciples as the commonly valid rule for any activity in Jesus' service. The new element, on the other hand, is a report regarding their success that is instructive regarding their relationship to Jesus.

What they experienced at their commissioning did not shake their faith in Jesus. While the commissioning discourses and the further course of Jesus' ministry indicate that their success was not great, they nevertheless returned rejoicing and reassured since Jesus' name had proved to them its power even in their dealings with demons. This provided the basis for their confidence in Jesus. Even if the larger Jewish community remained at a distance to him, their faith did not originate in the community's attitude but took its cue from the power given to Jesus by God.

Jesus linked what his disciples were capable of with what he himself did for them before the Father and what he saw occur in heaven, for the disciples' power was based upon what he himself had been given. That they overcame evil spirits had its basis in the fact that Satan was now barred from heaven, so that he could not appear before God as their accuser.[11] This, however, was not their greatest joy but that their names were recorded in the book of life. As indispensable as their participation in Jesus' work was, it was even more necessary for them to free themselves continually from the consideration of their power and success and to remind themselves of the major issue: they were given salvation through their communion with him. Having God's pleasure was the great and the entire blessing.

The struggle in Jerusalem grew more intense with every new feast. In the fall, Jesus went from Galilee to the Feast of Tabernacles, and in December he traveled from the region east of the Jordan into the holy city to the Feast of Dedication. Since the Feast of Tabernacles attracted a large portion of the nation, Jesus' brothers wanted him to force the decision at that time and to gather his disciples around himself in such a way that the community established by him would be revealed. Jesus, however, saw in their counsel resistance toward God's will, which was already being revealed with sufficient clarity. If he forced a decision from the people, it would lead him to the cross. But Jesus was authorized to postpone this, being guided by the conviction that the Passover, the feast of Israel's redemption, would be the right hour for his death. Therefore he did not go to Jerusalem with the throngs of pilgrims at the beginning of the feast but arrived at the temple only in the middle of the festive week.

11. We should hardly imagine Jesus to have watched Satan's fall passively; the meaning of the saying appears to be that, since Jesus interceded for the disciples before God, Satan was denied access to God's throne of judgment. The saying has no overtones, however, of being some admiring meditation upon Jesus' greatness.

The dispute arose through the fact that Jesus demanded faith from the community. This meant internal, free, and therefore complete allegiance to him. He substantiated this claim by the messianic promise, not by describing God's rule that gave eternal life but by succinctly promising to the community gathered in the temple the fulfillment of the messianic hope. Since the credibility of his promise, however, depended on his closeness to God, and since his opponents denied or doubted it, his divine sonship became the target of their attack and gave rise to his defense. The dispute found its conclusion in the fact that Jesus, on the one hand, told the Jews that they had become the children of Satan on account of their lying and murdering and that he, on the other hand, revealed his divine sonship all the way back to its origin in God's eternal being. Thereby the division that separated them from each other was completely brought to light; it was as irreconcilable as the contrast between truth and lie, love and hate, God and the devil.

The way in which Jesus described to the inhabitants of Jerusalem their share in God was entirely new to them since it has no parallels in the human history of thought. Only in Jesus were the prerequisites for his consciousness of eternity fulfilled, merely in the fact that he knew his work to be given him by complete grace and that he sensed the unity of his will with God's will to be complete in a pure conscience. Since he served, free from self-condemnation and in complete obedience, that will of God which created the eternal, he could unite the concept of eternity with his practical life-setting illuminated by his human consciousness.

Without the messianic aim of being God's Son, however, his thought would have inevitably been pushed in a gnostic direction. In that case, he would have separated the divine power residing in him from his person, would have set it beside or above himself or into his substance or into his nature conceived as lying in his subconscious. Solely the one called to execute the divine work, who followed his calling in complete obedience, could consider his conscious acts of thought and volition to be caused by God and his human condition to belong to God. It was Jesus' concept of love alone that led to the fact that the concept of eternity did not cancel out his self-sufficiency in relation to the Father. No leveling with God resulted. The clear distinction of his life from God and his entire submission to God remained the characteristics of his communion with him. Since he had a vocation to which he devoted his entire will, he also had his own life as also did the Father. But he did not attribute that life to himself, as if it had been his own creation and the means to his own glorification, but considered it to be God's presence within him.

But the new element in his thought was precisely what intensified people's opposition to him. The concept of preexistence in the form that souls already existed previous to birth in the beyond was well known to Jerusalem's teachers. This preexistence, however, merely referred to the soul inherent in consciousness, not to a person's self. If Jesus had formulated his thought in gnostic fashion and distinguished a preexistent nature from his human person, his opponents would probably still have doubted and disputed his statement without, however, condemning it as blasphemy. Since Jesus, however, claimed in his humanity a heavenly origin and eternal glory, his thought amounted to blasphemy for his opponents.

In Jesus' dealings with the disciples, too, his concept of eternity emerged the more clearly the more completely he described his messianic work. Since the Christ introduced the community to its eternal fulfillment, giving it eternal life, his words of prophecy expressed in all accounts his concept of eternity. Yet this was not a theory steeped in speculation but the ground of his will that determined his way to the cross and his dealings with his disciples. By depicting himself before them as their eternal Lord through the prophecy of the parousia, the backward-looking concept of eternity by which Jesus attributed to himself life and glory in the Father before the inception of his human existence provided the complement that formed the basis for his promise.

Jesus also revealed the completeness of his divine sonship by appropriating the concept parallel to eternity, omnipresence. If he freed himself through the former concept from time, he distanced himself by the latter from space. He could think of himself as omnipresent, likewise, merely by attributing completeness to his relationship with God. He also did not conceive of his omnipresence in gnostic terms and did not promise that something of him or in him would be everywhere with the disciples, neither a power proceeding from him nor a nature residing in him. He himself would be with them. The concept was established simply by the fact that he was omnipresent as God was omnipresent. His concept of eternity had the same form: he was eternal since God was eternal.

To his verbal testimony at Jerusalem about his union with God Jesus added the deed by which he opened the eyes of the blind, in clear anticipation of intensifying the opposition of his antagonists and of closing the eyes of those who claimed to see. Subsequently he elaborated upon the purpose for which divine sonship was given to him and upon his concept of the Christ by the image of the shepherd. First he spoke of the fact that the ministry which gathered his community would be mediated by the ministry of his disciples since he, as the door, would lead the right shepherd to the community. Then he spoke of the fact that he himself as its shepherd would provide for its gathering and guidance, protection and care.

Although he revealed thereby his kingly aim openly and completely, substantiating it by the attestation of his divine sonship, he nevertheless did not use the messianic name even in Jerusalem. At the Feast of Dedication, the inhabitants of Jerusalem therefore reproached him for putting them deliberately in an uncertain position of wavering since he denied them a definitive statement regarding his regal status. By surrounding him in Solomon's colonnade they sought to force an explanation. Jesus, however, resisted any demand that sought to force him to present himself to the nation as its king. Likewise, however, he did not take on a mysterious air, as if he were the founder of a mystery religion who was too noble for the people. He rather expressed his intentions once again most explicitly by way of the image of the shepherd. But they were denied what they demanded and awaited: his application of the messianic name to himself. Thereby he acted in Jerusalem according to the same principle by which he had also conducted his work in Galilee.

9. The Ordering of Natural Relationships within the Community of Disciples

After Jesus' discourse in Capernaum informing the disciples what the purpose for their union with one another was to be, Matthew collected from Jesus' dealings with the disciples in Perea those actions by which he ordered their natural relations (Matt. 19:1–20, 16). While the community strongly seized its highest aim of giving to God what was God's, the ties of natural life did not lose their importance, and the disciples knew how decisively the lives of individuals and of the community would be affected by what Jesus had said about them. They also realized how profound the contrast was between their community and that of other Jews regarding their treatment of natural relations.

In contrast to the custom that had always existed among the people and that was expressly condoned and declared compatible with piety by the Pharisaic rabbinate, Jesus excluded divorce and required complete marital faithfulness from his followers. He thus acted as the protector of women against the abuse they suffered by being handed from one husband to another. The only limitation he gave his rule arose from the fact that love even then not lead to promoting sin but remain united with the ethical norm. Therefore the woman lost the protection granted her by Jesus in the case of license (Matt. 5:32).

By this rule Jesus prevented the community from avoiding marriage and from replacing it with brotherly communion. It consisted of families in which the husband was united with his wife in a permanent and wholesome communion. At the same time Jesus gave love toward God the freedom to renounce marriage according to the same principle that he applied to any property, right, and honor. The pure and effective renunciation of marriage was accomplished in the service of the divine lordship in obedience to God's government rather than out of selfish desires. It had its prerequisite in the fact that it can be achieved, not by a wavering will and by internal struggle, but in complete resoluteness. When it met those conditions, Jesus praised the single life.

Since he based the community on marriage, the question immediately arose how the community's relationship to children should be ordered. Jesus also opened it to children since God did his regal work for them and for those like them. He gathered neither a community of males, nor of sages whose insight enabled them to the service of God, nor of those who had renounced everything and were able to overcome nature, nor of workers who wrestled for the gain of the world in obedience to Jesus. He rather instructed all to have the same attitude toward God's grace as a child.

Matthew does not contain any special instruction regarding women's share in the community. John, on the other hand, deliberately showed by the example of a woman how Jesus' grace created faith. Moreover, ancient tradition already acquaints us also with female friends of Jesus. It indicates that the circle around Jesus did not consist merely of men but that female disciples, too, belonged to the community of those who followed Jesus (Luke 10:38–42; Matt. 27:55; 26:6–13; Luke 8:1–3; 7:36–50). John revealed why the woman's religious status immediately and entirely changed by encounter with Jesus. "If you had asked me, I would have given to you," Jesus told the woman (John 4:10). This was the rule of complete grace, which also enabled the child to be included in God's rule. Likewise, that same rule overarches the difference between men and women. Now the woman no longer stood as the weak person beside the strong, as the one exempt from obligation beside the one so obliged; for the calling to faith does not know such differences. The woman, too, was thirsty; thus God gave her the living water she sought. She, too, prayed; thus she likewise was called to that worship that proceeded in the Spirit and in truth. She, too, was able to listen to God's word and thus had the one thing that was necessary. In this respect, too, Jesus produced liberty and equality in his community.

It is profound that the disciples added Jesus' verdict regarding wealth to the saying regarding marriage and children, because the esteem of wealth received an obvious, ethically vigorous substantiation from what Jesus said about the family. Therefore it was now maintained, the natural relations having been sanctified, that the community had turned its desire completely away from wealth and that it had become free in relation to its possessions. For it knew that Jesus, when he required from a rich man the renunciation of his possessions, did not do this in the opinion that his requirement was harsh but on the basis of the explicitly expressed confidence that God was good. For the rich person was rich in God's sight when he gave away his possessions and was received by Jesus among his disciples. The offer of discipleship, too, was essential for Jesus' demand. But renunciation did not lose its own internal value on this account. Jesus gave it its own promise, since by it the rich person gained a treasure in heaven.[12] Whoever was rich with God was perfect, had the secured state of salvation, and thus also had the confirmed state of faith. Jesus did not merely demand renunciation from the rich apart from his entrance into the circle of disciples and did not merely require it on account of the apostolate so that his commandment arose just from the particular circumstances of the circle of his disciples. While placing great value in renunciation, he linked it with the positive decision by which the rich person gained a new vocation. He did not call him to become poor in order for him to sit on the street as a beggar; but the rich person was rather to embrace this renunciation because he was to come to Jesus and receive from him the greatest conceivable good. He could not give it to him before he had become free from his fortune. Renunciation, however, was valuable also in itself, since it provided a person with that genuine possession which an individual can receive from God in having a personal tie with God and by receiving his grace. By

12. The common misconception that one would someday in the future have great blessedness in heaven did not understand wherein Jesus saw the wealth of a person. He saw it not in the fact that a man or woman at some time in the future would enjoy great happiness but in the fact that God granted him his gift. Treasure in heaven is what one receives now.

renouncing his possessions he proved that he sincerely longed for God and for eternal life. It was love for God to renounce everything for God's sake, and Jesus gave his promise to this kind of love. Whoever had it was "perfect," had reached his goal, had seized eternal life, and was elevated above the anxious question whether it might be attainable for him or not and what he had to do in order to attain it. Now his relationship with God was clear and firm.

When the rich man did not find the courage to obey Jesus, he claimed that it was impossible for a rich person to enter God's kingdom. He expected the rich to choose the wrong thing, for he knew how completely possessions replaced God in a person's affections. Help for the rich came therefore solely by God's omnipotence that made possible what otherwise was impossible. For while the rich had little esteem for God, the latter did not therefore also reject the rich. God rather forgave them their attachment to wealth and freed them from it so they could learn to honor God.

Jesus did not conceive of the simultaneous validity of both statements—that it was impossible for the rich person to attain God's rule and that it nevertheless remained possible—as illogical nor as compromise by which he lowered his "ascetic ideal" closer to reality. Both statements rather resulted simultaneously and uniformly from the same assurance that provided the foundation for Jesus' actions, which was God's goodness. Since he alone was good, but since he was truly good, a person's entire love was due him, and it was guilt that separated the rich man from him when he loved other goods than the sole one who was good. Moreover, since he alone was good, even truly good, the rich man need not be lost due to his misguided affection. Rather, salvation was available also for him, namely the salvation granted him by the good God in his goodness.

His requirement that called others to the complete love of God would never have been able to find a hearing with them unless he had revealed with great clarity the characteristic of love also in his own relationship with the Father. By example he taught that love did not seek one's own will but that of the other person. If he wanted to liberate his own from their selfish desire, he himself had to stand before them as the selfless one, as the one who had whatever he was and had as the gift of the Father and who did not have his own wealth and success as his goal. Therefore the disciples also included in the Gospel the beginning of Jesus' conversation with the rich man. They recalled how he rejected the request for him, the good Master, to inform him what work he would be able to obtain eternal life since no one was good but God. But he added that God was truly good, and he recalled him to the divine commandments in their simple clarity rather than fulfilling his wish and giving him a commandment of his own (Matt. 19:16–17; Mark 10:17–18).

The desire to receive a new commandment instead of the old, one that would guarantee life right now, Jesus called godless. He considered this demand to be a denial of God, and it was not improved by the fact that it was addressed to him. Jesus could not allow himself to be praised as good while permitting at the same time and precisely on that account God's goodness to be denied. He always spoke out against that kind of religion as the son who protected the Father's goodness against any doubt and who completely honored his commandment. A glorification of his own worthiness at the expense of God, trust in his counsel coupled with distrust in God's commandment, the acknowledgment of his goodness together with the reproach of God, amounted for him to a complete impossibility.

At the same time, however, he put the entire consciousness of his power into the revelation of his selflessness without obscuring it or wavering in any way. For he did not send the one away who called him "good," as if he regretted that the good was as concealed for him as it was for the petitioner, but called him to himself and thus offered him perfection. He did not set his authority in the place of divine authority but had his authority solely in God, whereby he obliterated any doubt in God. In God, however, he did have authority, the authority of the one who gathered the eternal community, and therefore he called people to himself with the absolute promise and the no less absolute requirement.

Those who used Jesus' answer to the rich man, and the other actions of Jesus that revealed the selfless nature of his love for God, as proof for his sense of guilt sought sin at a place where Jesus revealed the purity of his will with particular clarity. By honoring God alone as the one who was good and by not issuing any commandment other than God's, he elevated himself above the entire history of religions that everywhere produces counselors, people who take others' confessions, and moralists who shape their ethical systems according to their own desires without any awareness of the godlessness of their own behavior, like the Jewish young man did. We consider this to be normal, "ethical," since we have a distant and unknown God whom we neither trust nor obey, thus aiding our aimlessness by our own ethical fabrications. It took the entire aliveness of Jesus' divine sonship to reveal the contempt of God contained in this kind of religion and in such good works. By distancing himself completely from it and by speaking as the Son who did not place his own will above God's commandment and who did not claim honor through the contempt of God but sanctified God's clear commandment as the sole way to salvation, he revealed by the selflessness of his love for God its authenticity and genuineness. There is no contrast but rather the strictest causal relationship between his abandonment of his own honor, by which he placed himself to the side so that God's goodness alone would be believed and God's commandment would be done, and his unity with the Father by which he knew himself given the entire divine love and power for the performance of a truly good service to God. By self-promotion over elevation against God his sonship would have been destroyed and his goodness a lie. He was Son and good precisely by virtue of the complete abandonment that desired nothing but God's rule.

Thus Jesus arrived at the ordering of the natural relationships in which we live by making love fruitful for others and free from material things.

While the disciples, according to established custom, considered it possible to sever the union with their wives while considering the bond with their possessions as indissoluble, Jesus bound them to the mates God gave them and drew them away from the things that constituted their property. Through perfect love, from which he took the standards for the ordering of all natural relations, marriage received its inviolable nature, while all rationales regarding its benefit or happiness clashed with its indissolubility. Since Jesus required from the husband a kind of love that was not consumed by a crass desire for erotic enjoyment, children, or other advantages, but which was devoted to the wife and honored and esteemed her as himself, marriage provided this complete bond. By this God's will was done. For the same reason Jesus commended together with those who were married those outside of marriage. For the kind of love directed toward others was not the first or only thing that mattered but was exceeded in importance by the great commandment. Based on this commandment a renunciation of marriage could arise that was wholesome, because it was truly rooted in the highest love.

Through love the child was incorporated into the community as an equal member, since rights in the community were not established by the accomplishments of its participants but by the greatness of divine grace. Through that grace, however, the community's freedom toward money also remained intact, and the determined struggle against its overpowering force continued to be its duty. For love toward God liberated from any other bond and enabled a person to any sacrifice. Therefore, however, there also was no need for casuistry and legislation in these respects. There is no commandment by Jesus regarding the baptism and the instruction of children, just as there is no ruling on the economic system to be adopted by the community. It has everything it needs for the accomplishment of its tasks when it has love.

By directing God's rule to those who were like children and at the same time to those who renounced their possessions, he graced his disciples in two ways at once. He made them recipients of God's gift freely given to them, and he rendered them complete, persons who invested complete love into God's rule and who were able to suffer and to act. On account of this, however, there arose no question for Jesus that caused him to elaborate how reception and production, how childhood and adulthood, related to one another. In Jesus' discipleship there was no room for a "synergistic dispute."[13] He placed them before God's grace as children, since grace was God's and since he gave it and transformed them into liberated men, and because God's grace must be entirely seized and his word completely done. These two movements of will, like all of these antitheses, were united in the concept of God. Jesus viewed God as the one who gave and who ruled over him, for which reason the recipient of his gift stood before him like a child. He did, however, see in God a genuine love that granted the individual a good, determined will. Therefore he led him to that love of God that was able to say good-bye to all other (and lesser) goods.

13. Only thinkers who had been influenced by Hellenism considered this a mystery and sought formulas for the relationship between the human and the divine will, since to them God's will, owing to its might, appeared to suspend human will.

On the other hand, he allowed bright light to fall on the danger of the kind of arrogance that attached itself to the free, active power of love. It demonstrates the clarity by which the disciples observed these actions of Jesus that they linked the condemnation of the rich directly with the struggle against the consciousness of those who denied themselves. When Peter cheerfully clarified the contrast between the disciples and the rich man who decided in favor of his own wealth and against Jesus' calling, Jesus initially confirmed to them the value of their sacrifice by a promise to which he assigned the highest formulation for the present and for the future. Since he wanted renunciation, he also wanted it to be exercised and borne cheerfully, not as a misery and misfortune but as gain.

He described the distinction they drew between themselves and Israel by renouncing their possessions and by following him as so real that it would provide the ground for their share in the power of judgment over Israel. Moreover, all they renounced would be given back to them many times over since a genuine and complete fellowship would develop in his community that would be their wealth. In order for the disciples' joy and confidence not to lead to sin, however, Jesus coupled his promise with the condemnation of religious arrogance, showing them by the example of the laborers who had been hired at different times how first became last and last first. The refutation of any arrogance resulted from the fact that the share in God's gift was not calculated by the rule of merit, which granted the appropriate reward in proportion to human performance, but was determined by God's grace, which forgave and gave in its own liberty above and beyond all rules of remuneration.

Precisely because he grounded the disciples' confidence in the generosity of divine grace, his promise was accompanied by a sharp call to repentance. For that call made clear not merely that God's grace reached down into all the depths of human need but also that it resisted those who tied it to the greatness of their own achievements and thus denied it to those who were weaker than themselves. If the disciples forgot that those who did not presently match up to them might still be called at a later time, and so transformed the grace given to them into the basis for their own honor, they became the cause of their own fall. For in this case, too, the first could become the last.

In similar terms as in the conversation with Peter, the power keeping the disciples with Jesus and fueling their communion with one another was revealed in the request of the two brothers who asked for the complete communion with him in his glory (Matt. 20:20–23). In them dwelt a strong love and glowing hope that desired to rule and to judge with Jesus and that was likewise determined to drink the cup with him. The same train of thought stood behind the disciples' request that Jesus recognize which of them was greatest. It likewise informed their naively optimistic appraisal of the renunciation they had achieved. Their thinking provided Jesus with a foil for addressing his ethical demands to them.

Jesus did not entertain the thought that he had to shake or sober their confidence. By confirming to them their share in his regal and juridical work, he nurtured and strengthened their love and hope, for the purity of which he provided by depicting for them thrones as God's gift and by submitting them to his ruling will. In this way, too, any dispute was avoided that might have arisen between their desire for thrones and their duty to serve. Their thoughts of glory did not prevent them from exercising sacrificial love if they understood their share in Christ's judgment sincerely in terms of the revelation of God's righteousness.

When the disciples subsequently rebelled against the thought that James and John might have been destined for a special share in the regal glory, Jesus again shattered the conventional ideal of power, thus differentiating their community from all others by prohibiting any rule that originated in the elevation of one over another. He took from them the greatness that was established in the humiliation of others, the honor that resulted from the abuse of others, and the power that was acquired by the slavery of others and that originated from making others powerless. In his community greatness was achieved by bearing, liberating, and elevating others, not by binding and humiliating them. Thereby Jesus injected a powerful tension into the disciples' aspirations, because he assigned them thrones and gave them the office effective before God and producing eternal yields, while simultaneously denying the bearers of the office the rule and the passion to rule and by lifting the distinction between the privileged and the disowned, between the esteemed and the despised. For he united all through the selflessness of love that used whatever God provided for God in the service of others.

10. The Disciples' Instruction Regarding the Purpose of Jesus' Death

Jesus substantiated the prohibition against that rule which was typically exercised by the rulers of the nations by his surrender to death (Matt. 20:28). The disciples had long observed that he did not demand others to serve him but that he served them. He made this attitude complete by acquiring his lordship through the surrendering of his life. Therefore the disciples were thinking like he did only when they desired no greatness save for the distinction of service. How Jesus served others by his death and how he gained his lordship through his cross he expressed by the statement that he would give his soul as a ransom for many.

With this saying, likewise, he subjected all of his thoughts pertaining to the cross to the rule of obedience. The topic of his instruction was not how the disciples had to conceive of his death but how they order their relationship to one another. The salvific power of the cross he considered self-evident; the outcome would reveal it when the many would be liberated from their bondage. On the other hand, he saw the danger that threatened to confuse the disciples' thoughts in the fact that they were lured by a false concept of rulership, and if they were blinded by it, his cross would, of course, became a dark mystery for them. He also used the instruction regarding his cross to keep them from a misguided craving for power, showing them that he did not ask great things merely from them but that he himself did even greater things.

The community described the Promised One as the "redeemer and liberator."[14] Jesus related to these conceptions by comparing the surrender of his life to the payment of a ransom, by which a person subject to punishment was freed from the penalty or by which a slave was set free from slavery. By this he based his death simultaneously upon God's righteousness and upon God's grace, which he considered to reflect a unified will. God's righteousness that rejected the sinful will of man and consigned him to death subjected him to arrest from which he was unable to free himself. Jesus honored God's righteousness as valid and therefore acted simultaneously in the assurance of divine grace. For the purpose for which God led him into death was that a community would be born through him, one free from guilt and death. Since people resembled prisoners, Jesus served them by freeing them, and through his death he received the ability to place them into God's grace and into life despite their guilt. Just as he promised his disciples that they would not deprive themselves of honor and power by serving others but that they would thus find their greatness, he also had in view regarding his own will to the cross the result that he would achieve by it. He would thus gain as his own possession the large community that possessed freedom from guilt and death as the fruit of his death.

The new pronouncement did not deviate from the saying that he would die in order to give God what was God's. He would die so that God's truth, righteousness, grace, and rule would be revealed and effective through his death. For with this pronouncement, too, he derived his will to the cross from the obligation that arose from his relationship to the Father and that described his death as his form of worship. He paid the ransom to God that was due him in order for his righteousness to be intact and his verdict regarding mankind to be valid. At the same time, however, he expressed how his love for the Father would become fruitful for others, how he transformed into one and the same will love for the Father and love directed toward others. Since he gave to God what belonged to him through his death, it served as a ransom for people who needed a redeemer. Therefore he placed beside the prophecy of his death the promise that he would build his community, which had eternal life despite its share in guilt and death, and therefore he called his flesh the bread that the community might eat unto eternal life. When he became the bread that gave life to the dying and the ransom that provided liberty to the guilty, these were not two separate events or two incompatible concepts. Just as life and liberty were joined, bread and ransom likewise were related.

This word also does not go beyond God's will and does not demand any justification for him. Even now, Jesus did not seek to find a necessity apart from the divine commandment that would have induced God to give the commandment, thus providing Jesus additional certainty regarding his duty. He knew only one question: What kind of exercise of authority would meet with God's good pleasure; how might he gain it by thinking in divine terms and by remaining one with God's righteousness and love? From this followed

14. Firmly attested are the terms *goel, parok, g(e)ulla,* and *purkan.*

for him that he did not allow others to die while wanting to live himself, that he did not demand life from others so that their unrighteousness would be atoned for, but that he gave his own life for them in order that they would be forgiven, being certain of the fact that he thought in divine terms, in a way that comported with God's gracious righteousness. Thereby his decision took on firmness, since death possessed for him a necessity by which he could pull himself together freely and completely. Doubts may always emerge in response to theories. Ethical norms, on the other hand, are perennially valid. Since Jesus acted in full assurance, that he was preserving good will and doing what love does, he bore his cross cheerfully and freely. Therefore he also made his will to the cross the norm for the disciples, to which also their action must conform.

Rationalism has spread the view that this pronouncement of Jesus regarding the fruit of his death was incompatible with the offer of forgiveness to the repentant and that it sank below the assurance of God usually evident in Jesus. The argument runs as follows. While he otherwise had considered God's grace to be the will present in God that did not yet need to be awakened in him, the concept of God was obscured by his supposed demand of a ransom in order to liberate prisoners, which is what demanded Christ's death. Against this argument, however, we note that by the images Jesus used to illustrate his call to repentance—the two sons, the slave pardoned by the king, the justified tax-collector—Jesus portrayed what God did through him for those who repented. These images contain therefore the concept of a mediator no less than the words regarding the cross, for that concept is always contained in the Christ concept, since the community receives God's gifts from the Christ.[15]

Such parables also combine God's righteousness with God's grace as completely as the words regarding the cross. When Jesus acted upon the guilty and righteous in such a way as he described it there, he represented God's opposition toward evil as poignantly as when he derived his cross from God's verdict against the sinner. The righteous are separated from God's good pleasure, and the prodigal son is placed in a state of misery without hindering the father who gave him his grace only by converting him through Jesus. For God the guilty party became the one who was dead and lost. It was the same with the prison term ended by Jesus' ransom.[16] Jesus likewise drew his activity from God's grace in the same perfection.

15. Rationalism completely failed to grasp the Christ concept and therefore avoided it. Moreover, since this concept emerges unambiguously from his words regarding the cross, these, too, were offensive for it. Of course, if one transforms the parable of the prodigal son into a timeless abstraction and into a mood separated from history, reading in it the admonition that the guilty party should place himself into a joyful mood by deciding not to think any more about his own fall, one receives a message incompatible with Jesus' will to the cross. Such interpretations, however, are useless for historical research.
16. Jesus did not ask why God demanded a ransom, just as he did not ask why he left those who had fallen away with the pigs rather than bringing them home. As strange as it may seem for us that Jesus did not rebel against God's righteousness, the fact remains.

Jesus' will to free by his death those who were bound and his will to give them the name of sons and to clothe them with honor—these two wills are one and the same. The festive meal he prepared for the guilty by calling them to himself is nothing but the freedom he provides for the many through his death. The words regarding the purpose of his death are spoken for the purpose of excluding the thought that his call to repentance was going to be denied or refuted by his cross. By acting upon the community as those images portray and by justifying those who repented while rejecting the righteous, he also provided death for himself.[17]

When he thus was crucified, would that prove his verdict wrong and render his gift worthless? Jesus did not permit these thoughts. He called the following of him by penitent sinners their institution into God's sonship, not although he died, but because he died. Since he never conceived of his divine sonship in terms other than that he gained by it the obedience that bore the cross, he had the authority to justify the praying tax-collector and to make the penitent person a son of God, just as he had, for the same reason, the authority to reject the proud righteous person. New in Jesus' exiting of the earthly scene by the cross and in the words interpreting him in the disciples' insight was merely how Jesus revealed God's grace to them and how he gave his gifts to them, how they received the festive meal, sonship, and justification. He did so not merely by giving them his word but also by the fact that he bore the cross for them, not merely by giving them his bread, but also by giving his life for them.

The cross, however, did not introduce a change in the union of God's righteousness with God's grace and of Jesus' work with God's activity. The imminent end did not obscure God's grace for him, nor did it make him merely the preacher of the divine wrath and judgment, just as he remained free from a selfish version of God's love at the beginning of his work. He had always been ready to sanctify God's righteousness, even by his own death, and had always seen in the execution of justice the complete act of grace.

Therefore Jesus had no occasion to attach to his death a special purpose beyond the one served by his work as a whole. He died in order to be able to do in eternal perfection what he had always done: to call, to forgive, to set free by revealing the glory of God's grace. He did not have room for two doctrines of salvation, one regarding the healing effect of his life and another concerning the healing effect of his death. For God's grace was not shown in him by things and thus did not consist of segmented blessings. God was completely good for those for whom he was good. Whoever had him, has him completely.

Therefore he also did not put together his own work out of various segments. He lived as one called to die and died as the one going into life. When he called the individual to himself, he connected him with the one who bore the cross and with the one who lived forever. What he was before the Father and for the world, he was through the life that gave him the sonship and

17. The conception is untenable that these parables temporally precede Jesus' will to the cross so that Jesus at that time did not yet think of his death.

through the obedience by which he seized the cross. These things were not separated in Jesus' consciousness. Therefore his teaching of the cross did not need any particular substantiation in his view. He rather used it to substantiate what he commanded his disciples. Since it was clear that God had commanded him to take up his cross, its saving effect was equally clear. While he gave his soul to God, God gave him the community in exchange. On this account his soul was a ransom.

When during discussion with the nation at the Feast of Tabernacles he portrayed wherein he saw his work and God's gift through the parable of the shepherd, he used the parable to help the people realize the connection between his death and the office of the Christ (John 10:12–18). Beside the hired hand who guards the flock merely for his wages he placed the shepherd who owns the flock. They act differently when the wolf attacks the flock. The determined, strong love that binds the shepherd to his property shows itself in the fact that he gives his life for it. The success of his act—that the shepherd dies but does not remain in death and thus protects his flock effectively—could not be described by the image of the shepherd; but this does not rob the parable of its power. By this image Jesus showed both his opponents and his disciples, not the benefit of his death, but the inner necessity that called him with compelling power to the cross, and by this was clearly revealed how he conceived of the outcome. He gained it by the surrender of his life and thus became the savior of the community. He preserved his possession without harm and saved it from all danger by dying.

It is always the same train of thought that the disciples depict as Jesus' inner certainty. The two statements—that he would give his life as a ransom for many whom he thereby would give liberty and that he would bring his community security and life through his death—are parallel. The imprisonment that requires a ransom and the danger arising from the wolf's attack aim at the same human condition, and in both images it is his death that is the means by which he provides salvation for the community.

The regal majesty that gave Jesus his will to the cross achieves clear expression in John. He dies for the flock because it belongs to him and thus remains his possession. The regal will of Jesus revealed itself in this glimpse of how the one who will die views the community he founded. By his will he drew it to himself as his possession. This has parallels in the fact that he surrendered his life to the rebellious vinegrowers because the vineyard was his inheritance and belonged to his Father, and to the fact that he acquired by the many the community that belonged to him by leading them from slavery into freedom.

The renunciation and humiliation, however, which he took upon himself through his surrender to death lost thereby nothing of their veracity. His concept of lordship, precisely because it included the cross, remained free from all taint of selfishness. Since people were bound, since the flock was in danger, and since those who fought against God were headed for disaster, he did not want to protect his own life but to die so that they would be helped. After all, he wanted to show his disciples precisely through his death that he did not permit any rift between majesty and service or between the selflessness of love and its glorious power, even when at present both elements were entirely separated.

According to the Johannine word, danger arises for the shepherd and for the flock through Satan. By his death, Jesus overcomes the murderer who wants to rob the community of its life and thereby acquires life for it. By this he also continued the call to repentance, since he always conceived of God's rule in terms of God's opposition against Satan's power and since by the call to repentance he fought not merely against human sin but also against Satan's rule.

In his view of the cross, too, it was not merely a general theory that occupied him, a theory dealing with the relationship between sin and death on the one hand and the afterlife on the other. He rather waged the battle with Satan with his will and his action (John 12:31; 14:30; 16:11; cf. Matt. 12:29). In the case of the ransom paid by Jesus, on the other hand, he thought of God whose judgment caused the misery in which man was caught and whose grace freed those in prison. No inconsistency arose, however, from this in Jesus' thought so that he regarded his surrender to death as a matter to take up with God one moment and with Satan the next. His rendering of obedience to God and his resistance against Satan are rather his single indivisible resolve. He overcame Satan by obeying God (John 10:18).

Again, his soul was the ransom since he opposed Satan unto death. The affirming will by which he yielded to God and the denying will by which he eluded Satan resulted in a uniform act. From Jesus' consciousness of power his gaze fell downward upon the adversary who kills men and therefore also would seek to kill him, and whom he would overcome by dying. From Jesus' mercy that placed him in the service of those who were bound, his gaze ascended to God, whose judgment gave man over to death and whose grace granted him life. Therefore Jesus harbored an intense desire for his own death. The disciples were moved by a saying by which he made his desire for his own end the example for the hope in which they were to wait patiently for his glorious revelation (Luke 12:49–50; cf. Luke 22:15; John 14:28).

He called his death his "baptism" at that time (cf. Mark 10:38) and thereby compared his outcome with the beginning of his ministry. As he placed himself at his baptism in communion with the guilty, he did so again as the one who would die. As the Father gave him his communion through his Spirit when he took the guilt of the people upon himself at his baptism, his cross, too, would bring him complete unity with the Father. Then everything that separated him from the Father would fall away, and he would be consecrated for service and enabled to complete it in divine glory. Therefore he could speak of his "exaltation" when he pondered being lifted up from the earth and dying on the cross, raised up above onlookers. For he saw in all this at the same time his entrance into the glory of God.

11. The Signs Preceding His Entry

Every one of the Gospel accounts, according to its own particular way of thought, places before Jesus' final trip to Jerusalem an act of Jesus that revealed God's will as a shining sign that led him through the severity of the up-coming events to his goal. Matthew narrated that in Jericho blind men did what no one else dared to do by calling upon Jesus as the Son of David. While the larger community did not allow itself to be raised to faith in his regal sta-tus, the begging blind men sought in him the promised Lord, and Jesus con-firmed the name given to him by granting their request. Thereby he placed before his entry a regal act that proved him to be a giver of the helping grace of God precisely when he seized the cross.

The account preserved by Luke told of Jesus' entry into Jerusalem in such a way that Jesus won the head tax-collector in Jericho so that he made Jesus his guest. Since he had the entirety of the nation against himself, he proved himself to be the Christ by lifting the individual out of it. And this was not just any individual but one whom the community had written off as guilty and lost. Jesus acted upon him in the authority of God's grace that was able to forgive and, by forgiving, effected repentance. In such a way he did not yet reveal that grace in its full dimension yet did show its internal completeness. Thus he confirmed, precisely at the time when Jerusalem decided against him, the eternal validity of the divine promise that assigned "the son of Abraham" a share in God's kingdom.

Since the disciples and the crowd that followed Jesus were moved by the thought that he would fully reveal himself at his entry into Jerusalem, he purged their expectation from its overenthusiastic hopes. Luke showed how Jesus did this; he addressed the story about the stewards managing their Lord's possessions to those who spoke of the imminent revelation of God's rule as Jesus departed from Jericho (Luke 19:11–27). Those who thought merely of God's rule and wanted to experience it immediately needed to look at the slaves to whom their master gave a small amount in order that they should prove their faithfulness in what they themselves had been entrusted with.

The other image that is tied to the major part of the parables, the citizens' rebellion against the one who departed in order to get the kingdom, made Jesus' contradiction against overenthusiastic hopes complete. Thereby the se-riousness of the present was entirely revealed, a seriousness arising from the fact that Israel would fall because of its resistance to the Christ. The disciples must maintain their loyalty in the service given to them, as small as it may be.

By the raising of Lazarus John revealed the greatness of the deed Jesus ac-complished by his surrender to death. Through the triumphant certitude of life that filled him and that he exemplified at the tomb of his friend, his death became a free renunciation and thereby the perfection of his love, by which he praised the Father and drew the disciples to himself. John thereby revealed why the cross of Jesus separated him completely from the Jews and why it tied him completely to Jesus. The Jews killed him because he proved to be the giver of life: this severed John completely from Israel and tied him entirely to Jesus, since he saw God's love in the one who gave his life to others and who therefore bore the cross.

The fact that Jesus' crucifixion had on his disciples the effect of demonstrating perfect love requires corroborating facts that Jesus did not merely act with words but actively exercised his love as the one who died. His cross would never have given the impression that God's perfect love had been revealed if Jesus had not had such love and if he had not been able to prove it by his actions. John places the meal in Bethany at the evening before the entry. Here Mary, the female disciple and sister of the one raised from the tomb, proved her grateful love to Jesus by the giving of her precious ointment.

Jesus stated once again how he conceived of God's kingdom and of his messianic office by subsuming her deed under the message of God that had to be told to all of humanity (Matt. 26:13). It had to be proclaimed that he was rejected and killed; for he accepted her ointment as preparation of his body for burial. But it should also be proclaimed that faith and love were devoted to him and that he did not labor in vain. By this statement he expressed, precisely at a time when with his royal name he called Jerusalem and the entire nation to a decision, that he recognized his aim to be in the internal, personal effect that created faith and love in a person. What the Father desired had been brought about when a woman showed her gratitude to him from a pure love.

12. The Triumphal Entry

Jesus linked the proclamation of his regal office with the final entry into Jerusalem. He now also needed the public testimony of the disciples for himself. We must not burden Jesus with the thought that he could still be the Christ even if no one followed him; the acknowledgment of his legitimacy belonged to his office. He desired the community that would praise his rule, and because God gave him those who celebrated his messianic identity, he was able and ready to go to death for them. The public acknowledgment of his office, however, was also indispensable for the community. Secrecy and his messianic identity were incompatible in the long run. If he maintained the secret indefinitely, he surrendered his regal status. The nation must comprehend that the Christ was with it and that God's promise would be obtained or rejected with him. Thus he completed his obedience toward the one from whose hand he had received his office, assuring those for whom it became their salvation of his commission and confirming his verdict regarding those who rejected him.

The new act symbolized by his entry remained internally and qualitatively the same as his deeds in Galilee. He did not make a single move to seize power. He was hailed as king without, however, making claims to be king himself. For those who believed in him, he made it their obligation not to remain silent, thus confirming their witness. More than this he did not do. The manner by which he procured the donkey shows how he balanced his concept of kingship with his poverty. He made no preparations for the entry; he did nothing to give it a festive aura. For he lived in complete trust in the providential activity of the Father. He would not lack what he needed, and since he now needed an animal to ride on for the entry, it was there for him, and he sent his disciples to get it.

This is the first of numerous details in the passion story that are connected by the same perspective: it shows God's guidance in all its events, no matter how small they were. Thereby the final days of Jesus' earthly life became God's revelation for the disciples. They did not seek it in the fact that Jesus was shielded from pain or that he was raised above it. The outcome of his life rather retains for him the gravity of suffering and for Israel the severity of guilt. But precisely because he ended up forsaken by God, the perceptible character of the divine guidance in external circumstances took on strong religious significance for the disciples, because they recognized by this God's work in Jesus' death.

Thus their certainty grew that he bore the cross according to God's will.[18] By the fact that the first of the events, the provision of the prepared donkey, occurred by Jesus' own instruction, it becomes evident that the disciples did not thereby inject into the passion story an element that was foreign to Jesus. He himself already faced his final days in the solemn confidence that the Father would provide everything that was needed and that also in his suffering everything that happened to him was determined by the Father.

John said that Zechariah 9:9 was not explicitly referred to at that time but that it only became significant for the disciples subsequent to Jesus' death (John 12:16). This is unobjectionable. The disciples' acknowledgment of Jesus' kingdom was not based on Jesus' ride into Jerusalem on a donkey but on their inner allegiance to him, which was devoted to his divine sonship and to the righteousness of his ethical aims. Whether Jesus' thoughts were occupied with Zechariah's saying or not cannot be determined. His action should not be understood merely as an enactment of the passage. It therefore also did not need to grow out of the memory of it but was based on the conviction that he owed the disciples and Jerusalem the proclamation of his kingdom.

The selflessness that controlled his behavior also rendered it a mystery for the leaders of the nation. When the messianic acclamation was taken up merely by lads, they pressured him to suppress it (Matt. 21:16). His passive attitude appeared to justify them in this, since, after all, he was not doing anything regal. By answering them, to their surprise, with Psalm 8:3, Jesus expressed his agreement with what was happening, both the children's acclamation and the silence of the elders.

Thus God's will was done. He did not need the elders; God was praised through the mouth of children and in this had the glory he desired. This was the same Christ who thanked God for the illumination of babes and who saw God's revelation in his followers' acknowledgment of his regal office. His answer united the unshakable regal will with abandonment of any hope of re-

18. Such a manifestation of providence is never artificially attained by accounts of Jesus' work; when his ministry moves into the realm of suffering, the account receives its formative principle from the idea of this providential working.

ceiving the larger community's acclaim. It united his ability to rejoice in small and hidden things with readiness for the cross.

According to the Lucan account, there were immediate objections against the messianic celebration (Luke 19:40), and this should be expected in the light of the weight of the messianic name. His detractors here, too, assume that Jesus could not be in agreement with his disciples' gesture but that he had to know that he was not suited for this role. His answer is parallel to the saying preserved in Matthew: when adults remain silent, boys testify. He called the confession of his regal status a divine necessity. He put his entire will into his action.[19]

He would have deviated from his earlier action if he had staged the entry in hope that he might move the nation after all and that he might get it to unite around himself as the Anointed. In this case he would have abandoned the conviction that repentance alone would lead to God's rule and that Israel did not want to repent. Up to that point he had linked proclamation of the kingdom with the word of repentance by demanding confession of his kingdom only from his disciples.

If, on the other hand, he were now to base himself on a jubilant crowd that was not internally committed to him but allowed itself to be swept along by nationalistic ideas and sought in the king the one who would make his glory fruitful for all, regardless of how they stood toward him internally, this would have revealed an altered approach on his part. All witnesses claim, however, that he did not just hang on to the will to the cross at that time but that he based his confidence in it. Through that will all norms of his word of repentance remain fully in force.

In John, there is no room at all for such a question, since Jesus there calls his anointing on the previous evening the preparation of his body for burial. According to the Lucan account, he wept when he saw the city since it was doomed to fall after he had come to it in vain (John 12:7; Luke 19:41). Not even here may we attribute to the disciples an enthusiastic excitement that led to a wavering in their state of faith. Doubtless they praised God with the messianic name for the fact that he would reveal his glory in unimaginable greatness.

But for those who were familiar with Jesus, this rejoicing was united with determined readiness for suffering. When John told Jesus that he was prepared to drink his cup, he was serious, as was Peter when he got ready to go into death with him (Matt. 20:22; 26:35; cf. John 11:16). The account did not become a part of Gospel tradition because the disciples looked back on their former conduct with regret or as an enthusiastic hour that had been contradicted by later events, but because they were convinced that they had done at that time what their obligation required from them as disciples.

---

19. Whoever thinks of Jesus as internally averse to the concept of the Christ speaks of the entry as a calamity, as an outburst of his followers' enthusiasm, over whom he had lost control. In that case, one has to eliminate, not merely the story, but also the two sayings that embody Jesus' originality in the highest degree.

13. Final Conflict in Jerusalem

Even now when the regal name was proclaimed publicly in the city, Jesus, by what he said and did, directed people's view entirely to what the call to repentance demanded of them. He renewed the demand for them to remove the market in the temple[20] and not to despise John's baptism, cutting off those who wanted to question him regarding the Baptist's authority.[21] Even then he did not speak for himself but revealed the community's guilt and need, calling it to turn back to God.

The demand he addressed to the community receives its most profound expression through the three parables by which Matthew recounts Jesus' final word to Jerusalem (Matt. 21:18–22:14). The two disobedient sons, of whom the one initially promised obedience and subsequently became disobedient and the other initially refused obedience and then relented, are followed by the vinegrowers who rob their master. Later the son seeks to confront them, but in vain. The last parable tells of guests who are invited to a feast. Israel is depicted as God's sons, God's laborers, and God's guests. After the concept of the son has expressed the great good granted to the community, Jesus unfolds this idea in two directions: the Son serves God and receives the divine gifts through which he is blessed. We are here confronted with Jesus' entire concept of religion. The divine sonship, which includes the obedience that does God's work and which contains the blessedness that arises from God's gifts, this sonship Jesus called the aim of the establishment of Israel. Therefore it was also the aim of his own commission, an aim providing the substance of his first and final words to Israel.

Through him the community is confronted with the demand to relate to God as his sons with the obedience that is the duty of sons. Whoever obeys him confirms his sonship; whoever contradicts him surrenders it. The second parable deepens the call to repentance, since it accuses the community of rebellion against God, because it keeps for itself what is God's, thus robbing God. By identifying with rebels in order to reconcile them to God, Jesus forces them to choose, and by the nature of their choice they will determine their destiny. By the third portrayal of the call to repentance, the invitation to the festive meal, the community is likewise shown the decision with which it is confronted by Jesus. His invitation confronts it with the divine gift that it must seize. Yet it cannot grasp it apart from rejecting what hinders their calling. Until the end, Jesus' work remained different from that aim which may be called "enlightenment" on a merely rational level. The sons who refuse to obey God, the slaves who use God's property for themselves, and the guests

---

20. See, pp. 137–38,145–46. The two similar accounts regarding Jesus' attack on the market in John 2:14–22 and Matt. 21:12–13 may relate to one another as do the similar stories regarding the Sabbath controversy. Just as Jesus showed the Pharisees insistently regarding the Sabbath that they distorted God's commandment, there is a transparent reason for the fact that Jesus repeatedly showed the priesthood at the market why he rejected their worship. Assimilations of the individual events to one another can easily occur in the tradition.

21. See p. 74.

who reject his invitation do not need and do not receive any instruction that
would prove to them that their opposition was not permitted. Jesus' word was
directed toward their will; he wanted them to judge and end their own conduct and to go the way he showed them.

Subsequently Matthew reveals the ethical contrast between Jesus and
Jerusalem more powerfully than could be done by the harshest accusation as
he brings each of the major religious parties before Jesus (Matt. 22:15–40).
Also here the struggle did not arise in the realm of the intellect but had the
complete seriousness of a dispute that divided the will. Each party suspected
him of belonging to its opponents; the Pharisees ascribed to him Zealot elements, the Sadducees accused him of Pharisaic attitudes. Each sought to expose him through means that had proven effective in conflict with their opponents. Thereby the process became completely hypocritical. As they fought
one another in hypocrisy, inasmuch as each party covered its selfishness and
resultant hate by lofty phrases, they also attacked Jesus with the air of those
who want to discuss Israel's privilege and obligation and what God's Law prescribed. All was pretense, and the desires for which they fought were exclusively selfish ones. They fought for money and women.

In contrast to a piety that required and produced pretense and untruthfulness, Jesus stood as the one who was true, the one who honored God truly as
God without subsidiary purposes and who placed him above everything else.
Meanwhile, the religion of his opponents was a mixture of selfish and pious
wishes, of earthly and divine elements. Therefore they misunderstood him
and took offense at him. The Pharisees who could imagine the Christ only as
a Zealot did not understand that he could grant Caesar what he required since
he was sincerely concerned for God. His aims were God's truth, God's will,
and God's honor. In the robbery Israel committed toward God he recognized
Israel's guilt and abject need. Neither the Sadducees nor the Pharisees knew a
hope that desired more than the restitution of what death took from man.
Jesus, on the other hand, elevated hope above people's earthly existence; what
God would give to the resurrected was a new life for God.

Matthew placed the teacher who put Jesus' regal status to the test by asking
him what was good in the sight of God at a higher level than the parties that
fought with one another for power. But here, too, a complete contrast came
to light between him and Jesus. The teacher saw himself confronted with
many commandments of God, and therefore no longer knew what was great
or small, and how they should be arranged so that the important stood above
the unimportant. As a result, with all his zeal for the Law he remained unsure
of what God's will actually was. By way of reply Jesus pointed to a first commandment that did not need to be discovered but that was clearly indicated
in Scripture: to value and esteem God in such a way that man stood at his disposal with everything he had.

This was the good will desired by God from which all true worship came.
That a second commandment was added did not obscure the uniformity and
clarity of the Law; for God did not merely connect us with himself but also
with one another, and what he required from us regarding the neighbor was

readily apparent, namely, that we should esteem him and value him as we do ourselves. This follows directly from what God desires from us regarding himself. We cannot honor God and dishonor man, nor are we able to serve God and to corrupt man. The love that places us below God places the neighbor beside us. What was a mystery for the theologian was therefore no mystery for Jesus, because God was for him completely different from who Jesus' interrogator pictured God to be. From the perspective of the questioning teacher, loving God was an ambiguous, ineffective matter. For Jesus, on the other hand, it was that will which drew the entire person to God. Therefore all good things resulted for him from the love of God, also the goodness by which he elevated the neighbor to himself.

After these vignettes showing what separated Jesus from all those Jews who struggled with particular zeal for religious aims, the account tells how Jesus distinguished his kingly aim from what Jewish hope desired. Now he attacked the leaders of the community and made the messianic question his topic. He did not speak of secondary matters but of the main thing that determined his relationship to the community: Who was the Christ according to prophecy? For he wanted to ask his opponents how the Christ's rule over David that was assigned to him by Psalm 110:1 related to the Christ's origin from David. But he did not ask them how it was possible for the Son of David to be elevated as his Lord, but how David's Lord could become his son, so that he could become a part of his family and his heir even though he stood above David.

The purpose of this question cannot lie in the fact that Jesus wanted to defend himself against the accusation that he lacked descent from David. If this accusation had been leveled against him, he could not merely have quoted a verse from the Psalms, since a statement from Scripture could not be contradicted by an appeal to Scripture. One was spoken "in the Spirit" as much as the other. The way in which Jesus here used Scripture is an instance of those occasions where he limited Scripture by Scripture according to the formula, "On the other hand, it is written." Thereby, however, he never canceled one passage out, nor did he differentiate between valid and invalid elements of Scripture, but the authority of Scripture remained unshakable and comprised both sayings that were compared in equal measure. By this process it was merely stated how far the applicability of a given Scripture extended.

This interpretation also did injustice to Jesus' opponents, for they did not substantiate their decision against him by appeal to trivialities. What separated them from Jesus was not that he lacked pedigree but that he lacked power. Their concept of rule was different from his, and they considered their own understanding to be supported by the Scripture that made the Promised One David's son and heir. Thereby the expectation that took its cue from the name "the Son of David" became an obstacle for Jesus that barred his access to the nation. Therefore he confronted those who despised him with David's testimony, which honored him as his Lord and did not promise him his own but God's throne. Now it becomes, of course, a miracle that he actually is the Son of David, placed into his progeny and thus connected with Israel in complete communion. But this was no longer the basis for his glory but the reason for his cross. In the face of this miracle they ought to have shown themselves to be wise, but they understood neither Scripture nor God's work.

Jesus' question looked like the beginning of the development of the messianic idea that would unfold the entirety of his stature. Jesus gave an absolute interpretation of the verse in the Psalms, free from any symbolic limitation or historic shortening. Although he stood before the cross, he looked toward God's throne as the place destined for him, and he expected God to subject all his enemies to him. Israel rejected him, but David served him; therefore he bore Israel's rejection whose resistance God would break. He made him king even above all who crucified him. It appears that his messianic statement now gains large proportions. But he restrained himself and merely posed the question to silence his opponents. Even then he did not move from the messianic work to Christology, from waiting for God's glorifying witness to self-attestation. He could not show those who fought for money and women why the Christ did not act according to their ideas. It was sufficient for them to realize that their judgment regarding the Christ's glory was sinister and beclouded, not only when they judged him but already when they interpreted Scripture. What they considered to be the greatest thing, the inheritance of David's throne, was for him the small element. He looked toward the true greatness promised to him by Scripture that God would grant him with himself.

The connection between this pericope and the preceding one that portrays Jesus' dispute with the parties is probably deliberate. The conflict between Jesus and his opponents always arose at the same point. What God had and gave was real for him and was what he desired, while it was null and void for his opponents. They esteemed a king in David's likeness; to sit on God's throne was an empty image for them. Therefore they considered glory what he saw as his humiliation and despicable agony what he viewed as the path to glory.

In all these passages it became apparent how the word of repentance and Jesus' will to the cross reinforced each other. When he refused to give an answer when asked for his authority, he acted in the assurance of his death; for the necessity of his death resulted from the unbelieving, unrepentant attitude of Israel, which allowed not even a discussion of his communion with God, much less true communication. By the series of parables regarding the sons, workers, and guests of God he explained how he revealed God's righteousness and God's grace in their unity and perfection through his death. Since he did not hand over God's possession to those who robbed it, he suffered; thus he sanctified God's righteousness while establishing the new community that truly served God and celebrated God's feasts.

Likewise, it became clear through the words by which he rebutted the attack of the parties why he was able to retain the will directed toward the cross. If he had argued with Caesar regarding taxes, he would have had to fight and prevail, not suffer and die. Since, however, he wanted to give to God what was God's, he surrendered his life to him and thereby sanctified God's name and Law. If he had allowed people to perish as the Sadducees did, he could not have wanted to die. For this he needed the assurance that God would remain his God, as he was, and remained Abraham's God so that he would live in him.

And if he, with the Pharisees, had thought of a resurrection that would merely preserve what was earthly, he could not have been ready for the cross, since it would be futile if the resurrection merely restored the old order of things. But his aim lay above the earthly state of existence, and he reached it for himself and for the world through his death. If he had not known what was good before God and if he had not loved him with all his strength, if he would have had to despise others and could not have loved them as himself, his surrender to death would have been meaningless. In such a way, however, he fulfilled through his death the great commandment and thereby the entire Law.

And if his calling had consisted of the restoration of the Davidic throne, his path could not have led him to death. Since, however, he sought his rule at God's throne and saw in his present condition his humiliation, he faced the cross without fear. Israel would not overcome the one whom David considered to be his Lord. He also did not need to fight; God would subdue his enemies, for death for him was the way to God.

Because Jesus attributed the community's distance from him to the religious conduct of the Pharisees and rabbis, by pronouncing his verdict over them he revealed what it was in Pharisaism that he rejected. He expressly stated once again that he did not differ from the rabbinate on account of doctrine, but because it freed itself from God's commandment with regard to its actions and thus introduced into its piety the contradiction that destroyed it.[22] Therefore Jesus also explicitly called his final word a word of repentance.

The condemnation of the community is not grounded in its theology or lack of insight, although Jesus' recognition of the rabbinate did not entail his approval of all of its pronouncements. Much of what one heard in the synagogue was childish in his view. But the fact was not thereby done away with that the rabbinate represented God's Law and that it instilled into the community what Scripture required. What it added to it of its own thoughts did not constitute the reason why Jesus separated himself from it. He did not separate from the rabbinate on account of its heterodoxy but because what it did was blameworthy and corrupted the community. The struggle was played out in the ethical arena until the final word.

The same inconsistency that tore apart the word and the deed of the teachers Jesus also demonstrated to be present in Pharisaic conduct, linking doing what is right with sin. On the one hand stood the incredible precision by which the Pharisee dispensed of his obligation to tithe, on the other the open rebellion against the main focus of the Law: justice, kindness, and faithfulness. On the one hand was a concern for purity that was exaggerated to the extent of the most tedious washings, on the other the crass impurity of their meal. On the one hand was their glowing missionary zeal, on the other the evil to which they enticed those who fell into their hands.

22. See pp. 225–26.

On the one hand was the great fear of oaths, on the other a casuistry regarding oaths that deliberately showed ways of taking oaths without actually doing so. On the one hand was veneration of the prophets whose tombs were celebrated, on the other the inner indifference toward those who killed them, which drove them to repeat the murder of the prophets, not only in Jesus' case but also in the case of those he sent. Therefore Jesus created for them the powerful image of the white-washed tomb that contained only dead bones. This pairing of righteousness and sin, of obedience and disobedience, was not abnormal for Pharisaic piety. And it did not experience this dichotomy as a deficiency that humbled it and brought it to repentance. Rather, obedience produced and justified disobedience, and righteousness led to sin. On this account Jesus saw in Pharisaism the guilt that would be the death of Judaism.

John portrayed in the three events he told after Jesus' entry into Jerusalem how Jesus unwaveringly went to his end, overcoming everything that stood in the way of his will to the cross (John 12:20–36). The desire by several Greeks to see him reminded him of the significant amount of work that had not even begun among the nations. This, however, did not make him despair of the necessity of his cross. Precisely by dying he would establish the large community, as the harvest grew from the grain of wheat through its death, and the same rule he also postulated for his disciples. Then a wave of pain washed over him that took him aback for a time. But he prayerfully rose to obedience and received through a divine voice the assurance that his life and his death would reveal God's glory.

The suffering connected with his end brings to light the judicial side of his death. Now divine righteousness is executed. This, however, is the condition of his rule; for judgment is directed toward the world and its prince and makes room for him so that he can draw all people to himself. Therefore Jesus wants the cross and the execution of righteousness entailed by it. At this his hearers wanted to argue with him concerning the meaning of messianic prophecy. Since Scripture assigns to the Christ an eternal rule, Jesus' concept of death appeared to be in contradiction to it.

Although this objection struck at the root of Jesus' train of thought, because he supported himself in his death by the conviction that Scripture would show him this way, he nevertheless did not answer this objection, as little as in the words preserved by Matthew, by way of an exegetical discussion that would have produced a christological doctrine. His answer consisted merely of the call to repentance that received here a particularly poignant expression at the end of his work in its contrast to Jewish intellectualism. While they wanted to argue with him about exegetical problems, he confronted them with the fact that they had to use the light as long as it would shine for them, and the purpose for which it was to be used was not the illumination of exegetical riddles. It rather consisted of the fact that they were to become sons of light and thereby be renewed in their own human existence.

14. The Disciples' Work Subsequent to Jesus' Death

Jesus linked the pronouncement that the community would emerge in new form after his death with the judgment of Jerusalem. After the cornerstone was rejected by the builders, the building nevertheless would be erected in such a way that he would be the cornerstone. After the punishment of the rebels, God would create "another nation" for the performance of his will, a new community that would serve him. Then those who had not yet had access to his feast would be invited into the king's presence (Matt. 22:8–10; Luke 14:21–24).

This is not rendered uncertain even by the Lucan form of this image. The force of Jesus' judgment is even enhanced there by the fact that it immediately rejects the Pharisees' hope, which confidently grasped for the glory of the kingdom. They were, of course, invited; but since they rejected the feast, it was prepared for those who had not been invited. The image is not thereby limited to the present condition of the community, as if the Pharisees were being contrasted with the ethically corrupt class of people, because in Jesus' view, the invitation to the feast was a matter, not of Pharisaism, but of one's belonging to Israel.

If now those who had been invited were replaced by those who had not yet been called, both periods of the administration of the word are juxtaposed as they are in Matthew: formerly the limitation to the old community, now the calling in unlimited wideness; and thereby Jesus' opposition to Pharisaism received its entire depth. What they considered to be completely impossible would happen, not merely that other sons of Abraham whom they detested would be preferred to them but that those would receive God's grace to whom they denied it, while they themselves would lose it.

By the image of the shepherd, likewise, Jesus announced a new order of the community. Now the sheep that belonged to him were united in the same flock with those who were not his own. The shepherds, however, whom he now provided, would gather the sheep that were the possession of the Christ, separate those that did not belong to him, and unite with them also those who belonged to him from among the nations (John 10:3, 16). After his death the good news proclaiming God's work would be preached to all the nations (Matt. 26:13; 24:14).

If this idea had been missing, it would have been a sign that Jesus had abandoned his final thoughts in the face of the cross. No observer, however, talks about this. For Jesus, God's kingdom did not waver; thus there would be no lack of those to whom he would reveal his regal activity. The petition for God's name to be hallowed always embodied the assurance that there existed those who knew God, if not in Israel, then among the nations, and his assignment of the apostolate to his own was not revoked or weakened by his cross; it was rather confirmed and deepened.

It seems to be a matter of course that this change of the image of the future evoked a multitude of questions. The question we ask first of all is this: "Mission to the Jews or mission to the Gentiles?" From Jesus' perspective, the question regarding the relationship of his community to Israel was probably the more difficult one. The whole of Jewish thought could be summarized in the pronouncement that there was only one holy community, just as there only was one God. The idea of "two churches" appeared to be an impossible thought, as if God's rule created different kingdoms and not all who belonged to him were of necessity therefore united with one another because they were subject to him.

For Jesus, too, the uniqueness of God and the uniqueness of the Christ resulted directly in the one community (Matt. 23:9–10). Now it was, of course, certain that Jerusalem would have to fall. Jesus expressed the judgment of the old community. This verdict was, however, not yet executed, and as long as it continued to exist, how did a new community have room beside it or within it? The question did also not merely arise regarding the disciples' relation to Israel and to the Gentiles. Did not those who converted to him need a new worship, a new custom, new regulations for their common life?

Jesus' word of farewell, however, serves in all Gospel records exclusively his central will, solely the issue of salvation that took on a more profound seriousness for the disciples through his departure. He showed them how they would then enjoy his good pleasure and how they would preserve their communion with him. His death did not bring him into a different mode of operation than the one in which his dealings with them had occurred up to that point: they would perform their service by remaining his disciples and by preserving what he had given to them.

Therefore they also did not receive any instructions now regarding evangelism or the establishment of the church. There is no church law in Jesus' words of farewell. All attention is rather directed toward the internal processes by which the disciples would retain their internal allegiance to Jesus. Nevertheless, the thought regarding their duty to serve controlled all of Jesus' words. The disciples, however, did not have to carry out a special service beside their status as Christians and did not receive an office apart from their own personal identity. Their status as Christians and their work for Christ in the world were entirely complementary. As long as the disciple remained joined to Christ, he fulfilled his calling.

Their commission to Israel was not altered by Jesus' cross and occurred now also in service of God's grace. The disciples were not to proclaim Israel's rejection to it after Jesus' execution and go to the Gentiles instead of to it. The pen into which now shepherds enter instead of thieves and robbers—shepherds brought through the gate by the gatekeeper to the sheep—is Israel (John 10:1–3; only 10:16 speaks of the Gentiles). The duty imposed on the disciples in Matthew 10:5 remained in effect.[23] The call was again directed toward the nation as a whole, but the judgment resting on it excluded the old community's preservation in its former form. Individuals were won out of it.

---

23. Matt. 10:5 cannot be limited to the time before Jesus' death; since the discourse demands from the disciples martyrdom on account of Israel, Jesus' will is clearly delineated.

Regarding the issue of how they should be united and separated from the old community, the shepherd metaphor in John merely says that the sheep that belonged to the Christ would hear the voice of the shepherd when he led them out of the pen and when he separated them from the other sheep. Thereby Jesus gave the disciples the comforting assurance that God's will would be surely and truly accomplished at this separation by their service.

Since Israel, however, had rejected and crucified him, the call was now issued also to the nations.[24] How the disciples could combine persistent faithfulness toward Israel with preaching that was freed from all limitations, God's government would show them at the proper time. Jesus did not create a formula regarding this and did not anticipate the course of history by a pronouncement. He thereby effectively challenged the disciples to faith, to an attentiveness to God that turned the will toward him and that followed his activity.

In Matthew, Jesus testifies to the indestructible sanctity of the word of repentance in the new community. He does so in issuing the call to God's feast to those who had previously had no share in his promise especially at the end of the parable. Even when the call was issued without conditions or limitations, the one who stepped into the dining room without festive clothes would suffer in prison for his contempt of the regal grace. While one may doubt whether the pieces of the parable were always connected in this manner, it is clear that precisely this conclusion of the image created a powerful expression of Jesus' central will. That will executed the principle by which he knew the entire divine government to be in agreement even in the new form of calling, even when free grace was offered to those who had not known about it until that time. Grace always presses to be recognized and desired in its value. By this image Jesus did not express a single ethical requirement but rather the central demand he always saw flow from divine grace: that it determine our will and substantiate an activity that esteemed it and was grateful for it.

Or was the occasion for such an image missing when Jesus pronounced Jerusalem's condemnation?[25] If a new community should be established apart from Israel, free from any doctrine of merit, by the proclamation of divine rule brought to all, the question immediately arose whether God's will had changed and whether his Law was subject to alteration. Was he angry with the Jews while forgiving the Gentiles? Jesus maintained that he did not speak of two different ways of salvation, of a comfortable, gracious one for the new community that would be gathered, and of a hard, difficult one for Israel.

---

24. The contention that Jesus excluded the nations even from the eschatological form of God's rule need not be discussed here. The other thesis, that he thought the contemporary situation would remain until his parousia and that only through it would the kingdom be expanded while until then the word belonged to Israel alone, eliminates the parables of the vinegrowers and of the festive meal and the Easter account.

25. It is often said that the image could only belong to a later period, only to the institutional church, which in seeking to issue the call of free grace to all often was jolted by the realization that the call did not produce the desired result.

He did not speak of two wills of God, of which the one required obedience from Israel while the other permitted sin for Christianity. Rather, now and in the future, God's grace would reveal itself in the same unity with righteousness. With the same kindness it invited those who had been called first and those who had been called later and rejected any abuse with the same seriousness. The reason for the rejection of the first group of people also brought condemnation for the second one. The same divine righteousness stood in unshakable unity above the great change Jesus saw ushered in by his death, preserving his eternal holiness also in the new community.

The disciples' internal disposition toward Christ was now determined by their waiting for him. All words attribute this hope to them as their secure possession; for it arose directly from the recognition of his status as king. Therefore there also is no mention anywhere of any doubt regarding his return, even though hope was rendered difficult for the disciples by the fact that the coming events would place them into a hard and long period of suffering. Since their hope stood in complete contrast to their circumstances, it would only be preserved through patience.

It is, however, mentioned with genuine concern that their hope might be in vain, not because the promise would remain unfulfilled, but because they might combine their hope with the sinful will that robbed them of its fulfillment. Therefore a series of parables parallel to the word of repentance to Jerusalem served the purpose of confirming the disciples' decisive turning away from evil (Matt. 24:45–25:46). The temptation always occasioned by the received divine gift was enhanced for them, since they needed to prove themselves now as faithful and wise.

In the community they were assigned a role similar to the steward charged with caring for his master's house during his absence. If they grasped for power and earthly passion, their hope would die, and they would (wrongly) suppose themselves to be secure. He, however, would come and condemn them. Separation from him can occur even though their status as disciples appeared assured, while it was in fact destroyed. Therefore Jesus distinguished between hope that would find fulfillment and hope by which the disciple deceived himself, that hope in which the disciple rejoiced at the coming blessedness without, however, allowing such a prospect to move him to get ready for it.

The disciple had to place a genuine, complete will into his hope that controlled his actions in the same way that Jesus required such will for repentance, love, and faith. Only then hope would reach its fulfillment. As for Israel, so also for the disciples, the parable of the laborers applied simultaneously to the festive image. Those who cherished the anticipation of his rule with great joy stood at the same time in his service by the fact that they were to give to others what they had received from him rather than merely preserving it for themselves. By bringing his word to others they would increase the talents given to them. The grace granted to them occasioned the danger of a fall, since they could render unfruitful what had been given to them for others' sakes. If they unlovingly refused help to others, lovelessness toward Jesus was thereby revealed, which rendered the service worthless since it was not the slave but the master who was to receive the proceeds of the service.

Thus Jesus' words of farewell proclaimed to the disciples, in conformity with the word of repentance addressed to Jerusalem, the same righteousness that did not permit his grace to favor the selfish, dreamers, and loveless, but rather rejected evil in complete obedience and bound its recipients in complete obedience to him. Since the grace given to them was greater, it increased their guilt when they refused to obey. The fact alone that he had given them his promise rendered their disobedience a grave offense (Luke 12:47). The parables given to the disciples, on the other hand, are different from those portraying Israel in that they never make the entire circle of disciples subject to condemnation but always reveal the contrast separating the faithful from the faithless and the wise from the foolish. Jesus spoke in the conviction that his community would not corrupt entirely. Otherwise his work would have fallen apart.

Among the concepts that form the basis for the work of the disciples is also the conviction that the complete community inheriting the kingdom would be greater than their small fellowship. The final portion of Matthew recounting Jesus' instruction expresses this idea. It does so not in such a way that the greatness of the divine kingdom appeared as a new truth that was only then communicated to the disciples, but rather by placing emphasis on the norm according to which Jesus would deny or grant a share in God's kingdom to all regardless of their membership in a particular nation. He would call to himself all those who were kind to others, and he would reject all those who refused kindness to others. He assigned such weight to their kindness or harshness since it was rendered to him, for he considered even the least his brother. Regarding the manner in which the disciples evaluated and administered their community it mattered much that their relationship to Jesus was based on the conviction that his regal office made him the giver of grace to all who were kind.

The Lucan portrayal of Jesus' promise, likewise, makes note of the fact that the disciples used it exclusively for the purpose of procuring for their hope ethical integrity and fruitfulness. For the two prophetic discourses placed by Luke before the final words in Jerusalem (Luke 12:35–53; 17:20–18:8) have their aim neither in embellishment of the apocalyptic image, nor in the portrayal of the disciples as without hope, so that the compilation of the discourses would have served the purpose of lifting them up to hope. These discourses rather recognize the great main thing toward which Jesus' word was directed and for which the disciples were to be concerned: that their hope be pure and effective in order to bring the disciples to the goal of their aspirations.

After having liberated the disciples from the desire for visible goods, and having called them to a carefree attitude, Jesus' expectation united their positive obligation with this negative pronouncement. Both instructions are linked with one another as cause and effect: the disciple cannot keep himself free from earthly things without hoping for the Christ, and he cannot hope in the Christ without keeping himself free. By their hope they are given the power to resist sensual lust, and they have in God's love the element that controls their conduct.

Subsequently, Jesus freed the disciples' hope, in contrast to that of the Pharisees, from all visible crutches. God's work does not tolerate any calculation but comes suddenly and miraculously. Hope is placed in Jesus alone and stands in complete contrast to what the disciples experience in the world. Since they would initially long in vain to see Christ, they received a picture of their own situation by the widow who had to protect herself from an unjust judge through the persistence of her requests. This illustration discouraged the thought that they should expect a triumph over Israel's resistance or over the Gentile world, yet invested their hope with considerable excitement together with peace since it gave promise to their prayer for God's rule. The disciple should not be concerned about whether God was about to bring the glorious consummation to pass. Jesus depicted this end as perfect, whereby he sealed hope against doubt. His concern, however, was people's inability to exercise adequate faith, for in this he saw a great, important issue: that he find faith even in the circumstances that would be brought about through his death.

15. The Promise of the Spirit

Jesus knew he had been given the word in such a way that he thereby effected the calling to God. Jesus expected the Spirit for his disciples, on the other hand, only in the future. The issue of the Spirit, of course, had accompanied his ministry from the beginning since it resulted already from John's preaching of baptism. John had distinguished his own work from that of the one who was to come by acknowledging that he himself was not yet the one who would give the Spirit to the community. He was only the means of the regal ministry of the coming one. The word summoning hearers to repentance and to God, on the other hand, was already issued by the Baptist and was continued by Jesus, not merely as promise, but as God's call by which God invited man to himself. He did this in the conviction that God would also give his Spirit to those who received his word.

However, he still waited for the Spirit, in agreement with the fact that the gathering of the new community likewise remained to be accomplished in the future. For "the Spirit" and "the community" are concepts that are firmly connected with one another. The concept of the Spirit therefore appears only in such words that speak of the time subsequent to his death. Here, too, he kept himself from any violence or artificiality. Imagine Jesus agonizing over how he might make Spirit-filled supermen out of his disciples. As if God's rule could be revealed through cleverly devised tricks! God's Spirit was God's gift, and for Jesus he was God's greatest gift. If we reflect on his condemnatory word to the pious Israelites and to his disciples, it becomes clear that no one knew with equal clarity that the concept of the Spirit had a destructive effect on the human consciousness unless certain ethical conditions were present.

First the message of his reconciliation had to transform the consciousness of human separation from God with faith-inspiring power. Otherwise what remained in control of man was a will craving distance from God. The terror before him had to be overcome, the forgiveness of sins must be experienced, and this in such a way that pride is destroyed at its root. Otherwise, the most devastating corruption arose from the concept of God's activity in one's inner life. An arrogance would arise by which man made himself a god, claiming his own will to be God's and his opinion to be God's Law.

Thus the greatest grace would become the greatest fall, and the most bitter separation from God would result from the most effective union with God. By his word of repentance, a word that he completed through his cross, Jesus created the prerequisites for the concept of the Spirit, both by placing the assurance of reconciliation above terror before God and by replacing arrogance with the total humbling of complete obedience and the selflessness of genuine love for God. Therefore he saw in the Spirit the gift he would procure for the community once he had ransomed them from the bonds that still held them fast.

Jesus thought of his disciples as possessing the Spirit when they would do his work without him after his death. When he returned, they would stand before him as those who had preserved the greatness of his name by prophecy and by power over the spirits. Before magistrates the Spirit would have given them the words needed to carry out Jesus' mission in the face of the enemy. The promise of the Spirit appears as a promise given to all in Matthew and Luke where we should expect it, after the resurrection, when the Christ himself would have completed his work and when the new community was established. It would assume possession of the messianic largesse, including the Spirit. Then baptism would be performed in the name of the Spirit as well (Matt. 7:22; 10:20; 28:19; Luke 24:49).

With this John concurred. The means by which people are given life is initially the word, because life is given to those who believe and since word and faith cannot be separated. The word effects this since it is accompanied by a divine activity that determines the individual's life from within and thereby gives him relationship with God. Therefore Jesus already in the first discourse named the regeneration of man through the Spirit his aim. But John, like Matthew and Luke, did not directly link the life-generating work of the Spirit with Jesus' earthly work. The statement regarding birth by the Spirit remained initially a promise, albeit one that would soon be fulfilled. Before this he would through the cross establish faith and thereby the possession of eternal life. He would receive his own glorification prior to the time that the sons of God were generated by the Spirit (John 3:14–15 in connection with verse 5; 7:39; 14:16).

Therefore in the final words of Jesus the promise of Jesus' inner reunion with the disciples is coupled with that of the Spirit who would come to them at that time. What he would provide for them is indicated by the designation "advocate, paraclete." The main idea is not the fact that he would argue their case before God but, as Matthew expresses it clearly at the occasion of the promise of the Spirit, that he would be the disciples' advocate in their struggle with the world. The concept is related to their duty to serve, to the difficult struggle into which they are placed by proclaiming the crucified and invisible one as the Christ. The legitimacy of their witness would be confidently disputed by the world, so that they would appear to be lost and foolish by being Jesus' disciples. However, they do not need to conduct this struggle for the legitimacy of Jesus' kingship by themselves, as if its outcome depended on their wisdom, eloquence, or energy. Rather, the commissioned Spirit would cause truth to prevail and give victory to Jesus' regal claim and glory to his name, not without them, but through them. Jesus staked his cause on the fact that they would be bearers of the Spirit. He did not desire any other proof or grant the disciples any other protection.[26]

One should not think here of ecstatic or otherwise peculiar circumstances but of the fact that the Spirit reveals truth. What renders him a fitting advocate of the disciples, one who is able to give them victory in their struggle with the world, is his ability to reveal and to effect truth. John states that Jesus' strength in the face of the cross was based on his unconditional respect for truth. Therefore no doubt is admitted regarding whether the disciples would fulfill their task; for truth overcomes everything. Nothing is added to it, neither money nor weapons, neither intelligence nor power. The truth alone will bring it about; "the Spirit is truth." Therefore the disciples' word will establish faith, for when the Spirit seizes man in his internal disposition, when he puts pretense and lies to flight and grants vision to see the truth, then faith is present. And to those in whom faith does not emerge, the Spirit makes their guilt visible and judges their unbelief (John 16:8). The disciple is not able to accomplish this with his proofs of Christ or by his admonitions—the Spirit is.

This esteem for truth, that honors it as invincible and that recognizes in it God's gift which subjects the disciple to God in his thought life and volition, does not represent a new development only introduced into Jesus' character by John or arrived at by Jesus himself only at the end of his work. By describing the word as the means by which the individual was connected with God's rule and by making the work of God now occurring through him the word's exclusive content, he based the work of his disciples also completely on the truth which divulged God's activity to the human eye. His work had been from the beginning a struggle against pretense and lie, and he had separated his disciples from the old community by not tolerating in them any untruthfulness but by helping them to complete obedience and genuine love. Since he had the Spirit who gave him the ability to cast a penetrating look into people's innermost being, they remained subject to truth in everything. This, however, did not get lost for them through his death. The protection against all temptation, by which they were kept in the truth, and the victory above all

---

26. The accuracy of the information given about Jesus by the Evangelist is confirmed by the fact that the disciples began their apostolic work only when they had the conviction that the Spirit was with them. The disciples' conduct is based on Jesus' instruction. The converse supposition, that Jesus' words were created after the fact with the disciples' conduct as its starting point, is perverse.

that opposed them was given them by the fact that, since the Spirit was in them, so also was the truth.

Regarding the doctrine of the Spirit it can be observed with particular clarity, both in its earlier and in its Johannine forms, how completely Jesus rejected any self-centered interpretation of communion with God. Now, when Jesus prepares to allow God's Spirit to enter people's innermost being, one could expect Jesus to dwell at least with a few words on the increased quality of life mediated through the Spirit to those who received him. But the disciples are merely instructed to recognize in the Spirit the preparation for their service. They are not able to carry it out by their own ability but in order for them not to despair, Jesus pointed them to the Spirit. If, on the other hand, self-admiration was attached to the possession of the Spirit, this would result in the deepest fall.

The concept of the Spirit did not push aside or replace Christ's union with the disciples. Both ideas stand side by side: that the Christ lives and is active in them, and that the Spirit is in them as the giver of truth. Therefore the promise of the Paraclete did not replace the eschatological promise. The goal remains the disciples' new union with him. Through the idea of the Spirit both Jesus' call to repentance and his statements regarding the disciples' duty received their conclusion. The call to repentance and the promise of new birth by the Spirit did not have in common merely that both condemned the existing condition of human life, but also that both promised as attainable a new form of life.

Conversion does not merely alter individual thoughts and aspirations; if so, it would reveal itself only as long as the sole focus were the performance of the repentant person. It produces an effect that transcends this, since God accepts and forgives the repentant person and makes him his own son. Jesus did not base this on the repentant person's performance according to a doctrine of merit, nor did he conceive of a change of human nature by a person's own will power. He rather invested repentance with the effect of granting salvation and life, since God's gracious act upon man answered it and gave him a share in the divine sonship and eternal life. This occurred by the Spirit.

The issuing of the commission to the disciples was based on the thought that his death would not immediately be followed by the consummation through the glorious rule of the Christ and the glorification of the community but by the disciples' need to perform their service in the struggle with Judaism as the bearers of the cross. They would also bring God's grace to the individual, call him effectively to God, free him truly from his guilt, and sanctify him. That their office and work would reach its religious purpose in the full sense of the term would be substantiated and clarified by God's Spirit working through them.

He described his communion with them as complete, granting them parity with him. At the same time, of course, the master's superior position was never in doubt. But his dealings with them do not have their purpose in their continued dependence on him. They rather should think and choose as he did. "The disciple should be like the master" (Matt. 19:24): he considered this to be an applicable rule even for the disciples' suffering and dying, since he required of them the surrender of their lives. He did not do this as an end in itself, nor merely for the sake of the final end at which he would assign them a place on the thrones beside him. But he did not exclude their internal relationship with God from this rule. Since the disciple was what he was internally through the Spirit, he came to resemble him by the fact that God gifted and guided him through the Spirit as well.

Jesus never separated God's fatherhood from the kingdom of God. The promise to the disciples would disintegrate if he could not also attribute divine sonship to them. The idea that this sonship arose by human will power, however, as if there were individuals who were able to elevate themselves to it by their religious greatness, must not be imposed on Jesus after he judged the pious pride of the synagogue. When he frames his promise, "You should love completely in order to become God's sons" (Matt. 5:45), this did not obscure for them the fact that God's fatherly dealings with people arose from God's own will and not from human love. By his love man remains in God's grace. This love is granted to him, however, by God.

Therefore a divine sonship that did not originate from the gift of the Spirit cannot be reconciled with Jesus' teaching. Jesus always elevated what God's rule gave to man above what nature made man. Therefore those do not attain it who merely have their life by the flesh. What nature provides is not God's entire gift or complete revelation. Above nature stands God, above the flesh stands the Spirit. Therefore those who live by the Spirit attain his kingdom. This was a permanent foundational feature of Jesus' consciousness.

It is, of course, clear that the seriousness by which in Matthew Jesus' word of repentance addresses the will of his audience must not be overlooked. Jesus categorically testified to their responsibility and to the causal power of their will, both regarding their will to sin and to do good. He did not permit any evasiveness regarding the question of the will, not even an evasiveness that grasped for divine help in order to turn attention away from ethical imperatives in the hope for some substitute. Jesus' call to repentance demanded from man the exercise of his own will and obedience to God; only thus was he given help. But Jesus' assurance that the Father would act upon man in complete kindness was not shaken by this requirement addressed to a person's will. He did not entertain a concern regarding whether God would be gracious and grant help to others or not. His concern was directed toward whether or not man would hear, decide, and leave his evil. This concern had for him the entire seriousness of an open question that could not be solved by compulsion or skill. But that the Father would reveal himself to man in his divine power and grace he never doubted, and in this lay for him the assurance that God's Spirit would be active in his disciples.

Jesus did not use his assurance of God to deny or to weaken the individual's obligation and will power, but neither did he emphasize it, as if he sought in morality a substitute for a weakened consciousness of God. It was not that a low esteem of divine activity produced an esteem for human conduct, but neither did the emphasis on divine giving amount to a devaluation of our own decision. God's willingness to receive the prodigal son was completely present. This willingness, however, did not free the son from the obligation of returning home. If he did, a feast was prepared for him that did not merely consist of a friendly outworking of his destiny but united the one who came home internally with God. This is the starting point for the concept of the Spirit.

It is equally clear that an esteem for the word which attaches complete certainty to it, so that the word is seen to contain the full measure of God's gift, must not be weakened by the concept of the Spirit. This does not happen in John even through his stronger emphasis on the motif of the Spirit, since there, too, the word is judged to be the completely adequate presentation of God's gift, with allegiance to Jesus consummated by its reception. That the motif of the Spirit is added is not caused by doubt that the word by itself would be insufficient to establish communion with God. It does, however, develop from the limitless confidence that truly hears in the word God's call by which God turns to man. Thereby man enters into that relationship with God by which God's Spirit accomplishes his work in him.[27]

16. Jesus' New Commission

The disciples' ministry was entirely dependent upon the fact that Jesus went to his death with the promise that God would send him again to the disciples and to humanity. Therefore the only longer discourse of Jesus recorded by Mark and the final of the five discourses into which Matthew arranged Jesus' word make this promise the basis for the disciples' communion with one another and for their entire ministry. It is, however, not the opinion of the Gospel account that Jesus represented this thesis only in his final days. Jesus' great prophetic discourse in Matthew does not give this promise to the disciples for the first time. They already had it and at that time asked merely for greater certainty. Jesus had already bound them by calling them to martyrdom and by placing upon them the obligation to service after Jesus' death. Moreover, the disciples' request regarding their share in Jesus' judgment shows that this call lived powerfully within them (Matt. 24:3; 10:23: 16:27; 20:22–23). Luke, likewise, in the two prophetic discourses he places before the entry into Jerusalem, set the promise of Jesus' return directly beside the prediction of his death (Luke 12:35–59; 17:20–18:8).

By this promise Jesus maintained the kingly aim in its highest, eschatological version even when he died. He indicated thereby how he would reveal God's righteousness and grace to humanity and how he would establish the eternal community despite his death. Regarding his own destiny, he was content to make the statement that he would go to the Father in death. Just as he did not give any presentation of his heavenly glory to the disciples, he also did

27. John conceived of a tension between the validity of the word and the effectiveness of the Spirit as little as of a tension between that of the Father and of the Son. The Johannine God does not struggle with himself.

not occupy himself with the future history of the world. His prophecy merely expressed how he would complete the office for which he died.

It therefore consisted of two statements. First, Jesus addressed his disciples by telling them how he would come for them and to them and how he would renew his communion with them and make it eternal. This would not happen in such a way that they would be lifted up to him, perhaps by death and ascension into heaven, but by his return to them. Second, and at the same time, Jesus' view was directed toward the world and maintained the universal aim of the Christ. When he returned, he would bring God's highest revelation to humanity by which the perfect community would be established that would receive the name that stood above all national and personal differences: the chosen ones (Matt. 24:31). All to whom God's election and love were extended would at that time be gathered to him and have their Lord in him.

In both instances, the difference between his new commission and his present work consisted of the fact that he would execute judgment. Now he waited and suffered; then he would judge and rule. Then the disciples would receive from him the verdict regarding the service rendered by them (Matt. 16:27; 20:8; 25:19–30). But upon the nations, too, he would execute divine justice. The final portion of the prophetic discourse in Matthew describes how he brings God's grace to all the righteous from all the nations and how he separates all the wicked from the eternal community (Matt. 25:31–46; cf. John 5:28–29). A difference between his present and his future activity is seen solely in the fact that he will use divine power for the execution of justice. In the portrayal of the future judgment he does not separate justice and grace.

By acting as judge on his community and on humanity, he rather reveals the glory of God's grace. By the fact that his verdict confirms their faithfulness, the disciples receive their desired share in his feast, and his judgment regarding the nations lends highest expression not merely to God's justice that opposes all evil but also to his grace, since he rejoices in any act of goodness regardless of human differences, since they are rendered to him and since he rewards it with the eternal gift. Thus the Christ concept finds complete expression. By acting then in the omnipotence of God, he will reveal the perfection of his sonship in a way that excludes any selfish motive. He will stand before the Father as the one who served him, the one who executed his blessing and his curse. Before the community, on the other hand, he will stand in absolute power to rule as the one who called all who did God's will to himself and who separated all who opposed him.

The expectation of his resurrection and his ascension to God was the prerequisite by which Jesus was able to promise his return. He would come since he himself had eternal life, and he would come from heaven as the one who ruled in God's glory. If his expectation had comprised no more than that he would be raised and exalted to God after the completion of his earthly work, he would have jeopardized his statements regarding God's rule. For those statements did not relate God's promise to the after-life but to the community that lived on earth, and he secured the conclusion for ongoing history through God's work. Jesus assumed responsibility for the fulfillment of this promise by portraying it as his office to return to humanity, to complete upon it God's will through the execution of justice, and to give to it the eternal gift of divine grace. Therefore he juxtaposed also in his answer to the high priest the two passages of Scripture of which the one expresses the exaltation of the Christ to the throne with God and the other the sending of the Son of Man on the clouds of heaven, since here one thought provided the rationale for the other.

In the earlier account of Jesus' prophecy, the announcement of the parousia overshadows that of the resurrection and exaltation, even though the latter has its prerequisite in the former. This can be explained in part by the fact that the community did not come to know his resurrection merely through prophetic words but through the Easter account while the proclamation of the return stipulates what they may still expect from Jesus. But we will do justice to the facts only when we trace them back to Jesus' own will and to the power by which he confronted his disciples with his universal aim. If he had merely been concerned with dispelling for himself and the disciples the darkness of the passion, the Easter account would have been sufficient. But he did not give his disciples a shining picture of glory in order for them to elevate it above his image of the cross. He put his entire will into his office, which he completed through the parousia. Only through it will his communion with the disciples reach its fulfillment. It is true that the completeness of the union he established between himself and them is also proven by the fact that he promises them his omnipresence. From heaven he is the Lord and present with them, and he unites them internally with himself. But his communion with them controlled only their internal life, without defending them against the persecution faced in the world. Therefore he lifted their hope higher to that communion with him that would no longer be impeded by his invisible nature and that would also bring them a share in his judgment and rule.

However, in the image of the parousia, too, he appears as their Lord before whom they are placed as his servants. The uniqueness of his sonship and rule is not obscured by the completion of their communion with him, and the purpose of his appearance is never presented merely in terms of their salvation and glorification. He came in order to take possession of his property, which he had entrusted to their faithfulness, and in order to rule himself in the house that had been given to them. He was the bridegroom who wanted to celebrate his feast. Even when he reversed his relationship with them and when he promised that he would serve them as if they were the masters and when he told them that the Father would give them thrones at his side where he would once again give to them the festive cup, it always remained clear that he was the one who gave, the one who disclosed to them the riches of his grace (Luke 12:37; Matt. 20:23; 26:29). He made their need the basis for his parousia, using the example of the afflicted widow. But there, too, their longing was elevated above their own salvation, since it was grounded in the revelation of God's justice (Luke 18:1–8). The execution of justice was not merely a human but a divine aim. The norms that shaped the petitions of the Lord's Prayer and that elevated one's desires above one's own blessedness, remained in effect for the disciples with respect to even the highest promises.

With the community's reunion with him, we stand merely at the threshold of the new world. What, then, is eternal life? It is a notable characteristic of Jesus' prophecy that it ends with the fact that he reveals himself to his community once again. Thus he subordinated also his final word completely to the execution of the calling that he had to complete. By wanting to awaken hope in the disciple, he spoke out of love that was concerned for him not to fall nor to despair nor to become unfaithful but to do his duty and to find salvation. This was his only concern. Therefore his prophecy does not extend beyond the time when his reunion with them would be achieved.[28] Now the struggle was over, and there remained no more reason for concern. What followed was the new world full of God's eternal grace and glory. What it would be like, they would see when it arrived. He did not make his prophecy subservient to merely intellectual wishes.

But his prophecy also had great didactic value for the disciples, because it gave the word that preceded it its transparency and substantiation. Matthew made this clear by the arrangement of his discourses. He began with the ethical obligation the disciples took upon themselves by their decision to follow Jesus. This was followed by their duty to testify as his messengers. Then he showed them God's rule in that which they experienced. The discourse regarding the kingdom received its development by the statements regarding the Christ and his obligation to death. This led to the portrayal of the community that was now united in his name. All of this would remain an enigma if the disciples did not hear how Jesus would reveal his rule and what conclusion he would prepare for their work and suffering. So now Jesus explained how he would still achieve his kingly aim as one who was crucified and how he would bring the community to completion. The mystery did not arise merely through the conclusion of his own work but also by the obligation he gave the community. Their work was turned in an inner direction; removed from glitter and rule, it was called to pure, selfless service, and it, too, passed through suffering. Would it nevertheless be preserved and obtain the perfect outcomes that it expected for itself as the messianic community? Jesus' prophecy provided the answer to this question: by his renewed arrival it would reach its goal.

Since only the concept of the parousia provides the conclusion of all that preceded it, the thought is impossible that it had been lacking in the original Gospel tradition. This is confirmed also by the fact that from Pentecost on the Christian message never consisted merely in a look back to Jesus' earthly work, but that it always concluded with the prediction of his return. A prediction of Jesus' return only made up by the disciples would contradict the basic idea upon which their ministry was based: that they spoke as Jesus' messengers. Since we know that the disciples proclaimed his return, we also know that he promised it to them.

---

28. It may be concluded from the fact that Paul also described the parousia only until the point where the community is reunited with the Returning One (1 Thess. 4:16–17) that in this respect, too, the word of the Lord available to him possessed the same form as the one available to us.

By his promise Jesus provided their hope with a thoroughgoing simplification. He thus set back a multitude of ideas that were found in the community regarding the final aim and that rendered their hope rich and colorful. No statement dealt with the restoration of Jerusalem,[29] with the gathering of the Diaspora, with the relationship between Israel and the Gentiles, with the fate of Rome and of its ruler, with those resurrected from the dead and their new entrance into the community, with the glorification of nature and its adaptation to the eternal state, with the opening of heaven and the union of the heavenly spirits with humanity to a community, not even with theophany, with the new manner of perceiving God. The disciples' expectation was directed toward only one aim: the renewed presence of Jesus and their reunion with him. Thereby they were given complete salvation; all further questions were referred calmly to God's government. The pouring of the entire hope into the expectation of Jesus was parallel to the devotion of one's entire love and faith to him. It became thereby religious in the same strict sense as the faith and love directed toward Jesus. If the disciple was granted the view of Jesus, the promise was also fulfilled that he would see God. The king himself stepped into the celebration hall, and the landlord himself determined his laborer's wages (Matt. 5:8; 22:11; 20:8). But the mediation of God's activity by the Christ was also maintained in hope. The completeness of his sonship appeared in the fact that the image of the parousia did not establish two thrones but let God's judgment occur through the judgment of Jesus. It revealed God's rule by Jesus' rule. The blending of hope into one expectation was a religious act of great historic consequence that required someone who acted. Careful historical consideration indicates that it was not the disciples who first arrived at this insight.[30]

Thereby there arose a profound contrast to Jewish eschatology, not merely since its theoretical and fantastic attitudes were absent from Jesus' outlook but more profoundly by the fact that the center of the entirely expectation shifted. Since the synagogue hoped for the glorious transformation of the community, and since it combined with this also the arrival of the promised ruler, this was a particularly significant part of the events that would bring glory to it. But the glory remained for them and lent their hope its content. The hope given by Jesus to his disciples, however, had in the Christ's arrival its foremost and indispensable subject, and from it alone arose the new community of the coming world. The relation into which the hope set the Christ and the community was thereby altered by Jesus. Jewish hope desired to have a share in the eschatological community; from this resulted also enjoyment of the Christ's rule. The disciples' hope was directed toward being united with the

---

29. The words pertaining to Israel (Matt. 19:28; 23:39) have in view simply the beginning of the time to come, as does the entire prophecy treating the revelation of the Christ for all and the execution of judgment upon all. What further results there would be for Israel remains subject to God's rule. The identity between the tradition available to us with that known by Paul is confirmed here once again: Rom. 11:25 shows that the community did not possess any prophecy of Jesus regarding Israel's and Jerusalem's restoration.

30. Paul already found this form of hope; his prophetic words have it as their prerequisite.

Christ; from this resulted being numbered among the glorified community. This turn of events came about through Jesus, through the fact that he shattered the old community by his word of repentance and his cross (while maintaining his own calling) and by linking the fulfillment of God's promise with his return. From now on hope had only one sole object: union with him.

The limitation of hope resulted in its strengthening. It thus became possible for that hope to become a genuine, complete will; for it was based on certainty. The disciples were certain that Jesus had regal status and that they had experienced union with him. From this arose genuine hope that longed for the fulfillment of their communion with him, not merely a "doctrine of the last things" or apocalyptic poetry. Thereby the danger was also averted that prophecy turned into a dualism by which the will directed toward the future was separated from present piety and obligation. Jesus did not expose his disciples to an after-life that remained separated from the present but linked them firmly with the present through his expectation.

In religious history there always is the danger of dualism emerging from strong hope, since the goods desired by it transcend the present existence. If they coexist independently, the hope depreciates the present, since only the tomorrow has value, and corrupts the life given to us through passivity and pessimism, since it is not the perfect life. Jesus attacked this use of hope not merely in retrospect through the admonitions given in the parables but at the root. For he gave hope but one aim by linking people's longings to him alone and to his rule. The new union with him and the closeness that now existed with him resulted in a close unity. Now hope led to the grateful appreciation of what the community had been given through its call to the Christ. It therefore enhanced the value of the present, prohibited people from wasting it by daydreaming, raised the value of life, and expelled all despair from the present. It sharpened the attentiveness and energy available for present duty. With this hope alone it becomes intelligible that the disciples were able to accomplish the greatest ethical results that any human community has ever achieved. Through it alone the fact becomes possible what the Johannine account submits to us regarding Jesus: that a proclamation of Jesus emerged in the circle of disciples that had its aim not in hope, but in the faith that now united the community with him. This, in turn, happened without resulting in a denial or weakening of hope.

Jesus' prophecy had therefore neither the purpose nor the result of replacing or marginalizing the yields of his earlier work. It did not want to establish a new, unprecedented concept of God's rule but confirmed everything that had been achieved up to that point. Jesus did not replace the gospel with a prophecy. The message of what God has done remains. He has sent the Christ; the key to God's kingdom is here; the guilty are justified; the feast of God is celebrated; the service of God is occurring; eternal life is obtained; and the eternal community is gathered. The cross of Jesus, too, becomes a part of the gospel; for the cross, likewise, is the revelation of God's rule and of his perfect grace. His return has its prerequisite in his earthly work; therefore the disciples preserve their hope in that return only as hope provides them with the very marrow of their religion.

17. Signs of Jesus' Return

The interim between the present and the end did not leave Jesus' prophecy in complete obscurity. He did not add to what the disciples had now become through him simply the major content that should bear their hope, the guarantee of his new revelation. He also drew a connecting line from the present to the end by speaking of "signs" that would signal his return. The people and the disciples asked him continually when his rule would be revealed. He resisted this question resolutely and persistently (Luke 17:20–37; 19:11; Matt. 24:3; cf. Luke 13:23; Matt. 20:22; Acts 1:6). It concealed the major component of the hope: not when, but what would happen, was the most important question for Jesus, to which he demanded complete attention. Jewish expectation stumbled over this since the question regarding the "when" possessed for it uppermost significance. For Jesus, the reception of salvation was based on conditions that awakened people to complete seriousness. Questions by which the apocalyptic mood of the community confronted him tended to counteract it. That mood extended its concerns arrogantly and prematurely to what belonged to God, while forgetting what man's duty was in order to see God's rule. But since Jesus bore within himself a genuine hope by which he turned his will to the highest aim, and since he sought to awaken such a hope also in his disciples, the term "sign" possessed significance for him. For whoever desired the Coming One longed for indications by which it was confirmed that the promised event was approaching.

Jesus' preview depicted what would precede his second appearing as a time of dire need. The preservation of one's Christianity and therefore also that of hope would require the disciples' entire effort and patience. Had he invested his preview merely with the contrast that placed the dark period of sin and need before the day of redemption, the community's religious history would inevitably reveal pessimistic moods that despaired at the present. But even the great seriousness placed on the coming years by the prophecy of his parousia did not take away anything from the gain of his earthly work and thus did not detract in any way from what Matthew 13 said about the manner of God's rule.[31]

The statements regarding the near future made by the proclamation of the parousia differ, of course, significantly from those contained by the discourse regarding God's kingdom. There the sower does his work; wheat and weeds grow side by side, and the net is cast. Work that brings Jesus' word to people fills the time while the disciples wait for him. Patience still allowing time for

---

31. In Mark there is strongest ground for the impression that prophecy applies merely to the contrast between the dark present and the coming day, since Mark has the parallel to Matthew 24 but no such parallel to Matthew 25. But even Mark records the Sermon at the Lake (4:1–31), and this is not cancelled out by Mark 13.

evil flavors the character of that time, and the call is indiscriminately issued to all. The depiction of the signs preceding Jesus' arrival, on the other hand, does not direct the disciples' view toward their work but toward their suffering. No great expectations regarding their successes in Israel and the nations are awakened in them. They are rather severely tormented by the pressure of the world. The portrayal of the time of travail awaiting the disciples does not, however, do away with their obligation to work, which is rather reiterated once again by the final parables and whose significance is explained. Nevertheless, they resemble those who wait joyfully for their master at the evening before the feast and who cannot neglect his service, since he gave them what was his own. Moreover, the message that the Christ has come is now proclaimed among all peoples.[32]

Critical operations do not bring about the lifting of this contrast. The connection between the disciples and the obligation to serve cannot be removed. Likewise, Jesus' conviction cannot be done away with that the establishment of God's rule is not a human matter, that it is not the disciples who glorify and complete the world but that they need to wait for the new act of God. The severity of the struggle awaiting them was once for all shown by Jesus' cross. But Jesus' power, not to elude the pain but to transcend it and to preserve activity in suffering and gratitude and joy under pressure, showed itself also in his prophecy by the fact that he rendered the disciples' shameful destiny of suffering not a weakening but a strengthening of their hope by placing it under the signs of the coming redemption. For Jesus and his followers, the greatest pain was attached to the thought that "the abomination that causes desolation" would stand in the temple; but this, too, becomes the sign of the coming glory.

In Jesus' prophecy Israel's conflict with the disciples becomes the world's conflict with them. Now Judaism, too, is merely a part of the world. Owing to Jesus' cross the boundaries are obliterated that separated them from the other nations up to that point. Of course, by the fact that its history and that of humanity present themselves as one for prophecy, Israel's privilege comes to the fore even then, so that Jerusalem's destiny becomes a factor in the divine world government. Therefore the final promises converge directly with the statements regarding Jerusalem's end. It is, however, no longer awarded an inner privilege. Rather, it is now that part of the world that has sinned with particular gravity and that is hit by God's judgment with particular severity. This, however, did not have the consequence that prophecy turned to another nation such as the Greeks and transferred Israel's election to it. After the fall of Judaism Jesus did not institute a new nationalism in the place of the old. The only distinction within humanity that had significance for Jesus resulted from the special calling of Israel. After it had surrendered it, however, by the rejection of the Christ, an absolute universalism provides the horizon for an

---

32. The direction of the prophetic discourse can therefore not be used as an objection to the thesis required by the parables about the vineyard and the festive meal, that Jesus had freed his proclamation from all limitations subsequent to his death.

anticipation of the future, and the opposition into which Jesus' cross brings the disciples against Jerusalem is extended to all of humanity. It is not expected that the Jews would lose their religious character. Their rebellion against God does not reveal itself in their apostasy to paganism, gross indifference, or even contempt of its tradition. Jesus rather expects an acceleration of messianic hope until the formation of an arbitrary prophetic office and the false claim of messianic royalty. The same religious powers that disputed him will also fight the disciples, and precisely this renders their condition precarious and their persecution harsh (Matt. 24:11, 24; John 16:2; 7:34; 8:21).

Therefore the end of Jerusalem belongs to the signs of the time of salvation. Prophecy is directed solely against the holy city and the temple due to their sacramental significance. When the sign of grace given by God to the community is broken, judgment has come over Israel. Jesus did not consider the removal of the old sanctuaries to be a part of his own work; he did not come to abolish the temple. Divine righteousness does, however, demand that the desecrated sanctuary should disappear and that Israel's guilt be exposed. Therefore the end of Jerusalem receives its place among the signs of the parousia.

The gospel tradition provides two sayings regarding the fall of Jerusalem. The fall of Jerusalem is already mentioned in the introductory word to the prophetic discourse. The veneration with which the disciples still viewed the temple is completely removed by Jesus. The sanctuary will fall. How judgment is performed upon it is described in Matthew and Mark only by the word of Daniel: abomination would be found in the temple, for which reason desolation would come upon it (Matt. 24:1–2, 15–22). When the holy place is desecrated by the abomination, the disciples should flee and not be devastated together with Judaism. For from this would result a time of great misery. It was considered to be limited to Judea since one could save oneself from it by hastily crossing its borders. The words remain mysterious. It is only said that the time of misery would be extended and that it would threaten to become intolerable on account of its length. God's grace would shorten it, however, for the sake of the elect.

In place of these words, Luke records teachings that announce the siege and conquest of Jerusalem. The narrator used by Luke places particular emphasis on the fact that Jesus had prophesied this; for he also linked such words with Jesus' entrance into Jerusalem and with his final exit from the city (Luke 21:20–28; 19:41–44; 23:27–31; cf. 13:1–5; 19:27). Jesus wept at the sight, since he had its demise in view, and when he left it, laden with the cross, he called those who followed him to weep since horrible misery would come upon them. As he had the siege at his coming in view, he deplored its horrible end at his departure. The new portion of the prophetic discourse is parallel to this.[33]

33. To interpret Luke 21:20 merely as Luke's own exegesis by which he perhaps extended Mark's text in view of the destruction of Jerusalem is contradicted by the parallel portions. These should not be depreciated as free compositions of Luke but regarded as given to him through his source, if for no other reason than on account of their strong Semitisms.

In Matthew's version of the prophecy, no concrete historical events appear to be portrayed. There is no mention of Rome, and it is not indicated whereof the abomination consisted by which the temple would be desecrated. There remain several possibilities of how the prophecy could find fulfillment. An image of a god or of the emperor could be put into the temple, or it could become the dwelling of the antichrist, or a Roman army could bring destruction over it, or godlessness and crime could occur at the holy place, similar to the way in which Jesus drew attention to the murder of the prophet Zechariah between the temple and the altar. Only one thing is said: that the sanctuary would no longer remain under divine protection and that its desecration would bring the most severe misery upon the nation. The disciples were permitted and encouraged to flee. The other narrator indicated who would execute God's judgment over Jerusalem: armies who besieged it, whereby one thinks of the Roman army. This expectation, however, was not foreign to Jesus. Should the collapse of the walls of the temple of which Jesus spoke happen in a miraculous fashion? If it was people who caused this destruction, then war and the siege of the city were also involved; for that Judaism would give its life for the protection of the temple was known to everyone in Palestine.[34]

Immediately after this act of judgment, which transformed the holy place into its opposite and made Judea the place of deep grief, the signs would occur that reveal the arrival of the Christ. They emphasize the absolute authority of God over the state of the world and indicate that the fulfillment of humanity also entailed a restoration of the entire world. Nevertheless, the phrase "end of the world" does not accurately express the meaning of the prophecy. It is not the destruction of the existing order that Jesus envisions. He did not look at heaven and earth thinking that they would remain as they were, but neither did he believe that they were created to be destroyed. The fundamental pronouncement of the prophecy already excludes this: the Christ comes to humanity, albeit in order to elevate it to a completely new existence; but this, likewise, does not stand only in contrast to the present (Matt. 5:18; 24:35; cf. Matt. 19:28: *palingenesia*).

The depiction of signs uses ideas that were widespread also in Judaism, since it, too, expected that the course of history would become particularly dark before "the days of the Christ," both through the calamity that would befall the nations and through the disintegration of the community. The misery that reached highest proportions then would precipitate the coming of divine aid. The signs accompanying the coming of the Christ—the movements

---

34. There is no clear reference in the Gospels to the events that accompanied the beginning of the revolt in the year 66 and the fire in the temple in the year 70. It is more probable that Matt. 24:15 relates to the grave danger into which the emperor Caligula brought Jerusalem by intending to bring his statue into the temple. At that time, one surely thought in Christian circles seriously of Daniel's "abomination of desolation" and of Jesus' words against the temple, and it is not impossible that the version of Matt. 24:15–20 has been influenced by those events. The delimitation of the prophecy that emerged in the community from the prophetic words of Jesus was hardly as firm as the one that distinguishes the pronouncements of Jesus from the apostolic teaching, since the prophecy of prophets is also regarded as a word of the Lord.

in heaven, the falling of the stars, the sounds of the sea—likewise have parallels in Jewish portrayals of the end. They illustrate what we can observe with the entire message of Jesus: he thought using concepts that his native community mediated to him as confirmed conviction. Moreover, the commonality is effected here primarily through the canon, by Daniel's word regarding the abominations in the temple, by Micah's lament regarding the coming disintegration of the community, by Joel's description of the signs of the Day of the Lord. But the basic concept of even this portion of this prophecy belongs exclusively to Jesus, not only because he sees in these things the signs of his return but also because it makes Judea the place of the most severe judgments of God. No rabbi said, "Flee from the holy land as quickly as you can." Only in Jesus' judgment was Jerusalem's guilt greater than that of the Gentiles and God's judgment harsher than in the rest of the world.

While Jesus, by speaking of the signs, told the disciples that they could not be surprised by his arrival as long as they were awake, he juxtaposed with equal emphasis the other pronouncement that the end would come suddenly and that it could not be calculated. With that pronouncement he kept the disciples from an excited fear and put them calmly at the place given to them; one learns from the fig tree when the summer is near (Matt. 24:32). By this he resisted their tendency to attribute greatest significance to the question of when he would come. They would not be able to guess or calculate when he came. Their protection consisted merely of their constant readiness and alertness. It is not true that he did not want to tell them the time simply for pedagogical reasons; he could not do so since it was determined by the Father (Matt. 24:36). The question regarding the time of his coming therefore does not transcend merely the authority due the disciples but also what he himself had and desired for himself. Since he carried out God's will through his new coming, and since the Father alone presided over this will, he would wait until the Father sent him and come when the Father wanted him to do so.

Whether he gave the disciples one or the other idea, whether he protected them and calmed them by referring to the greatness of the signs against excitement or temptations or whether he alerted them in view of God's sudden and inscrutable work, the idea remained absent from his prophecy that there remained a long period of time before his return. He spoke of the completion of what had already been begun, and this completion would not fail. This generation had heaped great guilt upon itself; it had rejected the Christ, and it also rejected his messengers. Therefore this generation would also see God's judgment. Moreover, this generation had received the greatest thing, the sending of the Son, his cross, his exaltation, and the new calling through his messengers. It would also see the completion of these things.

Even genuine hope essentially disregards the time between "now" and what is hoped for, drawing it "soon" to itself. This tendency becomes the more powerful the stronger the deprivation and suffering are that give rise to it. The connections to the prophecy of the parousia clearly reveal this relationship. When the disciples' hard and painful struggle with the synagogue is considered, when they flee from town to town as those marked for death, the promise of his return is given; before the last refuge was barred to them, he would come to their rescue. When Jesus portrayed the greatness of temptation, the gravity of sacrifice, and the sanctity of the obligation imposed on the disciples by virtue of their apostolic office, he reminded them at the same time, as a warning and as an encouragement, of the imminence of his second coming. When he considered the end of Israel—that its sanctuary would fall and wrath would heavily weigh on it so that even the elect would be tempted—he promised that the Christ would come immediately after this time. In Jesus' judgment, it was inconceivable that God would let the community ask for its salvation in vain. He was ready to grant the complete gift (Matt. 10:23; 16:27, 28; 24:29; Luke 18:7–8). He did not give his disciples instructions to differentiate various components in the prophecy of which one related to the immediate and others to a more remote future. It is said of the entire picture of the future, right down to its final aim, that it was destined for this generation (Matt. 24:34).

It is equally impossible to extricate from one another the different aims interwoven in Jesus' prophecy and to distribute them to different periods and groups within the early church. These contrasts are just like others embodied within Jesus' will. Should we take the confident "as soon as" away from Jesus by which he moved his return closer to the present? It is said that he knew no such crush of events intent on the end. It is said that for him the entire world was in God's hands and that he looked cheerfully at everything the Father would do. Then where did the ardor of such a hope come from that can be so supremely aloof from the state of the entire world? The reply of some: it is a mirroring of the passion with which the disciples waited for the revelation of his rule. Or should we deny that he spoke the words that warn of calculating when the end will come and that prepare us for the possibility that the time would be extended? It is replied that those words stem from a time when the first fierce anticipation of necessity had calmed down; the strong tone of the prophecy, unchecked by any reservation, is the original one because the closeness of God's rule had been the ground of Jesus' entire work from the beginning. The theorizing continues: Jesus had extended the time twice already, at the beginning of his work when he transformed it into the call to repentance and again when it found its conclusion through his death and he set the promise once again into the future, after a long period of misery. The original form of his preaching had already rendered it impossible to sever the promise from "this generation." The rule of heaven was promised to him and thereby also the parousia. That explains why Jesus sought to grasp his final victory and the complete messianic work before his death as a near prospect, and drew the last and loftiest expectation closer to the present. The calming words counseling patience, in contrast, stem from the church, which anticipated that the time would be extended and that it would find large and fruitful labor even in this world.

All such constructions, however, that can just as easily be turned in opposite directions, offer much less certainty of approximating the true course of events than the statements of the texts. For the movements of will the above theories separate from one another are inseparably interwoven in the individual pronouncements. Israel's punishment serves as a sign for the parousia and guarantees its closeness; but any exact prediction is missing. For example, it is not said regarding the fire in the temple that the Christ would come immediately, but that the misery would be extended indefinitely, and while any calculation of the end must seek its basis necessarily in earthly history, the signs announcing the parousia are entirely supernatural. If the return resembles a flash of lighting, this attests to its suddenness but simultaneously to its plain visibility. From the former results the continual tension, from the latter the peace that can wait. The same saying serves both purposes. If the generation to which the Christ comes resembles the one that was surprised by the flood or the one that was judged in Sodom, the parousia comes unexpectedly; but the disciples' obligation to serve is thereby in no way denied. It is rather explained by these words why their testimony serves merely as an accusation of this generation and why it brings martyrdom for them. If the parousia separates the two who work together in the field or at the millstone, a strong image of its surprising suddenness is created, and all human calculations and guarantees are thereby destroyed. God's eye alone recognizes his elect ones, while the same majesty of God also assures that any impatience quiets down and that his hour is awaited (Matt. 24:27, 37–39; Luke 17:26–29; Matt. 24:40–41).

We need to connect the different aims of the prophecy with the double movement that we observe everywhere in Jesus' inner life. On the one hand, there is the deference to God, Jesus' restriction to humble conditions, to ignorance and obedience. On the other hand, we find the absolute consciousness of power that sees in the Father the omnipotent ruler of the world who is ready to save his elect quickly and to glorify his Son by bringing complete redemption into the near future. From the Son's obedience results the abandonment of omniscience, the refusal to replace constant alertness by a calculation of the end, the instruction that the disciple should accept the course of events in whatever way God's rule would arrange it. From the assurance of his commission arises the promise that the work begun by God would quickly be brought to its completion and that the Crucified would soon be revealed in his glory.

Prophecy is not construed according to logical standards. Its aim lies in the realm of the will, in the fact that Jesus wanted to give hope to his followers, a hope that was connected with their aims in all respects and that gave their will fulfillment in every direction. He united that hope with their faith; for now they awaited the complete revelation with its eternal glory solely from him and at the same time with their own work. For hope became the root of the faithfulness that esteemed God's gift and that did God's will. It brought its love for Jesus to completion. It showed them its greatest happiness in their union with him. Likewise, it strengthened their love for the brethren, since he would come in order to reward the love they rendered him in them. It created joy, since it transformed the present life into an anticipation of the feast, and fear, since it excluded the foolish and the faithless from the feast. Thus hope established the same form of will that Jesus had given to his disciples through his communion with them earlier. In Jesus' view, however, in order to create this effect it had to incorporate two characteristics: assurance that aspired to the highest level and restraint that bowed before God's mystery and honored his rule.

The Gospel account received strong confirmation also at this point from the fact presented to us by the apostolic Epistles, since in these Epistles hope has the same apparently contrasting characteristics as those evoked by Jesus' prophecy: the assurance of hope that links Jesus' revelation with one's own lifetime and the absence of any calculation of the end; the supernatural universalism that combines an all-transforming effect of omnipotence with the parousia and the peace that stands firmly on earthly ground and that builds the church; the juridical seriousness of the parousia together with its use as the source of joy; the clear consciousness of the inadequacy of one's own work since the Christ alone can bring about his kingdom; the unbroken devotion to one's obligation. Rigorous historical consideration has no occasion to reverse here the relationship between the master and the disciples and to judge their hope as its own creation, which they transferred to him only in retrospect. Here, too, their testimony must be that he was their master and not they his.

18. The Last Supper

Jesus' death remained his own free act until his arrest. One cannot speak of an external necessity that brought him to the cross; all depended on his own decision. Since Judas's betrayal to the priests, which gave them the courage to destroy Jesus, happened before his own eyes and since he himself helped determine Judas's action by exposing his treacherous intentions, he was not led away from the midst of his disciples without any previous warning. He rather determined the timing of his separation from them himself and thus was able to arrange his farewell from them in a festive way. In this, too, he proved the liberty with which he went to death.

He arranged it in such a way that his death fell at a time of celebration, and not only because the feast freed his presence in Jerusalem from the appearance of arbitrariness, explaining it by the obligation to praise God with the entire community for his covenant. He arranged it as he did also not simply because the decision by which their old relationship with God was ended was made before the gathered community. But Jesus acted when he did because in his death he would exercise the office of the Christ, combining its gracious effect with the ancient revelation of God. In a word, he instituted the new covenant on the day commemorating the old.

He held a meal of farewell with the disciples that was already distinguished by the fact that it did not occur in Bethany. He went with them into the holy city where he had asked for a room according to the custom common for the Passover, and there he united the disciples once more around his table. Since the differences between the disciples evoked a disturbance of community during the meal, he prohibited them once again from all glory-hungry striving for their own greatness and power and placed the value of their choices and actions in the service rendered to others. The exchange Luke received from his particular source (Luke 22:24–27) has complete transparency, since the desire for greatness is rooted deeply in the human psyche and in Jewish piety, and since Jesus' rule gave direction to the entire conduct of the community. John, likewise, by beginning the account of Jesus' final dealings with the disciples with the story of the footwashing, described the rule of service in glorious clarity as the final and complete will of Jesus by which the disciples had the constitutive law for their relationship with him and with one another.

During the meal Jesus stated that one of those he had chosen, one who was united with him in continual table fellowship, would hand him over to the power of his judges. Since he as the head of their community distributed the pieces of bread to the disciples, he used this for the purpose of showing Judas that he knew his intentions. Thereby he separated him from himself by revealing to him at the same time the entire seriousness of the condemnation that his death would bring, urging him, since he was now expelled from his fellowship, to fulfill the promise he had given to the priests without delay. Thereby Jesus surrendered freely and actively to death and did what he required of the disciples: he himself seized the cross with his own grasp. Silently Judas departed.

Now Jesus gave the disciples the bread that had been distributed in pieces with the explanation that this was his body; likewise the cup of wine with the words that it was his blood. Both words were preceded by the blessing of God, the word of thanksgiving that praised God for his gift according to the continual custom that we should always imagine to have been the norm at Jesus' meals. Whether at that moment Jesus spoke a prayer that was prescribed by custom or whether he formed it freely, we do not know. The disciples merely said that Jesus first thanked God for his gift as was customary for him before passing it to them.

Thereby he acted upon them as the Christ by showing them once more at the farewell how he united the office of the Christ with the will to the cross. He did not leave them with merely words, doctrine, or commandments but acted upon them as the one who gave to them. This alone was commensurate with his kingly aim. The other event, too, that lent significance to Jesus' final dealings with the disciples together with the Last Supper, the exposing of the betrayal, possesses all the characteristics of the finished act. Through it he pronounced judgment. Now he placed the act of grace beside the execution of justice and united the other disciples with himself by his gift, he himself being what he was able to give them. As always, he did not transfer the fruit of his labor from himself to a material good or leave them any possessions, powers, institutions, ideas, or laws, but his gifts for them were his body and his blood.

As always, he remained the one who was completely poor also in his final act. He did not have anything he could leave them, nothing to distribute; the only thing he had were his body and his blood. But he did not consider his poverty to be an obstacle or evil so that he deplored it. If he had wanted to present himself merely as impoverished, one whose last will did not dispense any wealth, there would never have been the exhortation: "Eat my body, drink my blood." His poverty rather reveals his wealth. He fulfilled his office by uniting the disciples with himself; for their share in God and in his kingdom consisted of their union with him, hence also their equipment for their work. Therefore he described his body for them as the food that gave them life and his blood as the drink that would provide festive celebration for them. By giving those gifts to them in order that they might enjoy them, he placed them before his cross gratefully as those who received life through his death.

By giving the Last Supper to the disciples he did not merely confirm his prophecy to them, which promised them his communion in the future. Nor did he merely add to the meal they now enjoyed the preview of what was to come and what he would prepare for them after his new revelation. As important it was that he awakened hope in them, he was able and wanted to give them more than a hope; for what happened then was already God's saving act and filled with the glory of God's rule. For his communion with them he needed words and concepts; otherwise it would remain mysterious to them and would cease to be communion. However, it did not merely consist of words and concepts, or it would have been broken. Therefore he did not simply clarify for them what he desired and worked with his death but simultaneously gave it to them as his gift. He died for them, gave his body and his blood for them, and this "for them" he revealed to them in its truth and reality by giving his body and his blood for the purpose that they should eat and drink it.

The conviction that his body would become food for believers and that his blood would become their drink did not move him only in the final night; he had made it explicit since the time he started preparing his disciples for his death. But the new element that could take place only in the final night was now added to the intention: the deed. Now that he went to death and actively fulfilled the will to the cross, he granted them all that was effected by the cross, and therefore he brought them now, through the offer of the bread and the wine, to an eating and drinking that was devoted to his life and to his blood. As he completed his grace in the gift, he did not leave their faith on the level of an idea or a wish but brought it to the finished completion of the deed.

That we should relate Jesus' action to his death is confirmed by the fact that he did not retain the body and the blood for himself but passed it on to the disciples. As long as he had to live in an earthly form, he possessed the ground of his life in his body and in his blood. Only as one who died could he give them away, and only by his death did they pass over into the property of the disciples. By the act of the Last Supper he anticipated what he did immediately thereafter by dying and showed them by this act what he wanted and established through the cross: he surrendered his body and his blood for them. This was confirmed by the fact that he set his blood beside the body since only death separated the blood from the body. He suffered death by the shedding of his blood and thus gave it to them so that they might drink it as the blood that was shed for many.

This does not become doubtful even when the narrator quoted by Luke, and perhaps Luke himself, depicted what Jesus did merely by the one act, merely by the fact that he designated the bread as his body and that he told them to eat it without having a cup follow it whose wine he depicted as his blood.[35] Jesus' action was completely defined for the disciples with the surrender of his body so that it clarified for them what he granted them through his death. The distributing of the cup did not add anything new but merely lent greater clarity to his thought.

According to both Matthew's and John's accounts, Jesus' final words to his disciples did not deal simply with the reason and success of his death but portrayed for them their entire task, giving content to their hope and the rule for their obedience, determining their relationship to the Christian community and to the world. The fact is assured that the idea of death was not so prevalent at Jesus' farewell that it chased away and overshadowed all other concerns. It was, however, entirely reasonable in his situation that this was the time when the question arose regarding the purpose and the blessing of his death, and that he answered this question in a way that based the disciples' communion with him on what his death provided for them.

He interpreted his directive to drink his blood for them by designating it as the blood of the covenant, by saying of it that it would be poured out not merely for the disciples but for many, with the result that their sins would be forgiven. These statements also depict Jesus' death as the fulfillment of the messianic office. The success of his death for the disciples comes from what God created through him. As the one who died Jesus stood in God's service and transformed his body and his blood into the instrument by which God accomplished his work.[36] By his death the community's new relationship to God was born, to which God granted a new revelation of his will. The act of God by which he initiated the new community into its close relationship with him was the Christ's surrender to death. Jesus gave his blood cheerfully so that the new covenant would come into being. In such a way he revealed God and executed the glorious will of his grace by which the community called to him was brought into a new relationship with God. Therefore the consequence arising from the surrender of his blood was the pardon of the many who were forgiven their sins on account of his death.[37] Now he paid the ransom to the Father of which he had spoken, liberating the many. This God-given success

---

35. Luke 22:19b–20 stands in close relationship to the Pauline formula regarding the Last Supper in 1 Cor. 11:23–25. It remains unclear whether they were linked already by Luke or only later with the short account of his special source.

36. That Jesus puts himself into God's service for the purpose of surrendering his life can, of course, be called a sacrifice in the highest sense of the term. But the concept of sacrifice is not used by Jesus himself. It fell short of the directness and immediacy by which he knew himself to be the one who brought God's work to fruition.

37. The thought that the surrender of his blood occurred for the forgiveness of sins cannot be denied Jesus because only Matthew reports it. To begin with, the granting of forgiveness constituted a firm element that was continually present and effective in Jesus' consciousness. Furthermore, the terms "new covenant" and "forgiveness of sins" are firmly linked with each other through Jer. 31:31–34. It would be a vapid notion to propose that Jesus had never considered what Jeremiah said about the new covenant, and that Matthew was the first to see this link.

of his death explained why the blood should be drunk by the disciples and why the body should be eaten by them. They were for them the means to life, which entered them with effective power, since his death provided for them the new relationship with God that had its characteristic feature in the forgiveness of sins.

Jesus ended his work as he had begun it. He began it with the call to repentance that granted them the forgiveness of sins. He ended it with the deed at the cross by which they received forgiveness. The only thing that had changed was that Jesus' right and power to forgive them, so that they had God's forgiveness, now found its complete substantiation and revelation. God gave him this power since he accepted the cross from him.

Whoever does not attribute the concept of the Christ to Jesus must attempt to trace the act of the Last Supper to general human ideas or to ones he could glean from his religious tradition.

Jesus' act is derived from general human ideas when its content is placed into the community that produced the meal between him and the disciples; thus it can be traced to the concept "farewell and love meal." This idea, of course, radiates clearly from Jesus' action. This already becomes apparent in the holding of a special meal in Jerusalem on his final evening. Likewise, the disciple who had broken faith was shown the greatness of his guilt by the fact that he possessed table fellowship with Jesus and that he nevertheless betrayed him unto death. Subsequently Jesus raised the disciples' thoughts from this meal to the one that would be prepared for them when God's rule would be revealed. The meal he shared with them now was not their last, since he described for them the coming new communion as a table fellowship characterized by the use of the festive cup, which he would drink with them again. If this, however, is the only train of thought contained in Jesus' action, the surrender of his body and blood merely serves the disciples' enjoyment and drops from the account. If the meal was designed merely to reveal the love and community that united them at that time, this did not require the eating of his body and the drinking of his blood.

The preceding history of religions did not create any concepts that could have given rise to Jesus' action. If we think of brotherhood sealed by blood at which two friends establish ties by drinking each other's blood or of magically tinged theories of sacrifice in gnostic unions or oriental religions that linked with the enjoyment of a sacrifice a union with God to whom the sacrifice had been brought, a union that was somehow conceived of as real, we once again do not arrive at the particular characteristics of Jesus' act. For those kinds of acts did not tolerate any surrogates. Brotherhood sealed by blood came into being by the drinking of blood, not of wine instead of blood, and a mystical communion with the sacrificial animal or with the God to whom it was sacrificed was accomplished by the eating of its flesh, not by bread that replaced the sacrifice. If the effectiveness and value attributed to his gift by Jesus were to be explained by such parallels from the pagan cult, they would invest Jesus' act with a foul crassness that would require the actual material substance for its expression. But such material substance is missing in Jesus' action. If, on the other hand, Jesus' action is accommodated to general forms of the human will, it becomes the expression of ideas without connection to the body and the blood. In Jesus' action we are presented neither with materialism, since the surrogates of bread and wine replace body and blood, nor spiritualism, since he did not speak of his continual love but of the giving and eating of his body. Jesus' action possessed complete individuality, because it lent expression to his special relationship with God and with the community now being brought into being through his death. Jesus' vocational will in its uniqueness lent his death and therefore also the act at the Last Supper a uniqueness that makes it unfit for comparison.

Jesus probably did not hold his meal at the same time as the Passover of the entire community but on the evening before, so that the Passover lamb was no longer sacrificed for Jesus and for his disciples (this is rendered probable by the data given by John 13:1, 29; 18:28; 19:14, 31). Thereby the celebration was not sidetracked from thoughts of the Passover. They influenced the entire procedure no less strongly when Jesus, in order to die on the day when the Passover lamb was slaughtered, revealed Judas's betrayal already during the preceding night, thus preparing the meal for those with whom he joined himself. In this way his body and his blood replaced the old meal with particular force. He denied that his meal was devoid of any divine gift due to its lacking the lamb and since it did not repeat the institution of the old covenant. The disciples were not to long for Israel's Passover, for now a new demonstration of God's grace occurred for them that reconciled them with God through Jesus' cross.

Paul renders Jesus' word at the Last Supper in the following words: "Do this in remembrance of me." He claims that the entire church has its foundation in this word of Jesus, not merely his own celebration of the Last Supper (1 Cor. 11:23–25). Since Jesus gave his disciples through his meal a share in the saving power of his death, he saw therein an imperishable gift that was granted not only to them but to his entire community and that would never again be taken away from them. God's new covenant would remain forever and was in effect for all who belonged to the Christ, and forgiveness of sins was acquired for them all by his death. They also were not to experience the blessed power of his death in such a way that they would forget its basis and origin. It reminded them of his human life and of his earthly deed, therefore making what he then did for them a means by which they could direct their memory to him again and again. Thereby he made direct connection with the way in which the old covenant possessed its continual attestation in the annually repeated covenantal meal.

It was a sacrament, not a sacrificial act, that originated here. It had fundamental significance for the religious history of his disciples that the center of their common cult was not a sacrifice but a sacrament.[38] This came about because Jesus did not part with God by surrendering the cross but knew himself

---

38. Sacraments are acts by which God's love is manifested to us and his gift is mediated to us. Sacrifices are acts by which we testify our love to God by our gift.

to be united with him and therefore stood before the disciples as the one who gave. In this way what he gave to them became a sign and a bearer of God's grace and therefore his meal did not occasion a sacrificial act but a sacrament. This is evident also by the fact that Matthew and Mark, while doubtless thinking in their accounts of the meal by which the community continually renewed and testified to its communion with Jesus, did not talk about what the disciples should do but solely about what Jesus did for them. Not a trace of sacramental legislation attached itself to Jesus' act by which the manner of its performance by the disciples would be regulated. Even the simple formula by which Paul links the community's celebration with Jesus' act is missing. This is how exclusively the view is directed toward what Jesus did for the disciples. By not placing the value of the Last Supper in what they did there but in what Christ did, the disciples proved that they celebrated their last supper as a sacrament. The meaning of their action was that it granted them the share in what Christ's death provided for them.

This is paralleled by the lack of any account of the institution of the Last Supper in John. Through Jesus' discourse in Capernaum and through his words of farewell, he witnessed to the church merely of Jesus' abiding association with believers, without speaking of the special act by which he transformed his body into their food. Likewise he does not speak of the church's celebration. If polemical thought has any part in the shaping of the Johannine text, it may be directed against the manner in which the church began to transform the sacrament into a sanctuary for itself. This he can oppose by directing attention away from the mere bread and wine, to the flesh and blood of Jesus which he gave for them unto death and thereby made the bread of life. But the account received its form most of all through its positive aim, since this is what he explicitly revealed and not a polemic thrust. John says that the fundamental idea underlying the Lord's Supper was the determined resolve of Jesus, by which he explained to his disciples his will to endure the cross already when he approached the end of his work in Galilee.

On the other hand, John repeated the message Jesus gave to his disciples at his farewell in a rich presentation. By describing Jesus' dealings with his disciples at this precise juncture and by expressing what his communion with them provided for them at this time and not some other, John indicated that it was at that very time that he received from Jesus what determined his condition of faith. Thereby he does not assign second place to the preparatory steps and the first stages of Jesus' work and its results but expresses the conviction that the disciples' relationship to Jesus had become entirely new through Jesus' death. This is why the basis for their faith was given to them only through the words that explained what he was for them by and after his death. It can easily be seen that it was out of consideration for the church, for which John described Jesus' work, that this version of his account took shape. Since one cannot believe in a dead person, and since it is baffling how one can have an invisible person as one's Lord and leader, it was all-important to show the Christian communities that Jesus' death did not bring an end to his association with them. It rather provided the basis for it. Yet this does not prove that the motives supplied to John by his situation at the time he wrote detracted from the memory of what constituted the decisive experience for himself at Jesus' farewell. Whether or not Jesus' communion with them would transcend his own death had already at that time been his disciples' question and was posed with urgent seriousness. Jesus assured them that it was indestructible. He elevated them above his own death and above their separation from him to the promise that their faith and love would continue to reach him when he was separated from them, and that their communion with him possessed eternal security.

John first portrayed through an action of Jesus why the disciples would be associated with him forever. He thereby did not, however, place a miracle before the word. He did not explain by an act of power how his communion with them arose and what it granted; he rather revealed this through the footwashing. Jesus humbled himself to any service for their sake. A shameful, humble service issued from his relationship to them, since they needed to be cleansed, and since he was able to provide cleansing for them, he accepted humiliation to the point of the cross. Therefore the disciples' entire community was based on this attitude of Jesus. If Peter had finally rejected this service, he would have severed his relationship with Jesus. From this originated also for the disciples an obligation to serve. They were to cultivate their relationships with one another in such a way that they corresponded to his conduct.

The words attached to this action show the disciples how they would be able to preserve their communion with him. Through faith they are internally associated with him. Faith is linked with the preservation of his word and thereby also with the obedience that does his commandment. Through obedience they prove their love to him. His will is expressed by the commandment that they should love one another. This does not lead us away from the warning parables, by which Jesus depicted their fall for the sinning disciples. Those who waited for the bridegroom and those who worked with his talents believed in him. They appreciated what he gave to them as their highest and eternal good, and this did not merely remain an idea for them but entirely determined their conduct. Of course, precisely what gives the parables their exhorting thrust is Jesus' intention to move the disciples and rule their behavior. Whoever wanted to participate in the feast had to get the jar of oil and put on the festive garment. The disciple who managed the talents for the master did not live and work for himself; he loved him, and his love was one with the obedience that kept his commandments. If we translate the parables into didactic formulas, we get what John calls believing in him, loving him, and keeping his word, and therein Matthew, likewise, sees the entire duty of discipleship.

In John, too, Jesus' final words extend to equipping the disciples for persecution. Now the struggle with the world would begin for them, bringing death for some. This is parallel to the preparation of the disciples for the gravity of the coming events in the older account. In the Lucan narrative, too, Jesus' final meal concludes with his command for them from now on to take their bag of provisions and to make sure they had a sword. For the time where the disciples could face the Jewish communities without bag or sword was now over. Israel severed fellowship with the disciples of the Crucified, and from now on their lives would be threatened continually.

In John, on the other hand, all words are missing that interpret the course of divine government. There is no discussion of Jerusalem, of the nations, or of the direction of the universe. The thought is foreign to John that Jesus, by his final words, had given his disciples a doctrine of the last things. Likewise foreign to him remains any enjoyment-oriented occupation with the promise, and this constitutes a fundamental agreement with Matthew. He does not submerge the glory of the Coming One into imagination and longing. For him everything is subordinated to the central aim to keep the disciple in communion with Jesus. His position in humanity is described to the extent that it impinges directly on his relationship with Jesus. For his disciples Jesus is not one who takes them out of the world and keeps them from persecution but the one for whose sake they must suffer. However, they also have with them his complete joy and peace.

John takes a step beyond Jesus' word of farewell as reported in the other Gospels by letting Jesus describe not only the duty of the disciple but also his own close communion with him. In the parables they are portrayed in their separation from Jesus as the ones who waited for him and who did his work in the interim according to their own discretion and faithfulness. What linked them with him was his word that he had given them. Thereby, however, his promise was not recanted that he would be with them everywhere and that he himself would build his community through their service. In view of the community's new situation, however, the sense of separation and responsibility prevails that now provides them with their own work. In John, the relationship between these two ideas is reversed. While he completely neglects to invest the hope with a strong sense of its value and its blessedness by embellishing the promise, he wants to provide faith with an eye for the greatness it is granted. John, too, provides us with words of farewell; Jesus departs to the Father, and the disciples now stand in the world without him and wait for him. But next to this stands what one often calls the "Johannine mysticism," the certitude that Jesus is nevertheless present to the disciples so that he protects, guides, and rules them. Their association with him is not based solely on their faithfulness nor merely on the fact that they believe in him and love him, so that it is merely the power of their faith and love that unites them. He himself keeps them close to himself. They resemble the branches on the vine not merely by growing out of it but also by being linked with him forever through a living bond, and from this effective union arise their vocational obligation and the ability to carry it out. Therefore they are the ones by whom he produces the community, as the vine produces its fruit only through the branches.

The thought that Jesus' death did not abolish his union with his disciples is common to all texts; John does, however, indicate more strongly than others that Jesus' death completed his communion with the disciples. In this way he enters into them, and they are placed into him. This idea radiated directly from Jesus' concept of God; above the thought of "being in the Christ" stood the other thought of "being in God." "Being and living in God" was a familiar thought for Jesus; not even the life of a bird ended without the Father. For him it was those whom he had brought to the Father who live fully. The address to Nicodemus concluded with the pronouncement, "Do your works in God." From this "in God" arose the "in me" on the basis of Jesus' complete sonship,[39] and his death would enable him to this "I in you and you in me."

This oneness with the disciples expresses a mystery. But although mysteries excite efforts to interpret them, we do not receive a single formula that seeks to explain the Christ's presence in the disciples. How the Christ who was with the Father would make it possible to be in human beings, and how this would be revealed in their existence, does not become the subject of instruction. Any question in this regard is muted in the face of the assurance that he himself was in the Father. Since nothing hindered God from being present, Christ, likewise, is close to his own since he is in the Father. John, in his own way, expresses no less clearly than Matthew how strong Jesus' antipathy was toward the formation of religious theories. Nevertheless, the center of John's piety lay in this thought. For the love that united him with Jesus was completed by the assurance of its complete association with Jesus.

This thought did not displace the expectation of Jesus' return (John 14:3; 17:24). Nevertheless, John used Jesus' word of farewell primarily to establish believers' lives already at this time firmly in the Christ. The community was not merely to have a hope and an empty present. It had Jesus and would not merely have him in the future; it was with him and would not merely be with him one day. The hope, however, can thereby not be replaced or weakened. Rather, the present possession forms its basis, since the goal is always described in absolute terms that cannot be separated from the messianic idea. Therefore Jesus' intercession also turns to final aims and asks regarding the disciples that they would one day be where he is and that they would see his glory.

The community into which Jesus brings his disciples is completed by the fact that he can pray for them. Even now, at the end of his life, he continues his communion with them before the Father. His sonship and unity with the Father also provide the basis for the Father's love for them. Jesus' act by which John began the account of Jesus' final dealings with the disciples portrayed the way he stepped from his majesty into communion with them. The act with which John concluded it portrayed Jesus as one who addressed the Father on their behalf and effectively used his sonship for them. Both actions together demonstrate how his communion with them continues beyond his death. It originates from the fact that he provides for them cleansing and reconciliation by dying, and that he places them, through his intercession with the Father, with him in his love.

---

39. Linguistically, too, the "in" in relation to the Christ is linked with the preceding "in God."

19. The Decision in Gethsemane

Since Judas had gone away from the meal to the priests, Jesus' arrest was imminent after the meal. The Last Supper makes, however, clear why it was inconceivable for Jesus to think of using the time to escape. He also did not speak to his disciples regarding the question why he did not save himself but about the sin to which his suffering would lead them and of which Peter's denial was the particularly visible sign. By it the disciples gained a lasting perspective of the gravity of the burden that Jesus bore and of the necessity of his death.

Peter's conduct is entirely transparent. Everyone understands why he refused the priest's maid information regarding his relation to Jesus in that night. Only Jesus' unconditional ethical sincerity and his absolute valuation of faith caused the event to be judged by the disciples as sin before all of Christianity. Thereby it is attested once again that Jesus' work had its aim in faith. Nothing material or external was able to replace that effect of Jesus of seizing the human being internally and turning it to Jesus. The personal internal association with him in complete truthfulness and therefore also with the unlimited obligation to testify constituted the essence of discipleship. The denial of fellowship with Jesus, however, stood in complete contrast to this. When Peter did not dare to confess him, he did not believe in him at that time and thus broke his discipleship. From a human perspective, Jesus' work was thereby destroyed. This completed the renunciation into which his end led him. The leaders of the community rejected him, and the leader of his disciples denied him. In Jesus' consciousness, however, this did not constitute any contradiction to the saving power of his death but rather substantiated it. Since his disciples were not a flock that was firm in its faith but rather a wavering group of people capable of denial, they needed the Father's forgiveness, and the Father led him into death in order to be able to give it to them.

This part of his suffering which came about through the disciples' sin he did not bear merely because he could not avert it. He rather determined his relation to it freely and rose above it by virtue of his sonship, which made him the giver of grace also for the one who would deny him. Thereby he kept Peter and the entire group of disciples in his fellowship and prevented them from being shattered by their fall. For they already learned about his forgiveness from the way in which Jesus spoke to them. Jesus gained the right for this in his interchange with God in prayer (Luke 22:31–34), in which he subjected the disciples' fall to God's righteousness and grace in the same way that he saw God's righteousness and grace uniformly effective in his cross. Jesus was neither able nor willing, whether for the disciples or for himself, to violate God's providence, which assigned to the particularly gifted also the test by which they needed to prove the determination of their obedience. But he was concerned for them regarding the outcome of the testing they faced, particularly Peter. Therefore he countered Satan's demand with his intercession, by which he preserved him in the faith. The way in which he made his action effective in the spiritual realm according to this word of Jesus eludes our understanding. But it shows us the inimitable will characteristic of Jesus: the most earnestly truthful exposure and attribution of guilt joined with complete forgiveness, by which the community is renewed beyond its guilt, and together with this the use of grace received for the help of others: "When you have turned, strengthen the brothers." The grace he experienced upon himself had the intention of enabling him to support the wavering and the weak. The fact that Jesus offered him forgiveness even before the fall detracted nothing from the sincerity of his repentance. It rather strengthened it and had the result that he sensed the gravity of his sin. But it could not result in a separation from Jesus, after Jesus had already spoken to him about it beforehand, not as the judge but in his gracious sincerity.

By doing what they had done during earlier nights at Gethsemane, namely, sleep, they avoided the pressure and the pain of suffering. This is included in the tradition, since the disciples' opposition to suffering shows Jesus' greatness in bearing his cross willingly. At the same time, he thus remained toward them the one who forgave until the last moment. The admonishing word he issued to them remained free from all harshness; it expressed no complaint but merely concern for them. Now that all bitter aspects of suffering, the pain and shame of the cross, shook them and demanded them to deny themselves in the deepest sense, his merciful verdict emphasized the connection between the perverted desire of man with human nature. Since, by being "flesh," he was materially different from God, the Spirit's desire and the desires originating from the flesh were in conflict with one another. Therefore, since the willingness of the Spirit was opposed by the weakness of the flesh, the disciple was not to approach his duty with a fearless sense of power but had to be alert and ask. For only God's protection and gift preserves him in what Jesus' communion gives despite the opposition proceeding from the flesh.

While waiting for his arrest, the pain urged him to request liberation from suffering to God. Before and thereafter he acted in the assurance of his sending, both when he gave his body to his disciples and when he stepped calmly before his enemies. This assurance did not arise merely from a yielding to the inevitable but embodied the regal consciousness of power, since the Father would send the heavenly host if he requested it. The verdict that the intervening suffering and the resulting petition contradicted his regal will misjudged how a personal relationship to God affected the will. Jesus did not set an impersonal fate in the place of God and God's will, no natural power that would assign him his fate in place of the free relationship of the Son to the Father. He rather expected the decision from God's will, not from a chain of physical causes nor from a logical necessity nor from a compulsion proceeding from human beings. It was his opinion that he would die when the Father wanted his death; if he did not want it, then no power of the world would kill him. Therefore the suffering never became mere suffering for him, and his attitude toward his death was never merely surrender. The Father's will made him, too, one who chose, and the act by which he accepted his death received all the characteristics of the free decision that did not occur by itself but needed a rationale, an answer to the question of whether God wanted his death at that time or not. Only prayerful interchange with God could yield that answer. With this interchange he filled the time as he waited for his arrest. He thereby transferred his decision to die into the deed for which everything that had preceded was merely preparation. It was not weakness but shows the ethical greatness of Jesus that he based the will that acted not merely on an earlier certainty or on an abstractly conceived necessity but by appropriating it through prayer which received the complete weight of the question, because he suffered. Therefore he could make his decision only through the formation of a greater will that powerfully subdued his initial strong desire for life, victory, and glory. Such desire was present and was based not merely on nature but at the same time also on his status as God's Son.

By their account of his prayer, the disciples revealed once again the nature and the root of his divine sonship. They maintained that the sufferer lay before God without the claim to possess special insight or a unique form of will but with a unique characteristic, namely, the ability to obey God and to overcome the inevitable resistance to pain through union with God's will. He first became cognizant of his will in complete truthfulness and then expressed it to God. Suffering and death resulted also in him in an aversion. Only a second, higher will was able to choose it. When the Father, however, did not answer and confirm that first preference, Jesus overcame his aversion in victorious superiority, although he was shaken to the core. He achieved this not through a natural process nor through a passionate flash of pathos that replaced the conscious decision. Rather, we have him before us with all the characteristics of practiced obedience, so that he confronted his initial desire with an opposite desire, one gained through a new and higher will by which he agreed unconditionally with the will of God.

The picture we receive of his inner life agrees with the one revealed by his prayer in the temple (John 12:27–28). There also it was the aversion seizing him that initially produced a wavering. This hesitation was, however, subsequently ruled by a powerfully intervening higher will that possessed its aim in the glorification of God's name. This aim was seized with complete devotion. His thanksgiving for the illumination of the ignorant (Matt. 11:25) likewise shows the same movement of his will. Yet there it was not the emergence of obedience but the ready union with God's will that came to expression. But in that prayer, too, Jesus rose above the painful, disturbing fact that the wise remained aloof from him to grateful agreement with what was revealed to be God's will.

These events reveal nothing of a resistance to God. That initial desire, which he kept subject to God and to himself, was not sinful, not even in an only human fashion, but grounded with equal power and truth in his communion with the living and self-glorifying God. That Jesus' conscience did not attach any contempt to the desire for life is revealed by the fact that it presented it in prayer to the Father with the question whether he might fulfill it or not. Jesus never made a sinful desire the subject of prayer, nor did he ever consider it to be possible for God to fulfill it. He joined a good conscience with the will that he was able to transform into prayer. If the question for which he sought a decision had originated from his own will, so that the issue would have been whether he would obey or not, we would be confronted with that temptation which presupposes and manifests Jesus' loss of normalcy. We would see that temptation in which love and lovelessness wrestle with one another. Prayers would have arisen from it demanding information from God and an account of the burden laid on him, why he excluded the wise, why he had put him into that hour, why he did not spare him the cup. But he did not ponder whether or not he wanted God's will but what God's will was. He desired only the assurance that made God's will clear to him: Would he send him into death or not? Would he take his illumination away from the wise or not? However, he did need assurance since his behavior was obedience, and because obedience is based on clear apprehension of God's commandment. By seeking and receiving such insight through prayer, he revealed that he based his will on God's guidance.

Jesus' prayer does not reveal any turning away from his commission or a breach of love, no desire to throw away his office or to leave people to their own devices. The reason for this is that he did not conceive of any liberation from the cup than the one that occurred when the Father took it away. In the Father, however, he saw the completeness of grace in everything he did, and he expected that he would work his glorification, effected through the revelation of his grace to the world, in whatever way he chose to arrange it. Jesus' prayer therefore left untouched whatever he had accomplished in word and deed up to that point, and its result consisted therefore of the fact that he took the cup from the Father.

It was part of Jesus' powerful influence on the disciples that they remembered clearly that he suffered rather than being lifted into a blessedness that excluded pain through his divine sonship, in which he had the assurance of victory. He was thereby not separated from reality, becoming untouchable and inviolable so that his suffering turned into a mere illusion. The sincerity by which Jesus saw in his death the judging act of God excluded any attempt to elude the pain, and the disciples continually reminded themselves in their memory of his end that he felt the gravity of what happened with complete sobriety, suffering death as death, shame as shame, the end of his work as the end, and judgment as judgment, not with the smile of the enchanted but with deep sighing, over which he gained control through prayer.

The suspicion has often been expressed that the profound shaking Jesus underwent had its basis in a particular event. It was not merely that he must take up his cross immediately but involved a mysterious encounter with the beyond, an attack of Satan, a visualization of the world's sin in its entire gravity, a glimpse of God's wrath in its power directed against evil. Jesus' will to the cross does, of course, possess a depth we do not comprehend; this also came to light in his dealings with Peter when he bore him beyond the approaching denial with the promise that he had prayed for him even though Satan had accused him. But such deliberations cloud our judgment if they suggest that the plain circumstances of Jesus known to us were insufficient to shake him to the core, as if another misery and bitter need invisible to us were required in addition to it. The step he had to take entailed the complete renunciation by which he yielded everything in obedience, not the trivialities of a vocationless life but the office of the Christ, God's revelation and rule, his community, the salvation of humanity from evil, the absolute values that his life had served and that he connected inseparably with his own person. He admittedly bore within himself the certainty that he would receive everything in return. First of all, however, he faced death, which took everything away from him for the sake of humanity's sin, because Israel was unrepentant and incapable of faith. These things, the things that were brought to him by his plain circumstances, were powerful enough to move him profoundly. The comparison with others said to have died cheerfully never was more than thoughtless speculation.

At his arrest his concern was directed only toward the preservation of his disciples. This thought alone determines the Johannine presentation (18:1–11). Therefore he kept them from any act of violence and made sure that he alone was arrested. This, too, reveals that he maintained and achieved his kingly aim. If he had surrendered it, the preservation of his disciples would no longer have been of concern. By protecting his own, however, he protected his own work and brought it to completion by dying while preserving the disciples who would carry out his commission.

As in his entire ministry, he once again acted on the basis of two convictions, one that the Father's will determined everything, the other that the individual had the power of his own will that made him the doer of his deeds. When he prayed, he arose above all human rulers, above all historical or natural necessities, and made his need to die solely contingent upon the Father's will. Yet he did remind those who arrested him of their responsibility and told them that they acted in the service of darkness. He confronted them with the contradiction that rendered their actions inconsistent: they had only recently had him with them as one who taught publicly. Now they treated him like a robber (Matt. 26:55).

20. Jesus' Death Sentence

Jesus suffered his crucifixion as the act of the nation, and this understanding of events controls the entire Gospel record. Not the resistance of individual persons or parties, nor the sin of Caiaphas or of the priests, nor the passion of individual teachers or of the rabbinate, are singled out as the cause of Jesus' death. Israel proved to be a unified community in this decision; for it had in common the thoughts about God that led it into the struggle against Jesus and the will that rejected his word. These thoughts and will were the power that bound them together. That he was delivered into the hands of the Gentiles and that he met his end at the cross, likewise, was felt to be particularly weighty, because Israel thereby expelled him from the community. Therefore the guilt for his death is not placed on Pilate, and Israel is not left with the excuse that Roman rule was guilty of injustice that led to the Christ's cruci-

fixion. All Evangelists expressly emphasize the events that required the Jews
to take an effective part in Jesus' execution until the end.

The arrest was commanded by the priests who ruled in the temple and
was executed by the temple guard accompanied by Judas. According to John,
the officer who commanded the occupation of Jerusalem's fortresses had
been briefed and was present with a division of soldiers, because it was considered possible that Jesus' and his disciples' resistance against his arrest
might find support among the multitudes gathered for the feast. But since
Jesus did not permit his disciples any kind of resistance, bringing also the disciple who seized the sword to obey the divine will, the Roman troops had no
occasion to intervene. Accordingly, Jesus was brought to be tried by the
heads of Judaism, Caiaphas the high priest and Annas. The latter had remained the most powerful man in the priesthood even after the procurator
urged him to yield the high priesthood. In Israel, however, it was never the
high priest as a single judge who pronounced a verdict. The principle stood
firm that the proclamation and execution of law would occur through him
and his counselors, through him and his Sanhedrin. Whom he wanted to
consult was subject to his own discretion. His pronouncement did, however,
receive the more weight, the more of those who participated possessed authority among the priesthood, in the rabbinate and among the elders, and
among the city administrators.

The very existence of Jesus' circle of disciples depended upon whether or
not, and how, Jesus represented his regal status before those who had gathered
as his judges (cf. Paul: 1 Tim. 6:13). His behavior remained the same as it had
been up to that point. Even now he did not testify to or defend his kingdom.
"You said it, not I," he could tell the high priest when the name of Christ had
been pronounced (Matt. 26:64). He did not make any kingly claims before
his judges but remained intent on the will to the cross, expecting his glory
from God. Since, however, he was now no longer able to prevent questions
pertaining to his kingly status, he acknowledged without any reservation the
entire content of his messianic vocation.

A Jewish verdict was inconceivable without previous testimony and proof,
and the religious height that Jesus' opponents occupied gave the hearing a direction that exposed freely what divided them from Jesus. It was not political
considerations or calculations of necessity that lent direction to the hearing
but merely the question whether or not Jesus was a sinner. No witnesses were
called to confirm that he had appropriated the messianic name, for this did
not need to be proven. This, however, did not yet suffice to condemn him.
What needed to be established was that he had appropriated the designation
falsely in dispute with God. If it could be proven that he had denied and
transgressed God's Law, then his claim to the messianic name was false. The
Christ is just and obedient to God; Jesus and his judges shared this conviction
in common.

The disciples saw Jesus' justification in the fact that the witnesses wanted
to prove his opposition to God and to the Law by his word regarding the temple (Matt. 26:61). Not his attack on the market, which could easily be dem-

onstrated, was used for that purpose; for by it he had been zealous for the holiness of the temple, and it was at any rate not clear that he had thus proven to be a sinner. On the other hand, his judges considered any thought of the temple's destruction to be blasphemous, particularly when he himself wanted to replace it by a new sanctuary. The suspicion that he thought of a new relationship to the community on God's part that made the temple dispensable since a new worship of God arose from the Christ, rendering the service of the temple obsolete, made all of them his opponents.

Thereby that word was used against him by which he had linked his death with the deepest need of Israel, not with its ignorance of God's rule nor with any particular error, but with the fact that it did not tolerate him, since he was God's temple for it. Since he revealed God and made his grace present for the community, it did not grant him room in its midst. At the same time he stated by this word why he considered himself to be invincible. His victorious joy and his immovable assurance of life arose from his closeness with God that made him the genuine temple. God does not allow human hands to destroy his temple; if they tear it down, it will be restored. According to Jesus, this word received its fulfillment precisely here. He therefore did not protect it by any further explanation, even though the witnesses no longer testified with certainty regarding what he had said concerning the sanctuary. The meaning of his word became clear precisely through what happened at that time. God closed the old temple and created the new, the risen Christ by whom the new community came into being.

Therefore the hearing came to a close by the high priest's own admonition for Jesus to declare whether he was the Christ, the Son of God, or not. The connection between the messianic name and the divine sonship lent the question and the answer their weight. Whoever desired the kingdom because he was the Son of God truly was the Christ, and if Jesus therefore claimed to possess it because he stood in divine sonship, he raised an unconditional claim to rule and required religious obedience from all (cf. Luke 22:70). He did not avoid the high priest's attack but declared that the power of the Promised One was now granted to him. From now on, after he suffered death, he would be exalted to God's throne and be revealed in glory through his new sending. He deliberately did not express with his own words what he expected from God but used only two passages of Scripture (Ps. 110:1; Dan. 7:13) that even his judges could not impugn. He spoke solely of his power, not of his ethical aims, nor of the Spirit and of the truth by which he ruled, since he did not establish his regal office at that time nor defend, excuse, or "spiritualize" it but maintained solely that he had it, and that he had it in the entire scope Scripture assigned to the activity of the Promised One. The opponents asked about his power and only his power; therefore Jesus, too, spoke only of it. By appropriating both words of Scripture as having been written regarding him, he simultaneously expressed the uniqueness and perfection of his divine sonship. Since he had it, God's promise is fulfilled upon him from that time on, and this was his blasphemy in the view of his judges. In their mind the question of power was decided. His powerlessness proved that he did not have this closeness to God. He was forsaken by God. Since Jesus did not admit this but claimed communion with God that exalted him to God's throne, he committed blasphemy. Thereby Jesus' destiny alone was made the basis for his condemnation. Because he suffered, he had to die. For Israel's God was a God of power who protected his Anointed One, who exalted him and led him to power. That he, the one whom God did not protect but allowed to die, nevertheless appealed to God—that was his blasphemy.

Here Jesus' thought and that of his opponents parted ways. Both agreed on one thing: that the Christ was righteous. But for his opponents, this resulted in the fact that he would triumph since he was the righteous one. For Jesus this meant that he suffered since he was the righteous one. The respective concepts of the Christ now stood in clear contrast to one another. The council's concept of the Christ had its content in the success effected by the Anointed One, in the value of his accomplishment for the nation and in the power he had at his disposal. The Christ's internal, personal relationship to God remained a secondary issue. Of course, he had to have such a relationship since God otherwise would not assist him; but that God helped him was the essential characteristic that determined his regal status. Jesus' concept of the Christ, on the other hand, was based on his sonship, on his internal closeness to God. Above the power stood the Spirit by which the love of God and obedience arose. From this resulted the share in God's power, since God was with him with the complete glory of his divinity. His regal status, however, did not spring into being at his use of power. He rather gained, through his internal closeness to God, independence from success and the ability to be certain as the one given by God to death. He was able to testify to his sonship and rule not despite but because he suffered, suffered because he rejected evil, fulfilled God's Law, and remained obedient to God, even when he had to die. The Sanhedrin would have had to reverse its entire religious theory and practice, had it been open to a concept of God that considered the divine sonship and the rule over people compatible with a will that included the cross. This would have been possible only by yielding to Jesus' word of repentance; but for this it was now too late. His judges therefore immediately furnished proof for the truth and justice of their verdict by abusing him. For the fact that Jesus was a defenseless object of their abuse proved with indisputable clarity that he was forsaken by God and that his appeal to God was delusion and sin.

The same consideration led them to urge Pilate to hang him on the cross and to foil all Pilate's attempts to extricate himself from participating in this verdict. Since the rule was valid for the Roman administration of the country that the procurator did not interfere with the religious struggles within Judaism, Pilate made major concessions to the Jewish leaders, permitted Herod to pronounce the verdict over Jesus, authorized the Sanhedrin itself to execute it, and offered Jesus' pardon according to festive custom. The determination by which Jesus' accusers forced his crucifixion revealed the fear of his spiritual power that had humbled them up to that point. Only then would he finally be destroyed and faith in him entirely extinguished: when he died on the cross

by the Romans. Then it would clearly be proven for every Jew that he was forsaken by God.

Jesus represented his kingdom also before Pilate not with words that must
have remained unintelligible for him and therefore not by appeal to the Scripture and its eschatology, but by showing him how he possessed and executed
his rule by his word (John 18:37). Thereby he gave Pilate the answer to his
question; for Pilate was not concerned with what would be but with what
Jesus had done and who he was, and how he now intended to rule. By designating himself as a witness to the truth, he made clear to him how he united
the will to rule and the will to the cross, why his kingdom rendered him defenseless and obliged him to suffer while nevertheless granting him a power
that remained unaffected by his cross. His presentation of his rule by testifying to the truth led as little to a slanting of Jesus' aim toward gnostic thought
as when he allowed God's rule to be executed by the word. For truth revealed
God's relation to man and therefore provided not only material for thought
but also the rule for love and work. Precisely at the time he died, and since he
died, Jesus was the truth. He was the truth not merely by what he said but on
account of the fact that he devoted himself to the Father with complete obedience, going to the cross.

As he does concerning the farewell from the disciples, John also says regarding Jesus' final hours when the verdict against him was pronounced, that
the thought of truth filled him and gave him strength. Precisely at the moment when pretense, hypocrisy, and lie fought against him, when the priests
fought for God's honor in pretense and persecuted him with the lie that he
was a blasphemer, when Israel appeared in pretense to be the holy nation that
would not tolerate a false Christ while simultaneously in pretense subjecting
itself to the Roman as if it was concerned for the rule of the emperor, when
even Pilate acted in pretense as a judge although he despised truth and righteousness, Jesus saw what separated him from all and elevated him above all
in the fact that he had been put into the service of the truth and that he had
his vocation in being its mouthpiece, testifying to it before humanity. This
gave him firmness that could not fear the struggle nor avoid the cross; the witness cannot remain silent. At the same time he explained thereby as far as it
was possible in conversation with a Roman why he did not consider his patience a deviation from his office as a ruler and why he did not violate it by
the way to the cross but rather fulfilled it. For truth cannot be served by violence. Whoever wanted to reveal it had to be ready for suffering; he would be
opposed in the world of pretense and lie by those who fought the truth. His
power would, however, not be taken away from him through this struggle
since truth was not foreign to man but touched and moved him within so that
his life could grow out of it. All those who had in the truth the basis for their
conduct were his community. They gathered around the witness to the truth
and had in his voice what ruled them. Thus his rule attained to universal
greatness. For it reached as far as the power of truth extended. Nevertheless,
at the same time its unity with God's righteousness remained clear, the righteousness that divided humanity and that separated those from Christ's own-

ership who broke with the truth. In all this Jesus made what he considered to
be his regal work before the cross and at the cross clear for every state of
knowledge. He made it easy to understand, yet still profound and undiluted.
By describing himself as witness to the truth, he once again revealed the unity
he found between grace and judgment, between repentance and the kingdom,
and therefore also between the cross and his kingly aim.

In their memory of Jesus' end, the disciples dwelt on the fact that Jesus received at that time the insignia of the kingdom, albeit in a form that entirely
contradicted the human conception of rule. For the eyes of the disciples, however, these signified not simply mockery of his kingly aim but possessed the
full truth, since he became the Christ indeed through his suffering. Therefore
the crown of thorns and the worship of him as the Anointed One and the
public announcement of his regal name were for them an integral part of the
passion story. They saw in this not merely a measure of his humiliation but
God's witness regarding him. He obtained the regal insignia in the exercise of
his messianic commission since he gained his messianic office by his death.
The fact that Jesus already interpreted his anointing by a woman in a similar
perspective reveals that their perspective does not stray from his.

21. Jesus' Death

The disciples did not avoid the image of the dying one as a horrible memory but gave it a visible dimension for the entire community. Great poetic
power was active in the way this happened. Since the image of the cross was
linked internally with the narrators' state of faith, they also developed the personal dimension of their faith in its portrayal, particularly in their account of
Jesus' final words.

Matthew only reports that Jesus loudly prayed Psalm 22:2, thereby confronting the church with the truth and depth of his suffering. This may support the notion that a verse of Scripture was made a word of Jesus in retrospect. However, the fact that this word and Jesus' final word of prayer
recorded by Luke (Luke 23:46) are the only instances where this question can
even be entertained requires a cautious evaluation of this idea. And the content of the quoted passage in the psalm further counsels against it. The account shows that the narrators strongly felt the contrast between Jesus' prayer
and his regal vocation. For they linked it with the mockery that it was now
time for Elijah to appear from heaven to serve the Christ and to effect his un-
veiling. The prayer shows that Jesus did not float above suffering even at the
cross, whether unconsciously or in the blessed assurance of divine closeness.
It further shows that he paid attention, even then, only to what the Father did
for him. The disciples did not hear any complaint regarding men at the cross.
What rendered his suffering difficult was that God had forsaken him, and this
happened not only through the helplessness into which he had been thrown
by his circumstances but also in his internal existence. Dying is not merely an
external change; it also affects the person. God had taken his hand away from
him.

Thereby he himself expressed the thought by which his judges had substantiated his conviction. It was as they had said: God's protection and gift were no longer with him. This was, however, no new idea in the sense that Jesus would have had no room for such a thought given the way he had previously related to God. For he never used his sonship to acquire power; he had never measured it by its strength and blessedness. His entire conduct was based on the fact that the sonship arose for him at a deeper point: in the community of will with God. This bears even the absence of divine power and gift and does not break apart even in God-forsakenness. Therefore he prayed even now with the messianically understood word from the Psalms as the one for whom Scripture was also written, in what it depicted as the deepest misery of the Righteous One. Moreover, he did not choose a verse in the Psalms that spoke of the guilt of the one who prayed, lamenting that God had left him. The certainty of being obedient to God determined his prayer even now. He suffered as the Righteous One and therefore asked lamentingly why God had forsaken him. This was what was difficult in his dying, that he had to keep close to God even though God had removed his power and aid.

Luke, on the other hand, reports words that show Jesus' forgiveness and messianic office even in the hour of death, the intercession for those who crucified him, and the promise to the one who died beside him at the cross. As he begins the passion story with Zacchaeus's conversion, he concludes it with that of the crucified; between those two actions of Jesus lies the surrender of Jerusalem that will flare up as dry wood on the day of God's judgment. Thus God's judgment and grace are revealed in Jesus' cross. He singles out individuals from the community falling away from its God, not righteous but guilty ones, whom he helps when they repent and believe in him. In such a way he reveals perfect grace. Whether or not Israel is blind and the temple falls, to save the tax-collector and to unite the criminal eternally with himself was his profession and his blessedness during his affliction at the cross. I cannot consider this to be a myth. This is the way he was.

A tension with the God-forsakenness would only result from the promise, "Today you will be with me in Paradise," if consciousness of guilt were revealed by it. Then, of course, the promise would be invalid which opened Paradise for others; the power of reconciliation would be invalid which was certain that his will was sufficient to institute the guilty one in the Father's grace. Jesus, however, did not rebel against God in his prayer, and he did not throw away the confidence that God had led him to the cross and that he was obedient to the Father in dying. This, of course, was, according to his cry of lament, the most difficult and most devastating part of his suffering: that God surrendered him to death. Therefore he also had the assurance that he would grant the request as soon as it was directed toward him.

Luke linked Jesus' final moment with that verse in the Psalms that was suitable as no other for the prayer of a dying person, Psalm 31:6. Here it is more plausible that the image given by Scripture of how a pious person could die might have influenced the passion story. The simplicity of the presentation remains, however, in any case an important testimony to the way in which

Jesus' end continued to linger in the disciples' memory. He did not seek any special form of prayer, nor did he desire any special demonstration of grace. He shaped his request by the word from the Psalms, and what he asked for was that the Father would take his spirit that now departed from him into his care.

John elevates the form of the dying one completely above the teeming surroundings of the cross and directs the view solely on him. By Jesus' final word to his mother and to John, the dying one released himself from the deepest relationships his earthly life had brought him. The painful side of dying is thereby revealed, for now the earthly bonds are broken. The words, "I thirst," too, illustrate the awkward misery of the dying one. Then it is only a brief cry that expresses the assurance that he had completed his commission and overcome, sensing that death was imminent.

From a Greek perspective, and one may as well say, from a human perspective, the passion account poetry would have turned into tragedy, which showed the will that rebelled against pain and its defeat by fate. But there is no trace of this in the way in which the disciples portray the image of the Crucified. Pain is felt and expressed, but Jesus' will is completely united with it. He does not rebel against suffering; he wants it, bears it, and completes it. The poetic element in the image of the cross is unparalleled, since it portrays the one who suffered wholeheartedly. This would have been impossible, unless the disciples had been entirely reconciled with Jesus' cross, and this, in turn, was only possible if they saw in it God's grace and Christ's love.

Therefore even the passion narrative shows how God's providence at Jesus' death extends to the smallest details, so that God's rule is revealed in everything precisely when God gives him to death. It is manifested in the fact that he is not crucified alone, that his clothes are distributed and that lots are cast for his garment, in what he was given to drink, in the way in which Pilate formulated his guilt and characterized him to the people as a human being, in how the elders mocked and Jesus himself prayed, in the darkening of the sun, in the tearing of the temple veil, in the earthquake, and in the way in which his corpse was kept from destruction and how he was buried. This took nothing away from the gravity of his end; it rather explained why all of these detailed circumstances took on such significance for the disciples, the witnesses of the fact that God prepared this outcome for him and that everything happened according to his will.

The Easter Account

1. The Continuation of Jesus' Life beyond the End of His Earthly Ministry

Later effects of Jesus we meet frequently, not merely in the circle of his followers, but into the present. But later effects are not yet the continuation of his history, since history entails the act, that effect upon others that the person itself produces by his will.

The simplest way of categorizing the Easter account among Jesus' later effects appears to be the one of interpreting the Easter reports as legends. That the poetry arising with those reports has a lofty quality need not be disputed by the one who represents this thought. This is not a crude, impure legend, but perhaps still nothing more than a legend, a series of ideas that doctrine produced by itself. The disciples believed that Jesus was and continued to be the Christ, that he would continue to live and remain in contact with them, and this concept gave birth to legend. Now a sound historian will not speak of a "necessity" for the legend to develop. For there is no "necessity" that faith in the Christ had to perpetrate itself once he was contradicted by the cross. But to speak much of necessities is a task for dreamers; they alone claim to have a complete understanding of all the conditions that gave rise to a process. The accomplishment of the historian is great enough when he achieves the perception of an event. The legend seeks to bring together the fact that the disciples did not view merely Jesus' spirit as rising to the Father—in fact, they also transcended the mere expectation of his return—with the fact that the doctrine of the resurrection was a given for the completion of the community. From this, it is argued, the conclusion arose that the Christ already now possessed the existence that all attain in God's kingdom. He has become "the firstborn of those who have fallen asleep."

This theory, however, eliminates together with the Gospels also the statement by Paul. For Paul the assertion that Jesus had risen came to him not as a legend from an already established theory but from the fact that he saw him.

375

No interpretation that we may provide for Paul's claim leads us to fiction; he always confronts us with what happened, with what he experienced. But Paul did not attribute the appearance of Jesus solely to himself while denying it for the other apostles; he rather claimed for himself merely what he found with the others, thus putting himself, on account of the appearance granted to him, on the same level as them. Since Paul's conversion leads us back to the beginnings of the community, his testimony makes clear that the Easter account was told from the beginning as the apostles' experience. It never consisted of the explanation that Jesus "must have risen" but rather appeared as a testimony that they had seen him.

This the Gospel accounts reveal by providing a geographical locale for the dealings of the risen one with the disciples. He did not receive this limitation merely on account of the messianic concept. Postulates that conclude apart from experience that Jesus "must have risen" and "must have appeared to others" embody no limitations. The Easter account, however, was never that Jesus revealed himself from time to time. It was never promised to anyone who entered the community that he would now see the Christ, as if the thought were present that Christ might crop up out of nowhere at, say, the community gathered at Corinth. This theory could be deduced from the prior theory with which we are dealing regarding the Easter account as easily as the one that he appeared to the disciples in Jerusalem or at the Sea of Tiberias. The limitation of the Easter report can only be accounted for by the actual course of events. When there were no more appearances of the Risen One, they were no longer claimed or invented. There emphatically did not arise a legend that construed appearances for the purpose of proving his messiahship. The Easter account as we know it had this form from the beginning, for it always appeared as the "testimony" of those who had experienced the days of Easter. Just as the Easter report is based on testimony, it is geographically constrained.

The power evoked by the Easter account, according to this theory, is "faith." This faith, however, had to be there at the beginning in order to be able to produce something. Whoever eliminates the Easter story will also eliminate miracle from Jesus' ministry, and probably also the regal will. He will acknowledge only a moralist or an apocalypticist with shreds of ideas that differ little from those of his contemporaries and that crumbled entirely by the countervailing power of the cross. Nevertheless, he was the Christ for his followers only a few weeks later, the Christ around whom a community gathered with a faith whose genuineness it proved by thinking, choosing, and acting in him. The Jews could not suppress it nor the Greeks resist it. Here history occurred; and this requires causes for its effects, not legends. And even when this theory is aware of the fact that it is futile to empty Jesus' history, putting in his mouth a firm messianic testimony and surrounding him with a number of somewhat miraculous events, it is always the cross that deals the fatal blow to such theories. The disciples, however, did not work with memories of the great events that now belonged to the past but spoke as apostles. Is it really possible that they acted as apostles of someone of whom they were able to say merely that he had been crucified? This idea would be one of the most curious monstrosities ever created by speculative conjecture.

The necessity of establishing the transition from the cross to the establishment of the community, not by poetry or theory, but by a series of events filling the days of Easter, is met by that interpretation of the Easter account that considers it to be a series of visions. Like the prior theory, it categorizes the report under Jesus' later effects and does not admit to the continuation of his history beyond death. It does, however, differ from the fiction theory by allowing for experiences on the part of the disciples, thereby stepping onto the ground of history, albeit not Jesus' history, but that of the disciples. In them, it is said, one should find the conditions for these events so that they arose from their wishes and moods. They desired for Jesus not to be dead and wanted him to rise, longing for his appearance. From this, it is claimed, arose the appearances, caused merely subjectively, yet with a vividness that made them real for their consciousness and authorized them to assert that they had seen him.

This idea finds support in the fact that visions also occur later in the apostles' lives, so that one could assume a certain predisposition for these. It is also true that Jesus' crucifixion deeply agitated the disciples.[1] They were not in a calm, calculating mood that was capable of sober observation, least of all the women who have such a great part in the Easter account. Yet our sources reveal nothing of such a passionate mood but are characterized by a solemn calmness that is becoming for certitude. This, it is argued, is only the mood of a later time that has become accustomed to the concept of the resurrection and that now treats it as an assured fact. The disciples entered the Easter account in a mood oscillating between despair and hope, unable to give up their faith in view of Jesus' earlier words and deeds, and unable to retain it in view of his death; and from these waves of emotions visions emerged that ended all doubt, experiences of highest value for the disciples although they were found merely in their own subjective realm. This interpretation of the events has against it that the appearances are not narrated in terms of visions but, if such visions are assumed, can have received their present form only by deliberate transformation that camouflaged their visionary character. Paul did not judge differently here than the other disciples. He distinguished his later visionary experiences from that appearance of Jesus which made him an apostle, precisely as John distinguished the visionary view of Jesus that he experienced on Patmos from the encounters with the risen one. Again, Paul concluded the series of witnesses who saw the risen one, adding to them only that appearance of Jesus he himself had been given (1 Cor. 15:1–11). This does not imply that there could not be any continual "revelations" of the Lord that would bring him close to his own in form of a vision, since the ministry of his Spirit should not be limited in this way. Visions and the Easter report are, however, most

---

1. The contention that the disciples were deeply agitated can find support in the claim that they did not merely see Jesus during the days of Easter but also other dead people (Matt. 27:53).

definitely distinguished. The latter remains limited to the days subsequent to Jesus' death and therefore is restricted to those who followed Jesus.

The accounts' content corresponds to this. As far as the empty tomb is involved in the events, they are at any rate not conceived of as vision. Those accounts that do not occur at the tomb, such as Jesus' appearance to the twelve or to the two who walked to Emmaus or at the Sea of Tiberias, likewise are unlikely to be descriptions of visions, since they always involve a multitude of disciples at the same time who are simultaneously part of the action. What one individual sees the others see as well; what one person hears is heard by all. Whoever speaks of visions that were experienced by several at the same time distorts the accounts, since they do not claim that several disciples bore impressions of Jesus within them simultaneously but that, when they saw the Lord, they at the same time saw not only him but also one another and the world, and that they were in contact with one another and acted jointly. Simultaneous visions of this description, if we call them visions, become virtually inexplicable.

The reports are told in such a way that Jesus' form steps before the disciples as objectively as any other appearance without separating them from one another or from the world, so that their entire consciousness retains its natural state. The risen one remains, of course, a mystery for them, as is strongly stressed by the accounts; he lives in a different order of things and comes and goes as someone who is placed into nature is not able to do. But the accounts do not thereby render doubtful the event's rootedness in a reality other than merely the disciples' spiritual condition.

The vision theory therefore needs to resort to legend and to suppose that the community's tradition surrendered the original Easter accounts, forming new ones in their place that are scarcely still in connection with the earlier versions. This result, it is argued, came about through apologetic motives. But this alteration of the accounts cannot merely be transferred to a later period, since Paul did not receive an Easter report made up of visions. He was told that Jesus first appeared "to the Twelve," then "to more than five hundred brothers," then "to all the apostles"; thus he was not told of visions. The commonality of the event and experience that brought the disciples jointly into contact with the Lord is not of a visionary nature.

According to this theory, opposite effects need to have arisen immediately subsequent to the visions; through them, faith in Jesus' resurrection developed. At the same time they did not suffice for it but left the impression that more than a vision was necessary to be certain of Jesus' resurrection. Accordingly, their memory was replaced by other accounts. If that memory created faith by appearing to the disciples as the revelation of the Christ, where then came the doubt? If doubt arose, how did it produce the proclamation of the risen one?

One proposal seeks to do justice to this question by alleging a difference between whether the faith originated within the circle of disciples itself or whether it had to be represented and proven to others. For the disciples themselves, visions were sufficient; before their critical audience, on the other hand, they felt their inadequacy. In the case of the latter, one appealed to the empty tomb rather than speaking of the vision experienced by Peter, which Paul nevertheless called the first appearance of the Lord, since what an individual thought to have seen did not have sufficient power of proof for others. That is why the entire group of apostles quickly rallied around the "risen" one. Therefore, it is argued, we no longer have the resurrection account in such a way as it had created faith but as it had been prepared for Christianity at large in order to provide for it as much insight and certainty as possible.

This distinction between an original faith and the one to be established by the New Testament account alerts one to a fact that is not adequately accounted for by the vision theory. The distinction between a faith that arises through a vision and the one represented by the disciples is so great that one could not emerge from the other. Visions are always connected with the consciousness that they belong to the internal history of the one who experienced them. They were present to a person as his own psychological state.[2] If it becomes the basis for his faith, it is based on what the believer senses, perceives, and desires within himself. This is precisely not where New Testament faith looks for its foundation. If the disciples had looked for the basis of their faith in Jesus to the internal movements of their soul, the church would have turned into a gathering of mystics who spent their time trying to produce within them the ecstatic condition by which the Christ would become visible also to them. The idea, however, that it was Christianity's calling to enhance its emotions to such a degree that it would culminate in a vision of Jesus wherein the assurance of salvation was rooted or completed is not interwoven with early Christian history. The disciples always and solely, by a sober use of the idea of truth, understood faith in such a way that what happened showed them what God was and did, so that the objectiveness of an accomplished fact would present the basis for their conviction and the goal for their will. From this will their inner life received its content. The Easter account did not create the effort in the disciples to retreat into their inner lives and to seek there the revelation of God that world history denied them. Conversely, their lives rather received its basis and its power from the event that came to them externally. Precisely for this reason they considered the act of faith to be what constituted the foundation of all Christian piety. If the disciples' conviction of having seen Jesus once more subsequent to his death was derived from visionary states of being, the consequences of this process would have had to be revealed in the entire state of piety. As a result, we would have received in the place of Christianity a religion in which the individual elevated himself to God one way or another.

---

2. The objection that this is not true when the vision is linked to a strong awareness of God, as was the case with the prophets, distorts the events. The power by which the recipient of a vision knew himself touched from above, by God, by the Christ, by the Spirit, or by an angel, did not extinguish the consciousness that what had been shown him did not have its origin beyond his soul. Neither Paul in his vision of the man from Macedonia, nor Peter in the case of the sheet containing various kinds of animals, nor John in his vision of the Christ on the white horse, transposed their visions into nature or into heaven. If the limitation was missing that affirmed the subjective character of the experience, one no longer spoke of a "vision."

This interpretation of the Easter events also brings them in sharp contrast to the way in which the disciples acted. Whoever speaks of the vision's contagious power that, it is argued, was capable of repeatedly transferring all of the apostles jointly into ecstasy, and finally also a great assembly, injects a passionate flaring up of emotion into the disciples that renders the course of their work impossible. They kept great calm in it, as befits the rule of obedience that was valid for their entire conduct. Their practice of mission constitutes clear, albeit not the only, proof. It does not know anything of a stormy, passionate exclamation of Jesus' messiahship. One used the occasion courageously and did not remain silent even before the Sanhedrin, yet did not intrude into council affairs by, say, confronting the high priest with the fact that he had killed the Christ. We no longer arrive at this determined firmness that did what the situation required when the beginnings of the community are invested with an excitement that drove several hundred jointly into a vision. Such consequences would also have had to become evident in the Easter report. That account as we have it, however, is the complete opposite of mere fantasy in the pure reverence with which it conceals the miracle and in the concentration of the will on the obligation to service given to the disciples.

The desire to produce an Easter narrative for later generations that was more useful than the one possessed by those who participated in it cannot be shown anywhere from the form of our documents. The Pauline account demonstrates that the Easter account was from the start considerably richer than the concluding words of the Gospels. There can be no discussion that the disciples made every effort to enumerate the witnesses for Jesus' resurrection as completely as possible and that they wrote down all appearances of the risen one in order to strengthen the certainty of the account. If such motives were present, why is there no mention of Jesus' appearance before the five hundred brethren? If this account was spawned by apologetic considerations, its apologetic value for the Gospel records is no less great than it was for Paul. The deviations of the texts from one another and the difficulty of putting them together confirm that no apologetic skill was used in compiling them. In their incompleteness and in their relationship to the personal motives of the narrators, they are similar to the account preceding the passion, so that one should adopt the same attitude to the passion narrative as to the earlier history experienced by the disciples.[3]

3. The significant differences in the Easter account that arise from the fact that Matthew places Jesus' encounter with the disciples in Galilee while Luke locates it in Jerusalem does not necessitate reflection upon new motives that nowhere else emerge in the portrayal of Jesus. Matthew effects the disciples' separation from Jerusalem's holy ground by his entire presentation; therefore he begins with Jesus' transport to Nazareth, portraying only his work in Galilee and describing his dealings with Jerusalem only through the passion narration. This now finds its conclusion in the fact that the risen one sends his disciples from Jerusalem back to Galilee and from there to all the nations. In Luke, however, the conclusion of the Gospel includes a preview of the apostles' work: Jesus places his disciples in Jerusalem in order for them to gather his community and to go from there to the nations. The texts give no grounds to the suspicion that the transposition of the appearances to Jerusalem was designed to cover up the disciples' faithless flight to Galilee.

The consciousness that in telling of Jesus' resurrection the disciples narrated something incredible is expressed in all accounts by the fact that the disciples themselves are depicted as those who doubt and who only tediously arrive at certainty by really seeing him. Among the disciples gathered in Galilee are those who doubted when Jesus appeared to them. Mark said regarding the women that they did not dare to tell the Easter message to the disciples. Those who traveled to Emmaus considered this message incredible, and John portrayed the same process movingly in the case of Thomas. The later account, too, that is now used as the conclusion to Mark stresses the unbelief with which the disciples initially stood before Jesus (Matt. 28:17; Mark 16:8; Luke 24:22–24,37–43; John 20:25; Mark 16:11, 13–14). Therein one may see an apologetic intention, since the suspicion is countered that the disciples merely imagined Jesus' appearance because they desired it; the desire might have suggested the message to them. The accounts, on the other hand, emphasize that the disciples themselves were surprised by the event, that they resisted acknowledging it, and that they believed and proclaimed it only since they were convinced by the reality of Jesus' resurrection. This kind of apologetic, however, provides no occasion for suspicion. It explicitly rejects the procedure that the vision hypothesis suspects regarding the disciples. By this, however, talk of the narrators' apologetic skill has come to an end, since the remainder of their accounts is completely dependent upon the prerequisite that everyone in the community knew that the disciples' conviction regarding Jesus' resurrection was firm and not subject to any wavering. It is therefore not presented to the audience by any special proofs but constitutes in the same way as the other portions a part of the gospel that is secured by the apostles' witness and their commitment to truth.

This gives preference to a third type of explanation rather than the supposition of visions. This theory resorts not to an ecstatic alteration of consciousness but to a preoccupation with illusions. It differs from the previous two by not interrupting the normal course of events and by allowing the consciousness to function in its normal manner, injecting concepts into early Christian consciousness by the effect of an objective factor, such as a strong will. These concepts are completely characterized by a normal way of perception. This theory has the advantage that events of the kind of which it conceives lead, not to mysticism, but to faith, and may happen to many people at the same time, just as the power inherent in illusions may simultaneously control the attention of many.

Thereby, however, the theory approximates miracle, and this all the more, the more it distances itself from the pathological processes assumed by vision theories, and the more it recognizes, in those illusions brought to the clarity of seeing, the source of effective and valuable powers that shape the progress of history. By the fact that those curious processes operate in the disciples, Jesus' word becomes fruitful for them, and not merely for them but for the world. Thereby the church's opening to all nations develops, the dying off of paganism in the entire Hellenistic world, and the victory of the Christian ethic in the public consciousness of great peoples. Whoever recognizes value in this and somehow bears a concept of God within him, also will not allow those unusual influences and effects to develop apart from the divine government, perhaps not even without the collaboration of the Christ himself, and thus that way of looking at things emerges that is characterized by the ambiguous term "objective vision." It believes that the conditions that produced in the disciples a vision of the present Christ had been ordained by the divine government and gave to the entire process the value of a divine revelation. In this view a picture of Christ developed within them, but only his picture, this, however, in such a way that the disciples could not perceive any distinction separating his image from his person, so that they could only conclude from the course of events that he had showed himself to them once again.

This interpretation of the Easter narrative deviates from the disciples' account by eliminating the elements in it that touch on nature. Accordingly, one should not speak of Jesus' body and of his empty tomb. It retreats exclusively to the sphere of the internal event, but in such a way that the event is supposed to have been affected by stimuli coming from outside and above it. This theory's deviation from New Testament principles does not have historical but doctrinal reasons. It results from the ideas that the historian develops regarding the end of human life and the relation of the internal life to nature. Its discussion therefore transcends historical observation. For the latter, one may merely mention, in order that one's own consciousness not gratuitously revise history, that what this interpretation assigns to the onlooker's subjectivity as an illusion possessed a serious causal power for the religious history of early Christianity. It was essential for it that the disciples did not conceive of Jesus' end in terms of a translation into a world beyond, not as surrender of the earthly sphere so that he continued to exist merely as "spirit" without connection with his earthly existence, but that they saw in his resurrection the fulfillment, but thereby also the preservation, of his preceding life.

All theories using the concept of vision or illusion to interpret the Easter story are open to a dualistic tendency, since they surrender the natural world to destruction and allow the glorification to occur through the elimination of the earthly. But the Easter concept of the disciples, according to which the Christ experienced in his entire human condition, including his body, the life-giving and glorifying work of God, resulted in that complete faith that knows itself not to be cut off from God in the natural realm, in interaction with earthly matter, and in circumstances conditioned by the body. Precisely in these connections and spheres, this faith knows simultaneously that it is integrally linked with God. This is significant for the development of a hope that conceives of the ultimate goal of man and of the world in terms of the Christ and therefore longs, not for immortality with the separation of this world from the world beyond, but the fulfillment of the world that will grant to humanity, including the nature bearing it, entrance into an eternal glory.

The apostolic concept of Easter was the prerequisite for the fact that the disciples placed a genuine, strong-willed hope in the idea of the parousia. Their concept of the resurrection, however, was also successful in the way in which it helped them conceive of their religious task in the present. It elevated their desire

above the natural sphere so that it transcended what impinged on "the flesh," seeing the divine activity not merely in the natural process. By following the risen
one the disciples directed their love and their ministry with clear determination
toward a transcendent aim. Since this aim, however, did not merely stand in contrast to their present existence on account of their conception of Easter, bringing
them, not destruction, but fulfillment, their supernaturalism retained in all circumstances a sober naturalness that was open to reality. The concept of resurrection was a strong bulwark against all enterprises that sought to open heaven by
despising the earth and to strengthen the spirit by trampling down the natural
life, seeking to honor God by demeaning humanity.

2. The Content of the Easter Report

The disciples do not provide an account of Jesus' resurrection; they do not
recount how Jesus awakened to new life and left his tomb. Once again it is
evident at an important point that imagination must not be given free rein.
The act of resurrection offered a fascinating topic to the one who was inter-
ested in fiction, and undisciplined writers of the Gospel story such as the one
operating under the name of Peter also immediately filled this gap in the disciples' account while, similar to the Christmas narrative or the account of
Jesus' miracles, making no attempt to explain the creative act by which God
gives life. They retreated from what was God's and spoke of what they had
supposedly experienced.

Moreover, it is common to all accounts that the Easter narrative did not ex-
pand Jesus' ministry beyond his circle of disciples. He returned as the Risen
One to those whom he had previously called and placed into his community.
Whoever trusts in his own conclusions will expect the Easter account to transcend and thus overshadow Jesus' earthly work, particularly Jesus' cross, which
now was a thing of the past and could be forgotten in the light of the glory of
the Risen One.[4] Following this line of reasoning, the memory of Jesus' previous
ministry, too, must have suffered from the perspective of the concept of Easter,
since the hour of the complete revelation of God had come only when he stood
before the disciples in the glory of eternal life. Only now, the argument goes,
was he the complete witness of God's grace and of God's will.

Such an effect did not proceed from the Easter account. That part of Jesus'
history that proceeded within his earthly conditions of life is confirmed, not
depreciated, by his resurrection; it is brought to fruition rather than being surpassed. Only the gnostic movement created gospels that made the risen one's
dealings with his disciples the major emphasis, pushing back his suffering and
teaching as merely preparatory, since at that time he was still invested with
naturalness, being determined by earthly circumstances. The circle of disciples, however, never allowed for the gnostic viewpoint. For them his previous

---

4. The passion narrative includes just as much reflection and creative poetic power as the
Easter account. This proves that the community did not regard the image of Jesus' cross with
any less seriousness than that of the Risen One.

ministry and his cross rather received from his resurrection the basis upon which their relationship to Jesus was built. The prerequisite for this was provided by the fact that Jesus included his death as part of his salvific work, recognizing in it the fulfillment of his earthly labor. Had he regarded his cross as the destruction of his ministry, the Easter account would have become a new revelation lacking any connection with previous events. Since Jesus, however, completed his commission through his cross, placing it into the gospel, the Easter message likewise combined with the reminiscences about his earthly work and formed the gospel together with them.

In the risen one's dealings with the disciples the major issue appears to be his claims regarding himself. This issue is the focal point of the entire process. He does not come to them as a silent figure but produces a complete, personal relationship with them by speaking with them. What he tells them consists of the statement that makes him recognizable to them in his commission from God.[5] The actions that are added when he eats before or with them have the same purpose: he reveals himself to them. With the disciples of Emmaus he speaks about the promises of Scripture and about their relationship to Christ's sufferings. This, however, was mere preparation. As long as he spoke with them, they did not yet recognize him. The aim of that act consisted, however, of the fact that they would recognize him, and when he had achieved this, he left.

Thus the resurrection account remains internally and qualitatively similar to the preceding ministry of Jesus. Even now no doctrine develops independently of his person. That he had been sent to them by the Father is the presence of God's rule and the revelation of his grace. Likewise, the personal framing of his aim is not replaced by eschatological instruction or by a legislation designed to govern the church. During the days of Easter there arose neither an apocalypse nor a church law; what corresponded to Jesus' claims regarding himself and what actually developed was faith in him. The entire process has its aim and its success in the establishment of faith. Faith arises from the clear recognition that he whom they know from his earthly work now stands in the glory of eternal life and unites himself with them in precisely this way. John clarified the inner value these events possessed for the disciples by leading the Easter narrative to the point where the doubting Thomas believes in Jesus, and the older presentations yield the same result. The success of the Easter account was that faith was no longer merely a goal for the disciples for which they struggled but that it was present and confirmed in them. Now Jesus' messianic office had become reality for them. When they had him before them as the risen one, they were certain that he was the Christ. And since the community was now connected with the risen one no longer by seeing but solely by believing, faith was now singled out from all other indicators of piety and became the foundation of Christianity.

5. This was already the case in the Easter account received by Paul. The essential element in the process was that the Christ revealed himself to the disciples. His Easter report did not have a gnostic character. Therefore the Easter account heard by Paul, too, was the final word of the passion narrative.

This meant the assurance of God's grace that was now complete, just as the passion narrative had brought to light the power of sin, not merely in Israel but also in the disciples. They are forgiven. The risen one enters into communion with them beyond all their transgressions. As was the case during Jesus' earthly work, reconciliation with God is not so much taught or defined but effected and received; its necessity or possibility are not established but its reality created. The disciples' separation from God is overcome. For the Glorified One relates to them as their friend and has a meal with them. John portrayed this by Jesus' dealings with Peter, who was authorized to love him more than the others and was therefore given his office as shepherd. This, however, was not a gift reserved for Peter alone. For the one whom God's glory sent to the entire group again became for all the disciples the messenger of peace in the spirit of reconciling grace.

At the same time, the execution of righteousness he accomplished by his cross for Israel and all humanity was confirmed and completed in the Easter account. The new revelation did not occur for Israel. Its will that had been accomplished with the crucifixion of the Christ was confirmed and determined the course of history. Matthew said that even the leaders of the nation were immediately impacted by the Easter report, since the guards at the tomb told them what had happened. This, however, was not followed by an appearance of the Christ before the Sanhedrin. The risen one made his disciples his possession, and his community was separated from Israel.

The assurance of forgiving grace and the redemption from evil rooted in it were linked as a result of the Easter account with that assurance of life that is a characteristic of the New Testament. There is rejoicing confidence: "Death, where is your sting?" "The life became manifest." The community had this confidence from the very beginning, as is immediately shown by its willingness to suffer martyrdom (cf. Acts 7:55–59). How closely liberation from the thought of death is linked with the Easter report is revealed by the fact that the community did not produce any theories regarding immortality nor give any indications regarding the place where souls would go. It created nothing that resembles a proof for immortality, demonstrating by the nature of the soul the prerequisite and ability for eternal life, and this in the midst of a tradition that was vividly moved by those questions and that offered a variety of materials for its discussion. The first community's joy of life is grounded exclusively in its view of the Christ and can be summarized by the one sentence: since he has risen, we will be with him. "Through Jesus' resurrection we are born anew to a living hope." This is a direct result of the Easter events.

The demonstration of Jesus' regal status is linked in all accounts with the confirmation of the apostolate. On a higher level, that process is repeated which we observed at the first revelation of the Christ and at the confession of his regal office in Galilee: the apostolic office of his disciples is always placed side by side with Jesus' regal office. In Matthew, the commissioning of the disciples constitutes the core of the entire account. In Luke, Jesus' walk to Emmaus with the two disciples portrays him as the comforter of his own who helps them to faith once again; but the aim of the Easter narrative is also in

Luke the establishment of the apostolate. In John, the major portion of his Easter account serves directly his central thought: he shows how the Risen One united the disciples with himself through faith and how he gave them authority for their work. But also the second segment with its warm, intimate tone telling of an encounter between Jesus and the disciples that renewed his previous dealings with them on a higher level, so that he was with them once again as their friend, caring for their work and preparing their meal, is dominated by the vivid consciousness of office evidenced by the first segment. From the fact that the one who has entered eternal life keeps communion with them, the obligation to serve arises with its absolute seriousness, until either the cross or his return. The different positions held by the two major disciples, Peter and John, in the community are determined by the Risen One. In Paul, the Easter account is exclusively viewed from the perspective that Jesus created his messengers through it.

Therefore Jesus' appearance is bestowed upon the gathered disciples. The individual traits and the participation of a larger circle in these experiences are pushed back. Paul names only the two leaders of the community, Peter and James, as recipients of a particular appearance, and the Gospel account shows that the community's Easter faith was not grounded in what Peter experienced for himself but on what Jesus gave to all apostles. His resurrection is not established merely or particularly through Peter's testimony; Peter represents it together with the entire apostolate. We are not told of a special appearance for any other disciple. The one where Thomas learns to believe has its purpose clearly in gaining this final disciple as well. This, however, is effected not by the granting of a special appearance of Jesus to Thomas but by the fact that he gathers with the others and there receives the word that puts his doubt to shame and establishes his faith.

The characteristics of the apostolic office given to it by Jesus' preceding ministry all remain in effect. The equipment of the disciples consists of faith in him that is now grounded in the fact that they know him as the one who lives forever. Their power obliges them to services that they fulfill by calling all to repentance. To this end they receive the authority to forgive sins and to judge, since the call to repentance has its aim in the renewed fellowship of man with God. As the means of directing the call to repentance to all they are given baptism.

For the community's religious history it was important that the final appearance, that seen by Paul, remained of the same kind as the previous events. Admittedly, he saw the Christ as the bearer of heavenly glory in the light, not in the familiar human manner in which the other Easter stories feature him. But Paul's experience, too, has its center exclusively in the Christ's self-attestation. He does not receive any other revelation from him than the one that helped him recognize the Christ in Jesus. Thereby he is granted the grace that unites him, absolved of his guilt, with the Christ and with God. The obligation to service is brought into an indissoluble connection with that union, so that any selfish abuse of his experience is excluded. Thus the final appearance did not surpass the older Easter story, nor did it turn it toward a new goal. It rather followed it in firm uniformity and confirmed it.

In a new and in any case more definite way than at an earlier time, humanity's universal destiny is tied by the Easter account to the apostolate. As the Christ is Lord over all the nations, his messengers are sent to all. Matthew, after describing Jesus' faithfulness to the cross that was entirely devoted to Israel, records in the Easter account Jesus' universal mandate to his disciples, not as a disavowal of the commission previously given to them but in such a way that their commission to humanity also includes the one to Israel, albeit not to Israel alone (Matt. 28:18–20).[6] In Luke, too, Jesus' commission to the disciples has universal greatness, and in John there can be no doubt, because from the very beginning he juxtaposes the Christ and the world. The certainty by which the disciples relate their office and gospel to the entire world is to be characterized as an acquisition of the days of Easter, when Israel had rejected the Christ after he testified unto death of God's faithfulness to the old community, after he now stood before the disciples in the glory of God as the one who had a share in God's rule in heaven and on earth and who was always and everywhere with his community. Universalism had always been at home in eschatology. In Jesus' resurrection, however, the disciples already had a final aim as reality before them. They had experienced something that belonged to the fulfillment of the course of the world; now universalism was in effect.

No objection can arise from the fact that world mission does not follow immediately after the Easter account. For the greatness of its aim obliged it to a sober respect for the existing situation and did not legitimize it to fantastic enterprises. Prevailing circumstances were always regarded as divine providence, according to which one's work has to be arranged. The community was therefore first established in Jerusalem; from there the gospel was extended step by step to humanity. The disciples' claim is not thereby contradicted that the aim directing their work toward all of humanity was given them by Jesus in the days of Easter.

The Easter account also was confirmed and sealed by the promise of the Spirit. At the cross Jesus had given his body and his blood for the disciples. Now that he was elevated above mortal nature and lived in the Spirit, he also gave his Spirit to them, without which they could not perform their apostolic

---

6. If we seek to understand the convictions that guided the disciples, the Easter account constitutes the place where we should expect to find their statements regarding the extent of their commission. Now the Christ is consummated and that community emerges which he establishes. Now Israel, too, has received its full due because the Christ has served it to his death. Even if the historian considers the resurrection account to be a mere legend, this does not remove the fact that the disciples traced the universal mission to Jesus' commandment. By the way, the supposition that the words of the Easter account could or must necessarily originate from a subsequent period is without merit. What is certain is that there never existed an Easter report without Easter words, a tale that described Jesus as a silent shadow, like a ghost who cannot talk. For its effect always depended on the fact that Jesus subsequent to his death entered again into contact with his disciples and that he renewed and confirmed his communion with them. The supposition, however, that there ever were some other words where one now finds the commission to the apostles is unfounded.

office. In John he shows this to them by breathing on them. In Luke the promise of the Spirit belongs to the words of the Risen One, and in Matthew Jesus grounds baptism not merely in God's fatherhood and in his own sonship but also in the presence of the Holy Spirit with whom the community lives from now on in fellowship, to the extent that and since it is united with the Christ and with the Father (John 20:22; Luke 24:49; Acts 1:4; Matt. 28:19). There is a connection between the fact that the disciples' work receives its basis in the Spirit's presence and that the public proclamation of the Christ does not yet begin in the days of Easter. Whoever puts confidence in extrapolations may judge that the gathering of the messianic community would originate immediately from the events at the time of Easter. But this did not come about by the message, "We see the risen Christ among us," but only by the proclamation that the Christ was in heaven and had revealed himself by sending his Spirit. Not the view of the Risen One but the share in the Spirit was considered to be the gift that was granted to all and that provided for all the motive to faith.

Since the Easter narratives and Jesus' appearances were always limited to a certain place and time, they were from the start and everywhere tied to the concept of Jesus' ascension. Nowhere is there a trace that Jesus' community sought him anywhere but in heaven. He was with God, at his right hand, at his throne (Matt. 22:44; 26:64; 28:18; John 6:62 and parallels; likewise, Paul, Peter, Hebrews, and Revelation; the expectation of the parousia by itself indicates that Jesus' ascension everywhere belonged to the gospel). The fact that the expectation that the Easter appearances could be repeated is entirely missing confirms Luke's claim that Jesus' final appearance was revealed clearly as his farewell from the disciples and as his exaltation into heaven.

How profoundly the events of Easter touched the disciples' entire relationship with God and renewed their concept of God is evident in the fact that the Trinitarian name of God is tied to the events of Easter. John provides a parallel to the baptism in the name of the Father and of the Son and of the Holy Spirit by noting that the disciples' faith in the presence of the Risen One is completed by the adoration of him as their Lord and God (Matt. 28:19; John 20:28). Jesus became the creator of the Trinitarian concept of God by placing his office into the eternal and complete revelation of divine grace, setting the sending of the Spirit beside himself as a second testimony to God. Thereby it became the religion of his community that it possessed its communion with God in fellowship with the Christ and with the Spirit. Jesus never thought of this merely as a temporary form of divine activity, since he conceived of his sonship as being personal and therefore eternal. Moreover, with the clear recognition of the Risen One the thought of a disappearance of his office and work was completely ruled out. While it always remained a profound mystery how the earthly Christ could claim eternity for himself, the concept of eternity was confirmed by the view of the Risen One and the completeness of his sonship, which united him with the Father, was revealed. Inherent to the Spirit were always the characteristics of eternity and divinity; the idea that God could ever be without his Spirit never existed.

By the fact that the formula "tri-unity" truly described to the relationship with God into which the disciples knew themselves to be placed, Jesus' entire work found its ripe fruit. He never spoke of himself in such a way that the thought could be attached to his work that he replaced the Father's activity, so that he contained in himself the entire divine activity. Since the Father was active, the Son was active, too. This is the thought that Jesus confirmed to his disciples. The same principle also determined Christ's relationship to the divine Spirit and excluded any tension between them. Christ did not retire since the Spirit was active. He rather exercised his own rule through him and was revealed by the Spirit's testimony. Likewise, his word did not allow for any divergent parallelism regarding their activities, as if the Father might rule nature, the Son humanity, and the Spirit the holy community.

Through Jesus the community became in the highest sense the place where the Father was active. As he himself lived through the Father as the Son, the community was transferred into light and life by the Father. Likewise, the work of the Spirit formed a complete unity with that of the Christ. Both held possession of the called community and simultaneously performed a universal work upon humanity, and both effected righteousness and grace in complete unity. As the Spirit illumined and convicted, the Christ reconciled and judged. The disciples did not receive three names of God from Jesus. Neither did they, however, receive only one name for a hidden God; rather he was now present with them and was revealed to them in the two bearers of his grace.

Subject Index

Abomination of desolation, 348, 349
Abraham, 30, 64, 205, 227, 328
  sons of, 320, 330
Acceptance by God, 157
Accommodation
  of Jesus, 102
  theory, 283–84
Accuser. *See* Satan.
Acts of God, 142–43, 192, 205, 254,
    288, 341
  gospel of, 120, 121–22, 190, 356–57,
    358
  revealed, 213, 337
Adam, 136
Admiration for leaders, 235
Adoption, 247, 317
Adulteress brought to Jesus, 146, 147,
    150, 155
Advocate. *See* Holy Spirit.
After-life. *See* Eternal life.
"Ages," 27–28, 63, 93
Alexander Jannaeus, 48
Alexandria, 49, 71
Allegiance
  to Christ, 107, 164, 166, 237, 239,
    275, 295, 302, 306, 322, 331
  to God, 204
Alms-giving, 167, 172, 211
Altar, 45, 94, 95, 97, 138, 145, 215
Andrew, 105
Angels, 37, 43 n. 11, 93, 121, 233. *See
    also* Demons; Satan.
Anger, 142, 144, 164
  of God. *See* Wrath of God.

Annas, 368
Anointed One. *See* Identifications of
      Jesus Christ; Messianic
      concept.
Anointing
  by Spirit, 133
  of Jesus, 235, 321, 323
Anti-Christ, spirit of, 57. *See also* Satan.
Apocalyptic books, 232–33, 235 n. 56
Apocalypticists, 232–34, 259–60, 261
Apostle's Creed, 12 n. 11
Apostles, 18, 241 n. 61. *See also* Disciples.
  commission of, 234–48, 251, 304–5,
      334, 338, 387
  establishment of, 279–80, 284, 386
  interpretation of prophets, 211–12
  judgment of, 285–86, 313, 314, 386
  persecution of, 286, 287, 331 n. 23,
      335, 347–48, 350, 352, 360
  mission of, 209, 226, 337, 356
  "myth makers," 31
  office of, 314, 351, 386, 388
  suffering of, 242, 250, 252, 266, 268,
      292, 323, 339, 347
  testimony of, 375–76, 377–78
  thrones for, 342
  transcendent ministry of, 382–83
  visions of Christ, 376–78
Aramaic language, 48
Archelaus, 37
Aristotelian instruction, 49
Arrest of Jesus, 363–68

391

grace to, 94–96, 98, 129, 239, 258,
  275–76, 290, 293, 294, 309,
  312, 332, 373, 385
holy, 94, 117, 156, 281, 301–3,
  331, 333, 334
Holy Spirit in, 84 n. 7, 387–88, 389
inheritance of, 334
Jesus present in, 274, 275, 333, 364
liberated, 75, 294, 299, 303–4, 309,
  312, 364
Lord's supper in, 275, 359
love in, 94, 295, 298–304, 360
mercy in, 242, 298, 300, 301, 333–
  34
organization of, 237, 239, 241, 259,
  298–304
separated from old community,
  331, 332, 385
united, 229, 246, 279–80, 299, 300,
  301, 308, 330–31, 332, 333
covenant, 119, 213 n. 42, 276
temple, 369
Testament theology, 17–20, 21
worship, 214, 215
Nicodemus, 139, 142, 217, 264, 362
Noah, 227

Oaths, 227, 329
Obedience. *See also* Submission.
  Jesus', 209–10, 306, 352
    in prayer, 196
    in temptation, 88, 89, 90, 132
    of cross, 317–18, 319, 365, 370,
      373
    teaching on, 96–97
  kingdom, 53, 333–34
    in discipleship, 103, 105–7, 137,
      151, 227, 293, 336
    in faith, 171, 201, 227
    in repentance, 64, 141, 339, 340
    in joy, 56, 294
    in unity, 299, 380
    to Christ, 60, 236–39, 278
    to law, 44–47, 197, 209, 214, 244,
      245
  national, 46, 68, 215, 324–25
"Objective vision," 382
Offense of Jesus, 275, 274
Office, messianic, 210, 212, 253–58,
  269, 367, 369–70, 388

priestly, 93, 185–86, 284–85, 293,
  321, 341–42, 372, 373
prophetic, 95 n. 13, 211–12, 215–16,
  278–80, 326–27, 329
kingly, 125–36, 230–31, 262, 281–82,
  283, 296, 307
Old
  community. *See* Covenant
    community.
  nature. *See* Nature, old.
  Testament, 28, 39, 178
Omnipotence of Father, 69, 72, 186,
  191, 236, 341, 352, 353
Omnipresence of Christ, 38–39, 260,
  300, 302, 307, 341, 342, 361,
  364
Omniscience, at incarnation, 352
Only One. *See* Identifications of Jesus
  Christ.
Opposition. *See* Rejection of Jesus.
  by Jesus
    to arrogant, 78, 152, 197, 218, 235,
      283, 313
    to evil, 202, 316
    to hero-admiration, 235
    to intellectualism, 292
    to God's word, 259, 260
Ownership of disciples, 253

Paganism, Greek, 381, 357
Pan, god, 276
Parables, 43, 125, 137, 142, 210, 258–
  62, 280–81, 299, 320
  as dramas, 360
  final, 324–25, 327, 347
  of repentance, 333
  of separation, 361
  purpose of, 118–19
Paraclete, 43 n. 11
Paraclete. *See* Holy Spirit.
Paradise, promise of, 373
Pardon. *See* Justification.
Passover, 40, 304, 305, 353, 358
Patience
  of disciples, 247, 259, 346–47, 352,
    353
  of Jesus, 156, 164, 236, 243, 298
Patriarchs, 118, 127
"Patriotism," 102
Paul, 18, 31, 84 n. 7, 172 n. 31, 212, 384
  n. 5, 386
  visions of, 375–76, 377, 379, 386

basis for, 116
  Christ, 26, 305, 318
  gift, 338, 351, 352
  repentance, 146
  way of, 311, 332, 199, 200
  works and, 123–24
  in new community, 98, 239, 258, 309,
    385
  plan of, 293, 320, 351
  power of, 273, 275, 314
  standards for, 333–34. *See also* Conver-
    sion; Eternal life.
Samaritan
  parable of, 142
  people, 139, 236, 242, 304
  woman at well, 139–40, 147, 150,
    308, 309
Samson, 35
Samuel, 35, 40
Sanctification, 158, 317
Essenes, 232
Sanhedrin, 189, 368, 370, 380, 385
Satan, 175, 182, 189, 202, 264, 305 n.
    11. *See also* Demons.
  accuser, 43 n. 11, 120, 305, 363, 366
  murderer, 101, 319
  service to, 287, 306, 367
  warfare against, 120, 124, 319
    on believers, 228
    on Jesus, 87–88, 89, 90, 192, 291,
      366
  wolf, 318–19
Schlatter
  Adolf, 9–17, 22, 23–24
  Theodor, 9
Scribes, 224–29. *See also* Rabbinical Juda-
    ism; Teachers of the Law.
Scripture. *See also* Interpretation.
  authority of, 92, 141, 209, 210, 213
  confirmation of, 209–10
  heroes of, 234–35
  inspiration of, 44, 45, 59, 129, 213
  integrity of, 9, 44, 45, 60, 85, 175,
    213, 216, 278, 326
  Jesus'
    fidelity to, 42–43, 44, 48, 92–93,
      111, 209–16, 248
    fulfillment of, 209–16, 326–27
    weapon of, 210–11
    zeal for, 270
  Jewish canon of, 210

Scythopolis, 48
Sea
  of Galilee, 48, 111, 175, 258
  of Tiberias, 376, 378
  signs in, 349–50
Second coming of Christ, 174, 207, 210,
    266, 333, 341, 342, 343–44
  signs of, 346–53
  timing, 346, 350, 351, 352
Seleucids, 48
Self. *See also* Selfishness; World, Renunci-
    ation of.
  -centered
    community, 58, 59, 119–20, 154–
      55, 230, 325, 334
    desires, 289, 298
    discipleship, 235, 238, 241
    religion, 72, 154, 164, 169 197,
      218, 252, 274
  -denial, 172–73, 250–51, 364–67
  -glory, 115, 157, 223, 292, 311, 329,
    354
  -love, 161–62, 286, 310
Selfishness, 141, 160
  of disciples, 162, 248, 342, 343, 264
  of nation, 115, 140
  of rejecting God, 265
Selflessness of Jesus, 91, 126, 127, 154,
    268, 269, 278–79, 318–19
  in humanity, 40
  in love, 77, 162
  in prayer, 196
Separation
  from evil, 65, 77, 78, 79, 238
  from God, 286, 336, 358
  from God on cross, 372–73
  from Jesus by sin, 364
  from Jewish community
    Jesus, 213, 216, 240, 244–45, 265
    disciples, 250
  from sin, 77, 78, 79, 123, 137, 138,
    140, 142
  of Israel, 206
  of Jesus
    from crowd, 271
    from Father, 319, 358, 372–73
    from Jewish Community, 213, 216,
      217, 265, 274, 279, 320, 328
Sepphoris, 37, 111
Septuagint, 29, 48, 98

Scripture Index

Genesis
1:26—136 n. 18
6—233
15:6—196

Exodus
1—39 n. 9

1 Samuel
21:6—43

Psalms
2—128
8:3—322
8:4—134
22—216
22:2—372
31:6—373
69—216
82:6—210
110—43, 98, 99, 131, 216
110:1—210, 326, 369
110:3—98

Isaiah
9—216
11—216
40—94 n. 11
40:3—60, 72
52:7—115 n. 2
53—98

61—94 n. 12
61:1—108

Jeremiah
31:31–34—356 n. 37

Daniel
7:13—134, 369

Hosea
6:6—145, 210

Zechariah
9:9—322

Malachi
4:3—210

Matthew
1:21—27
3:3—60
3:6—68
3:7—62 n. 21
3:8—63–64
3:11—56, 57, 58, 59, 114
3:14—255
3:15—80, 81
4:3—100
4:6—100
4:13–16—111
4:18–22—103

4:19—107
4:25—234 n. 54
5:1—234, 234 n. 54
5:3—100
5:3–4—237
5:3–10—121
5:6—155
5:7—159
5:8—344
5:9—159
5:11–12—242 n. 64
5:12—152, 277
5:13–16—239
5:16—160, 191, 237
5:17—210
5:17–19—77, 209
5:18—349
5:20—47, 217, 238
5:21—142, 150, 211
5:22—144, 153, 264
5:23–24—145
5:24—215
5:25—264
5:27—211
5:28—150
5:29—144, 244, 264
5:32—308
5:33—211
5:35—215
5:38—211
5:39—174

419